Agricultural Business Management

Agricultural Business Management

Prof. H.L. Nagaraja Murthy

M.A. (Psy), M.Phil. (Psy), PGDPM&IR, Ph.D. Pursuing,

Assistant Professor,
Bharati Vidyapeeth Deemed University,
New Delhi Campus,
A-4 Paschim Vihar, New Delhi-110063.

(OB/HR- Agri.Bus.Mgt-Bus.Com-Psy-Journ-IB-PR-Mass Com.)
Academic Co-ordinator/Visiting Professor, IGNOU Study Centre,
JIMS Institute, Rohini, Delhi-110085.

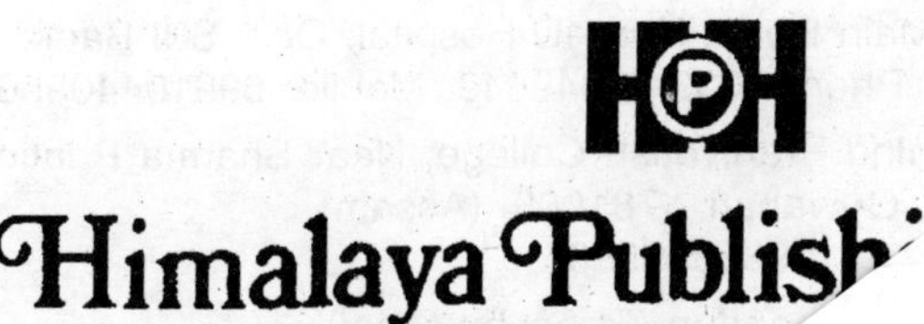

MUMBAI • NEW DELHI • NAGPUR • BENGALURU • HYDERA
• ERNAKULAM • BHUBANESWA

First Edition : 2013

Published by : Mrs. Meena Pandey for **Himalaya Publishing House Pvt. Ltd.,**
"Ramdoot", Dr. Bhalerao Marg, Girgaon, **Mumbai - 400 004.**
Phone: 022-23860170/23863863, Fax: 022-23877178
E-mail: himpub@vsnl.com; Website: www.himpub.com

Branch Offices :

New Delhi : "Pooja Apartments", 4-B, Murari Lal Street, Ansari Road, Darya Ganj, New Delhi - 110 002. Phone: 011-23270392, 23278631; Fax: 011-23256286

Nagpur : Kundanlal Chandak Industrial Estate, Ghat Road, Nagpur - 440 018. Phone: 0712-2738731, 3296733; Telefax: 0712-2721215

Bengaluru : No. 16/1 (Old 12/1), 1st Floor, Next to Hotel Highlands, Madhava Nagar, Race Course Road, Bengaluru - 560 001. Phone: 080-32919385; Telefax: 080-22286611

Hyderabad : No. 3-4-184, Lingampally, Besides Raghavendra Swamy Matham, Kachiguda, Hyderabad - 500 027. Phone: 040-27560041, 27550139; Mobile: 09848130433

Chennai : No. 8/2, 2nd Madley Street, Ground Floor, T. Nagar, Chennai - 600 017. Mobile: 09345345055

Pune : First Floor, "Laksha" Apartment, No. 527, Mehunpura, Shaniwarpeth (Near Prabhat Theatre), Pune - 411 030. Phone: 020-24496323/24496333

Lucknow : House No 731, Shekhupura Colony, Near B.D. Convent School, Aliganj, Lucknow - 226 022. Mobile: 09307501549

Ahmedabad : 114, "SHAIL", 1st Floor, Opp. Madhu Sudan House, C.G. Road, Navrang Pura, Ahmedabad - 380 009. Phone: 079-26560126; Mobile: 09327324149, 09377088847

Ernakulam : 39/104 A, Lakshmi Apartment, Karikkamuri Cross Rd., Ernakulam, Cochin - 622011, Kerala. Phone: 0484-2378012, 2378016; Mobile: 09344199799

Bhubaneswar : 5 Station Square, Bhubaneswar - 751 001 (Odisha). Phone: 0674-2532129, Mobile: 09861046007

Indore : Kesardeep Avenue Extension, 73, Narayan Bagh, Flat No. 302, IIIrd Floor, Near Humpty Dumpty School, Indore - 452 007 (M.P.). Mobile: 09301386468

Kolkata : 108/4, Beliaghata Main Road, Near ID Hospital, Opp. SBI Bank, Kolkata - 700 010, Phone: 033-32449649, Mobile: 09910440956

Guwahati : House No. 15, Behind Pragjyotish College, Near Sharma Printing Press, P.O. Bharalumukh, Guwahati - 781009, (Assam). Mobile: 09883055590, 09883055536

: HPH, Editorial Office, Bhandup (Rupeshri Misal)

Jayalakshmi Enterprises Offset Printers, Hyderabad. On behalf of HPH.

FOREWORD

The ongoing structural changes in the economy have resulted in major shifts in the Indian agricultural scenario. The primacy of subsistence orientation is yielding place to commercialization, opening up vast opportunities for value addition, packaging and exports of agricultural products, with strikingly high levels of technology. The policies of globalization have taken Indian agriculture into the global village, opening up unprecedented opportunities as well as great challenges.

India is the seventh largest country in geographical level and second largest country in population wise and twelfth largest country in economic wise .The economy of India is as diverse as it is large, with a number of major sectors including manufacturing industries, agriculture, textiles and handicrafts, and services but more than 75 per cent of population maintaining their livelihood in agriculture.

The Five Year Plans (FYP) has given importance to the agriculture sector, rural development and rural people's employment. Nearly 21.1 per cent of the entire rural population of India exists in difficult physical and financial predicament but poverty ratio in urban remain at 15 per cent and there is great disparity between rich and poor.

According to latest Economic Survey Report, Indian agriculture including crop and animal husbandry, fisheries, forestry and agro-processing provides the underpinnings of our food and livelihood security. Agriculture provides significant support for economic growth and social transformation of the country and provides employment to around 52 per cent of workforce.

The public investment in agriculture in real terms has witnessed steady decline from the Sixth Five Year Plan to the Tenth Plan but trend in public investment in agriculture seems to be declining but after tenth FYP this was reversed and stood positive which is positive sign in the Indian economy.

According to latest statistics, Investment in agriculture and allied sector since 2004-05 the Gross Capital Formation (GCF) in agriculture and allied sectors as a proportion of total GDP stood at 2.66 per cent in 2004-05 and improved to 3.34 per cent in 2008-09.Similarly, the GCF in agriculture and allied sectors relative to Gross Domestic Product (GDP) in this sector has also shown an improvement from 14.07 per cent in 2004-05 to 21.31 per cent in 2008-09.

Agribusiness explores production, marketing and trading of products related to agriculture. It also covers improved growing techniques, agricultural machinery, fertilizer, pesticides, pre- and post-harvest handling, storage, transportation, packaging and labeling. Critical management issues as financing and technical assistance, preparation of products for exports, overseas marketing issues and government policy.

Keeping this in mind, this book has been devised and authored to motivate agribusiness managers to contribute substantially to the development of diverse activities in this sector. And many universities have devised the PG programs in such areas such as production and marketing seeds, fertilizers, pesticides, farm machinery and equipment, livestock feed, irrigation, export and import, cooperatives, rural banking, agricultural projects, insurance, logistics, land management, water management and irrigation, and sustainable energy. The curriculum is different in different institutions.

The course module includes one trimester for summer internship during which the students undergo an assignment given by agribusiness companies. The academic curriculum covers 39 subjects broadly distributed into basic, functional, sectoral and general courses during the period of two years. In addition, the students also participate in live projects assigned to the institute along with faculty members during their stay in the institute. The program also provides opportunities to students to take up an industrial visit for closer interaction to understand the latest developments in the industry as a part of the course curriculum.

Similarly, Logistics and Infrastructure Management in Agriculture, Marketing of Agricultural Inputs, Management and Finance of Agro Food Projects, Market Research for agribusiness, Managerial Communication for Agribusiness, Management of Contract Farming, Management of Technology for Sustainable Agriculture, Franchising in Agribusiness (FAB) Private-Public Community Partnership for Inclusive Agribusiness, Rural Advertising, Strategic Food Agro Marketing, and Sales and Distribution Management for Agriculture.

Further, it is the intention of providing detailed study materials to students of BBA and MBA who have little exposure in this field to provide them first hand information on agriculture business management with basic concepts while efforts have been made to elucidate the managerial and marketing skills in this era of competition. More and more information will be added to this edition in due course as and when I get some study materials on this subject and I hope this book will serve as handy for all management students as ready reckoner.

Dr. Nitin Nayak
Director - BVIMR
Bharati Vidyapeeth Deemed University,
Institute of Management & Research, New Delhi Campus,
A-4 Paschim Vihar Near Paschim Vihar (East), Metro Station
New Delhi-110063

PREFACE

Agriculture Business Management plays an important role in India's economic scenario and developmental strategy, and in particular in the areas of rural development, farming practices, introduction of innovative and indigenous technologies that are economical, viable and feasible easily adoptable in Indian farming sector. Further in the field of modernization globalization and self-reliance.

Rural India is evolving, dynamic and stood on its own for centuries. Country's rural area's population is more than one-tenth and it has become necessary to understand their lifestyles, livelihood, and standards of living in agrarian economy. Further this book outlines how agricultural business management and agricultural marketing can give multiplier effect for continuous advancement of the Indian economy in all aspects. Rural segments in Indian economy are under backwardness, illiteracy, ignorance, and living in unhygienic conditions without any basic amenities and sanitation.

The government at the centre headed by UPA steered under the able guidance of Ms Sonia Gandhi and Prime Minister of India Dr. Manmohan Singh has taken umpteen initiatives to develop rural sector by undertaking various programs. To name few Integrated Rural Development Programme, Wage Employment Programme, Employment Assurance Scheme, Food for Work Programme, Rural Housing, Social Security Programmes, and Land Reforms. Further Integrated development of rural areas is one of the abiding tasks before the Government of India. The National Common Minimum Program (NCMP) of the Central government reiterates the cardinal importance of villages to the overall development of the country and commits to work towards development of rural areas, which for various reasons could not keep pace with urban areas in the past.

In conformity with this commitment of the Government, the Ministry of Rural Development accords foremost priority to development in rural areas and eradication of poverty and hunger from the face of rural India. A number of initiatives have been taken in the recent years for creation of social and economic infrastructure in rural areas to bridge the rural-urban divide as well as to provide food security and fulfill other basic needs of the rural populace. The renewed emphasis on rural development is also visible in the commensurate progressive increase in the allocation of resources for implementation of poverty alleviation programmes. For the Tenth Five Year Plan, the allocation of funds for rural development programmes has been enhanced to ₹ 76,774 crore as against ₹ 42,874 crore in Ninth Plan.

Further UPA led government had addressed the challenges of unemployment in the rural areas of the country, thereby pledged itself to the development of rural sector for ameliorating the economic condition of the people. Wage employment is provided in rural areas under: National Rural Employment Guarantee Act (NREGA) and Sampoorna Grameen Rozgar Yojana (SGSY). Whereas self-employment is provided under Swarnajayanti Gram Swarozgar Yojana (SGSY). Besides generating employment, these wage employment schemes also ensure creation of durable assets in rural areas. Initiatives are also taken by the Ministry to build and upgrade the basic rural infrastructure through various schemes.

Similarly, under Pradhan Mantri Gram Sadak Yojana (PMGSY), construction and repairing of rural roads are taken up to ensure rural connectivity. It is expected under the scheme that an expanded and renovated rural road network will lead to an increase in rural employment opportunities, better access to regulated and fair market, better access to health, education and other public services so as to accelerate the pace of economic growth in rural areas. Similarly, basic amenities for housing, drinking water and toilets, etc. are provided under Indira Awaas Yojana (IAY), Accelerated Rural Water Supply Programme (ARWSP) and Toral Sanitation Campaign (TSC) to enhance the welfare and well-being of the vulnerable sections of rural population. Area Development is encouraged through Watershed Programmes to check the diminishing productivity of waste land and loss of natural resources.

Agricultural Business Management has been introduced as core subject to MBA and BBA students course curriculum by Bharati Vidyapeeth University and also many other agriculture universities in India in their Post Graduate and Graduate courses. From my side, I have made an humble effort to fulfill the needs of our students and teachers of the subject by covering necessary topics explaining the concepts.

Extensive efforts have been made to collect relevant information from various literatures, brochures, leaflets, reference and text books available on the subject and Government of India's website Planning Commission's website, Department of Agriculture, Ministry of Agriculture websites, and other sources including Economic Surveys brought out by Government of India for the past two years and Research reports by few research organizations, Newspaper clippings, have been studied thoroughly and essence of the topics have been so simple for students to comprehend the essence of the concepts and are motivated to dig out more information and knowledge available on these topics. I invite more suggestions from all the readers for further improvement of this book.

I am grateful to my wife Mrs. Jivan Lata and my son Amrit Lal Murthy, B.A. (Hons.) in Psychology from University of Delhi and now pursuing his Master's Programme in Applied Psychology from Jania Millia Islamia University, New Delhi who remained guiding spirit in providing me required information and piece of knowledge for inclusion in this book and stood with their helping hands throughout my hectic task of compiling this book to make it more attractive. I am also indebted to publishers of this book M/s Himalaya Publishing House Pvt. Ltd. in general and to Mr. V.S. Rawat – Sales Manager in particular for his linking me with network of Himalaya Publishing House Pvt. Ltd., which is rendering in the world of publishing by bringing out books on relevant topics making students' life more comfortable by providing required information timely.

Prof. H.L. Nagaraja Murthy

FARMING INDIA

During his visit to India, the US President, Mr. Barack Obama pointed out that India is fortunate to have over half of its total population of 1.2 billion under the age of 30. Out of the 600 million young persons, over 60 per cent live in villages. Most of them are educated. The 'Father of the Nation' Mahatma Gandhi considered the migration of educated youth form villages to towns and cities as the most serious form of bran drain adversely affecting rural India's development. He, therefore, stressed that we should take steps to end the divorce between the intellect and the labour in rural professions.

The National Commission on Farmers stressed the need for attracting and retaining educated youth in farming. The National Policy for farmers placed in Parliament in November 2007, includes the following goal of the new policy —"to introduce measures which can help to attract and retain youth in farming and processing of farm products for higher value addition, by making farming intellectually stimulating and economically rewarding". On the other hand, the pressure of population on land is increasing and the average six of a farm holding is going down to below one hectare.

Farmers are getting indebted and the temptation to sel prime farmland for non-farm purposes is growing. Over 45 per cent of farmers interviewed by the National Sample Survey (NSS) Organization wanted to quit farming. Under these conditions, how are we going to persuade the educated youth, including farm graduates, to stay in villages and take to agriculture as a profession? How can youth earn a decent living in villages and help shape the future of our agriculture? This will require a three pronged strategy.

1. Improve the productivity and profitability of small holdings through appropriate technology and market linkages.
2. Enlarge the scope for the growth of agro processing, agro-industries and agribusiness.
3. Promote opportunities for the service sector to expand in a manner that will trigger the technological and economic upgradation of farm operations.

Some years ago, the government of India launched a programme to enable to enable farm graduates to start agri-clinics and agri business is yet to attract the interests of educated youth to the degree originally expected. It is hence time that the programme is restructured based on the lessons learnt.

Ideally a group of four to five farm graduates, who have specialized in agriculture, animal husbandry, fisheries, agribusiness and home science, could jointly launch an agri-clinic-cum-agribusiness centre in every bloc of the country. Agri-clinics will provide the services needed during the production phase of farming while the agribusiness centre will cater to the needs of farm families during the post-harvest phase of agriculture. Thus, farm women and men can be assisted during the entire crop cycle, starting with sowing and extending up to value addition and marketing.

The home science graduate can pay particular attention to nutrition and food safety and processing and help a group of farm women to start a food processing park. The group should also assist farm families to achieve economy and power of sale both during the production and post-harvest phases of farming.

Opportunities for such young entrepreneurs are several. Climate resilient agriculture is another area that needs attention. In dry farming areas, methods of rainwater harvesting and storage and watershed management as well as the improvement of soil physics, chemistry and microbiology, need to be spread widely.

The cultivation of fertilizer trees which can enrich soil fertility and help to improve soil carbon sequestration and storage, can be promoted under the Green India Mission as well as the Mahatma Gandhi National Rural Employment Guarantee Programme.

A few fertilizer trees, *a jal kund* (water harvesting pond) and a biogas plant in every farm will help to improve enormously the productivity and profitability of dry land farming.

The "Yuva Kisans" or young peasants (farmers) can also help women's self-help groups to manufacture and sell the biological software essential for sustainable aquaculture. The fisheries graduate can promote both inland and marine aquaculture, using low external input sustainable aquaculture (leis) techniques. Feed and seed are the important requirements for successful aquaculture and trained youth can promote their production at the local level.

Similar opportunities exist in the fields of animal husbandry. Improved technologies of small-scale poultry and dairy farming can be introduced. Codex alimentarius standards of food safety can be popularized in the case of perishable commodities. For this purpose, the young farmers should establish, Gyan Chaupals or Village Knowledge Centres. Such centres will be based on the integrated use of the Internet, FM Radio and mobile telephony.

In the service sector designed to meet the demand-driven needs of farming families, an important one is soil and water quality testing. Young farmers can organize mobile soil-cum-water quality testing work and go from village to village in the area of their operation and issue soil health and water quality cards to every family. This will help rural families to utilize in an effective manner the nutrient based subsidy introduced by the government from April 2, 2010.

Similarly, educated youth could help rural communities to organize gene-seed-grain-water banks, thereby linking conservation, cultivation, consumption, and commerce in a mutually reinforcing manner. Young farmers can also operate climate change risk management centres, which will help farmers to maximize the benefits of a good monsoon and minimize the impact of unfavourable weather. Educated youth can help to introduce the benefits of information space, nuclear, bio and eco technologies.

Eco technology involves the blend of traditional wisdom and frontier technology. This is the pathway to sustainable agriculture and food security and agrarian prosperity. If the youth choose to live in villages and launch the new agriculture movement based on the application of science and social wisdom, our untapped demographic dividend will become our greatest strength.

Prof. H.L. Nagaraja Murthy

CONTENTS

UNIT 1

CHAPTER 1

INTRODUCTION TO THE INDIAN AGRICULTURAL ECONOMY

(CHARACTERISTICS, IMPORTANCE AND ECONOMIC PLANNING)

Characteristics

Need of the Hour – Passion for Farming

Role and Importance of Agriculture in Indian Economy

Role of Agriculture in Indian Planning System

Disparities in Agricultural Planning

Overall Achievement in Five-year Planning

Agrarian Reforms and Green Revolution

General Overview of Indian Economy

Key Features of 11th Five Year Plan (2007-12)

How Can Agriculture Sector be Strengthened?

General Overview on Indian Agriculture

Reasons for Low Agriculture Productivity

Agriculture is developing agrarian economy in the world characterized by high population growth, abundant natural resources and optimal rate of capital formation with average standard of living that makes the country's economy so radiant and vibrant. The primary sector of Indian economy and agriculture along with the ancillary sectors like forestry, horticulture, and fishing employed over 50 per cent of the country's total population.

Although in the GDP the share of agriculture is constantly falling, still it remains the largest economic sector and plays a major role in the socio-economic development of India. In India, the State governments are responsible for the output of agriculture and the financial policies are formulated by the central government. India is the largest producer in the world of milk, cashew nuts, coconuts, tea, ginger, turmeric and black pepper.

According to recently presented Economic Survey Report, Indian economy pegged the country's agriculture growth at 5.4 per cent for the fiscal year 2011-12 as against – 0.4 per cent in the previous year. The recent achievement in agriculture sector has made the country so proud that this era has been metaphored as a "Second Green Revolution with technological breakthrough in the agriculture sector" to boost farm output and ensure the food security of the country. Stagnant agriculture, combined with a population growth rate in the continent that is higher than the world average, is obviously leading to food insecurity.

Agriculture is likely to grow at 5.4 per cent in 2010-11, and the growth of agriculture and allied sectors is expected to be higher this year on the back of a revival in foodgrains production in the 2010-11 crop year (July-June) following a good monsoon. Further foodgrains production is estimated to rise to 232.07 million tons in 2010-11 crop year from 218.11 million tons last year.

The country is all set to harvest a record of wheat, pulses and cotton crop this year. In the 2009-10 crop year, farm sector growth was only 0.4 per cent due to severe drought in 2009, which hit almost half the country, reducing food grain production by 16 million tons.

India is the second most populous country in the world. In 2003, the total population of 1.068 billion persons, representing 17 per cent of the world's population, occupied 2.4 per cent of the world's land mass. The proportion of the rural population is at 72 per cent in 2003. The overall population growth rate is also falling from 2.2 per cent in 1981 to 2.09 per cent in 2003. Unfortunately, the (female to male) sex ratio has been declining from 972 in 1901 to 927 in 2001.

India's average GDP growth rate at present is 8.5 per cent and per capita income increased from USD 260 in 1980 to USD 1000 in 2007. But the agriculture sector, which contributed 57 per cent of GDP in the early fifties, became less important and its share dropped to 17.5 per cent in 2007-08. Its performance continues to decline. It is said that unless the agriculture sector grows at over 4 per cent, an overall economic growth rate of 10 per cent plus may not be achieved.

The overall goal of the agriculture business management is to contribute to the development of resilient production, sustainable and diversified households, on-farm and off-farm livelihoods, allowing households to face production and market risks without falling back into poverty and distress throughout the country.

The main objectives of Agribusiness management are to: (i) improve household incomes from diversified farming and from off-farm activities; (ii) render farming systems resilient with the introduction of organic and low-input contract farming; (iii) facilitate the involvement of farmers groups in primary processing, quality enhancement and marketing; (iv) empower women through microfinance and micro-enterprises; and (v) convergence of government programmes and resources.

CHARACTERISTICS

Agriculture is the production, processing, marketing, and use of foods, fibers and byproducts from plant crops and animals. Agriculture was the key development that led to the rise of human civilization with the husbandry of domestic animals and plants (i.e., crops) creating food surpluses that enabled the development of more densely populated and stratified societies. The study of agriculture is known as agricultural science and it is also observed in certain species and termite.

Agriculture encompasses a wide variety of specialties and techniques, including ways to expand the lands suitable for plant rising, by digging water channels and other forms of irrigation. Cultivation of crops on arable land and the pastoral herding of livestock on rangeland remain at the foundation of agriculture. In the past century, there has been increasing concern to identify and qualify various forms of agriculture. In the developed world, the range usually extends between sustainable agriculture (e.g., permaculture or organic agriculture) and intensive farming (e.g., industrial agriculture).

Modern agronomy, plant breeding, pesticides and fertilizers and technological improvements have sharply increased yields from cultivation, but at the same time have caused widespread ecological damage and negative human health effects. Selective breeding and modern practices in animal husbandry such as intensive pig farming, and similar practices applied to the chicken have similarly increased the output of meat, but have raised concerns about animal cruelty and the health effects of the antibiotics, growth hormones, and other chemicals commonly used in industrial meat production.

The major agricultural products can be broadly grouped into foods, fibers, fuels, and raw materials. In the 21st century, plants have been used to grow biofuels, biopharmaceuticals, bioplastics and pharmaceuticals. Specific foods include cereals, vegetables, fruits, and meat. Fibers include cotton, wool, hemp, skills, and flax. Raw materials include lumber and bamboo. Other useful materials are produced by plants such as resins. Biofuels include methane, from biomass, ethanol, and biodiesel. Cut flowers, nursery plants, tropical fish and birds for the pet trade are some of the ornamental products.

In 2007, one-third of the world's workers were employed in agriculture. The services sector has overtaken agriculture as the economic sector employing the most people worldwide. Despite the size of its workforce, agricultural production accounts for less than 5 per cent of the gross world product (an aggregate of all GDP).

Agriculture played pivotal role in the development of human civilization. Until the industrial revolution, the vast majority of the human population laboured in agriculture. Development of agricultural techniques has steadily increased agricultural productivity and the widespread diffusion of these techniques during a time period is often called an agricultural revolution. A remarkable shift in the agricultural practices has occurred over the past century in response to new technologies.

Indian agriculture including crop and animal husbandry, fisheries, forestry and agro-processing provides the underpinnings of our food and livelihood security. Agriculture provides significant support for economic growth and social transformation of the country.

As one of the world's largest agrarian economies, the agriculture sector (including allied activities) in India accounted for 15.7 per cent of the GDP (at constant 2004-05 prices), in 2008-09, compared to 18.9 per cent in 2004-05, and contributed approximately 10.2 per cent of total exports during 2008-09. Notwithstanding the fact that the share of this sector in the GDP has been declining over the years, its role remains critical as it provides employment to around 52 per cent of the workforce.

The growth rate has been 8.6 per cent in 2010-11 and is expected to be around 9 per cent in the next fiscal year. The growth has been broad based with a rebound in the agriculture sector which is expected to grow around 5.4 per cent. However, food, inflation, higher commodity prices and volatility in global commodity markets have been a cause of concern underscoring the need of fiscal consolidation and stronger reserves.

Further, the agriculture sector growth in the first four years of the 11th Plan (2007-12) is estimated at 2.87 per cent. The foodgrain production went up to 232.1 billion tons from 218.1 billion tons in 2009-10. With a relatively good monsoon, the agriculture sector is expected to grow at 5.4 per cent during 2010-11. The rising food inflation and the critical role of agriculture underline the need for a larger investment in agriculture *en route* to the second green revolution.

Challenges of every kind are being faced by the agricultural sector for which serious policy methods are to be initiated to achieve the growth of 4 per cent in agriculture. Government has adopted methods like availability of wants, credit at reasonable rates for more private investments in the field of agriculture.

NEED OF HOUR — PROFITS — PASSION IN FARMING

If we needed further proof of the pernicious social consequences of persisting inflation, there are ample evidence to prove this. Umpteen studies have been carried out by rating agencies to this effect and reverberating country is facing soaring inflationary cost.

Indian households had added burden of ₹ 5.8 lakh crore over the last three fiscal years. And it is primarily owing to food inflation that annual private consumption spending grew to almost 17 per cent during this time from 14 per cent earlier. Spending mainly on eatables, low income groups with little or no disposable income — have been hardest by scorching food prices. Yet, there is marked official apathy — *vis-à-vis* the broader structural problems flood inflation highlights.

Take the fact that a bumper wheat harvest should normally bring cheer. But courtesy official unpreparedness compounded by export bans, ill-equipped granaries stretched beyond capacity. Foodgrain stocks exceed the manageable amount for warehouses countrywide. In some Food Corporation of India (FCI) godowns, wheat is being kept out in the open because covered facilities have been full up, thanks to non-clearance of grain. And due to lack of adequate policies, private capital has flowed towards building modern silos and storage.

We are in anomalous situation, 'problem of plenty', now co-exists with a psychology of want linked to high food costs. The case with fruits and vegetables is similar, courtesy inadequate cold chains, nearly 40 per cent goes waste annually even as shop prices of onions or potatoes soars high.

Given food prices are major inflationary trigger, supply side issues must be tackled urgently. That means embracing agricultural reforms in all its aspects — productivity, marketing and distribution. Only then we access the multifarious benefits of creating infrastructure raising output and introducing effective delivery systems that will supplement — or even replace, the PDS from where subsidized foodgrain routinely rots or gets siphoned off.

In this context, there has been a reassuring signal recently that the government plans to liberalize multi-brand retail. Greater private investment will help build capacity. Plus it will strike a blow against predatory middlemen in the supply chain who eat into farmers' incomes while inflating retail prices.

Private funds are critical to farming's overall modernization, whether for innovating with water-efficient irrigation, promoting research in agricultural inputs and transgenic crops or boosting agro-processing. In view of unviable farm sizes across India, policymakers of our country must incentivize cooperatives and contract farming. Where supply is concerned, let us lift barriers on transport and marketing of commodities.

Our antediluvian mandi system enriches commission agents, not growers who need direct, competitive access to processors and sellers. Finally, our country should discourage corruption spearheading rampantly for handing distribution towards well-targeted, personalized instruments like food coupons or cash transfers. That will bitterly ensure food gets to the needy even while giving them sense of agency and greater choice.

In recent years, the agricultural growth rate has tended to be lower than the population growth rate. This year the former is nearing the target of 4 per cent, but we still have very large per centage of undernourished children, women, and men. Poverty and destitution also remain stubborn. The Indian food security enigma rises from the mismatch between the grain mountains and the hungry millions. What are the prospects for ensuring food and nutrition security for a population that is expected to hit 1.4 billion by 2020, given the diminishing per capita availability of arable land and irrigation water and the expanding biotic and abiotic stresses?

Climate change will further compound our difficulties in achieving the balance between human numbers and the human capacity to produce the necessary. In addition, we will need a major effort at social engineering, involving Panchayat Raj Institutions (PRIs), Gram Sabha or Village Councils across the country to effect a small farm management revolution. Special programmes will be needed for women and young peasants. Packages of technology, services and public policies will have to be delivered in an integrated manner.

"Deliver as one" should become the norms for the interdepartmental functioning. Conservation, cultivation, consumption and commerce should become parts of an integrated system of biodiversity management. The bio-village paradigm of sustainable human security developed by Father of India's green revolution Dr. M.S. Swaminathan Research Foundation (MSSRF) should be widely adopted, so that every village becomes a bio-village. Similarly, every watershed should become a bio-industrial watershed, so that the job opportunities are created in the secondary and tertiary sectors of economic activity.

There are number of areas that need to be addressed for the next few years to accomplish country's goal which is eradication or reduction if not and hunger free India. They are reaping the demographic dividend. The National Commission on Farmers (2004-06) stressed the need for attracting and retaining educated youngsters in farming. The National Policy for Farmers placed before the Parliament in November 2007 depict the goal "to introduce measures which can help to attract and retain youth in farming and processing of farm products for higher value addition, by making farming intellectually stimulating and economically rewarding".

We are currently deriving very little demographic dividend in agriculture. On the other hand, the pressure of population on land is increasing and the size of the average farm holding is dipping below one hectare. Farmers are getting trapped in debt and as real estate rates continue to rise, the temptation to sell prime farmland for non-farm purposes is growing.

Over 45 per cent of farmers interviewed by the NSSO (National Sample Survey Organization) want to quit farming. Under these conditions, how are we going to persuade educated youngsters, including farm graduates to stay in villages and take to agriculture as a profession? How can youngsters earn a decent living in villages and help shape the future of India's agriculture sector? It will take a three-pronged strategy; we must improve the productivity and profitability of small holdings through appropriate technologies and market linkages. Enlarge the scope for the growth of agro-processing and agri-business.

Promote opportunities for the services sector to expand in a manner that will trigger the technological and economic upgradation of farm operations.

Yuva Kisans or young peasants can also help women's self-help groups manufacture and sell the biological software essential for sustainable agriculture. These would include biofertilizers, biopesticides and vermiculture composting.

A fishery graduate could promote both inland and marine aquaculture using low external input sustainable aquaculture techniques. Feed and seed are the important requirements for successful aquaculture and trained youngsters could promote their production at the local level. They could also train rural families in induced breeding of fish and spread quality and food safety literacy.

Similar opportunities exist in the fields of animal husbandry. Improved technologies can be introduced in small-scale poultry and dairy farming. The Codex Alimentarius (Latin word for 'food code') a set of internationally recognized standards for food safety could be popularized in the case of perishable commodities. For this, young farmers should establish gyan chaupals or village knowledge centres. Such centres would be based on the integrated use of the Internet, FM Radio and mobile telephony. For example, the artisan fishermen those fishing in tiny boats on a small scale or merely for subsistence could be empowered with information on wave heights and the location of fish shoals. Such techniques would help transform the lives of these families.

Another area is seawater as a solution. No discussion on food security can be complete without bringing in water security. There is an urgent need for a sustainable water security system with concurrent attention to two areas — supply augmentation and managing demand. The major sources of irrigation water are rainfall, rivers, tanks, reservoirs, and other surface water resources, groundwater, industrial and domestic effluents and seawater.

Seawater is almost 97 per cent of the global water resource and an important social asset. With the melting of Arctic and Antarctic ice, sea levels will go up with disastrous consequences. The tsunami of December 26, 2004 gave us a glimpse of this.

To augment supplies, we must harvest rainwater and store it carefully both above and below ground. We should also ensure that all waste water — industrial and domestic — is purified and recycled. Rainwater harvesting should become a way of life. Seawater is an invaluable resource for agriculture and aquaculture and seawater farming should become normal activity for coastal communities. Seawater farming involves an integrated approach to agro-forestry, horticulture, aquaculture and marine fisheries.

MSSRF is establishing a research and capacity building centre for seawater farming near Chidambaram in Tamil Nadu. Another one, for below sea-level farming is being developed in Kuttanad in Kerala.

The second element to water security is by managing demand. Unfortunately, water is generally measured in quantitative terms alone. There is not much interest in getting the best out of the available water by emphasizing the economy and efficiency of water use. These are great opportunities for minimizing demand through increased efficiency of water use in the agricultural and industrial sectors. We should launch a Water Literacy Movement using modern information and communication technologies to make economy and efficiency the bottom line of water use policies.

Another area which is of interest to the country is Food Consciousness by 2020 and if the above strategic plan is adopted through a fusion of political will, professional skill and people's participation, feeding a population of 1.4 billion with nutritious food will not be a difficult task. Fortunately, we have a large untapped production reservoir because of the wide gap between potential and actual yields in most of the farming systems. Therefore, we can safeguard our food technology divides and the male-female gender divide. Above all the proposed Food Security Bill, which confers on every citizen the right to food, will once again arouse consciousness of the fact that we live as guests of the green plants that convert sunlight into food, and of the farm women and men who cultivate them.

ROLE AND IMPORTANCE OF AGRICULTURE IN INDIAN ECONOMY

Agriculture is a very important sector for the sustained growth of the Indian economy. About 70 per cent of the rural households and 8 per cent of urban households are still principally dependent on agriculture for employment. Agriculture and allied sectors contribute one-fifth of GDP while about 65-70 per cent of the population is dependent on agriculture for their livelihood.

In terms of composition out of the total share of 15.7 per cent in GDP in 2008-09 for the agriculture and allied activities sector, agriculture alone accounted for 16.3 per cent of GDP followed by fishing at 0.8 per cent and forestry and logging at 0.7 per cent of GDP.

Since some three-quarters of the population live in rural areas, a majority of households thus depend principally on this sector. Though industrialization of the Indian economy has adversely affected the share of agriculture in the GDP, the fact cannot be ignored that India has undergone a series of successful agricultural revolutions — starting with the 'green' revolution in wheat and rice in the 1960s and 1970s, the 'white' revolution in milk to the 'yellow' revolution in oilseeds in 1980s. As a result, India has achieved self-sufficiency in agriculture.

Share of Agriculture in National Income

Year	Agriculture (in % terms)
1950-51	55
1970-71	44
1990-91	31
2000-01	26
2005-06	20
2010-11	15.7

Note: Agriculture includes agriculture, forestry and fishing.

Source: Economic Survey.

Figures provided by the Central Statistical Organization (CSO) reveal that in 1950-51 the share of agriculture in GDP was around 55 per cent and as the process of industrialization and economic growth gathered momentum under the FYP with manufacturing and service sector growing rapidly and agricultural sector limping along the percentage share of agriculture in GDP declined and reached a level of 20 per cent in 2005-06. According to some authorities, it could now be around 16-17 per cent.

Two important facts must be emphasized here: One is agriculture contributed a major share of the national income in India at one time. Secondly, the share of agriculture in national income however has been decreasing continuously while the shares of the manufacturing and service sectors are increasing.

Comparison can be made between the positions of agriculture in India with that in the other countries as regards the share of agriculture in national income. The backward and less developed countries that the working population engaged in agriculture is quite high.

Role of Agriculture in International Trade

Importance of Indian agriculture also arises from the role it plays in India's trade. Agricultural products – tea, sugar, oilseeds, tobacco, spices, etc. constituted the main items of exports of India. Broadly speaking, the proportion of agricultural goods which were exported came to 50 per cent of our exports, and manufactures, jute, cloth and sugar contribute another 20 per cent or so and the total comes to 70 per cent of India's exports. The Tenth Plan estimates that the agriculture contributes about 15 per cent of total export earnings. This has great significance for economic development. For, increased exports help the country to pay for the increased imports of machinery and raw materials.

ROLE OF AGRICULTURE IN INDIAN PLANNING SYSTEM

Till recently, Indian planning regarded higher investment as the kingpin of economic growth and in such framework resource allocation or investment pattern becomes main source of expressing the plan objectives and of implementing the actual planning strategy. Unfortunately, in India, regional variables did not form part of the overall planning strategy and all models that formed the basis of planning strategy and all models that formed the fundamentals of planning were sectoral in its features.

In the Five Year Plans, the planners of the economy have divided the developing economy into three core sectors — agriculture, industry and infrastructure. Here, the main thrust was focused on agriculture as India is agrarian country and 70 per cent of people depend on agriculture sector for their livelihood. But owing to gradual economic development and modernization, processes were closely monitored and evaluated periodically. Any country which aspires to become fully developed economy has to concentrate on the agriculture sector.

Further, Indian agriculture has passed through three different phases. One is conventional (traditional) agriculture, another is mixed agriculture (semi-subsistence) and third is pre-independence period. It has come a long way towards visualizing the tremendous potential for the commercial and export-oriented agri-business.

Initially, the agricultural economy in India suffered huge setbacks due to umpteen number of problems such as lack of appropriate technology, predominance of small and marginal farmers, high harvest losses and inadequate infrastructure facilities. Since the 1st FYP (1951-56) recognized the agriculture as a priority sector on whose development, the overall economic development of the nation was dependent.

The objectives of the **1st FYP** was to increase agriculture production through the intensive and extensive cultivation, besides transformation in the institutional framework through land reforms and cooperative form of organization, aid the process of agricultural development through the setting up of national extension and community projects so as to accelerate the process of community development.

The **2nd FYP** (1956-61) allocation to agriculture and allied sectors declined from 14.8 per cent under the First Plan to 11.7 per cent under the 2nd FYP and in absolute terms it approximately doubled from ₹ 290 crore to ₹ 549 crore. Further 2nd FYP aimed at diversified agricultural economy as it included the development of livestock and other allied sectors in addition to the increased crop production. Even though the outlay was higher as compared to the first five plans, the percentage of outlay for agriculture to the total outlay came down to 11 per cent as compared to 15 per cent in the 1st FYP but higher targets for different crops were fixed for the second plan period.

The **3rd FYP** (1961-66) was approximately the double the size of the 2nd FYP. The outlay on agriculture and allied sectors was doubled from ₹ 549 crore in the 2nd FYP to ₹ 1089 crore in the 3rd FYP as agriculture production being one of the most important limiting factors in the development of the Indian economy. The 3rd Plan once again aimed at the production of enough foodgrains to be self-sufficient and to produce enough commercial crops to meet the needs of the export and industry. During 3rd FYP, the government introduced Intensive Agricultural District Programme and the plan was conceived as first phase of a period of intensive development leading towards self-reliant and self-generating economy.

The **4th FYP (1969-74)** wherein the approach to this plan emphasized the necessity to create favourable economic conditions for the promotion of agriculture – systematic effort to extend the application of science and technology to agriculture and in general to intensify the agricultural programmes to the maximum possible extent in the selected areas. The priority programmes of the 4th FYP had the twofold objectives of maximizing production through a 5 per cent growth per annum.

And secondly to reduce the economic imbalances through involving as many people in the rural areas as possible in the development programmes. The production targets were to be achieved through intensive agriculture based on mechanization, use of improved varieties of seeds and judicious use of fertilizers and pesticides. Soil conservation measures were undertaken, plant protection measures provided to wide area of the land and consumption of fertilizers was aimed to cross three times the prior consumption.

The industrial programmes and policies for 4th FYP, however, conceived keeping in view the need to correct imbalances in the industrial structure and to bring about the maximum utilization of capacity already built up. Strangely village and small-scale agriculture business activities irrigation and flood control accounted for ₹ 2320 crore (14.7 per cent) and ₹ 1354 crore (8.6 per cent) respectively. The planners, therefore, rightly decided to increase resource allocation to agriculture under the 4th FYP in percentage terms as compared to that of under the 2nd and 3rd FYP.

5th FYP (1974-79): In this plan in the agriculture sector, the thrust was towards land development and improved agricultural horticultural and livestock practices. Special programmes meant for the rural poor sectors, like the drought-prone area programmes were given due emphasis.

6th FYP (1980-85): The Sixth FYP emphasized greater significance on agricultural and rural development with a view to tackling the problems of unemployment and poverty. Therefore, it was in the fitness of things that the agricultural sector was allocated larger resources than in the past. However, in percentage terms, the share of this sector was only marginally higher than that in the 5th FYP. Under the successive plans, the share of education in the public sector expenditure had declined and this trend was maintained under the 6th FYP also as education accounted for only 3.6 per cent of the total expenditure under it as against 4.4 per cent of the total expenditure under the 5th FYP.

Sectoral Allocation of Resources under the First Six Five Year Plans

(₹ in crore)

Head of Development	1st FYP (1951-56)	2nd FYP (1956-61)	3rd FYP (1961-66)	Annual Plans (1966-69)
Agriculture and Allied Sectors (in %)	290 14.8%	549 11.7%	1089 12.7%	1107 16.7%
Head of Development	**4th FYP (1969-74)**	**5th FYP (1974-79)**	**6th FYP (1980-85)**	**7th FYP (1985-90)**
Agriculture and Allied Sectors (in %)	2320 14.7%	4865 12.3%	5201 13.9%	10574 5.9%

Head of Development	8th FYP (1992-97)	9th FYP (1997-02)	10th FYP (2002-07)
Agriculture and Allied	22,467	37546	58933
Sectors (in %)	5.2%	4.4%	3.9%

Note: Figures of plan expenditure in this chapter is not strictly comparable to those given in the chapter on *'Financing of Plans'*.

Figures in brackets indicate percentage of the total.

Source: Economic Survey.

7th FYP (1985-90): There was paradigm shift in lieu of developmental strategy in favour of agriculture sector. Under the 7th FYP, relatively smaller allocations to industry and minerals 13.4 per cent evidently make it clear that new development in this country completely drifted away for more than two decades and provided the framework.

8th FYP: In this plan, agriculture including rural development, special areas programmes, and irrigation was allocated 22.2 per cent of the resources, i.e., more than one-fifth of total resources. There was increased emphasis on the agriculture and rural development was also due to the reason that this sector has greater employment potential as compared to the industrial sector and creation of employment opportunities happened to be the most important objective in the 8th FYP.

9th FYP: The agricultural sector including agriculture and allied activities, irrigation activities and flood control. Rural development and special area programmes has recently received greater attention on account of its importance from the point of view of maintaining food security and employment generation.

10th FYP: In this Plan, the agriculture sector defined to include agriculture and allied activities, irrigation and flood control. Rural development special areas programmes was allocated 20.1 per cent of the total outlay (i.e., one-fifth of total resources). In contrast, industry and minerals were allocated just 3.9 per cent of the total outlay. This is due to the reason that the State is withdrawing rapidly from the industrial sector giving more space to the private sector to expand its activities. In this Plan period, the agriculture accounted for 20.2 per cent of Plan Expenditure.

DISPARITIES IN AGRICULTURAL PLANNING

As far as regional disparities in agricultural sector is concerned, the disparities have increased over time with the states of Punjab and Haryana and parts of UP states pushing well ahead of others. This is due to the reasons that the success of the programme of High Yielding Varieties of seeds known as HYVP or New Agricultural Strategy) was largely limited to wheat growing areas. In fact, due to HYVP, the combined share of Punjab and Haryana in total output of foodgrains rose from 7.5 per cent in 1964-65 to 18.3 per cent in 2007-08 while these states account for a mere 4.4 per cent of the country's population (as per 2001 census) is 2006-07 productivity of foodgrains in Punjab was 4.017 kgs per hectare which was about two-and-a-half times and the national average of 1,756 kgs per hectare.

Productivity of foodgrains in Haryana was 3,393 kgs per hectare which is about twice the national average. Disparities in this respect would be clear from the fact that productivity in the state ranked third in terms of yield per hectare Tamil Nadu was only 2610 kgs per hectare in 2006-07. The prosperity of agriculture in Punjab and Haryana, in 2005-06 was impressive.

In 2005-06, gross irrigated area as percentage of gross cropped area was 97.6 per cent and 85.2 per cent respectively as against all-India average of 45.5 per cent. Likewise, fertilizer consumption per hectare of cropped area was 210.1 kgs in Punjab and 166.7 kgs in Haryana in 2005-06 as against the national average of 104.50 kgs in the same year.

OVERALL ACHIEVEMENT IN FIVE YEAR PLANNING

Let us now turn to the agricultural sector – performance of the First Plan on this front was satisfactory. Production of foodgrains rose from 54 million tons in 1950-51 to 64.8 million tons in 1955-56 against the target of 61.6 million tons. Achievement was well above target in the case of oilseeds and was marginally less than target in the case of cotton. However, it was considerably below the target in the case of jute and sugarcane. Target for foodgrains production was kept at 75 million tons in the Second Plan while achievement was 76 million tons.

The achievement was greater than the target for oilseeds and sugarcane while it was less than the target for Jute. Target for foodgrains production for the terminal year (1965-66) in the Third Plan was kept at 100 million tons but actual production was merely 72.0 million tons because 1965-66 happened to be drought year. The production in 1964-65 was 89 million tons. The performance of the Third Plan on the agricultural front can be considered quite unsatisfactory keeping in view the fact that achievements were below targets for most of the targets.

The Fourth Plan kept the target of 129 million tons for foodgrains production in 1973-74 while actual production was merely 104.66 million tons. Achievements were below targets in most of the commercial crops, like jute, sugarcane, cotton, oilseeds, etc. Taking agricultural production as a whole, the rate of growth was only 2.8 per cent per annum in the Fourth Plan against the target of 5 per cent per annum. The Draft Fifth FYP kept the target of 140.0 million tons for foodgrains production for the terminal year 1978-79. Target for sugarcane was kept at 170 million tons and for cotton at 80 lakh bales. However, the actual production of foodgrains production in 1978-79 was 131.90 million tons and of sugarcane and cotton was 151.7 million tons and 79.6 lakh bales respectively.

During the 6th FYP period, actual production of foodgrains rose to 152.4 million tons due to exceptionally good crops in 1983-84 against Plan target of 153.6 million tons. The production of foodgrains, however, declined to 146.2 million tons in 1984-85 that is in the terminal year of the Sixth Plan. The production of cotton jute and sugarcane also remained much below the Sixth Plan targets. The production target for oilseeds was however realized. The performance of agriculture during the Seventh Plan period was once again not very satisfactory.

Against foodgrains production, the actual production was only 171.0 million tons in the terminal year of the Plan. Under the 7th FYP while the production levels of oilseeds and jute were below the targets, the production targets for sugarcane and cotton were realized. In the terminal year of the Eighth Plan period, foodgrains output was 199.0 million tons against the target of 210 million tons.

Further the output of oilseeds, sugarcane, cotton, and jute also increased only at modest rates during the Eighth Plan period and foodgrains output rose to 212 million tons in the last year of Ninth Plan period while the output of oilseeds, cotton and jute did not register any growth. Output of sugarcane was only marginally higher in 2001-02 as compared to its output in 1996-97.

In line with the New Agriculture Policy 2000 which envisaged a growth rate exceeding 4 per cent per annum in the agricultural sector and Tenth Plan aimed at 4 per cent per annum growth. The demand for foodgrains was put at 236 million tons by the end of Plan, i.e., 2006-07 while the supply projection for foodgrains in that year made by the Planning Commission ranged from 225 million tons to 243 million tons. The actual production of foodgrains in 2006-07 was however only 217.3 million tons in

2007-08 and further to 233.9 million tons in 2008-09. However, the rate of growth of the agricultural sector fell from 4.7 per cent in 2007-08 to just 1.6 per cent in 2008-09 and is estimated to have fallen still further to only 0.2 per cent in 2009-10.

Thus, the importance of agriculture in the national economy is indicated by many facts. Further good crops implying large purchasing power with the farmers lead to greater demand for manufacturers and therefore better prices. In other words, prosperity of the farmers is also the prosperity of industries. Likewise bad crops lead to a depression in business. Generally, it is the failure in the agricultural farming that has led to failure of economic planning in particular periods.

Agricultural growth has direct impact on poverty eradication and it is also important factor in containing inflation, raising agricultural wages and for employment generation. Rural domestic savings are an important source of resource mobilization. Any change in the agricultural sector, positive or negative will have a multiplier effect on the entire economy. Horticulture, animal husbandry, dairy and fisheries have an important role in improving the overall economic conditions and health and nutrition of the rural masses.

AGRARIAN REFORMS AND GREEN REVOLUTION

Planning has contributed to agricultural development mainly in two ways. At the time of independence, conditions conducive to development in agriculture did not exist on account of the presence of exploitative land relations which permitted the landlords or zamindars to appropriate the economic surplus for their wasteful expenditure. Since tenants were subjected to the worst kind of exploitation, they hardly had any resources for investment in agriculture. Further they lacked the will for making any permanent improvements in the soil and the farm techniques since they knew that their efforts would benefit only the landlord.

Seeing a large surplus, the landlord would have increased the rent while the earnings of the tenants would have remained where they were. Hence, in the early phase of economic planning, the State paid attention to land reforms. No doubt, land reforms in this country were not properly carried out and failed to deliver the desired results. Nonetheless with all their limitations, land reforms did create congenial environment for agricultural development.

Since 1966 the main emphasis has been on the introduction of new technology for raising the agricultural productivity. This work was the first undertaken in some selected areas covered under intensive agricultural areas programme in the form of increased use of fertilizers along with high yielding varieties of seeds. This was followed by the High Yielding Varieties Programme (or the New Agricultural Strategy as it is called). The phenomenal increases registered in foodgrains production following the adoption of NAS resulted in what is known as green revolution. However, in the initial period, the benefits of green revolution were confined only to the wheat growing area of Punjab, Haryana and western UP state. Accordingly, it accentuated regional inequalities and in recent decades green revolution has spread to new crops and new regions.

11th FYP: The 11th Five Year Plan started on April 1, 2007 and covers the five year period 2007-12. The 11th FYP document starts on an optimistic note pointing to the robust economic growth registered in the Tenth Plan which was 7.8 per cent per annum (higher than the rate of growth registered to any other Plan). In fact, the last four years of the Tenth Plan recorded a rate of growth of as high as 8.6 per cent per annum making India one of the fastest growing economies of the world. However, according to the Plan, the major weakness in the economy is that the growth is not perceived as being sufficiently inclusive for many groups especially SCs, STs and minorities. Gender inequality also remains a pervasive problem and some of the structural changes taking place have an adverse effect on women. The lack of inclusiveness is borne out by data on several dimensions of performance.

As monitorable target of the 11th FYP sectoral target fixed for agriculture sector was to achieve a 9 per cent per annum rate of growth in the Tenth Plan (2002-07), the 11th FYP notes that although GDP from agriculture has more than quadrupled from ₹ 1,08,374 crore in 1950-51 to ₹ 4,81,547 crore in 2006-07 (both at 1999-2000 prices), the increase per worker has been rather modest. GDP per agricultural worker is currently around ₹ 2,000 per month which is only about 75 per cent higher in real terms than in 1950 compared to a fourfold increase in overall real per capital GDP.

"While slower growth of GDP in agriculture than non-agriculture is expected, the main failure has been the inability to reduce the dependence of the workforce on agriculture significantly by creating enough non-farm opportunities to absorb the labour surplus in rural areas and equipping those in agriculture to access such opportunities. In this context, it may be pointed out here that even growth of agricultural GDP decelerated from over 3.5 per cent per annum during 1981-82 – 1996-97 to only around 2 per cent per annum during 1997-98 – 2004-06 and 3.8 per cent in 2006-07. The Eleventh Plan hopes that some of the causes of poor agricultural growth are being reversed. Accordingly, it sets a target of 4 per cent growth in the agricultural sector. According to the Plan, achievement of this growth rate requires action in the following broad areas: bringing technology to the farmers, improving efficiency of investments, increasing systems support and rationalizing subsidies, diversifying and also protecting food security concerns, fostering inclusiveness through the group approach by which the poor will get better access to land, credit and skills.

In the field of technology, the Eleventh Plan identifies the immediate action. They include priority in agriculture. Research should be given to strategic research. Research priorities have to shift towards evolving cropping systems suited to various agro-climatic conditions and towards enhancing the yield potential in rainfed areas through the development of drought and pest resistant varieties.

The Indian Council for Agricultural Research (ICAR) needs to restructure accordingly and to increase its accountability. And state agricultural universities also need to be made more accountable and strengthened to develop, refine and promote location-specific technologies. Their teaching capacity also needs to be strengthened. Public expenditure research will need to increase from around 0.7 per cent of agriculture GDP at present to 1 per cent by end of 11th FYP.

To improve the efficiency of investments, the 11th FYP Plan proposes a number of steps to improve the efficiency of investments and increasing systems support particularly in the field of irrigation like improving the utilization of funds under AIBP (Accelerated Irrigation Benefit Programme) more emphasis on PIM (Participatory Irrigation Management) exploiting the abundant availability of groundwater in Assam, Bihar, Chattisgarh, Orissa and parts of Jharkhand, UP, and WB states.

As far as rationalizing subsidies is concerned, the Plan notes that the present unbalanced and irrational system of fertilizer subsidy is an important cause of deteriorating soil quality. It therefore calls for rationalizing subsidy across nutrients and also examine methods by which the delivery of some part of the presently huge subsidies can be transferred from fertilizer producers to farmers or group of farmers directly.

According to the 11th FYP, demand for foodgrain including for uses other than for direct human consumption is expected to grow at 2 per cent to 2.5 per cent per annum and livestock and horticulture at 4 per cent to 6 per cent per annum and 3 per cent to 4 per cent per annum respectively. Diversification towards horticulture and livestock therefore will have to be a very major element in the strategy. The Plan advocates a number of steps to improve the agricultural marketing system.

Given that 80 per cent of farmers are small and marginal, and increasingly female the 11th FYP advocates number of steps to improve their effective access to inputs, credit, extension services and output markets. The Plan argues that the best way to empower the poor is to encourage 'group approach' that is to encourage poor to function as a group rather than individuals.

In this context, it advocates redesigning the subsidies in the current schemes giving greater benefits to farmer groups rather than individuals, so as to incentivize group formation particularly amongst small, marginal and female farmers. To promote gender equity, the Plan advocates steps to ensure women's rights to land and infrastructure support.

We can say in this introductory chapter, you will be able to learn about the *abracadabra* of agri-business and its definition, interpretation and various shades of meanings. The major agricultural products can be broadly grouped into foods, fibers, fuels, and raw materials. In the 21st century, plants have been used to grow biofuels, biopharmaceuticals, bioplastics and pharmaceuticals. Specific foods include cereals, vegetables, fruits, and meat. Fibers include cotton, wool, hemp, skills, and flax. Raw materials include lumber and bamboo. Other useful materials are produced by plants such as resins. Biofuels include methane, from biomass, ethanol, and biodiesel. Cut flowers, nursery plants, tropical fish and birds towards for the pet trade are some of the ornamental products.

There are two aspects where agriculture sector is contributing its contribution to national income. One is agriculture contributed a major share of the national income in India at one time. Secondly, the share of agriculture in national income, however, has been decreasing continuously while the share of the manufacturing and service sectors are increasing.

Similarly at the international trade arena the agriculture is playing its pivotal role. Thus, importance of agriculture in the national economy is indicated by many facts. Further, good crops implying large purchasing power with the farmers lead to greater demand for manufacturers and therefore better prices. In other words, prosperity of the farmers is also the prosperity of industries. Likewise, bad crops lead to a depression in business. Generally, it is the failure in the agricultural farming that has led to failure of economic planning in particular periods.

Agricultural growth has direct impact on poverty eradication and it is also important factor in containing inflation, raising agricultural wages and for employment generation. Rural domestic savings are an important source of resource mobilization. Any change in the agricultural sector, positive or negative will have a multiplier effect on the entire economy. Horticulture, animal husbandry, dairy and fisheries have an important role in improving the overall economic conditions and health and nutrition of the rural masses.

GENERAL OVERVIEW OF INDIAN ECONOMY

Is India really shining? Or is it mere propaganda?

Some Encouraging Statistics

India is the second fastest growing major economy.

India is already the fourth largest economy in the world at Public-Private Participation (PPP).

During 2010, **India's Foreign Exchange** reserves touched the figure of US$ 277.04 billion, an increase of US$ 24.71 billion over same period last year, according to the Reserve Bank of India's Weekly Statistical Supplement.

India received **Foreign Direct Investment** (FDI) worth US$ 20.92 billion during April-December 2009, taking the cumulative amount of FDI inflows from August 1991 to December 2009 to US$ 127.46 billion, according to the Department of Industrial Policy and Promotion.

The total number of **Foreign Investment Institutions** (FIIs) came for registration was 1713 as on March 31, 2010.

Indian companies have gone **on a buying rampage**, with Tata Steel acquiring Corus, Mittal buying Arcelor and Tata also buy Jaguar and Land Rover from Ford.

The **Bombay Stock Exchange's value** has been consistently rising, currently worth 1.61 trillion dollars, the largest in South East Asia.

Unemployment ratio in the country has dropped by 2 per cent annually, and illiteracy and mortality rates have also been falling, indicating that India is not only growing but developing too.

India's poverty level is decreasing by 10 per cent annually.

Every year population in **India's middle class** segment **is increased** by 40,000,000 new members which show that the wealth is truly entering society.

The **number of billionaires** in the country was 3 in 1999; 23 in 2006; and now they are 48.

India ranks 49th among 133 countries in 2009-10 in the **global competitiveness index** (GCI) prepared by the World Economic Forum (WEF), an improvement of one position from last year and its performance is measured on 12 categories of GCI. Some of them are as follows:

Exports from India were worth US$ 16.09 billion in February 2010, 34.8 per cent higher than the level in February 2009, according to the Ministry of Commerce and Industry. India's imports during February 2010 were valued at US$ 25.05 billion representing a growth of 66.4 per cent over February 2009.

Foreign tourist arrivals in India during the month of February 2010 were 601,000, an increase of 9.9 per cent over February 2009.

Foreign exchange earnings during February 2010 were US$ 1.43 billion, an increase of 55.4 per cent over February 2009, according to data released by the Ministry of Tourism.

The **total telephone subscriber base** in the country crossed the 600-million mark to touch 600.69 million in February 2010, taking the overall tele-density to 51.05, according to the figures released by the Telecom Regulatory Authority of India (TRAI). Also the wireless subscriber base increased to 563.73 million.

According to data released by Society of Indian Automobile Manufacturers, the **cumulative production data** for April-February 2010 shows production growth of 24.34 per cent over same period last year. Passenger vehicles production crossed 2 million and two-wheelers' production touched almost 9.5 million.

According to the Gem and Jewellery Export Promotion Council, the **exports of gems and jewellery** from India including rough diamonds, rose by 10.48 per cent during April-February 2010 to touch US$ 28.84 billion.

The **Indian drug retail market** grew by a 29.24 per cent in value terms in October 2009 over the year ago period, more than double the average monthly revenue growth rate of 13-14 per cent in the recent past, as per market research firm ORG IMS.

India has **joined an elite group of six countries** which have successfully **decoded the human genome indigenously**. The discovery, which was announced by the Council of Scientific and Industrial Research (CSIR), will bring pharmaceutical companies a step closer to designing drugs accounting for the specific characteristics of the Indian physiology.

Merger and acquisition (M&A) activity involving Indian small and medium enterprises (SMEs) are on the rise. During the first two months of 2010, M&A transactions worth US$ 155 million have been concluded in the SME sector, up by 66 per cent over the US$ 93 million in transactions in the corresponding period of 2009, according to Venture Intelligence, a Chennai-based research firm focusing on M&A and PE transactions.

KEY FEATURES OF 11TH FIVE YEAR PLANNING (2007-12)

Main Points:

- To accelerate GDP growth from 8 per cent to 9 per cent.
- To reduce educated unemployment to below 5 per cent.
- To reduce IMR to 28 and maternal mortality rate to 1 per 1000 live births.
- A second green revolution is urgently needed to raise the growth of agricultural GDP to around 4 per cent.
- Reduction of poverty, aim to less than 10 per cent by 2011-12.
- Aim to provide essential services like education, health, clean drinking water, electricity.

Growth Target

Agriculture — 4 per cent per annum while industry — 10-11 per cent per annum and services — 9-11 per cent per annum.

Total Outlay: 36,44,718 crore (at 2006-07)/approx. 36 trillion.

Central Plan Outlay: 21,56,571 crore (at 2006-07)/approx. 21 trillion.

Outlay of States and Union Territories: 14,21,711 crore (at 2006-07)/approx. 14 trillion.

GDP Composition by Sector

Services: 62.6 per cent

Industry: 20 per cent

Agriculture: 17.5 per cent (2009 estimation)

Forex Reserves: US$ 285.1 billion (in the week ended January 15, 2010)

Cumulative Value of Exports: US$ 104,247 million (April-November, 2009)

Exports Commodities: Minerals, fuels, petroleum products, gems and jewellery, iron and steel, organic chemicals, nuclear reactors, heavy machinery.

Export Partners: US 12 per cent, UAE 10.8 per cent, China 5.1 per cent, Singapore 4.8 per cent, Hong Kong 3.7 per cent, UK 3.6 per cent (April 08-February 09)

Cumulative FDI Inflows: US$ 19.38 billion (April-November 2009)

Top Investing Countries: Mauritius, USA, Singapore, Cyprus, Japan (during April 2009 to October 2009)

Major Sectors Attracting Highest FDI Equity Inflows: Services Sector, Telecommunications, Housing and Real Estate, Agriculture Services, and Power (during April 2009 to October 2009).

(***Projected Source:*** *The Economic Times*)

Growing GDP

Contribution of Services - increased from 48 per cent to 62.6 per cent in 2009-10 (as on January 2010)

(**Projected Source:** India Brand Equity Foundation (IBEF))

Growing Exports

Cumulative Value of Exports: US$ 104,247 million (April-November, 2009)

Exports projected at $188.9 billion in 2009/10 (Eco Outlook for 2009-10)

(***Source:*** Ministry of Commerce & IBEF)

Growing Imports

Imports projected at $306 billion in 2009/10

Increasing Forex Reserves

Forex Reserves: US$ 285.1 billion (in the week ended January 15, 2010)

Steadily increasing Forex reserves offer adequate security against any possible currency crisis or monetary instability.

(***Source:*** Reserve Bank of India and India Brand Equity Foundation (IBEF)

Growing FDI Inflows

India is ranked second in AT Kearney's FDI Confidence Index (2007)

Electronic equipment, manufacturing and telecom have witnessed significant FDI inflow

- Provisional
- FDI inflows from August 1991 to December 2009 to US$ 127.46 billion, according to the Department of Industrial Policy and Promotion.

(***Source:*** Department of Commerce.)

Increasing Per Capita Income

Per Capita Income (constant prices) in 2008-09: US$ 653.13

(***Source:*** India Brand Equity Foundation (IBEF) and Economic Survey 2007-08)

India Inc. Investing Overseas

Main Destinations: China, UAE, UK, North America is emerging as a destination.

- Exports to US

  India's Trade with USA

  USD Billion

  Imports from US

  (***Source:*** Department of Commerce, Govt. of India)

- Export Partners: US 12 per cent, UAE 10.8 per cent, China 5.1 per cent, Singapore 4.8 per cent, Hong Kong 3.7 per cent, UK 3.6 per cent (April'08-February'09)

  Major Items Exported to USA

  (***Source:*** US Department of Commerce)
- Major Items Imported from USA

  (***Source:*** US Department of Commerce)

Share in GDP

- Agriculture is one of the strongholds of the Indian economy and accounted for 15.7 per cent of the country's gross domestic product (GDP) in 2008-09.
- 60 per cent of population still depends on agriculture for their livelihood.
- Occupied 43 per cent of India's geographical areas.
- According to the Centre for Monitoring Indian Economy (CMIE), crop production is expected to rise by 1.7 per cent during FY 10 and food grain production is expected to increase by 1.1 per cent.
- All other sectors are growing at much faster rate.

India has become the world's largest producer across a range of commodities due to its favourable agro-climatic conditions and rich natural resource base.

India is the largest producer of coconuts, mangoes, bananas, milk and dairy products, cashew nuts, pulses, ginger, turmeric and black pepper.

It is also the second largest producer of rice, wheat, sugar, cotton, fruits and vegetables.

According to the government's agri-trade promotion body, Agricultural and Processed Food Products Export Development Authority (APEDA), India's exports of agricultural and floricultural products, fruits and vegetables, animal products and processed food products was worth US$ 7.98 billion in 2008-09, an increase of 13.88 per cent from US$ 7.01 billion in 2007-08.

India's agri-export turnover is expected to double in the next five years, according to APEDA. Agri-export turnover is set to rise to nearly US$ 18 billion by 2014.

At present, around 70 per cent of the country's agricultural and processed food exports are to developing countries in the Middle East, Asia, Africa and South America.

The National Cooperative Development Corporation (NCDC), a statutory corporation under the Union Ministry of Agriculture, is to take up various cooperative development programmes in the country.

In Budget 2010-11, the Finance Minister, Mr. Pranab Mukherjee has made the following announcements for the agriculture sector. US$ 88.02 million is provided to increase the Green Revolution to the eastern region of the country comprising Bihar, Chattisgarh, Jharkhand, Eastern UP, West Bengal and Orissa.

US$ 66.02 million has been provided to organize 60,000 pulses and oilseed villages in rainfed areas in 2010-11 and provide an integrated intervention for water harvesting, watershed management and soil health to improve productivity of the dry land farming areas.

Banks have been consistently meeting the targets set for agricultural credit flow in the past few years. For the year 2010-11, the target has been set at US$ 82.53 billion.

In addition to the 10 mega food park projects already being set up, the government has decided to set up five more.

External commercial borrowings are available for cold storage for preservation or storage of agricultural and allied products.

(***Source:*** The *Economic Times*, India Brand Equity Foundation, Reserve Bank of India and Ministry of Commerce)

Government Initiatives

India is expected to spend around US$ 14.05 million for the development of organic spices, particularly turmeric, chilly, and ginger, by 2012.

The government has already approved 60 Agricultural Export Zones (AEZs).

The National Food Security Mission was launched in 2007, with an outlay of US$ 979.51 million over the 11th Plan (2007-2012). It aims at enhancing the production of rice, wheat and pulses by 10 million tons, 8 million tons and 2 million tons respectively, by the end of the 11th Plan.

Services related to agro and allied sectors have been thrown open to 100 per cent foreign direct investment (FDI) through the automatic route.

The Cabinet has approved 2 per cent interest subsidy on bank loans taken by farmers. The subsidy would cost the exchequer about US$ 826 million in the fiscal year 2009-10.

Indian agriculture still suffers from:

- Monsoon based agriculture (60 per cent agriculture depend on rain).
- Poor productivity (small landholding, soil quality).
- Falling water levels.
- Expensive credit.
- A distorted market.
- Many intermediaries who increase cost but do not add much value.
- Laws that stifle private investment.
- Prices fluctuations.
- Poor infrastructure (loss of ₹ 500 billion/year).
- Produce that does not meet international standards.
- Inappropriate research.

HOW CAN AGRICULTURE SECTOR BE STRENGTHENED?

- Agricultural marketing (market information, sorting-grading of the produces and products, improvement in transportation) and setting up of cooperative institutions, Apni mandi, Big Bazar etc.
- Retailing.
- Wasteland development (e.g., Indira Gandhi Canal).

- Risk management (watershed, linkage of rivers).
- Farm extension (agriclinic, IVLP, lab to land programme).
- Technological measures, Biological (seed, fertilizer) and Mechanical innovations (tractors, harvesters) etc.
- Further encouragement of contract farming and finance.
- Reduction of cost of production, aversion of natural hazards and social uncertainty to maximum extent.
- Regulating the market fluctuation and ensuring constant flow of market intelligence reports.
- Shift from less profitability to more profitability of crops.
- Increase in exports and competitiveness in both domestic and international markets.
- Protecting environment and creating congenial and favourable conditions for combing agriculture-fishery-forestry-livestock.
- More crops for diversification to existing cropping system that will lead to horizontal diversification.
- But in vertical diversification, various other downstream activities which could be referred to as vertical diversification.
- Further intensification of agriculture.

CONCLUSION

Major Areas of Reforms Needed

Business environment: Lowering the barriers to entrepreneurship; ending reservation of products for SSI; need for bankruptcy law, faulty practices; easing of service sector; FDI restrictions and more privatization of public sector enterprises.

Financial sector: More liberalization and privatization of public sector banks.

Infrastructure: Electricity reforms to be speeded up transport. More private sector involvement.

Public Finances: Better targeting of subsidies.

GST Education: Higher public expenditure on primary and education. Addressing financing of higher education.

Modern agriculture: Condition to produce surpluses in order to enhance economic growth.

FINAL NOTE

If these problems are solved, then the future for India looks bright. India might well become one of the superpowers of the 21st Century India — A country with potentials for sustaining development.

GENERAL OVERVIEW ON INDIAN AGRICULTURE

Agriculture is the mainstay of the Indian economy. Agriculture and allied sectors contribute nearly 17.8 per cent and 17.1 per cent of Gross Domestic Product (GDP of India) during 2007-08 and 2008-09 respectively. The agricultural output, however, depends on monsoon as nearly 55.7 per cent of area sown is dependent on rainfall.

An all-time record in production of foodgrains of 233.88 million tons is estimated in 2008-09 as per 4th Advance Estimates. This is about 13.10 million tons more than last year's production of foodgrains. The production of rice is estimated at 99.15 million tons which is about 2.46 million tons more, production of wheat is estimated at 80.58 million tons which is 2.01 million tons more, production of coarse cereals is estimated at 39.48 million tons which is 1.27 million tons more and production of pulses is estimated at 14.66 million tons which is about 0.99 lakh tons more than the production during 2007-08.

The sugarcane production is estimated at 2,712.54 lakh tons which is about 769.34 lakh tons less than the production during 2007-08. Cotton production is estimated at 231.56 lakh bales (of 170 kg. each) which is 27.28 lakh bales more than the production during 2007-08. Jute and mesta production during 2008-09 is estimated at 104.07 lakh bales (of 180 kg each) which is about 8.04 lakh bales less than the production during 2007-08.

The total area coverage under foodgrains in 2008-09 has been reported as 123.22 million hectares against 124.07 million hectares in 2007-08. The area under rice is estimated at 453.52 lakh hectares which is significantly higher about 1,437 lakh hectares. However, the area coverage under wheat during 2008-09 estimated at 278.77 lakh hectares is slightly lower by around 1.62 lakh hectares. The total area coverage under coarse cereals during 2008-09 is estimated at 276.17 lakh hectares which is slightly lower by 8.64 lakh hectares as compared to 2007-08. The increase in Minimum Support Price (MSP) in 2008-09 over 2007-08 amongst cereals has ranged between 8.0 per cent wheat to 52.6 per cent (ragi). The percentage increase in case of paddy (common) is 31.8 per cent. In case of pulses, the increase has ranged between 8.1 per cent (gram) and 48.2 per cent (urad and moong).

Centrally Sponsored Scheme on National Food Security Mission has been launched in the country to enhance the production of rice, wheat and pulses by 10, 8 and 2 million tons respectively by the end of the 11th Plan. The Mission covers 312 districts in 17 States and has become operational from Rabi 2007-08. The focused and target oriented technological intervention under NFSM has made a significant impact since inception which is reflected by the fact as per the third advance estimate of 2008-09, the production of rice has raised to a level of 99.37 million tons thus depicting increase of 2.68 million tons when compared to 2007-08 and 6.02 million tons against 2006-07. Similarly, the situation is also promising in case of wheat, wherein the production of wheat showing an increase of 2.76 million tons over the last year. Consequently, as per the third advance estimate of 2008-09, the production of wheat is estimated to the level of 77.63 million tons which is 1.82 million tons more than 2006-07. In case of pulses, the production was recorded at 14.20 million tons during 2006-07. Accordingly, as per the third advance estimate of 2008-09, the production of pulses is estimated at 14.18 million tons, which is almost a stagnated production trend when compared to 2006-07.

The Union Government has constituted a National Rainfed Area Authority (NRAA) on 03-11-2006 to give focused attention to the problem of the rainfed areas of the country. The Authority is an advisory, policy making and monitoring body charged with the role of examining guidelines in various existing schemes and in the formulation of new schemes including all externally aided projects in this area.

A scheme of debt waiver for small and marginal farmers and debt relief for other farmers has been announced by the Government in the Union Budget for 2008-09. Against the target of ₹ 2,25,000 crore for agriculture credit flow for 2007-08, the achievement was ₹ 2,43,569 crore. Agricultural Extension has been strengthened and Agricultural Technology Management Agencies (ATMAs) have been set up in 565 districts by the end of 2007-08.

Under NHM, an area of about 8.25 lakh hectares has been brought under horticulture crops, 1.17 lakh hectares of senile plantations have been rejuvenated and 1710 new nurseries have been set up since launching of NHM in 2005. An area of about 6 lakh hectares has been covered under the Scheme of Micro Irrigation since it was launched in 2006. Current year's target is coverage of 4 lakh hectares.

REASONS FOR LOW AGRICULTURE PRODUCTIVITY

An inquiry into their work attains significance, for modern economic theory does not know how to accommodate dichotomies in an economy, such as the rural-urban divide or the formal-informal separation, in a comprehensive manner.

An increase in quantity and/or quality of land or an increase in quantity and/or quality of labour would increase the social surplus. Alternatively, a reduction in the costs would also lead to a rise in the social surplus. Another perspective, is that of social division of labour. It points out that the entire population in a country is socially divided between villages (*rural*) and towns (*urban*). Largely, the rural population engaged in agricultural activities and the urban population involved in manufacturing activities. As long as adequate land and labour was available, agricultural production would go unhindered.

Also, an increase in agricultural surplus meant that there was more raw facilitated by an increase in agricultural surplus, would provide additional incomes to the labour in the urban areas which also would be spent on consumption. In this manner, an increase in agricultural surplus would foster economic growth via increase in income and consumption, which would motivate an increase of production in the following period. In short, the presence of a sizable agricultural surplus was necessary for market towns and cities to grow, i.e., for urbanization. However, it will be shown below that the presence of agricultural surplus alone is not sufficient for growth to take place in the rural areas.

The interaction between the villages and towns signifies one of the "oldest and most revolutionary division of labour: the fields on one hand and the activities described as urban on the other". Such migration of people and the disproportionate attention received by the towns led to a drain of wealth from the countryside to the towns.

This policy measure was based on the state's notion of a peasant. The peasant is looked upon as a slave of the state. Rural life is made out to be the hardest, most troublesome and contemptible possible because rural dwellers are reserved for work only fit for animals. When a peasant tills the soil himself, it is a token of his poverty and his usefulness. Because of such a negative view, the state had of rural dwellers/agriculture, Quesnay argued that "of all the occupations by which gain is secured, none is better than agriculture, none more profitable, and none more delightful.

In fact, primary objective underlined here is the importance of agriculture as an important sector in economic growth. This objective was able to convincingly show the demerits of a growth policy which favours a particular class – in this case, it was the urban manufacturers. One of the primary contributions of economists of yesteryears to economic theory was the depiction of the economy as a circular flow. This implied that the economy was an interconnected system. Therefore, a disproportionate flow of wealth in one sector at the cost of the other sectors would ultimately result in economic ruin.

Hence, many economists maintained that it was essential for wealth, contained in the urban or manufacturing sector, to flow back into agriculture, so that production of food and raw materials could take place in the following period of production. By highlighting the interdependence in an economy, specifically in the production process, economists were able to show that, the neglect of rural sectors/ agriculture would prove detrimental to the entire economy in the long run. In fact, as even Smith notes, "The inhabitants of a city, it is true, must always ultimately derive their subsistence, and the whole materials and means of their industry from the country.

From the preceding discussion, it becomes clear that agricultural surplus, which arises mainly from the rural sector, is a necessary condition for overall economic growth and prosperity. However, it is crystal clear that sustained growth can only take place if the social surplus which is produced by the agricultural sector, in the form of landlords' rents and entrepreneurs' profits, flow back to the rural areas. However, as pointed out earlier, the presence of a large agricultural surplus is not sufficient to attain, what is now known as "inclusive growth".

From the works of economists, it becomes clear that we need to examine the channels through which the rising incomes of the urban populace flow into the rural sector. In other words, it calls for a detailed study of the way in which the commodities as well as the people circulate between the rural and urban sector — the location of markets, the availability of good infrastructure, the number of intermediaries, the nature of production undertaken, the structure of earnings, the employment situation — which has been attempted at through the concept of the intersectoral terms of trade. However, this interaction or "struggle" between the rural and urban areas is much more complex that it calls for a far richer analysis.

Further, the interdependence in the production structure of an economy, the prevalent economic theory divides the economy into smaller parts, and studies them in isolation. That is, agricultural economics, industrial economics, urban economics, etc. are considered to be legitimate areas of independent inquiry. This is one cause for concern.

Another cause for concern is that the mainstream neoclassical/marginalist theory ascribes undue importance to the sphere of exchange, at the cost of almost a complete neglect of production structures and conditions. Whereas, only a study of production will throw light on the actual producers, their relation to the employer, the conditions of work, the compulsion to work, their incomes, etc.

Production structure, in mainstream economic theory, pertains to market structure. Issues pertaining to property rights, role of gender, role of caste, environment, common property resources, technological change, unorganized markets, etc. are not incorporated in the core study of microeconomics and macroeconomics; instead, these extremely significant aspects of economies are extensively taught and researched separately — law and economics, feminist economics, social exclusion, environmental economics, growth theory, etc.

Basically, the crucial element of interdependence present in an economy, at various levels, have been neglected by mainstream economic theory. Owing to such misguided tools, it becomes extremely difficult to understand an economy where around 60 per cent of the population is employed in agricultural activities and where around 90 per cent of the economy falls under the unorganized sector, let alone frame policies!

So, what is the way forward? The major change has to occur in the way economics is taught across India. A narrow focus on microeconomics and macroeconomics does not aid in making sense of the changes nor does it help in understanding the structure of the Indian economy.

First, the curriculum should be tailored in such a way that non-mainstream approaches to economics are included. Secondly, research should adjust to the problems thrown up by the Indian society and economy at large; for, India cannot afford to do research which merely copies the West. Third, economics education should pay more attention to tools such as village studies and case studies, which aid in understanding the production process and consumption structure in a context-dependent manner. Last of all, it must be remembered that economic theory is and should ultimately be a servant of economic policy.

Land acquisition spree curbing agriculture production

India's 1.5 per cent or more than 21 lakh hectares net sown area between 1990 and 2003 have gone to non-farm activity. The actual figures could be much higher. If we accept 21 lakh hectares of crop land which is diverted to non-agricultural uses and if this area was brought under wheat, then it would amount to a mind-boggling 57 lakh tons of produce, which could have fed more than 43 million hungry people every year. For instance, in Uttar Pradesh, 68.6 per cent land is cultivated and 31.4 per cent land is under non-farm uses. Only seven per cent land is under forest, when according to forest policy there should be one-third forest cover for healthy environment.

Adverse environmental impact is now reflected in falling yield and increasing other fallow and current fallow land as it is becoming uneconomical to cultivate. For example, according to Economic Survey reports and few monthly Economic Monthly Status reports in Sultanpur, Pratapgarh, Lucknow and Unnao districts, other and current fallow lands have increased up to 15.0 per cent. In UP, cereal production was 41.8 million metric tons in 2001-02 which has fallen to 37.6 million metric tons in 2004-05 due to land degradation.

In Central region of UP the growth of land put to non-agricultural use in rural areas has risen to 19.1 per cent during 2001-08. Similarly, growth rate of land put to non-agricultural uses in Bundelkhand has gone up to 17.6 per cent in rural areas. In Lucknow division, we find that during 2004-05 from an area of 2420134 hectare, the production was 4958114 metric tons, while during 2005-06 the area decreased to 2314603 hectare and with it the production also decreased to 4721101 metric tons.

Therefore, it is most essential to identify the non-agricultural infertile land through satellite imageries and on the basis of data the area available should be compulsorily utilized for urbanization. Million plus cities should not be allowed to further grow by putting ban on expansion of industries or any kind of activities which are not directly required for the cities. In this way, urbanization would grow in unurbanized areas and thus barren waste lands would be easily available for urban use.

Agricultural land should not be fallowed at any cost to be used for non farm activities. There should be strict check and control on the basis of clear-cut formulated policies at the state and local level so that an all-round sustainable development should be achieved and that too within a short period of time.

If at all it is so essential to acquire the agricultural land, then on the basis of average cost of the produce at present and future prices, it should be calculated for 30 years and paid to farmers every year. During 30 years, farmers would be able to adopt non-farm livelihood as it is already in practice in Haryana State.

The increasing size of land put to non-agricultural uses and recently decline in net area sown in rural areas is an indication that the prime agricultural land is fast being encroached by fringes of towns and cities and in due course of time they would become the part of urban land.

Earlier land put to non-agricultural uses was generally meant that the land is being used as a common land for thrashing the harvested crops, exhibition grounds, playgrounds and other amenities and it was well within eight percent of the geographical area. Now with the beginning of the 21st century, it is especially found that around some of the fast growing cities and towns a large chunk of fertile land is being purchased and left by the industrialists, colonizers and individual entrepreneurs for future use as urban land. It is generally found that the expansion of cities is taking place on commercially viable areas ignoring the importance of environment and land meant for cultivation purposes.

Around every city and town and in every district, there are plenty of wastelands, which could have been brought under urbanization if there was any such law to restrict and spare the agricultural land and also to protect environment. The farmers on urban fringes are compelled and lured to sell their land to urban people and they loose their centuries old traditional livelihood from farming forever. Farmers are left only with their dwellings and it is found that once they become landless, for generations they do not become capable to earn their proper livelihood from non-farm occupations.

Mostly they work as casual labourers in their neighbourhood of city and their socio-economic condition remain deplorable for decades together.

It is an interesting study to survey few villages and their households, enquiring about the value of land received and its utilization, their changing occupation and income and their overall socio-economic and living conditions. This would guide us how to control the agricultural land brought to non-agricultural uses and how to plan the rehabilitation of agricultural farmers and their families before the city encroaches in an unplanned manner.

SUMMARY

India is the seventh largest country in geographical level and second largest country in population wise and twelfth largest country in economy-wise. The economy of India is as diverse as it is large, with a number of major sectors including manufacturing industries, agriculture, textiles and handicrafts, and services but more than 75 per cent of population maintaining their livelihood in agriculture.

Agriculture is developing agrarian economy in the world characterized by high population growth, abundant natural resources optimal rate of capital formation with average standard of living that makes the country's economy so radiant and vibrant. The primary **sector of Indian economy** and **agriculture** along with the ancillary sectors like **forestry, horticulture, and fishing** employed over 50 per cent of the country's total population.

Although in the GDP the share of **agriculture** is constantly falling, still it remains the largest economic sector and plays a major role in the socio-economic development of India. In India, the state governments are responsible for the output of **agriculture** and the financial policies are formulated by the central government. India is the largest producer in the world of milk, cashew nuts, coconuts, tea, ginger, turmeric and black pepper.

Agriculture encompasses a wide variety of specialties and techniques, including ways to expand the lands suitable for plant rising, by digging water channels and other forms of irrigation. Cultivation of crops on arable land and the pastoral herding of livestock on rangeland remain at the foundation of agriculture. In the past century, there has been increasing concern to identify and quality various forms of agriculture. In the developed world, the range usually extends between sustainable agriculture (e.g., permaculture or organic agriculture) and intensive farming (e.g., industrial agriculture).

QUESTIONS

1. Describe salient features and basic characteristics of Indian agricultural economy.
2. Explain in brief the key role of Agricultural Economy in developing countries and with special reference to Indian context.
3. What was the achievement of agriculture sector during Planning period?
4. Enunciate essence of Agrarian Reform and Green Revolution.

ooo

CHAPTER 2

RELEVANCE OF AGRIBUSINESS MANAGEMENT

Relevance of Agriculture Business Management

Overview of Indian Agriculture: Bird's Eye View

Career Options in Agriculture Business Management

About the Course Curriculum Course Contents of Agribusiness Management

Optional Courses Offered in Agribusiness Management

Institutions Offering Courses in Agribusiness Management

Courses Offered by Agriculture Universities

How this Course Curriculum can be Studied?

RELEVANCE OF AGRICULTURE BUSINESS MANAGEMENT

For any living being, food is the basic necessity. As the societies grew from Stone Age, agriculture became an important component of the sources of food. Till today, it is the most important source of food. Agriculture has gained further importance by becoming a business and a part of economy. Therefore, there is a requirement of formal education in the field of agriculture. MBA in Agribusiness Management is a great option for individuals seeking career in agriculture. Before entering this field, it is often helpful to have a background in science. Students of life science often find MBA in agribusiness management as a great option to continue in their area of interest.

Agribusiness management is not limited to only farm production and processing, it extends in tillage, supplying of agriculture inputs, improved growing techniques, storage, labelling, transportation and marketing of agriculture products. Advancement in science and biotechnology has further increased the importance of agribusiness management. Now, there are also more choices of seeds, fertilizers, pesticides, etc. thus, this complexity has to be managed well. The management of this complexity is achieved by agribusiness management. The area of export of agricultural products and government policy is well managed in agribusiness management.

Agribusiness sector has evolved into a huge sector including fertilizer manufacturing, import-export of agricultural products, pesticides production and usage, manufacturing of agricultural machinery, food retailing, agricultural insurance, horticulture and the list goes on. This tremendous growth gives opportunity to people interested in agriculture sector. Agriculture is being globalized extensively. Therefore, MBA in Agribusiness Management becomes an interesting option.

Entrepreneurs in the field of agriculture are evolving and contributing a good chunk of share in global economy. The work is not just profit but also environmental concerns, a responsibility to eradicate hunger, give a new light to farmers and help government in forming agriculture-friendly policies. Agribusiness management also involves a strong line of planning which includes the future lines of action depending on past experience and present trends. A sound organization makes the growth stable and makes the objective achievable. Research and finance are other obvious areas where the reach of agribusiness management is there.

Agribusiness is a valuable extension of a standard business degree in many markets, and offers students a chance to learn about public policy, business models, agribusiness marketing, and the basics of agricultural economics. Agricultural business and economics help to organize business processes and procedures for agribusiness firms in accordance with federal and state guidelines. Students completing an agribusiness degree may also receive hands on training through a cooperative work placement program or internship as part of their educational career. Each degree program can continue into graduate studies or specializations for research.

Agricultural business professionals can pursue a wide range of careers in Agricultural Economics, Agricultural Business and Business Administration. Even though a standard business degree offers a strong foundation for a career in this growing industry, the specializations with an agribusiness degree enable students to learn about natural resource economics, production management, farm and ranch management, and commodity trading. Students who wish to pursue a specialization beyond the standard agribusiness degree program can choose areas of agricultural management, international agriculture, or agricultural supply.

OVERVIEW OF INDIAN AGRICULTURE: BIRD'S EYE VIEW

India ranks second worldwide in farm output. Agriculture and allied sectors like forestry, logging and fishing accounted for 15.7 per cent of the GDP in 2009-10, employed 52.1 per cent of the total workforce, and despite a steady decline of its share in the GDP, is still the largest economic sector and a significant piece of the overall socio-economic development of India. Yields per unit area of all crops have grown since 1950, due to the special emphasis placed on agriculture in the five-year plans and steady improvements in irrigation, technology, application of modern agricultural practices and provision of agricultural credit and subsidies since the Green Revolution in India. However, international comparisons reveal the average yield in India is generally 30 per cent to 50 per cent of the highest average yield in the world. Indian states like UP, Punjab, Haryana, MP, AP, West Bengal and Maharashtra, are key agricultural contributing states of India.

India receives an average annual rainfall of 1,208 millimeters (47.6 in) and a total annual precipitation of 4000 billion cubic meters, with the total utilizable water resources, including surface water and groundwater amounting to 1123 billion cubic meters. 546,820 square kilometers (211,130 sq. kms) of the land area, or about 39 per cent of the total cultivated area, is irrigated. India's inland water resources including rivers, canals, ponds and lakes and marine resources comprising the east and west coasts of the Indian Ocean and other gulfs and bays provide employment to nearly six million people in the fisheries sector. In 2008, India had the world's third largest fishing industry.

India is the largest producer in the world of milk, jute and pulses, and also has the world's second largest cattle population with 175 million animals in 2008. It is the second largest producer of rice, wheat, sugarcane, cotton and groundnuts, as well as the second largest fruit and vegetable producer, accounting for 10.9 per cent and 8.6 per cent of the world fruit and vegetable production respectively. India is also the second largest producer and the largest consumer of silk in the world, producing 77,000 million tons in 2005.

Slow agricultural growth is a concern for policymakers as some two-thirds of India's people depend on rural employment for a living. Current agricultural practices are neither economically nor environmentally sustainable and India's yields for many agricultural commodities are low. Poorly maintained irrigation systems and almost universal lack of good extension services are among the factors responsible. Farmers' access to markets is hampered by poor roads, rudimentary market infrastructure, and excessive regulation.

India's population is growing faster than its ability to produce rice and wheat. The low productivity in India is a result of several factors. According to the World Bank, India's large agricultural subsidies are hampering productivity-enhancing investment. While overregulation of agriculture has increased costs, price risks and uncertainty, governmental intervention in labour, land, and credit markets are hurting the market. Infrastructure and services are inadequate.

Further, the average size of land holdings is very small, with 70 per cent of holdings being less than one hectare in size. The partial failure of land reforms in many states, exacerbated by poorly maintained or non-existent land records, has resulted in sharecropping with cultivators lacking ownership rights, and consequently low productivity of labour. Adoption of modern agricultural practices and use of technology is inadequate, hampered by ignorance of such practices, high costs, illiteracy, slow progress in implementing land reforms, inadequate or inefficient finance and marketing services for farm produce and impracticality in the case of small land holdings.

The allocation of water is inefficient, unsustainable and inequitable. The irrigation infrastructure is deteriorating. Irrigation facilities are inadequate, as revealed by the fact that only 39 per cent of the total cultivable land was irrigated as of 2010, resulting in farmers still being dependent on rainfall, specifically the monsoon season, which is often inconsistent and unevenly distributed across the country.

The low productivity in India is a result of the following factors:

- According to World Bank, Indian Branch: Priorities for Agriculture and Rural Development, "India's large agricultural subsidies are hampering productivity-enhancing investment. Overregulation of agriculture has increased costs, price risks and uncertainty. Government intervenes in labour, land, and credit markets. India has inadequate infrastructure and services". World Bank also says that the allocation of water is inefficient, unsustainable and inequitable. The irrigation infrastructure is deteriorating. The overuse of water is currently being covered by overpumping aquifers, but as these are falling by foot of groundwater each year, this is a limited resource.
- Illiteracy, general socio-economic backwardness, slow progress in implementing land reforms and inadequate or inefficient finance and marketing services for farm produce.
- Inconsistent government policy. Agricultural subsidies and taxes often changed without notice for short-term political ends.
- The average size of land holdings is very small (less than 20,000 m²) and is subject to fragmentation due to land ceiling acts, and in some cases, family disputes. Such small holdings are often overmanned, resulting in disguised unemployment and low productivity of labour.
- Adoption of modern agricultural practices and use of technology is inadequate, hampered by ignorance of such practices, high costs and impracticality in the case of small land holdings.
- Irrigation facilities are inadequate, as revealed by the fact that only 52.6 per cent of the land was irrigated in 2003-04, which result in farmers still being dependent on rainfall, specifically the monsoon season. A good monsoon results in a robust growth for the economy as a whole, while a poor monsoon leads to a sluggish growth. Farm credit is regulated by NABARD, which is the statutory apex agent for rural development in the subcontinent. At the same time, over-pumping made possible by subsidized electric power is leading to an alarming drop in aquifer levels.

Status of Agriculture in India

In 2007-08, India achieved a record food grain production of 227 million tons, posting a growth of 10 to 12 million tons in excess of the previous fiscal.

With an added two to three million tons during the Rabi season, it would touch 230 million tons a landmark in foodgrain production.

The agri-biotech sector in India is growing at a whopping 30 per cent since the last five years, and it is likely to sustain the growth in the future as well.

The food processing sector, which contributes 9 per cent to the GDP, is presently growing at 13.5 per cent against 6.5 per cent in 2003-04, and is going to be an important driver of the Indian economy.

India is the largest producer of coconuts, mangoes, bananas, milk and dairy products, cashew nuts, pulses, ginger, turmeric and black pepper. It is also the second largest producer of rice, wheat, sugar, cotton, fruits and vegetables.

Agricultural production is likely to increase significantly during fiscal year 2009. Centre for Monitoring Indian Economy (CMIE) has projected a growth of 3.2 per cent during fiscal year 2009, for the GDP of agriculture and allied sectors.

The allied sectors comprising livestock, forestry and logging, and fishing are likely to see a growth of 4.8 per cent during fiscal year 2009.

India's exports of agricultural and processed food products posted a 38 per cent increase in the 2007-08 fiscal, bolstered by an increase in shipments of coarse cereals like maize, jowar and barley.

Export figures for agricultural products touched US$ 6.59 billion in 2007-08, against US$ 4.79 billion in the previous fiscal.

- Acreage under horticulture which includes fruits, vegetables, spices, floriculture, and plantations was around 20 million hectares in 2006-07. India is the second largest producer of both fruits and vegetables in the world and the National Horticulture Mission (NHM) aims at doubling horticulture production by 2012.
- India is the largest producer of milk in the world, and is likely to become the second largest dairy products producer in the coming years.
- It is the second largest producer of fruits and vegetables.
- It is home to the largest number of livestock in the world.
- It is the third largest producer of foodgrains.
- It has the third largest output of fish.
- With above 9500 spices from medicinal and aromatic plants, India is truly a treasure trove of spices, accounting for 25-30 per cent of the world's production.
- India is the largest producer consumer and exporter of spices, with major spices produced being black pepper, cardamom (small and large), ginger, garlic, turmeric, chili etc.

What is Agricultural Economics and Agricultural Business?

Agricultural economics takes into account three critical areas; these include finance, accounting, and supply control management. Many basic business principles are used to understand the scope of agricultural economics, and students with an agribusiness degree can work in a position where they are required to extend decision-making and problem solving in the areas of agricultural production. Agricultural economics requires the ability to read reports, conduct statistical analysis, make effective decisions based on patterns and trends, and design strategic business models.

Agricultural business allows students to enter management levels within the industry. They may be in charge of food systems regulation, environmental policy-making, agricultural equipment production, along with general agricultural management procedures. Agricultural business combines basic management training with specialized studies in horticulture, trade, and food supply.

Skills Needed for an Agricultural Business Career

A successful career in agricultural business requires basic business skills, as well as the ability to understand agricultural systems and processes within the industry. For example, agriculturally supply training provides students with information on the retail and wholesale aspects of trading; this may lead to agribusiness sales, management, or learning emergency response. Agricultural business and management training teaches students how to operate successful farms and stay ahead in the industry by making use of the latest developments in technology. An agricultural economics career also focuses on the challenges of protecting natural resources—all while making the agricultural business profitable.

Key skills needed for a successful agricultural business career include:

- Strong communication skills
- Agricultural mathematics
- Strong decision-making skills
- Understanding systems based thinking and concepts
- Direct application of basic mathematics and accounting principles
- Computer skills
- Proficiency in marketing and finance
- Understanding the importance of natural resources
- Strategic planning

CAREER OPTIONS IN AGRICULTURE BUSINESS MANAGEMENT

An agribusiness degree can open up multiple opportunities in the field of agricultural business, agricultural economics, and related enterprises within the field. The most common types of positions with an agribusiness degree include:

- Agricultural Production Management
- Food Systems Analyst
- Agricultural Marketing
- Agricultural Economics Statistician
- Natural Resource Protection Management
- Public Policy Management
- Agricultural Finance Analyst or Management

An agribusiness degree program can lead to work with government programs and agencies, community cooperatives, philanthropic organizations, food supply firms, financial service firms, or marketing firms specializing in promoting agribusiness.

Programmes and Courses in Agricultural Economics and Agricultural Business

Common programmes and courses to complete an agribusiness degree include:

- Animal Science
- Communications
- Agricultural Business Management
- Natural Resource Management
- Food Supply and Statistics
- Agricultural Finance
- Farming Equipment, Production, and Supply

Agribusiness Degree Requirements

Both an associate's degree programme and a bachelors' degree are available through most colleges and universities in the field of agribusiness. An agribusiness degree can be earned through the School of Agriculture and/or an extension of the School of Business and related departments. Students may also have a chance to choose a concentration or specialization such as:

- Agricultural Education
- Plant and Soil Science
- Animal and Poultry Science
- Agricultural Production and Manufacturing

Most agribusiness degree programmes include a cooperative or internship requirement. This enables students to work side-by-side with an agricultural business professional in the industry, where they can gain significant experience before entering the field. Today's competitive job marketplace requires students to learn how to formulate public policies, keep with technology and trends, and make effective decisions. Learning how to maximize natural resources is another fast-growing area of agribusiness, and offers many opportunities for students interested in policy-making and public welfare.

Employment Prospects and Career Outlook with an Agribusiness Degree

Employment prospects with a career in agribusiness look promising, as the technological and business developments of the industry demand skilled professionals within the field. Agricultural research, especially in the fields of agricultural economics and agricultural business policy, is especially valuable to the government sector and both public and private firms. Many farms and large-scale agricultural operations need professionals who can help build and lead their organization in the global market. With the increasing costs associated with trade and marketing within the industry, skilled industry leaders are becoming even more valuable.

The scope of MBA in agribusiness management is rising in extractive industries which aim at extraction and best utilization of natural resources. Genetic industries also demand agribusiness management as the research in genetics is rapidly progressing. MBA in agribusiness management also has scope in manufacturing industries concerned with the processing of raw agricultural products likc cotton industry, silk industry, honey and sugar industries, etc. There are many NGOs that are related to the field of agriculture and post-graduates in agribusiness management can seek career there too. These industries and organizations need skills in critical thinking, research skills, active learning, economics skills, communication and science training. MBA in Agribusiness Management provides these skills.

Commercialization of agriculture calls for specialized production, post-harvest management, expansion of processing, transportation and packaging activities and positioning of products both in domestic and international markets. The need for agribusiness management (ABM) programmes both at under-graduate and post-graduate levels has become important. Now, agribusiness is taught as a separate course in most of the State Agriculture Universities (SAUs) at the under-graduate level in various degree programmes.

The concept of agribusiness denotes the activities of agricultural sector integrated in terms of production, processing, marketing and shipments (exports/imports) under different organizational networks. Agribusiness, thus, explores production, marketing and trading of products related to agriculture. It also covers improved growing techniques, agricultural machinery, fertilizers, pesticides pre- and post-harvest handling, storage, transportation, packaging and labeling. Critical management issues as financing and technical assistance, preparation of products for exports, overseas marketing issues and government policy will also receive attention in agribusiness management.

There is no doubt that the agribusiness activities are on the increase. The liberalization policies of the Government and the establishment of WTO have created more opportunities for globalizing our agriculture.

There are clear indications that certain sectors such as floriculture, aquaculture, poultry, processing of fruits and vegetables are reaping the benefits of advanced technology. The entrepreneurs or organization engaged in such ventures are on the look for competent and trained agri-business managers.

But, who can provide them the required manpower? Obviously, the SAUs should take a lead in this direction. The Indian Institutes of Management (IIM), no doubt, have the competency and facilities to turnout such trained personnel. However, their priorities and mandates are different. Moreover, those trained by IIM rarely go into the agribusiness sector. The time is, thus, ripe for SAUs to start post-graduate programmes in agribusiness management.

Most of the SAUs are offering post-graduate programmes in agricultural economics and agricultural extension. Tamil Nadu Agricultural University, Coimbatore was the first in the country to start masters programmes in agricultural marketing management and agribusiness management.

These two new programmes have been well received by the corporate sector. University of Agricultural Science, Bengaluru was the first in the country to introduce Agricultural Marketing and Cooperation programme at under-graduate level. Now, a PG programme in sericultural marketing and cooperation is also in operation. Our experience of human resource development in specialized areas had met with relatively good degree of success. However, we have to be cautious since it takes time for the employers to accept new degree holders especially in the public sector.

Two major constraints in initiating new programmes such as ABM in SAUs are there is resource crunch and lack of trained manpower. These could be addressed to some extent by pooling resources on multi- and inter-disciplinary basis. Wherever possible, a separate PG department in agri-business management could be created so that the expertise could be built over a period of time. If not, the Department of Agricultural Economics be strengthened by recruiting trained personnel in identified areas and also by training the existing staff members.

It is possible to operate the ABM programme as a multi- and inter-disciplinary subject in the SAUs. All the SAUs can take the benefit of existing basic science and humanities departments such as economics, sociology, psychology, mathematics and statistics.

Agricultural engineers and horticulturists could be used for teaching post-harvest management and food technologists for food science.

The ABM programme mainly intends to cater to the emerging needs in the agri-food sector. In general, it should aim at producing following categories of trained manpower.

(i) Management personnel for the agri-food firms, entrepreneurs and cooperatives.

(ii) Policymakers for government, financial and parastatal agencies.

(iii) Teachers and research workers.

(iv) Agribusiness consultants and self-employed persons.

This programme is mainly designed for graduates coming out of the SAUs comprising of agriculture, horticulture, forestry, sericulture, agricultural marketing and cooperation. We may also think of admitting graduates in veterinary, fisheries, dairy and agricultural engineering. The scheme, therefore, assumes that all students will have knowledge of agricultural production so that instruction can concentrate exclusively on agribusiness aspects.

The post-graduate course aims to provide students with an understanding of:

(i) the public policy framework within which business operates.

(ii) the business and marketing management techniques necessary for graduates to operate as managers

(iii) the theoretical framework together with analytical techniques for decision-making

(iv) conduct of research on a subject of topical interest.

The proposed course is offered for the M.Sc. programme in ABM. Clearly, this is only a model for masters' course, but is flexible enough to incorporate location-specific requirements.

The main focus of the proposed programme is to produce specialists who have understanding of production technology as well as business aspects of agriculture. This specialized type of training is even more useful when it comes to dealing with farmers who have been often told of production technologies with very less of marketing extension. It is therefore reasonable to believe that agribusiness firms or organizations will provide employment to such post-graduates at middle management levels. Presently, the SAUs are keen to establish linkages with industry. This will provide us an opportunity to convince the industry that we are making effort to meet their requirement.

The pay scale can vary from industry to industry and individual to individual. But there is a certainty that this field will always be in demand as agriculture is one of the basic needs of human beings.

Why Agriculture Business Management Course Preferred by All?

The Post-Graduate Programme in Agribusiness Management (PGP-ABM) prepares students for careers in management related to agriculture, food, agribusiness, rural and allied sectors of the economy. PGP ABM programme aims at enabling meritorious agricultural graduates to acquire the critical competencies to function as effective agribusiness managers. It also prepares students for managerial and entrepreneurial careers in enterprises serving or dependent on agriculture and allied activities.

Agriculture plays a dominant role in the economy of a nation. The growing need for professional manpower to execute various functions in the agricultural sector has enhanced the importance of agribusiness management courses. There are several institutes which offer post-graduate diploma programmes in agribusiness management for the students who wish to build up a career in this field of work. The comprehensive courses offered by various institutions help the individuals acquire modern technical skills to implement in the areas of production, supply chain management, harvest management and other areas of the sector. The duration of the courses offered is generally two years.

The minimum eligibility criteria required for admission to this post-graduate diploma programme in agribusiness management is graduation. Candidates who have completed their graduation in any of the following subjects like agriculture, food technology, agricultural engineering, dairy technology, animal husbandry, horticultural fisheries and forestry from any recognized university are eligible to apply for the Agribusiness Management Courses. At least two years of work experience in the relevant field is also required for taking admission in some of the institutes. Students are selected on the basis of the scores obtained in the admission test conducted by the institutes. Short-listed candidates are also called for a personal interview session.

ABOUT THE COURSE CURRICULUM

Course Contents of Agribusiness Management

Agribusiness explores production, marketing and trading of products related to agriculture. It also covers improved growing techniques, agricultural machinery, fertilizer, pesticides pre- and post-harvest handling, storage, transportation, packaging and labelling. Critical management issues as financing and technical assistance, preparation of products for exports, overseas marketing issues and government policy.

The PG programmes touch areas such as production and marketing seeds, fertilizers, pesticides, farm machinery and equipment, livestock feed, irrigation, export and import, cooperatives, rural banking, agricultural projects, insurance, logistics, land management, water management and irrigation, and sustainable energy. The curricula is different in different institutions.

Role of Agribusiness Managers

Agribusiness Managers have a big role to play in Indian economy as agriculture is a main part of Indian economy. Agribusiness Management is application of management principles for agriculture. Indian agriculture is rapidly changing due to globalization, competitive environment and changing role of government. It was found that fresh agricultural graduates were facing problems as managers in agribusiness firms. This became need for properly designed special management programmes.

The work of agribusiness managers is to contribute substantially to the development of diverse activities in this sector. To achieve this, Agribusiness Management Education was established — the National Institute of Agricultural Extension Management (MANAGE), Rajendranagar, Hyderabad - 500 030 (website: www.manage.gov.in). It is an apex national institute set up in 1987 as an autonomous society under the Ministry of Agriculture, Government of India.

Agribusiness Management Course Curriculum

The agribusiness management programmes offered by the reputed institutes help the students acquire the professional competence to deal with the various problems in the agricultural sector. Candidates can learn a lot about statistics for management, principles of general management, organizational behaviour, financial management, marketing of agricultural inputs, agricultural output marketing, business laws and ethics and economic environment and policy. Moreover, students can also collect knowledge on marketing research, agricultural extension and rural advantage, human resource management, agricultural development policies and production and marketing rural advertising. For more information on professional courses, you may browse through the site.

Institute of Agribusiness Management (IABM) was set up in 2000, with the financial assistance from the World Bank. Located in Bikaner (Rajasthan), the institute is an integral part of Rajasthan Agricultural University, Bikaner. IABM Bikaner is committed for the upliftment of agriculture in India and rural development. It is approved by the All India Council for Technical Education (AICTE) and Ministry of Human Resource Development, Government of India. Institute of Agribusiness Management offers a post-graduate degree level course, that is, Master of Business Administration (MBA) in Agribusiness. It is a two-year full-time residential programme, which is conducted as per the guidelines of AICTE.

OPTIONAL COURSES OFFERED IN AGRIBUSINESS MANAGEMENT

- Agribusiness and Carbon Finance
- Agricultural Development
- Agricultural Finance/Banking
- Agricultural Futures and Options Markets
- Agro-industries
- Agro Processing
- Econometrics for Agribusiness
- Food Processing
- Forest-based Industries
- International Agriculture and Trade Policy
- International Marketing
- Logistics and Infrastructure Management in Agriculture
- Marketing of Agricultural Inputs
- Management and Finance of Agro-food Projects
- Market Research for Agribusiness
- Managerial Communication for Agribusiness
- Management of Contract Farming
- Management of Technology for Sustainable Agriculture
- Franchising in Agribusiness (FAB)
- Private-Public-Community Partnership for Inclusive Agribusiness
- Rural Advertising
- Strategic Food Agro Marketing
- Sales and Distribution Management for Agriculture

INSTITUTIONS OFFERING COURSES IN AGRIBUSINESS MANAGEMENT

1. Indian Institute of Management, Ahmedabad
2. Indian Institute of Management, Lucknow
3. Amity Business School – MBA – Agriculture and Food Business
4. Aligarh Muslim University (AMU) – Master of Agri Eco. and Bus. Mgt. (MAEBM)
5. L.N. Welingkar, Mumbai – 6 month's Part-time Dip. in Agri. Bus. Mgt.
6. FMS, Varanasi – Banaras Hindu University – Masters' Programme in Agri. Bus. Mgt.
7. National Instt. of Agri. Marketing, Kota Road Bambala, near Sanganer, Jaipur

8. Instt. of Agribusiness Mgt. (IABM) – World Bank Funded – Bikaner
9. Indian Institute of Management – Vastrapur – Ahmedabad 2-yr Resi. Programme
10. Indian Institute of Mgt. – Lucknow: 2-yr Resi. Program in ABM.
11. Univ. of Mumbai – Garware Institute of Career Edn. PGD in ABM
12. GB Pant Univ. of Agri. and Tech. Pantnagar – 2-yr PG Prog. MBA – Ph.D. in ABM
13. Acharya NG Ranga Agri Univ. Hyderabad – Master degree in ABM
14. Symbiosis Group of Bus. School – MBA in ABM
15. National Instt. of Rural Dev. – Hyderabad Training Programmes in Rural Dev.
16. Instt. of Agribusiness Mgt. regd under Centre for Agri. & Rural Dev. Society
17. Kerala Agri Univ. – MBA in ABM
18. Center for Food & Agribusiness Mgt. (CFAM) Courses in ABM.

COURSES OFFERED BY AGRICULTURE UNIVERSITIES

- Allahabad Agricultural University – Post-graduate Diploma in Agribusiness (The Institute also has two other courses: MBA and PG Diploma in Business Administration)
- Dr. Y.S. Parmar University of Horticulture and Forestry – MBA (Agribusiness)
- Forest Research Institute (Dehradun) – M.Sc. Forestry (Economics and Management)
- G.B. Pant University of Agriculture and Technology (College of Agribusiness Management) – MBA (Agribusiness)
- Indian Institute of Forest Management (Bhopal) – PG Diploma in Forest Management (Equivalent to Master's Degree in the subject)
- Jawaharlal Nehru Krishi Vishwavidyalaya – Master of Agricultural Business Management (MABM)
- Kerala Agricultural University – B.Sc. and M.Sc. (Cooperative and Banking)
- Mahatma Gandhi Chitrakoot Gramodaya Vishwavidyalaya – MBA (Agribusiness)
- Mahatma Phule Krishi Vidyapeeth – PG Diploma in Farm Business Management (Two-year duration)
- Mysore University – Master of Food and Agricultural Marketing Management (MFAMM)
- National Institute of Agricultural Extension Management (MANAGE), Hyderabad – PG Diploma in Agriculture-Business Management
- Punjab Agricultural University (College of Agribusiness Management) – MBA (Agribusiness Management)
- Tamil Nadu Agricultural University – Master of Business Management (MBM), M.Sc. (Agricultural Marketing Management)
- Tamil Nadu Veterinary and Animal Sciences University – Post-graduate Diploma in Business Management (Animal and Fisheries Sciences)
- University of Agricultural Sciences, Bangalore – B.Sc. (Agricultural Marketing and Cooperation), M.Sc. (Agricultural Marketing)
- University of Agricultural Sciences, Dharwar – B.Sc. (Agricultural Marketing and Cooperation)

HOW THIS COURSE CURRICULUM CAN BE STUDIED?

This subject Agribusiness Management can be divided into various segments for the study purposes and they are furnished hereunder:

Introduction to Agricultural Economics I:

Introduction to Agricultural Economics – Scope and Method, Price Theory and the Functions of the Market with particular reference to Agriculture, Theory of Agricultural Production, Cost Analysis with respect to Agricultural Production, Theory of Distribution.

Introduction to Agricultural Economics II:

Macroeconomic Theory as it relates to Agriculture emphasizing the components of agriculture in National Income and in international trade; fiscal and monetary policies as they affect Agriculture, Inflation and the Rural Sector.

Statistics and Biometrics:

The nature of Statistics and Statistical Method; Methods of Data Collection; Sampling and Presentation; Measures of Association; Regression Analysis; Analysis of Variance; Elementary design of experiments.

Introduction to Farm Management:

Nature and scope of farm management, management functions in traditional agriculture, organization of the farm set-up, farm records and accounting, farm business analysis, capital budgeting, farm and enterprise budgeting, farm decisions and long-term investment, linear programming (maximization). Analysis of various food crops interplanted with cocoa; reasons for inter-planting; density of inter-planted food crops; costs and returns in agro-forestry. Evaluation of alternative technologies in livestock production.

Principles of Agricultural Economics I:

Theories of production (resource allocation), consumer behaviour and price determination with emphasis on agriculture.

Principles of Agricultural Economics II:

Theory of income determination with emphasis on the impacts of the product, money and employment markets and of macroeconomic policies on agriculture.

Fundamentals of Econometrics:

Introduction to Econometric Methods; Simple linear regression; violation of basic assumptions of the classical normal linear regression model, estimation with bad or deficient data, multiple regression; statistical demand analysis; statistical production and cost analysis.

Land Resource Economics:

Study of Man and Land: Economic Principles relevant to Land Economics; population pressure and the demand for land; control of land use, spatial and location concepts of urban land, etc. Land Tenure Systems and ownership of property rights, land reforms: economic returns to land resources, real estate taxation of landed property, land development, conservation of land, institutional factors in land use; property rights in land resources; introduction to real estate finance and real estate market, natural resource economics.

Mathematics for Agricultural Economics Analysis:

Revision of basic algebraic manipulations, solution of simultaneous, quadratic and cubic equations including production, cost and utility functions; sets and sample spaces, functions, differentiation and derivatives, techniques of maximization and minimization, integration and difference Equations. Series and Progressions. Elements of Matrix Algebra and economic applications, e.g., in national income models. Solving systems of equations and comparative statistics.

Agricultural Economic Analysis II:

Consumption, saving and the theory of income determination; the general equilibrium level of employment, the price level and the theory of interest, inflation and deflation, Macroeconomic policies; monetary and fiscal.

Agricultural Development and Policy:

Objectives of Economic Development; Theories and Models of Economic Development; Agriculture's contributions to Economic Development; Appropriate Technology in Agriculture; Economic Institutions; Population Pressure; Consumption, Savings and Capital Formation, Agricultural Policy; Case Studies in Agriculture.

Production Economics:

Location of Agricultural Production; The physical environment of agricultural production, comparative advantages and localization of production, the technical knowledge, capital, human and institutional factors; Traditional Indian cultivation systems, which discusses shifting cultivation, ridge cropping, multiple cropping systems.

Input-Output relationships in agricultural production including principles of diminishing returns, optimal use of factor inputs, opportunity costs and output, factor combination and least cost combination of factor inputs and linear programming; Risk and uncertainties and enterprise combination, risk uncertainty and innovation;. Economies of size and scale and their applications; Farm appraisal and valuation.

Management Information System:

Management Information System – an Indian perspective, Information, data and Communications; Systems Concepts Structure and Elements; Systems Concepts – Objectives and Types; Organizations – Principles and Structure; Organizations – Adaptability and Behaviour in organization — configuration, culture and information, management levels and functions. Motivation and Leadership, Organizing and coordinating, Planning, Decision Making and control, Concepts, Loops and information, control in organizations, information technology and Management information Service, with influences on MIS design.

Agricultural Business Management:

The scope of Agricultural Business and Management, Types of Agricultural Business, Management and Organizations, Management Accounting, Production Planning, Public Policies affecting growth of agricultural business, organization of large-scale farms, legal organization and tax strategies, Economics of Agricultural Processing and Marketing Management Financial Control, Case Studies of Agricultural Businesses in India.

Research Method in Agricultural Economics:

Introduction to scientific methods, defining a research problem; developing hypotheses and objectives; research design, measurement and data collection; statistical analysis of data, data presentation and report writing.

Agricultural Finance:

Principles of Agricultural Finance, types of credit extended to agriculture; the basis of interest rates; sources of loanable funds and collateral security for loans; specialized institutions for the extension of agricultural credit in entire India including cooperative loan and thrift societies; financial management concepts for managing growth, leverage, liquidity, risk and capital investment in agricultural businesses; Inventory, balance sheet, cash book analyses an examination of financial markets, principles of accounting.

Agricultural Economics Analysis I:

The theory of Consumer behaviour, price theory and resource allocation; analysis of market structure; market equilibrium analysis (partial and general) for outputs, inputs and prices; welfare economics.

Agricultural Marketing:

The role of marketing in agricultural development; marketing functions, channels and costs; the nature of competition in agricultural marketing; cooperative marketing of agricultural products; the process of analyzing marketing problems; Agricultural demand and Price analysis; marketing research, techniques for evaluating marketing efficiency. Domestic marketing of agricultural commodities; international trade in agricultural commodities.

Farm Management and Accounting:

The decision-making process in farm management. Organization of resources, organization of enterprises, Principles and procedures in planning enterprise combinations. Budgeting and programme planning. Cash-flow budget and its uses. Break-even analysis. Measurement of resource productivity. Principles of labour management and wage administration. Farm decisions and long-term investment. Linear Programming. Farm records and accounts.

Research Project:

Steps in the research process and their application, evaluation and treatment of economic data in agriculture. Methods of sample survey design, questionnaire design and administration. Techniques of data analysis including multiple regression and techniques of research report writing. Time-series analysis: secular trend, seasonal variations, cyclical and irregular fluctuations; application to agricultural economic problems.

Demography and demographic data analysis, Social Accounts and the Measurement of National Income, Real Domestic Product and indexes of production. Quality Control (Statistical Control of quality).

Statistics for Agricultural Economists:

Statistical analysis as a scientific method. The role of statistic in agricultural planning. Sample design in agricultural economic research; Agricultural price analysis: price determination (theory and practice); price variation through time, empirical price analysis; index numbers (types and methods of construction).

SUMMARY

In this introductory chapter, you will be able to learn about the abracadabra of agribusiness and its definition, interpretation and various shades of meanings. The major agricultural products can be broadly grouped into foods, fibers, fuels, and raw materials. In the 21st century, plants have been used to grow biofuels, biopharmaceuticals, bioplastics and pharmaceuticals. Specific foods include cereals, vegetables, fruits, and meat. Fibers include cotton, wool, hemp, skills, and flax. Raw materials include lumber and bamboo. Other useful materials are produced by plants such as resins. Biofuels include methane, from biomass, ethanol, and biodiesel. Cut flowers, nursery plants, tropical fish and birds for the pet trade are some of the ornamental products.

There are two aspects where Agriculture sector is contributing to national income. One is agriculture contributed a major share of the national income in India at one time. Secondly, the share of agriculture in national income, however, has been decreasing continuously while the shares of the manufacturing and service sectors are increasing.

Similarly, at the international trade arena, the agriculture is playing its pivotal role. And importance of agriculture in the national economy is indicated by many facts. To add here good, crops implying large purchasing power with the farmers lead to greater demand for manufacturers and therefore better prices. In other words, prosperity of the farmers is also the prosperity of industries.

QUESTIONS

1. Why management students' fraternity prefers Agriculture Business Management?
2. List out career options in Agriculture Business Management?
3. Just sketch the detailed course curriculum of Agriculture Business Management?

OOO

CHAPTER

3

Agribusiness: Meaning, Nature and Importance

Scope of Agribusiness

Objectives of Economic Planning for Agriculture

Forms of Agribusiness

Agri Processes in India

What is Agribusiness?

The word 'agriculture' indicates plowing a field, planting seed, harvesting a crop, milking cows, or feeding livestock. Until recently, this was a fairly accurate picture. But today's agriculture is radically different.

SCOPE OF AGRIBUSINESS

The scope of Agribusiness is vast and it is treated as a sunrise industry, human resources (HR) for meeting the marketing challenges, meanwhile strengthen industry-institution linkages, and to meet the stakeholders' requirements.

The career opportunities in the field of agribusiness are vast and resourceful. The careers are abundant and growth oriented: sales manager in super and hypermarkets, agribusiness credit officer, commodity trade and technical analysts, farm/plantation management, procurement personnel, marketing of financial products and services, agribusiness credit manager, HR Manager, Supply Chain managers, Marketing research and analyst, and logistics managers.

Learning of agribusiness management can be through class lectures, group discussions, case studies, individual and group projects, internship opportunities, industry visits, e-learning and outsourcing.

OBJECTIVES OF ECONOMIC PLANNING FOR AGRICULTURE

While planning to develop the agriculture sector, the Planning Commission has generally kept four broad objectives in view:

1. Agri-business increases agricultural production. The aim has always been to bring more and more land under cultivation.
2. And it will raise the yield per hectare yield through intensive application of such agricultural inputs as irrigation, improved seeds, fertilizers etc. and thus bring about increased agricultural production.
3. Agribusiness will increase employment opportunities.

FORMS OF AGRIBUSINESS

The second generation society realized agriculture as viable proposition focusing only on production and purchasing farm inputs from other sources. This changing mindset opened new avenues for others to focus on input supply business to the large farming community, and agriculture started widening its scope as a business. This was an era of shifting from subsistence to commercialized agriculture. It was the time when institutes for marketing, finance, transportation, research and development and storage started functioning. The government also started promoting agriculture by providing a better place for planning in order to feed the growing population. Agribusiness includes all interrelated activities (production and services) involved in farm production and value addition to agri-products.

People in gradual course of time also started realizing the need for value-added products. This phase of processing and transporting agri-produce was technology driven due to unique characteristics of agri produce and are in the form of bulkiness and perishability. Sequel to Liberalization, Privatization and Globalization (LPG) and in line with global demand, agribusiness entrepreneurs became professionals with the ability to improve products so quickly. Thus, this is an era of agribusiness revolution, where important changes are taking place especially after the international pacts on agriculture The input supply, product processing and distribution systems are passing through major structural changes and will continue to face ups and downs in future.

Food is basic need of human beings and makes agriculture the vital industry all over the world and is most important sector. The agriculture is the single contributor to the economy of each country and provides employment to unemployed people. India is the world's third largest agricultural commodities after US and China. India is the third largest in livestock and cattle population possess huge potential for dairy and meat export. India is largest fruit and vegetable producer but only 1 per cent of these produce will get processed and remaining will be sold and wasted as they are perishable in nature.

Agri-business is a complex and massive business sector and one can find complexity in understanding this sector as it relies on interdependency with other subsectors. These are four sectors namely input supply, farm business, processing and service.

The input supply plays vital role in the performance of farm business which is the centre for the entire sector. Quality, quantity and timelines of input supply to the farm businesses are very crucial as all are equally responsible for the success of the whole system. Second sector is farm sector which is the complete system as the sector provides raw materials to the processing sector and takes raw materials from the input supply sector. But this sector has limitations like climatic factors.

Conversion of farm produce to consumer commodities is called agro-processing and any activities or processes that reduce wastage and increases shelf life resulting in value promotion, is called agriprocessing. Therefore, agriprocessing includes agro product processing, packaging, storing, transporting, and distribution and these can be further classified into following groups:

1. Foodgrains — pulses milling
2. Fruits/vegetable processing
3. Bakery products
4. Sugar industry
5. Edible Oils/Fats
6. Milk and milk products
7. Beverages
8. Fish/Poultry products
9. Meat and meat products
10. Alcoholic Beverages/soft drink

Allied agriculture processing consists of Cotton Textiles, Jute Industry, Paper Industry and Silk industry. The entire system of agribusiness works under public, private or cooperative organizational culture.

Farming Business consists of activities of farm production through various linkages give complete shape to agribusiness. It is an art of managing scarce farm resource profitably. The farm business is the usage of scarce farm sources namely – land, labour, capital and management having an alternative use to obtain maximum sustained profit. In the farm business, the options available to produce are very much limited and mainly governed by the lifestyle and preference of the society. And also it depends on demand and supply of the product along with other non-market forces, decide the price of the product which ultimately provide solutions to what and how much to produce from given land.

Then decisions that were to be taken on farm business which are dynamic and flexible and entirely rely on following variables:

- Biological nature
- Weather dependency
- Changing input supply situations
- Changing taste/lifestyles of consumers

Wide fluctuations in prices	Changing socio-economic environment
Changing technology	Changing government policies.

Significance of Rural segment: If farmers are more concerned about agriculture, agriculture produce and production, then the country can provide farmers better quality of life and livelihood in the rural sector. In other words, the agricultural business leads to the overall development of the agriculture sector.

Many more facilities can be expected by the farmers if they want better management of agricultural land they should have adequate knowledge on how to improve the irrigational facilities, to explore lucrative export market. They should be more familar in finding solutions and apply suitable technologies to increase more produce. Further, farmers should also be able to mobilize cooperative societies for better yields of produce and marketability, besides developing road network and keen to reduce poverty to some extent if not fully.

The agriculture business is untapped resource and many developing countries have been taking part actively in the process of economic growth on the expansion of non-traditional agro-exports. Active participation in the global market exposes the rural sector to the latest technologies being used in other countries. Many developing countries are actively participating in the task of their country's economic growth with an ambition of expanding non traditional agro-exports.

AGRI PROCESSES IN INDIA

Agricultural process and practices in India are going on smoothly and service sector in agribusiness is accountable for exploring new and efficient ways to produce, to market and to provide customer-friendly service to all other stages of the product cycle. This sector plays a very important role in commercializing agribusiness and it is to the tune of the business through appropriate R & D facilities in the era of changing global economy.

Prior to independence it was decision of PSU to facilitate agribusiness in major service sectors, R & D, finance, communication, infrastructure and also storage besides regulation of middlemen by government while all these activities were carried through private sector.

Public Services include activities related to research, education, communication and regulation while Ministry of Agriculture through its ICAR (Indian Council of Agricultural Research) supports R & D sector in agriculture. Provision of credit facilities in agribusiness is crucial as more than 80 per cent of farm holdings are less than two hectares which will result in capital intensive business. The agribusiness needs adequate finance, timely credit facilities, and leading commercial banks should take initiatives for fulfilling these needs. Financial institutes are also becoming more and more popular as their main motto is to earn reputation as well as their business by acceded to by providing timely loans to farmers for their agribusinesses. Many NGOs (Non-governmental Organizations) are also involved in assisting the farmers in getting their loan requirements fulfilled and also other essential services for the farmers. Public sector units are also indulged in managing and exploring marketing facilities to farmers and helping them in commercializing the agriculture business thereby impressing the government to become responsible and accountable for protecting farming community.

Similarly, private sector is also second to none as they are involved in industrialization of agribusinesses. Many reputed private companies have started gearing up their resources to invest in the agriculture sector aiming at producing high quality of genetically modified crops and seeds for better yield and also providing better communication with improvized services for farmers to gain profits.

Further, private sector is also involved in contract farming and modern technology, the private sector is innovating new techniques to solve finance related problems. MNCs are also bringing new technologies from advanced countries to assure good quality of raw materials to reap more produce for agriprocessing industries, which are being set up in developing countries because of cheaper skilled manpower.

SUMMARY

India has abundant natural resources with varied climatic conditions, consequently producing a large variety of agricultural and horticultural produce. India ranks first in vegetable production and second in fruit production. Agribusiness started expanding its scope beyond its horizon with the integration of sequential activities like inputs supply and processing and retailing with service sector. Green Revolution steered by world renowned Agriculture scientist Dr. M. S. Swaminathan who made farming more easier by attaining high yielding of wheat and rice varieties, with more fertilizer responsive. This initiative had created huge demand for fertilizer, high demand for irrigation and plant protection chemicals and more demand for high yielding genetically modified seeds of various crops.

The food and agriculture processing industry has gained momentum with the initiatives from Government of India's plans by creating new ministry for this sector and this sector has great future in the days to come in catering to the needs of people whose lifestyles are frequently under change according to their tastes and preferences. Strong linkage between agriculture and industry resulted in increased high tech cultivation of improved varieties of crops, fruits and vegetables through contract farming. These technological advancements resulted in reduction of post-harvest losses, and improvement of quality. The agriculture sector is booming for its vast employment and export potential.

Further commercialization and modernization of agriculture sector in India has brought new vista to the service sector to agribusiness. The farmers' fraternity decided to withstand the risky situation from the banking sector but now it is considered with great potential and unexploited sector. Both public and private sector financial institutions are now offering many attractive schemes.

QUESTIONS

1. What do you mean by the term and concept 'agriculture business'?
2. Examine the objectives of Economic Planning for Agriculture Business Management.
3. Outline the activities taking place in agriculture processes in India.

ooo

CHAPTER 4

STRUCTURE AND FORMS OF AGRIBUSINESS AND ROLE OF WTO

- World Trade Organization
- Ministerial Conferences
- Organizational Structure
- The WTO Agreement on Agriculture and Concerns of Developing Countries
- Proposals of Developing Countries with Comparative Advantage in Agriculture
- Proposals of Major Industrialized Countries
- Proposals to Address Food Security, Development and Related Issues
- Other Proposals for Meeting Food Security and Development Objectives
- Salient Features of Agro Products
- Why Agri-Based Service Sector is in Demand?
- Government's New Initiative - 2011
- Ban on Pulses Export
- Government Favours PPP in Seeds Processing

This unit deals with structure and forms of agriculture business and agriculture based industrial units. The industry sector in the agriculture segment focus on value-added agriculture products and residues both food and non-food by way of food processing exercise for easy marketing purposes. Further, these value-added products besides marketing can be made reusable and edible. Also there are many technologies which have proven in improving the quality of these processed food products with modernized storage facilities have made the food more freshened, packagable and exportable.

The agro based industries in India are equipped with modernized way of fertility, plough of fertilized land and wasteland with less water requirements that can increase the yields of produce known as high tech agriculture technology, that are under greater use for vegetable and fruit produce, floriculture, (flower growing) using flower leaves for value-added food products for consumption purposes and medicine purpose, and also using flowers for preparation of refined edible oil for cooking purpose and some flower leaves are under use for preparation of bio diesel for use of automobile vehicles.

1. WORLD TRADE ORGANIZATION

The **World Trade Organization** (**WTO**) is an organization that intends to supervize and liberalize international trade. The organization officially commenced on January 1, 1995 under the Marrakesh Agreement (Morocco), replacing the General Agreement on Tariffs and Trade (GATT), which commenced in 1948. The organization deals with regulation of trade between participating countries; it provides a framework for negotiating and formalizing trade agreements, and a dispute resolution process aimed at enforcing participants' adherence to WTO agreements which are signed by representatives of member governments and ratified by their Parliaments. Most of the issues that the WTO focuses on derive from previous trade negotiations, especially from the Uruguay Round (1986-1994).

The organization is currently endeavouring to persist with a trade negotiation called the Doha Development Agenda (or Doha Round), which was launched in 2001 to enhance equitable participation of poorer countries which represent a majority of the world's population. However, the negotiation has been dogged by "disagreement between exporters of agricultural bulk commodities and countries with large numbers of subsistence farmers on the precise terms of a 'special safeguard measure' to protect farmers from surges in imports. At this time, the future of the Doha Round is uncertain."

The WTO has 153 members, representing more than 97 per cent of total world trade and 30 observers, most seeking membership. The WTO is governed by a ministerial conference, meeting every two years; a general council, which implements the conference's policy decisions and is responsible for day-to-day administration; and a director-general, who is appointed by the ministerial conference. The WTO's headquarters is at the Centre William Rappard, Geneva, Switzerland.

The WTO's predecessor, the General Agreement on Tariffs and Trade (GATT), was established after World War II in the wake of other new multilateral institutions dedicated to international economic cooperation — notably the Bretton Woods Institutions known as the World Bank and the International Monetary Fund (IMF). A comparable international institution for trade, named the International Trade Organization (ITO) was successfully negotiated. The ITO was to be a United Nations specialized agency and would address not only trade barriers but other issues indirectly related to trade, including employment, investment, restrictive business practices, and commodity agreements. But the ITO treaty was not approved by the US and a few other signatories and never went into effect.

The GATT was the only multilateral instrument governing international trade from 1948 until the WTO was established in 1995. Despite attempts in the mid 1950s and 1960s to create some form of institutional mechanism for international trade, the GATT continued to operate for almost half a century as a semi-institutionalized multilateral treaty regime on a provisional basis.

Seven rounds of negotiations occurred under the GATT. The first real GATT trade rounds concentrated on further reducing tariffs. Then, the Kennedy Round in the mid-sixties brought about a GATT Anti-dumping Agreement and a section on development. The Tokyo Round during the seventies was the first major attempt to tackle trade barriers that do not take the form of tariffs, and to improve the system, adopting a series of agreements on non-tariff barriers, which in some cases interpreted existing GATT rules, and in others broke entirely new ground. Because these plurilateral agreements were not accepted by the full GATT membership, they were often informally called "codes". Several of these codes were amended in the Uruguay Round, and turned into multilateral commitments accepted by all WTO members. Only four remained plurilateral (those on government procurement, bovine meat, civil aircraft and dairy products), but in 1997 WTO members agreed to terminate the bovine meat and dairy agreements, leaving only two.

Well before GATT's 40th anniversary, its members concluded that the GATT system was straining to adapt to a new globalizing world economy. In response to the problems identified in the 1982 Ministerial Declaration (structural deficiencies, spill-over impacts of certain countries' policies on world trade GATT could not manage etc.), the eighth GATT round — known as the Uruguay Round — was launched in September 1986, in Punta del Este, Uruguay.

It was the biggest negotiating mandate on trade ever agreed: the talks were going to extend the trading system into several new areas, notably trade in services and intellectual property, and to reform trade in the sensitive sectors of agriculture and textiles; all the original GATT articles were up for review. The Final Act concluding the Uruguay Round and officially establishing the WTO regime was signed during the April 1994 ministerial meeting at Marrakesh Morocco, and hence is known as the Marrakesh Agreement.

The GATT still exists as the WTO's umbrella treaty for trade in goods, updated as a result of the Uruguay Round negotiations (a distinction is made between *GATT 1994*, the updated parts of GATT, and *GATT 1947*, the original agreement which is still the heart of GATT 1994). GATT 1994 is not however the only legally binding agreement included via the Final Act at Marrakesh; a long list of about 60 agreements, annexes, decisions and understandings was adopted. The agreements fall into a structure with six main parts:

- The Agreement Establishing the WTO
- Goods and investment — the Multilateral Agreements on Trade in Goods including the GATT 1994 and Trade related Investment Measures.
- Services — the General Agreement on Trade in Services.
- Intellectual Property — the Agreement on Trade Related Aspects of Intellectual Property Rights (TRIPS).
- Dispute Settlement (DSU)
- Reviews of governments' trade policies — Trade Policy Mechanism (TPRM)

A. MINISTERIAL CONFERENCES

The topmost decision-making body of the WTO is the Ministerial Conference, which usually meets every two years. It brings together all members of the WTO, all of which are countries or customs unions. The Ministerial Conference can take decisions on all matters under any of the multilateral trade agreements. The inaugural ministerial conference was held in Singapore in 1996. Disagreements between largely developed and developing economies emerged during this conference over four issues initiated by this conference, which led to them being collectively referred to as the "Singapore Issues". The second ministerial conference was held in Geneva in Switzerland. The third conference in Seattle, Washington ended in failure, with massive demonstrations and police and National Guard crowd control efforts drawing worldwide attention. The fourth ministerial conference was held in Doha in Persian Gulf nation of Qatar. The Doha Agreement was launched at the conference. The conference also approved the joining of China, which became the 143rd member to join. The fifth ministerial conference was held in Cancun, Mexico, aiming at forging agreement on the Doha round. An alliance of 22 southern states, the G-20 developing nations (led by India, China and Brazil), resisted demands from the North for agreements on the so-called "Singapore issues " and called for an end to agricultural subsidies within the EU and the US. The talks broke down without progress.

The sixth WTO ministerial conference was held in Hong Kong from 13-18 December 2005. It was considered vital if the four-year-old Doha Development Agenda negotiations were to move forward sufficiently to conclude the round in 2006. In this meeting, countries agreed to phase out all their agricultural export subsidies by the end of 2013, and terminate any cotton export subsidies by the end of 2006. Further concessions to developing countries included an agreement to introduce duty free, tariff free access for goods from the Least Developed Countries, following everything but arms initiative of the European Union — but with up to 3 per cent of tariff lines exempted. Other major issues were left for further negotiation to be completed by the end of 2010. The WTO General Council, on 26 May 2009, agreed to hold a seventh WTO ministerial conference session in Geneva from 30 November-3 December 2009. A statement by chairman Amb. Mario Matus acknowledged that the prime purpose was to remedy a breach of protocol requiring two-yearly "regular" meetings, which had lapsed with the Doha Round failure in 2005, and that the "scaled-down" meeting would not be a negotiating session, but "emphasis will be on transparency and open discussion rather than on small group processes and informal negotiating structures". The general theme for discussion is "The WTO, the Multilateral Trading System and the Current Global Economic Environment".

The WTO launched the current round of negotiations, the Doha Development Agenda (DDA) or Doha Round, at the fourth ministerial conference in Doha, Qatar in November 2001. The Doha round was to be an ambitious effort to make globalization more vibrant and help the world's poor, particularly by slashing barriers and subsidies in farming. The initial agenda comprised both further trade liberalization and new rule-making, underpinned by commitments to strengthen substantial assistance to developing countries.

The negotiations have been highly contentious and agreement has not been reached, despite the intense negotiations at several ministerial conferences and at other sessions. Disagreements still continue over several key areas including agriculture subsidies.

Principles of the Trading System

The WTO establishes a framework for trade policies; it does not define or specify outcomes. That is, it is concerned with setting the rules of the trade policy games. Five principles are of particular importance in understanding both the pre-1994 GATT and the WTO:

1. **Non-discrimination.** It has two major components: the most favored nation (MFN) status, and the national treatment policy. Both are embedded in the main WTO rules on goods, services, and intellectual property, but their precise scope and nature differ across these

areas. The MFN rule requires that a WTO member must apply the same conditions on all trades with other WTO members, i.e., a WTO member has to grant the most favourable conditions under which it allows trade in a certain product type to all other WTO members. "Grant someone a special favour and you have to do the same for all other WTO members." National treatment means that imported goods should be treated no less favorably than domestically produced goods (at least after the foreign goods have entered the market) and was introduced to tackle non-tariff barriers to trade (e.g., technical standards, security standards *et al.* discriminating against imported goods).

2. **Reciprocity**. It reflects both a desire to limit the scope of free-riding that may arise because of the MFN rule, and a desire to obtain better access to foreign markets. A related point is that for a nation to negotiate, it is necessary that the gain from doing so be greater than the gain available from unilateral liberalization; reciprocal concessions intend to ensure that such gains will materialise.
3. **Binding and enforceable commitments**. The tariff commitments made by WTO members in a multilateral trade negotiation and on accession are enumerated in a schedule (list) of concessions. These schedules establish "ceiling bindings": a country can change its bindings, but only after negotiating with its trading partners, which could mean compensating them for loss of trade. If satisfaction is not obtained, the complaining country may invoke the WTO dispute settlement procedures.
4. **Transparency**. The WTO members are required to publish their trade regulations, to maintain institutions allowing for the review of administrative decisions affecting trade, to respond to requests for information by other members, and to notify changes in trade policies to the WTO. These internal transparency requirements are supplemented and facilitated by periodic country-specific reports (trade policy reviews) through the Trade Policy Review Mechanism (TPRM). The WTO system tries also to improve predictability and stability, discouraging the use of quotas and other measures used to set limits on quantities of imports.
5. **Safety valves**. In specific circumstances, governments are able to restrict trade. There are three types of provisions in this direction: articles allowing for the use of trade measures to attain non-economic objectives; articles aimed at ensuring "fair competition"; and provisions permitting intervention in trade for economic reasons. Exceptions to the MFN principle also allow for preferential treatment of developing countries, regional free trade areas and customs unions.

B. ORGANIZATIONAL STRUCTURE

The General Council has multiple bodies which oversee committees in different areas, and they are the following:

Council for Trade in Goods

There are 11 committees under the jurisdiction of the Goods Council, each with a specific task. All members of the WTO participate in the committees. The Textiles Monitoring Body is separate from the other committees but still under the jurisdiction of Goods Council. The body has its own chairman and only 10 members. The body also has several groups relating to textiles.

Council for Trade-related Aspects of Intellectual Property Rights

Information on intellectual property in the WTO, news and official records of the activities of the TRIPS Council, and details of the WTO's work with other international organizations in the field.

Council for Trade in Services

The Council for Trade in Services operates under the guidance of the General Council and is responsible for overseeing the functioning of the General Agreement on Trade in Services (GATS). It is open to all WTO members, and can create subsidiary bodies as required.

Trade Negotiations Committee

The Trade Negotiations Committee (TNC) is the committee that deals with the current trade talks round. The chair is WTO's director-general. The committee is currently tasked with the Doha Development Round.

The Service Council has three subsidiary bodies: financial services, domestic regulations, GATS rules and specific commitments. The General Council has several different committees, working groups, and working parties. There are committees on the following: Trade and Environment; Trade and Development (Subcommittee on Least Developed Countries); Regional Trade Agreements; Balance of Payments Restrictions; and Budget, Finance and Administration. There are working groups on the following: Accession Trade, debt and finance; and Trade and technology transfer.

The WTO oversees about 60 different agreements which have the status of international legal texts. Member countries must sign and ratify all WTO agreements on accession. A discussion of some of the most important agreements follows. The Agreement in Agriculture came into effect with the establishment of the WTO at the beginning of 1995. The AoA has three central concepts, or "pillars": domestic support, market access and export subsidies. The General Agreement on Trade in Services was created to extend the multilateral trading system to service sector, in the same way the General Agreement on Tariffs and Trade (GATT) provides such a system for merchandise trade. The Agreement entered into force in January 1995. The Agreement on Trade-related Aspects of Intellectual Property Rights sets down minimum standards for many forms of Intellectual Property (IP) regulation. It was negotiated at the end of the Uruguay Round of the General Agreement on Tariffs and Trade (GATT) in 1994.

The **Agreement on Agriculture** is an international Treaty of the WTO. It was negotiated during the Uruguay Round of the General Agreement on Tariffs and Trade and entered into force with the establishment of the WTO on January 1, 1995. The Agreement on Agriculture has three central concepts, or "pillars": domestic support, market access and export subsidies.

Domestic Support

The first pillar of the AoA is "domestic support". The AoA structures domestic support (subsidies) into three categories or "boxes": a Green Box, an Amber Box and a Blue Box. The Green Box contains fixed payments to producers for environmental programmes, so long as the payments are "decoupled" from current production levels. The Amber Box contains domestic subsidies that governments have agreed to reduce but not eliminate. The Blue Box contains subsidies which can be increased without limit, so long as payments are linked to production-limiting programmes.

The AoA's domestic support system currently allows Europe and the USA to spend $380 billion every year on agricultural subsidies alone. "It is often still argued that subsidies are needed to protect small farmers but, according to the World Bank, more than half of EU support goes to 1 per cent of producers while in the US 70 per cent of subsidies go to 10 per cent of producers, mainly agri-businesses". The effect of these subsidies is to flood global markets with below-cost commodities, depressing prices and undercutting producers in poor countries – a practice known as dumping.

Market Access

"Market access" is the second pillar of the AoA, and refers to the reduction of tariff (or non-tariff) barriers to trade by WTO member-states. The 1995 AoA required tariff reductions of:

- 36 per cent average reduction by developed countries, with a minimum per tariff line reduction of 15 per cent over six years.
- 24 per cent average reduction by developing countries with a minimum per tariff line reduction of 10 per cent over ten years.

Least Developed Countries (LDCs) were exempted from tariff reductions, but either had to convert non-tariff barriers to tariffs—a process called tariffcation—or "bind" their tariffs, creating a "ceiling" which could not be increased in future.

Export Subsidies

"Export subsidies" is the third pillar of the AoA. The 1995 AoA required developed countries to reduce export subsidies by at least 35 per cent (by value) or by at least 21 per cent (by volume) over the five years to 2000.

Criticism

The AoA has been criticised by civil society groups for reducing tariff protections for small farmers – a key source of income for developing countries. At the same time, the AoA has allowed rich countries to continue paying their farmers massive subsidies which developing countries cannot afford.

The Agriculture Agreement has been criticised by many Non-Governmental Organizations (NGOs) for categorizing subsidies into trade-distorting domestic subsidies (the amber box) which have to be reduced, and non-trade distorting subsidies (blue and green boxes) which escape disciplines and thus can be increased. Third World Network states that "This has allowed the rich countries to maintain or raise their very high subsidies by switching from one kind of subsidy to another... like a magician's trick. This is why after the Uruguay Round the total amount of subsidies in OECD countries have gone up instead of going down, despite the apparent promise that Northern subsidies will be reduced." Moreover, Martin Khor argues that the green and blue box subsidies can be just as trade-distorting as "the protection is better disguised, but the effect is the same".

WTO Negotiations on Agriculture and Developing Countries

The Doha Round of trade talks has been deadlocked since July 2006 mainly on account of differences relating to agriculture. If the negotiations eventually succeed in establishing a fair and harmonious agricultural trading system, it will have far-reaching implications for trade and economic prospects of developing countries.

To understand the reasons underlying the protracted stalemate and to assess the prospect of agreement on various proposals, the trading community needs to be initiated into the intricacies of the WTO rules and modalities of the negotiations. This volume provides an authoritative analysis of the provisions of the WTO agreements and of their evolution and fills an important gap in the existing literature.

The study examines the implementation experience of key members of the WTO and traces developments in the negotiations up to the recent impasse. Using India as a case study, the authors suggest ways of negotiating and strategizing for developing countries. They offer tough but realistic recommendations regarding market access, subsidies, special and differential treatment of developing countries, and other issues in negotiations.

The World Trade Organization's Doha Round of trade talks has been plagued by a lack of concrete progress toward establishing a fair and harmonious agricultural trading system. Because the results of the Doha Round could have far-reaching implications for the trade and economic prospects of developing countries in the twenty-first century, it is critical for these countries to fully understand the issues involved in the negotiations on agriculture.

However, there has been no authoritative analysis of the rules and modalities on which governments of developing countries can rely. This book, coauthored by an insider to the trade talks that led to the establishment of the WTO, fills this gap. The volume begins with a detailed analysis of the provisions of the WTO's Agreement on Agriculture and the modalities of the negotiations. It examines the implementation experience of key members of the WTO.

Then WTO traces the developments in the negotiations up to the recent impasse. In light of these considerations, and on the basis of a case study of India, the authors propose various elements of a negotiating position and strategy for developing countries. The authors offer tough but realistic recommendations regarding tariffs, market access, treatment of sensitive or special products, and other aspects of international trade.

This book will be of particular interest to researchers and practitioners as well as students seeking in-depth knowledge of the recent history of agricultural trade talks.

C. THE WTO AGREEMENT ON AGRICULTURE AND CONCERNS OF DEVELOPING COUNTRIES

1. Market Access: Main Features of the Agreement

The biggest advance made in the Agreement on Agriculture (AoA) in respect of market access for agricultural products was to prohibit the use of quantitative restrictions on imports and measures such as variable levies, minimum import prices, voluntary export restraints and similar border measures other than ordinary customs duties. AoA stipulated that all these measures should be converted into tariffs and subjected to binding and/or reduction.

Measures maintained under non-agriculture-specific provisions of GATT 1994, such as balance-of-payments restrictions, were exempted from the tariffication requirement. WTO members were required to reduce, over six years, customs duties on all products, including those resulting from tariffication, by 36 per cent on a simple average basis, with a minimum rate of reduction of 15 per cent on each tariff line. Where there were no significant imports, members were required to establish minimum access opportunities, set at a level of 3 per cent of the corresponding domestic consumption in the first year, rising to 5 per cent by the end of the implementation period.

While current access opportunities in excess of the stipulated minimum were to be maintained a time-bound exception from the tariffication requirement was made in respect of many primary products where imports comprised less than 3 per cent of domestic consumption. No export subsidies were being granted and effective production-restricting measures were in place. However, the condition was imposed that enhanced minimum access opportunities would be provided, beginning with 4 per cent of domestic consumption and rising by 0.8 per cent each year during the implementation period (only Japan availed itself of this exception). Members that had tariffied non-tariff measures were given access to the Special Safeguard provision of the Agreement.

This provision entitled these members to impose additional duties on a product in any year when either the volume of imports exceeded, or the price of imports fell below, the designated trigger levels. Developing country members were accorded special and differential treatment in the modalities for binding/reduction of tariffs. The reduction required was only 24 per cent on a simple average basis, subject to a minimum of 10 per cent for each tariff line.

The period of implementation for them was 10 years instead of 6 years. Further, in the case of unbound tariffs, they were given the option of binding the tariffs at ceiling levels while eliminating all non-tariff measures not covered by non-agriculture-specific provisions of GATT 1994. They were also given a time-bound exception from the rule on tariffication in respect of the main staple food of the country. (Only a few members, including the Philippines and the Republic of Korea, availed themselves of this exception.)

2. Market Access: Concerns of Developing Countries

Developing countries point out that agricultural tariffs have become very complex and non-transparent, with a high degree of reliance on specific tariffs, and the use of compound tariffs with *ad valorem* and specific components. This situation is complicated further with the use of factors such as sugar or alcohol content to determine the incidence of tariff.

Developing countries also point out that the process of tariffication resulted in an increased level of protection. Not only did the choice of the base period of 1986-1988 entail that protection would be captured at its historically high level, but also many countries used the flexibility in the modalities for the conversion of non-tariff measures in a manner that overstated the tariff equivalent.

Furthermore, the requirement for tariff reduction by a simple average of 36 per cent resulted in a shallower reduction in tariffs for sensitive products. Tariff peaks, therefore, continue to be a characteristic feature of the agricultural sector. Tariffs remain prohibitively high on many temperate-zone products and, despite the progress achieved, tariff escalation still remains prominent in tropical products.

Implementation of tariff rate quotas (TRQs), established for maintaining current access and granting minimum access, has also been problematic. The administration of TRQs has been such that there have been many instances of quota under-fill even when domestic prices were higher than international prices, and the practice of allocating quotas on the basis of aggregated commodity groups has increased the problems of exporters. In many cases, TRQs representing current access have been allocated to preferential and traditional suppliers, denying enhanced access to new efficient suppliers.

3. Domestic Support: Main Features of the Agreement

AoA targeted for substantial reduction those practices, such as market price supports that cause the most distortion to trade and production. It first identified measures that have no, or at most minimal, trade-distorting effects or effects on production, and exempted them from reduction requirements. These measures have come to be known as the **Green Box** measures. AoA was also exempted from reduction in commitments with other set of measures, namely, direct payments made conditional on limitation of production, as these are considered less distorting than open-ended price support. These measures constitute the **Blue Box**. A third category of measures, comprising investment subsidies that are generally available to agriculture, agricultural input subsidies generally available to low-income and resource-poor farmers and domestic support to encourage diversification from growing illicit narcotic crops, was also exempted from reduction commitments to be undertaken by the developing countries. The measures not included in the exempt categories described above, popularly referred to as **Amber Box** measures, were subject to reduction commitments.

The modalities agreed during the negotiations required by Governments first to compute the Aggregate Measurement of Support (AMS), which was the annual level of non-exempted measures provided to agriculture, expressed in monetary terms. The calculations had to be made separately for product-specific and non-product-specific support.

Whereas the product-specific support, expressed as a percentage of the value of the production of the relevant basic agricultural product, or the non-product-specific-support, expressed in terms of percentage of the value of the entire agricultural production, came to less than the *de minimis* level of 5 per cent (10 per cent for developing countries), there was no requirement to undertake reduction commitments. In other cases, WTO members were required to reduce their total AMS by 20 per cent over a period of 6 years (13.33 per cent over 10 years for developing countries).

The reduction of commitments are reflected in the schedules of each WTO member, and they are mandated not to exceed AMS permitted for each year of the implementation period. For members with no reduction commitment, the requirement is that the support must not be provided to agriculture in excess of the *de minimis* level separately for product-specific and non-product-specific support. The modalities provided for the initial AMS calculations to be based on the levels that existed during the period 1986-1988. Market price support was calculated using the gap between a fixed external reference price and the applied administrative price. Certain other forms of subsidies had also to be included in the AMS calculation.

No allowance has been made in AoA for normal rates of inflation in compliance with domestic support commitments. However, if the rate of inflation is excessive, its influence on the ability of a member to abide by its commitments has to be taken into consideration. Furthermore, in proving compliance with the AMS commitments during the implementation period, a member has to follow the same methodology, including the choice of currency, as was adopted at the time of making the commitments or submitting the data.

Article 13 of AoA, popularly known as the "peace clause", exempts all Green Box measures from actionability against injury to domestic industry, nullification or impairment of GATT benefits and serious prejudice to the interests of other members to which agricultural products would have been otherwise liable under the WTO Agreement on Subsidies and Countervailing Measures. Blue Box measures are similarly exempted, if the support to a specific commodity does not exceed the level of the 1992 marketing year. While Green Box measures are not liable for the imposition of countervailing duties, in respect of Blue Box measures it is provided only that due restraint must be shown while initiating countervailing duty investigations.

4. Domestic Support: Concerns of Developing Countries

Developing countries pointed out that the lack of financial resources limits their ability to subsidize their agriculture sector, and in this respect, they suffered from an inherent disadvantage as compared with the developed countries. However, AoA institutionalizes the disparity by allowing high subsidizing developed countries to maintain 80 per cent of their base-level AMS, while prohibiting the developing countries from going beyond the *de minimis* level of 10 per cent set for them. While AMS has been reduced, the overall level of subsidization of agriculture has increased in the developed countries as a result of re-instrumentation of support from field of measures subject to reduction commitments with those measures not subjected to such commitments.

Consequently, the total support estimate (TSE) of the countries belonging to OECD rose from US$ 308 billion in the period 1986-1988 to US$ 361 billion in 1999. Furthermore, developing countries question whether Green Box measures are as minimally trade-distorting as was originally assumed. Such payments even when decoupled from production levels, have an impact on the income and wealth of farmers and provide the means for them to invest more in production. They reduce the perception of risks associated with future production and increase land values, resulting in the maintenance of land in farming, rather than putting it to other uses.

For these reasons, despite the reduction of AMS, there has not been any decrease in the uneconomic production of cereals, for instance, in the developed countries. On account of the perceived trade-distorting effect of Green Box measures, developing countries have expressed concern at the exemption of these measures from the imposition of countervailing duties.

While most developing countries of the ESCAP region did not undertake any reduction commitments on domestic support, some have experienced problems in complying with AoA commitments, because of stipulations which fix the external reference price, make the methodology for calculation of the AMS unchangeable and give no allowance for normal rates of inflation. The problems of these countries arise from the prevailing high levels of inflation in their economies and the depreciation of their exchange rates. The ceiling of 10 per cent on product-specific support has also been a source of concern.

5. Export Competition: Main Features of the Agreement

While AoA did not prohibit the use of export subsidies, it made a major advance by requiring members to undertake reduction commitments in respect of six types of export subsidy practices which were most prevalent at that time and which have been listed in the Agreement. Members were required to reduce their budgetary outlays on these subsidies by 36 per cent of the base period outlays (1986-1990) and the quantities of subsidized exports by 21 per cent over a period of six years. Commitments in terms of the reduced budgetary outlay and reduced subsidized quantities for each year of the implementation period have been incorporated in the WTO schedules of the members. AoA originally gave some flexibility to members to carry forward unused export subsidy outlays and subsidized exports in the initial years.

AoA prohibits the use of listed export subsidies, except in accordance with the commitments incorporated in the schedules. It also stipulates that non-listed export subsidies must not be applied to circumvent the commitments. Members have also undertaken to work towards the development of internationally agreed disciplines on export credit, export credit guarantees or insurance programs.

In respect of International Food Aid scheme, it is stipulated that, its numerous provisions must not be tied to commercial exports of agricultural products to recipient countries. Further, the food aid transactions must be carried out in accordance with the "Principles of Surplus Disposal and Consultative Obligations" of the Food and Agriculture Organization (FAO) of the United Nations, and that such aid must be provided to the extent possible in fully grant form or on terms no less concessional than those provided for under Article IV of the 1986 Food Aid Convention.

AoA also contains disciplines on export prohibitions and restrictions. Before a member institutes a new export prohibition or restriction, it must notify the measure and discuss with any other member having an interest as an importer and any other matter related to the measure. AoA exempts developing countries from the requirement to undertake reduction commitments in two of the six listed export subsidy practices, namely, subsidies to reduce the cost of marketing exports and subsidies on internal transport and freight charges on export shipments. Furthermore, developing countries are required to reduce their budgetary outlays by 24 per cent and the subsidized quantities by 14 per cent over a period of 10 years. Developing countries are not covered by the obligation to notify new export restrictions unless they are net exporters of the product in question.

6. Export Competition: Concerns of Developing Countries

The absence of internationally agreed rules governing the use of export credits, export credit guarantees and insurance programmes have enabled some countries to circumvent and reduce the value of export subsidy reduction commitments. Developing countries also point out that the use of a rollover facility, permissible in the past, allowed members to carry forward unused subsidy credits from the years when international prices were high to years when these prices were low, thereby aggravating the problem of low prices.

Another concern expressed is that members that were subsidizing exports in the base period and had notified export subsidies in their schedules are permitted to use them, although to a reduced extent, while members that had no export subsidies in the base period are not permitted to introduce them.

7. Clause of Food Security and Development in the Agreement

As discussed above, AoA has a number of provisions for the special and differential treatment of the developing countries in recognition of their development needs. Special provision has also been made for buffer-stocking operations for food security purposes and for domestic food aid in these countries.

In addition, AoA has provided that non-trade concerns, including food security and special and differential provisions for developing countries must be taken into consideration in the WTO negotiations for the continuation of the reform process. A separate declaration adopted by ministers at Marrakech envisages, among others, the consideration of enhanced food aid and technical and financial assistance for the least developed and net food-importing countries to enable them to improve their agricultural productivity and infrastructure.

D. PROPOSALS OF DEVELOPING COUNTRIES WITH COMPARATIVE ADVANTAGE IN AGRICULTURE

The developing countries of the ESCAP region have made proposals in most cases jointly with countries outside the region and in only one or two cases individually. There are differences in these levels for lack of detailed ambitious proposals. Those proposals represent the mainstream and are summarized below. Special and differential treatment of the developing countries is dealt with mainly in the next section on proposals to address the issues of food security and development concerns.

1. Market Access

(a) Deep cuts to all tariffs using a harmonization formula that achieves greater reduction on higher level tariffs, including tariff peaks, eliminates tariff escalation and establishes maximum levels for all tariffs.

(b) Additional steps to eliminate tariffs, in particular for tropical products.

(c) Tariff quota volumes to be increased substantially, strengthened rules and disciplines to be provided to ensure that tariff quota administration does not diminish the size and value of market access opportunities provided by such tariff quotas

(d) Provisions to make tariff regimes simpler and more transparent, elimination of specific minimum entry price schemes and of practices containing elements resembling the erstwhile variable levy system;

(e) Elimination of special agricultural safeguard mechanism as well as of special treatment, as provided in Annex 5 of AoA.

(f) Down payment in the first year of the implementation period by way of substantial tariff reduction and expansion of tariff quota volumes.

2. Domestic Support

(a) Termination at the end of 2003 of the "peace clause" that restricts action against domestic support under GATT 1994 and the Agreement on Subsidies and Countervailing Measures.

(b) Adoption of a formula approach to reduce substantially and eventually eliminate trade and production support, including AMS and Blue Box measures.

(c) Review of basic and policy-specific criteria for Green Box support to ensure that the measures included in the box meet the fundamental requirement of no, or at the most minimal, trade-distorting effects or effects on production and/or imposition of an overall cap on the budget allocated to Green Box measures.

(d) Ensuring that trade and production-distorting support is reduced for all agricultural products by requiring commitments on a disaggregated basis.

(e) Down payment in the first year of the implementation period through a substantial initial education.

(f) Collapse all domestic support measures into one general subsidies box, allowing a common level of support of 10 per cent to be non-actionable for all countries.

(g) Direct payments under production-limiting programmes as well as decoupled income support falling under paragraphs 5, 6 and 7 of Annex 2 (Green Box) to be combined with AMS and reduced to 5 per cent by developed countries in three years and 10 per cent by developing countries in five years.

3. Export Competition

(a) Elimination and prohibition of all forms of export subsidies for all agricultural products.

(b) Substantial down payment in terms of reduction of outlays and volumes of export subsidies during the first year of the implementation period.

(c) Additional and strengthened rules and disciplines to be developed to prevent the circumvention of the elimination and prohibition of all forms of export subsidies including export credits, export credit guarantees or insurance programmes and non-commercial transactions.

(d) Termination of rollover flexibility granted for the original implementation period.

(e) Termination of the due restraint provision with respect to action against export subsidies.

(f) Development of improved disciplines on export restrictions and taxes.

E. PROPOSALS OF MAJOR INDUSTRIALIZED COUNTRIES

While some developed countries have submitted proposals for liberalization very broadly on the same lines as developing countries, others have emphasized the multifunctional role of agriculture, covering, among others, the protection of the environment, maintenance of the vitality of the rural areas, food security and consumer concerns. The proposals of those developed countries that lay emphasis on the multifunctional role of agriculture are summarized below.

1. Market Access

(a) Maintenance of the modality for tariff reduction of the Uruguay Round for an average overall reduction of bound tariffs and a minimum reduction per tariff line.

(b) Tariff reduction commitments should recognize the individual situation of each member country and special consideration should be given to the key staple crop.

(c) No sector-specific reduction of tariff.

(d) Review of the minimum access opportunities on the basis of the latest volume of consumption and other relevant factors.

(e) While TRQ administration needs to be made transparent, members must retain flexibility depending on market conditions and the characteristics of each product.

(f) Retention of special agricultural safeguards and introduction of a new safeguard for seasonal and perishable products.

2. Domestic Support

(a) Retention of the current basic framework of rules and disciplines of domestic support with Amber, Blue and Green boxes.

(b) Revisiting the criteria to be met by measures falling within the Green Box to ensure minimal trade distortion.

(c) Improvement and easing of requirements in some cases "in order to promote agriculture policy reform by reflecting the real situation of agriculture".

(d) Extension of coverage of the Green Box to include compensatory payment for multifunctionality of agriculture, support for enhancing income safety net.

(e) Support for small-scale family farm households and support for agricultural and rural development in developing countries.

3. Export Competition

(a) Need for level playing field in export competition by covering officially supported export credit by specific rules and disciplines.

(b) Revision and strengthening of rules on food aid and elimination of practices of cross-subsidization, price-pooling and similar practices by state trading enterprises.

(c) Binding the level of unit value of export subsidy; strengthening of discipline on domestic support that has similar effect as export subsidy.

(d) Tariffication of export prohibitions and restrictions and binding of export taxes.

(e) For products subject to export taxes, establishment of quotas for exports free of tax.

(f) Emergency measures to restrict exports to be of short duration and to maintain the proportion of exports to domestic production at the level of the preceding years.

F. PROPOSALS TO ADDRESS FOOD SECURITY, DEVELOPMENT AND RELATED ISSUES

The concerns related to food security and development over-arch the three pillars of AoA, but for analytical purposes they are best considered under these pillars. The proposals of the developing countries usually call for special and differential treatment of developing countries to address these concerns.

1. Market Access

The proposals made by the developing countries for special and differential treatment to address their food security and development concerns cover a broad spectrum. Some proposals call for faster and deeper cuts in, or elimination of, tariffs on all agricultural products, including value-added products, produced and exported by developing countries, provision of improved opportunities for exports from developing countries, preservation of the current special safeguards for developing countries and differential treatment in respect of commitments to be undertaken by them.

Other proposals demand greater flexibility in the market access commitments of developing countries. They call upon for developing countries to be allowed to maintain appropriate levels of tariff bindings, keeping in mind their development needs as well as high distortions prevalent in the international markets so as to protect the livelihood of the large percentage of the population dependent on agriculture.

They call upon for the right to raise low tariff bindings committed during the Uruguay Round to ceiling bindings. They call upon for the establishment of a separate safeguard mechanism on the lines of the existing one, but envisage also the imposition of quantitative restrictions in the event of surges in imports or declines in prices in order to ensure the food and livelihood security of the people. One proposal calls for special consideration for key staple crops and greater flexibility in reducing border protection measures, especially on products related to non-trade concerns.

One developed country of the region has proposed a wide range of flexibility for developing countries on broader measures and their application in order to ensure their food security. Another developed country has proposed that multilateral liberalization should be supplemented by preferences for developing countries and undertaking an examination to impart stability to preferences.

2. Domestic Support

One proposal calls for enhanced Green Box provisions for developing countries that would address specific concerns regarding food security, rural development and poverty eradication. It endorses a differentiated formula for commitments by developing countries, including the continuation of existing provisions on investment and input subsidies, and domestic support to encourage diversification from growing illicit narcotic crops.

Another proposal envisages more general provisions to give developing countries an effective and meaningful degree of autonomy on policy instruments to address food security concerns. It proposes extension of the existing *de minimis* concept only for developing countries. Another proposal is to exclude from AMS calculations product-specific support to low-income and resource-poor farmers.

A proposal of general application but of potential relevance to developing countries is that, while product-specific support should be calculated at the aggregate level, support to any one commodity should not be allowed to exceed double the amount of the *de minimis* limit. The proposal also calls for allowing negative product-specific support to be set off against the positive non-product-specific AMS figures.

It proposes that, after the expiry of the peace clause, developing country measures under the Green Box and domestic support measures conforming to AoA must be exempted from countervailing duties and from actions based on non-violation nullification or impairment of the benefits of tariff concessions. The suggestion also calls for all measures of special and differential treatment in respect of market access and domestic support to constitute a "food security box" for developing countries. Another proposal envisages the establishment of a "development box" constituted by measures, including broader measures, to encourage developing countries to maintain or increase their current domestic production capability as well as to protect the livelihood of small farmers.

Another developing country has proposed alleviation of reduction commitments and additional flexibility relating to the use of Green Box measures, especially for measures to improve food security and rural employment, even if they have an impact on trade. A developed country of the ESCAP region envisages flexibility being given to developing countries concerning domestic support in order, not to affect the support necessary to increase food production for domestic consumption.

Another developed country calls for enhancement of the Green Box to cover measures, among others, for poverty alleviation and food security in developing countries. It proposes additional flexibility to developing countries, including through a revision of the *de minimis* clause for them. One other developed country proposes the creation of additional criteria for exempt support measures deemed essential to the development and food security objectives of developing countries in order to facilitate the development of targeted programmes to increase investment and improve infrastructure.

3. Export Competition

One proposal calls for a longer implementation timeframe for the developing countries and the maintenance of the existing provision of special and differential treatment until the elimination and prohibition has been completed. Another proposal calls for the retention of the existing measures of special and differential treatment in their entirety and additionally proposes the extension to agriculture the dispensation of Article 27 read with Annex VII of the Agreement on Subsidies and Countervailing Measures to developing countries.

It proposes further that, after the expiry of the peace clause, export assistance measures permitted to developing countries must be exempted from countervailing duties and actions based on Article XVI of GATT 1994 and the Agreement on Subsidies and Countervailing Measures. Yet another developing country has proposed the expansion of export subsidies exempt from reduction commitments for developing countries and alleviation of export subsidy reduction commitments. A developed country of the ESCAP region has proposed that, while strengthening rules and disciplines on exports and state trading, measures to exempt or ease obligations must be taken so as not to cause an excessive burden on developing countries.

G. OTHER PROPOSALS FOR MEETING FOOD SECURITY AND DEVELOPMENT OBJECTIVES

A developed country of the ESCAP region has proposed the examination of a possible framework for international food stockholding in order to complement existing food aid schemes. Another developed country has recognized that food aid provided to the least developed and net food-importing countries is an important means for achieving food security in developing countries, so long as it is provided in fully grant form and in ways that do not damage local production and marketing capacities.

Yet another developed country recognizes that liberalization alone will not address food security needs in all developing and least developed countries. International food aid and credit programs must play a continuing role in providing for food to people of needy countries.

Possible Benefits for India:

Some positive avenues are opened up for our country to carry out agricultural trade commodities and for value added products in all the member countries. It has been argued that as a result of such a rule based practice our country may reap benefits:

1. Prices of agricultural commodities at the global level would move upwards which is in favour of domestic producers.
2. Sequel to this there is sharp increase in the production of exportable commodities
3. The benefit also covers introduction of new technology for its application in agriculture.
4. Consumers can have more options in terms of quality, safety, variety, size and packing.
5. There will be more capital resources in the field of agriculture.

Present Status in Indian Agriculture:

Above all these benefits, still there is apprehension that Indian farmers will get affected under the WTO's AoA but this apprehension of concern is baseless and unwarranted. Because India is under no obligation under WTO's AoA to decrease any subsidies that were being enjoyed by farmers as aggregate value of subsidies given to the Indian farmers are beneficial and well below the ceiling prescribed under AoA. Moreover, developing countries like India have been provided with three additional concessions from the calculation of aggregate value of subsidies.

These subsidies are mainly investment subsidies, which are generally available to agriculture. Further agricultural input subsidies, generally available to low economic and or resourceful to poor farmers who are under BPL (below poverty line). In addition to this, government's support to producers to encourage them to diversify from growing illicit narcotic crops.

But still India opine there is nothing to worry for any developing country(s) and they are at liberty to negotiate on agriculture and no developing country will feel disappointed with the outcome on agriculture in the negotiations.

SALIENT FEATURES OF AGRO PRODUCTS

In this era of globalization, urbanization and awareness among consumers' ever growing demand for storage facilities of agricultural produces, their quality, and safety are being exported and are being consumed in many countries who are also self-sufficient in agricultural produces.

But there is change in the dimension of consumers' perception which is evident as they are willing to pay for the consistency, safety of the value-added foods they purchase. Many of the safety and quality standards of value-added foods are influencing the consumers which they purchase. Many of these are largely determined by handling and treatment of commodities at the farm gate. This new demand not only requires products to meet the standards, but also certification from authorized organizations.

But in view of many agriculture experts, agricultural commodities are important sources of income generation and also important in terms of consumption. These are field crops, fruits and vegetables, milk and its products, livestock products, marine products, plantation crops. But majority of farming community are engaged in field activities and plantation of crops. Maximum amount of income comes from export of various produce and in particular plantation crops like coffee, tea, rubber, jute, cotton, and other commercial crops.

Field crops mainly consists of small grains like sesame, oilseeds, pepper, wheat, rice, corn, sorghum, soybean, cotton as well as pasture, sugar and forage crops are few to say.

Features of Field Crops: These small grain crops are sown and grown in wider areas, normally planted under subsistence farming for self consumption as well as for the market. And most producers applying age old and traditional practices and they do have large and spacious storage facilities. These crops are sown and grown in irrigable and cultivable area of the country. Majority of farmers are now interested in growing these agro products. Further these small grain crops are need of the hour for the government as majority of farmers depend on this segment.

Features of Products of Field Crops: Indian markets for these products are very much supportive and have continuous demand throughout the year. Many of the products are produced in the growing area itself. For instance, flooring of wheat, pulses, maize, jowar, millets, etc. Many of the products are raw materials for agro based industry in India. These crops are mainly inevitable for day-to-day consumption and so their prices are more or less stable throughout the country. But ultimately food security of India depends on these crops and products, as most of them are non-perishable in nature. Loans are easily available for these crops, their produce with products on contractual trade is also on anvil throughout the year. Albeit this, similar high value products are also manufactured from these products. Each product made up by these crops have different level of markets. Many area-wise markets in the close vicinity of the farm lands where these crops are grown will be available with transportation facilities.

Plantation Crops: These crops require large land holdings and mainly grown for economic significance, rather than for subsistence farming with adequate number of labour force carry out their part of work. These crops on the whole are grown in the form of plantation and monitored by well managed people with wider market network. For instance, tobacco, coffee, cotton, sugarcane or eucalyptus tree, and teak wood tree.

Some crops are used as high value-added crops grown are used as raw materials for beverage like tea, coffee, rubber, fruit orchards, black pepper, sunflower orchard, and some spices and includes sales, consultancy and support activities from crop producers.

Features of Plantation Crops: Plantation are carried out under monoculture farming. These crops are grown by a number of labours who are residents of that area, and many crops include herbs and shrubs besides they are new to the ecological serenity and environmental friendly. But the features of products made up of these plantation crops are of high value and contributing to GDP and National Income. These products are mainly commercial and not for subsistence farming. These products are available in free market and some of the products are export oriented and can earn enormous profits and foreign exchange. The products of these crops are non-perishable and seasonal, but continuous consultancy, marketing facilities branding and distribution are indispensable.

WHY AGRI-BASED SERVICE SECTOR IS IN DEMAND?

Post-independence era witnessed slow but steady progress in the agriculture sector and this slow progress was due to lack of adequate measures from government in those days. The production of milk has increased drastically due to increase in population and thus making India as largest milk producer in the world. But still India needs irrigable land for growing agriculture products and for its processing and India has long way ahead to become self-sufficient in catering to its people.

Shrinking resource base: The groundwater table is receding frequently and vacant lands are being used for urbanization, construction of shopping malls and residential complexes. The situation get worsen day by day if urbanization is not prevented timely. Further inappropriate technologies are applied for small land holdings, resulting in low yield of produce which poses threat of famine.

Changes in demand and consumption pattern: Day-to-day shift in lifestyles, tastes, preferences and consumption pattern the average land holdings of farmers are declining everyday during last five decades and has reached alarming level. And many water resources that are available from canals and other channels are receding thereby water scarcity and poor water management problem.

Change in demand-consumption pattern: Nowadays, people are more health conscious and have changed their consumption pattern of food intake and there is decline in per capita consumption of cereals, in the states but consumption of vegetables, fruits, meat, fish, eggs, and dairy products have increased. This trend also increased the demand for livestock products.

Change in farming systems: Due to frequent changes in consumption pattern and people's tastes, preference and lifestyles, the areas under food cultivation is going down drastically but for non-foodgrains the land usage is under increase. Similarly, there is ever growing demand for vacant land for its use in horticulture and agriculture, thus proved to be unending problem because of increasing demand for vacant land.

Diminishing public investment: Many states as well as centre have decreased their investment in agriculture considerably due to channelizing of funds to R & D for finding appropriate technological solutions for irrigation, rural roads, rural electrification, storage, marketing, agricultural research and education besides in the field of land development, cooperation. Further extension of agriculture related activities need to be addressed as researchers face problems during evaluation of technological options. Thus, there is constant need for pooling of resources to develop and maintain necessary infrastructure through increased efforts and investments.

GOVERNMENT'S NEW INITIATIVE - 2011

Government of India in its new initiative aiming for qualitative growth in Food Processing Sector had extended Financial Assistance for setting up/upgradation of existing quality control/ Food Testing Laboratories with following objectives:

1. To establish a surveillance system to monitoring the quality and composition of food.
2. To analyze the samples received from food processing industries and other shareholders.
3. To reduce the time of analysis of samples by reducing transportation time samples.
4. To ensure compliance of international standards on food in case of exports as well as imports.

Pattern of Financial Assistance:

1. Central/State government and its organizations/Universities including Deemed Universities will be eligible for grant-in-aid of entire cost of laboratory equipments required for labs. In addition, they would also be eligible to 25 per cent of the cost of technical inaccessibility for civil works to instal the equipments and furnitures with fixtures associated with the equipments for general areas and 33 per cent for difficult areas.
2. All other implementing agencies/private sector organizations will be eligible for grant-in-aid of 50 per cent of cost of laboratory equipments and 25 per cent of the cost of technical civil works to house the equipments and furniture and the fixtures associated with the equipments for general areas and 33 per cent for difficult areas.

The applications can be submitted directly to the Ministry of Food Processing Industries through Joint Secretary (Administration), Ministry of Food Processing Industries, Government of India, Panchsheel Bhawan, August Kranti Marg, New Delhi-110049 and telephone Number is 011-26492176 and official website is http://mofpi.nic.in.

BAN ON PULSES EXPORT

In an effort to ease the burden of rising food prices, the Government of India recently extended the ban on export of pulses for an indefinite period and released additional quota of wheat and rice for various states to be sold at the subsidized rates through ration or PDS shops.

The Empowered Group of Ministers (EGoM) on Food, headed by Finance Minister, Mr. Pranab Mukherji in its recent meetings during beginning of this year reviewed the price situation in the country and also decided to allow duty free import of pulses until March 2012. The government had banned export of pulses which have a weight of pulses, which have a weight of 0.72 per cent in the wholesale price index, in June 2006.

In the said meeting, it was also decided to give additional 25 lakh tons of wheat and rice quota at the BPL (Below Poverty Line) rates to the states. The agriculture minister Mr. Sharad Pawar in turn reciprocated to the gesture of the government and agriculture ministry, ordered the BPL families have to pay ₹ 4.15 per kg for wheat and ₹ 5.65 per kg of rice. The 25 lakh ton in addition to the normal quota available to this category, it was decided to release another 25 lakh tons of additional quota of wheat and rice to APL (Above Poverty Line) families.

APL families pay ₹ 11.85 per kg for rice and ₹ 8.45 per kg for wheat and the total 50 lakh tons of additional quota of wheat and rice has been approved to the states. In view of soaring food prices, the government of India had taken several steps to ease the soaring prices of onions and other essential commodities. Food inflation rising day by day heaping more pressure on government to check spiraling food prices.

GOVERNMENT FAVOURS PPP IN SEEDS PROCESSING

As a result of simplification of procedures in the agricultural products, processing country witness greater participation of Public-Private Participation (PPP) in domestic seed business. In a report submitted to the Prime Minister, the working group on agriculture production headed by Chief Minister of Haryana recommended public-private participation (PPP) for production of seeds, setting up of processing facilities and complete revamp of state seed corporations. These suggestions could form a part of the National Seeds Plan and Seeds Bill 2004 which was awaiting enactment.

So far the private sector has been quite active in the manufacturing of seeds, especially the hybrid variety, but their participation in the seed processing segment was needed to improve the seed replacement ratio (SRR). The SRR is the ability of the seed to prove yield of a crop used more than once.

The report is of the view that seed processing facilities could be created in state seed corporations, agriculture universities and private seeds agencies with the help of Rural Krishi Vikas Yojana funds. In this regard, the National Seed Corporation and the State Farms Corporation of India are likely to set up processing facilities with the help of private sector companies.

For production and supply of seeds, the report has recommended state seed corporations and private corporate cooperatives of farmers to enter into long-term contracts. The report has been categorical in suggesting either a large-scale revamp or restructuring of public sector seed producing undertakings or closure of these to allow alternative mechanisms to grow. Restructuring and streamlining the public sector seeds producing undertakings are required to product diversification, upgradation, and for improving governance, core competence, and competitiveness as per the guidelines of the Report.

The restructuring, if approved by the government will involve addressing issues of undesirable equity board structure, poor professional management and heavy workload. The Report has also suggested that capital assets of the state seed firms can be optimally utilized if state farms and farmers partners to produce certified seeds. While states can procure the foundation seed and provide the land, actual seed multiplication can be entrusted to farmers under contractual arrangements with assured price and purchase. Farmers could be selected under a bidding arrangement on annual basis, or for a short period of two to three years.

This will enhance productivity of state seed farms manifold, without forcing the state farms management to work with temporarily or casually employed farmers.

SUMMARY

This unit deals with structure and forms of agriculture business and agriculture based industrial units. The industry sector in the agriculture segment focuses on value-added agriculture products and residues, both food and nonfood, by way of food processing exercise for easy marketing purposes. Further, these value-added products besides marketing can be made reusable and edible. Also there are many technologies which have proven in improving the quality of these processed food products and with modernized storage facilities that will make the food more fresh.

The agro-based industries in India are equipped with modernized way of fertility, plough of fertilized land and wasteland with less water requirements that can increase the yields of produce known as high tech agriculture technology that are under greater use for vegetable and fruit produce, floriculture, (flower growing using flower leaves for value-added food products for consumption purposes and medicine purpose, and also using flowers for preparation of refined edible oil for cooking purpose and some flower leaves are under use for preparation of biodiesel for its use in automobile vehicles.

QUESTIONS

1. What pivotal role WTO plays in the structure of Agriculture Business Management?
2. Write short note on: Domestic Support and Market Access.
3. Explain present status of Indian Agriculture in the global scenario.
4. Explain salient features of Government's new initiatives for Indian Agriculture to make it more vibrant and radiant.
5. Why is government emphasizing on PPP approach in agriculture sector and also in seeds processing?

OOO

CHAPTER 5

BASIC INFRASTRUCTURAL FACILITIES FOR AGRIBUSINESS

Warehousing Technology in Agribusiness

Agri-Clinics

Agribusiness Centres

Soil, Water Quality and Input Testing Labs

Plant Protection Services Centre

Vermi Composting Unit

Horticulture Clinic Business Centre

Agro Service Centre -Farm Machinery

Agro Service: Farm Machinery & Primary Processing

Private Veterinary Clinic

Private Veterinary Clinic with Retail Outlet

Private Veterinary Clinic - Small Dairy Units

Private Artificial Insemination Centre

Economic Hatchery for Car Seed Production

Food Processing Training Centre: (FPTC)

Agribusiness - Under Rapid Transformation

WAREHOUSING TECHNOLOGY IN AGRIBUSINESS

Need for agricultural processing, storage and transportation: Processing of agricultural products increases its utility and this is more important for agricultural products as almost all products are perishable and seasonal in nature but are required throughout the year. The industry has been noted as one of the foreign earning segment, Special Economic Zones (SEZs), and Agricultural Export Zones (AEZs), Free Trade Zones (FTZs) and Export Processing Zones (EPZs), are in existence by the government to promote exports.

To improve the value of the product, it should be kept in safe and cool place to make it more freshener and so storage facility is required to preserve the products during off-season for better price realization. High-tech storage facilities are essential for agriculture commodities because of their distinctive nature and for commodities consumed without processing like potatoes and onions. But care is to be exercised for milk products and milk to keep in cool place. Transportation plays important role in agriculture sector and acts as a catalyst to enhance the place value of the product. It is important factor in the agriculture sector because of the unique character of the agricultural products.

Need for storage and warehousing: A cool house or storage facility should be developed for storage and protection of agricultural products, processed foods, seeds, crops and other food items until they are dispatched to the customers.

There is constant need for storing goods so as to make them available to buyers on demand. Storage facilitates the corporate to carry out its processing for future demand to fetch good market price. The need for warehousing also arises because some foods are produced only in some seasons but demand arises throughout the year. In the meantime, the food items are produced throughout the year but have a demand in particular season while it helps to collect them with other similar products.

Advantages: Warehousing helps in preservation even in odd season and available on demand. This will have direct effect on price stabilization by balancing supply and demand. It will help in safe custody resulting in minimizing the risk to goods from loss, damage, fire, and theft etc. Cold storage prevents perishability of goods while some warehousing companies extend insurance cover to the products that are under storage against instances of fire, theft etc. Cold storage available for processing, blending, grading and packing, labeling, of the goods for sale and prospective buyers. Some banks provide loans as security known as pledge finance. Sometime the businessmen have to pay heavy customs duties in installments wherein pledge financing make easier for the businessmen to pay their encumbrances promptly.

Limitations: Loss in quantity due to rodents, fire, dehydration and theft, deterioration in quality due to insects, improper storage, dehydration and chemical reaction, and price risk. Similarly, cost of storage/warehousing – depreciation, repairs, insurance, interest on declining capital and rent also causes heavy losses. Also interest on investment for cold storages in the stored products while cost of quantitative and qualitative loss will cause loss. Other causes are cost of protective materials, change in taste, preferences and fashion together with risk of price change, and tax and labour payment.

Types of Warehouses

They are private warehouses, public warehouses, bounded warehouses and public warehousing agencies.

Private Warehouses: These are owned and operated by big businessmen and manufacturers to fulfill their storage needs. They have adequate funds to build the warehouses after buying vacant lands.

Public warehouses: These are under public agencies that provide storage facilities to general public on chargeable basis. They are also known as duty paid warehouses, and located generally near railway station, national and state highways, and waterways.

Bounded warehouses are licensed by the government and are located near main sea/air ports. They are either operated by government or private sectors but the products preserved inside the warehouse is not to be removed without the permission of custom authorities.

Public warehousing agencies:

(i) **Food Corporation of India (FCI):** The country's premier regulatory body of food and agricultural products is Food Corporation of India. It controls fair distribution of food grains and ensure its quality. FCI has countrywide network of warehouse facilities maintained scientifically with the method of CAP (Cover and Plinth) which is indigenous method developed by it.

(ii) **Central Warehousing Corporation (CWC):** It is premier warehousing agency of the country and biggest public warehousing operator and offers logistics service to diverse group of clients and has more than 500 warehouses across the country.

(iii) **State Warehousing Corporation (SWC):** Warehousing Corporations have also been set up in different states of the country like AP, MP, Haryana, Rajasthan, and Kerala. This sector has gained momentum ever since future trading and spot trading in agricultural commodities by big corporations started in a big way.

In all hypes and buzz, we can say agriculture sector and agro based industry can increase total income of rural households through value-added activities, institutions and through the agro food based rural manufacturing systems. Such increase in income can play a significant role in poverty reduction, sustainable growth and food security in the country. Further, India is an interested party to the WTO and therefore it is necessary to implement with the conditions set under the three broad areas – AoA, market access, domestic support, and export subsidies. In India most, farmers are dependent on field and plantation crops. Domestic trade of both these group of crops is very important and plantation crops are a good source of export earnings.

Grant-in-aid of 50 per cent of cost of laboratory equipments and 25 per cent of the cost of Technical civil works to house the equipments and furniture and the fixtures associated with the equipments for general areas and 33 per cent for difficult areas.

The applications can be submitted directly to the Ministry of Food Processing Industries through Joint Secretary (Administration), Ministry of Food Processing Industries, Government of India, Panchsheel Bhawan, August Kranti Marg, New Delhi-110049 and telephone Number is 011-26492176 and official website is: http://mofpi.nic.in

AGRI-CLINICS

Agro-clinics are envisaged to provide expert services and advise to farmers on cropping practices, technology dissemination, crop protection from pests and diseases, market trends and prices of various crops in the markets and also clinical services for animal health etc. which would enhance productivity of crops/animals.

AGRIBUSINESS CENTRES

Agribusiness centres are envisaged to provide input supply, farm equipments on hire and other services. In order to enhance viability, agriculture graduates may also take up ventures in agriculture and allied areas along with Agriclinics/Agribusiness centres.

An illustrative list of activities that can be financed under Agriclinic/Agribusiness centres is furnished below for information. The scheme is open to Agriculture Graduates/Graduates in subjects allied to agriculture like horticulture, animal husbandry, forestry, dairy, veterinary, poultry farming, pisciculture and other allied activities.

SOIL, WATER QUALITY AND INPUT TESTING LABS

Soil, water quality and input testing labs services centre can be opened to undertake testing and analysis of soil, irrigation, water and other inputs etc. Project cost will approximately estimate at ₹ 5,23,500 with recurring cost of ₹ 1,54,800 and repayment period of 6 years including grace period of one year.

PLANT PROTECTION SERVICES CENTRE

Launching of plant protection services centres are also technically viable with an objective of providing guidance and consultancy services for control of various pests and diseases weeds, etc. and to undertake plant protection services as a package deal from seeds to harvest. To undertake regular visits to provide advice, respond to enquiries, undertake control operations using own equipments etc. The project cost estimated approximately capital cost of ₹ 6,75,000, recurring cost out of ₹ 2,46,000 with repayment period of 6 years including grace period of one year.

VERMI COMPOSTING UNIT

It is also technically and economically feasible and viable with an objective to provide culture material of the desired species and train farmers and entrepreneurs to demonstrate practically the production methodology on the unit that can be more useful in the rural settings. The project cost estimated approximately — capital cost ₹ 2,77,000, recurring cost of ₹ 3,68,000 and repayment period of 8 years including grace period of one year.

HORTICULTURE CLINIC BUSINESS CENTRE

This kind of clinic business centre seems to be having high profitable business with objectives to create facilities for provision of technical guidance, custom hiring services, including grading and packing up to the fruit growers under a single roof. And to ensure easy availability of various horticultural inputs and technical/extension services to the orchardists or fruit growers to increase their productivity. To provide plant protection services, project costs estimated approximately ₹ 40,000 as capital cost and recurring cost ₹ 2,86,000 with repayment period of around 7 years including grace period of one year.

AGRO SERVICE CENTRE – FARM MACHINERY

Objectives: To hire out farm machinery for various farm operations like ploughing, leveling spraying etc., to provide services for repair and maintenance of farm machinery, and the project cost estimated at ₹ 6,56,400 as capital cost and recurring cost of ₹ 2,53,000 with repayment period of 10 years including one year of grace period.

AGRO SERVICE: FARM MACHINERY AND PRIMARY PROCESSING

This kind of service centre is profitable business to provide custom hire service facilities to farmers to improve post-harvest processing facilities and profitability of farmers. The project cost estimated as capital cost approximately of ₹ 7.08 lakhs, and recurring costs of ₹ 2.62 lakhs and the repayment period of 10 years including one year grace period.

PRIVATE VETERINARY CLINIC

This kind of clinic is essentially aiming at providing veterinary services to the farmers at their door-step with project cost of ₹ 1.46 lakhs approximately with repayment period of 8 years including one year grace period.

PRIVATE VETERINARY CLINIC WITH RETAIL OUTLET

Objective: In addition to providing veterinary servies, supplying feed and medicines also at the doorsteps of farmers. The project cost approximately of ₹ 2 lakhs with repayment period of 5 years.

PRIVATE VETERINARY CLINIC – SMALL DAIRY UNITS

Objective: Rearing of cattle by the beneficiary in addition to providing veterinary services at the doorsteps of the farmers. The project cost of ₹ 3.30 lakhs approximately with repayment period of 5 years.

PRIVATE ARTIFICIAL INSEMINATION CENTRE

Objectives: To provide improved artificial insemination services at the farmers' doorsteps to undertake breed improvement programme for indigenous cattle and buffalo breeds so as to improve their genetic quality. The project cost of approximately ₹ 56,000 to ₹ 91,000 with repayment period of 7 years including grace period of one year.

ECONOMIC HATCHERY FOR CROP SEED PRODUCTI ON

The objective is to breed commonly cultivated crop seeds varieties and other crop varieties. And the project cost estimated approximately of ₹ 4,55,000 and recurring cost would be ₹ 1,48,850 with repayment period of 5 years including a year of grace estimated period.

FOOD PROCESSING TRAINING CENTRE (FPTC)

The government at the centre had launched recently the financial assistance scheme for rural entrepreneurs to set up the Food Processing Training Centre (FPTC). The benefits of this scheme are to develop the rural entrepreneurship and transfer of technology for processing of food products.

And by utilizing locally grown raw material and providing "hands-on" experience at such production-cum-training centres while giving approval to government's priority for SC/ST/OBC and women entrepreneurs will get utmost priorities.

Pattern of financial assistance is through single product line centre for any one group of processing activity and ₹ 4 lakhs for fixed capital cost and ₹ 2 lakhs as revolving capital cost. The

Multiproduct line centre for more than one group of processing activity is ₹ 11 lakhs as fixed capital and ₹ 4 lakhs as revolving seed capital. Centre or State government organizations, educational and training institutions, schools and colleges, ITI, NGO, and Cooperatives will be eligible for grant to set up FPTC.

The applicants can visit for detailed information at http://mafpl.nic.in and e-mail ID for inquiry – while suggestions can be sent to Joint Secretary (Administration), Ministry of Food Processing Industries, Panchsheel Bhawan, August Kranti Marg, New Delhi-110049 and Fax No. would be 26492176.

Further applicants can apply in the proper format for any aforesaid schemes with complete details of the project indicating cost of land, building, equipments, and recurring expenditure, copy of quotation for equipments and duly forwarded by the respective state nodal agency (SNA).

The SNA in turn may process and forward their recommendations to the Ministry along with duly filled in checklist in the case of Central/State government organizations and departments universities and in case of autonomous bodies the proposal can be submitted directly to the Ministry with a copy to SNA.

The project may be taken up either individually or on joint/group basis by agriculture graduates. The outer ceiling for the cost of the project by individual would be ₹ 10 lakhs and for the project by the group would be ₹ 50 lakhs. The group may normally be of 5, of which one could be a management graduate with qualification or experience in business development and management.

AGRIBUSINESS – UNDER RAPID TRANSFORMATION

Agriculture has evolved into agribusiness and has become a vast and complex system that reaches beyond the farms to include all those who are involved in bringing food and fiber to consumers. Agribusiness include not only those that of farm lands but also the people and firms that provide the inputs (for e.g., seed, chemicals, credit etc.), to process the output (for e.g., milk, grain, meat etc.), to manufacture the food products (for e.g., ice-cream, bread, breakfast cereals etc.), and to transport and sell the food products to consumers (for e.g., restaurants, supermarkets etc.).

Agribusiness system has undergone a rapid transformation as new industries have evolved traditional farming operations and have grown larger and more specialized. The transformation did not happen overnight, but came slowly as a response to a variety of forces. Knowing something about how agribusiness came about, makes it easier to understand how this system operates today and how it is likely to change in the future.

Initially, agriculture being the major venture it was easy to become a farmer, but productivity was low. Average farmer produced enough food to feed just four people. As a consequence, most farmers were nearly totally self-sufficient. They produced most of the inputs they needed for production, such as seed, draft animals, feed and simple farm equipment.

Farming families processed the commodities they produce to make their own food and clothing. They consume or use just about everything they produce. The small amount of output not consumed on the farm was sold for cash. These items were used to feed and cloth the minor portion of the country's population that lived in villages and cities. A few agricultural products made their way into the export market and were sold to buyers in other countries.

Farmers found it increasingly profitable to concentrate on production and began to purchase inputs they formerly made themselves. This trend enabled others to build business that focused on meeting the need for inputs used in production agriculture such as seed, fencing, and machinery and so on.

These farms involved with the industries that serves as "agricultural inputs sector", and play major part in agribusiness and produce variety of technologically based products that account for approximately 75 per cent of all the inputs used in production agriculture.

At the same time, the agriculture input sector was evolving, a similar evaluation is taking place, a commodity processing and food manufacturing moved off the farm. The value-added forms of most commodities (wheat, rice, milk, livestock and so on) must be changed to make them more useful and convenient for consumers. For e.g., consumers would rather buy flour than grind the wheat themselves before baking a cake. They are willing to pay extra for the sake of buying the processed commodity (flour) instead of the raw agriculture commodity (wheat).

During the same period, technological advance were being made in food preservation method. Up until this time, the perishable nature of most agricultural commodities meant that they were available only at harvest. Advance in food processing have made it possible to get those commodities all throughout the year.

Today, even most farm families use purchased food and fiber products rather than doing the processing themselves. The farms that meet the consumers demand for greater processing and convenience also constitute a major part of agribusiness and are referred to as the processing manufacturing sector.

It is apparent that the definition of agriculture had to be expanded to include more than production. Farmers rely on the input industries to provide the products and service they need to produce agricultural commodities. They also rely on commodity processors, manufactured food products, and ultimately food distributors and retailers to purchase their raw agricultural commodities and to process and deliver them to the consumer for final sale. The result is the food and fiber system.

The food and fiber system is increasingly being referred to as "agribusiness". The term agribusiness was first introduced by Davis and Goldberg in 1957. It represents three part system made up of: (1) the agricultural input sector, (2) the production sector and (3) the processing-manufacturing sector. The caption and the full meaning of the term "agribusiness" is important which visualizes these three sectors as interrelated parts of a system in which the success of each part depends heavily on the proper functioning of the other two.

Thus, we can say in all hypes and buzz, the Agri-business management can be interpreted as types of activities with agriculture including, farming, management, financing, processing, marketing, growing of seeds and nursery stock, manufacture of fertilizers, chemicals, implements, processing, machinery and transportation equipment and the process of transportation itself.

The agri-business management has been treated as pure and applied science as coordinating scientific formulae of supplying agricultural production inputs and subsequently producing, processing and distributing food and fiber. This science includes all business enterprises that buy from or sell to the farmers – the transactions including either a product – commodity or a service and encompass items such as productive resources (feed, seed, fertilizers, equipments, energy and machinery) and also agricultural commodities with all food and fiber besides facilitative services credit, insurance, marketing, storage, processing, transportation, packaging and distribution etc.

The government's initiative to inject and pump required amount of budgetary allocation in the form of economic reforms that have necessitated professionalism in vital sectors of the Indian economy. Transformation of the agriculture sector into a competitive sector calls for professional management and use of modern technologies in areas such as specialized production, post-harvest management, promotion of value-added agri products, supply chain management, etc., so as to position these competitively both in the domestic as well as in international markets. Agribusiness Management Education is now a priority area in the country, as several State Agricultural Universities and Agricultural Institutes have added MBA (Agribusiness) and equivalent programs to their educational systems over the past one decade.

SUMMARY

Agriculture and agro-based products and processed value-added products are to be conserved and protected in scientific manner. To improve the value of these products, these should be kept in safe and cool place to make it more delicious and so storage facility is required to preserve the products during off-season for better price realization. High-tech storage facilities are essential for agricultural commodities because of their distinctive nature and for commodities consumed without processing like potatoes and onions. But care is to be exercised for milk products and milk to keep in cool place. Transportation plays important role in agriculture sector and acts as a catalyst to enhance the place value of the product. There is constant need for storage and warehousing. A cool house or storage facility should be developed for storage and protection of agricultural products, processed foods, seeds, crops and other food items until they are dispatched to the customers. There is constant need for storing goods so as to make them available to buyers on demand. Storage facilitates the corporate to carry out its processing for future demand to fetch good market price. The need for warehousing also arises because some foods are produced only in some seasons but demand arises throughout the year. In the meantime, the food items are produced throughout the year but have a demand in particular season while it helps to collect them with other similar products.

QUESTIONS

1. What basic infrastructural facilities are indispensable for agriculture business?
2. Write in your own words and critically analyze why agriculture business is still underpaid despite umpteen government's initiatives?
3. "Emergence of Retail outlets led to overall growth in Indian Dairy small units." Examine.
4. Explain why setting up of agriculture service centre and distribution of Farm Machinery equipments are necessary for desired yields.

ooo

UNIT - 2

CHAPTER 6

ROLE OF CORPORATE SECTOR AND AGRI EXPORT

Agro-based activities are plenty and interrelated. The productivity and production of food grains is vital for peace and prosperity of India. Many infrastructural factors like finance, technology, storage, transport, cooperatives, import-export policies, banking loans, basic facilities like electricity and water, are vital and are very much favourable for corporate sector to make investments and to generate adequate revenue for their part as well as to contribute to country's GDP.

Due to this, trade at the international level has become easier with many world-renowned corporates are eyeing India as their business destination. These corporate conglomerates are expected to fulfill the shortages in the process of economic development of India while they will control the prices in the market.

The New Economic Policy of 1991 and its aftermath, gradually the government in power has realized of late to adopt more flexible and favourable policies of economic liberalization, privatization and globalization (LPG). Government of India under the stewardship of Dr. Manmohan Singh – steering the agriculture sector in excellent way while making efforts to increase agricultural exports through various policy changes and investment in infrastructure development.

Thus, UPA government's decision are more vibrant in permitting the private sector corporates in direct purchasing and developing infrastructure for marketing and has boosted them to develop export market in all angles of the country. Many policies are being drafted and initiated by the centre in export segment to market new products leaving behind most of the traditional agro-based products because of stiff competition in the international arena.

In these days of commercialization in every step of human life, there are more employment opportunities and today agricultural sector is in need of able, capable and efficient competitive executives to chalk out timely strategies for marketing agro-based products at the local, zonal, national, regional and global level to earn good income and also contribute to India's GDP.

The executives are needed in this sector to take the mansion of agriculture marketing to decide production pattern and usage of resources for effective agriculture produce in given period of time. They also needed to think of factors that will change the present scenario of agriculture market significantly while they should also guide, advise and direct the agricultural farmers and the agriculture producers to properly use the optimal or uniformly inputs for agriculture production – that is equal amount of inputs like use of electricity, frequent water supply, fertilizers, manures, pesticides, better quality of seeds, and recommends or suggests useful decisions for financial assistance to the farmers from financial institutions.

MANAGEMENT DECISIONS

There are two types of management decisions. The first one Organizational management decision and second one is Operational Farm management decision. In the first instance, the farm managers or owners of agricultural lands are supposed to take initiatives to keep the agricultural sector on the right sector so as to increase the produce as well as profit while attracting the unemployed towards agriculture as unemployed youths are blindly rushing to urban areas in search of employment in the industry sector which is highly saturated with competition in every step.

There is demand for less investment of money in agriculture production and aim for huge profitable gains and this dream will become true only if management professionals will take initiative to enter into agricultural sector and take operational decisions 'how to produce gainful agriculture produce aiming at cost minimization'. One element 'principle of factor substitution' which will guide and direct managers to choose most useful method of production or technology that gives maximum financial gains with minimum investment.

This principle says it is useful, economical and appropriate to substitute one part of resource with another resource as long as the cost will be reduced to extreme minimum extent. Say for example if you are sowing wheat, then it will cost ₹ 100/- per acre, then you will have to invest ₹ 100 for wheat and get maximum benefit of about ₹ 300 or ₹ 400. Next you will have to reduce this amount of investment to ₹ 75/- by sowing sugarcane, or soybean etc. so that you will spend ₹ 75 for sowing soybean per acre and will be able to reap maximum profit of ₹ 300 or ₹ 400 per acre and so on. This will prevent any cost increase due to increased use of replacing resource.

Then comes 'how much to produce'? Which is more important and here management professional or farm manager or farm owner should be much careful in the investment. That is to say the owner or manager will have to examine the quantities of various inputs (electricity, water, fertilizers, pesticides, manureseeds etc.) used in the production as the output or produce coming out from land will depend on the input used. If you invest amount of ₹ 100 and if you get the revenue it generates as ₹ 250, then it means investment has generated one-and-half times more and if you want more produce then you will have to double the investment or you will have to spend ₹ 200.

Next comes what to produce? Which is also important? This question entirely depends on manager or owner of the land and availability of input resources under the custody of manager or land owner. In other words, manager or landlord can act as entrepreneur and be able to spend as much as he can, the resources which is available with him to gain more profits in a given period of time. This is important step to determine most profitable combination of enterprises as to think whether the combination is complimentary, supplementary or more competitive in long run. One underlying principle is that so long the inputs are in constant usage it is more economical to substitute for different products or crops to sow.

OPERATIONAL FARM MANAGEMENT DECISIONS

Strategic farm decisions are crucial and important. It involves heavy investment to have maximum output and maximum profits. Then comes the size of the land purchasing, many machinery inputs like tractors, tiller, plough machines, and other scientific farming implements, etc. which are taken frequently. Decision on the size of land is sensitive because small sized farm land will have better management, because investment as well as maintenance on small land holdings will be easier and cost-effective. Whereas bigger lands needs heavy investment and large manpower for its day-to-day maintenance. But due to economic development of the country, large sized agriculture land needs huge investment – but it will meet with lower cost of production, but maintenance of big land holdings will be risky and uncertainty looms large as constant inflow of financial assistance, poor management and inappropriate type of farming will not bring desired results.

Machinery and labour are better substitutes but the best combination of these two can be taken on the basis of economic principles, but it will create problems in managing the labour and manpower which will have adverse impact on the economy. But the decision on construction of structure in the vacant land, cattle sheds, irrigation projects, dams, ware-housing facilities, storage facilities will have to be given second thought before final decision will be taken.

Administrative Management Decisions: Many gigantic tasks like financial assistance to the agricultural business, supervision of farm labours, farmers, accounting and legal aspects are important tasks for the land owners or agricultural managers. Managing the required finance to the agriculture land for irrigation, canal water supply, arranging fertilizers, manures, seeds etc. is crucial task indeed. Before applying for financial assistance from the bank or any financial institution(s), its terms and conditions will have to be seen and understood properly or otherwise the very purpose of getting loan easier will become nightmare till its repayment as many hidden terms and conditions will destroy the peace of mind of farm managers or land owners.

Financial entries must be properly entered in the ledgers and day books so that if any problem creeps in the same problem will be attended to and decisions will be taken promptly. Government recently formulated and revised certain regulations in the interest of society as well as farmers' condition and a manager should be familiar with all legal action and formalities.

Marketing Management Decisions: Managers will have to be more vigilant and alert while taking suitable market decisions with all skills and close monitoring the situations. The time and quantity of inputs to be purchased are important marketing decisions. Price will be determined by the market as well as consumers' demand and nothing to do with farm managers. The important decisions regarding what to sell, whom to sell, where to sell, and how to sell are the important decisions made by the managers who should be more vigilant on their decisions.

EXPORT OF AGRICULTURAL PRODUCTS

India is agriculture based country where 70 per cent of villages are depending on the agricultural produce and employed over 60 per cent of population and having contribution of 25 per cent to the GDP of the country. But recent survey shows India has only 1 per cent of its share towards world trade in agriculture. The total agriculture export during last two years was around US$ 10.5 billion and its main produce included coffee, tea, and fisheries.

India has entered into an agreement with General Agreement on Trade and Tariff (GATT) under Uruguay Round Agreement for exporting agricultural produce but in this era of LPG (liberalization, privatization and globalization) many countries are creating utter and stiff competition and India is now facing stiff competition in the export trade of commercial crops like tea, oil mills, rice, wheat, coffee, cashew and sugar are dominating India's agricultural exports. Presently, agriculture trade in the national and inter-regional and international level shows healthy sign and so it can be encouraged further by taking special initiatives to export large quantity of basic agricultural produce.

A new scheme has been initiated namely Vishesh Krishi Upaj Yojana (Special Agricultural Production Scheme) to encourage export of cereals, tea, coffee, cashew fruits and vegetables flowers and minor forest produce, NTFP (Non Timber Forest Products) were sent as value-added products at the international level.

But import of capital goods were waived off by heavy duty and customs levies under Export Promotion of Capital Goods (EPCG) scheme along with import of capital goods under EPCG for agriculture and permission to install them anywhere in the agriculture export zones.

Traditional agriculture has suffered badly because of the production constraints, which in turn is holding our agri exports. "Agriculture has to be competitive and it is important that what our farmers are producing". Lack of research and development, inadequate infrastructure, lack of commercial agriculture, small land holdings, etc. serve as a constraint and there is a strong case for agriculture reforms.

Further the global trade in agriculture is most distressed and pressure is likely to stay on agri commodity prices in the backdrop of rising price of agricultural commodities and the pressure on agri prices is going to continue for some more time. I also think that domestically the pressure on prices are going to continue even more. However, the Government policies should not and will not reflect a "knee-jerk reaction".

Various issues related to agriculture sector are being discussed at length by mandarins (especially constraints to agriculture exports) and draw a roadmap in order to make India not only self-sufficient in agriculture production but also generate export surplus in agriculture.

Various issues related to Indian agriculture have been debated, and are being debated in various platforms especially, the impact of economic reforms, trade liberalization and commitments under World Trade Organization (WTO) on Indian agriculture. Trade liberalization under WTO has created both challenges and opportunities for the Indian agriculture sector. The liberalization of the Indian economy during the early nineties gave hope to the agricultural sector that the opening up of the economy would facilitate in removing discrimination against agriculture. It was expected that India would benefit by signing the Agreement on Agriculture (AoA) due to the comparative advantage in the production of agriculture commodities in early nineties.

However, the outcome of Agreement on Agriculture (AoA) has not been as beneficial to India as was expected due to external and internal factors. Numerous distortions and market access barriers in the developed countries have adversely affected Indian agriculture exports. On the domestic front, vast opportunities to harness agricultural potential still remain to be tapped for achieving higher agricultural growth.

But the main challenge for this sector – that is export will be to deal with emerging range of non-tariff barriers such as sanitary and phyto-sanitary measures. We have to address quality and technical issues more seriously. Further, it is beneficial to note here the traceability measures deployed in various agri products to meet with international requirements, but traceability may become another mode of banning.

To assist and develop the agriculture export zones, financial assistance was proposed by the government to all the states to boost the infrastructure development of exports. Government of India had liberalized the import of seeds, tubers, implements material for encouraging the domestic agriculture production in India. Also centre liberalized the extraction of plants, herbals, derivatives of plants and flowers, for the manufacturing of oil and cooking oil (edible) thus paved the way for agricultural produce trade at the international level.

EXPORT POTENTIAL

India's export policy before WTO's formation was for time being tentative and reaction oriented. The basic aim was only to stabilize or regulate domestic prices and trade was only permissible of the surplus after domestic consumption.

Thus, export figures showed dismal performance and policy makers seen this step from the angle of overall economic development and not from the view of flourishing export trade. Because economy was witnessed upheavals in exchange rate, price and non-price factors, unequal distribution of income and poor savings, poor market access were effected by export potential but were commodity specific in the overall export trade sector.

But gradually decision-makers and policy makers started to realize exports as means of earning foreign exchange. Domestic price structure and world price structure were mainly determining the competitiveness and price phenomenon. Above all subsidy, tariff and non-tariff measures were influencing the volatility of prices in international level for exporting as well as importing countries. During 1960s, Indian's share in world market was declined due to sensitive export policies. High cost of production, low productivity, greater domestic demand, trade policies, product quality, market efficiency, credit to exporters lowered Indian competency.

EXPORT POTENTIAL OF AGRO-BASED PRODUCTS

Government of India had undertaken Five Year Plans since 1951 till date, and there are 13 Five Year Plans which are implemented for the country's economic development. Here, agri-based products have huge export potential due to unique climatic diversity of our country. Policy reforms initiated by the Government at the centre with regard to agricultural products have undergone much oscillations or ups and downs. Export of agricultural commodities were considered as a source of income during the first and second FYPs.

Policy makers and decision-makers of India learnt and realized the need of international trade so quickly and started giving it priority in the subsequent FYPs. Rice, marine products and meat and meat products emerged as commercially viable and feasible and in this direction EXIM Policy was drafted and formulated to increase the share of export trade in the international trading scenario.

There was need for international trade during 1960s and government was keen to chalk out some strategies for boosting international trade. And in this direction government made fundamental shift for export trade at global level and decision-makers were told to formulate a pivotal policy in this direction and EXIM (Export and Import Policy) Policy was the outcome of this whole effort of government.

Further, in the economic sector, the Indian rupee was devalued to favour the export trade. This led to significant earning in the export sector from foreign countries the sale of tobacco, cashew nut, vegetable oil, oilseeds, and sugar. But in 1964-65, the export trade was dismal which was the result of Chinese aggression against India and its aftermath. Similarly, poor harvest, Pakistan invasion, draughts, flood etc. all resulted in dismal performance in agriculture export.

In 1969-74, India's 4th FYP was taken off in the same pace with anticipated export promotion. But to increase the agriculture exports, planners of Indian economy facilitated the quality of agriculture products for export. The Agriculture Ministry has launched quality control section through opening of AGMARK Research and Training Institutes and many initiatives to this effect were proposed in the FYP. Further, economy witnessed the birth of Export Promotion Council, Commodity Boards, Trade Development Authority and Indian Institute of Foreign Trade were opened but the export of agricultural commodities could not respond positively.

Government of India had appointed Retired Agriculture Secretary Mr. G.V.K. Rao to study the prevailing situation in the field of agriculture and to identify the problems. But his committee flayed the system of agriculture trade on tentative basis through export policies. The committee observed India's export policy was the result of domestic policies and pointed out main focus was on domestic requirements rather than global demand. And therefore this committee urged for export policies be forced to be sustainable for longer durations and came down heavily on frequent changes in the policies of agriculture.

But due to dismal performance in the agriculture trade at international level, another committee was constituted under the chairmanship of Mr. P. C. Alexander who has reviewed the agriculture policies and his report recommended for export is and should not be the function of domestic production as otherwise uncertainties will result in the heavy loss in the market share. The committee further recommended the export policies which will be valid for at least three years and licensing system should be replaced by tariff system.

But many recommendations of P. C. Alexander Committee were implemented during the 6th FYP and had promoted Indian agriculture, exports were boosted further at the international level trade. But to its dismay many policies and initiatives could not bring laurels to the country, and economy suffered heavy loss due to increase of balance of payments at geometric speed which resulted in flop of many targeted agenda in 6th FYP and remain unfulfilled. Dismal performance in exports was also partly due to financial crisis and recession during 1980-83 in many developed countries.

Later, Government of India appointed another new committee under the chairmanship of Retired bureaucrat Abid Hussein to study the recession and trade policy and to submit his report to the government. Accordingly, the Abid Hussein's Report favoured rationalization of agriculture related policies and changed the focus for profitability through exports of agricultural commodities at the global level. The committee further recommended the real effective exchange rate of rupee and stood neutral against the appreciation of Indian rupee as they pointed out utter competitiveness at the international level will not encourage the Indian export of agricultural products.

Since 1960 till 90, agriculture sector remains open in the economy and only after 1990 the agriculture sector was brought under protection regime in the economy and only surplus commodities were allowed for export. The export policy was monitored strictly through variety of measures such as taxes, customs, levies, ceilings, and levies for export prohibitions. Next comes the NEP (New Economic Policy) proposed and drafted by the then Finance Minister Dr. Manmohan Singh (presently the PM of India) witnessed shift in many rules and regulations in the agriculture sector.

Accordingly, there was total prohibition for canalizing agencies who were acting as middlemen in the agriculture trade. Next NEP also streamlined the trade policies and removed the restrictions that were placed on the export trade. Accordingly, any amount of agricultural products/produce can be exported and there were no restrictions. Thirdly, incentive schemes were abolished or removed after Indian rupee was devalued to earn huge profits from other countries at the international trade.

Then comes 8th FYP which was critical plan aimed at earning huge profits, removal of all restrictions on trade and radical shift for agriculture trade – at the time when GATT (General Agreement on Tariffs and Trade) was replaced by World Trade Organization (WTO) reforms. For the first time, Indian government was acting at the behest of WTO – an international regulatory body for agriculture trade.

Many parameters were chalked out in the WTO and all countries have been boosted to increase the agricultural products' trade to earn heavy profits. The Uruguay Round agreement was signed in 1994 and country's control was replaced by tariffs by WTO. From 1995 onwards, agriculture trade was revamped and put under direct control of WTO for all countries that heralded the WTO's rule over each country's trade of agricultural products.

It is a sad state of affairs that India's potential for exports was not fully utilized because of its size and diversity of agriculture sector. China dominates the export arena in the agricultural products and India is the second world's largest exporter and India is largest producer of fruits and vegetables. Agriculture experts and pundits suggested following measures to boost the export potential in days to come:

Implementation of quality control unit in all levels of agriculture products production. Market intelligence reports should be disseminated and circulated to all export units periodically. Each state in India and centre should make the launching of R & D section as mandatory so that variety of agricultural products can lead the country's exports towards excellence with huge margin of profits.

Private Public sector Participation (PPP) should be initiated at all levels for upgradation of technology skills and infrastructure. Priority for building cold supply chain, including air cargos, railway, roadways on priority basis.

All licensing and permit giving procedures should be simplified to avoid perishable nature of agricultural products and permission should be cleared within expiry of 20-24 hours.

Government of India should make clarion call to the world community to attract Foreign Direct Investment (FDI) so that foreign countries can come to India and invest in our country so that huge amount of money will come to our economy which can be utilized for various infrastructural developments.

EXPORT OF SEAFOODS

Seafood exports is all set to scale new heights with the remarkable breakthrough for ensuring the supply of high quality all male Scampi (Scampi: Giant Fresh water prawn) seeds. In April this year, The Scampi Broodstock Development Project of RGCA at Konathanapadu, Kankipadu Mandal, Krishna District, Andhra Pradesh, successfully developed the first proven neofemale in the country and achieved production of all male progeny of the giant freshwater prawn (Scampi – Macrobrachium rosenbergii) for the first time in the subcontinent – an enviable achievement unmatched by any research organization in the nation so far. The technology developed at RGCA involves sex reversal of healthy Scampi males into functional females (called as Neofemales) through microsurgical interventions and crossing these females with normal males to produce all male progeny. This technology does not involve any kind of genetic manipulations or hormonal treatments. This has the potential of increasing the unit area production by around 40 per cent.

AGRICULTURE EXPORT ZONES

EXIM Policy of 2001 brought the concept of Agricultural Export Zones to give priority to promotion of agriculture exports. Each state of India has been divided into different export zones. Accordingly, each zone was created in all the states identifying the potential products in that region which was as under:

State	Agri Products	State	Agri Products
J & K	Apple	AP	Mango and grapes
MP	Wheat, Apple	AP & UP	Vegetables Mango
UP – WB	Basmati Rice, Potato	Gujarat	Onion- Garlic
WB	Tea, Lichi, Potato, Mango	Karnataka	Flower-Vanilla
Uttarkhand	Basmati Rice, Flowers	Punjab	Potato, Basmati rice

AP	Mango Pulp, Chili	J & K	Apple, Walnut
Gujarat	Sesame seeds, onion	Orissa	Ginger, Turmeric
Rajasthan	Cumin, Coriander		

The 10th FYP aimed at identifying the new export potential of agri products and made efforts to monitor the R & D activities for increasing annual agriculture production – post-harvest management processing and value addition with marketing potential. The 11th FYP draft made some collective efforts to accomplish international goals and also to cater to the needs of the global demand.

All the efforts and requirements of how to meet the rising demands of the global market in the international trade were included in EXIM policy that came into being with effect from August 31, 2004. The main ideas of this EXIM Policy was to focus the trade on product-wise strategy, removal of restrictions on exports, extension of financial incentives and assistance for trading at global level, assistance and modernization of agriculture products processing, quality control, improving the quality of each agriculture product, and carrying out timely market survey periodically to give market intelligence reports to all countries so as to cater to the growing needs of the countries.

FOREIGN TRADE POLICY OR EXIM POLICY (2004-09)

Main purposes of EXIM Policy were as under:

- Creating a congenial and harmonious atmosphere of sincerity, faith, and without discrimination
- Rigid procedural formalities were simplified and reduction of processing fees.
- Levies and custom duties were minimized or waived off in export of agri products.
- The status of India was given new impetus as global centre for manufacturing trade and service.
- Rural areas of the country were upgraded and improved with more infrastructural facilities.
- New technological and infrastructural upgradation – green signal given to import of capital goods and farm equipments.
- Domestic sectors were protected from exploitation and removal of inverted duty customs structure on import of goods.
- India's infrastructure network was given new look and redefined export trade to meet global standard.
- India's Board of Trade was revamped – revitalized with more appointments of experts to give timely advice and suggestions periodically to exporters.
- Aggrandizement (giving more powers) of Indian Embassies in all countries in the world to carry out their role to help Indian exporters if they met with any hurdles or export or trade barriers.

NEW EXPORT PROMOTION SCHEME (NEPS)

This scheme was introduced to increase the export of fruits, veggies, and flowers, minor forest products, and value-added products with other countries at the global level which will be made duty free export trade, and export of these products will be made duty free equivalent to 5% of Free on Board (FOB) value of exports and can be transferable if required.

Disadvantages

This can act as temporary relief to exporters of agriculture products, lacks systematic production.

This scheme requires high money transactions and high costs poor infrastructural facilities for post-harvest process like storage, cold storage, handling at mandi. There are no timely and periodical market intelligence reports, poor quality of products without quality control, high use of pesticides in agriculture produce.

Poor quality of agriculture products cannot convince the global trading countries and cannot withstand the qualities desired by foreign buyers.

Substandard packaging, gradation, brand images and poor efforts in market development.

SUMMARY

Agro-based activities are plenty and interrelated. The productivity and production of foodgrains is vital for peace and prosperity of India. Many infrastructural factors like finance, technology, storage, transport, cooperatives, import-export policies, banking loans, and basic facilities like electricity, water, that are vital and are very much favourable for corporate sector to make investments and to generate adequate revenue for their part as well as to contribute to country's GDP.

Due to this, trade at the international level has become easier with many world-renowned corporates who are eyeing India constantly as their business destination. These corporate conglomerates are expected to fulfill the shortages in the process of economic development of India while they will control the prices in the market.

The New Economic Policy of 1991 and its aftermath, gradually the government in power is realizing of late to adopt more flexible and favourable policies of economic liberalization, privatization and globalization (LPG). Government of India under the stewardship of Dr. Manmohan Singh – steering the agriculture sector in excellent way while making efforts to increase agricultural exports through various policy changes and investment in infrastructure development.

Thus, UPA government's decision are more vibrant in permitting the private sector corporates in direct purchasing and developing infrastructure for marketing and has boosted them to develop export market in all angles of the country. Many policies are being drafted and initiated by the centre in export segment to market new products, leaving behind most of the traditional agro-based products because of stiff competition in the international arena.

QUESTIONS

1. Write in your own words the role of corporate sector that stimulates growth in exports of agriculture produce.
2. List out your suggestions to improve the growth in export of agriculture produce.
3. Write down the salient features of EXIM policy 2004-09.
4. What are the characteristics and features of New Export Promotion Scheme?

❍❍❍

CHAPTER 7

FARM BUSINESS MANAGEMENT

FARM BUSINESS MANAGEMENT

Agriculture business management is the lifeline of the country and India is not exception in the world. Our country faced many crisis since independence, witnessed famine, scarcity of food grains, floods that devastated precious agriculture produce, and drought had ruined the agriculture produce resulted in untimely death of poor farmers in various states. Further added to fuel, the rain gods were also played their havoc in maroon, submerge of precious agriculture properties, cattle and other animals.

Characteristics of Farm Business Management

The term 'farm business management' has three words, farm means cultivable land, business means profitable venture, and management means art of management of farm business. The agriculture science is living and pure science and is regarded as pure science all over the world. In India, agriculture science has been treated with utmost priority and importance and Government through Planning Commission had proposed number of agriculture science colleges in each states to give fillip to this subject to give wider knowledge and also to maintain R & D section to do practical experiments to provide the farming community all over the country with latest research knowledge and make the country self-sufficient in agriculture sector. It can be best defined as science which deals with important farming decisions for the use of scarce farm products and to maximize the sustained farming income over the years.

Agriculture business management is unique subject that deals with dynamic forces like price, supply, demand, dynamics of consumer behaviour, changing socio-economic needs, degrading environment and ecological balance, weather-climatic condition, climate change, pollution, deteriorating water tables, global warming etc. are also influencing the farm managers and landlords to be vigil and alert while taking crucial decisions on what to produce, how to produce and to how much to produce the agriculture products.

Following are few characteristics of Farm Business Management:

Profit oriented science: Farm Business management is pure science, deals in economic development of the country and farm managers are only interested in investing less money and desires more yields from their farmland. This means yields of prime importance and thus farm decisions are not only based on costs of investment – yields or returns but also on expenditure on post-harvest activities.

Multi-disciplinary science: This science will help in taking farming decisions effectively for the managers or landlords while guide them to make use of facts and figures with detailed statistics developed by the governmental departments, and research think-tanks through their scientific research activities. But farm managers or landlords are warned not to ignore the understanding of physical and biological sciences, economic theories, socio-political behaviour of consumers, policymakers, economic environment, and psychological behaviour of people should also be taken into account in this regard.

Applied Science: The farm business management is applied science having evidence and proofs for all physical and biological theoretical decisions. Farm decisions are always taken by comparing the alternative methods developed by different streams of science and all decisions are taken considering the farm as an accounting unit.

Thus, farming decisions are always controlled by people or society's attitude, values, ethics, goals of the farm managers and landlords. The skills of taking timely decisions by the landlords and managers will remain as continuous process.

SUPPLEMENTARY FEATURES

The farm business management deals with plants, animals and all living organisms – climatic conditions, influence of weather, climate changes, ecological and environmental factors, that are always subjected to greater risks and uncertainties. Living beings always to be treated and handled with proper care and particularly in the case of animals, cattle, sheep, and goats.

The farm production is carried out in larger areas as compared to other businesses, and is vulnerable in nature.

Agriculture production is a small-scale business where managers, landlords, land owners and labourers are one and same person or group of persons. And therefore division of labour is limited.

The degree of risk and uncertainty compels the farm business management to take frequent changes in the decisions made already because of climatic condition or protection of crop against insecticides or pests.

Farm Business management has no control over prices and hence production of agriculture produce and demand move in opposite directions.

There is no standardization of products and practices and no uniformity of agriculture products anywhere, no perfect grading, and no certifying authority of agriculture produce.

Capital turnover rate is relatively slow due to peculiar nature of production and it is fully biological.

The farm business is closely associated with food or raw materials for food items and if there is any rise in demand the supply cannot meet the demand – due to inelasticity of supply.

Agriculture produce are bulky and perishable in nature and hence not possible to postpone the use of the produce any longer.

Fixed cost of agriculture production is relatively higher out of total costs earmarked for the production and it is not possible to change the decision on financial matters.

Finally, the farm business is mainly dominated and occupied by illiterates who are farmers and not available for any statutory verification, accountability and checks and this is real challenge.

PROBLEMS FACED BY INDIAN FARMERS IN FARM BUSINESS

Indian agriculture and farm business in particular is facing severe problems which have kept the yield rate dismal or negligible resulting in frequent fluctuation or oscillation in price pattern of agriculture products and insufficient farm resources.

Indian farms are small in size: Compared to other parts of the world, Indian farm land size is small which is uneconomical due to ever-increasing population growth that needs lot of conversion farm land for urbanization. The average holding per hectare was more in olden days but it is declining further day by day and this is mainly due to frequent fragmentation.

Insufficient capital: Another challenge faced by Indian farm business management is lack of capital or farmers are not equipped with adequate financial aid because they are weaker monetarily and whatever loans they had availed still not paid or paid half while remaining half amount of loan they are unable to pay. For any new venture in the farm requires free flow of money which Indian farmers are unable to mobilize due to their indebtedness.

Underemployment: The factors that lead to underemployment in the farming community are small holdings, but family size is big and joint families and work will be available during sowing, pre-monsoon time, rainy season, pre-harvest, harvest and post-harvest season and after which the farmers will sit idle which means their employability is not fully and properly utilized.

This is the reason why Government of India has initiated National Rural Employment Guarantee Scheme (NREGA) for village unemployed farmers and unskilled-illiterate workers and provide 100 days' employment to eke out their livelihood which is foresighted and compassionate attitude of GOI.

Incompetent to withstand risks: Indian farming community is illiterate to some extent and financially weaker, are unable to bear the brunt of risks and uncertainty. This incompetent attitude of farming community makes them much lethargic and stubborn to face any eventualities.

Non-availability of inputs timely: Agriculture productivity will be sustainable and more profitable through its yearly produce that requires timely availability of inputs to reap the profitable revenue. But it is sad state of affairs that Indian farming community could not get the required raw material or inputs to make use in their fields.

Seeds are most important input for farmers and there is no better quality of seeds available as more and more private players are producing seeds for farming community and healthy competition is playing its role.

Poor infrastructure facility: Indian farming community facing problems to reach the market due to lack of good roads, water supply, sanitation, health, electricity, fertilizer, pesticides and manures which are not available timely and even available not of good quality and this will not give gainful produce.

FARM ACCOUNTING

Agriculture will be a boon for proper economic development provided if it is properly planned, and good record keeping. Therefore, farm business managers should plan the agricultural farming of given period in advance and take useful decisions. They should keep track and follow-up when they apply for financial assistance from any financial institution or commercial or nationalized banks. They should also keep checking the cash at hand each time, while identifying reasons for weak business and they should be made good.

Farm managers or landlords will have to keep close watch over the business and it is by proper bookkeeping and financial management. Bookkeeping refers to recording of each entries of transactions made during the period over computers. Recording each entry in the book, totaling, keeping monthly statements, and summarizing the financial data to be kept handy to have glimpse when they incur loss or forced to face any problem.

Accounting cycle refers to a sequence of accounting procedures, so that bulk of information provided in order to take better decisions and will have to follow few steps as under:

Classification of documents in an organized way like challans, bills, cash receipts, indents, invoice and promissory notes, etc.

Recording of all entries after money transactions have to be made while debit and credit changes in the account balance are posted from journal to ledger accounts. Similarly, they have to summarize periodically the transaction figures and keep checking the balance. Timely prepare the statement of accounts to know exactly how much amount spent and how much is available handy. Further take out income statement which will give profit and loss account in given period of time. Monthly statements will have to be taken out so that it will become handy information to forecast the farm business for next season.

FARM BUDGETING

Farm owners and farm managers should understand the society's need and should plan their farm business strategy according to that information and the course of planning to meet the future requirements will be known as Farm Budgeting. This is technique of evaluating a farm's plan for the use of agriculture use and in particular for a planned activity of plan. It can be accomplished by following three steps which are as under:

Operating budget: This budget relates to expected sales or production activities and related expenditure – sales-production activities and related costs for the year in the form of statement – sales income and anticipated fixed and variable costs.

Cash-flow budget statement: This statement depicts flow of income in a given period of time during the year. Income sources are dealing with sales proceeds, borrowing details, sales of capital goods and payments collected, expenses for goods and services, loan repayment, tax obligations, salaries, wages, and payment given for capital goods purchase. The statement gives more information about profitability of the business and basic purpose of this statement in this context is to ensure the availability of more funds for any future transaction or purchase or disposal.

Capital expenditure budget: This statement related to projected expenditure allocated among different division activities within the business. Farm business require regular investment under various heads, and budget is meant to keep watch and spend amount which is necessary at the first instance and later other payment obligations on the basis of need arise in given period of time to meet them timely.

The accounting task for farming sector is very difficult because of farming in our country is of subsistence in nature and our farmers are illiterate and have lack of awareness. The accounting period in agriculture normally begins from July to June of next year.

FARM PRODUCTIVITY INDICATORS

Financial statements serve as diagnosis and prescription for future planning for the farm business management. Further if any farmer applies for financial aid from any finance institution or banks, the banks will see status of solvency and then only release the loan for the farmers. Further sometime the lending institutions may also want detailed information of liquidity status, changes in the net worth of the unit, periodical performance charts etc. These information will be articulated in the form of bird's eye view so that they will be treated as indicators.

Ratio Analysis: This is powerful technique for studying financial performance of any unit/firm dealing with farm business in a given period time. This indicates the extent to which the money was borrowed from which bank and due to what problem the payment has not been made. Another element is debt ratio and **profitability ratio** which will indicate how effectively it will be used to reap normal or supernormal profits. And these ratios are also used to see to ascertain management's performance. Finally, **activity**

ratio that will measure, the key function of management that is converting the firm's resources into profits.

Historical Analysis: This element indicates healthy improvement.

Comparative Analysis may help in selecting the best alternative using all these ratios in farming needs special attention.

AGRICULTURAL COST AND PRICES

The Agricultural Prices Commission (APC) was set up in January 1965 and since March 1985 the Commission renamed as Commission for Agricultural Costs and Prices (CACP). And this Commission advises government on pricing policy for all major agricultural commodities and evolves as a balanced and integrated price structure, with a view to fulfill the needs of the economy and to take care of the interests of the farm land owners or managers and consumers as well. The Commission has its own representatives of the farming community as non-official members who are experts in their fields of professions and actively associated with the farming community.

The Commission has extended its recommendations to the government on initiation of Minimum Support Price (MSP) and Procurement Prices which have been working as forward contract for the farming community which will help the farmers to allocate their resources in efficient manner.

MSP are announced for foodgrains, oilseeds, fiber crops, sugarcane and potato before the start of the sowing season. At the time of procurement, the government procures food grains either from the producers or traders by imposing a fixed levy. For maintaining the surplus or buffer stocks for the Public Distribution System (PDS), procurement prices are announced before the harvesting time which is generally higher than MSP.

FARM PRODUCE PRICE POLICY

The main objectives of the Government's price policy for agricultural produce aiming at ensuring remunerative prices to the growers for their produce with a view to encouraging higher investment and production. Towards this end, minimum support prices for major agricultural products are announced each year which are fixed after taking into account the recommendations of the Commission for Agricultural Costs and Prices (CACP). The CACP, while recommending prices takes into account all important factors, viz.:

1. Cost of Production
2. Changes in Input Prices
3. Input/Output Price Parity
4. Trends in Market Prices
5. Inter-crop Price Parity
6. Demand and Supply Situation
7. Effect on Industrial Cost Structure
8. Effect on General Price Level
9. Effect on Cost of Living

10. International Market Price Situation
11. Parity between Prices Paid and Prices Received by Farmers (Terms of Trade).

Of all the factors, cost of production is the most tangible factor and it takes into account all operational and fixed demands. Government organizes Price Support Scheme (PSS) of the commodities, through various public and cooperative agencies such as FCI, CCI, JCI, NAFED, Tobacco Board, etc., for which the MSPs are fixed. For commodities not covered under PSS, Government also arranges for market intervention on specific request from the States for specific quantity at a mutually agreed price. The losses, if any, are borne by the Centre and State on 50:50 basis. The price policy paid rich dividends. The Government has raised substantially the MSPs in recent years as may be seen from the statement enclosed.

SUMMARY

The term 'farm business management' has three words, farm means cultivable land, business means profitable venture, and management means art of management of farm business. The agriculture science is living and pure science and is regarded as pure science all over the world. In India, agriculture science has been treated with utmost priority and importance and Government through Planning Commission had proposed number of agriculture science colleges in each states to give fillip to this subject to give wider knowledge and also to maintain R & D section to do practical experiments to provide the farming community all over the country with latest research knowledge and make the country self-sufficient in agriculture sector. It can be best defined as science which deals with important farming decisions for the use of scarce farm products and to maximize the sustained farming income over the years. Agriculture business management is unique subject that deals with dynamic forces like price, supply, demand, dynamics of consumer behaviour, changing socio-economic needs, degrading environment and ecological balance, weather-climatic condition, climate change, pollution, deteriorating water tables, global warming etc. are also influencing the farm managers and landlords to be vigil and alert while taking crucial decisions on what to produce, how to produce and to how much to produce the agriculture products.

QUESTIONS

1. What is meant by Farm Business Management?
2. List out the problems and challenges being faced by Indian farmers in their effort to increase the overall annual agriculture produce.
3. What do you mean by farm account budgeting?
4. List out farm productivity indicators.

OOO

CHAPTER 8

INDIAN AGRICULTURE IN HISTORICAL CONTEXT

- Indian Agriculture in Historical Context
- Drawbacks
- The New Economic Policy (NEP)
- NEP's Impact on Indian Economy
- Government's Intervention
- Slow Growth Crops
- Household Demand for Raw Food Materials
- Agriculture Mechanization Development
- Mechanization of Farm Power
- Adoption of Mechanization
- Use of Tillage — Plant Machinery Use of Tillage and Planting Machinery
- Inter-culture and Plant Protection Equipment
- Irrigation and Drainage Equipment
- Harvesting and Threshing
- Availability and Use of Farm Machinery

INDIAN AGRICULTURE IN HISTORICAL CONTEXT

Indian agricultural production (in most parts of the country) is its relationship (even dependency) on skilful and wise water management practices. One of the unique features of the Indian Subcontinent is how almost its entire rainfall is concentrated in the few monsoon months. During the monsoons, the Indian Subcontinent is usually gifted with bountiful rains. Although not infrequently, this bountiful monsoon can turn into a terror, causing uncontrollable floods in parts of the country. Conversely, every few years, the monsoon can be erratic and deficient, leading to drought and the possibility of famine.

Although historical development of Indian agriculture has been inextricably linked with effective water management practices that have either been taken up by the state, or by local village communities.

Water management has necessitated a certain degree of cooperation and collective spirit in the Indian countryside, and until the imposition of colonial rule, it precluded any widespread development of private property in India.

Regional rulers or local representatives of the state were generally obliged to allocate a certain percentage of the agricultural taxes on building and managing water-storage, water-harvesting and/or water-diverting structures which facilitated a second crop, and provided water for drinking and other purposes in the long dry season.

DRAWBACKS

Only a small percentage of Indian farmers have enjoyed the luxury of natural irrigation, although there are reports that in certain parts of the country, the soil used to retain enough moisture well beyond the monsoon months. However, it is equally true that the drying up of wells led to mass migrations, and sudden depopulation of old towns and villages.

Many flood-prone states (Assam, Bengal and Bihar) seen under massive network of canals that allowed both effective drainage to prevent flooding during the heavy monsoon months, and also provide for fishing, transportation and irrigation arteries in the dry seasons.

Intelligent water management, thus, allowed for the growth of a healthy agricultural surplus, that in turn facilitated steady urbanization (*albeit* at a much slower pace than seen in the industrial era), and the development of a variety of pre-industrial manufacturing in areas such as textiles, jewellery, wood/ metal working etc.

Because of the immense importance of effective water management, the entire revenue system of the state was structured so as to take into account both the necessity of water management and the inherent dependency that existed between Indian agriculture and the availability of water.

Most Indian states attempted to collect revenues in a manner that did not entirely destroy the village solidarity that was essential in proper sharing and management of common water resources. At the same time, urban tax collectors had to deal with mediating entities from the villages, sø that they did not tax at a rate that might lead to the destruction of water management facilities so essential for life and sustainable agriculture.

By and large, taxes were imposed on villages collectively (not on individual farmers directly), and the village elites were obliged to ensure that the burden of taxes did not destroy the complete viability of agriculture. Taxes were also adjusted keeping in mind whether the land was well-irrigated or not.

THE NEW ECONOMIC POLICY (NEP)

The New Economic Policy and its overall impact on the common man and in particular on the country's agriculture sector in its entirety. Globalization and India's willingness to join GATT (General Agreement on Trade and Tariffs) few years ago has seen Indian economy grown to manifold but at the same time it had an adverse effect on our fellow manufacturers.

We would see the advantages first and then come to the impact. World Bank has predicted the global economy will grow at the rate of 2.5% from the next year after it was massively affected by US Sub Prime Mortgage Crisis and it has predicted that India and China would be the major driving factors towards it.

Since most of the countries have already reached the saturation point in various fields (like automobiles, mining, raw materials etc.), India and China were the hottest destinations for the other countries since the purchasing power of our people has gone up because of employment opportunities. We had seen many Indian companies taking over foreign companies like Corus, Jaugar and Land Rover, Whyte & Mackay, Testley to name a few which has made the Indian Flags to high in various countries across the globe.

NEP'S IMPACT ON COMMON MAN

The impact was serious because our economy was opened for foreign MNCs, they started pouring in their products at cheaper price because they had the expertise with them already. And they also wanted to develop their products by giving discounts to their products which seems attractive but at the same time they suppressed the local traders here.

Though the competition is good for healthy markets in India and people getting good price at the moment, one cannot deny the fact that it would slowly eradicate our manufacturers leaving entire control to foreign companies which might then lead to Predatory pricing. We also come across Government of India's ideas of selling more of its stake in public sector companies which involves in many sectors in order to get the funds to bail out the government expenditure though these companies were running in profits. Many sectors have seen rising of price of essential commodities and many companies have started hoarding their stocks to reap supernormal profits.

GOVERNMENT'S INTERVENTION

One of the major areas in which the government intervenes is in the agricultural sector of the economy. The government has three ways it can intervene and help its producers. These ways include price policies, direct payments, and input policies. Price policies have the largest effect on producers. Tariffs, quotas, and taxes are just a few examples of price policies.

While these policies bring revenue into the government, in the end they hurt consumers. Each of these policies raise the prices of both imported and native goods. They are designed to help stabilize prices and give the native producers a chance to compete with foreign goods. Under the doctrine of laissez-faire, the government would not interfere with prices and the native producers would be forced to lower their prices, giving the nation's citizens a better deal in the market.

In a sense, the way the government is involved in the agricultural sector is a necessity. If these procedures and policies were not in place, the native producers would quickly go bankrupt. While the people are now forced to "pick up the bill" for these policies, it would be very difficult to completely dismantle the current system. If it were dismantled, the goods the producer produces would come at a much higher price to consumers, and yet government's spending in the sector would decline. Of course, through taxes, consumers had already been paying to have lower priced goods.

The government not only intervenes in the agricultural sector of the economy, it also intervenes in strict safety and health regulations, tariffs and subsidies and government loans. The use of tariffs is another way that government intervenes in the business sector. They help inefficient domestic producers by forcing consumers to pay unnecessarily high prices for imported goods. The use of tariffs forces people to pay higher prices for certain goods and thus resulting in less money the consumer has to spend on other goods and services. This results in less employment in the industries that produce such goods and services. The hidden reality is that a job protected by a government tariff is at the expense of a worker in another industry.

The negative effects of government intervention in the economic sector outweigh the benefits of policies and methods implemented to help the consumer. These policies are found in both the agricultural and business sectors of the economy. On the agricultural side, these policies range from price policies to direct payments to input policies. On the business side, the government can intervene by implementing strict safety and health regulations, tariffs, and subsidies and government loans.

While all of these policies seem to have beneficial short-term effects, they never have positive long-term effects. In the end, the government's spending and intervention in the economy is detrimental. So, should the government stay out of the economy and let it be run by the doctrine of laissez-faire, or is government intervention necessary to the survival of the economy? Many would argue that some intervention is necessary, but in a completely competitive market, there is no need for the government to intervene.

SLOW GROWTH CROPS

The 'slow growth crops' includes oilseeds and pulses. India is the fourth largest edible oil economy in the world. But, there has been no breakthrough in productivity in oilseeds. In fact, in the post-green revolution period, the growth rate of oilseeds production has been lower than in the years preceding it. The result is that, since mid-1970s, 30-35 per cent of total demand is met by imports.

The Technology Mission on Oilseeds in 1986 did bring about a breakthrough in oilseeds production for the next decade but since 1999-2000 there has been serious problems. Much of the oil production in the country is from dry and rainfed areas. In spite of genuine doubts about competitiveness of Indian oilseeds, there has been a relaxation of trade in oilseeds. The study points to the need for adequate tariff guards as well as region-specific focus for increasing oilseeds production.

Further, food and nutrition dimensions of certain oilseed crops like rape-seed and mustard with supplementary produce like greens rich in vitamins and iron, and also supply of domestic fuel. These are especially important for poorer sections who depend, to an extent, on non-monetary sources of food and fuel. Pulses are yet another important crop sector where the supply has been deficient to an extent of about 20 per cent. Like oilseeds, pulses are also mostly grown in marginal lands and here too there has been hardly any breakthrough in productivity over the years.

With agriculture being part of the liberalized trade regime under WTO, the question often raised is about the export potential of India's agriculture. The post-GATT regime is also marked by a number of regional or Preferential Trade Agreements (PTAs) since India is not a member of any major PTA, it does suffer disadvantage in global market.

However, there has been growth in overall agricultural exports from India, accounted for mainly by marine products. Tea, cashew nut and spices have maintained growth but coffee has been badly hit.

Spices form another important segment of agricultural export. India accounts for about 44 per cent of the world's area under spices, but as a study included here shows its share in production is only 14 per cent. Here, again a serious problem of low productivity. Horticultural products like fruits, vegetables and flowers are high potential areas still lacking a critical mass in terms of exports.

HOUSEHOLD DEMAND FOR RAW FOOD MATERIALS

Based on the statistics compiled by Directorate of Economics and Statistics Ministry of Agriculture, the foodgrain demand predictions for 2011-12 are 222.30 million tons (rice 100.71 million tons, wheat 76.51 million tons, and coarse grains 24.81 million tons and pulses 19.7 million tons). India produces about 650 million tons of food materials of plant and animal origin.

India is a large country with wide agro-ecological diversity having predominance of rainfed agriculture. The total land area is 328 Mha and about 142 Mha is under cultivation, of which about 55 Mha is irrigated and reminder 87 Mha is rainfed. Farmers are left with less time for field operations. Farm mechanization has positive relation with farm productivity; firstly through timeliness of field operation and, secondly, through good quality work.

Present-day need is to increase the productivity and profitability of production and post-production agriculture. Younger generation does not want to work in the field. So, mechanization is the need for timeliness of operation. Effective engineering interventions and inputs have the potential to result in further useful technology packages for timeliness and precision in farm activity. Use of zero till-drill method on 3 million has resulted in timeliness of operation and savings up to 200 million US$ (10000 million INR). Mechanization for dry land and hill agriculture and horticulture. Efficient use of water, fertilizer, seeds, pesticide, energy and other inputs.

AGRICULTURAL MECHANIZATION DEVELOPMENT

Efficient machinery helps in increasing productivity by about 30% besides, enabling the farmers to raise a second crop making the agriculture attractive. Raising more crops with high productivity is a path for meeting the future food requirement of population.

Development and introduction of high capacity, precision, reliable and energy efficient equipment is the need for judicious use inputs. For crop production, human, animal and mechanical energy is extensively used. In small and marginal farms, except for tillage, other operations such as sowing/transplanting, weeding, cotton picking harvesting and threshing (paddy) are normally manually performed.

Economic Advantage of Mechanization

in per cent

Increase in productivity	up to 12-34%
Seed-cum-fertilizer drill facilitates saving in seeds	20%
Saving in fertilizer	15-20%
Enhancement in cropping intensity	5-22%
Increase in gross income	29-49% of the farmers

Source: Report of the Sub-group on Agricultural Implements and Machinery for Formulation of 9th Five Year Plan.

Mechanization also imparts capacity to the farmers to carry out farm operations, with ease and freedom from drudgery, making the farming agreeable vocation for educated youth as well. It helps the farmers to achieve timeliness and precisely meter and apply costly input for better efficacy and efficiency.

MECHANIZATION OF FARM POWER

Over the years, promotion of agricultural mechanization has been directed towards the promotion of eco-friendly and selective agricultural implements and machines with the aims of optimal utilization of the available sources of human, animal and mechanical/electrical power, removing the drudgery associated with various agricultural operations.

Farmers have also been provided financial assistance for owning a wide range of agricultural equipment, viz., tractors, power tillers, bullock/tractor drawn implements, reapers, threshers, irrigation equipment, hand tools, etc.

Further, new equipment such as precision planter, zero-till drill, seed-cum-fertilizer drill, raised bed planter, improved weeders, plant protection equipment, harvesting and threshing machines, drip, micro sprinkler and sprinkler irrigation equipment have been made available to the farmers. As a result of the joint efforts made by the Government and the private sector, the level of mechanization has been increasing steadily over the years.

ADOPTION OF MECHANIZATION

At present in India, tractors are being used for tillage of 22.78% of total area and sowing 21.30% of total area. Although, utility of manually and bullock operated equipment has been established but the response of the farmers has been selective. The bullock drawn seed-cum-fertilizer drill and manual paddy transplanter have not been universally accepted in spite of financial incentive from the Government.

Due to limited use in a year and economic advantage of many items, some improved implements could not replace the local alternatives. The land levelers, seed-cum-fertilizer drills have also been accepted by the farmers but on limited scale. Major adoption of agricultural machinery in addition to irrigation equipment and tractor, was thresher for wheat crop.

Due to various applications of paddy straw, preference has been limited for paddy threshers. Self-propelled/tractor operated combines, reaper harvester, potato and groundnut mechanization machinery are also commercially available and accepted by the farmers in states where tractors were introduced. Now, combine harvesters are commonly used in different parts of the country, on custom hire basis, for wheat, soybean and paddy harvesting.

USE OF TILLAGE AND PLANTING MACHINERY

The traditional animal drawn country plough has low output (30-40 h/ha) whereas tractor drawn MB plough, harrows, cultivators and motivators are better machinery used by the farmers. There is need for high capacity machines for custom hire services.

For precise application of seed and fertilizer, mechanically metered seed drill and seed-cum-fertilizer drill operated by animal and tractors have been developed and are being manufactured to suit specific crops and regions. Zero till drill and strip till drill have also been developed to reduce energy inputs in crop production. 'CIAE' (Central Institute for Agricultural Equipments) has developed farm equipment like inclined plate-planter and pneumatic-planter for precision sowing.

INTER-CULTURE AND PLANT PROTECTION EQUIPMENT

Use of long handle wheel hoe and peg type weeders are being accepted as they reduce drudgery and weeding time to 25-110 hours from 300-700 hours in conventional practice. Animal drawn weeder and cultivator are also used for control of weeds. Self-propelled and power operated weeders are being increasingly accepted on limited scale. Different designs of low-cost hand-operated sprayers and dusters are available for application of plant protection chemicals. Low volume and ultra-low volume (ULV) sprayers, which require comparatively smaller quantity of water, are also in use.

IRRIGATION AND DRAINAGE EQUIPMENT

Diesel and electric pump sets are common. The shift from conventional flood irrigation to sprinkler, micro sprinkler or drip irrigation systems is apparently visible indicating the importance of water-use efficiency for covering more area under irrigation. The Government support in the form of subsidy is serving as a catalyst to compensate for the high initial cost of the system.

Importance of drainage for achieving improved productivity is being realized by the farmers and progressive farmers are going for subsurface drainage, which is high initial cost technology. The low-cost mole drainage technology and equipment has been developed for vertisols. The mole drain laying cost is about 70 US$/ha (3500 INR) and the same is recovered in one crop season.

The farmers are getting attracted in favour of this technology. However, it is just a beginning of adoption of the technology. In years to come, it is expected to be common feature among the farmers. Efforts are on to popularize this technology through demonstrations and awareness programmes.

HARVESTING AND THRASHING

Sickle is the major low-cost traditional tool for harvesting. Self-sharpening serrated sickle is finding adoption. Walk behind and self-propelled reaper harvesters, which facilitate quick harvesting is getting acceptance.

Traditional threshing by animal treading has been almost fully replaced by power threshers operated by 5-15 hp engine or electric motor. Pedal operated paddy threshers reduce drudgery and have become popular in India. Whole paddy straw is obtained by using rasp bar type axial flow thresher. Combined harvesters are being used for harvesting wheat, paddy, soybean and gram in few states.

AVAILABILITY AND USE OF FARM MACHINERY

Often, farm mechanization has been coupled with use of prime movers, tractor and power tillers, rather than adoption and availability of farm machinery, which perform the specific task.

Over the years based upon the requirements of the farmers of different regions, following different set of cropping patterns, Indian Council of Agriculture Research (ICAR) controlled Institutes and State Agricultural Universities have developed number of farm machines and, manufacturers have introduced few imported designs.

Although utilization of farm power in the form of tractor/power tiller has increased manifold but utilization of farm machines for specific purposes remained low. The rate of growth in animal operated machinery has remained low as compared to tractor or power operated machinery.

State-wise analysis of the farm machinery utilization revealed that few states were using mechanical power source while others still uses the animate sources and implements operated by them.

Main reasons are: low purchasing power and fragmented land holding of farmers, low annual use of specific machinery, lack of awareness among farmers especially in hilly, backward and tribal areas and proper sell outlets and maintenance facility in nearby areas.

Often buyer has to travel long distances for procurement, repair and maintenance. Quality and reliability of farm machinery being manufactured and supplied by various agencies and scale of manufacturers are yet to gain confidence of common farmer.

SUMMARY

Indian agricultural production (in most parts of the country) has its relationship (even dependency) on skilful and wise water management practices. One of the unique features of the Indian Subcontinent is how almost its entire rainfall is concentrated in the few monsoon months. During the monsoons, the Indian Subcontinent is usually gifted with bountiful rains, although not infrequently, this bountiful monsoon can turn into a terror, causing uncontrollable floods in parts of the country. Conversely, every few years, the monsoon can be erratic and deficient, leading to drought and the possibility of famine.

Although historical development of Indian agriculture has been inextricably linked with effective water management practices that have either been taken up by the state, or by local village communities.

Only a small percentage of Indian farmers have enjoyed the luxury of natural irrigation, although there are reports that in certain parts of the country, the soil used to retain enough moisture well beyond the monsoon months. However, it is equally true that the drying up of wells led to mass migrations, and sudden depopulation of old towns and villages.

Most Indian states attempted to collect revenues in a manner that did not entirely destroy the village solidarity that was essential in proper sharing and management of common water resources. At the same time, urban tax collectors had to deal with mediating entities from the villages, so that they did not tax at a rate that might lead to the destruction of water management facilities so essential for life and sustainable agriculture.

QUESTIONS

1. Explain salient features of New Economic Policy (NEP).
2. Explain in brief historical background of Indian agriculture.
3. Write down the impact of NEP on Indian economy.
4. To what extent agriculture sector getting improved with the help of mechanization?
5. Describe the overall growth of agriculture yield after introduction of mechanization.
6. What are the prevailing drawbacks in the field of Indian agriculture?

OOO

UNIT - 3

Disadvantages

[illegible] agriculture products, lacks systematic production [illegible] and high costs, poor infrastructural facilities for [illegible] handling at manufacture [illegible] no timely and periodical [illegible] without quality control, high use of pesticides in [illegible]

[illegible] cannot convince the global trading countries and cannot [illegible] by foreign buyers.

[illegible] brand images and poor efforts in market development.

SUMMARY

[illegible] plenty but [illegible]. The productivity and production of foodgrains [illegible] infrastructural factors like finance, technology, storage [illegible] banking loans, and basic facilities like electricity, water [illegible] private sector to make investments and to generate [illegible] contribute to country's GDP.

[illegible] with many world-renowned corporates [illegible] distribution. These corporate conglomerates are expected [illegible] of India while they will control the prices [illegible]

[illegible] government in power is [illegible] policies of economic liberalization, privatization [illegible] under the stewardship of Dr. Manmohan Singh – steering [illegible] making efforts to increase agricultural exports through [illegible] changes and investment in infrastructure development.

[illegible] decision are more vibrant in permitting the private sector corporates in [illegible] marketing and has boosted them to develop export [illegible] drafted and piloted by the centre for export [illegible] of the traditional agro-based products because of [illegible]

[illegible] growth in export of [illegible]

[illegible] the growth in export of agriculture produce.

[illegible] EXIM policy 2004-09.

[illegible] of New Export Promotion Scheme?

○○○

CHAPTER 9

FOOD PROCESSING UNITS AND AGRO-BASED INDUSTRIES

FOOD PROCESSING UNITS AND AGRO BASED INDUSTRIES

India's food processing mainly involves primary processing which accounts for 80 per cent of the value. As much as 42 per cent of the food industry is in the organized sector and 33 per cent in the small-scale, tiny and cottage sectors. The value addition to agricultural commodities is less than 10 per cent. Food habits in India are traditional in nature and varied across the country.

Busier schedules and a growing number of working women have collectively led to an increase in the demand for ready-to-eat traditional and/or newer foods. As a segment of the food industry, traditional foods are the largest, both in terms of quantity and value.

Most of the operations are manual, even in relatively large-scale units, causing variation in quality. The present level of post-production losses is: 5-15 per cent in durables, 20-30 per cent in semi-perishables and 30-40 per cent in perishables. About 50 per cent of these could be prevented using appropriate post-harvest approaches.

The challenges in processing lie in presenting the product in near natural form with added convenience. The poor segment of population needs to be provided with good quality food at a price affordable by them. Traditionally, agro-processing has been the source of income generation in rural areas. It gradually reduced due to establishment of high capacity processing industry by organized sector.

However, to check migration to cities, now the processing of agro-produce in production catchments is being emphasized for employment generation. The Central Institute of Agriculture Engineering (CIAE), Bhopal has addressed these issues and developed suitable equipment for processing of cereals, oilseeds, pulses and vegetables.

PROCESSING OF CEREALS-PULSES-OILSEEDS

All major grains — paddy, wheat, maize, barley and millets like jowar (great millet), bajra (pearl millet), ragi (finger millet), etc. are produced in the country. Wheat is processed for flour, refined flour, samilona, grits, and whole-wheat flour. There are 360000 wheat milling units consisting of burr mills. Roller flourmills process over 50 per cent of wheat production with a milling capacity of 810 million tons each.

Modern rice mills process 65 per cent of paddy production and rest by huller/Sheller mills. The recovery of whole grains in a traditional rice mill using steel hullers for dehusking is around 52-54 per cent whereas in modern rice mills rubber roll shellers for dehusking operation is around 62-64 per cent in raw and 66-68 per cent in parboiled paddy. The conversion ratio (i.e., recovery per cent of various final product and byproduct for every 100 kg feed of raw paddy) for these improved rice mills are: milled rice 62-68 per cent, rice bran 4-5 per cent, rice husk 25 per cent and germ wastages 2 per cent-8 per cent.

Thus, need to establish small capacity (150 kg per hour) modern rice mills, available in the market, in villages for employment generation. *Dal* (split pulse) milling is the third largest processing industry in India after rice and wheat milling. Pulses meet 15-30 per cent of protein requirement.

Dal recovery potential is 83-85 per cent, but at present, it is 68-70 per cent in conventional mills and 72-78 per cent in modern *dal* mills. The mills are processing more than 10.5 million tons of dal. By-products are generally used as cattle feed.

Oil extraction used to be a cottage level activity in the rural areas using animal power in rotary mode. Now mechanical oil expellers, oil mills, 725 solvent extraction plants, 300 oil refineries and over 175 hydrogenated fat units produce about 6.85 million tons of edible oils and 3.61 tons of non-edible oils. The capacity utilization generally ranges from 10 per cent to around 30 per cent in case of the organized sector.

Apart from oilseeds, the by-products obtained during the processing operation, viz., deoiled cake, oil meals and other minor oil products are also of high economic value. India is one of the leading oil meal exporters in the world. Export of soymeal alone gets Foreign Exchange Reserves (FOREX) of about 800 million US$ (40000 million INR).

Small capacity oil expellers are available for use in rural areas for promoting agribusiness. The residual oil content in the oilcakes is between 6-8 per cent. Thus, the cake obtained need to be solvent extracted for enhancing availability of edible oil for food uses.

Soybean packed with 40 per cent good quality protein, 20 per cent oil and other nutrients has a great potential to combat protein-calorie malnutrition at an affordable cost.

India is now the fifth largest producer of soybean at a global level with more than 10.0 million tons production. Soy foods are nutritious, economical and provide many health benefits. Use of 10-20 per cent of soybean along with cereals gives maximum nutritional advantages.

However, due to the presence of some old nutritional factors in soybeans, it requires careful processing to make it fit for human and animal consumption. Soybean Processing and Utilization Centre (SPU) at CIAE, Bhopal have developed a number of process technologies and equipments for soy products. These are being promoted in rural/urban areas for agribusiness and nutrition security and so far over 210 cottage scale units have been established throughout the country.

FRUITS AND VEGETABLES PROCESSING

India produces 126 Mt of fruits and 63 Mt of vegetables. Almost all varieties of vegetables are grown in India. It is estimated that only 2 per cent of the total produce is being processed in India. Fruits and vegetables processing industry is being promoted for minimization of post-harvest losses.

The installed capacity of fruits and vegetables processing industry has increased from 1.1 million tons in January 1993 to 2.1 million tons in 2006. The processing of fruits and vegetables is estimated to be around 2.2 per cent of the total production in the country. The major processed items in the fruit and vegetable segment are fruit pulps and juices, fruit-based ready-to-serve beverages, canned fruits and vegetables, jams, squashes, pickles, chutneys and dehydrated vegetables. Some recent products introduced in this segment include vegetable curries in retortable pouches, canned mushroom and mushroom products, dried fruits and vegetables and fruit juice concentrates.

The fruits and vegetables processing industry is highly decentralized, and a large number of units are in the cottage, household and small-scale sector, having small capacities of up to 250 tons per annum. Since 2000, the food processing industry has seen significant growth in ready-to-serve beverages, fruit juices and pulps, dehydrated and frozen fruits and vegetable products, pickles, processed mushrooms and curried vegetables, and units engaged in these segments are export oriented.

Exporters of Fruits and Vegetables

(Quantity in MT, Value in ₹ Mn)

	2001-02		2004-05		CAGR	
	Quantity	Value	Quantity	Value	Quantity	Value
Dried and Preserved Vegetables	209157.8	5371.5	351034.3	7657.5	18.8	12.5
Mango Pulp	76735.18	2413.4	90988.6	3008.6	5.8	7.6
Pickles and Chutney	38758.97	1203.4	67193.29	1205.8	20.1	0.1
Other Processed Fruits and Vegetables	61332.39	2017.4	80760.5	2755.3	9.6	10.9
Total	385984.3	11005.7	589976.7	14627.2	15.2	9.9

Source: Ministry of Food Processing Industries, Annual Report 2005-06.

The domestic industry has to change its preference in favour of processed foods. Consumption of value-added fruits and vegetables are low compared to the primary processed foods, and fresh fruits and vegetables. The inclination towards processed foods is mostly visible in urban centres due to a high purchasing power.

A remarkable push can be given to this sector by strengthening linkages between farmers and food processors. The poor and weak linkage between farmers and markets as well as farmers and processing companies has brought about inefficiencies in the supply chain and encouraged the involvement of middlemen leading price rise to the products. The Government of India's National Agriculture Policy envisages the participation of the private sector through contract farming and land leasing arrangements which not only assures supply of raw material for processing units, but also a market for agriculture produce, accelerate technology transfer and capital inflow into the agriculture sector.

Fruits and vegetables offer a significant potential for the organized processing players due to the low level of processing and a vast supply base, coupled with considerable international demand for certain fresh as well as processed fruits and vegetables. However, inefficient domestic farming, higher costs of product delivery, exports protection and demanding standards, intermediaries and inefficiencies in the supply chain are the biggest bottlenecks in the growth of the sector. The recent emphasis on fruits and vegetables in light of nutrition security, growing interest of food processors and more profitable land use has brought in a significant change in the outlook of the producers who started using the arid/semi-arid lands and the horticultural crops that have lesser demands on water and gives three to four times more remuneration than field crops.

Innovative practices like contract farming in wheat crop in Madhya Pradesh by Hindustan Lever Ltd. and by Pepsi Foods Ltd. in Punjab for tomatoes, foodgrains, spices and oilseeds are some successful examples of contract farming in India, which changed the farming landscape and promoted the cultivation of processable variety of farm produce. This will certainly power the fruits, vegetables and grain processing industry. Besides such initiatives, fiscal incentives and tax concessions will also give impetus to the sector. The five-year 100 per cent tax exemption announced by the Government in the financial year 2005 was one such incentive for upcoming fruits and vegetables processing units.

The installed capacity for fruits and vegetables processing in India has increased from 11.08 2 lakh tons in 1993 to 24.74 lakh tons in 2007, mainly due to the increasing demand from ready-to-serve beverage industry, fruit juices and pulps, dehydrated and frozen fruits and vegetable products, pickles etc.

	Fruits		Vegetables	
Year	Fruits (Mn Ha)	Fruits Prodn. (Mn. Tons)	Vegetables (Mn. Ha)	Vegetables (Mn. Tons)
2002-03	4.8	49.2	5.9	84.8
2003-04	5.1	49.8	6.7	101.4
2004-05	5.3	52.8	7.1	108.2
2005-06	5.3	55.4	7.2	111.4
2006-07	5.6	59.6	7.5	115.0
2007-08	5.8	63.5	7.8	125.9

India's share in world fruits and vegetables market remains grim or poor.

Source: National Horticulture Board.

FRUITS

India has a large range of varieties of fruit in its basket and accounts for 10 per cent of world's total fruit production. Mango, banana, citrus, pineapple, papaya, guava, sapota, jackfruit, litchi and grape, among the tropical and sub-tropical fruits, apple, pear, peach, plum, apricot, almond and walnut among the temperate fruits and amla, pomegranate, fig, phalsa among the arid zone fruits are important. India leads the world in the production of mango, banana, sapota and acid lime and in productivity of grapes per unit land area.

India is the largest producer of mango, banana, sapota and acid lime. About 39 per cent of world's mango and 23 per cent of world's banana is produced in the country. In grapes, India has recorded the highest productivity per unit area in the world. The overall production of horticultural crops registered an increase of 8.0 per cent during 2004-05 as compared to 2003-04. The percentage increase in fruit production has been to the tune of 1.5 per cent during the period.

VEGETABLES

More than 40 kinds of vegetables belonging to different groups, namely, solanaceous, cucurbitaceous, leguminous, cruciferous (cole crops), root crops and leafy vegetables are grown in India in tropical, sub-tropical and temperate regions. Important vegetable crops grown in the country are tomato, onion, brinjal, cabbage, cauliflower, okra and peas.

India is next only to China in area and production of vegetables and occupies prime position in the production of cauliflower, second in onion and third in cabbage in the world. The area and production of major vegetables during 2004-05 is estimated at 6.30 million tons per hectare with a production of 93.0 million tons and average productivity of 14.8 tons per hectar. The production has increased by 5.7 per cent.

SPICES

Spices constitute an important group of horticultural crops and are defined as vegetable products or mixture thereof, free from extraneous matter, used for flavouring, seasoning and imparting aroma in foods. The term applies equally to the product in the whole form or in the ground form. India is known as the home of spices and produces a wide variety of spices like black pepper, cardamom (small and large) ginger, garlic, turmeric, chilli and a large variety of tree and seed spices.

India is the largest producer, consumer and exporter of spices and spice products. The total production of spices was 4.3 million metric tons and the area covered was 2.56 million hectares.

PLANTATION CROPS

Plantation crops constitute a large group of crops. The major plantation crops include coconut, arecanut, oil palm, cashew, tea, coffee and rubber; the minor plantation crops include cocoa. Their total coverage is comparatively less and they are mostly confined to small holdings. However, they play an important role in view of their export potential as well as domestic requirements and in employment generation and poverty alleviation programmes particularly in rural sector.

India is also the largest producer and consumer of cashew nuts. It is estimated that total production of cashew is around 0.57 million tons from an area of 0.24 million hectares. The cultivation of vanilla in India started in 1990s and was confined mostly to Karnataka and Kerala and to a lesser extent in Tamil Nadu, Northeast region, Lakshadweep and the Andaman and Nicobar Islands. India's production of vanilla was about 101 metric tons from about 27,811 hectare in 2004-05. Coconut is grown in an area of 1.93 million ha with a production of 12,148 million nuts and productivity of 6285 nuts per ha. India is the third largest producer of coconut and leads 90 coconut-producing countries of the world. It occupies number one position in arecanut production. India has been considered as a treasure house of valuable medicinal and aromatic plant species. The Government of India has identified and documented over 9,500 plant species considering their importance in the pharmaceutical industry. Out of these, about 65 plants have large and consistent demand in world trade. As a result, horticulture is not only an integral part of food and nutritional security, but also an essential ingredient of economic security.

FLOWERS

Though flower cultivation has been practiced in India since times immemorial, floriculture has blossomed into a viable business only in recent years. The increased growing of contemporary cut flowers like rose, gladiolus, tuberose, carnation, etc., has led to their use for bouquets and arrangements for gifts, as well as decoration of both home and work-place. A growing market, as a result of improvement in the general level of well-being in the country and increased affluence, particularly among the middle class, has led to transformation of the activity of flower growing into a burgeoning industry. Availability of diverse agro-climatic conditions in this large country facilitates production of all major flowers throughout the year in some part or the other, and improved transportation facilities, have increased the availability of flowers all over the country.

India has made noticeable advancement in the production of flowers. Floriculture is estimated to cover an area of 1.14 lakh with a production of 6,70,000 metric tons of loose flowers and 13,009.3 million cut flowers.

MEDICINAL AND AROMATIC PLANTS

Medicinal and aromatic plants have been used in the country for a long time for their medicinal properties. About 2,000 native plant species have curative properties and 1,300 species are known for their aroma and flavour. The Indian systems of medicines, popularly known as Ayurveda, Unani and Siddha drugs are in great demand in the country. There is already a spurt in demand for plant-based drugs and lately many such native species of medicinal values are being brought under systematic cultivation.

India has been considered as a treasure house of valuable medicinal and aromatic plant species. The Ministry of Environment and Forests (external website that opens in a new window). Government of India has identified and documented over 9,500 plant species considering their importance in the has pharmaceutical industry. Out of these, about 65 plants have large and consistent demand in world trade. India, however, produces only limited quantities of these materials. In terms of market share in production value, India holds only the 6th place with a mere 7 per cent share. On the contrary, we are still importing about 10 types of essential oils to the tune of 8,000 tons per annum.

BEE KEEPING

In order to maximize agricultural production, honeybee can be used as an important input. About 85 per cent crop plants are cross-pollinated, as they need to receive pollen from other plants of the same species with the help of external agents. One of the most important external agents is the honeybee. A few colonies of honeybees are placed in the field when the crop is in flowering stage. When pressed into service, they would make several thousand forages for pollination. The abundance of pollinators helps in early setting of seeds resulting in early and more uniform crop yield. Honeybees also produce honey, bee wax and royal jelly thus giving additional benefits to the farmers. About 5 million hectares of land in the country are under bee-dependent crops like fruit, vegetables, oilseeds, legumes and pulses. Many of these crops require three to nine bee colonies per hectare.

The National Bee Board which is looking after the developmental activities of bee keeping has been recently reconstituted with Secretary (A&C) as Chairman and Horticulture Commissioner as Member Secretary.

ANIMAL HUSBANDRY

Cattle and Buffalo Development

India possesses 27 acknowledged indigenous breeds of cattle and seven breeds of buffaloes. Various central and centrally sponsored schemes are being implemented for genetic improvement of cattle and buffalo with a view to enhance the per capita availability of consumption of milk through increased milk production. Efforts are also made to protect and preserve the indigenous breeds of cattle and buffalo in their native tract, which are facing threat of extinction. The elite animals are selected and registered on the basis of their performance for production of superior pedigree bulls, bull mothers, frozen semen and frozen embryos for future breeding improvements.

The National Project for Cattle and Buffalo Breeding envisages 100 per cent grant in aid to implementing agencies. At present, 28 States and one Union Territory are participating in the project.

Financial assistance to the tune of ₹ 398.36 crore has been released to these States upto 2007-08. During the financial year 2008-09, against the Financial Assistance of ₹ 89.70 crore, an amount of ₹ 87.37 crore has been released.

A Central Herd Registration Scheme (External website that opens in a North Western window) for identification and location of superior germ plasm of cattle and buffaloes, propagation of superior germ stock, regulating the sale and purchase, help in formation of breeder's society and to meet requirements of superior bulls in different parts of the country is also being implemented. The Government of India has established Central Herd Registration Unit in four breeding tracts, i.e., Rohtak, Ahmedabad, Ongole and Ajmer. A total of 92 Milk Recording Centres are functioning to register these breeds of cattle, viz., Gir, Kankrej, Hariana and Ongole and in Buffalo Jaffrabadi, Mehsani, Murrah and Surti.

The seven Central Cattle Breeding Farms at Suratgarh (Rajasthan), Chiplima and Semiliguda (Orissa), Dhamrod (Gujarat), Hessarghatta (Karnataka), Alamadi (Tamil Nadu) and Andeshnagar (Uttar Pradesh) are engaged in scientific breeding programmes of cattle and buffaloes and production of high pedigreed bulls for National Project for Cattle/Buffalo Breeding Programme besides providing training to farmers and breeders. During 2008-09, these farms produced 346 bull calves and supplied 245 high pedigreed bulls for use under Artificial Insemination Programme in various parts of the country. 3,711 persons were trained in farm management practices and demonstration of scientific breeding. The CCBFS trained 2912 number of farmers during the training camp on farm management.

The Central Frozen Semen Production and Training Institute (CFSP&TI) located at Hessarghatta (Bengaluru) is producing frozen semen doses of indigenous, exotic and crossbreed cattle and Murrah buffalo/bulls for use in artificial insemination (Ae). The Institute also provides training in semen technology to technical officers of the State Governments and acts as a Centre for testing the indigenously manufactured frozen semen and AI equipments. The Institute produced 8.66 lakh doses of frozen semen and provided training to 227 persons in field of frozen semen technology and andrology during the year 2008-09.

POULTRY DEVELOPMENT

Poultry development in the country has shown steady progress over the years, primarily due to research and development schemes of Government as well as effective marketing and management by organized private sector.

India, with poultry population of 489 million and estimated more than 532 billion eggs production, ranks among the top three countries in egg production in the world. During 1980-81, egg production reached double-digit billion figures (10 billion numbers) and has increased over 5 times currently. Per capita availability has, during this period, also increased nearly 3 times from a mere fifteen numbers per person per annum to forty-two per annum.

The broiler production is growing at the rate of nearly 8-10 per cent every year and growth in production of poultry/chicken meat increased from mere 0.12 million metric tons in 1981 to 2.2 million metric tons presently. The annual per capita availability of eggs and chicken meat has also increased from a mere 10 eggs and 146 grams in 1970s to around 42 eggs and 1.6 kgs respectively presently.

India's share of the world trade in poultry and poultry products is very small. However, the country has come a long way during the last decade increasing its value of exports from nearly ₹ 11 crores in 1993-94 to around ₹ 441 crores during 2007-08. Poultry sector, besides providing direct or indirect employment to nearly 3 million people is a potent tool for subsidiary income generation for many landless and marginal farmers and also provides nutritional security especially to the rural poor.

To provide necessary services to the farmers of the country region-wise, four regional centres have been restructured on the principle of one-window service to the farmers. In these regional Central Poultry Development Organizations (CPDOs) located at Chandigarh, Bhubaneswar, Mumbai and Hessarghatta, training is also being imparted to the farmers to upgrade their technical skills. To monitor the production potential of various stocks in the country, the Central Poultry Performance Test unit at Gurgaon is conducting one layer and two broiler tests in a year.

Recently, Cabinet Committee on Economic Affairs approved the Centrally Sponsored Scheme. "Poultry Development" from third year of Eleventh Five Year Plan, i.e., 2009-10, at a total outlay of ₹ 150 crore. The Centrally Sponsored Scheme combines three components, viz., 'Assistance to State Poultry Farms', (which is a continuing component) and two new components 'Rural Backyard Poultry Development' and 'Poultry Estates'. The administrative approval and scheme guidelines are being issued.

The Scheme through its 'Assistance to State Poultry Farms' component aims at strengthening existing State poultry farms so as to enable them to provide inputs, mainly in terms of providing improved stocks suitable for rural backyard rearing. The 'Rural Backyard Poultry Development' component is expected to cover the needy Below Poverty Line section of society to mainly enable them to gain supplementary income and nutritional support. Entrepreneurship skills are expected to be improved through pilot component of 'Poultry Estates' which is meant primarily for educated, unemployed youth and small farmers with some margin money, for making a profitable venture out of various poultry related activities in a scientific, and bio-secure cluster approach.

SHEEP AND GOAT DEVELOPMENT

According to Livestock Census 2003, there are about 61.47 million sheeps and 124.36 million goats in the country. About five million households in the country are engaged in the rearing of small ruminants (sheep and goats) and other allied activities.

Central Sheep Breeding Farm, Hissar is engaged in production of acclimatized exotic/cross-bred superior quality rams. During 2008-09, the farm supplied 613 rams and 95 bucks. A total of 44 farmers were trained in mechanical sheep shearing and 633 farmers were trained in sheep management.

CONSERVATION OF THREATENED BREEDS

The population of purebred animals of some of the small ruminants, equines, pigs and pack animal breeds has come down considerably and below 10,000 in some cases, which has brought such breeds to the category of threatened breeds in the country.

A new centrally sponsored scheme for conservation of such threatened breeds was started during Tenth Five Year Plan with a budget outlay of ₹ 1500 lakhs. Farm/farmer's units in their respective breeding tract are established under the scheme with 100 per cent central assistance. The conservation projects are being implemented by State Governments, Universities and NGOs. During the Tenth Plan period, conservation projects for 27 breeds were taken up.

Eleventh Plan allocation has been enhanced from ₹ 16.00 crore to ₹ 45.00 crore during 2008-09. Poultry and duck breeds would also be covered during Eleventh Plan whose population is around 1000.

Allocation under the scheme during 2008-09 was ₹ 1.90 crore against which ₹ 194.95 lakh has been released up to March, 2009. The State of Gujarat has been assisted for conservation of Surti Goat (₹ 32.25 lakh), Kerala Livestock Development Board has been assisted for conservation of Attapaddy Goat (₹ 27.25 lakh) as well as Angamally Pig (₹ 9.20 lakh) and Government of Jammu and Kashmir has been assisted for conservation of Zanskari Pony (₹ 6.00 lakh). Guru Angad Dev Veterinary and Animal Sciences University, Ludhiana has been provided with ₹ 30.00 lakh towards conservation of Beetal Goats and ₹ 68.00 lakhs to the Govt. of Gujarat for conservation of Kachchhi Camel during 2008-09. NABCONS has been provided with ₹ 2.25 lakh towards completion of evaluation of the performance of the scheme.

MEAT PRODUCTION/PROCESSING AND EXPORT

There are 20 export-oriented modern abattoirs and 21 meat processing plants registered with Agricultural and Processed Food Products Export Development Authority exporting raw meat (chilled and frozen) to about 56 countries. During 2007-08, about 483478 metric tons buffalo meat and 8908.72 MT sheep/goat meat valued at ₹ 3549.79 crore and ₹ 134.09 crore respectively were exported. During April 2008 to February 2009, meat and its product worth ₹ 4859 crores have been exported indicating 31.91 per cent growth in rupee terms.

PIGGERY DEVELOPMENT

As per Livestock Census 2003, the pig population in the country was 139.19 lakhs of which 21.80 lakh were cros-bred/exotic pigs. Exotic breeds like white Yorkshire, Hampshire and Landrace are maintained at these farms. There are about 158 pig breeding farms in the country run by the State Governments/UTs. Efforts are being made in consultation with Planning Commission and other appraisal agencies to initiate Integrated Piggery Development Scheme under Macro Management Scheme during Eleventh Five Year Plan.

FEED AND FODDER DEVELOPMENT

For the development of the production potentiality of our livestock, availability of nutritious feed and fodder is essential. To facilitate fodder availability, several regional stations have been established in different agro-climatic zones of the country for production of high yielding varieties of fodder/fodder seed and transfer of scientific fodder production technology through training of officers/farms, demonstration of latest fodder agronomic practices and organization of farmer fairs. During 2008-09, these stations produced 212.50 MT of high yielding fodder variety seeds, conducted 6249 field demonstrations, organized 110 training programmes and 116 Farmer Fairs.

The Central Fodder Seed Production Farm located at Hessarghatta (Karnataka) working with the same objectives as of Regional Stations produced 66.01 MT fodder seeds of different varieties of grasses/legumes, conducted 605 field demonstrations, organized 12 training programmes and 12 farmers fairs. A Central Minikit Testing Program of fodder crops is under implementation for popularizing the high yielding fodder varieties on a large scale through Director Animal Husbandry of States. During 2008-09, 6.34 lakh minikits were allotted to the states for distribution to farmers free of cost.

Besides a centrally sponsored Fodder Development Scheme is being implemented from 2005-06 for establishment of Fodder Block making units, grassland development including grass reserve, fodder seed production and biotechnology research project, under which funds of ₹ 924.91 lakhs was released to various States during 2008-09.

In addition, Special Livestock Package for Suicide Prone Districts of Maharashtra, Karnataka, Andhra Pradesh and Kerala is implemented under which the sum of ₹ 1382.00 lakhs was released during 2008-09 for Feed and Fodder Supply Programme and establishment of Fodder Block making units.

DAIRY DEVELOPMENT

The Indian dairy industry has acquired substantial growth from the Eighth Plan onwards, achieving an annual output of over 104.8 million tons (provisional) of milk at the end of 2007-08. India's milk output has not only placed the industry first in world, but also represents sustained growth in the availability of milk and milk products. The Government is implementing following schemes for the development of dairy sector during 2008-09.

- **Intensive Dairy Development Programme (IDDP):** The Schemes modified as Intensive Dairy Development Programme on the basis of the recommendation of the evaluation studies was launched during Eighth Plan period and is being continued during the Eleventh Plan with an outlay of ₹ 32.49 crore for 2009-10. So far 86 projects with an outlay of ₹ 489.84 crore have been sanctioned in 25 States and one Union Territory. A sum of ₹ 373.82 crore has been released to various State Governments upto 31st March, 2009 and 207 districts have been covered. The scheme has benefited about 18.79 lakh farm families and organized about 26882 village level Dairy Cooperative Societies till 31st March, 2009.
- **Strengthening Infrastructure for Quality and Clean Milk Production (CMP):** A centrally sponsored scheme was launched in October 2003, with the main objective of improving the quality of raw milk produced at the village level in the country. Under this scheme, assistance is provided for training of farmers on good milking practices. The scheme is being implemented on 100 per cent grant-in-aid basis to District Cooperative Milk Unions and State Cooperative Milk Federation through the State Governments/UTs for components, viz., training of farmer member, detergents, stainless steel utensils, strengthening of existing laboratory facilities whereas 75 per cent financial assistance is provided for setting up of milk ceiling facilities at village level in the form of Bulk Milk Coolers. Since inception, 131 projects at a total cost of ₹ 195.17 crore with central share of ₹ 159.33 crore have been approved up to 31st March, 2009 under this scheme. A total sum of ₹ 128.11 crore as a central share has been released to the concerned State Governments for implementation of approved project activities up to 31.03.09. The scheme has benefited 5,30,468 farmer members by imparting training and by installing 21.05 lakh litre capacity of Bulk Milk Coolers to facilitate marketing of milk produced by them and keeping its quality intact as on 31.03.09.

ASSISTANCE TO COOPERATIVES

The scheme aims at revitalizing the sick Dairy Cooperative Unions at the district level and Cooperative Federations at the State level. Under the scheme, rehabilitation programmes are prepared by National Dairy Development Board (NDDB) in consultation with Milk Union Federation/State Government. A central grant is released to Milk Union/Federations through NDDB. The scheme is being continued

Eleventh Five Year Plan with a tentative outlay of ₹ 50 crore. Since inception in 1999-2000, 34 rehabilitation proposals of milk union in 12 States namely, Madhya Pradesh, Chhattisgarh, Karnataka, Uttar Pradesh, Haryana, Kerala, Maharashtra, Assam, Nagaland, Punjab, West Bengal and Tamil Nadu at a total cost of ₹ 230.94 crore with a central share of ₹ 115.66 crore have been approved upto 31.3.09. A total sum of ₹ 88.19 crore has been released till 31.03.2009. An amount of ₹ 9 crore has been provided in the fiscal year 2009-10 out of which a sum of ₹ 155.495 lakh has been released to the concerned Milk Unions during current financial year till 20.8.2009.

DAIRY VENTURE CAPITAL FUND

To bring about structural changes in unorganized sector, measures like milk processing at village level, marketing of pasteurized milk in a cost-effective manner, quality upgradation of traditional technology to handle commercial scale using modern equipments and management skills, a new scheme, viz., Dairy Venture Capital Fund was initiated in the Tenth Five Year Plan. The assistance under the scheme is provided to the rural/urban beneficiaries under a schematic proposal through bankable projects with 50 per cent interest free loan component.

The scheme is implemented through NABARD and the funds released by Govt. of India to NABARD are kept as revolving fund. Under the scheme, the entrepreneur has to contribute 10 per cent and arrange 40 per cent loan from local bank. Government of India provides 50 per cent interest free loan through NABARD. Government of India also subsidizes the interest component payable by the farmer's agricultural activities to the extent of 50 per cent only in case of regular/timely repayment.

This scheme was approved in Dec 2004 with a total outlay of ₹ 25.00 crore. The scheme is being implemented through NABARD and the funds released to NABARD to be kept as revolving fund. Since inception, a sum of ₹ 112.99 crore has been released to NABARD for implementation of the scheme up to 31st March 2009. There is a provision of ₹ 38.00 crore for implementation of the scheme during 2009-10, out of which ₹ 10.00 crore have been released till 31.07.2009.

MILK AND MILK PRODUCT ORDER-1992

The Government of India notified the Milk and Milk Product Order on June 1992. As per the provisions of this order, any person/dairy plant handling more than 10,000 liters per day of milk or 500 MT of milk solids per annum needs to be registered with the registering authority appointed by the Central Government. With the enactment of Food Safety Standard Act 2006, at present the work related to MMPO-92 is under Food Safety and Standard Authority of India (FSSAI), M/o Health and Family Welfare.

NATIONAL DAIRY PLAN

Government is also examining the launching a National Dairy Plan with an outlay of more than ₹ 17,300 crore to achieve a target of 180 million tonnes of Milk producing annually by 2021-22. Milk production is expected to grow at 4 per cent with an annual incremental output of 5 million tons in the next 15 years. Under this plan, the government is contemplating to enhance milk production in major milk producing areas, strengthen and expand infrastructure to production, process and market milk through the existing and new institutional structures. The plan envisages breed improvement through agricultural land and through nature service, setting up plants to augment cattle feed, bypass protein and mineral mixture. The plan also proposed to bring 65 per cent of the surplus milk produced under the organized sector for procurement as against the present 30 per cent. Efforts are on the tap for World Bank funding for this project.

The fisheries sector has been one of the major contributors of foreign exchange earnings through export. Export of fish and fishery products has grown manifold over the years. From about 15,700 tons valued at ₹ 3.92 crore in 1961-62, exports have grown to 5.41 lakh tons valued at ₹ 7621 crore in 2007-08.

DEVELOPMENT OF INDIAN FISHERIES AND AQUACULTURE

The ongoing scheme of Development of Freshwater Aquaculture and Integrated Coastal Aquaculture have been combined with four new programmes on Development of Coldwater Fish Culture, Development of Waterlogged Area and Derelict Water Bodies into Aquaculture Estates, Use of Inland Saline/Alkaline Soil for Aquaculture and Programme for Augmenting the Productivity of Reservoirs. This scheme broadly has two components: Aquaculture and Inland Capture Fisheries.

EXPORT OF SEAFOOD

Seafood exports is all set to scale new heights with the remarkable breakthrough for ensuring the supply of high quality all male Scampi (Scampi: Giant Freshwater Prawn) seeds. In April this year, The Scampi Broodstock Development Project of Rajiv Gandhi Centre Aquaculture at Konathanapadu, Kankipadu Mandal, Krishna District, Andhra Pradesh, successfully developed the first proven neofemale in the country and achieved production of all male progeny of the giant freshwater prawn (Scampi Macrobrachium rosenbergii) for the first time in the subcontinent – an enviable achievement unmatched by any research organization in the nation so far. The technology developed at RGCA involves sex reversal of healthy Scampi males into functional females (called as Neofemales) through microsurgical interventions and crossing these females with normal males to produce all male progeny. This technology does not involve any kind of genetic manipulations or hormonal treatments. This has the potential of increasing the unit area production by around 40 per cent.

One of the major challenges faced by the Scampi farmers today is that with the differential growth (among males and females) which causes low survivals and poor yields. To overcome this, the Scampi farmers presently segregate males and females painstakingly at the farm and grow only males that grow to larger sizes in quicker time when compared to the females. Therefore, the technology, now developed by RGCA could easily resolve this major challenge of differential growth faced by the Scampi farmers and provide the much needed boost to revive the Scampi farming in the country.

Having developed the technology for all male Scampi production, the project is now just a step away from large-scale production of Neofemales. Once this is achieved, the project would be able to ensure the supply of high quality all male Scampi seeds to the industry resulting in elevating the unit area production by around 40 per cent as well as boosting up the overall Scampi Aquaculture production from the country. As a result, the Scampi export from the country is expected to rise, with improved economic benefits to the farmers.

The Giant Freshwater Prawn is an important export commodity with great demand in the International Seafood market. This species also has great potential for Aquaculture in India and can be farmed in inland areas also with good freshwater resources. However, in the wake of several technical problems that besieged the industry, the Aquaculture production of this species in the country declined from a high of 43,000 tons in 2005 to 4000 tons in 20010-11. Marine products account for around 1.1 per cent of the total export earnings for India. Around 7.53 lakh tons of Seafood worth around ₹ 12100 crores (2.68 billion USD) has been exported from India during 2010-11.

As a part of this project, RGCA has also completed a diallel crossing experiment for the development of an improved strain of Scampi that performs well in farming conditions. The development of all male seeds would be taken up from this strain to maximize the benefits to the industry. It is envisaged that the project would be able to produce and supply all male freshwater prawn seeds on commercial basis within next two years. The technology for all male Scampi seed production would also be passed on to the Scampi hatcheries/entrepreneurs across the country.

Aquaculture has been contributing to the seafood exports from the country, in view of the dwindling natural fishery of commercially important varieties like shrimps. Farmed Shrimp and Scampi (Freshwater Prawn) accounted for 41 per cent share in exports in terms of quantity and 50 per cent in terms of value of the total Shrimp and Scampi exports from the country. However, contribution from Aquaculture to the total Seafood exports has been more or less stagnant over the last decade and aquaculture production contributed only 15.3 per cent in terms of quantity and 25.2 per cent in terms of value to the total Seafood exports from the country. This is pale in comparison with countries like China where contribution from aquaculture for export is significantly higher than the contribution from wild catches.

DEVELOPMENT OF FRESHWATER AQUACULTURE

The Government has been implementing an important programme in inland sector, viz., Development of Freshwater Aquaculture through the Fish Farmers Development Agencies (FFDAs). A network of 429 FFDAs covering all potential districts in the country are in operation. During 2007-08, about 24,752 hectare of water area was brought under fish culture and 35,000 fish farmers were trained in improved aquaculture practices through FEDAs.

DEVELOPMENT OF BRACKISH WATER AQUACULTURE

With the objective of utilizing the country's vast brackish-water area for shrimp culture, an area of about 30,889 hectares was developed for shrimp culture till 2007-08 through 39 brackishwater Fish Farmers Development Agencies (BFDAs) set up in the coastal areas of the country. The agencies have also trained 31,624 fishermen in improved practices of shrimp culture till 2007-08. Presently about 50 per cent of the shrimp exported from the country is from aquaculture.

DEVELOPMENT OF MARINE FISHERIES

The Government is providing subsidy to poor fishermen for motorizing their traditional craft, which increases the fishing areas and frequency of operation with consequent increase in catch and earnings of fishermen. About 46,223 traditional crafts have been motorized so far. The Government has also been operating a scheme on fishermen development rebate on High Speed Diesel oil used by fishing vessels below 20 meter length to offset the operational cost incurred by small mechanized fishing boat operators.

DEVELOPMENT OF FISHING HARBOUR

The Government has been implementing a scheme with the objective of providing infrastructure facilities for safe landing and berthing to the fishing vessels. Since inception of the scheme, six major fishing harbours, viz., Cochin, Chennai, Visakhapatnam, Roychowk, Paradip and Mazgaon dock (Mumbai), 62 minor fishing harbours and 190 fish landing centres have been taken up for construction in various coastal States/Union Territories.

WELFARE PROGRAMMES FOR TRADITIONAL FISHERMEN

Important programmes for the welfare of traditional fishermen are:

- Group Insurance Scheme for active fishermen
- Development of Model Fishermen Villages
- Saving-cum-relief Scheme, and
- Saving-cum-component financial assistance is provided to the fishermen during the lean fishing season.

About 3.5 lakh fishermen were assisted under the saving-cum-relief programme in 2008-2009.

SPECIALIZED INSTITUTES

The Central Institute of Fisheries, Nautical and Engineering Training, Kochi with units at Chennai and Visakhapatnam, aims at making available sufficient number of operators of deep-sea fishing vessels and technicians for shore establishments. Integrated Fisheries Project, Kochi, envisages processing, popularizing and test marketing of unconventional varieties of fish. The Central Institute of Coastal Engineering for Fisheries, Bengaluru, is engaged in techno-economic feasibility study for location of fishing harbour sites. Fishery Survey of India (FSI) is the nodal organization responsible for survey and assessment of fishery resources under the Indian Exclusive Economic Zone (EEZ).

NATIONAL FISHERIES DEVELOPMENT BOARD

National Fisheries Development Board was established to work towards blue revolution with a focus on to increase the fish production of the country to a level of 10.3 million tons, to achieve double the exports from 7,000 crore to 14,000 crore and direct employment to an extent of 3.5 million by extending assistance to the various agencies for implementation of activities under Inland, Brackish water and Marine sectors. It will become a platform for public-private partnership for fisheries, a mechanism for ensuring proper in self-availability to efficient marketing etc.

It is an autonomous organization under the administrative control of the Department of Animal Husbandry, Dairying and Fisheries, Ministry of Agriculture, and Govt. of India. It has been registered with the Office of the Registrar of Societies, Hyderabad on 10th July 2006 with the registration number of 933 of 2006. The Board was inaugurated on 9th September 2006. The office was established at Hyderabad.

The period of implementation of the various activities of the board is 6 years (2006-12):

- To bring major activities relating to fisheries and aquaculture for focused attention and professional management,
- To coordinate activities pertaining to fisheries undertaken by different Ministries/Departments in the Central Government and also coordinate with the State/Union territory Government,
- To improve production, processing, storage, transport and marketing of the products and culture fisheries,
- To achieve sustainable management and conservation of natural aquatic resources including the fish stocks,
- To apply modern tools of research and development including biotechnology for optimizing production and productivity farm fisheries,
- To provide modern infrastructure mechanisms for fisheries and ensure their effective management and optimum utilization,
- To generate substantial employment,
- To train and empower women in the fisheries sector, and
- To enhance contribution of fish towards food and nutritional security.

Major activities to be taken up by the National Fisheries Development Board:

- Intensive aquaculture in ponds and tanks.
- Enhancing productivity from Reservoir Fisheries
- Brackish water Coastal Aquaculture
- Mariculture
- Sea Ranching
- Seaweed Cultivation
- Infrastructure for Post-harvest Programmes
- Fish Dressing Centres and Solar Drying Fish
- Domestic Marketing
- Other Activities

PROCESSING OF COMMERCIAL CROPS

Sugarcanes, jute, cotton, tea, coffee and tobacco are major commercial crops grown in India. More than 50 per cent sugarcane is estimated to be processed by sugar mills and the balance by jaggery *(Gur) and Khandsari* industries. Although, the efficiency of jaggery *(Gur)* and *Khandsari* sector is low compared to sugar mills, but these units provide more employment opportunities to rural workforce hence requires further attention.

RURAL AGRO-PROCESSING

Decentralized value addition of farm produce helps in better waste management, less transportation, and more employment in rural areas. Primary processing facilities need to be created in rural areas for farm processing to:

(a) Use available raw materials for processing in the catchments area at reduced cost,

(b) Reduce cost of processing due to availability of labour, reduced cost of handling, and transport,

(c) Generate more employment for rural people to arrest the migration and reduce social problems in cities (mitigation of congestion in cities),

(d) Achieve overall development of rural areas with the creation of other infrastructure to serve these units in terms of education, health, communication, etc.,

(e) Utilize by-products after value addition as animal feed, compost, biogas feed, etc. to reduce pollution load of cities,

(f) Make better use of crop residues, processing of by-products and wastes in eco-friendly and economically rewarding fashion, and

(g) Appropriately pack and market the minimally processed and value-added products through food chain.

ENERGY USAGE IN AGRICULTURE

The 20th century has witnessed the phenomenal growth of various industries based on these energy sources and fossil fuel, in particular, has played the most significant role. By now, it has penetrated so deep into the mechanism of human living that man is not prepared to accept the fact that this useful source of energy is not going to last very long.

Thus, there is the compulsion and constant search for alternate sources of energy. Renewable energy sources — solar, wind, and biomass have potential to be utilized as supplementary energy source. Biomass and animate power meet the major energy needs of the rural sector, as it is available locally.

The decentralized production of electricity using biomass is being attempted through the producer gas route, in addition to photovoltaic solar system for lifting water, lighting and energy for household appliances. It is estimated that more than 600 million tons of biomass is available from various crop residues and agro-wastes of which about 60-65 per cent can be used for power generation. Besides about 27 million tons municipal waste is also available which has potential to be utilized for energy production.

Engineers have done immense service, modernizing agriculture and agro-processing. Studies under ICAR reveal that the gains in agriculture have come largely from direct and indirect use of commercial energies, diesel and electricity, fertilizers and chemicals, which are not only expensive but their availability is much wanting in rural areas especially in remote and hilly areas. Petroleum is largest import bill of India. Total installed capacity in India for electricity generation (2008) in India is 147965.51 MW.

TECHNOLOGY TRANSFER

The Centre for Indian Agriculture in Energy (CIAE) has a Prototype Production Centre equipped with modern machine tools for fabrication of farm equipment for multi-location verification, evaluation and supply to needy. The Institute developed 140 farm machines of which 78 have been made available to end-users.

The Ministry of Agriculture and Cooperation, Government of India has released 23 machines for popularization through the provincial governments under centrally sponsored implements subsidy scheme. Institute has strong linkage with State Agro-Industrial Development Corporations and small-scale farm machinery industries for commercialization of technology.

Technology diffusion is done to farmers, artisans, extension workers, subject-matter specialists and manufacturers through vocational training of farmers, crafts persons, rural youths and subject matter specialists. Entrepreneurship development programmes receive special consideration.

Extension wing of Agricultural Ministry alone cannot do this work as engineering interventions and output need special inputs to make it available to end-user. Approach for National Level Commercialization of already developed effective technologies/equipment is:

(a) Networking of R & D Institutes, manufacturers and farmers

(b) Interface with ministries

(c) Participation of farmers/end-users

(d) Registration of manufacturers

The following approaches were considered as other means of effective technology transfer:

Service in Agriculture

Unlike other advanced countries, India cannot afford to displace large percentage of rural population from agriculture to other sectors for the want of employment. We have, therefore, to generate more jobs in rural areas. Scope of entrepreneurship development for employment and income generation on agricultural mechanization and renewable energy through Agri-business is of high order.

This includes repair and maintenance support for farmers, custom hiring services, setting up of agro waste/biomass based enterprises for charring, briquette, improved sign, solar cafe, etc. Repair and maintenance of agricultural machinery, irrigation, biogas plant, agro-processing equipment, etc. can lead to timely service inputs to save crop and resources and generate employment for local youth thereby checking migration to cities.

CUSTOM HIRE – SERVICE CENTRES FOR MACHINERY

One of the major constraints of increasing agricultural production and productivity is the inadequacy of farm power and machinery with the farmers. The average farm power availability needs to be increased from the current 1.43 kilowatt per hectare to at least 2 kW/ha to assure timeliness and quality in field operations, undertake heavy field operations like sub-soiling, chiseling, deep ploughing, summer ploughing, etc. All these agricultural operations are possible only when adequate agricultural mechanization infrastructure is created.

Even farmers with small holdings utilize selected improved farm equipment through custom hiring. Each farmer can't purchase the machinery set-up of his requirement. Therefore, custom-hiring facility can be of significance to both unemployed youth and the farmers. Establishment of such facilities has potential for adoption of mechanization systems. This can be true for processing activities also. Repair and maintenance service providers for agricultural machinery are a need and developing countries may adopt that system by training the upcoming entrepreneurs.

The approach identified for employment/entrepreneurship development covers:

- Setting up of Agro-processing enterprises in the rural areas and motivate the farmers to adopt modern techniques.
- Service, repair and maintenance facilities for agricultural machinery.
- Agro-Service Centres establishment.
- Establishing Agricultural Implements' Bank by entrepreneurs to provide the machinery on customer's hire basis to farmers when needed.

SKILL DEVELOPMENT-TRAINING AND EMPLOYMENT

Entrepreneurship development in service, agriculture and allied sector has immense potential through engineering interventions. One such approach is skill development training in manufacture, repair, maintenance and related service support in farm machinery, irrigation, processing, energy equipment repair, maintenance and for primary processing of foodgrains, fruits and vegetables, etc.

This is the key approach targeted at ensuring hand and mind engagement, security to get productive output. Training programmes are organized regularly to empower unemployed youth, farmers, farmwomen and upcoming entrepreneurs. Some of the technologies identified are production agriculture, agribusiness in improved farm implements, setting up of household/cottage and small-scale food processing and soy processing unit.

Soya based technologies include full fat soy flour, soy fortified biscuits and soy *paneer* (TOFU). These are simple soy food products for use with cereals and food legumes. Adoption of these technologies provides direct employment to 6-8 persons per unit, higher income to farmers, higher value for the products and minimizes losses. The initial investment to enterprise varies from US$ 4000-20000 (INR 0.2-1 million).

INCOME GENERATION FOR WOMEN

Women constitute about 45 per cent agriculture workforce in India. In addition to their daily household activities, they contribute 50-75 per cent of the total labour required for various production and post-production agricultural operations in the developing countries. It causes lot of drudgery to them and thus low productivity. To empower, they need to be provided with: (i) women-friendly agricultural tools and equipment and (ii) opportunities for gainful engagement throughout the year.

Thus, we can say in this chapter you have to learn about agricultural business management. You will also be able to understand that product contribution in terms of food supplies is extremely important in maintaining the price stability as the impact of food prices is much more severe in a developing economy than high income country. Further, students will be able to realize that inflationary trends will rise with any downward trend in the food supplies thereby affecting the terms of trade of the industrial sector. And the prices of foodstuffs that will also rise in relation to the prices of manufactured goods and thus raise the cost of living.

Further, role of agriculture in agri-business management is pivotal in any economy and since economy is agriculture dominated they will bring about an improvement in agricultural productivity which will in turn result in the raising of sufficient surplus for further investment in the agricultural sector and an increase in the agriculture sector that will have cascading effect on increase in farm incomes mobilized for capital formation through imposition of different taxes and levies.

According to latest Economic Survey Report, Indian agriculture including crop and animal husbandry, fisheries, forestry and agro-processing provides the underpinnings of our food and livelihood security. Agriculture provides significant support for economic growth and social transformation of the country.

As one of the world's largest agrarian economies, the agriculture sector (including allied activities) in India accounted for 15.7 per cent of the GDP (at constant 2004-05 prices), in 2008-09, compared to 18.9 per cent in 2004-05, and contributed approximately 10.2 per cent of total exports during 2008-09. Notwithstanding the fact that the share of this sector in the GDP has been declining over the years, its role remains critical as it provides employment to around 52 per cent of the workforce.

There were some notable improvements in the performance of agro-processing and agriculture-based industries. And government at the centre also introduced some measures to extend helping hand to rural folks in the form of subsidies on raw materials and also through periodical notification of procurement prices aiming at benefiting the farmers' fraternity after studying carefully the rural economic scenario. In this direction, many useful foresighted developmental programmes like DPAR and FYPs have been implemented and which thereby brought some reformmes in the field of agriculture.

The public investment in agriculture in real terms has witnessed steady decline from the Sixth Five Year Plan to the Tenth Plan. Trends in public investment in agriculture and allied sectors reveal that it has consistently declined in real terms (at 1999-2000 prices) from the Sixth Plan to the Ninth Plan (Sixth Plan [1980-85] ₹ 64,012 crore, Seventh Plan [1985-90] ₹ 52,108 crore, Eighth Plan [1992-97] ₹ 45,565 crore and Ninth Plan [1997-2002] ₹ 42,226 crore). However, this trend was reversed in the Tenth Plan (2002-07) and public investment in agriculture registered an increase of ₹ 25, 034 crore and stood at ₹ 67,260 crore, which is a positive and welcome trend.

Further, during 1991 under the stewardship of the then Union Finance Minister Dr. Manmohan Singh's (now Honorable Prime Minister of India), New Economic Policy was introduced to bring overall developmental changes in the Indian economy in various sectors to reach the benefits to common man. But still government at the centre conceived that there is need to intervene in the affairs of agriculture sector by devising various developmental programmes, like introduction of mechanization, latest machinery in tillage and processing, cutting and harvesting, processing, seeds processing, cereals, oilseeds, fruits and veggies processing, etc.

All these measures were timely devised and well conceived plans by government at centre which made 20th century to witness phenomenal growth of various agro-based and agriculture industries with the usage of energy sources and fossil fuel which played significant role in the agriculture sector.

SUMMARY

India's food processing mainly involves primary processing which accounts for 80 per cent of the value. As much as 42 per cent of the food industry is in the organized sector and 33 per cent in the small scale, tiny and cottage sectors. The value addition to agricultural commodities is less than 10 per cent. Food habits in India are traditional in nature and varied across the country.

Busier schedules and a growing number of working women have collectively led to an increase in the demand for ready-to-eat traditional and/or newer foods. As a segment of the food industry, traditional foods are the largest, both in terms of quantity and value.

Most of the operations are manual, even in relatively large-scale units, causing variation in quality. The present level of post-production losses is: 5-15 per cent in durables, 20-30 per cent in semi-perishables and 30-40 per cent in perishables. About 50 per cent of these could be prevented using appropriate post-harvest approaches.

The challenges in processing lie in presenting the product in near natural form with added convenience. The poor segment of population needs to be provided with good quality food at a price affordable by them. Traditionally, agro-processing has been the source of income generation in rural areas. It gradually reduced due to establishment of high capacity processing industry by organized sector.

QUESTIONS

1. Distinguish between food processing units and agro-based industry units.
2. Explain in your own words how technology transfer and energy usage brought some developments.
3. How can you improve the skills of farming practice and farmers to attain maximum yield?
4. Why rural households prefer the agriculture sector rather run after industry for earning their livelihood?

OOO

CHAPTER 10

GOVERNMENT SCHEMES/PROGRAMMES IN THE AGRICULTURE SECTOR

Government Schemes/Programmes in Agriculture Sector

National Mission for Sustainable Agriculture

Macro Management in Agriculture

National Food Security Mission (NFSM)

Rashtriya Krishi Vikas Mission (RKVM)

New Export Promotion Scheme (NEPS)

Integrated Scheme for Oilseeds and Pulses

Drought Management in Allied Sectors

National Horticulture Mission (NHM)

Micro Irrigation

National Bamboo Mission (NBM)

Livestock Insurance

Status of Milk Production in India

Credit and Insurance Schemes

Agriculture Insurance

National Agriculture Insurance Scheme (NAIS)

Weather Based Crop Insurance Scheme

Coconut-Palm Insurance Scheme (CPIS)

Food Processing Training Centre

GOVERNMENT SCHEMES/PROGRAMMES IN THE AGRICULTURE SECTOR

Agriculture is a State subject. Hence, the primary responsibility for increasing agricultural production, enhancing productivity, and exploring the vast untapped potential of the sector rests with the State Governments. Central Government supplements the efforts of the State Governments through a number of centrally sponsored and Central sector schemes. The major schemes/programmes are as follows:

RAJIV GANDHI UDYAMI MITRA YOJANA

(A Scheme of "Promotion and Handholding of Micro and Small Enterprises")

1. Background

1.1. World over, micro and small enterprises (MSEs) are recognized as an important constituent of the national economies, contributing significantly to employment expansion and poverty alleviation. Recognizing the importance of micro and small enterprises, which constitute an important segment of Indian economy in terms of their contribution to country's industrial production, exports, employment and creation of entrepreneurial base, the Central and State Governments have been implementing several schemes and programmes for promotion and development of these enterprises.

1.2. The small-scale industries in India, including the tiny or micro industries and service/business entities, collectively referred as micro and small enterprises (MSEs), have a long history of promoting inclusive, spatially widespread and employment-oriented economic growth. In terms of employment generation, this segment is next only to agriculture.

1.3. Entrepreneurship development and training is one of the key elements for development and promotion of micro and small enterprises, particularly, the first generation entrepreneurs. Entrepreneurship Development Programmes (EDPs) of various durations are being organized on regular basis by a number of organizations, e.g., national and state level Entrepreneurship Development Institutes (EDIs), Micro, Small and Medium Enterprises Development Institutes (MSMEDIs) [earlier known as Small Industries Service Institutes (SISIs)], national and state level Industrial Development Corporations.

Banks and other training institutions/agencies in private and public sector etc., are aiming to create new entrepreneurs by identifying their latent qualities of entrepreneurship and enlightening them on various aspects for setting up micro and small enterprises. Besides, various Industrial Training Institutes (ITIs), other private training institutions are also organizing vocational training (VT) programmes, skill development programmes (SDPs) and entrepreneurship-cum-skill development programmes (ESDPs).

1.4. However, there are still widespread variations in the success rate, in terms of actual setting up and successful running of enterprises, by the EDP/SDP/ESDP trained entrepreneurs. It has been observed that entrepreneurs particularly new entrepreneurs, generally face difficulties in availing full benefits under available schemes of the Governments/financial institutions, completing and complying with various formalities. Further, there are legal requirements under various laws/regulations, in selection of appropriate technology tie-up with buyers and sellers etc. In order to bridge the gap between the aspirations of the potential entrepreneurs and the ground realties, there is a need to support and nurture the potential first generation as well as existing entrepreneurs by giving them handholding support, particularly during the initial stages of setting up and managing their enterprises.

2. Objectives

2.1. The objectives of **Rajiv Gandhi Udyami Mitra Yojana (RGUMY)** are:

(i) To provide handholding support and assistance to the first generation entrepreneurs, who have successfully completed or undergoing entrepreneurship Development Training Programme (EDP)/Skill Development Training Programme (SDP)/Entrepreneurship-cum-Skill Development Training Programme (ESDP)/Vocation Training Programmes (VT), through few selected lead agencies, i.e., 'Udyami Mitras.' These Udyami Mitras are involved in the daunting task of establishment and management of the new enterprise, in dealing with various procedural and legal hurdles and in completion of various formalities required for setting up and running of the enterprise.

(ii) To provide information, support, guidance and assistance to the entrepreneurs through an 'Udyami Helpline' (a Call Centre for MSMEs), to guide them in various promotional schemes of the Government, encouraging procedural formalities required for setting up and running of the enterprise and help them in accessing bank credit etc.

3. Udyami Mitras

3.1. Eligibility

Under RGUMY, financial assistance would be provided to the selected lead agencies, i.e., **Udyami Mitras** for rendering assistance and handholding support to the potential first generation entrepreneurs. Following agencies/organizations can be appointed as the lead agency, i.e., Udyami Mitra:

(i) Existing national level Entrepreneurship Development Institutions (EDIs).

(ii) Micro, Small and Medium Enterprises Development Institutes (MSMEDIs)/ Branch MSMEDIs.

(iii) Central/State Government public sector enterprises (PSEs) involved in promotion and development of MSEs, e.g., National Small Industries Corporation (NSIC) and State Industrial Development Corporations etc.

(iv) Selected State level EDIs and Entrepreneurship Development Centers (EDCs) in public or private sectors.

(v) Khadi and Village Industries Commission (KVIC).

(vi) Special Purpose Vehicles (SPVs) set up for cluster development involved in entrepreneurship development.

(vii) Capable associations of MSEs/SSIs.

(viii) Other organizations/training institutions/NGOs etc. involved in entrepreneurship development/skill development.

3.2. Role and Responsibilities of Udyami Mitras

The selected lead agencies, i.e., Udyami Mitras would be expected to render assistance and handholding support for following services:

(i) Networking, coordinating and follow-up with various Government departments/agencies/organizations and regulatory agencies on the one hand and with support agencies like banks/financial institutions, District Industries Centers (DICs), technology providers, infrastructure providers on the other hand, to help the first generation entrepreneurs in setting up their enterprise. Udyami Mitras are expected to help the first generation entrepreneurs in:

(a) Identification of suitable project/product/enterprise and preparation of bankable project report for the same;

(b) Creation of the proprietorship firm/partnership firm/Company/Society/Self-help Group (SHG) etc.

(c) Filing of Memorandum (as prescribed under MSMED Act 2006);

(d) Accessing bank loans, admissible capital subsidy/assistance under various schemes of the Central/State Government and other agencies/organizations/financial institutions/banks etc. by networking with respective agencies;

(e) Assistance and support in establishment of workshed/office;

(f) Sanction of Power load/connection;

(g) Selection of appropriate technology and installation of plant and machinery/office equipment etc.;

(h) Obtaining various registrations/licenses/clearances/No Objection Certificates (NOCs) etc. from the concerned regulatory agencies/ Government departments/local bodies/ Municipal authorities etc.;

(i) Allotment of Income Tax Permanent Account Number (PAN) and Service Tax/ Sales Tax/VAT registration etc.;

(j) Sanction of working capital loan from the banks;

(k) Arranging tie-up with raw material suppliers;

(l) Preparation and implementation of marketing strategy for the product/service and market development;

(m) Establishing linkage with a mentor for providing guidance in future; and

(n) Creation of web page and email identity;

(ii) Once the enterprise has been successfully set up, the Udyami Mitras would also monitor and follow-up on the functioning of the enterprise for a further period of minimum 6 months and provide help in overcoming various managerial, financial and operational problems.

3.3. Empanelment of Udyami Mitras

3.3.1. The organizations of Ministry of MSME engaged in the task of entrepreneurship development, i.e., the three national-level EDIs (i.e., NIESBUD Noida, IIE Guwahati and NIMSME Hyderabad) MSMEDIs/ Branch MSMEDIs, KVIC, NSIC, Coir Board and such other organizations, as approved by Ministry of MSME, would be empanelled as Category-I Udyami Mitras under the scheme. Such Category-I Udyami Mitras would be referred as Apex Organizations.

3.3.2. For empanelment as Udyami Mitra, the Central/State Government public sector enterprises (PSEs) involved in promotion and development of MSEs as well as state level EDIs (hereinafter referred as Category-II Udyami Mitras), Universities/Institutes etc. are required to submit application in prescribed format (**Annexure-I**) to the Ministry of MSME through the Director/ Commissioner of Industries of the State/ UT concerned.

3.3.3. Other agencies fulfilling the eligibility conditions under Para 3.1 (hereinafter referred as Category-III Udyami Mitras) are required to submit application in the prescribed format (**Annexure-I**) to the General Manager of District Industries Centre (GM, DIC) concerned. The application would contain details regarding background, objectives, past experience in conducting EDP/SDP trainings and providing handholding services to new entrepreneurs, audited accounts for the last three years, profile of team responsible for providing handholding services, etc.

3.3.4. Application submitted by Category-III Udyami Mitras would be scrutinized by the GM, DIC. He would verify the credentials and capability of the applicant agency through inspections/other forms of enquiry and forward the application to the Director/ Commissioner of Industries of the State/UT, along with his recommendations.

3.3.5. The Director/Commissioner of Industries of the State/UT concerned would shortlist the applications received directly (from Category-II Udyami Mitras) as well as applications received through GM, DICs (in respect of Category-III Udyami Mitras) and forward the short-listed applications along with his recommendations to the Ministry of MSME.

3.3.6. Training facilities set up by Partner Institutions (PIs)/Franchisees of the Apex Organizations (to be regarded as Category- I Udyami Mitra) would submit their application to the Ministry of MSME through their concerned Apex Organization, which would also act as their Claim Processing Authority (CPA).

3.3.7. The applications received from Director/Commissioner of Industries of the State/UT concerned or Apex organizations, as the case may be, would be considered by a Screening Committee. The recommendations of the Screening Committee would be placed before the Secretary (MSME) and after the recommendations are accepted by the Secretary (MSME), the decision about empanelment of Udyami Mitras would be communicated through Director/Commissioner of Industries of the State/UT concerned or Apex organization, as the case may be.

3.4. Screening Committee

3.4.1. All proposals under the Scheme would be considered by a Screening Committee headed by the Joint Secretary (MSME). The other members of the Screening Committee would include:

(i) Economic Adviser Member

(ii) ADC (EA), O/o DC (MSME) Member

(iii) Industrial Adviser/JDC O/o DC (MSME) Member

(iv) Director/US, IF Wing - Member

(v) Director, Ministry of MSME Member-Secretary

3.4.2. The Screening Committee would scrutinize the applications and recommend the eligible applicants for empanelment as Udyami Mitras. The recommendations of the Screening Committee would be placed before the Secretary (MSME) and after the recommendations are accepted by the Secretary (MSME), the decision about empanelment of Udyami Mitras would be communicated through Director/Commissioner of Industries of the State/UT concerned or the concerned Apex Organisation.

3.4.3. The Screening Committee would also examine and process all proposals for training of key functionaries of Udyami Mitras as well as Call Centre Agents for the Udyami Helpline, in respect of their content, duration, training provider, location and costing etc. and submit its recommendations to Secretary (MSME) for approval.

3.4.4. The Screening Committee would regularly review the progress of the scheme and whenever necessary for the smooth functioning of the scheme, issue suitable executive instructions, with the approval of Secretary (MSME).

3.5. Training of the Key Functionaries

3.5.1. At least two key functionaries from the lead agency, i.e., Udyami Mitra, responsible for implementation of this scheme, will have to undergo training on the modalities of the implementation of this scheme at one of the Training Institutions approved by the Ministry for this purpose. The training expenses, including expenses on boarding and lodging of the trainees shall be borne by the Ministry of MSME. The key functionaries/Call Centre Agents would also be required to undergo Refresher Training from time to time, as necessary.

4. Udyami Mitra Cell

4.1 An Udyami Mitra Cell would be set up by the Ministry of MSME, with services support from NSIC. The administrative expenses/service charges for these services would be reimbursed to NSIC on actual basis.

4.2 This Udyami Mitra cell would act as Secretariat of the scheme and would process the proposals, claims etc., maintain records and accounts and also monitor the progress of the scheme.

5. Udyami Helpline

5.1 In order to provide information about the various promotional and developmental schemes of the Government/other agencies and helping the MSMEs in accessing bank credit and resolving their credit-related problems, an Udyami Helpline would be set up. Udyami Helpline would provide the potential as well as existing entrepreneurs the much needed information and guidance and about various aspects of entrepreneurship/information on MSME schemes/procedures/credit related issues.

5.2 The Udyami Helpline would function as a Call Centre for MSME entrepreneurs and have a Toll-free number (1800-xxx-xxxx) accessible from all landline and mobile phones etc. The Udyami Helpline would function, to begin with, from 6.00 am in the morning till 10.00 pm in the evening. During non-working hours, the callers would get an IVRS message.

5.3 Call Centre agents at Udyami Helpline would be trained about the various schemes of the Government and other developmental organizations and banks etc. They would answer basic queries from the public, related to schemes of the Government and banks etc., over the phone and wherever necessary escalate the call to the relevant authority by establishing a conference call or forwarding the call to the Call centre of the concerned bank/organization or by email.

5.4 Every call/query received by the Udyami Helpline would be captured by the Call centre agent by recording its basic contents, assigned a unique Reference No. and tracked till its closure. The caller can also subsequently call back and track his grievance by mentioning this Reference No. Alternately, the Call Centre may contact the calling party, if required, to close a query.

5.5. In case the caller/entrepreneur wants to contact someone directly or meet in person for obtaining guidance, assistance and handholding support, the Call centre agent would put the caller in contact with one of the empanelled Udyami Mitras, who may then provide the caller the required handholding support and assistance.

5.6. Development Commissioner (MSME) would act as the implementing, managing and monitoring agency for the Udyami Helpline.

6. Targets

6.1. Annual targets will be allocated to the lead agencies, i.e., Udyami Mitras, for taking up of post-EDP/SDP/ESDP/VT activities in the form of handholding of potential first generation entrepreneurs trained under various EDPs/SDPs/ESDPs/VTs.

6.2. Allocation of targets for handholding support to Category-I Udyami Mitras would be done by the Ministry of Micro, Small and Medium Enterprises (MSME) directly after assessing their capacity and past performance.

6.3. Targets to the other lead agencies, i.e., Categories II and III Udyami Mitras would be allotted by the Ministry of MSME through State Directorates of Industries, on the basis of capacity and past performance of the lead agencies/Udyami Mitras and the recommendation of the concerned State Government, keeping in mind the availability of Budget as well as the number of EDP/SDP/ESDP/VT trainees available in the State.

6.4. Reservation for SC/ST would be provided as per the policy of the Government.

7. Registration of Beneficiaries with Udyami Mitras

7.1. The Udyami Mitras would enroll the potential entrepreneurs for providing them handholding support. Only those beneficiaries would be enrolled who have already successfully completed or undergoing Entrepreneurship Development Training Programme (EDP/Skill Development Training Programme (SDP)/Entrepreneurship-cum-Skill Development Training Programme (ESDP)/Vocation Training Programmes (VT) of at least two weeks.

7.2. The applicants would be required to submit their application for enrolment under the scheme, along with their own contribution, as applicable (explained in Para 8.1), with the concerned Udyami Mitra.

7.3. On receipt of application along with beneficiary contribution, as applicable, from the beneficiaries, the Udyami Mitra would upload the required details in respect of each beneficiary like name, age, category, particulars of the EDP/SDP/ESDP undergone by the applicant, along with certificate number, duration and name of the institution; particulars regarding payment of beneficiary's contribution etc. on the server maintained by Ministry of MSME with National Informatics Centre (NIC).

The expenses on web hosting and creation of IT infrastructure required for the scheme (including development of software, training, hardware and maintenance etc.) shall be reimbursed to NIC from the plan funds allocated for the scheme.

7.4. Once the application is successfully uploaded, an acknowledgement certificate with unique Registration number would be generated for the applicant. Udyami Mitra would issue the acknowledgement, so generated, and the receipt of the money received to the concerned applicant.

7.5. The applicant entrepreneur will also enter into an agreement with the Udyami Mitra (**Annexure - II**) regarding assistance to be provided by the Udyami Mitra and the roles and responsibilities/ obligations of both the parties.

8. Financial Assistance to Udyami Mitras

8.1 Rates of Financial Assistance

8.1.1. For setting up of service enterprises, the Udyami Mitras would be provided retaining charges at the rate of ₹ 4000/- (Rupees four thousand only) per trainee that would include a Central grant of ₹ 3000/- (Rupees three thousand only) under RGUMY and contribution of ₹ 1,000/- (Rupees one thousand only) by the beneficiary (to be deposited in advance).

8.1.2. For setting up of micro manufacturing enterprises, having investment (in plant and machinery) up to ₹ 25,00,000/-, the handholding charges would be ₹ 6,000/- (Rupees six thousand only), including ₹ 1000/- (Rupees one thousand only) to be contributed by the beneficiary.

8.1.3. For the beneficiaries from special category, i.e., SC/ST/physically handicapped/ women/ beneficiaries from North-Eastern Region, the beneficiary's contribution of ₹ 1,000/- shall also be provided as a grant under RGUMY.

8.1.4. For small manufacturing enterprises having investment (in plant and machinery) of more than ₹ 25,00,000/-, in addition to Government grant (₹ 5000/- or ₹ 6,000/-, as applicable), and entrepreneur's contribution (₹ 1000/- or nil, as applicable), the entrepreneur will also have to make additional contribution towards handholding charges at the rate of 0.1 per cent of the project cost in excess of ₹ 25,00,000/-, subject to a ceiling of ₹ 10,000/-.

8.2. Release of Handholding Charges to Udyami Mitras

8.2.1. Ministry would place funds in advance with Apex organizations and Commissioner/ Director Industries for release to Udyami Mitra in their jurisdiction. They would, in turn, release handholding charges to the Udyami Mitras in three installments on successful achievement of various milestones (as applicable) by the enrolled beneficiary, as under:

8.2.2. The Udyami Mitras would submit claim for release of handholding charges in the prescribed Performa.

8.2.3. Category-I Udyami Mitras would submit the claim to the concerned Apex Organization for release of handholding charges. The Categories II and III Udyami Mitras would submit their claims to the Director/Commissioner of Industries of the State/UT concerned.

8.2.4. The claims for handholding charges received from the Category-I Udyami Mitras would be scrutinized and processed by the concerned Parent Apex Organization (out of the advanced grant money placed at their disposal by M/o MSME). The handholding charges for Category-I Udyami Mitras will be released to them after adjusting the amount of beneficiary contribution available with the concerned Udyami Mitras.

8.2.5. The claims for handholding charges received from the Categories II and III Udyami Mitras would be scrutinized by the Office of Director/Commissioner of Industries of the State/UT concerned. Handholding charges against the eligible claims would be released to the Udyami Mitras by the Director/Commissioner of Industries of the State/UT concerned (out of the advanced grant money placed at their disposal by M/ o MSME), after adjusting the amount of beneficiary contribution available with the concerned Udyami Mitras.

Stage		Activity/Milestone	Release of hand-holding charge (as % of total)
1	(a)	Selection of entrepreneur.	25
	(b)	Identification of skills/interests of the entrepreneur.	
	(c)	Assessment of financial and managerial capabilities of the entrepreneur.	
	(d)	Selection of suitable project keeping in view the availability of necessary skills/expertise, financial and managerial capabilities, market survey and viability of the project.	
	(e)	Preparation of project report including linkage with available schemes for financial assistance (e.g. PMEGP, assistance schemes of Central/State Government, Banks etc.)	
	(f)	Creation of the Proprietorship firm/Partnership firm/ Limited Liability Partnership (LLP)/Company/Society/ Self Help Group (SHG) etc.	
	(g)	Sanction of term loan and application(s) under the concerned financial assistance scheme(s).	
	(h)	Filing of memorandum (part-I) with DIC.	

2	(a)	Identification and selection of appropriate technologies, plant and machinery/office equipment etc.	60
	(b)	Release of term loan.	
	(c)	Hiring/allotment of land and construction/hiring of work sheds/office space etc.	
	(d)	Power connection.	
	(e)	Allotment of PAN.	
	(f)	Registration under Sales Tax/VAT/Service Tax etc.	
	(g)	Completion of ESI and EPF related requirements.	
	(h)	NOC from pollution control.	
	(i)	Other clearances/NOCs from local bodies/Municipal authorities.	
	(j)	FDA license/other licenses as required under law.	
	(k)	Tie up with raw material supplier(s).	
	(l)	Installation/commissioning of the plant and machinery.	
	(m)	Trial run of plant and machinery.	
	(n)	Successful commencement of production/operations.	
	(o)	Preparation of Marketing plan/strategy.	
	(p)	Market tie up with buyers.	
	(q)	Creation of web page/e-mail identity.	
	(r)	Linkage with mentor.	
	(s)	Filing of memorandum (Part-II) with DIC.	
3	(a)	Monitoring and follow up for a period of six months since successful commencement of production/ operations.	
	(b)	Submission of follow ups/feedback report on the performance of the assisted enterprise to State Directorate of Industries/Ministry of MSME.	

8.2.6. For projects costing more than ₹ 25,00,000/-, after completion of Stage-1, i.e., after sanction of term loan and filing of memorandum (Part-I) with the DIC, the Udyami (entrepreneur) shall pay to the Udyami Mitra additional handholding charges, as stated in Para 8.1.4 above.

9. Monitoring and Evaluation

9.1. The progress of the scheme will be reviewed and monitored on a regular basis by the Ministry of Micro, Small and Medium Enterprises as well as by the Commissioner/Director of Industries of the concerned States/UTs.

The Category-I Udyami Mitras and the concerned Commissioner/Director of Industries would submit periodic (monthly/quarterly/half yearly) returns to Ministry of MSME. Further, the consolidated information and progress report compiled on the basis of above returns, if any, will be placed before the Screening Committee/Ministry for review and analysis.

9.2. The scheme would also be evaluated by an independent agency to assess its success/impact and to ascertain constraints/shortcomings, if any, after XI Plan.

(**Source**: Ministry of Agriculture – Department of Agriculture and MSME.)

National Mission for Sustainable Agriculture

While agricultural productivity is adversely affected by climate change, agricultural activity itself contributes to global warming. The adoption of 'ecological agriculture', which integrates natural regenerative processes, minimizes non-renewable inputs, and fosters biological diversity, has tremendous scope for reducing emissions and enhancing soil carbon sequestration.

At the same time, many ecological agricultural practices also constitute effective strategies for adapting to climate change, which is a priority for developing countries. This calls for more investment and policy support to be devoted to this productive and sustainable form of farming. Recognizing the challenge of climate change to Indian agriculture, the National Mission for Sustainable Agriculture (NMSA), which is one of the eight Missions under the National Action Plan on Climate Change (NAPCC) has been conceptualized.

It seeks to address issues regarding 'sustainable agriculture' in the context of risks associated with climate change by devising appropriate adaptation and mitigation strategies for ensuring food security, enhancing livelihood opportunities, and contributing to economic stability at national level.

While promotion of dry-land agriculture would receive prime importance by way of developing suitable drought and pest resistant crop varieties and ensuring adequacy of institutional support, the Mission would also expand its coverage to rainfed areas for integrating farming systems with livestock and fisheries, so that agriculture continues to grow in a sustainable manner. The Mission identifies ten key dimensions for promoting sustainable agricultural practices, which will be realized by implementing a programme of action.

The Mission also emphasizes the need to harness traditional knowledge and agricultural heritage for conservation of genetic resources. The Programme of Action (PoA) would be operationalized by mainstreaming adaptation and mitigation strategies in ongoing R&D programmes and in flagship Schemes including the Rashtriya Krishi Vikas Yojana (RKVY), National Horticulture Mission (NHM), and National Food Security Mission (NFSM) through a process of selective up scaling and course correction measures. This would further be supplemented by introduction of new programmatic interventions and by seeking convergence with other National Missions and collaborations with key Ministries/Departments for institutionalizing linkages in order to address cross-sectoral issues.

Macro Management of Agriculture

The Macro Management of Agriculture (MMA) scheme was revised in 2008 to improve its efficacy in supplementing/complementing the efforts of the States towards enhancement of agricultural production and productivity and provide opportunity to draw upon their agricultural development programmes relating to crop production and natural resource management, with the flexibility to use 20 per cent of resources for innovative components.

The revised MMA Scheme has formula-based allocation criteria and provides assistance in the form of grants to the States/UTs on 90 : 10 basis except in case of the North-eastern States and Union Territories where the Central share is 100 per cent. MMA assistance during 2010-11 has been used to treat 3.02 lakh hectares of land under the National Watershed Development Project for Rainfed Areas (NWDPRA) and 1.94 lakh hectares under River Valley Projects (RVP) sub-schemes and for financing acquisition of 10,208 tractors and 5766 power-tillers among other farm machinery.

The National Food Security Mission (NFSM)

The NFSM was launched in Rabi 2007-08 with a view to enhance the production of rice, wheat, and pulses by 10 million tons, 8 million tons, and 2 million tons respectively by the end of the Eleventh Plan. The Mission aims to increase production through area expansion and productivity; create employment opportunities; and enhance the farm-level economy to restore confidence of farmers. The NFSM is presently being implemented in 476 identified districts of 17 States of the country.

Besides, a series of activities for more vigorous promotion of pulse crops has been adopted under the NFSM to intensify the pulse production programme from 2010-11. These are:

(i) Merging of the pulse component of the Integrated Scheme of Oilseeds, Pulses, Oil Palm and Maize (ISOPOM) with the NFSM so as to increase the scope and area coverage of the pulses programme. Jharkhand and Assam have also been included under the programme since there is immense potential for pulse promotion in rice fallows.

Through a new programme under the NFSM called the Accelerated Pulses Production Programme (A3P), 1000 block demonstrations of technology have been launched from 2010-11. This programme will essentially promote plant nutrients- and plant protection-centric technologies in compact blocks of 1000 ha each for five major pulse crops, namely, tur, moong, urad, gram, and lentil.

Focused and target-oriented technological intervention under the NFSM has made significant impact since its inception, reflected in the increase in production of rice and wheat in 2008-09 and 2009-10. 8.38 From 2010-11, as a new initiative, the A3P has been launched as a part of NFSM pulses. Under the A3P, one million ha of potential pulses area, covering tur, urad, moong, gram, and lentil, has been taken up for large-scale demonstration of technology in compact blocks.

A total of 600 A3P units of tur, urad, moong, gram, and lentil have been proposed for 2010-11. For organizing A3P units at the farmers' fields, an amount of ₹ 54.66 lakh per unit has been proposed. Further, an amount of ₹ 300 crore has been provided in the Union Budget 2010-11 for promoting dry-land farming in 60,000 pulses and oilseeds villages in rainfed areas.

These funds have been provided as additional Central assistance under the ongoing RKVY to the States of Andhra Pradesh, Gujarat, Karnataka, Madhya Pradesh, Maharashtra, Rajasthan, and Uttar Pradesh. Another programme, namely Bringing Green Revolution in the Eastern States is operational in seven States—Uttar Pradesh, Jharkhand, Bihar, West Bengal, Assam, Orissa, and Chhattisgarh. The Rice Development and Organizing Pulses and Oilseeds Villages is another programme, beside the pulses promotion strategies and other initiatives undertaken to boost agricultural productivity in these States.

The progress reports received from the States indicate significant achievements under the NFSM during the course of its implementation in the last four years, i.e., during 2007-08 to 2010-11 (till date). New farm practices have been encouraged through 3.24 lakh demonstrations of improved package of practices.

As many as 63,273 demonstrations of the system of rice intensification (SRI), and 32,344 demonstrations of hybrid rice have been conducted. Nearly, 96.84 lakh quintals of high yielding variety seeds of rice, wheat, and pulses and hybrid rice have been distributed.

About 72.27 lakh ha of area has been treated with soil ameliorants, such as gypsum/lime/micro nutrients to restore soil fertility for higher productivity. An area of about 29.25 lakh ha has been treated under Integrated Pest Management (IPM).

Further, nearly 21.27 lakh improved farm machineries, including water-saving devices have been distributed. As a capacity-building initiative, 33,205 farmers' field school (FFS) level trainings have so far been held. In addition, about 353 (3.53 lakh ha) block demonstrations have been conducted during the 2010 kharif under the A3P.

Rashtriya Kisan Vikas Yojana

The National Development Council (NDC), in its meeting held on 29th May, 2007 resolved that a special Additional Central Assistance Scheme (RKVY) be launched. The NDC resolved that agricultural development strategies must be reoriented to meet the needs of farmers and called upon the Central and State governments to evolve a strategy to rejuvenate agriculture. The NDC reaffirmed its commitment to achieve 4 per cent annual growth in the agricultural sector during the 11th plan. The Resolution with respect to the Additional Central Assistance scheme reads as below:

Introduce a new Additional Central Assistance scheme to incentivize States to draw up plans for their agriculture sector more comprehensively, taking agro-climatic conditions, natural resource issues and technology into account, and integrating livestock, poultry and fisheries more fully. This will involve a new scheme for Additional Central Assistance to State Plans, administered by the Union Ministry of Agriculture over and above its existing Centrally Sponsored schemes, to supplement the State-specific strategies including special schemes for beneficiaries of land reforms. The newly created National Rainfed Area Authority will on request assist States in planning for rainfed areas.

Economic reforms initiated since 1991 have put the Indian economy on a higher growth trajectory. Annual growth rate in the total Gross Domestic Product (GDP) has accelerated from below 6 per cent during the initial years of reforms to more than 8 per cent in recent years. The Planning Commission in its approach paper to the Eleventh Five Year Plan has stated that 9 per cent growth rate in GDP would be feasible during the Eleventh Plan period. However, Agriculture, that accounted for more than 30 per cent of total GDP at the beginning of reforms, failed to maintain its pre-reform growth. On the contrary, it witnessed a sharp deceleration in growth after the mid-1990s. This happened despite the fact that agricultural productivity in most of the states was quite low as it were, and the potential for the growth of agriculture was high.

The GDP of agriculture increased annually at more than 3 per cent during the 1980s. Since the Ninth Five Year Plan (1996 to 2001-02), India has been targeting a growth rate of more than 4 per cent in agriculture, but the actual achievement has been much below the target. More than 50 per cent of the workforce of the country still depends upon agriculture for its livelihood. Slow growth in agriculture and allied sectors can lead to acute stress in the economy because the population dependent upon this sector is still very large. A major cause behind the slow growth in agriculture is the consistent decrease in investments in the sector by the State governments. While public and private investments are increasing manifold in sectors such as infrastructure, similar investments are not forthcoming in agriculture and allied sectors, leading to distress in the community of farmers, especially that of the small and marginal segment. Hence, the need for incentivizing states that increase their investments in the agriculture and allied sectors has been felt.

Basic Features:

The RKVY aims at achieving 4 per cent annual growth in the agriculture sector during the XI Plan period, by ensuring a holistic development of agriculture and allied sectors. The main objectives of the scheme are:

1. To incentivize the states so as to increase public investment in agriculture and allied sectors.
2. To provide flexibility and autonomy to States in the process of planning and executing agriculture and allied sector schemes.
3. To ensure the preparation of agriculture plans for the districts and the states based on agro climatic conditions, availability of technology and natural resources.
4. To ensure that the local needs/crops/priorities are better reflected in the agricultural plans of the states.
5. To achieve the goal of reducing the yield gaps in important crops, through focused interventions.
6. To maximize returns to the farmers in agriculture and allied sectors.
7. To bring about quantifiable changes in the production and productivity of various components of agriculture and allied sectors by addressing them in a holistic manner.
8. These guidelines are applicable to all the States and Union Territories that fulfill the eligibility conditions.

The RKVY will be a State Plan Scheme. The eligibility for assistance under the scheme would depend upon the amount provided in State Plan Budgets for agriculture and allied sectors, over and above the base line percentage expenditure incurred by the State Governments on agriculture and allied sectors.

The list of allied sectors as indicated by the Planning Commission will be the basis for determining the sectoral expenditure, i.e., Crop Husbandry (including Horticulture), Animal Husbandry and Fisheries, Dairy Development, Agricultural Research and Education, Forestry and Wildlife, Plantation and Agricultural Marketing, Food Storage and Warehousing, Soil and Water Conservation, Agricultural Financial Institutions, other Agricultural Programmes and Cooperation.

Each state will ensure that the baseline share of agriculture in its total State Plan expenditure (excluding the assistance under the RKVY) is at least maintained, and upon its doing so, it will be able to access the RKVY funds. The baseline would be a moving average and the average of the previous three years will be taken into account for determining the eligibility under the RKVY, after excluding the funds already received.

The RKVY funds would be provided to the states as 100 per cent grant by the Central Government. The process of determining eligibility under the RKVY is illustrated in Annexure-I. The states are required to prepare the Agriculture Plans for the districts and the state that comprehensively cover resources and indicate definite action plans.

Since the RKVY is applicable to the entire State Plan for agriculture and allied sectors, and seeks to encourage convergence with schemes like NREGS, SGSY and BRGF, the Planning Commission and the Ministry of Agriculture will together examine the States' overall Plan proposals for Agriculture and allied sectors as part of the Annual Plan approval exercise.

At this stage, in consultation with the Ministry of Panchayati Raj, it will also be decided if the requirements with respect to the District Development Plans have been met or not. Advice may also be taken from DAHD&F, Ministry of Water Resources, MoRD, DARE, and NRAA, if the convergence has been appropriately factored in. Once a state becomes eligible for the RKVY, the quantum of assistance and the process of subsequent allocation to the state will be in accordance with the parameters and the respective weights.

It will be permissible for the states to initiate specific projects with definite time-lines, and clear objectives for agriculture and allied sectors excluding forestry and wildlife, and plantations (i.e., Coffee, Tea and Rubber). For this purpose, the RKVY would be available to the states in two distinct streams. At least 75 per cent of the allocated amount shall be proposed under Stream-I for specific projects. The amount under Stream-II, will be available for strengthening the existing state sector schemes and filling the resource gaps. A review of the ratios between Stream-I and II will be made after a year's experience in the implementation of the scheme.

A State Level Sanctioning Committee (SLSC) headed by the Chief Secretary of the state will have the authority to sanction specific projects under the Stream-I. The Government of India's representative shall participate in the SLSC meetings and the quorum shall not be complete without the presence of at least one official from the Government of India.

There may arise a situation when a particular state becomes ineligible to avail of the funds under the RKVY in a subsequent year due to its lowered expenditure on agriculture and allied sectors. If this were to happen, the states shall be required to commit their own resources for completing the sanctioned projects/schemes under the RKVY.

The pattern of funding is 100 per cent Central grant and the eventual goal is that the additional investments made through the RKVY scheme will lead to at least 4 per cent growth in agriculture. The states are given sufficient flexibility under the scheme to make appropriate local choices so that the outcomes are as envisaged in the RKVY objectives.

Each District will formulate a District Agriculture Plan (DAP) by including the resources available from other existing schemes, District, State, or Central schemes such as BRGF, SGSY, NREGS and Bharat Nirman, etc. The District Agriculture Plans shall not be the usual aggregation of the existing schemes but would aim at moving towards projecting the requirements for development of agriculture and allied sectors of the district. These plans will present the vision for agriculture and allied sectors within the overall development perspective of the district.

The District Agriculture Plans would present the financial requirement and the sources of financing the agriculture development plans in a comprehensive way. Since RKVY is conditional to proper District Planning and since Planning Commission has already circulated guidelines for District Planning in line with Constitutional requirements, these requirements should be adhered to by the state as far as possible.

The states will have to specify the institutional mechanisms evolved by them for District Planning as resolved in the NDC and submit a status report at the stage of the Annual Plan exercise. The SLSC will monitor and ensure this. The DAP will include animal husbandry and fishery, minor irrigation projects, rural development works, agricultural marketing schemes and schemes for water harvesting and conservation, etc. keeping in view the natural resources and technological possibilities in each district.

Each state will prepare a comprehensive State Agriculture Plan (SAP) by integrating the District Plans. The state will have to, at the outset, indicate resources that can flow from the state to the district. The DAP will integrate multiple programmes that are in operation in the district concerned, include the resources and activities indicated by the state, combine the resources available from the other programmes and finalize the plan.

Centrally sponsored schemes, viz., NREGS (National Rural Employment Guarantee Scheme), BRGF (Backward Region Grant Fund), SGSY (Swaranjayanti Gram Swarojgar Yojana) and Bharat Nirman etc., also come under District Agriculture Plan's monitoring.

The preparation of the State Agriculture Plan could be a two-way process. In one method, the state nodal department (Agriculture Department) could obtain the draft DAPs from the districts in the first instance and examine if aspects of importance to the state are properly covered in the district plans or not. For example, at the state level, the vision could be to set up fertilizer quality testing labs in certain districts.

The state should, at this stage of scrutiny, ensure that establishment of the fertilizer testing labs is incorporated in the District Agriculture Plans of the districts concerned. Ensuring that the state's priorities with respect to agriculture and allied sectors are appropriately captured in the District Agriculture Plans would be the responsibility of the nodal department/State agency vested with the responsibility of preparing the SAPs.

In the other method, the State Nodal Agency could communicate to the districts in the first instance, the state's priorities that ought to reflect in the respective district plans and the districts may incorporate these in their district plans. The preparation of the District Agriculture Plan is an elaborate, exhaustive and iterative process so every care should be taken by the state nodal department and the district agriculture department officials in ensuring that the DAPs are properly and comprehensively made.

District Agriculture Plan

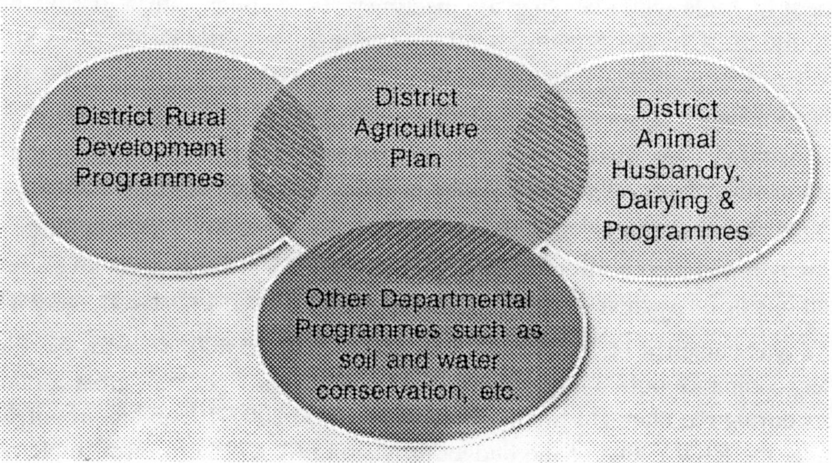

Source: Website of Department of Agriculture — Ministry of Agriculture

The district level potential linked credit plans (PLPs) already prepared by the NABARD may be useful in this regard. The state governments are advised to make best use of the PLPs and SREPs (Strategic Research and Extension Plans) developed under the ATMA programme.

The guidelines for preparing the District Development Plans have been communicated to the state governments by the Planning Commission. For the purpose of the RKVY, the District Development Plans so prepared, in accordance with the Planning Commissions Guidelines should be broadly sufficient. It should however be ensured that the convergence with other programmes as well as the role assigned to the PRIs are satisfactory.

For the year 2007-08, a clear indication should be given by the states that they are encouraging the preparation of the district agriculture plans that are integral to the District Development Plan. The interests of the States will be known by the number of districts already covered, and also the availability of a roadmap for covering the remaining districts. Eventually, from 2008-09 onwards, no assistance under the RKVY shall be made available unless all the districts are ready with the District Plans.

The finalized State Agriculture Plan will be placed before the Department of Agriculture (DAC) and the Planning Commission, as a part of the State Plan exercise, for Additional Central Assistance by the State Planning Department. The DAC and Planning Commission will approve the SAP with such suggestions as may be necessary. The states will provide complete rationale and justification for the assistance sought, well before the state plan discussions to give sufficient time to the DAC and the Planning Commission to firm up their views on the proposals and make such consultations as may be necessary with concerned departments.

The districts will be required to prepare a shelf of projects, for posing to the SLSC under Stream-I. At least 75 per cent of the total funds under the RKVY that a state gets entitled to, will be available under the Stream-I. The Nodal Department/Agency will undertake/compile such projects from each of the districts, prioritize them and place them before the SLSC. The SLSC is vested with the authority to sanction the projects under Stream-I in a meeting that will be attended by representatives of the Government of India. The Nodal Agency will give at least 15 clear days of notice to the representatives of the Government of India while sending the meeting notice, along with a gist of the agenda. The projects posed to the SLSC under Stream-I shall be consistent with the District and State Agriculture Plans. The balance of the total RKVY funds will be available for strengthening of the existing schemes and for filling resource gaps under the State Plans. This would be untied assistance to the states.

A State is permitted to use up to 1 per cent of its total RKVY funds for incurring the administrative expenditure that includes payments to consultants recurring expenses of various kinds, staff costs, etc. However, no permanent employment can be created, nor can vehicles be purchased.

The DAC may retain a proportion of 1 per cent of the RKVY funds at its level, so as to organize pan-India evaluations or for such administrative contingencies that may arise at various times.

The RKVY was launched in 2007-08 with an outlay of ₹ 25,000 crore for the Eleventh Plan to incentivize States to enhance public investment so as to achieve a 4 per cent growth rate in agriculture and allied sectors during the Plan. During the three year period 2007-10, an amount of ₹ 7895.12 crore was released under the RKVY. Out of the budget provision of ₹ 6722 crore for implementation of the RKVY in the States, an amount of ₹ 3986.76 crore has been released as on 25 November, 2010. Specific allocation has to be made for the following three new initiatives introduced under the RKVY in 2010-11:

(i) Extending the Green Revolution to the eastern region of the country, covering the States of Assam, Bihar, Chhattisgarh, Jharkhand, Orissa, eastern UP, and West Bengal, with the objective of increasing the crop productivity of the region by intensive cultivation through recommended agricultural technologies and package of practices.

(ii) Special initiatives for pulses and oilseeds in dry-land areas are mooted by organizing 60,000 villages for pulses and oilseeds in identified watershed areas where farmers are provided farm machinery equipments on hiring basis. These initiatives dovetailed with other schemes of the Government having components for promotion of oilseeds and pulses production. (iii) Implementation of the National Mission on Saffron – Economic Revival of Jammu & Kashmir Saffron Sector during 2010-11.

The RKVY has linked 50 per cent of Central assistance to the percentage of State Plan expenditure on agriculture and allied sectors. This has incentivized States to step up allocation to agriculture and allied sectors, which was 5.11per cent of total State Plan Expenditure in 2006-07, to 6.29 per cent in 2009-10. The RKVY has emerged as the principal instrument in financing development of agriculture and allied sectors in the country.

Its convergence with other schemes like the Mahatma Gandhi National Rural Employment Scheme (MGNREGA) is expected to boost development of the agrarian economy. The States will take up projects under the RKVY primarily from amongst those that appear in their District and State Agriculture Plans. There will be increased synergy between agricultural planning and implementation of schemes in the coming years, which will play a crucial role in promoting holistic development of agriculture and allied sectors.

New Export Promotion Scheme (NEPS)

This scheme was introduced to increase the export of fruits, veggies, and flowers, minor forest products, and value added products with other countries at the global level which will be made duty free export trade, and export of these products will be made duty free equivalent to 5 per cent of Free on Board (FOB) value of exports and can be transferable if required.

Disadvantages:

- NEPS can act as temporary relief to exporters of agriculture products lacks systematic production.
- This scheme requires high money transactions and high costs.
- Poor infrastructural facilities for post harvest process like storage, cold storage, handling at mandi.
- There are no timely and periodical market intelligence reports.
- Poor quality of products without quality control, high use of pesticides in agricultural produce.
- Poor quality of agriculture products cannot convince the global trading countries and cannot withstand the qualities desired by foreign buyers.
- Substandard packaging, gradation, brand images and poor efforts in market development.

The Integrated Scheme of Oilseeds, Pulses, Oil Palm and Maize (ISOPOM)

The ISOPM is being implemented in 14 major States for oilseeds and pulses, 15 for maize, and 10 for oil palm. The pulses component has been merged with the NFSM with effect from April 1, 2010. The ISOPOM scheme provides flexibility to the States in implementation based on a regionally differentiated approach for promoting crop diversification.

Under the Scheme, assistance is provided for purchase of breeder seed, production of foundation seed, production and distribution of certified seed, distribution of seed minikits, plant protection chemicals, plant protection equipment, weedicides, gypsum/pyrite/liming/dolomite, sprinkler sets, and water carrying pipes, supply of rhizobium culture/phosphate solubilizing bacteria and improved farm implements, publicity, etc.

The Oil Palm Development Programme under the ISOPOM is being implemented in the States of Andhra Pradesh, Karnataka, Tamil Nadu, Gujarat, Goa, Orissa, Kerala, Tripura, Assam, and Mizoram.

Its Maize Development Programme is under implementation in 15 States, viz., Andhra Pradesh, Bihar, Chhattisgarh, Himachal Pradesh, Jammu and Kashmir, Gujarat, Karnataka, Madhya Pradesh, Maharashtra, Orissa, Punjab, Rajasthan, Tamil Nadu, Uttar Pradesh, and West Bengal.

Drought Management

Due to deficit rainfall during south-west monsoon 2010 in Bihar, Jharkhand, Orissa, and West Bengal, the Central share of the State Disaster Response Fund (SDRF) for 2010-11 has been released to enable these States to expeditiously take the necessary drought-mitigation measures. In view of drought/deficit rainfall in certain regions, it was decided to implement a Diesel Subsidy during kharif 2010 (14 July 2010 to 30 September 2010) in drought/deficit rainfall areas to save the standing crops in the field.

ALLIED SECTORS

Agriculture is the mainstay of the Indian economy. Agriculture and allied sectors contribute nearly 17.8 and 17.1 per cent of Gross Domestic Product (GDP of India) during 2007-08 and 2008-09 respectively. The agricultural output, however, depends on monsoon as nearly 55.7 per cent of area sown is dependent on rainfall.

An all-time record in production of food grains of 233.88 million tons is estimated in 2008-09 as per 4th Advance Estimates. This is about 13.10 million tons more than last year's production of food-grains. The production of rice is estimated at 99.15 million tons which is about 2.46 million tons more, production of wheat is estimated at 80.58 million tons which is 2.01 million tons more, production of coarse cereals is estimated at 39.48 million tons which is 1.27 million tons more and production of pulses is estimated at 14.66 million tons which is about 0.99 lakh tons more than the production during 2007-08.

The sugarcane production is estimated at 2,712.54 lakh tons which is about 769.34 lakh tons less than the production during 2007-08. Cotton production is estimated at 231.56 lakh bales (of 170 kg. each) which is 27.28 lakh bales more than the production during 2007-08. Jute and mesta production during 2008-09 is estimated at 104.07 lakh bales (of 180 kg each) which is about 8.04 lakh bales less than the production during 2007-08.

The total area coverage under food grains in 2008-09 has been reported as 123.22 million hectares against 124.07 million hectares in 2007-08. The area under rice is estimated at 453.52 lakh hectares which is significantly higher about 1,437 lakh hectares. However, the area coverage under wheat during 2008-09 estimated at 278.77 lakh hectares is slightly lower by around 1.62 lakh hectares.

The total area coverage under coarse cereals during 2008-09 is estimated at 276.17 lakh hectares which is slightly lower by 8.64 lakh hectares as compared to 2007-08. The increase in Minimum Support Price (MSP) in 2008-09 over 2007-08 amongst cereals has ranged between 8.0 per cent wheat to 52.6 per cent (ragi). The percentage increase in case of paddy (common) is 31.8 per cent. In case of pulses, the increase has ranged between 8.1 per cent (gram) and 48.2 per cent (urad and moong).

Centrally Sponsored Scheme on National Food Security Mission has been launched in the country to enhance the production of rice, wheat and pulses by 10, 8 and 2 million tons respectively by the end of the 11th Plan. The Mission covers 312 districts in 17 States and has become operational from Rabi 2007-08. The focused and target oriented technological intervention under NFSM has made a significant impact since inception which is reflected by the fact as per the third advance estimate of 2008-09, the production of rice has raised to a level of 99.37 million tons thus depicting increase of 2.68 million tons when compared to 2007-08 and 6.02 million tons against 2006-07.

Similarly, the situation is also promising in case of wheat, wherein the production of wheat showing an increase of 2.76 million tons over the last year. Consequently, as per the third advance estimate of 2008-09, the production of wheat is estimated to the level of 77.63 million tons which is 1.82 million tons more that 2006-07. In case of pulses, the production was recorded at 14.20 million tons during 2006-07. Accordingly, as per the third advance estimate of 2008-09, the production of pulses is estimated at 14.18 million tons, which is almost a stagnated production trend when compared to 2006-07.

The Union Government has constituted a National Rainfed Area Authority (NRAA) on 03-11-2006 to give focused attention to the problem of the rainfed areas of the country. The Authority is an advisory, policy making and monitoring body charged with the role of examining guidelines in various existing schemes and in the formulation of new schemes including all externally aided projects in this area.

A scheme of debt waiver for small and marginal farmers and debt relief for other farmers has been announced by the Government in the Union Budget for 2008-09, against the target of ₹ 2, 25,000 crore for agriculture credit flow for 2007-08 the achievement was ₹ 2, 43,569 crore.

Agricultural Extension has been strengthened and Agricultural Technology Management Agencies (ATMAs) have been set up in 565 districts by the end of 2007-08.

Under NHM, an area of about 8.25 lakh hectares has been brought under horticulture crops, 1.17 lakh hectares of senile plantations have been rejuvenated and 1710 new nurseries have been set up since launching of NHM in 2005. An area of about 6 lakh hectares has been covered under the Scheme of Micro Irrigation since it was launched in 2006. Current year's target is coverage of 4 lakh hectares.

The National Horticulture Mission (NHM)

The Ministry of Agriculture has been implementing the centrally sponsored NHM for the holistic development of the horticulture sector since 2005-06, duly ensuring forward and backward linkages, and with the active participation of all the stakeholders.

All the States and the three Union Territories of Andaman and Nicobar Islands, Lakshadweep, and Puducherry are covered under the Mission except the eight North-eastern States including Sikkim and the States of Jammu and Kashmir, Himachal Pradesh, and Uttarakhand.

The latter are covered under the Horticulture Mission for the North East and Himalayan States (HMNEH).The scheme is being implemented in 372 districts in the country. During 2005-06 to 2009- 10, an additional 16.57 lakh ha of identified horticulture crops has been covered. Apart from establishment of 2192 nurseries for production of quality planting materials, 2.78 lakh ha has been covered under rejuvenation of old and senile orchards.

Organic cultivation of horticultural crops has been adopted in an area of 1.37 lakh ha. With the implementation of the NHM and other schemes, the production of horticulture crops has increased from 170.8 million tons in 2004- 05 to 214.7 million tons in 2008-09. The per capita availability of fruits and vegetables has increased from 391 gram/day in 2004-05 to 466 gram/day in 2008-09.

Micro Irrigation

The Centrally sponsored National Mission on Micro Irrigation (NMMI) was launched in June 2010 in addition to the earlier Micro Irrigation Scheme launched in January 2006. The Mission is being implemented during the Eleventh Plan period for enhancing water-use efficiency by adopting drip and sprinkler irrigation systems in all States and Union Territories for both horticulture and agricultural crops.

The scheme provides assistance at 60 per cent of the system cost for small and marginal farmers and at 50 per cent for general farmers. Since 2005-06, a sum of ₹ 2739 crore has been released by the Government of India under the scheme and 2.27 lakh ha brought under micro irrigation.

The system is beneficial for farmers in increasing crop productivity and water-use efficiency; reducing fertilizer consumption (fustigation through drip system) and electricity and labour consumption; and enhancing income.

National Bamboo Mission (NBM)

With a view to harnessing the potential of the bamboo crop in the country, the Ministry of Agriculture has been implementing the centrally sponsored NBM in 27 States in the country with a total outlay of ₹ 568.23 crore. The Mission aims to promote holistic growth of the bamboo sector by adopting an area-based, regionally differentiated strategy and to increase the area under bamboo cultivation and marketing.

Under the Mission, steps have been taken to increase the availability of quality planting material by supporting the setting up of new nurseries/tissue culture units and strengthening of existing ones. To address forward integration, the Mission is taking steps to strengthen the marketing of bamboo products, especially handicraft items. During the current year (2010-11), 7946 ha forest and 2079 ha non-forest area has been covered under bamboo plantation.

Accelerated Foder Development Programme (AFDP)

The livestock sector in India contributes to nearly 32 per cent of total agricultural output. India with 2.3 per cent share of global geographical area supports nearly 20 per cent of the livestock population of the World, notably among them are cattle (16 per cent), buffalo (55 per cent), goat (20 per cent) and sheep (5 per cent). The desired annual growth of agriculture sector at 4 per cent can also be accomplished by enhancing productivity from the livestock sector. This would require a steady supply of fodder for supporting the livestock population. Having only 4 per cent of total cropping area under fodder cultivation has resulted in a severe deficit of green fodder (36 per cent), dry fodder (40 per cent) and concentrates (57 per cent). The need of the hour is, therefore, to fulfill this shortfall in demand for fodder (which is over 55 per cent) from crop residues and agricultural by-products. Fodder deficit can mainly be attributed to our limitations in increasing the area under fodder crops, limited availability of good fodder varieties/hybrids, lack of quality seeds of improved varieties/hybrids, poor quality of dry fodder like paddy/wheat straw etc. Besides, low priority accorded to investment in fodder production, lack of post-harvest management for surplus fodder, poor management of grazing/pasture lands and inadequate research, extension and manpower support have only aggravated the situation.

Need for an Inclusive Fodder Development Programme

In the current scenario, where competing demands on land renders even expansion of food/cash crops a difficult proposition, the probability of increasing area under fodder crops is nearly impossible. It is therefore imminent to adopt a multi-pronged strategy for adequate availability of fodder in order to provide a buffer to the farmer even in times of climatic variability. This strategy *interalia* envisages supply of quality seeds, promoting production of fodder crops, extending fodder cultivation to currently fallow and unutilized lands, promotion of dual purpose varieties of crops which has the potential of meeting fodder requirements in season and off-season, promotion of non-traditional fodder, post-harvest technologies for preservation of fodder etc.

Besides, improving productivity in areas already under fodder cultivation, improving productivity of grazing and pasture lands, raising perennial fodder crops on field bunds and boundaries, peri-urban areas and exploiting unutilized and underutilized fodder crops are also some of the promising options to enhance fodder availability. Plant Breeders in India have also identified a number of varieties/hybrids which could give a better quality and higher yield of crop residue without any compromise in grain yield. This would provide an opportunity for augmenting the availability of fodder from crops like pearl millet, sorghum, maize and oats.

Objectives:

The programme envisages accelerating production of fodder through promotion of integrated technologies and processes for enhancing the availability of fodder throughout the year.

Strategies:

The programme proposes a multi-pronged strategy to achieve the stated objectives:

I. **Production of Quality Seeds**: Supporting/Strengthening State Agricultural Universities for production of breeder and foundation seeds of selected promising varieties/hybrids of fodder with participation of farmers.

II. **Production of Fodder:** Organizing fodder production programme based on cluster approach in the selected/targeted clusters preferably in dairy catchment areas of the potential States by promoting appropriate and region-specific fodder varieties.

III. **Adoption of appropriate technologies for Post Harvest Management**: Technologies like fodder block making units, chaff cutter for fodder processing and silage making would be promoted in the selected/targeted clusters.

Components and Pattern of Assistance:

Sl. No.	Name of the Component	Description	Pattern of Assistance
1.	Production of Quality Seeds and organizing Demonstration of Appropriate forage Equipment through State Agriculture Universities (SAUs)	Supporting institutions for organizing production of breeder and foundation seeds. The promotion of dual purpose varieties/ hybrids of sorghum and Pearl millet would be encouraged. Besides technical collaboration with specialized institution and IGFRI would also be supported for identification and multiplication of planting vegetative material like napier/guinea grass and cactus and seeds of fodder trees like prosopics. The institutions shall also organize field level demonstration of appropriate forage equipment. The beneficiaries would be SAUs.	100 % of total project cost limited to ₹ 50 lakh per SAU. (Maximum of one SAU in state will be permitted). Suggestive allocation as under: Production of breeder seeds ₹ 10 lakh, production of foundation seeds ₹ 30 lakh and demonstration of Technology and Practices ₹ 10 lakh. SAUs shall prepare detailed project proposals. The SAU shall also spell out targets and mechanism for sale/utilization of breeder seeds in the Project proposals. SAUs wherever feasible can have Public-Private Partnership (PPP) for production of fodder seeds.
2.	Fodder Production	Support to selected clusters preferably in dairy catch-ments areas in the beneficiary states. Each cluster comprise area of 500 ha under fodder/dual purpose crops. The interventions shall be in the form of distribution fodder production kit comprising of critical inputs like seeds of improved varieties/hybrids, nutrients, plant protection measures, fertilizers, fungicides etc. Supply of planting material for crops like napier/guinea/cactus would also be preferred in the kit. The beneficiaries would be individual farmers/ farmers' associations/	Fodder production kit ₹ 3200 per ha and kits will be distributed free of costs. States will choose the com-position of kits depending on the local needs. Maximum ceiling is restricted to 5 ha per beneficiary.

		Federations/Cooperatives and NGOs.	
3.	Adoption of Appropriate Technology for post-harvest Management	Distribution of low cost technology tools/products, e.g., manual chaff cutter – fodder block making units. Establishing silage making units comprising of silo pit and power-driven chaff cutter. The beneficiaries would be individual farmers/ Farmers' Associations/ Federations/Cooperatives/ dairy groups of ATMA and NGOs.	100% of procurement cost Subject to maximum ceiling of ₹ 4 lakh per cluster of 500 ha of area under fodder/dual purpose crops cultivation. The component will be operationalized in same cluster as identified under Sl. No. 2 (States also consult SAUs/KVKs/ATMA for identifying appropriate equipment for the region. and for finalizing source of supplies and quality of product.

The programme will be implemented on a location specific approach in selected states. For components 2 and 3, selection will be based on **Cluster approach comprising** an area of 500 ha under Fodder /Dual purpose crops.

Inclusiveness for Catering to the Weaker Sections of the Society

In order to cater to the weaker sections of the society, priority would be given to small and marginal farmers and/or SHG, Cooperatives formed by 'small and marginal farmers', Cooperatives of weaker sections of the society and women. Similarly, special emphasis would be accorded for adopting gender-friendly equipment to technologies practices.

Planning and Approval

The AFDP will be implemented as a sub-scheme of Rashtriya Krishi Vikas Yojana (RKVY). The programme will be operationalized through a three-tier planning-implementation-reviewing structure.

The planning process will follow a decentralized approach. Panchayati Raj Institutions or similar Local Government Institutions/line departments will select the beneficiaries and identify appropriate interventions in the villages/clusters in consultation with SAUs, ATMA, Watershed Committee (WC) and other similar agencies. The respective work plans for the year will be compiled by the District Agricultural Officer/Dy. Director (Agriculture) for inclusion in the District Agriculture Plan (DAP).

The DAPs will be appraised at the State Level for inclusion in the consolidated State Agriculture Plan (SAP). Respective SAUs will submit their project proposals directly to the State Department of Agriculture for inclusion in the SAP. The SAP will be finalized and consolidated in consultation with Department of Animal Husbandry. The consolidated SAP will be considered and approved by State Level Sanctioning Committee (SLSC) of RKVY as per standard procedures.

Implementation

At the National Level, Department of Agriculture and Cooperation, Ministry of Agriculture will oversee the activities of the programme and accord approval to the State's proposal. The Department of Agriculture will be the nodal agency at the State Level to implement the programme in collaboration with the State Department of Animal Husbandry, Dairy, Forest, Waste Land Development, State Milk Federations and Panchayati Raj Institutions etc. Indian Grassland and Fodder Research Institute, Jhansi with its Regional Stations/Centres would also be involved in implementation and in collaborating with SAU's on aspect of technological support. The services of SAUs may also be utilized by the States. The State Governments will further nominate, select or create suitable agencies for implementing the programme at the district level. Such agencies could be line departments, Zilla Panchayats, Agriculture Technology Management Agency (ATMA), Watershed Committee (WC), Self Help Groups, NGO's etc.

The proposed programme is expected to enhance the availability of green and dry fodder. The interventions in post-harvest technology would not only add to the availability of fodder during lean period, but also protect the environment from pollution due to burning of these crop residues. Besides, this programme would also help in contingency planning to mitigate the shortage of fodder caused by the natural calamities like droughts and floods.

LIVESTOCK INSURANCE

A Centrally sponsored scheme of livestock insurance is being implemented in all the states with twin objectives: providing protection mechanism to the farmers and cattle rearers against any eventual loss of their animals due to death; and demonstrating the benefits of insuring livestock to the people.

The scheme, which was introduced in 100 selected districts on pilot basis during 2005-06, has now been extended to 300 selected districts covering all states. The scheme benefits farmers and cattle rearers having much cattle and buffaloes. In 2010-11, 20.12 crore has been released up to December 2010 and 20.63 lakh animals were insured from 2006-07 to 2009-10.

STATUS OF MILK PRODUCTION IN INDIA

Annual milk production in India has grown more than six times since independence. The average annual growth rate in the production of milk in recent years has been close to 4 per cent. Even though the level of per capita availability at 263 gram/day for India in 2009-10 is much lower than that in developed countries, it is well above the developing country average. The Eleventh Five Year Plan envisages an overall growth of 6-7 per cent per annum for the sector.

As per an assessment made by the Planning Commission, the domestic demand for milk by 2021-22 is expected to be 172.20 million tons. As projected under the proposed National Dairy Plan, the production of milk in the country is required to increase to 180 million tons by 2021-22 to meet the demand. However, the country has not been able to keep pace with the domestic demand for milk. The domestic demand for milk is growing at about six million tons per year whereas annual incremental production over the last ten years has been about 3.5 million tons per year.

With higher growth of the economy, increase in population, and increased health consciousness among the populace, it is only natural that the demand for milk and milk products will increase leading the proportion of income spent on milk and milk products to increase. Further, urban centres will demand more and more processed and packaged dairy products but in the rural areas people may still prefer to purchase from the local milkmen.

About 80 per cent of milk produced in the country is still handled in the unorganized sector and only the remaining 20 per cent is equally shared by cooperatives and private dairies. Despite the appreciable growth in the milk production in the last six decades, the productivity of our animals is still low. Our marketing systems are also not modernized or developed to a satisfactory level. Other issues in this sector are ineffective breeding programmes, limited availability and affordability of quality feed and fodder, improper veterinary infrastructure, lack of vaccinations, inadequate access to formal credit mechanisms, inadequate research capacity, limited processing capacity, and lack of transport.

Considering that the requirement of milk in 2021-22 is expected to be 180 million tons and the current level of milk production is 112 million tons, the milk production must increase at around 5.5 per cent per annum in the next 12 years. If it fails to do so, India may need to resort to imports from the world market.

A large consumer like India entering the international market would have the potential to cause international prices to spurt. Hence, it is prudent that we depend on the domestic market and develop the milk sector with the right attention and focus and the required investment. Recent hikes in prices of milk and milk products have been a matter of concern. The gap between domestic demand for milk and production of milk has put upward pressure on milk prices in the country. A strong supply response with focus on production and productivity can only keep the prices stable.

CREDIT AND INSURANCE SCHEMES

Agricultural Credit

From Kharif 2006-07 to 2008-09, farmers were receiving crop loans up to a principal amount of ₹ 3 lakh at 7 per cent interest. In the year 2009-10, Government provided an additional 1 per cent interest subvention to those farmers who repaid their short-term crop loans as per schedule.

The Government has raised this subvention for timely repayment of crop loans from 1 per cent to 2 per cent from the year 2010-11. Thus, the effective rate of interest for such farmers will be 5 per cent per annum.

Revamping of Cooperative Credit Structure

In January 2006, the Government announced a package for revival of the Short-term Rural Cooperative Credit Structure involving financial assistance of ₹ 13,596 crore. The National Bank for Agriculture and Rural Development (NABARD) has been designated the implementing agency for the purpose. States are required to sign memorandum of understandings (MoUs) with the Government of India and NABARD, committing to implementation of the legal, institutional and other reforms as envisaged in the revival package.

So far twenty-five States have executed such MoUs. This covers 96 per cent of the primary agricultural cooperative societies (PACS) and 96 per cent of the Central cooperative banks (CCBs) in the country. As on November 2010, an amount of ₹ 8009.75 crore has been released by NABARD as Government of India share for recapitalization of 49,983 PACS.

Rehabilitation Package for Distressed Farmers

The Government is implementing a rehabilitation package for 31 suicide-prone districts in the States of Andhra Pradesh, Karnataka, Kerala, and Maharashtra involving a financial outlay of ₹ 16,978.69 crore. Special packages are being implemented in Kerala for the development of Kuttanad wetland ecosystem and mitigation of agrarian distress in Idukki district with an outlay of ₹ 1840.75 crore and ₹ 764.45 crore respectively.

Kisan Credit Card (KCC) Scheme

The KCC scheme was introduced in August 1998. About 970.64 lakh KCCs have been issued up to September 2010. The scheme includes reasonable components of consumption credit and investment credit within the overall credit limit sanctioned to the borrowers to provide adequate and timely credit support to the farmers for their cultivation needs.

Task Force on Private Moneylenders

A Task Force has been constituted under the chairmanship of Chairman, NABARD, to look into the issue of a large number of farmers who had taken loans from private moneylenders in the country. The Task Force on Private Moneylender hars submitted its report in June 2010. This has been circulated to stakeholders for furnishing their comments/views.

AGRICULTURAL INSURANCE

Four crop insurance schemes, namely the National Agricultural Insurance Scheme (NAIS), Pilot Modified NAIS (MNAIS), Pilot Weather Based Crop Insurance Scheme (WBCIS), and Pilot Coconut Palm Insurance Scheme (CPIS) are under implementation in the country.

(i) The National Agricultural Insurance Scheme (NAIS)

The NAIS is being implemented in the country from rabi 1999-2000 season. The Agriculture Insurance Company of India Ltd. (AIC) is the implementing agency (IA) for the scheme. The main objective of the scheme is to protect farmers against crop losses suffered on account of natural calamities.

The scheme is available to all the farmers—loanee and non-loanee—irrespective of their size of holding. It is operating on the basis of an area approach. It envisages coverage of all the food crops, oilseeds, and annual commercial/horticultural crops in respect of which past yield data are available for adequate number of years.

Premium rates for food and oilseeds crops are ranging between 1.5 per cent and 3.5 per cent. In case of annual commercial/horticultural crops, actuarial premiums are being charged. A 10 per cent subsidy is available for small and marginal farmers. All financial liabilities under the scheme are shared by the Central and State Governments on 50 : 50 basis. The scheme is at present being implemented by 25 States and two UTs.

(ii) The Pilot Modified NAIS (MNAIS)

Keeping in view the limitations/shortcomings of the existing scheme, the Government has approved the Modified NAIS for implementation on pilot basis in 50 districts from Rabi 2010-11 seasons.

The major improvements made in the MNAIS are: actuarial premium with subsidy in premium at different rates, i.e., 40 per cent to 75 per cent depending upon the slab, provided to farmers, all claims liability on the insurer, unit area of insurance reduced to village panchayat level for major crops, indemnity for prevented/sowing/planting risk. And for post-harvest losses due to cyclone, payment up to 25 per cent advance of likely claims as immediate relief, more proficient basis for calculation of threshold yield minimum indemnity level of 70 per cent instead of 60 per cent.

And private sector insurers with adequate infrastructure allowed (at present, ICICILombard, IFFCO-Tokyo and Cholamandalam-MS). Only upfront premium subsidy is shared by the Central and State Governments on 50 : 50 basis and claims are the liability of the insurance companies. Seven states have already notified the areas for implementation of the scheme during Rabi 2010-11. It is expected that the scheme will be notified by 14-15 states.

(iii) Weather Based Crop Insurance Scheme (WBCIS)

Efforts have been made to bring more farmers under the fold of crop insurance by introducing a Weather Based Crop Insurance Scheme (WBCIS) as announced in the Union Budget 2007 in selected areas on pilot basis. The WBCIS is intended to provide insurance protection to farmers against adverse weather incidences, which are deemed to unfavourably impact crop production. It has the advantage of settling claims within the shortest possible time.

The WBCIS is based on actuarial rates of premium but to make the scheme attractive, premium actually charged from farmers have been restricted on a par with the NAIS. In addition to the Agriculture Insurance Company of India Ltd. (AIC), private insurers have also been included for implementing the scheme in selected areas. During kharif 2007 to kharif 2010, about 81 lakh farmers have been covered under the pilot scheme.

(iv) Coconut Palm Insurance Scheme (CPIS)

The CPIS is being implemented on pilot basis since 2009-10 in selected areas of Andhra Pradesh, Goa, Karnataka, Kerala, Maharashtra, Orissa, Tamil Nadu, and West Bengal. The scheme is administered by the Coconut Development Board (CDB) through the AIC. As on 30 July 2010, 14.33 lakh palms of about 27,023 farmers have been covered under the scheme.

FOOD PROCESSING TRAINING CENTRE (FPTC)

The government at the centre had launched recently the financial assistance scheme for rural entrepreneurs to set up the Food Processing Training Centre (FPTC). The benefits of this scheme are to develop the rural entrepreneurship and transfer of technology for processing of food products.

Further by utilizing locally grown raw material and providing "hands-on" experience at such production-cum-training centres to give atmost priorities to SC/ST/OBC and women entrepreneurs.

Pattern of financial assistance is being released through single product line centre for any one group to undertake processing activity and ₹ 4 lakh as fixed capital cost and ₹ 2 lakh as revolving capital. The Multiproduct line centre for more than one group of processing activity is ₹ 11 lakh for fixed capital and ₹ 4 lakh as revolving seed capital.

Financial assistance is provided by Centre or State government organizations, to educational and training institutions, schools and colleges, ITI, NGO, and Cooperatives will be eligible for grant to set up FPTC.

The applicants can visit for detailed information at http://mafpl.nic.in and e-mail ID for inquiry – while suggestions can be sent to Joint Secretary (Administration) Ministry of Food Processing Industries, Panchsheel Bhawan, August Kranti Marg, New Delhi-110049 and Fax No. would be 26492176.

Further applicants can apply in the proper format for any aforesaid schemes with complete details of the project indicating cost of land, building, equipments, and recurring expenditure, copy of quotation for equipments and duly forwarded by the respective state nodal agency (SNA).

The SNA in turn may process and forward their recommendations to the Ministry along with duly filled in check list in the case of Central/State government organizations and departments universities autonomous bodies the proposal can be submitted directly to the Ministry with a copy to SNA.

The project may be taken up either individually or on joint/group basis by agriculture graduates. The outer ceiling for the cost of the project by individual would be ₹ 10 lakh and for the project by the group would be ₹ 50 lakh. The group may normally be of 5, of which one could be a management graduate with qualification or experience in business development and management.

SUMMARY

Agriculture is a State subject. Hence, the primary responsibility for increasing agricultural production, enhancing productivity, and exploring the vast untapped potential of the sector rests with the State Governments. Central Government supplements the efforts of the State Governments through a number of centrally sponsored and Central sector schemes. The major schemes/programmes are as follows:

While agricultural productivity is adversely affected by climate change, agricultural activity itself contributes to global warming. The adoption of 'ecological agriculture', which integrates natural regenerative processes, minimizes non-renewable inputs, and fosters biological diversity, has tremendous scope for reducing emissions and enhancing soil carbon sequestration.

At the same time, many ecological agricultural practices also constitute effective strategies for adapting to climate change, which is a priority for developing countries. This calls for more investment and policy support to be devoted to this productive and sustainable form of farming. Recognizing the challenge of climate change to Indian agriculture, the National Mission for Sustainable Agriculture (NMSA), which is one of the eight Missions under the National Action Plan on Climate Change (NAPCC) has been conceptualized.

It seeks to address issues regarding 'sustainable agriculture' in the context of risks associated with climate change by devising appropriate adaptation and mitigation strategies for ensuring food security, enhancing livelihood opportunities, and contributing to economic stability at national level.

QUESTIONS

1. List out various schemes introduced by government to bring total change in the agriculture scenario.
2. What are the essential features depicted in National Food Security Mission (NFSM)?
3. How government's kicked off program Rashtriya Krishi Vikas Yojana achieved success in the prevailing agriculture scenario?
4. How New Export Promotion Scheme has instilled confidence among Indian agricultural exporters to carry out their export trade so briskly?
5. Write down essential features of Integrated Scheme introduced in oilseed and pulses processing.
6. Write down characteristics of National Horticulture Mission.
7. How far rural households have heaved sigh of relief in the presence of Livestock insurance scheme?

ooo

11

Marketing – Agriculture Marketing

Marketing – Agriculture Marketing

General Features

Main Characteristics of Marketing

Benefits of Efficient Marketing

Importance of Agriculture Marketing in Economic Development

Options for Farmers

Direct Marketing

Contract Farming

Agriculture Marketing Intelligence

Marketable Surplus and Post-harvest Losses

MARKETING – AGRICULTURAL MARKETING

Agricultural marketing is the study of all the activities, agencies and policies involved in the procurement of farm inputs by the farmers and the movement of agricultural products from the farmers to the consumers. It includes organization of agricultural raw materials supply to processing industries, the assessment of demand for farm inputs and raw materials.

From the producer point of view, it is important to know whether the prices prevailing in the market enable him to continue to produce or not, and what he should produce and where and at what time he should sell it. Large-scale production requires skill to sell it at remunerative price. A consumer looks at marketing from the point of view of goods and the prices at which they are offered. Middlemen try to increase his profit margin by discharging various marketing functions.

Organized marketing of agricultural commodities is being promoted in the country through a network of regulated markets. Most of the States and Union Territories have enacted legislations (the Agriculture Produce Marketing Committee [APMC] Act) to provide for regulation of agricultural produce markets. Seventeen States/UTs have amended their APMC Acts and the remaining are in the process of doing so.

The agricultural marketing in any economy will give fillip for overall growth and development of the economy. Agricultural Marketing includes sowing of crops and their yield coupled with other activities like sowing commercial crops like cardamom, pepper, cotton, sericulture, horticulture, plantation of coffee – tea, fruits orchard, dairy products livestock, and fishing. Due to literacy through books, media (both print-electronic-online) radio, weather bulletins, and Kissan Call Centres scenario in village had undergone sea of changes. The rural peasants are focusing to grow more cash crops, fuits and vegetables, bio fuel plants, with application of indigenous and innovative farming technologies with drip irrigation and other methods of scientific farming.

The term "Agricultural marketing" was defined by National Commission on Agriculture (NCA) as 'a process starts with decision to produce saleable farm commodity encompass all aspects of marketing structure or system both functional and institutional based on technical and economic considerations and include pre-harvest and post-harvest operations of assembling, grading, storage, transportation and distribution'.

Agriculture marketing of any economy will indicate the level of growth or advancement of the economy. Agriculture marketing pushes the economic resources for the fullest utilization, development, it will increase the overall productivity, widen product ranges, will give insight to planners and policy-makers, changes in the lifestyle of people, consumer's satisfaction, and widen the talents and skills of Farm managers' fraternity.

Agriculture Marketing will play important role in keeping the economy in right track on the path towards development. It will give rise to cooperative movement through institutional structures, coordination with procurement agencies, leads to proper estimation of demand for agricultural produces thereby regulating time schedules, stimulates generation of proper market intelligence and market studies, regulates price policy and give insight to country's central bank Reserve Bank of India to control price policy to the whole country, gives more knowledge for farmers, peasants and market agents for grading of commodities, storage facilities and side by side educates peasants and farming community.

Agriculture Marketing had led the country to become more vibrant – radiant to steer the country towards development in the present-day scenario. Agricultural Marketing led to green revolution where it gives rise to total mechanization of marketing process, improved seed qualities, overall growth in the agriculture sector, instilled cooperative movement, improved the dairy products and poultry, scientific methods in irrigation, use of non conventional energy sources, and created awareness among farming community in educating them through books, street shows, radio hourly bulletins, and setting up of Kissan Call Center. Further agriculture marketing led to improvement of infrastructure, increased the life expectancy, changes in consumer tastes and livelihood standards.

Thus, creation of systematic agriculture marketing mechanism led the Indian economy towards overall development but marketing of agriculture produce ought to face some challenges. They are dilapidated condition of transport and distribution, low level of literacy among peasants community led to poor communication, poor state of road connectivity between village to village, lack of proper and adequate storage facilities in village, towns, and district headquarters.

Poor functioning of Financial Institutions, commercial banks, and national financial institutions due to lack of political interests, and procedural wrangling. Further absence of adequate financial facilities, variation of quality of agriculture produce from one place to another due to segmentation, perishability of commodities, presence of middlemen or brokers and agents, low irrigability and low productivity due to quality of soil, absence of updated market intelligence,

Apart from this, there are few special rural produce having high significance in its marketing at national as well as at international markets. They are tender leaves used as cover pipe for beedies at the cottage sector business but having potential market in its trade. Similarly natural gum, medicinal plants, beetle leaves (pan) that will cater to the pan lovers Indians mostly who are habituated to consume pans after the meals. Likewise sandalwood is also famous for its wider usage like bathing and toilet soaps, agarbathis.

The sandalwood is also used for manufacturing sandalwood oil, carvings of deities and Hindu Gods and Goddesses and manufacturing of garlands.

There are 7157 regulated markets in the country as on 31st March 2010. The country has 21,221 rural periodical markets, about 15 per cent of which function under the ambit of regulation. The advent of regulated markets has helped mitigate the market handicaps of producers/sellers at wholesale assembling level. Internet connectivity is being provided to important agricultural markets in the country to establish a nationwide information network for speedy collection of prices and market-related information.

GENERAL FEATURES

Agricultural marketing system can be analyzed by looking at the farmers' marketing practices, marketing channels and the structure of markets. The marketing system and farmers' marketing practices have undergone considerable changes during the last 50 years owing to the expansion of the size of the market, increased availability of infrastructure and changes in the pattern of demand and consequently introduction of new methods of processing, packaging, storage and transportation. Farmers' marketing practices and evolution of marketing system are guided by the shelf-life of the commodity. All agricultural products do not have the same shelf-life. Some products are perishable, some are less and some are even durable. Cotton and jute versus fruits, vegetables and milk are contrasting examples of agricultural products having long and short shelf-life. In between these two extremes are other agricultural commodities. Owing to the increase in marketed surplus and need to make these available in the off-season and at places other than production points, functions of storage, processing, transportation, packaging and grading are required to be performed either by the farmers or by market functionaries.

MAIN CHARACTERISTICS OF MARKETING

Optimization of input use and output produced: Agricultural marketing leads to the optimization of resource use and output management. An efficient marketing system can contribute to an increase in the marketable surplus by scaling down the losses arising out of the Agricultural Marketing inefficient processing, storage and transportation. A well-designed system of marketing can effectively distribute the available stock of modern inputs and thereby sustain a faster rate of growth in the agricultural sector.

Increase in farm income: An efficient marketing system guarantees to the farmers better prices for farm products and induce them to invest their surpluses in the purchase of modern inputs so that productivity may increase. This again results in increase in the marketed surplus and income of the farmers.

Widening of markets: A well-known marketing system widens market for products by taking them to remote corners of the country to areas far away from the production point, e.g., paddy produced in Punjab and Haryana are sold in remote tribal areas. Another example is potato. The widening of the market helps in increasing the demand on a continuous basis and thereby guarantees a higher income to the producer.

Growth of agro-based industries: The agricultural marketing system helps in the growth of agro-based industries and stimulates the overall development process of the economy. Many industries depend on agriculture for the supply of raw materials, e.g., sugar industry, cotton industry, and silk industry.

Price movements: An efficient marketing helps the farmers in planning their production in accordance with the need of the economy. This work is carried out through the price signals.

Adoption and spread of new technology: The marketing system helps the farmers in the adoption of new scientific and technical knowledge.

Employment: The marketing system provides employment to millions of persons engaged in various activities such as packaging, transportation, storage and processing.

Addition to National income: Marketing activities add to the Nation's Gross National Product.

Better living: Any plan of economic development that aims at diminishing the poverty of agricultural population, reducing consumer food prices, earning more foreign exchange or eliminating economic waste has to pay special attention to the development of an efficient marketing for food and agricultural products.

Creation of Utility: Marketing creates the following four types of utilities of the product:

(i) **Form Utility:** The processing function adds form utility by changing the raw material into finished products, e.g., paddy-rice; wheat-bread, biscuit, cake; milk/ghee, cream, cheese, skimmed milk, butter.

(ii) **Place Utility:** The transportation function adds place utility to products by shifting them to a place of need from the place of plenty, e.g., potatoes in plain, milk at urban places.

(iii) Time Utility: The storage function adds time utility to the products by making them available at the time when they are needed, e.g., tamarind, rice in off-season.

(iv) Possession Utility: The marketing functions buying and selling helps in the transfer of ownership of goods from one person to another in the marketing system. The points of view of producer, middlemen, and consumers are different, but each is individualistic and concerned with his profit. From the producer point of view, it is important to know whether the prices prevailing in the market enable him to continue to produce or not, and what he should produce and where and at what time he should sell it. Large-scale production requires skill to sell it at remunerative price. A consumer looks at marketing from the point of view of good and the prices at which they are offered. Middlemen try to increase his profit margin by discharging various marketing functions. Marketing has greater importance and significance for the society as a whole than for any of the individual beneficiaries of the marketing process.

BENEFITS OF EFFICIENT MARKETING

1. **Any increase in the efficiency** of the marketing process, which results in lower costs of distribution and lower prices to consumers, really brings about an increase in the National Income.
2. **A reduction in the cost** of marketing is a direct benefit to the society.
3. **Marketing process brings new varieties**, quality and beneficial goods to consumers. It provides connecting link between production and consumption. **Approximately one-third of all persons gainfully employed** in the country are engaged in the field of marketing and about one-fourth of National Income is earned by marketing profession.
4. **Scientific marketing has a stabilizing** effect on the price level. If producers produce what consumers want and consumers have a wide choice of products, there are no frequent ups and downs in price.
5. **Marketing is a catalyst** for the transmutation of latent resources into actual resources of desires into accomplishments and development of responsible economic leaders and informed economic citizens.
6. **Marketing brings to the farmers useful** implements, tools and fertilizers etc. and the benefits of the use of machines and free after sales service, and make them modern farmers. Scientific marketing also remedies the imbalance in the supply of making available the surpluses to the deficit areas. If the functions of marketing are not performed properly, the economic system may get out of balance resulting in piling up of goods with retailers, wholesalers and manufacturers, which leads to closure of factories and retrenchment of workers. Thus, it plays an important role in economic stability of a country.

IMPORTANCE OF AGRICULTURAL MARKETING IN ECONOMIC DEVELOPMENT

The students of agribusiness marketing should make a note that there are two sides of agricultural marketing. One side is the 'big picture' of agricultural marketing or macro marketing. This is the view of planners, economists, industry analysts, and senior government functionaries. The marketing, economic and social theories are used to analyze the situation. Analysis is also made as to how good the system is working to contribute to the public interest and serving all sections of society or stakeholders in the process. Macro marketing also views at how the agricultural systems are organized and how good it contributes to its social and economic goals and how agricultural system is adapting and changing over time.

The second side is micro marketing or commonly known as business marketing. The micro marketing consists of demand stimulation, competition, new product development, market research pricing and distribution strategies, customer service and other marketing inputs.

Micro marketing view is taken by an individual decision-maker in the agriculture industry. This could be a villager who produces, a business manager, a consumer who is making decisions about how, when, where and what to buy or sell. The marketing channels develop marketing strategies to satisfy customers at a profit by using the tools and principles of marketing management.

Both micro and macro marketing worlds are closely connected in the agricultural area. In developing countries, the national economies are also closely connected. To be a successful rural marketer, one must know how the changing macro marketing is affecting their decisions and creating new market opportunities. The marketer should know the changing public perceptions of performance of agricultural marketing.

The marketer must constantly plan new and better ways to attract and satisfy customers, outsmart their competitors and also make profit. In the complex market economy, each farmer, his seller, or consumer by their decisions contribute to the larger market picture and in turn to the national economy. Each one of them influence the other and become contributors to the macro picture of agricultural produce marketing.

The agricultural marketing helps in accelerating the pace of economic development of the economy by stimulating demand and production. Due to the green revolution, Indian economy is able to feed its large population and minimize starvation related deaths. The development of high yielding seeds, use of chemical fertilizers use of plant protection methods and use of modern agricultural implements are reasonable in increasing food production and generate large marketable surplus. A good marketing system only can guarantee the tempo of development and good prices to farmers for their produce. With large agricultural resources India can leverage its plus points to make India the next economic power house.

The Indian farmer has shifted his focus from traditional agricultural methods to modern farming. The development of agricultural economy has led to increase in demands for related products. Since 1970-71, the Indian population has doubled and foodgrain production has matched the demands. Since the last five years that is year 1997-2002, the food grain production has stabilized at 192 and 212 million metric tons. The year 2002 has seen 49 per cent less rainfall and less production to the level of 183.2 million metric tons.

Agricultural marketing helps in the development and specialization of crops which yield large profits. A good marketing system helps in giving price signals and development of non-agricultural sectors in the economy. Agricultural production and marketing must develop hand in hand and they are partners in progress.

The active government's interventions in the development of the agriculture in planned economy and its policies in 4th to 9th Five Year Plans have turned agriculture to market orientations. The plan outlays for agriculture in the Tenth Five Year Plans are high and lays emphasis on the agri-sector growth.

Some of the sectors where agricultural marketing plays its important role in the Indian economy are detailed hereunder:

1. **Contributor to National GDP Growth:** In developing economies in general and India in particular, agriculture is the mainstay. It is an employment provider to about 70 per cent of its population. To sustain growth of the non-agricultural sector, resources have to be obtained from the agricultural sector. Physical resources guarantee supply of food for the masses and raw materials for agro-based industries. It also provides financial resources for investment in economy and also for reinvestment in agricultural sectors and act as resource multiplier.
2. **Increase in Agriculture Produce and Incomes:** A good agricultural marketing system stimulates demand and helps in increasing production. The system also guarantees better prices of the produce and thus farmers increase their incomes. This acts as a multiplier effect in the economy for growth. The incentives increase production in qualities, varieties and quality.
3. **Reduce Middlemen:** The efficient marketing system reduces the middlemen by streamlining practices – remove malpractices – delays and restrict commission and service charges.
4. **Optimizer of Resources:** The efficient agricultural marketing leads to the optimal use of available resources that are inputs in the agriculture in addition to land and manpower. The losses are reduced by arranging timely processing, handling, transportation and storage. The increased output per rupee invested helps in the faster rate of growth in the agricultural sector.
5. **Stabilizer of Prices:** The knowledge of sharing and surplus availability of the agricultural produce gives a stabilizing effect on the price front to the commodities. The activities of middlemen get restricted and thus prices get stabilized.
6. **Demand Developer:** Marketing helps in the development of the demand for agricultural produce and thus widen the markets in the country and outside. Marketing helps in taking the produce to the consumer and expands marketing.
7. **Infrastructure Developer:** The geographical area of marketing activities has increased manifold due to greater facilities in transport and communications. The expansion has further generated interest and investment in infrastructure in India. The government is investing in infrastructure projects and helping the growth of the economy.
8. **Earn Valuable Foreign Exchange:** In the year 2001-02, the agricultural products valued at US dollars 5.8 billion were exported from the country over 20 per cent of which was contributed by marine products alone. Rice and wheat exports are around 10 million tons. Sugar was around one million tons and export of horticultural produce has also shown strong growth rate.

9. **Marketing Emergencies:** An efficient agricultural marketing is able to create sufficient surpluses to meet national emergencies in developing economies. Emergent relief measures help to mitigate problems.

10. **Developer of New Technologies:** The development of high yielding variety of seeds, increased use of NPK fertilizers, new pesticides and modern cultivation practices have increased farm output per acre.

Thus, the production increase has given more income for the same acreages. This has increased the economic development of the area. The result is confidence built up in agricultural marketing. The Royal Commission on Agriculture was set up in 1928 and an act for grading and standardization was made in 1935. The commercialization picked up in mid sixties. The development of markets grew up due to markets and result of its own dynamic nature.

The first commission on development of agriculture in India after independence called the National Commission on Agriculture and noted that 'there is an increasing awareness that is not enough to produce a crop of animal product, it must be marketed well. Increased production resulting in greater per cent increase in marketable surplus accompanied by increase in demand from urban population calls for rapid improvement in existing marketing system' with emphasis on the importance of agricultural marketing.

OPTIONS FOR FARMERS

There are several areas in which farmers will be required to remain proactive to derive benefits from emerging scenario of technological changes and marketing system. There will be need for adoption of varieties suitable for different times of sowing, different durations of maturity and those amenable to processing.

Farmers would need to learn the methods of preparing the produce for market, viz., cleaning, grading and packaging at the farm level which will not only fetch better prices for their products but also reduce physical losses during post-harvest handling. They will also need to keep track of the prices of different grades/varieties in nearby and other markets and sell the produce where the net prices realized by them are the highest.

The farmers also will have to keep track of the facilities like pledge-loan available to them and judiciously use such facilities. In the coming years, farmers would need to reduce their price risks by entering into advance agreements with processors or bulk buyers. In this context, the farmers would need to increasingly organize themselves into groups or cooperatives for the purposes of marketing of their products, value addition and processing.

DIRECT MARKETING

Direct marketing encourages farmers to undertake grading of farm produce at the farm-gate and obviates the necessity to haul produce to regulated markets for sale. Direct marketing enables farmers and processors and other bulk buyers to economize on transportation costs and to considerably improve price realization.

In South Korea, for instance, as a consequence of expansion of direct marketing of agricultural products, consumer prices declined by 20 to 30 per cent and producer-received prices rose by 10 to 20 per cent. This also provided incentive to large-scale marketing companies to increase their purchases directly from producing areas.

Direct marketing by farmers to the consumers has been experimented in the country through Apni Mandis in Punjab and Haryana. The concept, with certain improvements has been popularized in Andhra Pradesh through Rythu Bazars and in Tamil Nadu as Uzhavar Santhaigal.

At present, these markets are being run at the expense of the State exchequer, as a promotional measure, to encourage marketing by small and marginal producers of fruit and vegetables without the help of the middlemen. Considering the vastness of the country, more and more such markets need to come up in the organized sector so that they can be developed in tune with the backward and forward linkages.

The Agriculture Produce Marketing Committee (APMC) Acts will also have to be amended to permit private and cooperative sectors to take up direct marketing of agricultural commodities from the producing areas and the farmers' fields, without the necessity of going through licensed traders and regulated markets. Such a reform will spur private initiative in building consumer-oriented market infrastructure in the country.

CONTRACT FARMING

Contract farming arrangements of different types have existed in various parts of the country for centuries for both subsistence and commercial crops. The commercial crops like sugarcane, cotton, tea, coffee etc. have always involved some forms of contract farming. Even in the case of some fruit crops and fisheries, contract farming arrangements, involving mainly the forward trading of commodities have been observed. However, in the wake of economic liberalization, the concept of contract farming in which national or multinational companies enter into contracts for marketing of the horticultural produce and also provide technologies and capital to contract farmers has gained importance.

According to this, bipartite agreements are made between the farmer and the company and the latter contributes directly to the management of the farm through input supply as well as technical guidance and also markets the produce. The main features of this type of contract farming are that selected crops are grown by farmers under a buy back agreement with an agency engaged in trading or processing. In such cases, the centralized processing and marketing agencies supply technology and resources, including planting materials and occasional crop supervision.

Under such contracts, the farmer assumes the production related risks, which the price risk is transferred to the company. In some cases, the company also bears the production risk, depending on the stage of crop growth at which the contract is made. If the contract is made at flowering or fruiting stage, the company bears the production risks also.

In any case, the company bears the entire costs of transaction and marketing. It is this variant of contract farming which is said to be one of the ways by which small farmers can participate in the production of high value crops like fruits, vegetables, flowers etc. and benefit from market-led growth.

AGRICULTURAL MARKET INTELLIGENCE

Current Status

On the recommendation of the Agricultural Prices Enquiry Committee (1954), the Directorate of Economics and Statistics, Ministry of Agriculture (DESMOA) set up 14 Market Intelligence Units (MIUs) in the capitals of Andhra Pradesh, Assam, Bihar, Delhi, Gujarat, Karnataka, Kerala, Madhya Pradesh, Maharashtra, Orissa, Rajasthan, Tamil Nadu, Uttar Pradesh, and West Bengal.

The market intelligence units are intended to help the DESMOA in the formulation, implementation and review of the agricultural price policy relating to procurement, marketing, storage, transportation, import, export and credit, etc.

The units furnish regular reports on market arrivals, off-takes, stocks, crop prospects, and outlook of market prices. They are also required to give their appraisal of production of various kharif and rabi crops at regular intervals to help preparation of crop forecasts. Though the data to be supplied by the market intelligence units are of great utility, the units have ceased to be effective in discharging their functions mainly due to a lack of proper direction and control of their activities. Over the years, the staff strength of the units has been considerably reduced resulting in even worse performance.

Marketing Research and Information Network

Objectives

- To establish a nationwide information network by providing electronic connectivity to important Agricultural Marketing Boards and Directorates;
- To collect and disseminate price and market related data for its efficient and timely utilization by producers, traders and consumers to derive maximum advantage of their sales and purchases;
- To increase efficiency of marketing by effective improvement in the existing market information system; and
- To sensitize and sensitize and orient farmers to respond to new challenges in agricultural marketing by using Information Technology (IT) as a vehicle of extension.

Salient Features

The scheme aims at evolving an Information Communication Technology (ICT) based information network to link important agricultural produce markets spread all over the country and the State Agricultural Marketing Boards and the Directorates. With the support of National Informatics Centre, a user-friendly software package 'AGMARK' has been developed to facilitate organization and transmission of market data. The **AGMARKNET** portal **(http //agmarknet nic.in)** serves as a single window for accessing websites of various organizations concerned with agricultural marketing. It provides weekly/monthly trend analysis for important markets in respect of major commodities, spot prices, futures prices/Good Agricultural Marketing Practices, Minimum Support Prices (MSPs) and international commodity prices, commodity profiles and good agricultural market practices etc. Further, it provides information about schemes of Directorate of Marketing and Inspection, weather information, e-directory of markets, Codex Standards, etc. The portal is constantly being enriched.

Structure of Scheme

Under the scheme, computer hardware and software is provided to State Agricultural Marketing Boards/Directorates as also assistance under market-led extension activities for market level publications, accepted standards of grading, packaging and labelling, quality certification, sanitary and phyto-sanitary aspects, good farming practices, national level atlas, commodity profiles, CDs, training and educational modules, studies through outsourcing to professionals/experts and conducting farmers' awareness programmes.

Funding Pattern: 100 per cent Grant by Government of India

Eligibility: State Agricultural Marketing Boards/Institutes, Directorate of Agriculture/Agricultural Marketing of the State Governments.

Person to be Contacted: Agricultural Marketing Adviser/Joint Secretary (Marketing), Department of Agriculture and Cooperation, Krishi Bhavan, New Delhi-110114.

MARKETABLEM SURPLUS AND POST-HARVEST LOSSES

Current Status

The Directorate of Marketing and Inspection (DMI), Ministry of Agriculture has been conducting surveys on marketable surplus and post-harvest losses of foodgrains. The surveys provide information on marketable surplus ratios as well as on a variety of other important items like farm retention for family consumption, for seed, feed and wastage, etc. In this direction, it is worth to mention that one of the surveys is expected to be carried out where data would be collected and relevant information on certain reliable and viable parameters using the methodology approved by a Technical Committee constituted for the purpose under the Chairmanship of the Agricultural Marketing Adviser to the Government of India.

This survey covers the following crops: Paddy, Wheat, Jowar, Bajra, Maize, Ragi, Barley, Red Gram, Gram, Green Gram, Black Gram and Lentil. **The sampling methodology used is that of stratified multistage random sampling and consists in selecting 20 per cent of the districts in a State, 15 villages in each selected district and 10 cultivator households from each selected village with a maximum of 100 districts, 1,500 villages and 15,000 households.**

The fieldwork of the surveys is conducted by designated State Agencies through field investigators employed by them under the overall supervision of the Directorate of Marketing and Inspection. The data so collected are analyzed with the support of IASRI and published. The information collected through these surveys is used in the National Accounts Statistics, and Ministry of Commerce and Industry in fixing the weights for certain agricultural commodities while compiling the all-India Index Number of Wholesale Prices in addition to its uses in planning and procurement operations and market development programmes.

Marketable Surplus

The marketable surplus is that quantity of the produce, which can be made available to the non-farm population of the country. The marketable surplus is the residual left with the farmers after meeting his family consumption, farm requirements, social and religions payments. This may be expressed as:

$$MS = P - C$$

where, MS = Marketable Surplus;

P = Total Production; and

C = Total requirement of farm family.

The marketable surplus differs from region to region and within the same region, from crop to crop. It also varies from farm to farm. On a particular farm, the quantity of marketable surplus depends on the following factors:

1. Size of holding
2. Production of commodity
3. Price of the commodity
4. Size of family and
5. Requirements of seeds and feed

Marketed Surplus

Marketed surplus is that quantity of the produce, which the farmer actually sells in the market, irrespective of his requirements for family consumption, farm requirements, social and religious payments. The marketed surplus may be more, less or equal to the marketable surplus.

Marketed surplus is more than the marketable surplus when the farmer retains a smaller quantity of crop than his actual family and farm requirements. This is true especially of small and marginal farmers whose need for cash is immediate.

The situation of selling more than marketable surplus is termed as distress or forced sale. Such farmers generally buy the produce from the market in a later period to meet their requirements. The marketed surplus is less than the marketable surplus when the farmer retains some of the surplus produce. This situation holds well under:

(a) Large farmers generally sell less than the marketable surplus because of their better retention capacity. They retain extra produce in the hope that they would get a higher price in the later period. Sometimes farmers retain the produce even up to the next production season.

(b) Farmer may substitute one crop for another crop either for family consumption purpose or other farm requirements because of the variation in prices. With the fall in the price of the crop relative to a competing crop, farmer may consume more of the first and less of the second crop.

The marketed surplus may be equal to the marketable surplus when the farmer neither retains more nor less than his requirement. This holds true for perishable commodities and agricultural raw materials like cotton, jute etc. Given the average size of farms and consequently lower farm output, the farmers marketing practices are determined by the surplus available with the individual farmer.

The market structure and conduct on the other hand determine the incentives for the farmers to sell their surpluses. Also, the market structure and conduct depend on the quantity of surpluses available to be handled by the system. In this context, the estimates of marketed surplus assume critical importance both for the farmers as well as for the marketing system.

Volume of marketed surplus also affects the supplies of food for the non-farm population and fibre and raw material for the agro-industry and for exports. Naturally, the estimation of marketed surplus has attracted the attention of researches as well as the policymakers.

The marketed surplus and marketable surplus in the context of small farm agriculture are not the same. While the marketable surplus is the difference between farm output and family and farm needs, the marketed surplus is the actual quantity marketed by the farmers. The marketed surplus may be even higher than the marketable surplus. This is what is called distress sale, which is particularly true in food-grains and other food items on marginal and some small farms.

SUMMARY

Agricultural marketing is the study of all the activities, agencies and policies involved in the procurement of farm inputs by the farmers and the movement of agricultural products from the farmers to the consumers. It includes organization of agricultural raw materials supply to processing industries, the assessment of demand for farm inputs and raw materials.

From the producer point of view, it is important to know whether the prices prevailing in the market enable him to continue to produce or not, and what he should produce and where and at what time he should sell it. Large-scale production requires skill to sell it at remunerative price. A consumer looks at marketing from the point of view of goods and the prices at which they are offered. Middlemen try to increase his profit margin by discharging various marketing functions.

Agricultural marketing system can be analyzed by looking at the farmers' marketing practices, marketing channels and the structure of markets. The marketing system and farmers' marketing practices have undergone considerable changes during the last 50 years owing to the expansion of the size of the market, increased availability of infrastructure and changes in the pattern of demand and consequently, introduction of new methods of processing, packaging, storage and transportation.

Farmers' marketing practices and evolution of marketing system are guided by the shelf-life of the commodity. All agricultural products do not have the same shelf-life. Some products are perishable, some are less and some are even durable. Cotton and jute versus fruits, vegetables and milk are contrasting examples of agricultural products having long and short shelf-life.

QUESTIONS

1. Distinguish between 'marketing' and 'agriculture marketing'.
2. Elucidate general features and characteristics of Agriculture marketing.
3. Write down the importance of agriculture marketing in economic development.
4. What do you mean by direct marketing in agriculture marketing?
5. What are the uses of agricultural marketing intelligence network?
6. Distinguish between marketable agriculture surplus and post-harvest losses.

ooo

CHAPTER 12

Role of Government in Promoting Agricultural Marketing

- Role of Government in Promoting Agriculture Marketing
- Marketing Channels and Functionaries
- Main Features
- Common Marketing Channels Identified
- Market Functionaries Supervision
- State Agriculture Marketing Boards
- Council of State Agriculture Marketing Board
- Type of Cooperative Marketing Societies
- Sources of Finance
- Market Functions
- Approach to Marketing
- Function – Institutional – Commodities Behavioral
- Functions of Physical Supply/Distribution
- Road Transport – Rail Transport-Water Transport – Air Transport
- Market Classification
- Market Margins
- Making Market Information Relevant to Farmers
- Agmarknet (Internet Based Marketing Schemes)
- Database Management
- National Institute of Agriculture Marketing (NIAM)
- Information Technology in Agriculture Marketing
- Directorate of Marketing and Inspection (DMI)

ROLE OF GOVERNMENT IN PROMOTING AGRICULTURAL MARKETING

In the interest of public welfare, the government intervenes in the marketing system. The extent of intervention depends on the objectives of the government and the extent of defects and malpractices prevailing in the system. Government intervention may be direct or indirect, and it may take anyone or a combination of the' following forms:

1. Framing of rules and regulations for the protection of the interest of some sections of the population. This may include restriction on activities of traders, licensing and market regulation.
2. Promotional activities such as storage and warehousing, transportation and communication facilities, credit facility, grading and standardization, and encouragement of cooperative marketing.
3. Administration of prices at different levels of marketing, guaranteeing minimum support prices to producers, providing commodities at fair prices to consumers, and fixing the rates of commission charged by commission agents.
4. Influencing supply and demand by import, export, internal procurement and distribution.

MARKETING CHANNELS AND FUNCTIONARIES

Agricultural commodities move in the marketing chain through different channels. The channels are distinguished from each other on the basis of market functionaries involved in carrying out the agricultural produce by the farmers to the ultimate consumers. The length of the marketing channels depends on the size of market, perishability of the commodity and the nature of demand at the consumer level.

The marketing channels for agricultural commodities in general can be divided into following four broad groups:

1. Direct to consumers
2. Through wholesalers and retailers
3. Through public agencies or cooperatives, and
4. Through processors

MAIN FEATURES

The quantities moving in these sets of channels vary from commodity to commodity and state to state. But some general features of the importance of these channels can be summarized as follows:

(i) The proportion of marketed surplus going directly from the farmers to consumers continues to be small (around one or two per cent) and has decreased over the years due to the increase in marketed surplus, shifting of processing from consumer to the processors and increase in the demand for packed and branded products. As the price received by the farmer in this channel is higher (both in absolute term and as a proportion of consumer's price) than others, the government is encouraging direct marketing by the farmers through such schemes as **apni mandi, modern bazaar and uzhavar sandies**.

(ii) The private trade, despite government intervention, has continued to dominate the trade in agricultural commodities. The quantity of agricultural producers handled by the government agencies has been about 10 per cent of the total value of marketed surplus. Further, around 10 per cent of the marketed surplus was handled by the producers or consumers cooperatives. Thus, nearly, 80 per cent of the marketed surplus of agricultural products in India is handled by private sector.

(iii) The main functionaries in the marketing channel for agricultural commodities include village traders, primary and secondary wholesalers, commission agents, processors and retailers including vendors. Public agencies, farmers cooperatives and consumers' organizations also perform many of these marketing functions.

(iv) Marketing channels for various cereals in India are more or less similar.

COMMON MARKETING CHANNELS IDENTIFIED

(a) Farmer — consumer

(b) Farmer — village trader-consumer

(c) Farmer — wholesaler-retailer-consumer

(d) Farmer — village trader — wholesaler-retailer-consumer

(e) Farmer — wholesaler — wheat miller (flour-mill) — retailer of flour consumer

(f) Farmer — government agency (FCI) — wholesaler or flour miller tailer consumer

(g) Farmer — government agency (FCI) — fair price shop (FPS) — consumer

Majority of the States has Enacted the Agricultural Produce Market Acts

The States or Union Territories yet to enact their own legislation are Kerala, Manipur, Meghalaya, Nagaland, Sikkim, Andaman & Nicobar Islands, Dadra & Nagar Haveli, Daman and Diu and Lakhswadeep. Infrastructure in the regulated markets has been created as per the need in terms of volume of market arrivals. The regulated market with larger arrivals of produce have been designated as principal market yards and those with lower arrivals and turn over as sub-market yards. Each market yard is attached to one or the other principal market to minimize the establishment costs. On the whole, these are in the ratio of 1 : 2, i.e., on an average, each principal yard has two sub-yards.

The establishment of regulated markets helped in creating orderly and transparent marketing conditions in primary assembling markets. Further, increase in the number of regulated market yards, from a meagre 286 at the time of Independence to 7,161 in 2001 helped in increasing the access of farmers to such orderly marketplaces. This development, coupled with construction of approach roads and roads network linking primary markets with secondary wholesale and terminal markets, also improved the process of price discovery at the primary market level where most of the small farmers dispose off their produce.

Increase in physical access of farmers to marketplaces, apart from reducing transaction costs of farmers, helped small farmers more who have low marketed surplus and could not transport their surpluses to long distances. Though precise data on the proportion of benefits of regulated markets going to the small and marginal farmers are not available, there is evidence to show that expansion of such physical infrastructure in rural areas has helped small and marginal farmers more by increasing their excess to the markets.

The number of regulated markets is relatively more in geographically larger States like Andhra Pradesh, Bihar, Maharashtra, Madhya Pradesh, Uttar Pradesh and West Bengal. These six states together account for 61 per cent of total regulated markets in the country. The Punjab and Haryana States though geographically small, have a large number of regulated markets owing to sizable quantity of surpluses of rice and wheat. These two states account for 13.4 per cent of the total regulated markets in the country.

The number of commodities brought under the ambit of regulation varies from state to state. However, these include almost all the important agricultural commodities produced in that area/state. The commodities notified for this purpose generally include food grains (cereals and pulses), oilseeds and oils, fibre crops, fruits, vegetables, livestock products, seed spices, forest products, dry fruits, narcotic crops, sugar, gur, fodder and grasses. The state governments, by notification, add or delete the commodities from the list of regulations from time to time.

MARKET FUNCTIONARIES SUPERVISION

The officials of the market committee supervise the day-to-day functioning of regulated markets, i.e., the Secretary, auction-clerks and other staff. The administrative decisions are taken by the nominated/elected market committee. The market committee consists of representatives of all sections, i.e., farmers, traders, cooperative marketing societies, co-operative or commercial banks, autonomous bodies (Panchayat Samithi and Municipal Board of the area) and government officials. The number of farmer members is more than that of other interest groups. The sources of funds to market committee for meeting administrative expenditure, to create additional facilities in the market area are market fee, license fee/renewal fee and subsidy from the government.

Settlement of Disputes: Disputes arising between producer-seller and traders by reason of the quality of the produce, sub-committee of the market committee solves account and deductions of unauthorized charges. This avoids legal complications and unnecessary expenditure.

STATE AGRICULTURAL MARKETING BOARDS

These were established to supervise and provide guidance to market committees. The main functions of the board are:

(i) To carry out the training of officers and staff, create facilities for grading and standardization, construct market road and approach roads to the markets, construct market yard and sub-yard, establish and maintain the Board office and others as specified;

(ii) To tender advice to the government on the functioning of market committee and on improvement in agricultural marketing as and when referred to, and

(iii) To frame bye-laws, help in the functioning of market committees and supervise their operations.

STATE AGRICULTURAL MARKETING BOARDS

1. Identification of location of markets for connectivity under the Directorates of Marketing scheme based on importance of the market in commodity flow patterns.
2. Administration/implementation of the scheme at market level.
3. Provide necessary administrative and financial sanctions.

4. Markets for smooth implementation of the scheme.
5. Liaison with State NIC units and DMI offices for monitoring of progress, removal of impediments if any in day-to-day functioning of the scheme.
6. Undertake research for which information through computer network is to be provided to farmers. Transforming information available for practical use by farmers and undertake market-led extension.
7. Generate reports in local language at state level.

COUNCIL OF STATE AGRICULTURAL MARKETING BOARDS (COSAMB)

The COSAMB, an apex body of the State Marketing Boards was established in February 1988. The need for such a body was felt to coordinate the activities of State Marketing Boards, especially those connected with credit mobilization, central assistance for market development and some common problems.

Cooperative Markets

The efforts of the government to improve the marketing system of agricultural commodities have been only partially successful. The progress of regulated markets is not uniform in all areas. So, the establishment of cooperative marketing societies is another step taken to overcome the problems arising out of the present system of marketing agricultural produce.

A cooperative sales association is a voluntary business organization established by its member patrons to market farm products collectively for their direct benefit. It is governed by democratic principles, and savings are apportioned among members on the basis of their patronage.

The Main Functions of Cooperative Marketing Societies are:

(i) To market the produce of the members of the society at fair prices;

(ii) To safeguard the members from excessive marketing costs and malpractices;

(iii) To make credit facilities available to the members against the security of the produce brought for sale.

(iv) To make arrangements for the scientific storage of the member's produce. To provide the facilities of grading and market information which may help them to get a good price for their produce;

(v) To introduce the system of pooling so as to acquire a better bargaining power than the individual members having a small quantity of produce for marketing purposes.

(vi) To arrange for the export of the produce of the members so that they may get better returns.

(vii) To act as an agent of the government for the procurement of food grains and for the implementation of the price support policies.

(viii) To make arrangement for the transport of the produce of the members from the villages to the market on collective basis and bring out a reduction in the cost of transportation.

(ix) To arrange for the supply of inputs required by the farmers such as improved seeds, fertilizers, insecticides and pesticides.

Types of Cooperative Marketing Societies

On the basis of the commodities dealt in by them, the cooperative marketing societies may be grouped as:

(i) Single commodity marketing societies, e.g., Sugarcane Cooperative Marketing Society, Cotton Cooperative Marketing Society, Milk Cooperative Marketing Society.

(ii) Multi-commodity cooperative marketing societies.

(iii) Multi-purpose, Multi-commodity cooperative marketing societies.

Structure:

The cooperative marketing societies have both two-tier and three-tier structures. Two-tier structure/ Three-tier structure, State level marketing Federation, Primary co-operative marketing, District marketing societies (Taluk Level), Taluk Primary Cooperative marketing societies.

Three-tier structure is found in Assam, Bihar, Kerala, Madhya Pradesh, Karnataka, Orissa, Rajasthan and West Bengal. In all other States, two-tier structures is functioning.

Two Types of Members in Cooperative Marketing Societies

(a) **Ordinary Members:** Individual Farmers, Co-operative farming societies and service societies of the area may become the ordinary members of the cooperative marketing society. They have the right to participate in deliberations of the society share in profits and participate in decision-making process.

(b) **Nominated Members:** Traders with whom the society establishes business dealings are enrolled as nominated members. Nominated members do not have the right to participate in decision-making and share in profits.

SOURCES OF FINANCE

(i) **Share Capital:** Farmer members and state government subscribe to the share capital of the marketing societies.

(ii) **Loans:** The societies can avail loans from the Central and State cooperative banks and Commercial banks by pledging and Agricultural Marketing hypothecation and also by advancing credit to the extent of 50 per cent of owned capital.

(iii) **Subsidy:** Societies get subsidy from the government for purchase of grading machines and transport vehicles to meet their initial heavy expenditure. They also get a subsidy for a part of the cost of the managerial staff for a period of 3 years to make them viable.

Suggestions for Strengthening of Cooperative Marketing Societies

(i) The area of operation of societies should be large enough so that they may have sufficient business and become viable.

(ii) Storage facilities, transport facilities, accommodation and drinking facilities should be strengthened in the societies.

(iii) Cooperative feeling among members should be inculcated by proper education and adequate representation should be given to small and marginal farmers in their organizational setup.

(iv) In the selection process of officials of cooperative marketing societies, weightage should be given to business experience and qualification. After selection, proper thinking should be given.

MARKET FUNCTIONS

It includes the services and functions of different specialized institutions and middlemen. Different commodities have special marketing problems. Therefore, the results of the study of one commodity may not be applicable to other commodity.

Also the same commodity will have different problems in different regions. Various approaches have been suggested and used to study marketing problems. These are functional, institutional, commodity and behavioural approaches.

(i) Functional Approach: A marketing function is an act, operation on service by which the original producer and the final consumer are linked together. Marketing consists of many operations and an operation may be performed several times in the marketing process. The functional approach splits down the field of marketing into a few functions. This method analyses in detail the specific functions of marketing such as buying, selling, transportation, storage, standardization, grading, financing, risk taking and marketing research. The advantages of the functional approach in the study of agricultural marketing problems are:

1. We can make inter-functional comparison of the marketing costs.
2. Inter-agency comparison of the cost of performing a marketing function can be made.
3. Inter-commodity comparison of cost of performing the various functions can also be made.

The demerits of this approach are:

1. An undue emphasis on functions of marketing does not permit one to know how these functions are applied to specific business operations.
2. The marketing functions are so numerous that it is difficult to eliminate the unnecessary from the necessary functions.

(ii) Institutional Approach: The approaches aims to study of marketing problems which implies a study of agencies and institutions, which perform various functions in the marketing process. The nature and character of various middlemen and other related agencies involved in the movement of the product are studied.

The human element receives the primary emphasis, whereas the agencies and institution, which perform various marketing functions, are individuals, partnership, corporation, cooperatives, or government organizations, agencies and Institution, Individual Partnership Corporations, Cooperatives Government, Taluk Organization Commission, FCI, Cooperative, Coffee Board, Marketing Tea Board, Societies, NAFED, Wholesalers, APEDA, Retailer MPEDA.

These agencies vary widely in size and ownership. They get their reward in the form of marketing margins. This approach helps us to find answers to the problems of 'who does what' in the marketing process, whether the Marketing and Markets margin of the agency is commensurate with the services rendered, which government regulations are necessary so that their unlawful activities may be curbed, and how to simplify the procedural system.

The serious limitations of this method are that it leaves one with an inadequate understanding of marketing. Since the material presented is often largely descriptive and does not show effectively the interrelations of the institutions studied.

(iii) Commodity Approach: Under this approach, the commodity is the pivot around which all institutional and functional details are studied. The problems of marketing differ from commodity to commodity mainly because of the seasonality of production, the variations in its handling, storage, processing and the number of middlemen involved in them.

For example, potatoes are stored in cold storage, while wheat is stored in godowns. Paddy, pulses and oilseeds are processed at miller's level. The main advantage of this approach is that it is concrete since all work relates to a specific product but it is a time consuming process and often results in excessive repetitions.

(iv) Behavioural System Approach: This approach refers to the study of behaviour of firms, institutions and organizations, which exist in the marketing system for different commodities. The marketing process is continually changing in its organization and functional combinations. An understanding of the behaviour of the individuals is essential if changes in the behaviour and functioning of the system are to be predicted. Under the approaches to study of marketing, we have seen the marketing functions which can be broadly classified as:

1. Functions of exchange which includes selling and buying.
2. Functions of physical supply, which consists of transportation, storage and warehousing.
3. Facilitating functions: This function comprise of financing, risk taking, standardization and market information. The process of passing goods into the consumer's hands is called function of exchange. It includes buying, assembling and selling, where buying is the first step in the process of marketing. Buying involves careful planning and needs setting up of policies and procedures. The following points are to be considered before a particular product is bought.
   (a) What to buy (Product)?
   (b) When and how much to buy? (Time and quantity).
   (c) From whom and where to buy? (Source).
   (d) On what terms and conditions and prices? (Price).

Assembling starts after the goods have already been purchased. It is a function separate from buying. Buying involves transfer of ownership of the goods whereas assembling involves creating and maintaining of stock of goods purchased from different sources. The problems encountered in assembling of agricultural products are:

1. Seasonal production
2. Difficulties in controlling quantity and quality
3. Non-availability of information about sources of supply
4. Low quantity of marketable surplus.

(v) Selling Function: The function of marketing is to ensure that the right product is made available at the right place, in the right quantity, at the right price, at the right time and under the right impressions to the consumer. All these righteousness is made possible by performing the sales function.

Through selling function desires are created and hence it is called as creative function. Selling is also often referred to as distribution function because distribution makes good move from the place of production to the place of consumption. This is achieved through selling function.

Thus, buying, assembling and selling functions are directly concerned with change in the ownership of goods. They are complementary in nature. For every sale, there is a purchase and for every purchase there must be sale. And, assembling precedes a sale and assembling follows buying. Forms of sales of agricultural produce in India are:

1. Under Cover: Under this system, buyer or his representative indicates the price he is prepared to pay by clasping the hand of seller's agent under cover of cloth and pressing or manipulating the fingers, e.g., cattle sale.
2. By open auction: The broker invites bids for the produce and to the highest bidder is sold the produce, e.g., vegetables by commission agents.
3. By private agreement.
4. By quoting on samples.
5. Dara Sales: The heaps of grain of different quantities are sold at a flat price.
6. Close tender system: In regulated markets.
7. Moghum Sale: The sale is based on the verbal understanding between buyers and sellers without mentioning the rate as it is understood that buyer will pay the prevailing rate, e.g., flowers and vegetables by commission agents.

(vi) Functions of physical supply/distribution: It includes determining warehouse locations (establishing a material handling system, maintaining an inventory control system, establishing procedures for marketing and markets processing orders) and selecting mode of transportation. Transportation and storage account for the major share in the total distribution cost. Transportation is a necessary function of marketing because the most of the markets are geographically separated from the areas of production. It enhances the economic value through creation of place utility. The important functions of transport are:

1. It helps in the growth of industries whose products require quick marketing, e.g., vegetables, flowers, milk and fish.
2. It increases the demand for goods through widening of market
3. It creates place utility. As such transportation bridges the gap between production and consumption centres.
4. By virtue of improvement in the speed of transport, it offers time utility to products.
5. It helps in stabilization of prices by moving commodities from surplus area to deficit area.
6. Ensures continuous flow of goods into the hands of consumers.
7. It enables consumers to enjoy the benefits of many goods that are not produced locally.

8. Transport sector intensifies competition, which, in turn, reduces prices. Prices are also reduced because of the facilities offered by transport for large-scale production.

   Classification of transport:, Broadly speaking various modes of transport fall under the three categories: Land, Water and Air. These are further classified on the basis of the vehicles used.

Road Transport

Merits: It is cheap, safe and flexible.

Demerits: It has got limited carrying capacity, slow speed, and unstable rates.

Rail Transport

Merits: More suitable for transportation of heavy and bulky commodities. Long distance is quickly covered, cheap, all weather-friendly transport,

Demerits: Inflexibility, non-suitable for local transport and lesser accessibility.

Water Transport

Merits: Cheapest means of transport, high carrying capacity, creator of international trade and especially suitable for certain areas (forest products).

Demerits: Low speed, seasonal difficulties, longer journey required, international and political problems and limited area of operation, Agricultural Marketing.

Air Transport

Merits: Rapid speed, no barriers and boon to perishable commodities.

Demerits: High rate, low carrying capacity, dependence on climatic conditions and high rate of accidents.

MARKET CLASSIFICATION

The word market comes from the Latin word *"marcatus"* which means merchandise or trade or a place where business is conducted. The market, in economic sense, refers not to a place but to a commodity or commodities, and buyers and sellers are in free intercourse with one another. Components of a market for a market to exist, certain conditions must be satisfied. These conditions should be both necessary and sufficient. They may also be termed as the components of a market.

1. The existence of a goods for transactions (physical existence is, however, not necessary).
2. The existence of buyers and sellers.
3. Trading operations between buyers and sellers;
4. Geographical demarcation of area such as place, region, country or the whole world. The existence of a perfect competition or uniform price is not necessary.

Classification of markets: Markets may be classified on the basis of dimensions like area, time, commodities, volume and competition.

1. **On the basis of area**: On the basis of area from which buyers and sellers usually come for transactions markets:

   (a) **Local or Village Markets:** A market in which the buying and selling activities are confined among the buyers and sellers drawn from the same village or nearby villages. The village market exists mostly for perishable commodities.

   (b) **Regional Markets:** A market in which buyers and sellers for a commodity are drawn from a longer area than the local markets. Regional markets in India usually exist for food.

   (c) **National Markets:** A market in which buyers and sellers are at the national level.

   (d) **International Market:** A market in which the buyers and sellers are drawn from the entire world. These are the biggest markets from the area point of view. These markets exist in the commodities, which have a worldwide demand and/or supply such as coffee, machinery, gold, silver etc.

   The storage facility, transportation, preservation and processing techniques used can enhance the area dimension of market for a commodity, e.g., mushroom local to wider area by dehydration; milk pasteurization enhances the area dimension from local to regional.

2. **On the basis of time span:** Markets on the basis of time span can be grouped as follows:

   (a) **Short Period Markets:** The markets, which are held only for a few hours are called short period markets. The products dealt within these markets are of a highly perishable nature, such as fish, vegetables, milk and flowers.

   (b) **Long Period Markets:** These markets are held for a longer period than the short period markets. The commodities traded in these markets are less perishable and can be stored for some time, e.g., foodgrains and oilseeds. The prices are governed both by the supply and demand forces.

   (c) **Secular Markets:** These are markets of a permanent nature. The commodities traded in these markets are durable in nature and can be stored for many years. Example is markets for machinery and manufactured goods.

3. **Classifications of markets based on commodities:** It includes two aspects:

   (a) Number of commodities and

   (b) Nature of commodities.

   (a) **Number of Commodities:** A market may be general or specialized on the basis of the number of commodities in which transactions are completed.

      (i) **General Markets:** A market in which all types of commodities, such as food grains, oilseeds, fiber crops, gur etc. are bought and sold is known as general markets. These markets deal in a large number of commodities.

      (ii) **Specialized Markets:** A market in which transactions take place only in one or two commodities are known as specialized market. For every group of commodities, separate markets exist. The examples are food grain markets, vegetable market, wool market and cotton market.

(b) Nature of Commodities: On the basis of the type of goods dealt in markets may be classified into the following categories.

(i) **Commodity Markets:** A market which deals in goods and raw materials such as wheat, barley, cotton, fertilizer seed, gold etc. are formed as commodity markets.

(ii) On the basis of volume of transactions, there are two types of markets on the basis of volume of transactions at a time:

(a) Wholesale Markets: A wholesale market is one in which commodities are bought and sold in large lots or in bulk. Transaction in these markets takes place mainly between traders.

(b) Retail Markets: A retail market is one in which commodities are bought and sold to the consumers as per their requirements. Transactions in these markets take place between retailers and consumers. The retailers purchase in wholesale markets and sell in small lots to the consumers. These markets are very near to the consumers.

(iii) On the basis of degree of competition: On the basis of competition, markets may be classified into the following categories.

(a) Perfect Markets: A perfect market is one in which the following conditions hold good.

1. There are a large number of buyers and sellers.
2. All the buyers and sellers in the market have perfect knowledge of demand, supply and prices.
3. Prices at anyone time are uniform over a geographical area, plus or minus the cost of getting supplies from surplus to deficit areas.
4. The prices are uniform in any one place, over a period of time, plus or minus the cost of storage from one period to another.
5. The prices of different forms of a product are uniform plus or minus the cost of converting the product from one form to another.

(b) Imperfect Markets: The markets in which the conditions of perfect competition are lacking are characterized as imperfect markets. The following situations, each based on the degree of imperfect, may be identified.

(i) Monopoly Market: Monopoly is a market situation in which there is only one seller of a commodity. He exercises sole control over the quantity or price of the commodity, e.g., Railways.

(ii) Duopoly Market: A duopoly market is one, which has only two sellers of a commodity, e.g., two retailers in a village.

(iii) Oligopoly Market: A market in which there are more than two but still a few sellers of a commodity is termed as an oligopoly market, e.g., different airlines operating in our country.

(iv) Monopolistic Competition: When a large number of sellers deal in heterogeneous and differentiated form of a commodity, the situation is called monopolistic competition, e.g., Tea and Coffee by different companies, pump sets, fertilizers etc.

MARKET MARGINS

The Directorate of Marketing and Inspection (DMI) has also estimated costs and margins of a number of agricultural commodities. The DMI studies revealed that costs and margins account for 30 to 35 per cent of consumer's price in food grains, 45 to 55 per cent in fruits and vegetables and 12 to 36 per cent in oilseed crops. The results further reveal that the costs were higher when farmers adopted private channels in marketing of surplus produce compared to the institutional channels (Bhatia, 1996).

The gross marketing margins in marketing of agricultural products have also been worked out from National Accounts Statistics (Acharya, 1998). In this approach, difference between the total consumer expenditure on a particular farm product and the value of the output at the farm level has been used to estimate gross marketing margin.

Based on a aggregate accounting, the gross marketing margins (GMM) as percentage of consumer's price is 19.2 in cereals, 7.2 in oilseeds, 32.9 in fruits and vegetables, 6.7 in milk and milk products, 37.2 in sugarcane/sugar with an overall average of 19.3 per cent for all agricultural commodities.

The marketing efficiency can be increased by reducing costs and margins for given level of marketing functions. Obviously this can be achieved by: (i) reducing losses during storage, transportation and handling by providing scientific know-how and facilities for these activities to farmers; (ii) establishing farm-retail outlet linkages; (iii) establishing retail chains/supermarkets to achieve scale economies; and (iv) establishing farmer-processor linkages (backward and forward integration) by organization of marketing on cooperative lines.

The APMCs should take initiative in establishing such linkages on the basis of Mobilize, Organize, Operate and Transfer (MOOT). It may be mentioned here that in developed countries like United Kingdom, farmer's cooperatives handle 80 per cent milk, 54 per cent oilseeds, 40 per cent peas, 36 to 80 per cent fruits and 27 per cent cereals.

MAKING MARKETING INFORMATION SERVICES RELEVANT TO FARMERS

Accuracy, availability, applicability and **analysis** are the four "A's" of market information. If Maker Information Service (MIS) are to have any meaning for farmers, the information they provide must be accurate and farmers must understand to which product, quality, etc. the prices refer. Further, even if prices are completely accurate, they are of much use if they are only available to farmers and it will be too late for them to use effectively.

Farmers need to be able to apply the accurate information made available to them. This requires knowledge of how to convert prices they receive from the MIS into a realistic price at their local market or farm gate. Finally, farmers need long-term data, which has been analyzed in such a way that they can make decisions about when to plant and harvest and what new crops to diversify into.

Accuracy

Providing accurate information requires attention to a lot of different issues. Food and Agricultural Organization (FAO) has a publication on how to set up an MIS and this goes into considerable detail about how to ensure prices are accurate.

INTERNET BASED SYSTEM (AGMARKNET) — A NEW DIMENSION

1. Internet provides a completely new dimension to information utilization. Free electronic text, images, software, and many other forms of data are increasing the number, volume, diversity, as well as the number of server/host. Internet means free access, and has been, up till now operated by the "Internal Principle" that is fundamentally different from the "Conventional" commercial database distribution.

   Despite a growing awareness and attempt to commercialize the services and products within the internet, the market information has been regarded as a public good in India because of presence of large number of small and marginal farmers who are unable to pay for information. Exploring on the internet for the farmers would provide wider marketing opportunities and social acceptance for this new media, a derivation from earlier, needs promotion. Basic functions of transfer of knowledge, changing attitude, behaviour and skills to the farmers of earlier media needs to be incorporated in the new media—Internet, so that it takes over traditional media in the interest of the farmers.

2. Professor Eisuke Naito of National Centre for Science Information System, Tokyo, Japan defines information as "a dynamic process in which a solution to a problem is gained by consolidating knowledge judged to be matching the solution seeking". Knowledge recorded and stored on paper or any digital media is only in a static state without any action for solution.

   Without decision making and the corresponding action following a solution, the recorded knowledge and data gathering are not completely utilized. The agricultural marketing information service envisages utilization of recorded knowledge for solution—making it information. The distinct advantages of electronic, media, viz., instant access, remote access, simultaneous access and high speed search over volume of available knowledge form part of the internet based marketing information service envisaged to be developed.

3. A large amount of data with more accuracy can be stored in computer, analyzed and retrieved within shortest possible time. AGMARKNET will ensure dissemination of data through network to any distance with thc help of communication devices for the benefit of farmers, traders, consumers, etc. The improved communication system will enable the producers to know about probable markets where they can dispose of their produce more profitably. The traders and consumers can also derive maximum advantage out of their purchases at low communication cost. The modernization of market information system will lead to the efficiency in the markets and increased participation of the farmers.

DATABASE MANAGEMENT

Data on various aspects of agricultural marketing are important for policy formulation and conducting research leading to solution of different marketing problems faced by the farmer-producers and consumers. The non-availability of primary data from different market functionaries and secondary data of time series nature from published sources has limited the scope of research in this field.

There is difference in the coverage of data collected at the primary level and those published by different organizations. Published data include farm (harvest) prices at the district level, wholesale prices of selected crops for selected markets, retail prices of few selected markets of the states, market arrivals in important markets, market charges prescribed by the market committees, import and export of selected commodities at the national level and production and area of commodities at district and state level.

From raw price data, index numbers are also constructed with reference to a particular base year. Since most secondary data in respect of all crops and markets on a time series basis are not available, it becomes difficult for analysts and researchers to draw meaningful conclusion unless these are supplemented by other data from unpublished sources. The agencies engaged in collection of market information/statistics are:

(i) Directorate of Marketing and Inspection, Government of India, Faridabad and Nagpur

(ii) State Agricultural Marketing Boards

(iii) State Agricultural Marketing Departments

(iv) Directorate of Economics and Statistics, Government of India

(v) Corporations such as the Food Corporation of India, the Warehousing Corporation of India, Commodity Boards and other Corporations

(vi) The Agricultural Produce Market Committees (APMCs)

(vii) The Revenue Department of State Governments

(viii) The Directorate of Economics and Statistics (DES) of State Governments.

Marketing statistics/data are available in the following publications brought out by the concerned departments, viz.:

(i) Agricultural Situation in India — Monthly

(ii) Bulletin on Prices — Weekly

(iii) Reserve Bank of India Bulletin — Monthly

(iv) Agricultural Marketing — Quarterly

(v) Bulletin on Food Statistics — Bi-annual

(vi) Indian Agriculture in Brief — Bi-annual

(vii) Economic Survey — Annual

(viii) Commodity Survey Reports — Occasional

(ix) CMIE Publications — Occasional

(x) Indian Journal of Agricultural Marketing —Thrice a year

(xi) Indian Journal of Agricultural Economics — Quarterly

(xii) Reports of Various Commissions and Corporations

(xiii) Annual Reports of different Departments stating their progress

(xiv) Newspapers (especially the Economic Times and Financial Express) — Daily

(xv) Monthly Bulletins of Market Committees and State Agricultural Marketing Boards – Occasional.

Of the various organizations, Directorate of Economics and Statistics is the main agency collecting and compiling price statistics of agricultural commodities. This Directorate was set up in 1948 in the

Ministry of Agriculture. Three types of prices – wholesale, farm harvest and retail prices of various agricultural commodities, their sub-groups and groups are collected and compiled on a regular basis using a standard methodology.

NATIONAL INSTITUTE OF AGRICULTURAL MARKETING (NIAM)

The National Institute of Agricultural Marketing (NIAM) is a pioneering national level organization set up by the Government of India in year 1988 for offering specialized training, education and consultancy and for undertaking research in agricultural marketing. It is an autonomous body under the aegis of Ministry of Agriculture (previously of Ministry of Rural Areas and Employment), Government of India. The Institute is being developed as a Centre of Excellence in the field of Agricultural Marketing (NIAM, 2000). The following functions have been assigned to the Institute:

(i) To provide specialized training in agricultural marketing for entrepreneurs and institutions by offering and sponsoring specialized marketing courses at various levels as necessary to supplement existing facilities;

(ii) To undertake research in agricultural marketing for government, cooperatives and other institutions for demonstrating and replication of the advanced management techniques in this field;

(iii) To provide advisory and consultancy services to marketing enterprises (state, private and cooperatives) in the field of agricultural marketing; and

(v) To develop and formulate investment projects in the field of agricultural marketing for public, cooperative and private institutions.

The Institute has conducted more than 300 training programmes up to 1999-2000. The Institute has also undertaken long- and short-term research studies on various facets of agricultural marketing. The long-term projects handled by the Institute include formulation of master plans for the development of agricultural markets for the states of Jammu & Kashmir, Andhra Pradesh and Sikkim.

The Institute has also undertaken a collaborative research project on the formulation of Integrated Action Plan for the Promotion of Handicrafts and Handlooms in thc States of Uttar Pradesh and West Bengal in association with IRMA-Anand. The short-term research activities include case studies on various agri-business activities and commodity marketing studies.

The Institute has developed a data bank on various aspects of agricultural marketing including infrastructural facilities available in different market yards of Rajasthan, Delhi, Meghalaya, Jammu & Kashmir, Goa, Himachal Pradesh, Andhra Pradesh and others. The publication entitled "Statistical Abstract" containing data on post-harvest technology and different marketing aspects of national and international level is being brought out by the Institute since 1997.

INFORMATION TECHNOLOGY IN AGRICULTURAL MARKETING

Market information is needed by farmers in planning production and marketing, and is equally required by other market participants in arriving at optimal trading decisions. The existence and dissemination of complete and accurate marketing information is the key to achieving both operational and pricing efficiency in the marketing system and IT has an important role to play in the process.

There are several areas of agricultural marketing with which farmers need to be fully familiarized in order to improve price realization. Promotion of nationally and internationally acceptable standards of grading and standardization, packaging and labelling, storage and warehousing and sanitary and phyto-sanitary measures and quality certification in farm sector will enable trade and processing sector to undertake large-scale agricultural marketing operations in domestic as well as international markets.

Once the farm produce is standardized and labelled, backed by reputed quality certification, it can be directly offered for sale in national and international markets. Several Ministries in Government of India take decisions directly affecting the process of Agricultural marketing in the country. Important among these are Agriculture, Commerce, Food and Public Distribution, Consumer Affairs and Health. Several central institutions set up by Government of Indi, viz., NCDC, NAFED, TRIFED, NDDB, NHB, APEDA etc., are directly involved in implementing programmes to strengthen agricultural marketing in the country and to help farmers in the process of marketing of agricultural produce.

Then there are Commodity Boards and Export Promotion Councils for specific commodities and to promote exports. All the relevant programmes and policies of these institutions need to be disseminated to the farm producers and the target groups to enable them to take full advantage of newer opportunities made available by the Government. Although many of these organizations have their independent web sites hosted through NIC or other internet service providers, the portal developed by NIC (AGMARKNET) should provide linkages to these sites to access marketing related information to all market players.

Data on various aspects of agricultural marketing is important for policy formulation, infrastructure planning and research. To facilitate both the Government as well as the private sector in planning development of an appropriate marketing strategy in agriculture sector, it would be necessary to create at national level an 'Atlas of Agricultural Markets' which would provide information in respect of each commodity, major areas of production, movement and storage and of market and consuming centres.

In parallel, commodity profile should be prepared for all major commodities outlining the market requirements in terms of quality, standards, labelling, packing, storage, transport, regulations taxation, warehousing, forward and futures markets etc. This information has to be translated in local languages and uploaded onto the State level portals to facilitate market-led extension to farming community in local language through internet.

DIRECTORATE OF MARKETING AND INSPECTION (DMI)

The Directorate of Marketing and Inspection (DMI), headed by Agricultural Marketing Advisor to the Government of India (AMA), implements agricultural marketing programmes of the Central Government, under the supervision and control of the Central Ministry of Agriculture. DMI aims at bringing integrated development of marketing of agricultural and allied produce in the country, and maintains a close liaison between the Central and State Governments through its regional offices (11) and sub-offices (37) spread all over the country. DMI has a network of 22 regional AGMARK Laboratories with its Central AGMARK Laboratory at Nagpur. Its thrust areas functional responsibilities include:

- promotion of standardization and grading of agricultural and allied produce;
- market research and surveys;
- manpower training in Agricultural Marketing;
- market development through Regulation, Planning and Designing of physical markets;

- marketing extension to educate consumers/producers;
- administration of Meat Food Products Order (1973);
- promotion of Cold Storage; and
- market information network

SUMMARY

In the interest of public welfare, the government intervenes in the marketing system. The extent of intervention depends on the objectives of the government and the extent of defects and malpractices prevailing in the system. Government intervention may be direct or indirect, and it may take anyone or a combination of the' following forms:

Government at centre will indulge in framing of rules and regulations for the protection of the interest of some sections of the population. This may include restriction on activities of traders, licensing and market regulation. Similarly, government carry out promotional activities such as storage and warehousing, transportation and communication facilities, credit facility, grading and standardization, and encouragement of cooperative marketing. Side by side, it also regulates the economy by fixing administration of prices at different levels of marketing guaranteeing minimum support prices to producers, providing commodities at fair prices to consumers, and fixing the rates of commission charged by commission agents. Also it influences supply and demand by import, export, internal procurement and distribution.

Agricultural commodities move in the marketing chain through different channels. The channels are distinguished from each other on the basis of market functionaries involved in carrying the produce the farmers to the ultimate consumers. The length of the marketing channels depends on the size of market, perishability of the commodity and the nature of demand at the consumer level.

QUESTIONS

1. What is the role of government in promoting the agriculture marketing?
2. Write down various marketing channels and functionaries in agriculture marketing.
3. Explain what do you mean by common marketing channels and how they differ from agricultural produce marketing?
4. Outline the basic factors that are essential when agriculture marketing is being monitored.
5. Write down different types of cooperative marketing societies.
6. What are the functions of State Agriculture Marketing Boards?

CHAPTER 13

OUTLOOK — CHALLENGES IN INDIAN AGRICULTURE MARKETING

Outlook – Challenges in Indian Agriculture Marketing

Agriculture Business – Vast Complex System

Important Requisites for Success of Agriculture Business Management

Role of Commerce in Indian Agriculture Marketing

Economic Reforms in India

Achievements of Indian Agriculture Sector

Crop Production

Growth Rates of Area and Production with Yield

Exports and Imports

Price Policy for Agriculture Produce

Minimum Support Price (MSP)

Subsidies for Raw Materials

Procurement Prices

OUTLOOK – CHALLENGES IN INDIAN AGRICULTURE MARKETING

The country has made great strides towards increasing food grains production since the mid-sixties. Today, India ranks high in the production of various commodities such as milk, wheat, rice, fruits, and vegetables. However, the agriculture sector in India is at a crossroads with rising demand for food items and relatively slower supply response in many commodities resulting in frequent spikes in food inflation.

The technological breakthrough achieved in the 1960s is gradually waning. The need for a second green revolution is being experienced more than ever before.1894 Increasing agriculture production and productivity is a necessary condition not only for ensuring national food security, livelihood security, and nutritional security but also for sustaining the high levels of growth envisaged in the current Plan.

However, with very little growth in area and marginal growth in yields of many crops during the last decade, increasing agricultural production remains a challenge. Concerted and focused efforts are required for addressing the challenge of stagnating productivity levels in agriculture. A holistic approach, simultaneously working on agricultural research and development, dissemination of technology, and provision of agricultural inputs such as quality seed, fertilizers, pesticides, and irrigation, would help achieve the critical levels of productivity needed. Further, effective coordination and monitoring of the ongoing agriculture and allied sector programmes needs to be ensured for optimum results.

Capital investment in agriculture as a percentage of the GDP has been stagnating in recent years, although the capital expenditure in agriculture as a percentage of the GDP in agriculture has shown some improvement in the current Five Year Plan. It may, however, also be noted that the agriculture sector GDP has itself been stagnating during the last three years from 2007-08 to 2009-10. The real challenge in agriculture sector is to enhance capital investment in the sector both by public and private sector in a sustained way.

Sixty per cent of our net sown area is still rainfed. Various studies indicate that the potential of rainfed areas has not been fully utilized. A targeted development of rainsfed areas should be prioritized.

Enhancing the returns farmers get on their production is essential for incentivizing the farmers to produce more. Farmers need to realize the market price for their produce. Setting up of efficient supply chains is not only essential for ensuring adequate supplies of essential items at reasonable prices but also to ensure that producers get adequately compensated. Linking farmers to the market is, therefore, very important. The successful experience of cooperatives in the milk sector in managing the supply chain and providing remunerative prices to the producers may be emulated in the case of agricultural products.

The level of secondary food processing in India is very low compared to many western countries. With increasing income and population, demand for processed food is likely to increase. It is necessary to cater to this changing demand and at the same time enhance the income of farmers. So far the focus in food management has been on cereals, mainly rice and wheat. However, the demand for processed food is expected to increase. Investment in food processing, cold chains, handling, and packaging of processed food needs encouragement.

Declining per capita availability of food grains has been a matter of major concern. For ensuring nutritional security, it is not only important to increase the per capita availability of food grains but also to ensure that right quantities of food items are there in the food basket of a common man. A thrust on horticulture products is required for enhancing per capita availability of food items as well as ensuring nutritional security.

Addressing infrastructure requirements in the agriculture sector, especially storage, communication, roads, and markets should be a priority. Public-Private Partnership models can be of help in ensuring faster development of these requirements which are of vital importance for the growth of agriculture sector.

A higher growth rate of the economy and rising levels of income are putting pressure on products from the livestock sector. Many items such as meat, milk, and poultry are experiencing upward pressure in their prices adding to the wholesale food price inflation. A long-term strategy to increase the production of these items is the need of the hour. These steps would also help enhance rural income and supplement the livelihood options of the rural populace.

There has been substantial increase in the MSPs of various crops over the last few years. This is considered necessary for incentivizing farmers to increase production and productivity. At the same time, the MSP signals the floor price for the produce which, in turn, has the potential of increasing the prices. Addressing the welfare of the agricultural producers and of the consumers simultaneously poses a challenge.

Further, inability of a large number of small and marginal farmers to directly access the agri-market puts a question mark on increases in MSP actually benefiting such farmers. Record procurement of rice and wheat in the last few years has helped build up the buffer stock and strategic reserve of wheat and rice. There is, however, a huge cost involved in the process, which is met through budgetary sources in the form of food subsidy. The procurement operations linked with MSPs cause fiscal stress by way of increasing food subsidies. The issue of efficient food stocks management and offloading of stocks in time needs urgent attention.

One of the most pressing of emerging challenges is that of conservation. Enactment of laws for ecological foundations for climate resilient agriculture, management of agricultural waste, building carbon sequestration of soil and overall natural resource management is urgently needed.

To conclude, raising farm productivity with adequate focus on rainfed areas, diversification of Indian agriculture from just crop farming to livestock, fisheries and poultry and horticulture while simultaneously addressing environmental concerns should be the focus for the agriculture sector. Higher levels of investments are required for not only increasing farm productivity but also creating adequate infrastructure for transport, storage and distribution of agricultural produce.

AGRIBUSINESS — A VAST COMPLEX SYSTEM

Agriculture has evolved into agribusiness and has become a vast and complex system that reaches far beyond the farm to include all those who are involved in bringing food and fiber to consumers. Agribusiness includes not only those that farm the land but also the people and firms that provide the inputs (for example, Seed, chemicals, credit etc.), process the output (for example, milk, grain, meat etc.), manufacture the food products (for example, ice-cream, bread, breakfast cereals etc.), and transport and sell the food products to consumers (for example, restaurants, supermarkets).

Agribusiness system has undergone a rapid transformation as new industries have evolved and traditional farming operations have grown larger and more specialized. The transformation did not happen overnight, but came slowly as a response to a variety of forces. Knowing something about how agribusiness came about makes it easier to understand how this system operates today and how it is likely to change in the future.

Initially agriculture being the major venture it was easy to become a farmer, but productivity was low. Average farmer produced enough food to feed just four people. As a consequence, most farmers were nearly totally self-sufficient. They produced most of the inputs they needed for production, such as seed, draft animals, feed and simple farm equipment.

Farm families processed the commodities they grew to make their own food and clothing. They consumed or used just about everything they produced. The small amount of output not consumed on the farm was sold for cash. These items were used to feed and cloth the minor portion of the country's population that lived in villages and cities. A few agricultural products made their way into the export market and were sold to buyers in other countries.

Farmers found it increasingly profitable to concentrate on production and began to purchase inputs they formerly made themselves. This trend enabled others to build business that focused on meeting the need for inputs used in production agriculture such as seed, fencing, and machinery and so on.

These farms involved into the industries that make up the "agricultural inputs sector". Input farms are major part of agribusiness and produce variety of technologically based products that account for approximately 75 per cent of all the inputs used in production agriculture.

At the same time, the agriculture input sector was evolving, a similar evaluation was taking place a commodity processing and food manufacturing moved off the farm. The form of most commodities (wheat, rice, milk, livestock and so on) must be changed to make them more useful and convenient for consumers. For example, consumers would rather buy flour than grind the wheat themselves before baking a cake. They are willing to pay extra for the convenience of buying the processed commodity (flour) instead of the raw agriculture commodity (wheat).

During the same period, technological advance were being made in food preservation method. Up until this time, the perishable nature of most agriculture commodities meant that they were available only at harvest. Advance in food processing have made it possible to get those commodities all throughout the year.

Today even most farm families' use purchased food and fiber products rather than doing the processing themselves. The farms that meet the consumers demand for greater processing and convenience also constitute a major part of agribusiness and are referred to as the processing manufacturing sector.

It is apparent that the definition of agriculture had to be expanded to include more than production. Farmers rely on the input industries to provide the products and service they need to produce agricultural commodities.

They also rely on commodity processors, food manufacturers, and ultimately food distributors and retailers to purchase their raw agricultural commodities and to process and deliver them to the consumer for final sale. The result is the food and fiber system.

The food and fiber system is increasingly being referred to as "agribusiness". The term agribusiness was first introduced by Davis and Goldberg in 1957. It represents three part system made up of: (1) the agricultural input sector, (2) the production sector and (3) the processing-manufacturing sector.

To capture the full meaning of the term "agribusiness", it is important to visualize these three sectors as interrelated parts of a system in which the success of each part depends heavily on the proper functioning of the other two.

IMPORTANT REQUISITES FOR SUCCESS OF AGRIBUSINESS

Nevertheless, a farmer operator/farmer manager has to give proper thought to this consideration in order to make his business a successful one. The important requisites for success in a modern business are:

Clean Objectives

The determination of objectives is one of the most essential and crucial pre-requisites for the success of the business. The objectives set forth should be realistic and clearly defined. Then, all the business efforts should be geared to achieve the set objectives. In a way, objectives are destination points for the agri-business.

1. Destination: As a traveler must know here she or he has to reach that is destination, business also must know what are its objectives.

2. Planning: In simple words, planning is a predetermined line of action. The accomplishment of the objectives set, to a great extent, depends upon planning itself. It is said that it does not take time to do thing but it takes time to decide what and how to do. Planning is a proposal based on past experience and present trends for future actions. In other words, it is an analysis of a problem and finding out the solutions to solve them with reference to the objective of the farm.

3. Sound organization: An organization is built-up structure of business for service to society. Just as human frame is build up by various parts like heart, lever, brain, legs etc. Similarly, organization of business is a harmonious combination of men, machine material, money, management etc. so that all these could work jointly as one unit, i.e., "business", "the agribusiness". Organization is, thus a systematic combination of various related parts for achieving a defined objective in an effective manner.

4. Research: As indicated earlier, today the agricultural production philosophy "produces what the consumer want". Consumer's behaviour is influenced by variety of factors like cultural, social, personal and psychological factors. The business needs to know and appreciate these factors and then function accordingly. The knowledge of these factors is acquired through market research. Research is a systematic search for new knowledge. Market research enable a business in finding out new methods of production, improving the quality of product and developing new products as per the changing tastes and wants of the consumers.

5. Finance: Finance is said to be the lifeblood of business enterprise. It brings together the land, labour, machine and raw materials into production. Agribusiness should estimate its financial requirements adequately so that it may keep the business wheel on moving. Therefore, proper arrangements should be made for securing the required finance for the enterprise.

6. Proper plant location, layout and size: The success of agribusiness depends to a great extent on the location. Where it is set up. Location of the business should be convenient from various points of view such as availability of required infrastructure facilities, availability of inputs like raw materials, skilled labour, nearer to the market etc.

Hence, the businessmen must take sufficient care in the initial stages to be selected at the suitable location for his business. The size of the business is also important because the requirement for infrastructural facilities and inputs varies as per the size of the business. The requirement for raw materials, for example, will be less in a smaller sized firm than a larger size firm.

7. Efficient management: One of the reasons for failure of business is often attributed to as their poor management or inefficient management. The one man, i.e., the proprietor may not be equally good in all areas of the business. Efficient businessman can make proper use of available resources for achieving the objectives set for the business.

8. Harmonious relations with the workers: In an agribusiness organization, the farmer operator occupies a distinct place because he/she is the main living factor among all factors of production. In fact, it is the human factor who makes the use of other non-human factors like land, machine, money etc. Therefore, for successful operation of business, there should be cordial and harmonious relations maintained with the workers/labours to get their full cooperation in achieving business activities.

It was already indicated that agribusiness is a complex, system of input sector, production sector, processing manufacturing sector and transport and marketing sector. Therefore, it is directly related to industry, commence and trade. Industry is concerned with the production of commodities and materials while commerce and trade are concerned with their distribution.

ROLE OF INDUSTRY IN AGRICULTURAL MARKETING

Industry refers to the processes of extraction and production of goods meant for final consumption or use by individual or by another industry for its production. Thus, goods used by the final or ultimate consumers are called "consumer goods" such as edible oils, fruit jams, papaya, pickles etc.

Types of Industries

According to nature, the industries are broadly classified into following types:

(1) **Extractive Industries:** These industries are concerned with the extraction and utilization of natural resources. Example – fishing, fruit gathering, agro-based industries, forestation.

(2) **Genetic Industries:** These industries include breeding of plants, seeds, cattle breeding farm, fish hatcheries, and poultry farms. Of course, factors like nature, climate and environment play a dominant role in these industries, yet human skill involved in their production cannot be ignored. For example, intensive agriculture is possible with greater amount of capital and larger number of workers.

(3) **Manufacturing Industries:** These industries are engaged in the conversion of raw materials or semi-finished goods produced in the extractive industries. Some prominent examples are – cotton textile industry, spinning and weaving mills etc. Manufacturing industries can further be classified into five types: (i) Analytical industry, (ii) Processing industry, (iii) Synthetic industry, (iv) Service industry and (v) Assembly industry.

ROLE OF COMMERCE IN AGRICULTURAL MARKETING

Commerce is another major component of agribusiness. It includes all those activities which are necessary to bring goods and services from the place of their production to the place of their consumption.

Thus, it includes the buying and selling of goods and service and all those activities which facilitate trade such as storing, grading, packaging, financing, insurance and transportation. In simple words, commerce includes trade and aid to trade. The principal function of the trade (commerce) are to remove the hindrance of person, place, time exchange, knowledge etc. and ensure a free and smooth flow of goods from the producers to the consumers.

Trade, in fact, is a branch of commerce itself. In a way, it is the final state of business activity involving sale and purchase of commodities or goods. It does not include trades like transportation, insurance, banking, finance etc. On the basis of its coverage and volume, trades is normally classified into the following types: (1) on the basis of volume and (2) on the basis of coverage.

1. **On the basis of volume:**
   (i) Wholesale trade
   (ii) Retail trade
2. **On the basis of coverage:**
   (i) Regional trade
   (ii) National trade

ECONOMIC REFORMS IN INDIA

The economic reforms have necessitated professionalism in vital sectors of the Indian economy. Transformation of the agriculture sector into a competitive sector calls for professional management and use of modern technologies in areas such as specialized production, post-harvest management, promotion of value-added agri-products, supply chain management, etc., so as to position these competitively both in the domestic as well as in international markets.

Agribusiness Management Education is now a priority area in the country, as several State Agricultural Universities and Agricultural Institutes have added MBA (Agri Business) and equivalent programs to their educational systems over the past one decade.

The Economic Reforms process aimed at accelerating the economic development to lead the country on following ends:

- A higher rate of growth
- An enlargement of employment potential leading to full employment.
- Reduction of population living below the poverty line.
- Promotion of equity leading to a better deal for the poor and less well off sections of our society.
- Reduction of regional imbalance and disparities between the rich and poor states of India.

ACHIEVEMENTS OF INDIAN AGRICULTURE SECTOR

Pioneering work by agriculture scientists and the efforts of farmers had helped achieve a breakthrough in the agriculture sector in the 1960s, popularly known as the 'Green Revolution'. High agricultural production and productivity achieved in subsequent years has been the main reason for attaining food security to a large extent. The country has not witnessed any big technological breakthrough in agriculture since then.

The food safety net for each and every of the over a billion citizens — a number that is growing requires enhanced agricultural production and productivity in the form of a Second Green Revolution. Further, special attention is required for achieving higher production and productivity levels in pulses, oilseeds, fruits, and vegetables, which had remained untouched in the First Green Revolution but are essential for nutritional security. In this regard, achieving high production of poultry, meat and fisheries is also essential.

The relatively weak supply responses to price hikes in agricultural commodities, especially food articles, in the recent past brings back into focus the central question of efficient supply chain management and need for sustained levels of growth in agriculture and allied sectors. The choice before the nation is clear—to invest more in agriculture and allied sectors with the right strategies, policies, and interventions. This is also a 'necessary' condition for 'inclusive growth' and for ensuring that the benefits of growth reach a larger number of people.

The growth of agriculture and allied sectors is still a critical factor in the overall performance of the Indian economy. As per the 2010-11 advance estimates released by the Central Statistics Office (CSO) on 07.02.2011, the agriculture and allied sector accounted for 14.2 per cent of the gross domestic product (GDP), at constant 2004-05 prices.

During the period 2004-05 to 2007-08, the GDP for agriculture and allied sectors had increased from ₹ 5,65,426 crore to ₹ 6,55,080 crore, at constant 2004-05 prices; thereafter it stagnated at this level for two years (2008-09 to 2009-10) (Table 8.1). In 2009-10, it accounted for 14.6 per cent of the GDP compared to 15.7 per cent in 2008-09 and 19.0 per cent in 2004-05. its share in GDP has thus declined rapidly in the recent past.

This is explained by the fact that whereas overall GDP has grown by an average of 8.62 per cent during 2004-05 to 2010-11, agricultural sector GDP has increased by only 3.46 per cent during the same period. The role of the agriculture sector, however, remains critical as it accounts for about 58 per cent of employment in the country (as per 2001 census).

Moreover, this sector is a supplier of food, fodder, and raw materials for a vast segment of industry. Hence, the growth of Indian agriculture can be considered a necessary condition for 'inclusive growth'. More recently, the rural sector (including agriculture) is being seen as a potential source of domestic demand, a recognition that is even shaping the marketing strategies of entrepreneurs wishing to widen the demand for goods and services. In terms of composition, out of a total share of 14.6 per cent of the GDP in 2009-10 for agriculture and allied sectors, agriculture alone accounted for 12.3 per cent followed by forestry and logging at 1.5 per cent and fisheries at 0.8 per cent.

Table 8.1 Gross Capital Formation in Agriculture and Allied Sector

YEAR	GDP (in crore at 2004-05 prices)	GCF (in agriculture and allied activities)	GDP (in agriculture and allied activities)	GCF/GDP (in agriculture and allied activities)	GCF (in agriculture As % of total)
2004-05	29,71,464	76,096	5,65,426	13.46	2.56
2005-06	32,54,216	86,611	5,94,487	14.57	2.66
2006-07	35,66,011	90,710	6,19,190	14.65	2.54
2007-08	38,98,958	1,05,034	6,55,080	16.03	2.69
2008-09(P)	41,62,509	1,28,659	6,54,118	19.67	3.09
2009-10 (QE)	44,93,743	1,33,377	6,56,975	20.3	2.97

Source: Eco. Survey CSO Q = Quick Estimates P = Provisional

Gross Capital Formation (GCF) in Agriculture and the Allied Sector

The GCF in agriculture and allied sectors as a proportion to the GDP in the sector stagnated around 14 per cent during 2004-05 to 2006-07. However, there is a marked improvement in this figure during the current Five Year Plan.

It increased to 16.03 per cent in 2007-08 and further to 19.67 per cent in 2008-09 (provisional) and to 20.30 per cent in 2009-10 (quick estimates [QE]). However, the GCF in agriculture and allied sectors relative to overall GDP has remained stagnant at around 2.5 to 3.0 per cent.

As a result, the share of GCF in agriculture and allied sector in total GCF has remained in the range of 6.6 to 8.2 per cent during 2004-05 to 2009-10. There is need to significantly step up investment in agriculture, both by the private and public sectors to ensure sustained target growth of 4 per cent per annum.

CROP PRODUCTION

For four consecutive years from 2005-06 to 2008-09, foodgrains production registered a rising trend and touched a record level of 234.47 million tons in 2008-09.

Table 8.2 Share of Agriculture & Allied Sectors' GCF in Total GCF (Per Cent) (at 2004-05 Prices)

2004-05	7.5
2005-06	7.3
2006-07	6.6
2007-08	6.5
2008-09	8.3
2009-10	7.7

The production of food grains declined to 218.11 million tons during 2009-10 (final estimates) due to the long spells of drought in various parts of the country in 2009. The productivity of almost all the crops suffered considerably, which led to decline in their production in 2009. As per the second advance estimates released by Ministry of Agriculture on 9.2.2011, production of food grains during 2010-11 is estimated at 232.07 million tons compared to 218.11 million tons last year.

This is only marginally below the record production of 234.47 million tons of foodgrains in 2008-09. The country is likely to achieve record production of wheat (81.47 million tons), pulses (16.51 million tons) and cotton (33.93 million bales of 170 kg. each) this year. This high level of production has been achieved despite crop damage due to drought in Bihar, Jharkhand, Orissa and West Bengal and the effects of cyclones, unseasonal and heavy rains, and cold wave and frost conditions in several parts of the country.

GROWTH RATES OF AREA, PRODUCTION AND YIELD OF AGRICULTURAL CROPS

Growth in the production of agricultural crops depends upon acreage and yield. Given the limitations in the expansion of acreage, the main source of long-term output growth is improvement in yields.

Trends in indices of area, production, and yield of different crops for two periods 1980-81 to 1989-90 and 2000-01 to 2009-10 (base triennium ending [TE] 1981-82 =100) are given in Table 8.3 Following tabular form explains in brief about analysis of growth rates of area, production, and yield of various crops based on their respective indices.

Table 8.3 Agricultural Production 2010-11

(Million tons)

Crops	2nd advance Estimates 2010-11	Target 2010-11	% of 2010-11 to Target set for 2010-11	2009-10 Final Estimates	% of Change in 2010-11 Compared to 2009-10
Rice	94.01	102.00	92.17	89.09	5.52
Wheat	81.47	82.00	99.35	80.80	0.83
Coarse Cereals	40.08	44.00	91.09	33.55	19.46
Pulses	16.51	16.50	100.06	14.66	12.62
Total Foodgrains	232.07	244.50	94.92	218.11	6.40
Oilseeds	27.85	33.20	83.89	24.88	11.94
Sugarcane	336.70	315.00	106.89	292.30	15.19
Cotton*	33.93	26.00	130.50	24.22	40.09
Jute and Mesta**	10.08	11.50	87.65	11.82	–14.72

Notes: *million bales of 170 kg each **million bales of 180 kg each

Source: Economic Survey

Compound Growth Rates of Area, Production and Yield

Rice and Wheat: During the 1980s, the growth in area in rice was marginal at 0.41 percent but growth in production and yield was above 3 per cent. From 2000-01 to 2009-10, the situation changed with growth in area turning negative and in production and yield standing at 1.59 per cent and 1.61 per cent respectively.

In wheat too, during the 1980s the growth in area was marginal at 0.46 per cent but in production and yield was above 3 per cent. During 2000-01 to 2009-10, the growth in area in wheat was 1.21 percent and in production and yield was 1.89 per cent and 0.68 per cent respectively.

Table 8.4 Compound Growth Rates of Area, Production and Yield

(As per cent per annum with base TE 1981-82 =100)

Crop	1980-81 to 1989-90			2000-01 to 2009-10		
	Area	Production	Yield	Area	Production	Yield
Rice	0.41	3.62	3.19	-0.03	1.59	1.61
Wheat	0.46	3.57	3.10	1.21	1.89	0.68
Jowar	-0.99	0.28	1.29	-3.19	-0.07	3.23
Bajra	-1.05	0.03	1.09	-0.42	1.68	2.11
Maize	-0.20	1.89	2.09	2.98	5.27	2.23
Ragi	-1.23	-0.10	1.14	-3.03	-1.52	1.57
Small Millets	-4.32	-3.23	1.14	-5.28	-3.58	1.78
Barley	-6.03	-3.48	2.72	-1.41	-0.25	1.17
Total Coarse Cereals	-1.34	0.40	1.62	-0.76	2.46	3.97
Total Cereals	-0.26	3.03	2.90	0.09	1.88	3.19
Gram	-1.41	-0.81	0.61	4.34	5.89	1.48
Tur	2.30	2.87	0.56	0.26	1.82	1.56
Other Pulses	0.02	3.05	3.03	-0.34	-0.32	0.02
Total Pulses	-0.09	1.52	1.61	1.17	2.61	1.64
Total Foodgrains	-0.23	2.85	2.74	0.29	1.96	2.94
Sugarcane	1.44	2.70	1.24	0.77	0.93	0.16
Oilseeds	1.51	5.20	2.43	2.26	4.82	3.79
Cotton	-1.25	2.80	4.10	2.13	13.58	11.22

Source: Economic Survey

This suggests that in these two crops the yield levels have plateaued and there is need for renewed research to boost production and productivity. Given the constraints in area expansion, there is no other alternative. Both public and private sector investment in research and development (R&D) needs to be encouraged.

EXPORTS AND IMPORTS

Depending on domestic availability, Government allows exports and imports of food items especially wheat, rice, and pulses. Government has reduced the import duty on wheat to nil from 9th September 2006 to augment its supply. Export of wheat has been prohibited since 8th October 2007.

The import duty on semi-milled or wholly milled rice has been reduced to nil from 20 March 2008 to augment its supply. Export of non-basmati rice has been prohibited since 15th October 2007 except for a quantity of 10,000 tons per annum of organic non-basmati rice permitted since 7th December 2009.

Further, export of non-basmati rice is permitted on diplomatic/humanitarian considerations. Export of basmati rice is permitted with a minimum export price (MEP) of US $ 900 per ton or ₹ 41, 400 per ton. Government has reduced the import duty on pulses to nil from 8th June 2006 to augment their supply. Export of pulses except Kabuli chana (chickpeas) has been prohibited with effect from 1st April 2008.

PRICE POLICY FOR AGRICULTURAL PRODUCE

The price policy for agricultural commodities seeks to ensure remunerative prices to growers for their produce with a view to encouraging higher investment and higher production and safeguarding of the interest of consumers, by making sure that adequate supplies are available. The price policy also seeks to evolve a balanced and integrated price structure in the perspective of the overall needs of the economy.

With this aim, the Government announces minimum support prices (MSPs) for major agricultural commodities each season and organizes purchase operations. The designated Central nodal agencies intervene in the market for undertaking procurement operations with the objective of ensuring that the market prices do not fall below the MSPs fixed by the Government. Over the years, the MSPs have been raised reasonably to ensure that farmers are incentivized to enhance production of their crops.

These operations involving high costs have put considerable fiscal strain on the economy. In addition, Government has also notified the MSPs of commercial crops like copra, raw jute, dehusked coconut, and toria. The MSPs for fair average quality (FAQ) variety of milling copra and FAQ variety of ball copra for 2010 season have been fixed at ₹ 4450 per quintal and ₹ 4700 per quintal respectively.

Farm Produce Price Policy

The main objectives of the Government's price policy for agricultural produce aims at ensuring remunerative prices to the growers for their produce with a view to encouraging higher investment and production. Towards this end, minimum support prices for major agricultural products are announced each year which are fixed after taking into account the recommendations of the Commission for Agricultural Costs and Prices (CACP). The CACP, while recommending prices takes into account, all important factors, viz.:

1. Cost of Production
2. Changes in Input Prices
3. Input/Output Price Parity
4. Trends in Market Prices
5. Inter-crop Price Parity
6. Demand and Supply Situation
7. Effect on Industrial Cost Structure
8. Effect on General Price Level
9. Effect on Cost of Living
10. International Market Price Situation
11. Parity between Prices Paid and Prices Received by Farmers (Terms of Trade).

Of all the factors, cost of production is the most tangible factor and it takes into account all operational and fixed demands. Government organizes Price Support Scheme (PSS) of the commodities, through various public and cooperative agencies such as FCI, CCI, JCI, NAFED, Tobacco Board, etc., for which the MSPs are fixed. For commodities not covered under PSS, Government also arranges for market intervention on specific request from the States for specific quantity at a mutually agreed price. The losses, if any, are borne by the Centre and State on 50 : 50 basis. The price policy passed by the government of India paid rich dividends in the long run. The Government have raised substantially the MSPs in recent years as may be seen from the statement enclosed.

The National Agricultural Cooperative Marketing Federation of India Ltd. (NAFED), the Central Nodal Agency for implementing price support operations for commercial crops, entered the markets with a view to safeguarding the interest of coconut growers and procured 44,418 quintals of milling copra and 480 quintals of ball copra up to 4th October 2010, as the wholesale prices ruled below their MSPs for 2010 season. During the marketing season 2010-11, month-end wholesale price of TD-5 grade raw jute ruled above the MSP and therefore no procurement was made under the Price Support Scheme.

The considerations of equity, productivity and stability formed the basis for the price policy in India and the main objectives of the price policy in India are as under:

1. To draw reliable price level for the essential agricultural commodities that will have relative costs of the production.
2. To contain the prices of raw materials, equipments, fertilizers, pesticides, etc. utilized in irrigable land with the help of government's financial assistance or the price controls to bring out reasonable terms of trade between the agricultural raw materials and yields.
3. Also to recommend amicable channel for importing highly improvized methods of cultivation for growing commercial crops.
4. Finally establishing some kind of relationships between prices of different crops to make an impact on resource allocation.

MINIMUM SUPPORT PRICE (MSP)

On the domestic front, there has been disprotection of food grains by raising Minimum Support Price (MSP) close to the global market level. As a result, during the period 1993-94 to 1999-2000, prices of cereals in real terms increased at 1.6 per cent whereas prices of non-cereals actually declined. The growth rate of cereal prices was 50 per cent higher than the rate of growth of general prices.

Since cereals account for one-third of total food expenditure, there was adverse effect on cereal consumption, especially by the poor. There has also been an increase in undernourishment. It is cautioned, that unless proper corrective measures are taken to step up food grain production and purchasing power of the farming community, food security is likely to be under threat.

A study making a detailed analysis of the MSP of different crops in the 1990s, brings out clearly that policy decisions turned out to be discriminatory, favouring certain regions and certain crops. The declared MSPs have been in tune with the changes in the costs in the case of paddy, wheat, groundnut and gram. But, in the case of coarse grains like jowar, bajra and ragi, and cotton, the changes in MSP have been less than the rise in costs. Similarly, the regions that gained consistently have been Punjab, Haryana, Uttar Pradesh and Madhya Pradesh.

The MSP for de-husked coconut for 2010 season has been fixed at ₹ 12 per kg, for TD-5 variety of ex-Assam raw jute for 2010-11 season at ₹ 1575 per quintal, and for toria of FAQ variety for 2010-11 to be marketed in 2011-12 at ₹ 1780 per quintal.

SUBSIDIES ON RAW MATERIALS

Government for the past so many years is practicing incentives to farmers and their owners in the form of providing fertilizers, free water for irrigation, free electricity and financial assistance in the form of rural credit from the commercial banks to make the farmers happier. In addition to this subsidization of food grains distributed through Public Distribution System is also being under practice.

PROCUREMENT PRICES

The price fixation is undertaken by the government such that the productive resources are channeled into production of required food commodities and also generates enough income to farmers for decent living and provide for capital formation in agriculture for future production. For the consumers, especially people living below poverty line, it should be at affordable prices. To advice the government to fix minimum support prices and procurement prices, the Agricultural Prices Commission was set up in 1965. Later its name was changed to Commission for Agricultural Costs and Prices (CACP) in 1980 by broadening the terms of reference. The Commission is a statutory body. The Commission submits separate reports recommending prices for Kharif and Rabi season crops.

The Central Government after considering the report of the commission and views of the State Governments and keeping in view the demand and supply situations in the country, takes decision on the level of administered prices. The Commission recommended two sets of prices, minimum support prices and procurement prices.

Minimum Support Price has been fixed by the government to protect the farmers against excessive fall in price during bumper production years. Minimum support price has been assigned a statutory status in case of sugarcane and as such the announced price is termed as statutory minimum price. There is statutory binding on sugar factories to pay the minimum announced price at and all those transactions or purchase at price lower than this are taken as illegal. The minimum support prices for different agricultural crops, viz., food grains, oilseeds, fiber crops, sugarcane and tobacco are announced by the Government of India before the start of the sowing season of the crop.

This makes it possible for the farmer to have an idea about the extent of price insurance cover provided by the government for the crop.

The Directorate of Economics and Statistics, Ministry of Agriculture (DESMOA) is responsible for the collection, compilation and dissemination of the price data of agricultural commodities. The price data are collected in terms of (i) weekly and daily wholesales prices, (ii) retail prices of essential commodities, and (iii) farm harvest prices.

SUMMARY

Though India has made great strides towards increasing foodgrains production since the mid-sixties, still concrete steps have to be undertaken to improve the agriculture sector in India. Anyway today, India ranks high in the production of various commodities such as milk, wheat, rice, fruits, and vegetables. However, the agriculture sector in India is at a crossroads with rising demand for food items and relatively slower supply response in many commodities resulting in frequent spikes in food inflation.

The technological breakthrough achieved in the 1960s is gradually waning. The need for a second green revolution is being experienced more than ever before 1894. Increasing agriculture production and productivity is a necessary condition not only for ensuring national food security, livelihood security, and nutritional security but also for sustaining the high levels of growth envisaged in the current Plan.

However, with very little growth in area and marginal growth in yields of many crops during the last decade, increasing agricultural production remains a challenge. Concerted and focused efforts are required for addressing the challenge of stagnating productivity levels in agriculture. A holistic approach, simultaneously working on agricultural research and development, dissemination of technology, and provision of agricultural inputs such as quality seed, fertilizers, pesticides, and irrigation, would help achieve the critical levels of productivity needed. Further, effective coordination and monitoring of the ongoing agriculture and allied sector programmes need to be ensured for optimum results.

Capital investment in agriculture as a percentage of the GDP has been stagnating in recent years, although the capital expenditure in agriculture as a percentage of the GDP in agriculture has shown some improvement in the current Five Year Plan. It may, however, also be noted that the agriculture sector GDP has itself been stagnating during the last three years from 2007-08 to 2009-10. The real challenge in agriculture sector is to enhance capital investment in the sector both by public and private sector in a sustained way.

QUESTIONS

1. What challenges you foresee in Indian agricultural marketing sector?
2. Elucidate relevant pre-requisites for success in agricultural business marketing.
3. How new Economic Reforms has stimulated the overall growth of Indian agriculture economy?
4. How centre is grappling with the problem of fixing and regulate the price mechanism for agro produce?
5. Are subsidies a suitable mechanism to regulate the price of raw materials and procurement prices and if so in what way? Give your own views.

OOO

CHAPTER 14

GOVERNMENTAL PROGRAMMES FOR RURAL DEVELOPMENT

GOVERNMENTAL PROGRAMMES FOR RURAL DEVELOPMENT

The Government of India focused on various strategies and programmes undertaken for the purpose of rural development in India. These strategies and programmes constitute the "five year plan", for the purpose of simplicity the measures undertaken have been categorized in broad groups and then elaborated upon. In the end, an ideal model of rural development which is in contrast to the current model is proposed.

The rural economy, as much as urban economy, is an integrated part of the overall Indian economy. Any talk of overall development without rural development, particularly in a country where three-quarters of people below the poverty line reside in rural areas, is flawed.

Poverty is indeed a global issue. Its eradication is considered integral to humanity's quest for sustainable development. Reduction of poverty in India is, therefore, vital for the attainment of international goals.

Poverty alleviation has been one of the guiding principles of the planning process in India. This can be substantiated by the fact that anti-poverty programmes have been internalized in the (particularly the ninth) five-year plan. This article sheds light on the various "strategies and programmes" that form the instruments of the plan.

Integrated Rural Development Programmes

First introduced in 1978-79, IRBD has provided assistance to rural poor in the form of subsidy and bank credit for productive employment opportunities through successive plan periods. Subsequently, Training of Rural Youth for Self Employment (TRYSEM), Development of Women and Children in Rural Areas (DWCRA), Supply of Improved Tool Kits to Rural Artisans (SITRA) and Ganga Kalyan Yojana (GKY) were introduced as sub-programmes of IRDP to take care of the specific needs of the rural population.

WAGE EMPLOYMENT PROGRAMMES

Important components of the anti-poverty strategy, Wage Employment Programs sought to achieve multiple objectives. They not only provide employment opportunities during lean agricultural seasons but also in times of floods, droughts and other natural calamities. They create rural infrastructure to support further economic activity. These programmes put an upward pressure on market wage rates by attracting people to public works programmes, thereby reducing labour supply and pushing up demand for labour. It encompasses National Rural Employment Programme (NREP) and Rural Landless Employment Guarantee Programme initially part of 6th and 7th FYPs. In 11th FYP, another measure National Rural Employment Guarantee Act (NREGA) was launched successfully by UPA led government.

Employment Assurance Scheme (EAS)

EAS was launched in October 1993 covering 1,778 drought-prone, desert, tribal and hill area blocks. It was later extended to all the blocks in 1997-98. The EAS was designed to provide employment in the form of manual work in the lean agricultural season. The works taken up under the programme were expected to lead to the creation of durable economic and social infrastructure and address the felt-needs of the people.

FOOD FOR WORK PROGRAMME

The Food for Work Programme was started in 2000-01 as a component of the EAS in eight notified drought-affected states of Chattisgarh, Gujarat, Himachal Pradesh, Madhya Pradesh, Orissa, Rajasthan, Maharashtra and Uttaranchal. The programme aims at food provision through wage employment. Foodgrains are supplied to states free of cost. However, lifting of foodgrains for the scheme from Food Corporation of India (FCI) warehouse have been found to be dismal in their overall performance.

RURAL HOUSING

Initiated in 1985-86, the IAY is the core programme for providing free housing to families in rural areas, targets scheduled castes (SCs)/scheduled tribes (STs), households and freed bonded labourers. The rural housing programme has certainly enabled many BPL families to acquire pucca houses, the coverage of the beneficiaries is limited given the resource constraints. The Samagra Awas Yojana (SAY) was taken up in 25 blocks to ensure convergence of housing, provision of safe drinking water, sanitation and common drainage facilities. The Housing and Urban Development Corporation (HUDCO) has extended its activities to the rural areas, providing loans at a concessional rate of interest to economically weaker sections and low-income group households for construction of houses.

SOCIAL SECURITY PROGRAMMES

Democratic decentralization and centrally supported Social Assistance Programmes were two major initiatives of the government in the 1990s. The National Social Assistance Programme (NSAP), launched in August 1995 marks a significant step towards fulfillment of the Directive Principles of State Policy. The NSAP has three components: (a) National Old Age Pension Scheme (NOAPS); (b) National Family Benefit Scheme (NFBS); and (c) National Maternity Benefit Scheme (NMBS).

The NSAP is a centrally-sponsored programme that aims at ensuring a minimum national standard of social assistance over and above the assistance that states provide from their own resources. The NOAPS provides a monthly pension of ₹ 75 to destitutes and BPL persons above the age of 65. The NFBS is a scheme for BPL families who are given ₹ 10,000 in the event of the death of the breadwinner.

The NMBS provides ₹ 500 to support nutritional intake for pregnant women. In addition to NSAP, the Annapurna scheme was launched from 1st April 2000 to provide food security to senior citizens who were eligible for pension under NOAPS but could not receive it due to budget constraints.

LAND REFORMS

In an agro-based economy, the structure of land ownership is central focus to the well-being of the people. The government has strived to change the ownership pattern of cultivable land, the abolition of intermediaries, the abolition of zamindari, ceiling laws, security of tenure to tenants, consolidation of land holdings and banning of tenancy are a few measures undertaken. Furthermore, a land record management system is a pre-condition for an effective land reform programme. In 1987-88, a centrally-sponsored scheme for Strengthening of Revenue Administration and Updating of Land Records (SRA & ULR) was introduced in Orissa and Bihar.

Drought Prone Area Programme

Drought Prone Area Programme (DPAP) is the earliest area development programme launched by the Central Government in 1973-74 to tackle the special problems faced by those fragile areas, which are constantly affected by severe drought conditions. These areas are characterized by large human and cattle populations which are continuously putting heavy pressure on the already degraded natural resources for food, fodder and fuel. The major problems are continuous depletion of vegetative cover, increase in soil erosion and fall in groundwater levels due to continuous exploitation without any effort to recharge the underground aquifers.

Though the programme had a positive impact in terms of creating durable public assets, its overall impact in effectively containing the adverse effects of drought was not found to be very encouraging. In addition, many of the States had also been demanding inclusion of additional areas under the programme.

With a view to identifying the infirmities in the programme and also for considering the case for inclusion of additional areas under the DPAP for inclusion of additional areas under the programme, a High Level Technical Committee under the chairmanship of Prof. C.H. Hanumantha Rao, Ex-Member Planning Commission was constituted in April 1993 to critically review the contents, methodology and implementation processes of all area development programmes and suggest suitable measures for improvement.

The Committee in its Report submitted in April 1994 had attributed the unsatisfactory performance of the programmes to the following major factors: Implementation of programme activities over vast areas in sectoral and dispersed manner. Inadequate allocations to the programme and programme expenditures thinly spread over large problem areas. Programme implemented through government agencies with least or no participation of the local people. Taking up of a vast array of activities, which were neither properly integrated nor necessarily related to the objectives of the programme.

In Nutshell

Although these measures have been successful (to some extent) in curbing poverty, this model has a very basic flaw. Under this model, resources are transferred from urban economy to rural economy just for short-term political motives. This is affecting both areas, not letting rural economy develop on its own and hampering growth and investments in urban economy.

The subdivision of already small farms in an agricultural model whose profitability is greatly linked to economies of scale makes the survival of the small farmer very difficult. Although the introduction of tractors and other industrial implements, of chemical fertilizers and pesticides, greatly increased the productivity of land and labour, it has not come without considerable burdens for the small farmer who is finding it very hard to compete with large and medium farmers. In most industrial nations, the introduction of such practices in the countryside has been accompanied by a gradual reduction in the rural population so that those who remain on the land can enjoy so.

An ideal approach should include the government, panchayats and key village people, NGOs and private companies. This will not only help reduce this imbalance but will have a multiplier effect on the overall economy. By aligning the goals of the two parts, we can convert this seemingly zero sum game into a win-win situation. It would be a very long drawn and difficult battle with conventions but the reward is worth the effort.

ECONOMIC REFORMS IN AGRICULTURE

There is no doubt that economic reforms have been able to promote the relatively higher growth. After the teething troubles of the first two years – 1991-92 and 1992-93, the growth rate during 1993-94 to 1997-98 has averaged to more than 7 per cent per annum. After 1991-92, the momentum of growth has been maintained providing increasing evidence that the growth potential has improved as a result of the reforms initiated in 1991.

If we compare the annual average growth rate during the pre-reform period (1980-81 to 1990-91) which was of the order of 5.2 per cent per annum and then the post-reform decade (1990-91 to 2000-01) also shows a little higher average annual growth rate of 5.8 per cent of real GDP. However, there is distinct improvement in growth rate of GDP during the 6th Five Year Plan period (2000-01 to 2006-07) to an average of 7.6 per cent which is good sign indeed.

GDP Growth at Factor Cost at 1999-00 Prices

Year	GDP (₹ in crore)
1980-81	6,41,919
1990-91	10,67,694
2000-01	18,45,755
2001-02	19,51,935
2002-03	20,29,482
2003-04	22,04,913
2004-05	23,66,886
2005-06*	25,93,160
2006-07**	28,45,155
2007-08	37,00,328
2008-09	38,00,695
2009-10	40,00,745

Source: CSO/Economic Survey

Per Capita Income and Consumption at 2004-05 Prices

Year	Income		Consumption	
	₹	(%) Growth	₹	(%) Growth
2004-05	29,745		17,620	
2005-06	32,012	7.6	18,909	7.3
2006-07	34,533	7.9	20,168	6.7
2007-08	37,328	8.1	21,841	8.3
2008-09	38,695	3.7	23,012	5.4
2009-10	40,745	5.3	23,626	2.7

Source: CSO.

Note: Income is taken as GDP at market prices. Consumption is PECE.

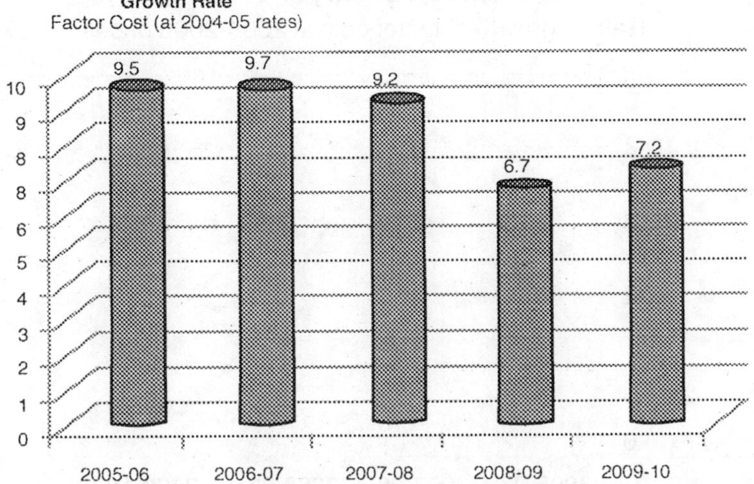

Source: Economic Survey
Graphics: www.gktoday.in

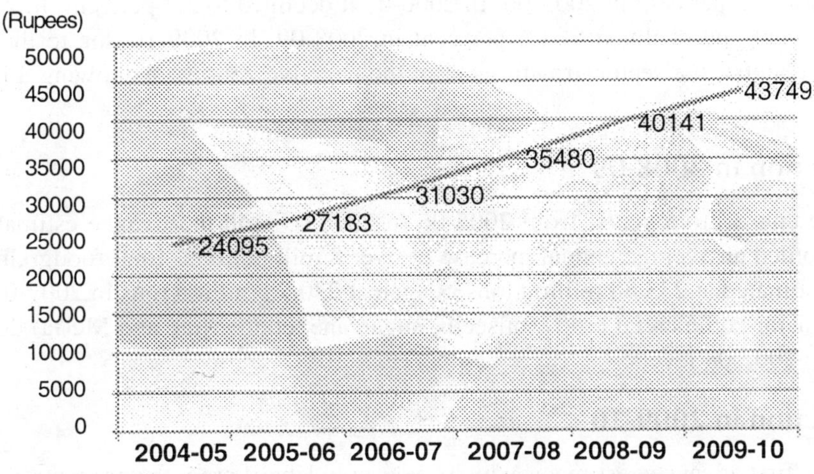

Source: Economic Survey 2009-10
Graphics: www.gktoday.in

In 2009-10, the Agriculture, Forestry and Fishing shows a **decline of 0.2** per cent while Service Sector shows maximum growth. The overall sectoral growth (Agriculture) rate at factor cost at 2004-05 prices is shown as follows:

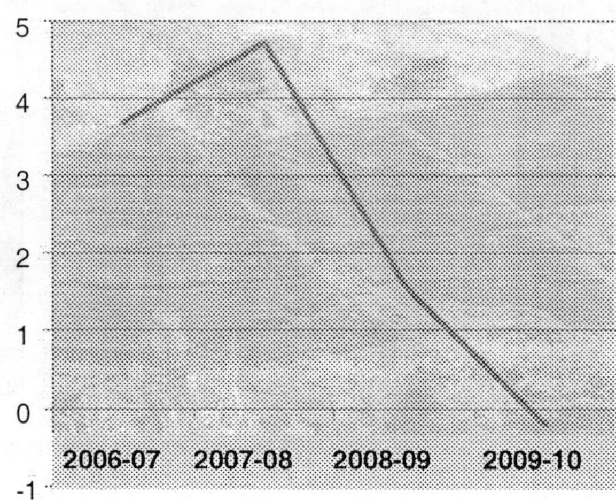

Source: CSO
Graphic: www.gktoday.in

The growth rate of Agriculture, Forestry and Fishing, which is also known as primary Sector of our economy, was 5.2 per cent in 2005-06. In 2006-07 it declined to 3.7 per cent. In 2007-08, it again rose to 4.7 per cent and declined to 1.6 per cent in 2008-09. In 2009-10 due to the poor monsoon throughout the country, the sector growth went in the negative zone with showing a negative 0.2 per cent growth.

Crop Production in 2008-09

For three consecutive years, from 2005-06 to 2008-09 (fourth advance estimates), foodgrains production recorded an average annual increase of over 8 million tons. Total foodgrains production in 2008-09 was estimated at 233.88 million tons as against 230.78 million tons in 2007-08. However, the production of major commercial crops (oilseeds, sugarcane, cotton, jute and Mesta) declined in 2008-09 compared to 2007-08 levels.

Crop Production in 2009-10

As per the first advanced estimates which cover only Kharif crop, the production of foodgrains is estimated at 98.33 million tons, as against fourth advanced estimates of 2008-09 and target of 125.15 million tons for 2009-10. Thus, there is an overall decline of 18.51 million tons over 2008-09.

Rice: As per the first advance estimates, the production of kharif rice is at 71.65 million tons in 2009-10, a decrease of about 15 per cent over 2008-09 levels and 17 per cent over the target for 2009-10.

Coarse Cereals: Total Kharif production of coarse cereals in 2009-10 is expected to decline to 22.76 million tons against 28.34 million tons in 2008-09 and a target of 32.65 million tons for Kharif 2009-10.

Cereals: The overall production of Kharif cereals in 2009-10 is expected to decline by 18.51 million tons over 2008-09.

Pulses: Total production of Kharif pulses is estimated at 4.42 million tons in 2009-10, which is 8 per cent lower than the production during 2008-09 and 32 per cent lower than the targeted production for 2009-10.

Oilseeds: Total Kharif production of the nine oilseeds is estimated at 152.33 lakh tons in 2009-10, which is about 15 per cent lower than the Kharif production in 2008-09.

Sugarcane: Sugarcane production in 2009-10 is estimated at 249.48 million tons, which is lower than the production of 273.93 million tons during 2008-09. This represents a decline of 9 per cent over the previous year and 27 per cent *vis-à-vis* the targeted production for 2009-10.

Cotton: Cotton production in 2009-10 is estimated at 236.57 lakh bales (of 170 kg each), which is higher than the fourth advance estimates of 231.56 lakh bales in 2008-09 by 2.2 per cent.

Jute and Mesta: The production of jute and mesta is estimated at 102.43 lakh bales (of 180 kg each) in 2009-10. This is lower than the targeted production of 112.00 lakh bales and also lower than the 104.07 lakh bales produced in 2008-09.

Area under Food Crops

1. The total area coverage of 667.84 lakh hectare under total foodgrains scheme during Kharif 2009-10 compared to 714.02 lakh hectares during Kharif 2008-09 shows a decline of 46.18 lakh hectares.
2. The area coverage under Kharif rice during 2009-10 is around 361.62 lakh hectares, which is 44.85 lakh hectares less than the 406.47 lakh hectares during Kharif 2008-09.
3. The area coverage under oilseeds during Kharif 2009-10 is 175.19 lakh hectares, which is lower by 9.49 lakh hectares than Kharif 2008-09.
4. The area coverage under sugarcane during the current year is 41.78 lakh hectares, which is also lower by about 2.18 lakh hectares than that in the previous year.

Role of Poor Monsoon

1. India received 23 per cent less rainfall compared to an average rainfall (LPA) India has received. (It is called Long period Average LPA).
2. The central India experienced a 20 per cent deficiency in the rainfalls, while, North-east India experienced 27 per cent decline, North-west India experienced 36 per cent decline (maximum) while Southern peninsula experienced 4 per cent decline (minimum).

Seeds:

1. In India, more than 4/5th of farmers rely upon farm saved seeds leading to a low seed replacement rate.
2. The Indian Seed program includes the participation of Central and State governments, ICAR, State agricultural Universities and the cooperative and private sectors.
3. India has 15 State Seed Corporations and 2 national level seed corporations, viz., National Seed Corporation and State Farm Corporation of India.

FERTILIZERS: NEW PROGRAMMES

Agri Ministry Favours Liquid Fertilizers

In an effort to revolutionarize sale of nutrient based fertilizers and with a view to increase the soil productivity, the union agriculture ministry recently express its interest to consider the proposal to introduce liquid fertilizers. This is based on the recommendation of a working group set up to study and recommend measures to increase agricultural production.

The report revealed micro irrigation can be combined with controlled application of fertilizers and other needed nutrients and to this effect the group has suggested usage of liquid fertilizers. Currently India does not have facilities for producing liquid fertilizers and therefore the group is of the view that liquid fertilizers should not only be freed from import duties but also be made eligible for subsidies in line with newly introduced nutrient based subsidy scheme.

The recommendation has cited the case of Tamil Nadu where productivity has considerably gone up by combining the usage of micro irrigation and liquid fertilizers otherwise known as precision farming. Liquid fertilizers usually the mixture of urea and ammonium nitrate dissolved in water, are directly used as plant and soil supplement. As with solid fertilizers, plants do not have to convert nitrogen into usable form. However, experts said it also had some disadvantages if the urea using the fertilizers was not protected. Liquid nitrogen swing into groundwater imbalanced the ocean ecosystem.

These recommendations have been made in the light of the fact that while average fertilizer consumption has gone up by 50 per cent since 2004-05 productivity of foodgrains grew only by 1 per cent during the period. The Government has introduced a nutrient based subsidy policy this year and thereafter has been introduced for micronutrients like boron and zinc.

The recommendations also include fortifying the infrastructure for soil testing so as to encourage farmers to buy the right kind of nutrient mix in fertilizers. For this, the report suggested the issuing soil health cards to all farmers by using resources under the National Project on Management of Soil Health and Fertility as well as the Rashtriya Krishi Vikas Yojana.

Besides this, private sector companies have been urged to intensify nutrient management efforts by the State governments by formulating and introducing new products, including crop and location specific customized fertilizers. These could be included under the Fertilizer (Control) Order 1985 in consultation with the Indian Council of Agricultural Research (ICAR).

Government's Initiatives

1. A number of measures have been taken by Government of India to improve fertilizer application in our country.
2. In this context. National Project on Management of Soil Health and Fertility (NPMSF), has been introduced in 2008-09 with a view to setting up of 500 new Soil Testing Laboratories (STLs) and 250 Mobile Soil Testing Laboratories (MSTLs) and strengthening of the existing State STLs for micronutrient analysis.
3. In order to ensure adequate availability of fertilizers of standard quality to farmers and to regulate trade, quality and distribution in the country, fertilizers have been declared an essential commodity as per the Fertilizer Control Order (FCO) 1985 promulgated under Section 3 of the Essential Commodity Act 1955.

4. The procedure for incorporation of new products has been liberalized and simplified to encourage manufacture and use of fortified fertilizers.
5. Eight fertilizers have been specified as fortified fertilizers in FCO 1985. To encourage balanced use of fertilizers, a new concept of customized fertilizers has been introduced.
6. These fertilizers are soil specific and crop specific. Organic fertilizers, namely city-based compost and vermin compost, and bio-fertilizers, namely rhizobium, azotobacter, azospirillum and phosphate solubilizing bacteria, have been recognized and incorporated in FCO 1985.

Fertilizers: Consumption

1. The following Graphic shows the consumption of fertilizers in India for the 2009-10 (only kharif season).

Fertilizer Consumption in Nutrient Terms during 2009-10

(Only Kharif Season)

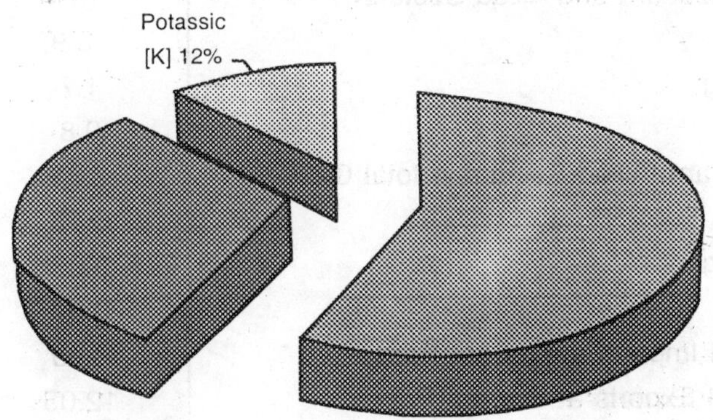

Quantitative Values (in lakh tons)
Phosphatic: 41.82 lakh tons
Potassic: 16.07 lakh tons
Nitrogeneous: 74.86 lakh tons

Source: Department of Fertilizers
Graphics: www.gktoday.in

2. **Overall Consumption:** Overall consumption of fertilizers per hectare has increased steadily from 105.5 kgs in 2005-06, to 111.80 in 2006-07, 116.80 in 2007-08 and 128.6 in 2008-09.
3. **India's Total Consumption:** India's total consumption of the fertilizers (N+P+K) has been 203.40 lakh tons in 2005-06, 216.51 lakh tons in 2006-07, 225.70 lakh tons in 2007-08 and 249. lakh tons in 2008-09. For the Kharif Season of 2009-10, it is 132.25 lakh tons.

In nutshell, there was good monsoon between 2005-06 and 2008-09 and the efforts of our farmers led to consistent increase in food production during the period and a record production of 233.88 million tons of foodgrains in 2008-09. Notwithstanding the fact that the south-west monsoon was the most deficient since 1972, by 23 per cent compared to the long period average (LPA), the overall agricultural gross domestic product (GDP) is estimated to have fallen by only 0.2 per cent in 2009-10 (advance estimates) as against the previous year's growth rate of 1.6 per cent.

Foodgrain area sown in kharif season declined by 6.5 per cent compared to last year and food production is expected to be short by 16 per cent compared to the fourth advance estimates of 2008-09. Rising food prices, spurred by expectations of shortfall in food production, have brought the issues of food security, food stocks management and need for improving food production and productivity to the forefront of national strategy.

Agriculture including crop and animal husbandry, fisheries, forestry and agro processing provides the underpinnings of our food and livelihood security. Agriculture provides significant support for economic growth and social transformation of the country as one of the world's largest agrarian economies.

Agriculture Sector: Key Indicators at Constant Prices (2004-05) in per cent

Item	2007-08	2008-09
1. Growth in GDP in Agriculture and Allied Sectors	4.7	1.6
Agriculture	5.0	1.1
Forestry and Logging	2.2	2.9
Fishing	6.0	6.3
2. Share in GDP – Agriculture and Allied Sectors	16.4	15.7
Agriculture	13.9	13.2
Forestry and Logging	1.7	1.7
Fishing	0.8	0.8
Share of Agriculture and Allied Sectors in total GCF	7.01	9.05
Agriculture	6.43	8.39
Forestry and Logging	0.07	0.09
Fishing	0.51	0.58
Share — Agricultural Imports at Current Prices	2.95	2.74
Share — Agricultural Exports at Current Prices	12.05	10.23
Employment in the Agriculture Sector		
Total Employment in 2004-05 as per CDS		52.1

Source: Central Statistical Organization (CSO) and Department of Agriculture as shown in Economic Survey

ACHIEVEMENTS FROM FIVE YEAR PLANS IN NUTSHELL

The Five Year plans have given prime importance to the agriculture sector and rural development and rural people's employment. Land and water management systems were developed with an aim of providing uniform growth. Our agriculture sector achieved green reveloution during 1970s after that we created white revolution in milk production.

Despite some stagnation during the later modern era, the policymakers were not concentrated on the development of comprehensive agricultural programmes and rural development compared to urban development and industrial development. Nearly 21.1 per cent of the entire rural population of India exists in difficult physical and financial predicament. But rate of poverty in urban population is 15 per cent. In general, the Government controls the Indian economy, and there remains a great disparity between the rich and the poor.

However, the service sector is greatly expanding and has started to assume an increasingly important role. The fact that the English speaking population in India is growing by the day means that India has become a hub of outsourcing activities for some of the major economies of the world including the

United Kingdom and the United States. Outsourcing to India has been primarily in the areas of technical support and customer services.

Other areas where India is expected to make progress include manufacturing, construction of ships, pharmaceuticals, aviation, biotechnology, tourism, nanotechnology, retailing and telecommunications. Growth rates in these sectors are expected to increase dramatically. But on the other side, the slowdown in agricultural growth has become a major cause for concern. India's rice yields are one-third of China's and about half of those in Vietnam and Indonesia.

Due to rapid urbanization and industrialization, use of agriculture land is reduced. During the last one decade, agriculture lands are converted in to residential houses and factories. Hence, the number of agriculture labours lost their work and moved to urban areas. This leads to low output in agricultural products, insufficiency and rise in food articles prices. Number of surveys said that the world will go to face food insufficiency in near future.

In India, maximum of landholders fall under the category of small farmers, so they are not able to meet out the increasing input cost and not able to introduce any new technological machineries in their farms, due to this reason our "*farmers are born in debt, live in debt and die in debt*".

Infrastructure is also a significant factor in the process of development but country like ours rural India has not possessed the required infrastructure such as roads, electricity, fertilizers and pesticides availability which caused the vulnerable damage to the growth of agriculture. While India has a wide network of rural finance institutions, many of the rural poor remain excluded, due to inefficiencies in the formal finance institutions, the weak regulatory framework, high transaction costs, and risks associated with lending to agriculture.

Farmers' access to markets is hampered by poor roads, rudimentary market infrastructure, excessive regulation and middlemen intervention in selling the products is very big problem in marketing the products. Hence, the Indian farmers need easily accessible and highly structured markets without middlemen interventions.

Indian agriculture policy allow some foreign companies to introduce dangerous genetic engineering technologies in seeds (GMS) and shift towards foodgrains to cash crops. It may be helpful to the farmers in one way in initial periods but using this type of GMS and by shifting our production system from foodgrains to cash crops in future we will loose our traditional seeds.

Now we are seriously talking about fuel and its importance and there are more arguments and problem will come for "***food or fuel***". An estimated 100 million tons of grain per year are being redirected from food to fuel. (Total worldwide grain production for 2007 was just over 2000 million tons. As farmers devoted larger parts of their crops to fuel production than in previous years, land and resources available for food production were reduced correspondingly. This has resulted in less food available for human consumption.

Irrigation is key to agricultural production. Irrigation facilities are inadequate, as revealed by the fact that only 52.6 per cent of the land was irrigated in 2003-04, which resulted in farmers still being dependent on rainfall, specifically the monsoon season. A good monsoon results in a robust growth for the economy as a whole, while a poor monsoon leads to a sluggish growth. The government must allocate funds to start the new irrigation projects to increase the cultivation.

creating a viable model of public-private partnership that allows private investors to invest in agriculture infrastructure in partnership with banks and financial institutions. This will help the farmers to access the high quality technologies and increase the output with international standards to meet the global market requirements.

The policymakers in India have a high responsibility on reducing poverty by raising agricultural productivity and developing the rural population economic status from deprived condition. However, bold action from policymakers will be required to shift away from the existing subsidy-based regime that is no longer sustainable, to build a solid foundation for a highly productive, internationally competitive, and diversified agricultural sector.

The government should instruct to the all universities, colleges, private and Government offices and manufacturing industries, canteens to sell agricultural products like tender coconut, cucumber, watermelon, fruits etc., to enhance and promote the agricultural products in these areas it will help the farmers to get good demand and price for their products.

We need more number of Agriculture universities and agriculture colleges in India to promote research and development in this area because majority of the population depends upon this sector for their livelihood. So, the government should concentrate and give more importance to the research and development in rural and agricultural sector.

Total population of India as well as total population of the world has been rapidly increasing. There is no question that improving standards of living for the current poor of the world, plus providing for the billions still to come, will increase global demand for food and levels of per capita consumption are so high. But the rate of foodgrains growth is substantially slower than the average population growth rate. Worldwide about two billion people have been starving without food security and 825 million people are chronically malnourished, according to a recent estimate by UN Food and Agriculture Organization (FAO).

Hence, there is urgent need for the policymakers and government to take responsible steps to improve the agricultural sector and eradicate poverty and food starvation in the world. Agricultural commodity futures are market-based instruments for managing risks and orderly establishment of efficient agricultural markets. These are used to hedge commodity price risks. The hedging and price discovery function of the future markets promote more efficient production, storage, marketing and agro-processing operations and help in improving overall agricultural marketing performance.

Commodity trading is just one step in solving the complex Indian agriculture problems. Although formalized future trading in agricultural commodities has been in place since 1918-19, the future trading in commodity through commodity exchanges came to its own very recently. But the trade was mostly in the form of forward contracts. Although India has a long history of trade in commodity derivatives, this sector remained underdeveloped due to government intervention in many commodity markets to control prices. Free trade in many agricultural commodities is restricted under the Essential Commodities Act (ECA) 1955 and Agriculture Produce Marketing Committees Act (APMC) of various states.

The forward and futures contracts till April 2003 was limited to only a few commodities items under the Forward Contracts Regulation Act (FCRA) 1952. However, in 2003, Government of India removed all restrictions on commodities which could be traded on commodity exchanges. At present, 25 commodity exchanges are in operation in India carrying out futures trading in as many as 81 commodity items. Most of these exchanges are regional and commodity specific. National Multi Commodity Exchange (NMCE) status has been accorded to four commodity exchanges, namely, National Multi Commodity

Exchange (NMCE), Ahmedabad; National Board of Trade; (NBOT), Indore, National Commodity Derivative Exchange (NCDEX), Mumbai and Multi Commodity Exchange (MCX), Mumbai during 2003. These exchanges have excellent financial backing, demutualized ownership structure and more transparent electronic trading system. The Forward Markets Commission (FMC) established under FCRA 1952 is the agency which regulates commodity derivatives trading in India in the same way as SEBI does for securities markets.

In some areas, farmers are gradually getting aware of futures prices which are disseminated through exchanges. In the capital market, spot market developed before the derivatives market which made the things easier. In the commodity space, the derivatives have come before the so-called integrated spot market. Future market is a boon to the farmers.

Under the prevailing scenario, Commission for Agricultural Costs and Prices (CACP) recommends Minimum Support Prices (MSP) with no guarantee that farmers will get that price. Generally, MSP acts as the maximum price that is paid to farmers. Open-ended purchase could continue to be made at MSP as floor price. Exchanges should be able to offer market-based options at strike prices higher than the MSP. Be able to offer market-based options at strike prices higher than MSP.

Budget fails to meet the expectations of participants in the commodity future markets as the needed reforms facilitating the growth of commodity markets have been avoided. Introduction of Commodity Transaction Tax (CTT) in line with Securities Transaction Tax (STT) is a negative move for the commodity market when market is still evolving seeking larger participants and volumes.

Moreover, the long- and short-term capital gains benefits extended to securities market has not been extended to commodities trading. On the other hand, the decision is significant in the wake of commodities markets regulator to institutionalize the development of market mechanism, support institutions, capacity building and development of strong forward and backward linkages between market, producers, traders and consumers and the Forward Markets Commission receiving more autonomy to deal efficiently with the challenges facing the commodities futures markets with the approval of Forward Contracts (Regulation) Act and Foreign Direct Investment (FCI)/Foreign Institutional Investors (FIIs) Investments in commodities sector.

It showed an increased interest of the government in expanding the commodity futures markets in line with the equity markets. Securities markets are eight times larger than the commodities market and hence the levy is premature. The functioning of securities markets is different from that of commodities markets. Commodities markets are global asset class and trade flowed to the most efficient markets that bore the least cost of trading.

Commodity markets are still in the nascent stage (4 years old) and a fraction of the size ($1/5^{th}$) of the securities markets. It would increase the cost of trading by at least four times. Future trading in wheat, rice, tur and urad had already been suspended by the FMC. Efficient functioning of futures markets pre-supposes the existence of efficient spot markets. Currently, physical spot markets have large numbers of infirmities. It will be difficult for the futures markets to function till these are removed. Commodity markets in India need structural changes for increasing depth and curbing of speculative activity.

Banks, FIIs and other institutions should be permitted to trade in the commodity markets. National Commodity spot markets need significant legislative and administrative support for taking off. Banks, FIIs and other institutions should be permitted to trade in commodity markets. Commodity options need to be developed. The setting up of national electronic exchanges by the national commodity exchanges is an attempt to create a national integrated market. The vibrant agriculture markets including derivatives markets are the frontline institutions to provide early sign of future prospect of the sector. Vibrancy in these markets gives signal about commodities which deserves flow of investment. All the regulators operating within the commodity markets scope work in cohesion.

SUMMARY

Agri-business management can be interpreted types of activities with agriculture including, farming, management, financing, processing, marketing, growing of seeds and nursery stock, manufacture of fertilizers, chemicals, implements, processing, machinery and transportation equipment and the process of transportation itself.

The agri-business management has been treated as pure and applied science as coordinating scientific formulae of supplying agricultural production inputs and subsequently producing, processing and distributing food and fiber. This science includes all business enterprises that buy from or sell to the farmers – the transactions including either a product – commodity or a service and encompass items such as productive resources (feed, seed, fertilizers, equipments, energy and machinery. Also agricultural commodities with all food and fiber besides facilitative services credit, insurance, marketing, storage, processing, transportation, packaging and distribution etc.

The government's initiative to inject and pump required amount of budgetary allocation in the form of economic reforms have necessitated professionalism in vital sectors of the Indian economy. Transformation of the agriculture sector into a competitive sector calls for professional management and use of modern technologies in areas such as specialized production, post-harvest management, promotion of value-added agri-products, supply chain management, etc., so as to position these competitively both in the domestic as well as in international markets. Agribusiness Management Education is now a priority area in the country, as several State Agricultural Universities and Agricultural Institutes have added MBA (Agribusiness) and equivalent programs to their educational systems over the past one decade.

QUESTIONS

1. How governments that are forming at the centre successively making their efforts by introducing different programmes of their own aiming at rural development and has it been successfully and if so in what way?
2. What do you mean by Integrated Rural Development Programme (IRDP)?
3. Elucidate whether Rural Housing scenario is in dilapidated condition or in vibrant condition. Give your own reasons.
4. How far land reforms policy has attained its success in Indian agricultural economy?
5. Why governments at centre prefer Liquid Fertilizer system than traditional manures and fertilizer system?

ooo

UNIT - 4

CHAPTER

15

LINKAGES OF AGRO INDUSTRIES TO INDIAN ECONOMY

Linkages of Agro Industries to Indian Economy

Agriculture-RNA Linkage

Consumption Linkages

RNEF Linkages

Uniqueness of Agro Industries

Agro Industrial Linkages

Historical Background

Village Industry Programmes

LINKAGES OF AGRO INDUSTRIES TO INDIAN ECONOMY

The progress of Indian economy depends to larger extent on the application of science and technology for the exploitation of agricultural raw materials into numerous consumer and industrial products thus accelerating the process of industrialization without sacrificing agricultural development resulting in the conversion of agricultural economies to industrial economies through the agri-industry linkages.

Primary agricultural commodity and organic residue, animal by-product and waste, fishery and forestry by-products etc., can contribute to the economic development of a series of industries if the primary commodity, its bi-products and waste matter are scientifically processed.

Discussions about the potential economic benefits of agriculture-industry linkages as instruments for achieving inclusive industrial development in the agriculture-dominated countries are common in the development literature emerged which estimated the magnitude of growth linkages between the agricultural sector and the rural non-farm sector in the context of selected East and South-east Asian countries.

These studies convincingly demonstrated that a broad-based growth of the rural economy based on close linkages between agriculture and rural non-farm sector encompassing both rural informal and formal manufacturing, trade and service activities, played, crucial role towards setting in motion or virtuous cycle of comprehensive economic growth in these countries.

In South Asian region, Indian agricultural prosperity needs to be deliberately stimulated to foster the growth of a dynamic rural non-farm activities sector (RNAs). The development of a vibrant RNA sector stimulates forward linkages with the rural towns and urban economy through growth of agro-processing and light manufacturing industries and service activities and subsequently produce for competitive export markets capitalizing on the cheap labour and low overhead expenses.

Most importantly, the growth of industries in the rural areas leads to a modernizing transformation in the rural economy, helps diversification of the rural production structure, establishment of backward and forward intra- and inter-sectoral linkages and facilitates the growth of rural townships which provides the incentives for spread of large-scale urban manufacturing and small-scale labour-intensive industries in the rural and peri-urban locations.

In a densely populated labour surplus Indian economy such agro-industrial linkages can play a crucial role in generating rural income and employment, earning foreign exchanges, and thereby igniting the process of a pro-poor, equitable and inclusive national economic growth.

AGRICULTURE-RNA's LINKAGES

Theoretical perspectives: In the process of transformation of the production structure in the rural economy, growth and expansion of the rural non-farm economy is one of the most important steps by which agricultural growth fosters economic growth. The farm sector can contribute to the growth of the non-farm sector through linkings via production, consumption, and labour markets.

On the production side, the linkages are both backward and forward. A growing agriculture using modern technology requires inputs such as fertilizer, seeds, pesticides, pumps, sprayers and machinery repairing services either produced or distributed by the non-farm firms. Further, increased agricultural output stimulates forward production linkages by providing raw materials that require milling, spinning, canning and other forms of processing and distribution by the non-farm enterprises.

CONSUMPTION LINKAGES

Consumption linkage (also termed as 'income' linkage) arise and become significant when growing farm incomes boost the demand for a range of consumer goods and services produced in the adjacent villages and rural towns. Diversification of the consumption of non-farm goods increases rapidly with rise in per capita incomes, with higher expenditure elasticity for home improvements, durables, services, transport, and education. Other than the level of per capita income, the strength of the consumption linkage also depends on the distribution of income and nature of technological change in agriculture across the geographical regions.

Agricultural growth also influences the supply side of the rural non-farm economy through the labour market. With increased productivity in agriculture, either labour is rewarded or wages will go up. Agricultural wages determine the opportunity cost of labour in the non-farm sector, while seasonality of labour demand in agriculture affects availability. Nevertheless, wages tend to increase if the non-farm economy expands due to increase in demand and in labour productivity. This is a push-pull situation where the non-farm sector is attracting labour out of the farm sector towards better-paying jobs. A converse or the 'push' situation can occur if there is a growing surplus of rural workers that the agricultural sector is unable to absorb at the prevailing wage rates. Workers in such cases are pushed out of agriculture into low productivity work in the rural non-farm economy.

Formal econometric studies required to look into the nature and magnitude of growth linkages between agricultural income and non-farm incomes and, or, employment are rather scanty. Most of the studies have been conducted in the Indian context in different regions of the country. The findings showed that the income multipliers had significant positive impacts (i.e., $1 dollar increase in agricultural value added led to an additional $ 1.0 value added in the rural non-farm economy (RNFE) etc.) on the growth of both non-farm employment and income.

The income multipliers resulting from high agricultural growth were found to be strong in the regions with better infrastructure (i.e., Punjab and Haryana), higher per capita agricultural incomes, pragmatic rural non-farm development policies and high population density.

AGRICULTURE-RNFE LINKAGES

Empirical perspectives and implications for Indian agriculture: A universal characteristic of economic development is the structural change in the productive sectors especially in agriculture towards a modernizing transformation. The onset of rapid economic growth in Asia which was stimulated significantly by a technology-driven agricultural growth precipitated a process of transformation of structure of production across economic sectors. Except few island states of Hong Kong, China and Singapore, all the rapidly growing Asian economies enjoyed successful agrarian revolutions prior to their industrialization.

An agricultural revolution is needed not only to overcome the food supply constraint but also to provide an engine of growth on the scale required to transform the national economy. Most Asian countries that experienced fastest growth were benefited significantly by the support provided by a dynamic and rapidly growing agricultural sector.

The broad-based and rapid growth in agriculture freed up labour and capital for the non-farm economy (through mobilizing rural savings while raising land and commodity-taxes) maintained a downward pressure on the food prices and key primary inputs for agro-industrial enterprises. This resulted in giving much-needed impetus in the form of foreign exchange earning through reduced food imports and increased agricultural exports. Further, this led to rapid growth in the rural non-farm economy but also contributed to the transformation of urban economy.

The agricultural growth fostered the development of the agro-industrial sector, particularly firms that supplied key inputs (machinery, fertilizer, cement etc.) and that processed agricultural output (food industry, textiles, jute etc.). These activities were often the breeding grounds for the development of private enterprises that later entered the export markets. Their growth also fostered the development of managerial skills and urban infrastructures which permitted subsequent diversification into new non-farm activities.

The rural non-farm economy emerged as a major driver of economic growth in its own sphere not only for the countryside but also for the national economy as a whole. Needless to say, such growth often has important welfare implication for woman and the poor households for achieving inclusive industrial growth helping to offset inequalities and unleashing forces of rural poverty reduction.

Agricultural growth, prior to urban-based modern manufacturing growth has transformed rural regions, providing thereby more diversified sources of income for the rural households with increased livelihood opportunities without encouraging large-scale migration into the urban cities. The growth of the rural non-farm economy led to development of small rural towns and surrounding economic hinterlands that dominated by agro-industrial firms and service establishments.

Another salutary spillover effect of healthy agricultural growth in Indian economy prior to its achieving an explosive manufacturing growth during mid 1970s and 1980s was its role in raising rural household incomes and living standards of rural population unleashed by a massive increase in domestic demand for the non-agricultural goods and services. This provided growing market for spawning growth of non-agricultural firms. Empirical studies depict links between agrarian growth and the rural non-farm sector growth in many states.

The rural non-farm activities (RNAs) defined to include everything except primary agricultural production assuring an increasingly important role in the economic landscape of India particularly in the rural areas.

RNAs in India account for 50% of total rural employment as well as similar proportion of rural household incomes. The average labour productivity in the RNAs appears slightly higher than the agricultural wage rate. The implication is that the rural poor, especially land-poor and landless would be better off by shifting from farms to non-farm occupations which entail higher earnings offering viable option for broad-based economic growth and poverty alleviation.

The policy will, therefore, formulate comprehensive proactive policies to develop appropriate institutional framework to ensure mainstreaming of RNA development in the overall national development strategies and policies. Unfortunately, RNA developmental policies still tend to be piecemeal effort or offshoot of policies targeted at other parts of the national economy. As a result, there remain huge knowledge and information gaps in the non-farm development as important missing pieces in developing an integrated rural development strategy for the country. Not surprisingly, in such a backdrop, macro, trade, labour, agricultural and industrial sector policies fail to identify critical constraints to non-farm sector growth and address them properly to facilitate their promotion and expansion.

UNIQUENESS OF AGRO-INDUSTRIES

Agro-industrial projects are unique because of the seasonality, perishability and variability of raw materials.

Unlike the nonfarm industrial sector, the farm sector have to deal with supply and demand together with imbalances problems of inventories, production scheduling and coordination of the production and the processing and marketing sections of the producer to the consumer chain.

Because of the perishable nature of the biological raw materials, agro-industrial products require greater speed and care in handling and storage which can effect the nutritional quality of the products by reducing the deterioration of the produce.

Additional pressure is exerted on the agro-industrial plants, production scheduling and the quality control operations on account of the variability in the quantity and the quality of the agricultural raw materials.

As the raw materials are the major cost component of the agro industries, procurement, operations fundamentally shape the economics of the operations.

AGRO-INDUSTRIAL LINKAGES

The application of science and technology has a snowball effect on the progress of industrialization and the economic development. Scientific information of the agricultural raw material and their commercial and industrial potential has led to the development of processing technologies, machinery and plant design and the establishment of agro processing enterprises. On the one hand, technologies were designed to suit the processing requirements of a particular raw material, while on the other hand varietal changes were introduced to suit the equipments of the post-harvest handling technologies thus leading to a two-way link between the agriculture and industry.

HISTORICAL BACKGRUOND

There are four phases – first one traces the socio-economic environment of the pre-independence era wherein Indian nationalist view on rural industries got crystallized. Traditionally, Indian agriculture depended in the main upon, input resources of its own. Agriculture provided raw materials to industry; industry's contribution to agriculture was, however, marginal. The agro-industry relationships were uni-directional due to British machine-made products, imported into India, offered a cheap substitute for the Indian cottage and rural industries and handicrafts in turn threatened employment opportunities in the countryside.

The second one provides a brief critique of the anti-machine, *Swadeshi* and pro-*Khadi* and village industries approach to rural industrialization pleaded for reservation of consumer goods sector for the cottage and small-scale production. This strategy saw employment angle as a significant factor along with a reduction of pressure on the limited capital resources of the economy. Specific programs and schemes were evolved for protection and promotion of village industries, crafts and specified rural activities.

The third one traces the developments of the eighties under which agro industries received a new impetus with Foreign direct investment that has now been invited to food processing sectors. The process of liberalization has resulted in reduction of regulations and controls thereby led to constitution of new Ministry for Food Processing Industries.

The fourth one discusses the place and role of agro-industries in the present-day context. It argues that there is a need to have a fresh and comprehensive review and to develop clusters of villages as complexes which specialize in production of specified types of crops along with multiple related activities. The objective of the area approach has to be the introduction of specialization in crop production, installation of wide scale and intensive processing to gain the maximum value addition within the region.

To pursue these objectives, it would be necessary to adopt a variety of new policies and have a plan for skill formation and information spread to evolve socio-economic and organizational institutions to make the new policies a success.

Traditionally, Indian agriculture drew most of its inputs locally from the village and the farm. Modern inputs like chemicals, fertilizers, pesticides, tractors and other agricultural implements, pump sets, diesel, gas and power had little impact in the overall agricultural inputs. Agro-industries were essentially perceived as first level post-harvest processing of farm produce. Agro, village, cottage and rural industries meant the same set of economic activities and expressions were interchangeable. Even when agro-industries have been assigned a special place in the successive Five Year Plans, a great deal of confusion continues to persist regarding their coverage. It is not very clear whether agro-industries are to denote only the activities directly related to agriculture or the total farm output and related activities. A broad-based classification on this would help appropriate classification of dairy farming, poultry, piggery and other farm activities. Similarly, a clear-cut view should be taken on whether tea, coffee, rubber, spices and other plantations are to be classified as a category separate from agricultural activity.

Indian political leadership identified itself with the Indian artisans and craftsmen were adversely affected by the competition from abroad. The call for *Swadeshi* and boycott of foreign made goods can be well understood only in this context. *Swadeshi* was the strategy to protect employment for millions of the Indian non-agricultural workers. Adoption of traditional consumer goods, made by the cottage and village industries, got associated with the Indian nationalist sentiment and the national struggle for political independence. The lead political party, the Indian National Congress, in fact, made it obligatory on all 'active' party workers to wear handspun and handwoven cloth which became symbol of patriotism, and nationalism.

The vision of agro-industries/rural industries as projected by the political leadership during the pre-independence era had some serious limitations. The most significant ones did not project itself to the impact on spread of literacy and technical education. Also availability of alternative technologies, growth of mass media with changing aspirations of people and youth in particular and easy availability of power and electricity. Being that it did not project itself to the likely impact of the spread of literacy and technical education, availability of alternative technologies, the growth of mass media, the changing aspirations of the people and the youth in particular, and easy availability of power and electricity.

The truth is that agro and village industries were seen in terms of production in a traditional village and not the village of the future in a free and modern India. It was not comprehended that occupational structure, employment of women and a variety of gainful employment opportunities, especially in the service sectors, could grow rapidly with cheap and efficient transport, recognition of environmental and other factors associated with large industrial complexes, and urbanization. Agro industries, as traditionally understood, could not accommodate regional specialization to exploit comparative and locational advantages.

Agro-industries have also been viewed as a safety valve that needs to be built within rural areas to absorb surplus labour and provide relief to the problem of large-scale disguised unemployment. Absence of employment opportunities within the village, it is suggested, the main push factor responsible for the rapid movement of youth towards cities. Emergence of slums in metropolitan towns of the country and arrival of unattached young without gainful employment is the direct and inevitable consequence. These developments have a variety of social, law and order, and political implications. There were hopes that promotion of agro-industries to help avoid furtherance of industrial concentration to achieve a more balanced regional dispersal of industrial activities and employment.

Then came Economic Programmes Committee under the leadership of the then Prime Minister Mr. Jawaharlal Nehru in 1948 with set of recommendations. Among them, some were dealt with industries those producing articles of food and clothing and other consumer goods to constitute decentralized sector of Indian economy to enable such industry units to run on cottage and small-scale level.

VILLAGE INDUSTRY PROGRAMME

The Planning Commission decided to draw up Village Industry Programmes in consultation with experts. For this, the industries covered were:

(i) Village oil industry;
(ii) Soap making with neem oil;
(iii) Paddy husking;
(iv) Palm gur industry;
(v) Gur and khandsari;
(vi) Leather industry;
(vii) Woolen blankets;
(viii) High grade hand-made paper;
(ix) Bee keeping; and
(x) Cottage and matches industry.

Other industries assigned special priority were: *Khadi*, coir, sericulture, fisheries, Forests, dairying and horticulture. Second Plan also assigned a special place to rural, cottage and small industries. This plan envisaged expanding demand for consumer goods which will reduce pressure on the capital and the limited savings of the economy. Next, the sixties witnessed the beginning of the green revolution in some parts of India – Punjab, Haryana and western Uttar Pradesh. Agricultural output per hectare rose markedly due to the enhanced canal and well irrigation, widespread adoption of new and improved seed varieties, enlarged inputs of chemical fertilizers and use of pesticides.

While managerial practices are important, green revolution was a direct consequence of high levels of agro-inputs per unit of land. The switchover to electricity, diesel and pumpsets was almost dramatic; the high-yielding seeds were brought in from research centres; and tractors and agricultural implements, supplied by national and international sources. The green revolution brought Indian agriculture in close contact with industry, the nature of agro-industry relationships extending themselves to supply of industrial inputs instead of agriculture playing the raw material supply function only. The prosperity of farmers was also bound to generate new consumer demands produced by industry.

Later Agro-industrial Corporation to focus on agricultural development was launched with following objectives:

(a) Promotion – execution of industries undertaking production, preservation and supply of food;

(b) Enabling persons engaged in agricultural and allied pursuits to own the means of modernizing their operations;

(c) Distribution of agricultural machinery and implements as well equipment pertaining to processing, dairy, poultry, fishery and industries connected with agriculture;

(d) Undertaking and assisting in the distribution of inputs for agriculture; and

(e) Providing technical guidance to farmers and persons concerned with the agro industries with a view to enabling efficient conduct of their enterprises.

The Agro-industrial Corporations were to promote agro-processing and generate additional employment opportunities in rural India. These objectives did not, however, find a priority in their actual working, for they chose the easier course of promoting sales of tractors, agricultural machinery, fertilizers, pesticides, etc. None could have been happier than the large enterprises manufacturing tractors and other agricultural machinery, when they found these State-sponsored corporations were most willing, even anxious, to undertake marketing for the private sector.

Most State Agro-industries Corporations make profits. In some states, beginning with the early seventies, subsidiary corporations were also set up to provide cold storage and crop processing facilities. The variety of activities undertaken by the Agro-industries notwithstanding, their main operations continue to be organizing modern inputs to agriculture.

The eighties witnessed a keen interest in investments in the area of food processing and soft drinks. For instance, Pepsi entered into collaboration with Punjab Agro-industries Corporation and the Tatas to establish processing facilities for tomato juice and paste along with soft drink concentrates. Though a failure, General Foods of US also entered India during this period. Kellogg has evinced interest in production of breakfast foods. Nestle, known for its interest in coffee, has started marketing "Maggie" convenience foods, ketchup, chocolates, etc. Hindustan Lever Limited (HLL), the first entrant to the hydrogenated edible oil industry in India, handed over the *Dalda* production and marketing to its sister company, Lipton.

The HLL, however, have acquired control over another large manufacturer of soap and oil products, TOMCO. They have also taken over Kissan, a company known nation-wide for jams and squashes, and are reported to have acquired rice-milling facilities. Brooke Bond, an associate of the Levers, has entered marketing of *masalas*.

Among the new entrants to the edible oil industry are ITC and Britannia. Parle, the market leader in the soft drinks segment, which had fought tooth and nail against the entry of Pepsi, was obliged to abandon its fight with TNCs and join hands with Coca-Cola. It appears that the withdrawal of restrictions on the use of foreign brand names has speeded up the process of domination of the Indian consumer goods market by transnational corporations.

Food processing industry in the modern sector is likely to have its main characteristic in "brand" domination. The poor hygiene, in which the traditional food processing is generally undertaken, does not help sustain high confidence in the processed food produced and packaged by the cottage and small units. Bulk food processing is amenable to standardization and offers certain economies of scale. It is no surprise, if brand names get associated with quality and standardized products. The consumer acceptability of branded goods is high. It is because of such wellknown advantages that brand names carry substantial premium.

Emergence of near monopoly situation in food processing is not unknown. And once a brand name gets accepted widely, it opens up possibilities for launching new products with a massive thrust. Indian consumers are well aware how 'Maggie' noodles were followed up by Maggie sauce and Maggie soups. It seems that, instead of offering more employment, the modern food processing plants can cause the closure of many cottage and small establishments. There is, however, a possibility that because bulk food processing enterprises cannot provide large varieties or cater to regional and personal tastes, there would remain a demand for products of the cottage, local and small enterprises which provide specialized services with personal care. The overall impact of the entry of large and modern units to the food processing sector can, however, hardly be creation of promising employment opportunities.

Location of a large food processing unit would bring in a substantial increase in the demand for the required farm produce. This would also provide better market prices to the farmers. Given the fact that there would be thousands of small farmers who would be suppliers of farm produce to one buyer/ processor, the market situation would invariably be of monopoly, the stronger one seeking to exploit the situation to its maximum advantage. The past experience in two important agro-based industries, viz., sugar and tobacco, shows that the processing units tend to thrive at the cost of the farmers. The sugar industry of UP and Bihar is a case in point.

On the other hand, whenever processing is undertaken in a cooperative framework, there is a faster growth both for the farmer and the industry. The sugar cooperatives of Maharashtra, Gujarat and Karnataka have won a name for themselves. The same holds true of the edible oil (groundnut) cooperatives of Gujarat and the Amul experiment of dairy development on cooperative foundations. Thus, location of large private sector agro-processing units may be accompanied by perpetual conflicts, supply or processing uncertainties, labour problems, farmers' agitations and political interventions. On the other hand, if there were large farms specializing in a crop to meet requirements of the agro-processing unit, there could be a more organized and stable relationship between the farms and the factory.

An important policy assumption is that agro-industries have a large potential for exports from India. One wonders, if at the present stage of India's level of food, vegetables and other farm production, there is a scope for generating export surpluses. Can India be a net exporter of food in the foreseeable future? The per capita availability of cereals, pulses, vegetables and fruit in India is so low that export surpluses can only be obtained at the cost of their consumption. The poor would, of course, suffer the most.

What is needed is a fresh and comprehensive approach, integrating the development of villages with agro-industries, with larger involvement of the farmers in processing their own produce. In a democratic set-up, one cannot ignore development of the majority of the people or keep them on subsidies. The fact also remains that Indian population is so distributed that migration from agriculture to industry or from rural to urban centres or from densely populated areas to scarcely populated ones is not an easy and sustainable alternative. Besides the physical dimensions involved, the very characteristics of the population are such that there are clear linguistic barriers, which limit large-scale population migrations. Gainful employment to the rural people has to be provided in their own locale.

Viewed in this perspective, agro-industries as a concept have to be dealt with very differently from the past approaches, policies and programs or other industries. In India, unfortunately, rural development, employment of the educated or the uneducated, equity, and phrases like social justice have not travelled beyond a pious demonstration of the good intentions of the state. Expressions such as these have found frequent entry into official policy announcements. The Indian Plan strategy was never operationalized for redistribution of wealth or for reduction of interpersonal or interregional disparities. Indian planning has, in the main, leaned more on investments than on the *policy* content. Consequently, old colonial and feudal institutions, social value systems, educational structures and citizen-state relationships have never undergone any marked change. Rural programs under the Five Year Plans, except land reforms during the fifties, though consolidated, were only extensions of the earlier individual rural development programs and there was no specific program designed for *area* development, where a region's resource endowment is sought to be optimally harnessed by relating Plan investment/Plan programmes or pattern of allocation to the nature and the magnitude of local resources. Agro-industry was never adopted as a concept for area development, wherein local resource endowment was sought to be utilized optimally.

Given the Indian reality, a number of factors should be taken note of in formulating policies mix for the agro-industries:

1. Promotion of agro-industries has to be seen in the perspective of inelastic nature of land available for cultivation. Future developments in agriculture will require more cropping intensity and better water management, adoption of new and improved varieties of seeds and crops, and use of appropriate quantities of manures and pesticides.
2. Indian agriculture continues to have low productivity. During the past few years, some progress has been made on this front, yet the productivity gaps are only too wide. For instance, the average yield of wheat in India during 1979-1981 was 1,545 kg/ha, which increased to 2,117 kg by 1990. During the same period, per hectare productivity of wheat in China increased from 2,047 kg to 3,179 kg while the UK, Germany and France managed to increase the yields to well beyond 6,000 kg. The gap in wheat yield in India and these countries increased substantially during the eighties. Similar is the case with paddy and a number of other crops. Should we not then address ourselves to the basic question of how land productivity can be raised? This may necessitate larger and newer varieties of industrial inputs and the creation of research infrastructure and farm information channels. Efforts at increasing agricultural productivity may also require regional specialization, as each of the crops cannot be grown profitably in all the locations of the country.
3. Coupled with low productivity, Indian agriculture suffers from substantial wastage. Estimates of waste differ for individual crops. There seems to be, however, a consensus that nearly 10-15 per cent of the grains and 20-25 per cent of the fruits and vegetables in India perish each year. This is substantial in terms of quantum as also as a percentage of the national agricultural output. In a country like India with 30-40 per cent of the population living below the poverty line, it seems a criminal waste. Systematic efforts should, therefore, be made to minimize wastage and perishing of farm output and to adopt practices and technologies that cut down processing losses. Efforts to improve quality and capacity of warehousing for grains and expansion of cold storage facilities for fresh vegetables and fruits is at best a part answer.

At this stage of India's development, it is necessary to undertake a thorough scrutiny of the post-harvest processes and technologies and identify appropriate programmes. For instance, the traditional technology in rice-husking is labour-intensive but it results in breaking of the rice grain. Also since manual husking is a cottage and small-scale operation, the husk is left as a waste, because the quantity at individual sites is not substantial enough to permit technically feasible and optimal use of the husk. In the case of sugarcane, the village cane crusher does not deliver the full glucose content and the open pan *gur* or *Khandsari* technology continues to be less efficient. Similarly, the modern solvent extraction technology can yield 8-10 per cent additional output of edible oil. One can multiply such instances. New technologies could help reduce the bulk of agricultural produce for easy storage, bring down transport costs and provide more efficient and convenient handling. Creation of cold storage capacities requires colossal investments with substantial demands on the energy sector, so the cold storage is not a convenient or long-term remedy to the problem of preservation. Fruits may be less perishable, when preserved as juice or pulp, and vegetables may have a longer shelf life, if stored after vacuum dehydration or packaged in saline water and other preservatives.

The poor in India suffer from food deficiencies on two counts, namely inadequate calories and absence of nutritional balance in food intake. Development of food processing industry would undoubtedly reduce wastage and make for better returns and production incentives to farmers.

The additional and associated advantage that the food processing industry offers is the possibility of affecting addition of appropriate vitamins and minerals in which the average Indian diet is considered deficient.

Avoiding the ill-effects of reliance on large private corporations, whether Indian or foreign, would be possible, only if cooperatives are encouraged to take up agro-processing in a big way. That would also enable them to realize the economies of scale. They offer, in addition, the best means of harmonizing the interests of the producer, the processor and the consumer. Also, given the pattern of land holdings in most States, it seems unrealistic to plan for large private farms, which would specialize in the production of a certain vegetable or fruit.

Problems of pest control, canal or underground water management and preservation of seed purity against pollen transfers would also require special coordination. The conflicts and technical problems can have solutions, but the Government found it particularly hard to pursue the objective of "market-oriented technology" especially in conditions prevailing in most regions of the country. Coordination, whenever sought by official agencies, proves a more difficult operation than in a cooperative system that brings farmers together as a result of enlightened self-interest. A publicly controlled and managed industrial system is more responsive to societal needs such as introduction of environment-friendly production processes. More importantly, introduction of harmless bio-fertilizers and bio-pesticides is easier in a cooperative setting. The farmers should be encouraged to form cooperatives to establish and run agro-industrial complexes for total processing of organic produce of specified types of crops.

Marketing is an area that requires a very special attention. Large corporations, Indian or foreign, have an edge in marketing. Without unduly hurting the interests of the consumers, one should be able to utilize the existing infrastructure to distribute the products of cooperatives. Besides, all the consumer cooperatives, including Super Bazars, could be made to provide a certain minimum shelf space for the products of cooperatives. One could also enlist the support of non-governmental consumer organizations to educate consumers about the inherent qualities of the products offered by the cooperatives.

The 'Fruit and Vegetable Shops' of the National Dairy Development Board indicates clearly the potential for such marketing machinery. Reservation of a certain portion of prime advertising time on the public television network at concessional rates is another step necessary to balance the marketing thrust of large corporations. Foreign brand names, whether original or in hybrid form, might be disallowed in agro-industrial products to give the local processors an equal chance of competing. Preferential treatment in purchases by public bodies might also be extended to cooperatives.

Advancement of agro-industries, fully integrated with the developmental needs of rural population, calls for bold and possibly unconventional measures. At the administrative level, it requires urgently the creation of a district level authority vested with wide-ranging powers and having majority representation of cooperative bodies. This authority would be the nodal agency for providing various support services such as information on crop varieties, weather, products, markets and coordination of technology acquisition.

SUMMARY

The progress of Indian economy depends to larger extent on the application of science and technology for the exploitation of agricultural raw materials into numerous consumer and industrial products thus accelerating the process of industrialization without sacrificing agricultural development resulting in the conversion of agricultural economies to industrial economies through the agri-industry linkages.

Primary agricultural commodity and organic residue, animal by-product and waste, fishery and forestry by-products etc., can contribute to the economic development of a series of industries if the primary commodity, its by-products and waste matter are scientifically processed.

Discussions about the potential economic benefits of agriculture-industry linkages as instruments for achieving inclusive industrial development in the agriculture-dominated countries are common in the development literature emerged which estimated the magnitude of growth linkages between the agricultural sector and the rural non-farm sector in the context of selected East and South-east Asian countries.

The contents incorporated in this chapter will convincingly demonstrate that a broad-based growth of the rural economy based on close linkages between agriculture and rural non-farm sector encompassing both rural informal and formal manufacturing, trade and service activities played crucial role towards setting in motion or virtuous cycle of comprehensive economic growth in these countries.

QUESTIONS

1. What are the needs for setting up of more agri-based units in the agricultural Sector?
2. Distinguish between Agriculture and RNA linkage.
3. Describe the uniqueness of agro industries in the light of value-added agriculture produce.
4. How supporting mechanisms like Village Industry programs helped the rural development?

OOO

CHAPTER 16

NATIONAL FOOD PROCESSING POLICY (NFP)

National Food Processing Policy (NFPP)

Introduction

Government's New Initiatives-2011

Pattern of Financial Assistance

Challenges, Constraints and Concerns

Creation of Enabling Environment

Infrastructural Development

NFPP's Promotional Policy

National Industrial Policy (NIP)

Objectives

Industrial Licensing Policy

Foreign Direct Investment

Foreign Technology Agreement

Public Sector Policy

MRTP Act

Decisions of Government

Small Scale Industry Policy 1991

New Agriculture Policy (NEP)

Salient Features

Sustainable Agriculture

Food and Nutritional Security

Generation and Transfer of Technology

Inputs Management

Incentives in Agriculture

Institutional Structure of Indian Agriculture Business

Risk Management

Management Reforms

EVOLUTION OF FOOD PROCESSING INDUSTRY

Introductory

Food processing industry is of enormous significance for India's development because of the vital linkages and synergies that it promotes between the two pillars of the economy, namely Industry and Agriculture. India is world's second largest producer of food and has the potential to become number one in due course of time with sustained efforts. The growth potential of this sector is enormous and it is expected that the food production will double in the next 10 years and the consumption of value added food products will grow at a fast pace.

The growth of the Food Processing industry will bring immense benefits to the economy, raising agricultural yields, meeting productivity, creating employment and raising the standard of very large number of people throughout the country, especially, in the rural areas. Economic liberalization and rising consumer prosperity is opening up new opportunities for diversification in Food Processing Sector. Liberalization of world trade will open up new vistas for growth.

The Food Processing Industry has been identified as a thrust area for development. This industry is included in the priority lending sector. Most of the Food Processing Industries have been exempted from the provisions of industrial licensing under Industries (Development and Regulation) Act, 1951 with the exception of beer and alcoholic drinks and items reserved for small-scale sector, like vinegar, bread, bakery. As far as foreign investment is concerned, automatic approval for even 100 per cent equity is available for majority of the processed food items.

The Food Processing Sector

Food processing involves any type of value addition to the agricultural produce starting at the post-harvest level. It includes even primary processing like grading, sorting, cutting, seeding, shelling packaging etc. This sector comprise of following areas:

1. Fruit and Vegetables
2. Beverages, Juices, Concentrates, Pulps, Slices, Frozen and Dehydrated products, Potato Wafers/Chips etc.
3. Fisheries
4. Frozen and canned products mainly in fresh form
5. Milk and dairy products include whole Milk Powder, Skimmed milk powder, Condensed milk, Ice-cream, Butter and Ghee
6. Grain and cereals: Flour, Bakeries, Biscuits, Starch Glucose, Cornflakes, Malted Foods, Vermicelli, Fast Foods, Beer and Malt extracts, Grain based Alcohol
7. Consumer industry confectionaries: chocolates, soft-aerated beverages drinks
8. Plantation: Tea, coffee, cashew, cocoa, coconut etc.

GOVERNMENT'S NEW INITIATIVE, 2011

Government of India in its new initiative during March 2011, aiming for qualitative growth in Food Processing Sector had extended Financial Assistance for setting up/upgradation of existing quality control/ Food testing Laboratories with following objectives:

1. To establish a surveillance system to monitoring the quality and composition of food.
2. To analyze the samples received from food processing industries and other shareholders.
3. To reduce the time of analysis of samples by reducing transportation time samples.
4. To ensure compliance of international standards on food in case of exports as well as imports.

PATTERN OF FINANCIAL ASSISTANCE

1. Central/State government and its organizations/Universities including deemed Universities will be eligible for grant-in-aid of entire cost of laboratory equipments required for labs. In addition, they would also be eligible to 25 per cent of the cost of technical civil works to house the equipments and furniture and the fixtures associated with the equipments for general areas and 33 per cent for difficult Areas.
2. All other implementing agencies/private sector organizations will be eligible for grant-in-aid of 50 per cent of cost of laboratory equipments and 25 per cent of the cost of technical civil works to house the equipments and furniture and the fixtures associated with the equipments for general areas and 33 per cent for difficult areas.

The applications can be submitted directly to the Ministry of Food Processing Industries through Joint Secretary (Administration), Ministry of Food Processing Industries, Government of India, Panchsheel Bhawan, August Kranti Marg, New Delhi-110049 and telephone number is 011-26492176 and official website is: http://mofpi.nic.in

CHALLENGES, CONSTRAINTS AND CONCERNS

India is a major producer of food (first in cereals, livestock population, milk and second in fruits and vegetables), producing over 600 million tons of food products, and in case the immense untapped potential of growth is achieved the country can emerge as the largest producer of major food items. Processing level presently being extremely low, the wastage levels are very high resulting in colossal wastage of national wealth running in thousands of crores.

Value addition to the raw produce in the country is only seven per cent, compared to as much as 23 per cent in china, 45 per cent in the Philippines and 188 in the UK. The small-scale and unorganized sectors today account for 75 per cent of the total industry having only local presence without much access to knowledge, technology and marketing network.

The difference between the farmer's realization and the final consumer price is very high in our country even in the case of fresh produce. In processed food products, there is high price on account of cumulative effect of low productivity, high cost of raw material, spoilage due to poor infrastructure, inefficient and costly transportation, high cost of finance and high incidence of taxes and duties. All these leads to the vicious cycle of low demand, low capacity utilization, high per unit cost and low demand.

Despite the existence of a strong and wide network of R&D institutions (CSIR labs, ICAR institutions, ICMR Establishments, Universities and Private institutions), their linkage with the users like farmers and industry, is not well established resulting in lack of technology flow, pure and academic research rather than applied and commercial, lack of involvement of industry in research work, and resource crunch.

This is due to unattractive nature and the high risk profile of food processing industry that has impeded the required flow of credit from financial institutions who are yet to acquire the proper understanding of this sector to attain the requisite levels of appraising skills. Further low margins, seasonality and high perishability being the distinct features of this industry, the access to seed capital and working capital is not easy. Despite having been declared a priority lending sector, there is hardly any growth in capital flow to this industry. Despite vast domestic market size, the present level of processed food marketability is very low. But by doing massive awareness and educational campaigns, this market could grow higher enough to consume substantial part of any quantum of our processed foods.

Indian brands are yet to establish in the international markets calling for a concerted effort to capture world market share in tune with our standing in the production front.

With the creation of World Trade Organization (WTO) regime, the country has to prepare for meeting the requisite quality standards in order to compete with imported goods in the domestic market itself. This calls for adoption of high tech machine and technologies as also development of entire chain of the infrastructure.

Weak database and lack of market intelligence are the prevailing features of this sector. Poor infrastructure of not only processing but even transportation, ports, airports, storage and handling etc. The backward linkage between the farmer and the processor is yet to take proper shape to tide over the impediments which exists on account of fragmented and small land holdings, erratic production due to natural factors, non-uniformity and inconsistent supply of raw material and longer chain of intermediaries.

Multiplicity of laws and regulatory authorities throttle the industry in its further growth calling for harmonization of laws, development and administration of standards in consonance with international standards like Codex through a single authority. Prevailing packaging system lacks requisite quality and presentability parameters creating handicap as compared to the imported products.

Cooperative institutions and other parallel organizations are weak and people's participation, either through Panchayat Raj Institutions or NGOs or farmers organizations, industries association in food sector remains far from adequate.

CREATION OF ENABLING ENVIRONMENT

The National Agricultural Policy will seek to create an appropriate atmosphere for entrepreneurs to set up Food Processing Industries through various measures. They include:

1. Fiscal initiatives/interventions like rationalization of tax structure on fresh foods as well as processed foods and machinery used for the production of processed foods.
2. Harmonization and simplification of food laws by an appropriate enactment to cover all provisions relating to food products so that the existing system of multiple laws is replaced and also covering issues concerning standards nutrition, merit goods, futures marketing and equalization fund etc.
3. A concerted promotion campaign to create market for processed foods by providing financial assistance to industry associations, NGOs/ Co-operatives, private sector units, state government organization for undertaking generic market promotion.

4. Efforts to expand the availability of the right kind and quality of raw material round the year by increasing production, and improving productivity.
5. Strengthening of database and market intelligence system through studies and surveys to be conducted in various states to enable planned investment in the appropriate sector matching with the availability of raw materials and marketability of processed products.
6. Strengthening extension services to farmers and cooperatives in the areas of post-harvest management of agro-product to encourage creation of pre-processing facilities near the farms like ashing, fumigation, packaging etc.
7. Efforts to encourage setting up of agro-processing facilities as close to the area of production as possible to avoid wastage and reduce transportation costs.
8. Promotion of investments both foreign and domestic.
9. Simplification of documentation and procedures under taxation laws to avoid unnecessary harassment arising out of mere technicalities.

INFRASTRUCTURAL DEVELOPMENT

The National Food Processing Policy has been devised by Government of India in order to **accomplish the following agenda** set forth by its mandarins. They include:

1. Establishment of cold chain, low cost pre-cooling facilities near farms, cold stores and grading, sorting, packing facilities to reduce wastage, improve quality and shelf life of products.
2. Application of biotechnology, remote sensing technology for environmental protection.
3. Building up a strong infrastructural base for production of value-added products with special emphasis on food safety and quality matching international norms.
4. Development of packaging technologies for individual products especially cut-fruits and vegetables so as to increase their shelf life and improve consumer acceptance both in domestic and international markets.
5. Development of new technologies in Food Processing and Packaging and also to provide for the mechanism to facilitate quick transfer of technologies to field through network of R&D institutions having central institute at the national level with satellite institutions located strategically in various states, regions to cover up the whole country and to make available the required testing facilities. This could be done by establishing new institution or strengthening an existing one.
6. Development of area-specific Agro Food Parks dedicated to processing of the predominant produce of the area – for example apple in J & K state, pineapple in North-East, Lichi fruit in Bihar, Mango in Maharashtra and AP state and orange in Maharashtra and Karnataka etc.
7. Development of nodal industrial centre and its linkage with anchor industrial units having network of small processing units.
8. Development of Agro-industrial multi-products units capable of processing a cluster of trans-seasonal produces.

NFP's Promotional Initiatives

1. Establishment of a sustained and lasting linkage between the farmers and the processors based on mutual trust and benefits by utilizing the existing infrastructure of cooperatives, Village Panchayats and such other institutions.
2. Development of futures market in the best interest of both the farmers and the processors ensuring minimum price stability to the farmer and a sustained supply of raw material to the processor.
3. Mechanism to reduce the gap between the farm gate price of agro-produce and the final price paid by the consumer.
4. Setting up of an Equalization Fund to ensure sustained supply of raw material at a particular price level and at the same time to plough back the savings occurring in the eventuality of lower price to make the fund self-regenerative.
5. Establishment of strong linkage between the processor and the market to effect cost economies by elimination of avoidable intermediaries.
6. Establishment of marketing network with an apex body to ensure proper marketing of processed products.
7. Development of marketing capabilities both with regard to infrastructure and quality in order to promote competitive capabilities to face not only the WTO challenges but to undertake exports in a big way.
8. The North-Eastern Region, the Hilly Areas islands and the Indo Tibetan Drought Prone areas in the country to be given not only special attention but also special consideration.
9. The fiscal incentives like excise duty/sales tax concession and the tax holidays to be provided not only to those units which are set up in these areas but also to those units which though set up outside these areas near the market centre are engaged in processing the produce coming from these areas.
10. Tax holidays for food processing units, with the exception of liquor, cigarettes and aerated drinks and similar luxury items for a period of ten years.

NATIONAL INDUSTRIAL POLICY (NIP)

Salient Features

The target of investment in heavy industries and mining fixed at ₹ 890 crores, under the Second Five-Year Plan Government of India had drafted New Industrial Policy and implemented on April 30, 1956. The salient features of the new Industrial Policy Resolution of 1956 may be summed up as under:

The Industrial Policy Statement of 1956 was issued to achieve the following important objectives: (a) to speed up industrialization and achieve a faster rate of economic growth; (b) to develop machine-making and heavy industries; (c) to build up a large and growing co-operative sector; (d) to expand the public sector; and (e) to reduce disparities in income and wealth and curb monopolies.

Threefold classification of industries: For the purpose of allocation between private and public sectors, the industries have been divided into three broad categories.

1. Those industries whose future development will be the **exclusive responsibility of the state** and under this category there are 17 types of industry units that were enlisted in Schedule A of the Policy. They include practically all the basic and key industries such as arms and ammunition, atomic energy, iron and steel, heavy machinery, coal, railway transport, telephone, ship building, generation and distribution of electricity, etc. Some industry units privately owned were expanded and allowed to operate.
2. Those **remaining industry units** which were progressively **state owned enlisted** in Schedule B of Resolution of this New Industry Policy – 12 industry units — aluminum, ferro-alloys, machine tools, chemical pulp, road and sea transport etc. The State will increasingly set up new units in these industries, though it will provide opportunities to the private enterprise to develop either independently or through its participation.
3. **Those units remaining were left to private entrepreneurs.** The government encouraged thereby to develop other industries in the private sector with programmes formulated in successive phased plans. These initiatives provided all kinds of facilities including development of power and transport with financial assistance through institutions specially fostered for this purpose.
    (a) **Those remaining industries apart from agribusiness which left to the private enterprises.** The government is committed to encourage development of other industry units in the private sector in accordance with the programs formulated in successive plans. It will provide all kinds of facilities including development of power and transport with financial help.
    (b) **Interdependence and cooperation between the sectors.** The Policy did not intend to place industries in water tight compartments. The previous governments have been given the freedom to undertake any type of industrial production. The private enterprises produced some of the items included in Schedule A which contains industries falling in the domain of the state – like generation of electricity.
    (c) **Role of small-scale and cottage industries:** On account of peculiar advantages with large employment potential and potentialities, Indian economy witnessed equal distribution of income and also mobility of labour and optimum utilization of capital resources while cottage and small-scale industries were given equal importance for their overall growth. Similarly, industrial estates and rural community workshops were given boost for their development with large-scale industries with permissible subsidies and tax concessions.
    (d) **Balanced regional industrial development**. The Policy recognized the need and carried out industrial development in various regions of country and industrial facilities (power and transport) were extended to remote corners which created employment opportunities.
    (e) **Sound regional relations with labour welfare**. The Policy resolution further extended benefits of sound and cordial industry relations across different regions of country and special emphasis was laid on power and transport sector generating thereby umpteen employments to many with congenial working conditions. They were kept under the constant monitoring of Public Sector Undertakings (PSUs).
    (f) **Training of personnel for rapid industrialization**. The Policy stressed the need for rapid industrialization of the country and in this direction initiatives were taken to pick up selected skilled personnel and imparted training at the university level.

(g) **Management of state enterprises**. In this context, this Policy aimed at decentralization of the authority and toned up efficiency of State Industrial Undertakings and enabled them to function with sound business principles to augment resources from surpluses.

POLICY'S OBJECTIVES

The then Prime Minister Jawaharlal Nehru laid the foundations of modern India. His vision and determination have left a lasting impression on every facet of national endeavor since Independence. It is due to his initiative that India now has a strong and diversified industrial base and is a major industrial nation of the world.

(a) The goals and objectives set out for the nation by Pt Nehru on the eve of Independence, namely, the rapid agricultural and industrial development of our country, rapid expansion of opportunities for gainful employment, progressive reduction of social and economic disparities, removal of poverty and attainment of self-reliance remain as valid today.

Any economy's industrial policy must contribute to the realization of rapid development in agriculture and industrialization, creation of employment opportunities, reduction of economic and social disparities – poverty if not eradicated completely at an accelerated pace.

Immediately after Independence, Government of India introduced the National Industrial Policy Resolution, which aimed at industrial growth and development and emphasized its relevance to economy and secured continuous increase in production and ensured its equitable distribution. The Industrial Policy was comprehensively revised and adopted later to meet new challenges. From time to time, it was modified through statements in 1973, 1977 and 1980.

(b) The Industrial Policy Resolution had as its objective the acceleration of the rate of economic growth and the speeding up of industrialization as a means of achieving a socialist pattern of society in the entire country. Though the capital was scarce in the economy, the base of entrepreneurship was strong enough to give primacy to the role of the State to assume a predominant and direct responsibility for industrial development.

(c) The Industrial Policy statement of 1973, *inter alia*, identified high-priority industries where investment from large industrial houses and foreign companies would be permitted.

(d) The Industrial Policy Statement of 1977 laid emphasis on decentralization and on the role of small-scale, tiny and cottage industries.

(e) The Industrial Policy Statement of 1980 focused for promoting competition in the domestic market, technological upgradation and modernization. The policy laid the foundation for an increasingly competitive export based and for encouraging foreign investment in high-technology areas. Sixth Five Year Plan bore the distinct stamp of the then Prime Minister Mrs. Indira Gandhi who emphasized the need for productivity as the central concern in all economic and production activities.

(f) These policies created a climate for rapid industrial growth in the country while Seventh Five Year Plan, a broad-based infrastructure had been built up. Basic industries were established with high degree of self-reliance in a large number of items — raw materials, intermediates, finished goods — had been achieved. New growth centres of industrial activity had emerged.

as had a new generation of entrepreneurs. A large number of engineers, technicians and skilled workers had also been trained. Numerous policies in this direction were conceived and introduced by the then Prime Minister Rajiv Gandhi aimed at increased quality, productivity, reducing costs and self-sufficiency.

(g) The public sector was freed from a number of constraints and given a larger measure of autonomy. The technological and managerial modernization of industry was pursued as the key instrument for increasing productivity and improving our competitiveness in the world. The net result of all these changes was that Indian industry grew by an impressive average annual growth rate of 8.5 per cent in the Seventh Plan period.

(h) Government pledged to launching a reinvigorated struggle for social and economic justice, to end poverty and unemployment and to build a modern, democratic, socialist, prosperous and forward-looking vibrant India.

(i) While Government continued to follow the policy of self-reliance, there was greater emphasis placed on building up country's ability to pay for imports through our own foreign exchange earnings. Government had also committed for development and utilization of indigenous capabilities in technology and manufacturing as well as its upgradation to world standards.

(j) Government continued to pursue a sound policy framework encompassing encouragement of entrepreneurship, development of indigenous technology through investment in R&D, bringing in new technology, dismantling of age-old regulatory system, development of the capital markets and increasing competitiveness for the benefit of the common man. The spread of industrialization to backward areas of the country actively promoted through appropriate incentives, institutions and infrastructure investments.

(k) Government provided enhanced support to small-scale sector so that it flourishes in an environment of economic efficiency and continuous technological upgradation.

(l) Foreign investment and technology collaboration were welcomed and obtained higher technology to increase exports and to expand the production base.

(m) Government committed to abolish the monopoly in all sectors and spheres of economy except on strategic or military considerations and thereby opened all manufacturing activities to competition.

(n) The Government motivated public sector to play its rightful role involving socio-economic, scenario of the country. Government further streamlined the public sector to run on business in lines as envisaged in the Industrial Policy Resolution and ensured to innovate to lead in strategic areas of national importance.

(o) Government was fully determined to protect interests of labour, enhanced their welfare and equipped them in all respects to deal with the inevitability of technological changes. Government extended stricture that no small section of society can corner the gains of growth, leaving workers to bear its pains. Labours made equal partner in progress and prosperity with motto "Workers' participation in management" with Workers' cooperatives.

(p) Government continued to visualize new horizons with major objectives of the new industrial policy package to build on the gains already made, corrected the distortions or weaknesses that crept in, maintained thereby sustained growth in productivity and gainful employment and attain international competitiveness. The pursuit of these objectives was tempered by the need to preserve the environment and ensure the efficient use of available resources. All sectors of industry whether small, medium or large, belonging to the public, private or cooperative sector were encouraged to grow and improve on their past performance.

(q) In pursuit of the above objectives, Government decided to take a series of initiatives in respect of the policies relating to the following areas.

A. Industrial Licensing.

B. Foreign Direct Investment (FDI)

C. Foreign Technology Agreements

D. Public Sector Policy

E. MRTP Act

Let us discuss in detail of all these above-said areas and examine one by one.

A. INDUSTRIAL LICENSING POLICY

Industrial Licensing policy was introduced by Government of India and is governed by the Industries (Development & Regulation) Act, 1951. The Industrial Policy Resolution of 1956 identified the following three categories of industries: (a) those that would be reserved for development in public sector, (b) those that would be permitted for development through private enterprise with or without State participation, and (c) those in which investment initiatives would ordinarily emanate from private entrepreneurs. Over the years, keeping in view the changing industrial scene in the country, the policy has undergone modifications. Industrial licensing policy and procedures have also been liberalized from time to time. A full realization of the industrial potential of the country calls for a continuation of this process of change.

In order to achieve objectives of the strategy for the industrial sector for 1990s and beyond, it is necessary to make a number of changes in the system of industrial approvals. Major policy initiatives and procedural reforms actively encouraged and assisted Indian entrepreneurs to exploit and met the emerging domestic and global opportunities and challenges. The attainment of technological dynamism and international competitiveness enabled the Indian entrepreneurs to swiftly respond to fast changing external conditions which is the characteristic of today's industrial world. Government policy and procedures thus geared to assisting entrepreneurs in their efforts.

The winds of change were seen in whole economy and in particular the industrial licensing system had been gradually moved away from the concept of capacity licensing. The system of reservations for PSU evolved towards an ethos of greater flexibility and private sector enterprise had been gradually allowed to enter into many of these areas on a case by case basis. Further provision of impetus to these changes pushed this country towards the attainment of its entrepreneurial and industrial potential.

Industrial licensing thus abolished for all industries, except those specified, irrespective of levels of investment, but will continue to be subject to compulsory licensing for reasons related to security and strategic concerns, social reasons, problems related to safety and over-riding environmental issues, manufacture of products of hazardous nature and articles of elitist consumption. This act of exemption from licensing will be helpful to many dynamic Small and Medium Entrepreneurs (SME) who have been unnecessarily hampered by the licensing system. As a whole the Indian economy will benefit by becoming more competitive, more efficient and modern and will take its rightful place in the world of industrial progress.

Industrial licensing was abolished for all projects except for a short list of industries related to security and strategic concerns, social reasons, hazardous chemicals and overriding environmental reasons, and items of elitist consumption. Industries reserved for the small scale sector were allowed to continue to be so reserved.

Areas where security and strategic concerns under predominance were permitted to continue and reserved for the public sector projects. Similarly imported capital goods that were required for manufacture was given automatic clearance.

The system of phased manufacturing programs run on an administrative case by case basis was made applicable to new projects. Existing units were provided a new broad banding facility to equip them to produce any article without additional investment and exemption from licensing was given to all substantial expansions of existing units. The mandatory convertibility clause was annulled in case of term loans required from the financial institutions for new projects.

B. FOREIGN DIRECT INVESTMENT (FDI)

Indian industry was freed from official controls, opportunities for promotion of foreign investments in India was fully exploited. In view of this significant development of India's industrial economy, the general resilience, size and level of sophistication was achieved, followed by significant changes taken place in the world industrial economy. Besides this, relationship between domestic and foreign industry was much more dynamic than it has been in the past in terms of both technology and investment. Foreign investment brought advantages of technology transfer, marketing expertise, modern managerial techniques and promotion of exports with economic cooperation and mobility of capital.

This policy also brought large investment strategies in prioritized industries with advanced technology while thrust was focused on FDI up to 51 per cent without any cognizable bottlenecks. Besides this FERA companies were allowed to invest on a discretionary basis. This served as landmark in the history of industry policy that made task of foreign investment transparent and attracted many giant corporate abroad to invest in India.

Promotion of exports of Indian products seen systematic exploration in the world markets through intensive and highly professional marketing activities. Government encouraged foreign trading companies to assist us in our export activities, with attraction of substantial investment and easy access to high technology to world markets over interaction with some of the world's largest international manufacturing and marketing firms. The Government nominated special Board to negotiate with such firms so that we can engage in purposive negotiation with such large firms to provide the avenues for large investments in the development of industries and technology in the national interest.

GOI approved for FDI up to 51 percent foreign equity in high priority industries without any bottlenecks and consequential amendments were made to easy availability of equity covers for imported capital goods. While the import of components, raw materials and intermediate goods, and payment of know-how fees and royalties were made to govern the general policy applicable to other domestic units. The payment of dividends were made to be monitored through the RBI so as to ensure that outflows on account of dividend payments are balanced by export earnings over a period of time.

The thrust was focused on export activities at par with domestic trading and export houses in accordance with the Import Export Policy. Special Empowered Board was constituted to negotiate with number of large MNCs and approved FDI in select areas to attract substantial investment that provide access to high technology and world markets.

C. FOREIGN TECHNOLOGY AGREEMENT

There was a great need for promoting an industrial environment with acquisition of technological capability that received priority. The relationship between the suppliers and users of technology became robust and continuous one without any government's meddling. Entrepreneurs were given full autonomy for commercial technology with foreign technology suppliers. Indian industry became competitive within such a regulatory environment.

Government injected desired level of dynamism in Indian industry to provide automatic approval for technology agreement within specified parameters. Similar facilities were made available for other industries as well. Indian companies were allowed to negotiate the terms of technology transfer with their foreign counterparts according to their own commercial judgement and viability.

The predictability and independence of action aimed at providing to Indian industry will induce them to develop indigenous competence for the efficient absorption of foreign technology. Greater competitive pressure also induced our industry to invest more in R&D. with hiring of foreign technicians with indigenously developed technologies.

D. PUBLIC SECTOR POLICY

In the pursuit of our development objectives, Power Sector Policy depicted public ownership with control over the economy played an important role in preventing the concentration of economic power, reduced regional disparities and ensuring that planned development serves the common good.

Massive investments made public sector in a commanding role in the economy. The key sectors of the economy dominated by PSUs those have successfully expanded production, opened up new areas of technology and built up a reserve of technical competence in a number of areas.

After initial exuberance of PSUs entered new areas of industrial and technical competence, number of problems have, begun to manifest themselves in many of the PSUs. Serious problems crept in the growth of productivity, poor project management, over-manning, lack of continuous technological upgradation, and inadequate attention to R&D and HRD. In addition, public enterprises have shown a very low rate of return on the capital invested.

Government adopted new approach to PSUs with greater commitment to support of PSUs which are essential for the operation of the industrial economy. Measures were taken to make the PSUs more growth oriented and technically dynamic. Units which may be faltering at present were made viable and restructured and given a new lease of life with a hidden agenda of essential infrastructure goods and services, exploration and exploitation of oil and mineral services with technology development.

Similarly building of manufacturing capabilities in areas which are crucial in the long run development were allowed while ensured manufacture of products in defence sector with strategic considerations.

Further Government reviewed existing portfolio of public investments with greater realism based on low technology, small-scale and non-strategic areas, inefficient and unproductive areas, where the private sector had developed sufficient expertise and resources.

Government strengthened those PSUs in the reserved areas of operation those are generating good or reasonable profits. These PSUs have been given greater degree of autonomy in management through the system of memoranda of understanding while competition was induced in these areas by inviting private sector participation. Some of the selected enterprises were disinvested in order to provide further market discipline to the performance of public enterprises.

E. MONOPOLIES RESTRICTIVE TRADE PRACTICES ACT (MRTP ACT)

Government drafted and passed MRTP Act with objectives of prevention of concentration of economic power to the common detriment, control of monopolies, and prohibition of monopolistic and restrictive and unfair trade practices.

The MRTP Act was effective from June 1970 with emphasis placed on productivity stipulated in the Sixth Plan, and was amended in 1982 and 1984 in order to remove impediments to industrial growth and expansion. This process of change was given a new momentum to Indian economy in 1985 by an increase of threshold limit of assets.

With the growing complexity of industrial structure, for ensuring high productivity and competitive advantage in the international market, the interference of the Government through MRTP Act in investment decisions of large companies became deleterious in its effects on Indian industrial growth. The pre-entry scrutiny of investment decisions by MRTP was abolished instead, emphasis was on controlling and regulating monopolistic, restrictive and unfair trade practices.

The thrust of policy was more on controlling unfair or restrictive business practices but later this Act was restructured by eliminating the legal requirement for prior governmental approval for expansion of present undertakings and establishment of new undertakings. New provisions relating to merger, amalgamation, and takeover were repealed and some provisions regarding restrictions on acquisition of and transfer of shares were appropriately incorporated in the Companies Act.

A. DECISIONS OF GOVERNMENT

In view of above achievements, Government has decided to take series of measures to unshackle the Indian industrial economy from the cobwebs of unnecessary bureaucratic control. These measures complemented other series of measures being taken in trade policy, exchange rate management, fiscal policy, financial sector reform and overall macro-economic management as under:

Procedural Consequences

All existing registration schemes for delicensed registration, exempted Industries registration, and DGTD registration were abolished. Entrepreneurs were asked to file an information memorandum on new projects and substantial expansions periodically.

Foreign Technology Agreements

Automatic permission was given for foreign technology agreements in high priority industries, 5 per cent royalty for domestic sales and 8 per cent for exports, subject to total payment of 8 per cent of sales over a 10 year period. In respect of industries other than those in Annex III, automatic permission was given subject to some guidelines. All other proposals were followed with specific approval under the general procedures that was in force.

Public Sector

Portfolio of public sector investments were subjected to periodical review with a view to focus the public sector on strategic, high-tech and essential infrastructure, whereas some reservation for the public sector is being retained.

One significant provision was included in the policy to refer public enterprises which were chronically sick to the Board for Industrial and Financial Reconstruction (BIFR). A social security mechanism was created to protect the interests of workers likely to be affected by such rehabilitation packages. In order to raise resources and encourage wider public participation, a part of the government's shareholding in the public sector was offered to mutual funds, financial institutions, general public and workers.

Greater thrust on performance improvement through the Memorandum of Understanding (MoU) was granted greater autonomy and will be held accountable and technical expertise was upgraded to make the MOU more effective. Another provision was made in the Policy and declared all food processing industries other than milk food, malted food and flour were categorized for small-scale sector. Similarly, all items of packaging food processing industries excluding others were reserved for small-scale sector included hotels and tourism related industry.

SMALL-SECTOR INDUSTRY POLICY, 1991

Features:

The government at the centre drafted and announced on 6th August 1991 new policy measures for promoting and strengthen small, tiny and village enterprises. The main thrust of the new policy is to impart more vitality and growth to employment and exports.

- Deregulation, debureaucratization and simplification on status, regulations and procedures.
- Increase in the investment limit in plant and machinery of tiny enterprise forms 21 lakh to ₹ 50 lakh, irrespective of the location of the unit.
- Inclusion of industry related services and business enterprises, irrespective of their location, as small-scale industries.
- Ensuring both adequate flow of credit on a normative basis and quality of its delivery for viable operation on the SSI sector.
- Setting up a special monitoring agency to oversee the genuine credit needs of the small-scale sector.
- Introduction of suitable legislation to ensure prompt payment of small industries bills.
- Introduction of a scheme of Integrated Infrastructural development (including technological back up services) for small-scale industries.
- Setting up a Technology Developed Cell in the Small Industries Development Organization.
- Market promotion of SSI products through cooperative/public sector institutions other specialized professional/marketing agencies and the consortia approach.
- Setting up of an Export Development Center in the Small Industries Development Organization.

NEW AGRICULTURE POLICY

Agriculture is a way of life, a tradition, which, for centuries, has shaped the thought, the outlook, the culture and the economic life of the people of India. Agriculture, therefore, is and will continue to be central to all strategies for planned socio-economic development of the country. Rapid growth of agriculture is essential not only to achieve self-reliance at national level but also for household food security and to bring about equity in distribution of income and wealth resulting in rapid reduction in poverty levels.

Indian agriculture has, since Independence, made rapid strides. In taking the annual foodgrains production from 51 million tons in early fifties to 206 million tons at the turn of the century, it has contributed significantly in achieving self-sufficiency in food and in avoiding food shortages.

Over 200 million Indian farmers and farm workers have been the backbone of India's agriculture. Despite having achieved national food security, the well-being of the farming community continues to be a matter of grave concern for planners and policymakers. The establishment of an agrarian economy which ensures food and nutrition to India's billion people, raw materials for its expanding industrial base and surpluses for exports, and a fair and equitable reward system for the farming community for the services they provide to the society, will be the mainstay of reforms in the agriculture sector.

The National Policy on Agriculture seeks to actualize the vast untapped growth potential of Indian agriculture, strengthen rural infrastructure to support faster agricultural development, promote value addition, accelerate the growth of agro business, create employment in rural areas, secure a fair standard of living for the farmers and agricultural workers and their families, discourage migration to urban areas and face the challenges arising out of economic liberalization and globalization. Over the next two decades, it aims to attain:

The Salient Features of the New Agricultural Policy are:

1. Over 4 per cent annual growth rate aimed over next two decades.
2. Greater private sector participation through contract farming.
3. Price protection for farmers.
4. National agricultural insurance scheme to be launched.
5. Dismantling of restrictions on movement of agricultural commodities throughout the country.
6. Rational utilization of country's water resources for optimum use of irrigation potential.
7. High priority to development of animal husbandry, poultry, dairy and aquaculture.
8. Capital inflow and assured markets for crop production.
9. Exemption from payment of capital gains tax on compulsory acquisition of agricultural land.
10. Minimize fluctuations in commodity prices.
11. Continuous monitoring of international prices.
12. Plant varieties to be protected through legislation.
13. Adequate and timely supply of quality inputs to farmers.
14. High priority to rural electrification.
15. Setting up of agro-processing units and creation of off-farm employment in rural areas.

Concept of Sustainable Agriculture

The policy will seek to promote technically sound, economically viable, environmentally non-degrading, and socially acceptable use of country's natural resources – land, water and genetic endowment to promote sustainable development of agriculture. Measures will be taken to contain biotic pressures on land and to control indiscriminate diversion of agricultural lands for non-agricultural purposes. The unutilized wastelands will be put to use for agriculture and afforestation. Particular attention will be given for increasing cropping intensity through multiple-cropping and inter-cropping.

Rational utilization and conservation of the country's abundant water resources will be promoted. Conjunctive use of surface water and groundwater will receive highest priority. Special attention will be focused on water quality and the problem of receding groundwater levels in certain areas as a result of overexploitation of underground aquifers. Proper on-farm management of water resources for the optimum use of irrigation potential will be promoted.

Erosion and narrowing of the base of India's plant and animal genetic resources in the last few decades has been affecting the food security of the country. Survey and evaluation of genetic resources and safe conservation of both indigenously and exogenously introduced genetic variability in crop plants, animals and their wild relatives will receive particular attention. The use of biotechnologies will be promoted for evolving plants which consume less water, are drought resistant, pest resistant, contain more nutrition, give higher yields and are environmentally safe. Conservation of bio-resources through their *ex situ* preservation in Gene Banks, as also *in situ* conservation in their natural habitats through biodiversity parks, etc., will receive a high priority to prevent their extinction. Specific measures will also be taken to conserve indigenous breeds facing extinction. There will be a time bound program to list, catalogue and classify country's vast agro biodiversity.

Sensitization of the farming community with the environmental concerns will receive high priority. Balanced and conjunctive use of biomass, organic and inorganic fertilizers and controlled use of agrochemicals through Integrated Nutrients Management and Integrated Pest Management (INM & IPM) will be promoted to achieve the sustainable increases in agricultural production. A nationwide programme for utilization of rural and urban garbage, farm residues and organic waste for organic matter repletion and pollution control will be worked out.

Agro-forestry and social forestry are prime requisites for maintenance of ecological balance and augmentation of biomass production in agricultural systems. Agro-forestry will receive a major thrust for efficient nutrient cycling, nitrogen fixation, organic matter addition and for improving drainage. Farmers will be encouraged to take up farm/agro-forestry for higher income generation by evolving technology, extension and credit support packages and removing constraints to development of agro and farm forestry. Involvement of farmers and landless labourers will be sought in the development of pastures/forestry programs on public wastelands by giving financial incentives and entitlements to the usufructs of trees and pastures.

FOOD AND NUTRITIONAL SECURITY

Special efforts will be made to raise the productivity and production of crops to meet the increasing demand for food generated by unabated demographic pressures and raw materials for expanding agro-based industries. A regionally differentiated strategy will be pursued, taking into account the agronomic, climatic and environmental conditions to realize the full growth potential of every region. Special attention will be given to development of new crop varieties, particularly of food crops, with higher nutritional value through adoption of biotechnology particularly genetic modification, while addressing bio-safety concerns.

A major thrust will be given to development of rainfed and irrigated horticulture, floriculture, roots and tubers, plantation crops, aromatic and medicinal plants, bee-keeping and sericulture, for augmenting food supply, exports and generating employment in rural areas. Availability of hybrid seeds and disease-free planting materials of improved varieties, supported by a network of regional nurseries, tissue culture laboratories, seed farms will be promoted to support systematic development of horticulture having emphasis on increased production, post-harvest management, precision farming, bio-control of pests and quality regulation mechanism and exports.

Animal husbandry and fisheries also generate wealth and employment in agriculture sector. Development of animal husbandry, poultry, dairying and aquaculture will receive a high priority in the efforts for diversifying agriculture, increasing animal protein availability in the food basket and for generating exportable surpluses. A national livestock breeding strategy will be evolved to meet the requirements of milk, meat, egg and livestock products and to enhance the role of draught animals as a source of energy for farming operations and transport. Major thrust will be on genetic upgradation of indigenous/native cattle and buffaloes using proven semen and high quality pedigreed bulls and by expanding artificial insemination network to provide services at the farmer's doorstep.

Generation and dissemination of appropriate technologies in the field of animal production as also health care to enhance production and productivity levels will be given greater attention. Cultivation of fodder crops and fodder trees will be encouraged to meet the feed and fodder requirements and to improve animal nutrition and welfare. Priority will also be given to improve the processing, marketing and transport facilities, with emphasis on modernization of abattoirs, carcass utilization and value addition thereon. Since animal disease eradication and quarantine is critical to exports, animal health system will be strengthened and disease-free zones created. The involvement of cooperatives and private sector will be encouraged for development of animal husbandry, poultry and dairy. Incentives for livestock and fisheries production activities will be brought at par with incentives for crop production.

An integrated approach to marine and inland fisheries, designed to promote sustainable aquaculture practices, will be adopted. Biotechnological application in the field of genetics and breeding, hormonal applications, immunology and disease control will receive particular attention for increased aquaculture production.

Development of sustainable technologies for fin and shellfish culture as also pearl culture, their yield optimization, harvest and post-harvest operations, mechanization of fishing boats, strengthening of infrastructure for production of fish seed, berthing and landing facilities for fishing vessels and development of marketing infrastructure will be accorded high priority. Deep sea fishing industry will be developed to take advantage of the vast potential of country's exclusive economic zone.

GENERATION AND TRANSFER OF TECHNOLOGY

A very high priority will be accorded to evolving new location-specific and economically viable improved varieties of agricultural and horticultural crops, livestock species and aquaculture as also conservation and judicious use of germplasm and other bio-diversity resources. The regionalization of agricultural research, based on identified agro-climatic zones, will be accorded high priority.

Application of frontier sciences like biotechnology, remote sensing technologies, pre and post-harvest technologies, energy saving technologies, technology for environmental protection through national research system as well as proprietary research will be encouraged. The endeavour will be to build a well organized efficient and result-oriented agriculture research and education system to introduce technological change in Indian agriculture. Upgradation of agricultural education and its orientation towards uniformity in education standards, women empowerment, user orientation, vocationalization and promotion of excellence will be the hallmark of the new policy.

The research and extension linkages will be strengthened to improve quality and effectiveness of research and extension system. The extension system will be broad-based and revitalized. Innovative and decentralized institutional changes will be introduced to make the extension system farmer-responsible and farmer-accountable. Role of Krishi Vigyan Kendras (KVKs), Non-governmental Organizations (NGOs), and Farmers' Organizations, Cooperatives, corporate sector and para-technicians in agricultural extension will be encouraged for organizing demand-driven production systems. Development of human resources through capacity building and skill upgradation of public extension functionaries and other extension functionaries will be accorded a high priority.

The Government will endeavour to move towards a regime of financial sustainability of extension services through effecting in a phased manner, a more realistic cost recovery of extension services and inputs, while simultaneously safeguarding the interests of the poor and the vulnerable groups.

Mainstreaming gender concerns in agriculture will receive particular attention. Appropriate structural, functional and institutional measures will be initiated to empower women and build their capabilities and improve their access to inputs, technology and other farming resources.

INPUTS MANAGEMENT

Adequate and timely supply of quality inputs such as seeds, fertilizers, plant protection chemicals, bio-pesticides, agricultural machinery and credit at reasonable rates to farmers will be the endeavour of the Government. Soil testing and quality testing of fertilizers and seeds will be ensured and supply of spurious inputs will be checked. Balanced and optimum use of fertilizers will be promoted together with use of organic manures and biofertilizers to optimize the efficiency of nutrient use.

Development, production and distribution of improved varieties of seeds and planting materials and strengthening and expansion of seed and plant certification system with private sector participation will receive a high priority. A National Seed Grid will be established to ensure supply of seeds especially to areas affected by natural calamities. The National Seeds Corporation (NSC) and State Farms Corporation of India (SFCI) will be restructured for efficient utilization of investment and manpower.

Protection to plant varieties through a *sui generis* legislation will be granted to encourage research and breeding of new varieties particularly in the private sector in line with India's obligations under TRIPS Agreement. The farmers will, however, be allowed their traditional rights to save, use, exchange, share and sell their farm saved seeds except as branded seeds of protected varieties for commercial purpose. The interests of the researchers will also be safeguarded in carrying out research on proprietary varieties to develop new varieties.

Integrated pest management and use of biotic agents in order to minimize the indiscriminate and injudicious use of chemical pesticides will be the cardinal principle covering plant protection. Selective and eco-friendly farm mechanization through appropriate technology will be promoted, with special reference to rainfed farming to reduce arduous work and to make agriculture efficient and competitive as also to increase crop productivity.

INCENTIVES FOR AGRICULTURE

The Government will endeavour to create a favourable economic environment for increasing capital formation and farmer's own investments by removal of distortions in the incentive regime for agriculture, improving the terms of trade with manufacturing sectors and bringing about external and domestic market reforms backed by rationalization of domestic tax structure. It will seek to bestow on the agriculture sector in as many respects as possible benefits similar to those obtaining in the manufacturing sector, such as easy availability of credit and other inputs, and infrastructure facilities for development of agri-business industries and development of effective delivery systems and freed movement of agro produce.

Consequent upon dismantling of Quantitative Restrictions on imports as per WTO Agreement on Agriculture, commodity-wise strategies and arrangements for protecting the grower from adverse impact of undue price fluctuations in world markets and for promoting exports will be formulated. Apart from price competition, other aspects of marketing such as quality, choice, health and bio-safety will be promoted. Exports of horticultural produce and marine products will receive particular emphasis.

A twofold long-term strategy of diversification of agricultural produce and value addition enabling the production system to respond to external environment and creating export demand for the commodities produced in the country will be evolved with a view to providing the farmers incremental income from export earnings. A favourable economic environment and supportive public management system will be created for promotion of agricultural exports. Quarantine, both of exports and imports, will be given particular attention so that Indian agriculture is protected from the ingress of exotic pests and diseases.

In order to protect the interest of farmers in context of removal of Quantitative Restrictions, continuous monitoring of international prices will be undertaken and appropriate tariffs protection will be provided. Import duties on manufactured commodities used in agriculture will be rationalized. The domestic agricultural market will be liberalized and all controls and regulations hindering increase in farmers' income will be reviewed and abolished to ensure that agriculturists receive prices commensurate with their efforts, investment. Restrictions on the movement of agricultural commodities throughout the country will be progressively dismantled.

The structure of taxes on foodgrains and other commercial crops will be reviewed and rationalized. Similarly, the excise duty on materials such as farm machinery and implements, fertilizers, etc., used as inputs in agricultural production, post-harvest storage and processing will be reviewed. Appropriate measures will be adopted to ensure that agriculturists by and large remain outside the regulatory and tax collection systems. Farmers will be exempted from payment of capital gains tax on compulsory acquisition of agricultural land.

INVESTMENTS IN AGRICULTURE

The agriculture sector has been starved of capital. There has been a decline in the public sector investment in the agriculture sector. Public investment for narrowing regional imbalances, accelerating development of supportive infrastructure for agriculture and rural development particularly rural connectivity will be stepped up. A time-bound strategy for rationalization and transparent pricing of inputs will be formulated to encourage judicious input use and to generate resources for agriculture. Input subsidy reforms will be pursued as a combination of price and institutional reforms to cut down costs of these inputs for agriculture. Resource allocation regime will be reviewed with a view to rechannelizing the available resources from support measures towards assets formation in rural sector.

A conducive climate will be created through a favourable price and trade regime to promote farmers' own investments as also investments by industries producing inputs for agriculture and agro-based industries. Private sector investments in agriculture will also be encouraged more particularly in areas like agricultural research, human resource development, post-harvest management and marketing.

Rural electrification will be given a high priority as the prime mover for agricultural development. The quality and availability of electricity supply will be improved and the demand of the agriculture sector will be met adequately in a reliable and cost-effective manner. The use of new and renewable sources of energy for irrigation and other agricultural purposes will also be encouraged.

Bridging the gap between irrigation potential created and utilized, completion of all ongoing projects, restoration and modernization of irrigation infrastructure including drainage, evolving and implementing an integrated plan of augmentation and management of national water resources will receive special attention for augmenting the availability and use of irrigation water.

Emphasis will be laid on development of marketing infrastructure and techniques of preservation, storage and transportation with a view to reducing post-harvest losses and ensuring a better returns to the growers. The weekly periodic markets under the direct control of *Panchayat Raj* institutions will be upgraded and strengthened. Direct marketing and pledge financing will be promoted. Producers markets on the lines of Ryatu Bazaars will be encouraged throughout the width and breadth of the country.

Storage facilities for different kinds of agricultural products will be created in the production areas or nearby places particularly in the rural areas so that the farmers can transport their produce to these places immediately after harvest in shortest possible time. The establishment of cold chains, provision of pre-cooling facilities to farmers as a service and cold storage in the terminal markets and improving the retail marketing arrangements in urban areas, will be given priority. Upgradation and dissemination of market intelligence will receive particular attention.

Setting up of agro-processing units in the producing areas to reduce wastage, especially of horticultural produce, increased value addition and creation of off-farm employment in rural areas will be encouraged. Collaboration between the producer cooperatives and the corporate sector will be encouraged to promote agro-processing industry. An interactive coupling between technology, economy, environment and society will be promoted for speedy development of food and agro-processing industries and building up a substantial base for production of value added agro-products for domestic and export markets with a strong emphasis on food safety and quality. The Small Farmers Agro Business Consortium (SFAC) will be energized to cater to the needs of farmer entrepreneurs and promote public and private investments in agri-business.

INSTITUTIONAL STRUCTURE OF INDIAN AGRICULTURE SCENARIO

Indian agriculture is characterized by predominance of small and marginal farmers. Institutional reforms will be so pursued as to channelize their energies for achieving greater productivity and production. The approach to rural development and land reforms will focus on the following areas:

- Consolidation of holdings all over the country on the pattern of north-western States;
- Redistribution of ceiling surplus lands and waste lands among the landless farmers, unemployed youth with initial start-up capital;
- Tenancy reforms to recognize the rights of the tenants and share croppers;
- Development of lease markets for increasing the size of holdings by making legal provisions for giving private lands on lease for cultivation and agribusiness;
- Updating and improvement of land records, computerization and issue of land passbooks to the farmers, and
- Recognition of women's rights in land.

The rural poor will be increasingly involved in the implementation of land reforms with the help of Panchayati Raj Institutions, Voluntary Groups, Social Activists and Community Leaders.

Private sector participation will be promoted through contract farming and land leasing arrangements to allow accelerated technology transfer, capital inflow and assured markets for crop production, especially of oilseeds, cotton and horticultural crops.

Progressive institutionalization of rural and farm credit will be continued for providing timely and adequate credit to farmers. The rural credit institutions will be geared to promote savings, investments and risk management. Particular attention will be paid to removal of distortions in the priority sector lending by commercial banks for agriculture and rural sectors. Special measures will be taken for revamping of cooperatives to remove institutional and financial weaknesses and evolving simplified procedure for sanction and disbursement of agriculture credit.

The endeavour will be to ensure distribution equity in the disbursement of credit. Micro-credit will be promoted as an effective tool for alleviating poverty. Self-help Group – Bank Linkage system, suited to Indian rural sector, will be developed as a supplementary mechanism for bringing the rural poor into the formal banking system, thereby improving banks outreach and the credit flows to the poor in an effective and sustainable manner.

The basic support to agriculture has been provided by cooperative sector assiduously built over the years. The Government will provide active support for promotion of cooperative form of enterprise and ensure greater autonomy and operational freedom to them to improve their functioning. The thrust will be on:

- Structural reforms for promoting greater efficiency and viability by freeing them from excessive bureaucratic control and political interference;
- Creation of infrastructure and human resource development;
- Improvement in financial viability and organizational sustainability of cooperatives;
- Democratization of management and increased professionalism in their operations, and
- Creating a viable inter-face with other grass-root Organizations.

The legislative and regulatory framework will be appropriately amended and strengthened to achieve these objectives.

RISK MANAGEMENT

Despite technological and economic advancements, the condition of farmers continues to be unstable due to natural calamities and price fluctuations. National Agriculture Insurance Scheme covering all farmers and all crops throughout the country with built-in provisions for insulating farmers from financial distress caused by natural disasters and making agriculture financially viable will be made more farmer-specific and effective. Endeavour will be made to provide a package insurance policy for farmers, right from sowing of crops to post-harvest operations, including market fluctuations in the prices of agricultural produce.

In order to reduce risk in and impart greater resilience to Indian agriculture against droughts and floods, efforts will be made for achieving greater flood-proofing of flood prone agriculture and drought-proofing of rainfed agriculture for protecting farmers from vagaries of nature. For this purpose, contingency agriculture planning, development of drought and flood resistant crop varieties, watershed development programs, drought prone areas and desert development programs and rural infrastructure development programs, will receive particular attention.

The Central Government will continue to discharge its responsibility to ensure remunerative prices for agricultural produce through announcement of Minimum Support Prices policy for major agricultural commodities. The food, nutrition and other domestic and exports requirements of the country will be kept in view while determining the support prices of different commodities. The price structure and trade mechanism will be continuously reviewed to ensure a favorable economic environment for the agriculture sector and to bring about an equitable balance between rural and urban incomes.

The methodology used by the Commission on Agricultural Costs and Prices (CACP) in arriving at estimates of cost of production will be periodically reviewed. The price structure of both inputs and outputs will be monitored to ensure higher returns to the farmers and bring about cost-effectiveness throughout the economy. Domestic market prices will be closely monitored to prevent distress sales by farmers. Public and cooperative agencies undertaking marketing operations will be strengthened.

The Government will enlarge the coverage of futures markets to minimize the wide fluctuations in commodity prices as also for hedging their risks. The endeavour will be to cover all important agricultural products under futures trading in course of time.

MANAGEMENT REFORMS

Effective implementation of policy initiatives will call for comprehensive reforms in the management of agriculture by Central and State Governments. Central Government will supplement/complement the State Governments through regionally differentiated Work plans, comprising crop/area/target group efforts specific interventions, formulated in an interactive mode and implemented in a spirit of partnership with States. Central Government will move away from schematic approach to Macro-Management mode and assume a role of advocacy, articulation and facilitation to help States in their efforts towards achieving accelerated agricultural development.

The Government will focus on quality aspects at all stages of farm operations from sowing to primary processing. The quality of inputs and other support services to farmers will be improved. Quality consciousness amongst farmers and agro-processors will be created. Grading and standardization of agricultural products will be promoted for export enhancement. Application of science and technology in agriculture will be promoted through a regular system of interface between S&T institutions and users/potential users, to make the sector globally competitive.

The database for agriculture sector will be strengthened to ensure greater reliability of estimates and forecasting which will help in the process of planning and policy making. Efforts will be made to significantly improve and harness latest remote sensing and information technology to capture data, collate it, add value and disseminate it to appropriate destinations for managing the risk and in accelerating the growth process. The objective will be to engage in a meaningful continuous dialogue with the external environment in the changing scenario and to have online and real-time system of 'Agriculture online' capacity to analyze signals emanating from the farms and markets for the benefit of farmers.

SUMMARY

Food processing industry is of enormous significance for India's development because of the vital linkages and synergies that it promotes between the two pillars of the economy, namely Industry and Agriculture. India is world's second largest producer of food and has the potential to become number one in due course of time with sustained efforts. The growth potential of this sector is enormous and it is expected that the food production will double in the next 10 years and the consumption of value-added food products will grow at a fast pace.

The growth of the Food Processing Industry will bring immense benefits to the economy, raising agricultural yields, meeting productivity, creating employment and raising the standard of very large number of people throughout the country, specially, in the rural areas. Economic liberalization and rising consumer prosperity is opening up new opportunities for diversification in food processing sector. Liberalization of world trade will open up new vistas for growth.

The food processing industry has been identified as a thrust area for development. This industry is included in the priority lending sector. Most of the food processing industries have been exempted from the provisions of industrial licensing under Industries (Development and Regulation) Act, 1951 with the exception of beer and alcoholic drinks and items reserved for small-scale sector, like vinegar, bread, bakery etc. As far as foreign investment is concerned, automatic approval for even 100 per cent equity is available for majority of the processed food items.

QUESTIONS

1. What are the salient features of National Food Processing Policy?
2. What are the characteristics of Government's new initiatives devised for Indian agriculture sector?
3. In what way you can create congenial and enabling atmosphere or environment to Indian agriculture for its success?
4. What are the essential factors governing the National Food Policy's promotional aspects?

OOO

CHAPTER 17

VARIOUS AGRO-PROCESSING INDUSTRIES

- Various Agro Processing Industries
- (R&D)
- Provisions of Technology Usage
- Value addition to Agriculture Food Products
- Crops
- Food and Vegetables
- Expected Development to Value Addition
- Processing of Cereals
- Bi-product and Waste Utilization in Rice
- Secondary Processing in Maize
- Steps for Starting SSI in Agri. Business Enterprises
- Process for Setting Up of SSI in Agriculture Business Units
- Crop and Commodity Wise Status of Agro Process Industry–Problems
- Indian Fruit and Vegetable Process Industry
- Rice Processing industry
- Coarse Cereals Processing Industry
- Indian Dairy Industry
- Indian Fish and Fish Products Processing Industry
- Preservation and Processing Industry Units
- Flavoring Agents and Extraction Industry
- Chemical Methods
- Pickle Industry
- Jams- Jellies and Marmalades
- Fermentation
- Constraints in Horticulture Industry
- Advantages of Floriculture
- Value Addition in Floriculture Industry
- Product Development
- Post-harvest Methods
- Processing and Marketing
- Indian Poultry Industry
- Indian Cotton Industry
- Increase in Domestic Cotton Consumption
- Cotton Exports from India
- Development of Entrepreneurship
- Occupational Mobility
- Rural Institutions
- Dynamic Development of Regions
- Pulse Processing Industry Units
- Oil Seeds Processing Units
- Sugar Cane Processing Units
- Jute Processing Units
- Animal Produce Processing Units
- Plantation Crops Processing Units
- Medicinal Aromatic Plants Processing
- Agriculture Produce Processing Units
- Traditional Foods Processing Units
- Quality Control and Standardization
- SWOT Analysis and Agro Processing Units
- Monetary Benefits in Agro Processing System

VARIOUS AGRO-PROCESSING INDUSTRIES

Introduction

Agro-processing could be defined as set of techno-economic activities carried out for conservation and handling of agricultural produce and to make it usable as food, feed, fiber, fuel or industrial raw material. Hence, the scope of the agro-processing industry encompasses all operations from the stage of harvest till the material reaches the end-users in the desired form, packaging, quantity, quality and price. Ancient Indian scriptures contain vivid account of the post-harvest and processing practices for preservation and processing of agricultural produce for food and medicinal uses. Inadequate attention to the agro-processing sector in the past put both the producer and the consumer at a disadvantage and it also hurts the economy of the country.

Agro-processing is now regarded as the sunrise sector of the Indian economy in view of its large potential for growth and likely socio-economic impact specifically on employment and income generation. Some estimates suggest that in developed countries, up to 14 per cent of the total workforce is engaged in agro-processing sector directly or indirectly. However, in India, only about 3 per cent of the workforce finds employment in this sector revealing its underdeveloped state and vast untapped potential for employment. Properly developed, agro-processing sector can make India a major player at the global level for marketing and supply of processed food, feed and a wide range of other plant and animal products.

RESEARCH & DEVELOPMENT (R&D)

R&D work in agro-processing carried out in India during the last 50 years categorized as follows:

1. Studies on physical, biochemical, nutritional, and engineering properties/characteristics of different food, feed, fiber, and industrial raw materials.
2. Response studies of different biological materials with reference to their storage, handling, and moisture conditioning.
3. Refinement of traditional equipment and processes for production of different foods, feeds, fibers and fuel materials for better quality, higher capacity energy efficiency, and reduced drudgery to workers.
4. Development of new produces and processes for better nutrition, convenience and taste and enhancement of shelf life of the produces, safe storage/packaging and development of better performing materials.
5. Better economic utilization of agricultural residues, by-products and recycling of wastes.
6. Design and Development of instruments and equipment for post-harvest operations and their evaluation, feasibility analysis, field trails/multiplication evaluation etc.
7. Design, layout planning and development of pilot plants, agricultural produce bulk handling systems and area specific agro-processing models.
8. Studies and modeling/simulation of post-harvest systems and industry for the purpose of optimization, forecasting and policy analysis.
9. Energy auditing and use of non-renewable sources of energy for post-harvest operations.

10. Product quality analysis, sensory evaluation and consumer acceptance studies.
11. Work conditions, safety and pollution control.

PROVISION OF TECHNOLOGIES USAGE

1. Agriculture produces refinement equipment such as, cleaners, graders and driers for on-farm operations as well as industrial operations.
2. Processes and equipment for parboiling of rice, preparation of puffed rice and flaked rice.
3. Development of processes and equipment for processing of pulses to produce dhal for higher recovery and better quality.
4. Development of driers using agricultural residues, by-products and solar energy.
5. Adoption and development of processes, and equipment for production of protein rich produces such as full fat soy flour, soy drink/soy milk, soy paneer (TOFU) and soy fortified baked products.
6. Development of equipment such as, leaf cup and *dona* making machine, multipurpose mills, mini flour mill, grain pearlers, maize dehuskers, shellers, groundnut decorticators, fruit graders, juice extractors, high recovery mechanical oil expellers and improved storage structures for cereals, pulses, oilseeds, onion and potato.
7. Processes and equipment for production of high quality ground spices and spice mix, development of raw materials and processes for production of instant sweets, curries, snack foods, instant soft drinks, *idli, dosa, sambhar* mixes/powders, egg. Powder, production and packaging of milk products such as *shrikhand*, butter milk, *paneer ghee* and sweets.
8. Equipment for high recovery of sugarcane juice processes for production of high quality jaggery and liquid jaggery.
9. Processes, equipment and pilot plants for production of various industrial raw materials from lac including dyes and pharmaceutical products.
10. Improved technology for processing of jute sticks to yield jute fibre and impregnation, preparation of jute based textile materials and bags.
11. Control of stored grain insects by using chemical and physical methods, storage structures for non-farm, Trade and process plant level operations.
12. Processing and canning of meat, meat products and fish. Some work has also been done in the area of processing forest produce such as oil extraction from oil bearing materials, collection and processing of resins and production of dyes, chemicals and pharmaceutical products.

The latest developments have been in the area of floriculture. Due to high export potential, R&D work has been initiated at some centres on pre-cooling, packaging, and transport of cut flowers and low-cost designs of greenhouses. Agro-processing models have also been developed for some of the agro-climatic regions in the country. In the area of agro-processing of fruits and vegetables, development of tools and techniques for harvesting, pre-cooling of freshly harvested produce, minimal processing, controlled ripening, juice extraction, concentration and storage has been done. Similarly, in the area of spices and condiments, floriculture, production of mushrooms, honey, eggs and fish, technologies have been developed for post-harvest loss reduction and value addition.

RECENT TRENDS IN AGRO PROCESSING TECHNOLOGIES

VALUE ADDITION TO AGRI FOOD PRODUCTS

CROPS:

Sl.No.	Crop/Item	Recent products, processes, trends and technologies
1.	Rice	Fully automatic modern rice mills particularly cooled quick cooking rice. Breakfast cereals and value added products. Attractive packaging and branding.
	Brown Rice	White Rice, Expanded rice and flaked rice
	Broken Rice	Pre-mixes, Alcohol
	Bran	Bran Oil, de-oiled bran, protein concentrate
	Husk	Husk ash, furfural, silica, fuel.
2.	Wheat	Fully automatic roller flour mills whole bran, wheat flour, Fortified wheat flour – attractive packaging and branding – Large number of baked products. Automatic Chapatti making machines.
	Maida	Noodle, biscuits, bread, cakes, pastries, traditional snacks, ready-to-cook mixes, self-rising flour.
	Atta	
	Semolina	Vermicelli, macaroni, spaghetti.
	Dallia	
	Bran	
	Other Products	Purified wheat, wheat flakes, shredded wheat, bran flakes
	Bi-products	Wheat stalks, wheatgerm, Wheatgerm oil, Gluten, Wheat stalks and husk are used as fodder. Wheatgerm Oil is rich in Vitamin-E and used in cosmetics.
3.	Maize Corn Flour	Packaged and branded corn flakes and value added products including ready-to-eat snacks (salted and sweetened) starch material, corn oil with specific consumer desired attributes. Cattle feed Baby corn. Large automatic corn processing plants
	Maize Dry milling (Primary Processing)	Maize flour, besan extender, grits.
	From Wet Milling	Starch, gluten, maize oil.
	Secondary processing	Corn Flakes
	Secondary processing from Starch	Dextrose, Dextrin, sorbitol, modified starch,High fructose corn syrup.
4.	Coarse Cereals	Value-added products including breakfast foods and extruded fortified tasty products industrial raw materials.
5.	Pulses	Automatic processing units for pulses with driers, colour sorters and packaging unit. Attractive consumer packaging

		with branding. Cold storing of processed pulses. Snack foods and other value-added products.
6.	Soya bean	Production of full fat soy flour/enzyme active soy flour for bakery and fortified foods ready-to-eat snack foods. Nuggets, so milk, soy paneer, soy biscuit and other soy based snack foods.
7.	Sugarcane	Sucrose and Syrup, fiber (cellulose) Folder
	By-products are Bagasse, molasses and press mud	Bagasse (cellulose) is used in cellulose industries like pulp, paper, particle boards, cattle-feed, etc. Molasses for commercial production of alcohol based chemicals, products and cattle feed.
	Sugarcane wax	for making carbon paper.
8.	Cotton-textile fiber	Cotton seeds are used as feed and stalks used as fuel, Paper and pulp industry raw material. Cotton willow dust is used for production of biogas. Cotton waste can also be used for mushroom production.
9.	Coconut	Copra, coconut oil, vinegar, jaggery, desiccated coconut powder, snowball tender coconut, bull copra, coconut, ball copra, coconut milk, handicrafts and coconut fiber products.

FRUITS AND VEGETABLES

1.	Apple	Juice, Jam, Apple slices, apple-cider	By-product Pomace
2.	Banana	Fruit, chips	Pseudo-stem for starch extraction and paper industry. Decoration, handicraft, Banana leaves for pattal and dis posable bio-plates, baking food items like adda and fish in steam.
3.	Citrus	Citrus-pulp-juice dried citrus, peel, extracts.	Squash dehydrated products.
4.	Guava	Jam, Jelly and Cheese, Juice, Canned Segments – Nectar, Carbonated Beverages.	Guava peel waste as substrate for protein and protease production, guava seed meal.
5.	Mango	Juice, Pulp, Jam, Leather, Canned products Pickles-aamchoor-dehydrated powder.	Stones, peeled skin etc.
6.	Papaya	Squash, sauce, pickle, leather, jelly, jam, candy, latex, for pappain extract pulp powder.	Fruit waste, leaves – stem pulverized to be used as animal feed, source of raw material to paper industry

7.	Pineapple	Candles-pickles-jelly	Waste can be utilized as ensilage for cattle feed or by industry for production of alcohol cellulose, actic acid.
8.	Tomato	Paste, juice, ketchup Pickle, sauce, sun dried products	
9.	Carrot	Peeled baby carrots Juice	Carrot pulp/pomace for extracting dietary home-made carrot based condemned milk, preparations like gazrella and burfee.
10.	Potato	Chips are most common home-made for market.	Potato peel waste utilization for extracting xanthan, product a thickening agent in salad dressings, yoghurts etc.

EXPECTED DEVELOPMENT TO VALUE ADDITION SECTOR IN CEREALS

Post-harvest Processes	Short Term	Medium Term	Long Term
Secondary Processing By-product and Waste Utilization in Wheat			
• Secondary processing of Wheat	Secondary processing of Wheat	More installations of Pasta plants	Further increase in use of enzyme based technology for fermentation
• By-product – waste utilization in wheat		Extraction of oil from wheat bran	Production of alcohol from damaged wheat
		Deoiled cake for animal/poultry feed	Extraction of gluten-starch from wheat
• By-product and waste		Gluten feed to be fortified	More gluten feed to be fortified
By-product and Waste Utilization in Rice			
Rice Bran	Gradual increase in Bran available for Oil extraction	Further increase in Bran availability Proteins	Higher % of oil Oil extraction Extraction may be commercialized
Rice Husk	Increased usage of Husk to generate	Increase in use of husk for furfural	Most modern mills to use husk as fuel.
Secondary Processing of Maize			
Secondary processing of Maize	Secondary processing of Wheat Rice in variety of secondary products	Gradual shift to Enzyme based technology	Further increase variety of secondary product including modified starch

STEPS FOR STARTING SMALL AGRI BUSINESS ENTERPRISE

The success of small-scale agribusiness industry solely depends upon doing the right thing at the right time. In other words, a small-scale agricultural business entrepreneur has to be conversant with the varied regulations governing the small-scale industry and the procedures to be followed in order to acquire the necessary assistance and incentives offered by the state government and central government.

Basic Objectives

The basic objectives underlying the development of small-and medium-scale industries are the increase in the supply of manufactured food processing goods, the promotion of capital formation for these industrial units, development of indigenous entrepreneurial talents and skills and creation of broader employment opportunities. In addition, they include the socio-economic goals such as decentralization and disbursal of manufacturing activities, marketing strategies in rural as well as urban areas, reduction of regional economic imbalances within the country, diffusion of entrepreneurial, managerial abilities, skills and technology throughout the economy.

In the Indian economy, cottage and small-scale industries in agriculture business units have a significant role to play. With the increasing pace of industrialization and sophistication of the large-scale industries, new orientation is inevitable in the relationship of the SSIs with the large and medium industries. This relationship calls for integration of the production methods, upgradation of the qualities of value-added agricultural products and their ability to meet the stringent delivery schedules with many other problems that arise in dynamic and changing environment not only in the country but also in the international field.

Steps to be Folllowed

1. Analyze and compile proposed SSI industry's objectives
2. List out newer ideas on this proposed SSI
3. Consult with various publications and agencies
4. Discuss with SSI office of state and central government and have more information
5. Choose type of ownership
6. Prepare project report
7. Make sure what laws will affect?
8. Obtain clearance certificates from state and centre
9. Financial Planning
10. Planning of machinery installations and other equipments
11. Identification of raw material requirement with suppliers
12. Financial arrangements
13. Chalking out appropriate marketing strategies
14. Deciding pricing policy
15. Recruit personnel

16. Organizing marketing channels
17. Identification of buyers
18. Maintenance of accounts ledgers
19. Diversification
20. Plough back profits
21. Ancillary development

Steps to be Followed for Analysis

Potential agri-business entrepreneur has to pass through various stages for setting up his small-scale unit and these are aiming at:

1. Decision for self-employment
2. Identification of opportunities in the agribusiness field
3. Idea generation-screening product-service idea
4. Concept testing and selection line of business

Business Analysis

- Market analysis
- Demand estimation-analysis-factors affecting demand
- Derived and autonomous demand
- Forecasting demand
- Marketing Methods
- Marketing Feasibility
- Market Research

Technical Analysis

- Proper location of the unit
- Proper size of the plant
- Suitable process of manufacture
- Factory layout
- Organizational set-up

Financial Analysis

- Fixed assets of units
- Requirement of working capital
- Manufacturing cost of the product
- Sources of finances
- Repayment schedule

- Profitability and production statements
- Cash flow statements
- Break-even point
- ROI in each year

Economic Analysis

- Social cost-benefit analysis
- Economic benefits and costs measured in terms of efficiency, impact of project on distribution of income in society level of savings and investment in society
- Contribution of project towards fulfillment of merit wants: employment, self-sufficiency, social orders

Market and Demand Analysis

- Selection of product/products
- Product Development
- Selection of site (location)
- Purchase/lease of land/shed in industrial estate
- Development of the plot
- Building of the factory
- Selection of ownership form
- Preparation of the project report with technical feasibility report

Comprehensive appraisal of proposed project should accompany the following:

(a) Technological aspect
(b) Financial aspect
(c) Economic aspect
(d) Managerial aspect
(e) Market aspect
(f) Break-even analysis
(g) Planning Commission's guidelines
(h) Project Life Cycle
(i) Project Manager — Role/Responsibilities
(j) Network Analysis – PERT and CPM
(k) Financial Appraisal methods
(l) Registration in case of company or partnership type of organization
(m) Agreement with collaborator
(n) Obtaining letter of intent

(o) Obtaining import license, customs, clearance, power/water connection, civil works

(p) Delivery of imported and indigenous machinery, erection of machinery-equipments

(q) Obtaining clearance from PUCB, Industrial license – SSI registration

(r) Acquiring manufacturing know-how, selection of personnel, technical and administration Unskill/skill

(s) Training to labors-designing and arranging financial schemes, arrangement of raw Material.

(t) Apply for grants-subsidies from government

(u) Trial run of the factory and commissioning of plant

(v) Start of commercial production, arrangement of sale of products

(w) Registration of designs and trade marks.

Winning Edge

The opening up of the Indian small industry sector to competition as well as the increase in the need to cater to the global market, demands fresh perceptions to respond to the radical changes in the 90s and 2010s. Consequently, this sector must change first to survive as well as restructure itself to meet the new challenges through a critical evaluation of the forces of free global trade and increased competition. These events demand quantum strategic changes in terms of industry culture, flattening of the organization structure employee empowerment so well as team building. Only those organizations which can respond to these changes will be able to survive and retain a winning edge.

Some of the important characteristics that differentiate the successful organizations from the unsuccessful ones are:

1. Most important aspect of successful business is leadership. It calls for clear vision, goals and objectives, well-defined mission and employees' participation.
2. Adequate but well-orchestrated control, constant feedback of results as well as setting and adherence of high standards give an organization cutting edge over others. Planning, foresight and analysis are other important qualities.
3. To be able to extract the best from its employees through total involvement, the organization puts a lot of emphasis on proper internal communication and on training of the employees.
4. The successful organization is one which is very close to the marketplace. The process of systematic market is used to develop products or process of systematic market research is used to develop products or process and to provide value for money to the customers. This helps to gain the market share.
5. The next most important characteristic of winning agricultural business management organization is "Zero Basing" or striking to the fast – knowing what business the company is in swiftly recognizing and preventing when it has diverted into an unsuitable path and preventing risks.

PROCESS FOR SETTING UP SMALL-SCALE AGRIBUSINESS UNIT

Guidelines

1. Selection of Industry:	
Small Industries Service Institute (SISI)	They provide entrepreneurs in the selection of industry, unit, areas, suitable raw material and machinery.
Indian Investment Centre, Parliament Street, New Delhi-110001 Ministry of Industrial Development & Company Affairs, New Delhi-110001	It advises on foreign capital participation and technical collaboration. Provides guidance to entrepreneurs regarding government privileges, policies and procedures, available incentives and facilities for investment, economic size of unit and magnitude of investments required.
2. District Industries Centre (DIC)	In each district, there would be one agency to deal with all requirements of small and village industries which would be called the District Industries Centre. Under the single roof of the Centre, all the services and support required by small and village entrepreneurs would be provided. The centre would have a separate wing for looking after the special needs of cottage and householdindustries as distinct from small-scale industry. The Rural Industries Project and Rural Artisans Program would be merged with program of District Industries Centre (DIC). Each DIC have GM and 7 managers for planning, economic investigations and marketing.
3. Factory Accommodation:	
DIC	They provide built-up factory space in industrial estates or developed factory sites, power, and water. The building designs have to be approved by Municipalities or Corporation, while power-water point are sanctioned by the State government/undertakings.
4. Industrial Estates	There are more than 600 industrial estates which give built-up plots in developed areas. Main facilities includes common facility services-workshops, sheds on hire-purchase, concessional charges on water-power, exemption from octroi duty on nudging materials.
5. Registration	Although it is not mandatory, it is certainly helpful to obtain SSI Registration Number from Director of Industries.
6. Machinery:	
SISI	They will advise different kinds of machinery-equipment used to manufacture of different value-added products.
National Small Industries Corporation (NSIC), New Delhi	It supplies indigenous and imported machinery on hire-purchase basis.
State Small Industries, New Delhi	They give indigenous machinery on deferred credit basis.
Chief Controller – Import/ Exports, New Delhi	They issue import licence for machinery of foreign origin on recommendation of Director of Industries.
Consultants	Install machinery as per layout drawn by them.

7. Raw Materials:

Dev. Commissioner SSI, New Delhi	He procures raw material for small industry and distributes them among State governments. He also arranges import of raw materials through MMTC and STC of India.
Director of Industries	They allot quotas of scarce raw materials.
SSI Corporation	They supply raw materials.
Chief Controller of Import/ Exporter	They issue license for import of raw material.

8. Finance:

SIDC	Small Industries Development Bank of India (SIDBI) started operations through its 25 offices in cities located in states of India. SIDBI set up under Act of Parliament as principal financial institution for promotion.
(SFC)	Financing and development of industry in tiny small-scale sector. The SIDBI expected to coordinate functions of institutions engaged in similar activities. SIDBI is wholly owned subsidiary of IDBI.
State Financial Corporation State Director of Industries	It has taken under State Aid to industries related to small-scale sector. They provide loans under State Aid Industries Act/Rules for block capital.
SBI and its subsidiaries	They sanction medium-term/installments credit loans for purchase of machinery, construction of factory buildings. They also provide working capital for purchase of raw materials to meet day-to-day requirements.
Commercial Banks – SISI	They sanction loans for working capital needs. They furnish tech reports to Institutes, the SBI on applicant units.

9. Technical know-how:

SISI	They prepare improved designs and Institute's drawings for products. They assist in making tools, dies, jigs, and fixtures.
National Small Industrial Corporation (NSIC), New Delhi	They help in optimum utilization of men and materials and machinery. They prepare management control charts for maximizing profits. They train managers, supervisors in industrial management. They train workers to upgrade their skills.
CSIR, New Delhi	They give advanced training in their prototype. Production-cum-Training centre in operation of modern machines.
National/State Productivity Council	It develops new technologies process and disseminates same to the industry. Train factory owners to increase productivity.
Small Industry Extension Training Instt, Hyderabad	It gives full-time management training to managers/ proprietors in small industry sector.
Central Institute of Tools Designs, Hyderabad	Specialize in provision, technical consultancy, tool facilities, training in design-manufacture of tools.
Instt. for Design of Electrical Measuring Instruments (IDEMI), Mumbai	Provides technical know-how, testing calibration. Laboratory-workshop-training facilities to Electrical Measuring instrument manufacturers.

10. Standardization:	
SISI	They provide technical guidance in production of goods according to prescribed standards.
Indian Standard Institution (ISI)	It prescribes specifications for products/issues ISI certification.
Directors of Industries Quality Control	They prescribe standards – give Q mark to small industry's products.
11. Marketing:	
SISI	They conduct distribution-surveys for benefit of small industrialists. They enlist units for the participation in the Central Government stores/purchase program. Competency certificates will be issued here to units on receipt of government orders.
National Small Industrial Corporation, New Delhi	They promote ancillary relationship with large and medium scale units in public-private sectors. It secures contracts from DGSD, Railways, Defence sectors for supply of manufctured goods by SSI units.
State Small Industrial Corporation	They secure orders from State government and other semi-government organisation for supply of stores materials.
12. Export:	
SISI	They enlist small units for meeting vide Export Aid to Small Industry Scheme of STC. They wll provide technical counseling for execution of export order and disseminate information, on exploring export markets. They maintain close liaison with Export Promotion Council to have updated information about products that has potential export markets.
Chief Controller of Import/ Export	Issues license for export to other countries and carry out exploration for latest information on market studies.
Directorate of Export Promotion, Udyog Bhavan, New Delhi	Publishes trade directories brochure bulletins. They organize exhibitions/showroom and liaison between Indian exporters and global marketeers.

CROP AND COMMODITY WISE STATUS

India's low level of processing is expected to change significantly in the future fuelled by sustained economic growth and steady urbanization. Processed food output is expected to grow at a strong 7 per cent CAGR in terms of value from 55.6 billion USD in 2005 to 95.6 1 billion USD in 2013. Premiumisation, especially among the young and rich urban population, is also a key factor helping value growth over the forecast period.

Key segments in Food Processing are as under:

- Fruits & Vegetables
- Meat & Poultry
- Dairy Marine
- Products Grains
- Consumer Foods.

Common features across segments:

Largely unorganized – Though the unorganized segment varies across categories that are mentioned above, approximately 75 per cent of the market is still in the unorganized segment.

The organized sector is relatively bigger in the secondary processing segment than the primary processing segment. Also, the primary processing segment is highly fragmented.

The following sub-sections provide a brief overview of the key segments.

While the opportunities and constraints at segment level are touched upon, a detailed analysis is provided in later chapters.

INDIAN FRUITS AND VEGETABLE INDUSTRY

This is one of the most important and fast growing sub-sectors of the food processing sector, as fruits and vegetables form an indispensable part of healthy diet. India accounts for 13 per cent of vegetables and 12 per cent of fruits production globally, with an enviable share in few categories like Mango, Banana, Cashew, Green Peas and Onion.

The productivity has also improved from 10.25 and 14.37 million tons/hectare for Fruits and Vegetables in 2002-03 to 10.94 and 16.14 million tons/hectare for Fruits and Vegetables respectively.

The share of the organized sector in Fruits and Vegetables processing is 48 per cent. Majority of the units are in the small-scale sector, having low capacities up to 250 tons/year though big Indian and multinational companies have capacities in the range of 30 tons/hour. Currently, only 2.2 per cent of the total produce in India is processed and the rest marketed as fresh fruits and vegetables. Globally, developed countries process fruits and vegetables in excess of 65 per cent.

Processing of Fruits and Vegetables

Joint effort of R&D institutions, farmers, government agencies and the trade has resulted in India emerging as a major producer of fruits and vegetables in the world. In the year 2000-2001, the country produced about 45 million tons of fruits and 80 million tons of vegetables. It was next to China in production of vegetables and topped in production of fruits. However, the growth in post-harvest sector has not kept pace with the production.

Even during the year 2000-2001, there were only 6,000 fruits and vegetable units in the country that had grown from a figure of about 1,000 during 1950-51. Less than one per cent of the total produce was processed, though the installed capacity of the processing industry has grown steadily from 0.27 metric tons in 1980 to about 3 metric tons in 2000-2001. Significant developments in technology include better understanding of the process of ripening of fruits, optimum harvesting time, pre-cooling of freshly harvested produce, cold storing of the raw fruits and vegetables, sorting, cleaning, waxing, packaging technology for fruits.

Bottlenecks

Inspite of the strong supply base, India has a low 1.38 per cent share of global trade. India's exports of fresh fruits and vegetables stood at INR 2,411.66 crore (534.97 million dollar) in 2006-07. It is estimated that around 30 per cent of the produce is lost due to lack of processing facilities (in flush season) and inadequate infrastructure for post-harvest treatment, packing, storage and transportation. The demand for processed fruits and vegetables is lower in India mainly on account of higher costs that can be attributed to higher duties and taxes on packaging material, inefficient supply chain with lot of intermediaries, absence of cost-effective latest technologies for processing, infrastructural bottlenecks and high cost of finance. Smaller units and their lack of marketing strength for end-products also is a major constraint for expansion of domestic market.

Fruits and vegetables offer a significant potential for the organised processing players due to the low level of processing and a vast supply base, coupled with considerable international demand for certain fresh as well as processed fruits and vegetables. However, inefficient domestic farming, higher costs of product delivery, exports protection and demanding standards, intermediaries and inefficiencies in the supply chain are the biggest bottlenecks in the growth of the sector. The recent emphasis on Fruits and Vegetables in light of nutrition security, growing interest of food processors and more profitable land use has brought in a significant change in the outlook of the producers who started using the arid/ semi-arid lands and the horticultural crops that have lesser demands on water and gives three to four times more remuneration than field crops.

India's has the largest livestock population in the world, however, most animals are not bred for meat, as a vast majority of the Indian population is vegetarian. People generally use Process Meat and Poultry, Dried fruits and vegetables and Fruit juice concentrates. Similarly, vegetable curries in restorable pouches, Mushroom products, Fruit pulps and juices, Ready-to-serve beverages, Canned/Frozen fruits, Pulp and vegetables, Jams, squashes, pickles and chutney.

The commodity-wise growth of agro-processing industries in the country during the years 1950 to 2000 has been as given below. **Rice Processing Industry** starting with 20.6 metric tons (Mt) of rice production during 1950-51, the country has come a long way to produce about 89.48 Mt of rice in the year 1999-2000. Similarly, in processing sector, the technology has undergone significant changes. Earlier, hand pounding, pedal operated system and Egle berg huller units were common for milling of paddy. By the year 1998-99, there were nearly 30,000 modern rice mills using rubber rolls for paddy dehusking. Of these, more than 5,000 are large rice mills with parboiling facility and nearly 100 have colour sorters for removal of discoloured rice for export market.

The industry could grow on account of R&D inputs starting from the design and development of a variety of threshing machines. Mud bins, wooden planks and mud plastered bins, gunny bags and metal bins have been in use by the farmers for storage of wheat for food and for seed purposes.

The traders and government agencies use gunny bags and godown type structures for storage of wheat. For transit level storage, CAP structures have been in use. Metal bins have gained popularity among farmers in the capacity range of 0.2-1.0 ton of grain storage. As wheat is usually harvested at low moisture content, drying has not been a major problem except for untimely rains.

A number of commercial organizations have been offering processing units for handling, cleaning, grading, drying, storage, treatment and bagging of wheat for seed and food applications. Wheat is now increasingly being used in the form of bread, biscuits, *suji* and *atta*. Wheat flakes and puffed wheat as breakfast cereals has been gradually picking up.

Traditionally used smaller size *atta chakkis* may face problems of declining clientele. Better mechanized Chakkis (with lower pollution level and better energy efficiency) are likely to increase in number. The number of roller flour mills is also likely to increase steadily. However, majority of the mills may continue facing the problems of low capacity utilization and working capital constraints.

These units would need to function through vertical integration of operations for sustaining profitability and achieve cost reduction through appropriate automation and computerization. Increase in demand is also expected in grain handling machinery, silo systems in grain markets and seed processing machinery. Trends in consumer preferences suggest increasing demand for baked products.

Demand for bread is likely to grow faster than the demand for biscuits. Presently bread is consumed mostly in large cities. Its consumption is expected to grow in smaller towns also. States with higher per capita income would continue to lead in the consumption of baked products. Among diversified products, full bran wheat bread has also been gaining popularity.

PROCESSING OF COARSE / CEREALS

Production of coarse cereals has risen from 15.4 to 32.0 metric tons between 1950-51 and 2000-2001. The growth has not been as rapid as in case of wheat and rice. It is because of low profitability of these crops for farmers. Till 1950s, we were dependent on manual methods of harvesting of these crops, bullock treading, storage in mud bins and gunny bags and milling by manual chakkis or water mills. By the year 1998-99, power operated equipment were available for all operations including threshing, pearling and milling.

The trends indicate that coarse cereals are now increasingly used as cattle feed, speciality/occasional foods, and industrial products such as starches. Efforts are required to develop high yielding varieties of coarse with desired characteristics for different uses and to explore new food uses. Safe storage of the flour produced from most of the coarse cereals has been a problem due to its high degree of perishability. This problem needs to be solved.

INDIAN DAIRY INDUSTRY

INDIAN DAIRY has been involved in the Dairy Business since many years in Delhi, India. INDIAN DAIRY take pride in introducing as one of India's leading **Manufactures**, **Exporters** and **Suppliers** of wide range of Dairy Products. We at INDIAN DAIRY have shown a new way of living – a healthy way of Dairy Industry for Dairy Business to improve the way of living. **INDIAN DAIRY** is on the edge of ISO 22000:2005 and HACCP Certified Company for further growth in our core competency areas — Dairy Products Manufacture, Exporter and Supplier in Delhi, India. We have extensive range of Milk Product and Dairy Product catering to people of all age and food industry. **INDIAN DAIRY** are continuously striving between Technology, System, and Human Recourse to provide Dairy Product and Dairy Business that meet the quality of Milk Product, performance and pride aspiration of Customers for Dairy Industry.

India is the largest producer of milk in the world. Milk products production is expected to increase from 99.9 million tons equivalent in 2006 to 108.8 million tons in 2009 growing at a CAGR of 2.89 per cent. The milk surplus states in India are Uttar Pradesh, Punjab, Haryana, Rajasthan, Gujarat, Maharashtra, Andhra Pradesh, Karnataka and Tamil Nadu with majority of the manufacturing of milk products also concentrated in these states.

India's unique pattern of production, consumption, processing and marketing of dairy products consist of over 11 million farmers organized into about 0.1 million village Dairy Cooperative Societies (DCS). These cooperatives form part of a national milk grid which links the milk producers throughout India with consumers in more than 700 towns and cities handling about 18 6 million kg of milk per day. The dairy sector ranks first in terms of processed food, with 37 per cent of the produce being processed, but the organized sector accounts for a mere 15 per cent, processing about 13 million tons annually while the unorganized sector 7 processes about 22 million tons per annum.

Ghee is the most widely marketed and branded product with a nationwide penetration of 24.1 per cent and growing at a rate of 8 per cent per annum. The dairy whitener market comprises of sweetened milk powders, condensed milk and creamers. The organized cheese market is dominated by processed cheese which accounts for 74 per cent market share. In the Ice-cream segment, organized sector accounts for a high 70 per cent and is growing at 20 per cent per annum.

Few problems like the packaged milk segment is dominated by the regional and national level Dairy Cooperative Societies. These Dairy Cooperative Societies collect milk from the various small-scale vendors, pack it and distribute it under their brand name. Despite the high production, the per capita consumption of milk in India is still lower at 229 grams/day compared to the world average of 285 grams/day. The farmers are not allowed to sell milk to new players outside the cooperatives preventing huge investments from large foreign players. Less than 0.4 per cent of the total milk and milk products are exported and virtually none imported. Most of the production is consumed in the domestic market. Also, the organized segment accounts for a lower 15 per cent share. There is tremendous potential for the organised players if the restrictions on the sale from farmers are removed and a level playing field is created for all.

Still we can say INDIAN DAIRY, one of the front runner of **Manufacture and Exporter**, **supplier** of **Skimmed Milk** Powder, Desi Ghee, Condensed Milk, Cased-in full cream milk, Full Cream Milk Powder, Dairy whitener, Cheese, Cheese Powder, Cheese mozzarella, Dairy Creamer, Butter Milk Powder, Skimmed White Powder, Sweet Cream, Whey Protein, Dairy Creamer, Palm kernal Oil, **Dairy** Mix, Non-dairy Creamer, Spray Milk Powder, Evaporated Milk, Maltodextrin, Protein Powder, Fat Fitted Powder, White Butter, Lactose (Edible and Pharma Grade), Glucose, Dematerialized Whey Powder and all kind of Dairy Products, has emerged as the indubitable winner of Dairy Industry.

Overview of the Indian Dairy Sector

- The country is the largest milk producer all over the world, around 100 million MT.
- Value of output amounted to ₹ 1179 billion (in 2004-05) (approximately equals combined output of paddy and wheat).
- 1/5th of the world bovine population.
- Milch animals (45 per cent indigenous cattle, 55 per cent buffaloes, and 10 per cecnt cross bred cows).
- Immensely low productivity, around 1000 kg/year (world average 2038 kg/year).
- Large number of unproductive animals, low genetic potency, poor nutrition and lack of services are the main factors for the low productivity.

- There are different regions – developed, average, below average (eastern states of Orissa, Bihar and NE region) in the dairy industry.

INDIAN FISHING INDUSTRY

In India, fishing is considered as a bright and prosperous industry. With short supplies of fish on land, India looks to the sea that holds huge promise and it can supply vast quantity of fish. Fish is a rich source of high grade proteins. It is quite surprising that fishing industry in India is almost in a primitive stage in spite of having a really long coastal line of near about 6100 kms and a broad continental shelf particularly in several parts along the West Coast.

Another probable reason is that modernization on a limited scale began after the independence of the country.

Fishing in India suffers from several climatic disadvantages. Firstly, India being a tropical country, fish does not keep fresh for long time without proper refrigeration. Modernization in this context means replacing fishing craft by power driven boats, providing facilities of quick refrigeration of fish to avoid its putrefaction. It also includes arranging canneries for surplus fish, utilizing discarded portions of fish for making fertilizers, etc., providing refrigerated road transport facilities to inland markets and the marketing of fish on cooperative lines. Hence, steps are being taken to introduce modernization in the fishing industry of India in order to bring better results in this particular area.

India has several mechanized boats as well as numerous commercial deep sea fishing vessels. Moreover, fishing harbors have been constructed on the East Coast and the West Coast. In ocean, fish is caught in shallow waters whose depth is moderately less. The fishing boats remain near the coast and they rarely go beyond a distance of around 11 kms from the coast. Coastal fisheries are not significant in the country as Indian coastline is not indented. Fish is mainly caught in the back waters of Kerala as well as Tamil Nadu, in deltas of Ganga River, Mahanadi River, Krishna River, Godavari and Kaveri river, Chilka Lake and a huge number of creeks on the West Coast.

The fish processing industry in India, during the past ten years has been rather exclusively concerned with shrimps largely because of the easy market which the shrimps provide abroad. The impact of shrimp export has not been very healthy, as the industry failed to diversify itself to other fish and fish products. Shortage of shrimps as raw material in some areas or in certain seasons has led to underutilization of the freezing and canning plants.

Surely the future of the processing industry in India does not lie in shrimps alone, for these constitute only about 12 per cent of the country's total catch. Therefore, all other fishes including the trash fish should be considered first as, important by the industry. The Central Institute of Fisheries Technology has made considerable advance on the economic utilization of many other varieties of fish. These include marketing of the entire fish, fish fillets and picked meat. Other products such as fish flour, fish protein concentrate, fish hydrolysate, and fish soup powder, fish flakes and fish sausages seem to have great possibilities. Little known products such as bacteriological peptone prepared from trash fish are also important.

INDIAN HORTICULTURE INDUSTRY

In India, we have several agro-ecological regions. Hence, there are ample opportunities to grow a variety of horticulture crops. Approximate estimates reveal that nearly 11-6 million hectares of land is covered by horticulture crops and the annual production is about 91 million tons. Horticulture crops, though they occupy hardly 7 per cent of the cropped area, they contribute over 18 per cent to the gross agricultural output of India.

India produces almost 28.2 million tons of fruits and 66 million tons of vegetables and is next only to Brazil and China. Though the per capita consumption of fruits and vegetables in India is only around 46 kg and 130 g against a minimum of about 92 g and 300 g respectively recommended by Indian Council of Medical Research and National Institute of nutrition.

At the present growing rate, the requirements of fruits and vegetables, on a yearly basis would be nearly 32.58 million tons and 83 million tons respectively.

The need for attaining nutritional security and for more profitable use of land has made the growers aware of greater utilization of available wastelands and focussed their attention towards horticultural crops that demand less water and other inputs. They also earn 3 to 4 times more remuneration than other field crops. Abundant sunshine throughout the year, surplus labour and varied agro-climate conditions offer high potential for commercial horticulture in the estimated 240 million acres of cultivable wasteland that is lying idle at present.

VALUE ADDITION IN HORTICULTURE

Value addition to horticultural produce through preservation and the processing play a very important role in the agro-industrial development of the country. Horticulture based processing industries can stimulate the commercial growers to cultivate high quality crops for better economic returns and also through the generation of enormous employment opportunities in production, processing, grading, storage and marketing etc.

High degree of perishability of certain fruits and vegetables particularly those produced and grown in the inaccessible pockets of the region warrant the scientific post-harvest management and processing to contribute higher value to the produce.

Processing is also undertaken to convert the unmarketable surplus in the form of low grade produce, overripe and the underripe fruits, windfall and drops and the bulky produce such as jackfruits into products of economic value.

Processing also acquires further importance as the estimated post-harvest losses of the fruits and vegetables are around 25-30 per cent. There are also several high value low volume products needing special processing technologies such as mushroom, ginger, turmeric, cardamom, mechanical and aromatic plants, cashewnut etc.

The total installed capacity of fruits and vegetables in the country has shown a steady increase and is currently estimated to be around ten lakh tons. The major processed items include fruit juices and the pulps fruit based drinks, canned drinks, vegetable jams, jellies, marmalades, and pickles and dehydrated vegetable produce.

PRESERVATION AND PROCESSING INDUSTRY UNITS

Several methods of food preservations are prevalent, the main being the physical methods, the chemical methods, and by fermentation.

Physical Methods

The physical methods can be classified into two types – thermal processing and the short wave exposure which involves the heating or the cooling under aseptic conditions to inactivate bacteria and the fungi-thermal processing is through:

Removal of heat – the prevention by cold through refrigeration freezing, de-hydro freezing and carbonation. Preservation of the food by freezing takes care of the two major aspects that the microbes do not grow below the freezing point and there is sufficient reduction in the rate of biochemical deteriorative changes so that the product can be stored for a long period.

Thermal processing by the addition of heat through stationary pasteurization, agitation pasteurization and the flash pasteurization.

Evaporation or dehydration by the removal of water through sun-drying low temperature evaporation or the concentration, freeze drying, foam mat drying and puff-drying. Drying means the removal of heat through non conventional energy resources such as the sun and the wind and dehydration implies retorting to the mechanical devices such as hot air, vacuum and the infra red radiation.

Onions, and the garlic are peeled and dried without blanching and are then used as seasoning for such products as canned tomatoes – tomato ketchup tomato sauce etc. Three main dehydrated potato products are the granules, flakes, and the cubes. Mushrooms are also processed through the drying.

Bananas are also peeled sliced and dried to fry or to cook. Unripe mangoes are peeled sliced and dried which is then used for the preparation of the mango powder. Sprays drying are used to dry the tomato products. Tomato flakes are used for the dry soup mixes etc.

Dry ginger is used whole in pickles and ground in cakes and the puddings and from dry ginger the ginger extracts and ginger cordial are extracted.

Flavouring Extracts

Flavouring extracts are concentrated and the synthesized forms of the flavouring substances substance of certain horticultural produce such as cirrus, spices, and aromatic herbs and are used in processed food industries as natural additives. Flavouring substances from these present sources are extracted and isolated from the inert dried residues and are more widely used in the pharmaceutical industries and the perfumeries. The flavouring extracts have different proportions of the aromatic essential oils and the non-volatile matters. Vanilla essence is prepared by extracting the minced vanilla beans with the alcohol and are commercially used in the cakes, ice-creams and the chocolates. The short wave exposure method consists of subjecting the product to ultraviolet or the gamma radiations.

Chemical Methods

The chemical methods normally adopted for the preservation of horticultural produce are:

By the addition of acids such as vinegar or the lactic acid for the pickling of the vegetables, fish and meat.

Pickles

Pickles are the edible products that have been preserved and flavoured in a solution of brine and the edible acid such as vinegar. Pickles are generally made from the cucumber, fenugreek, onions, cauliflower, cabbage, carrot, tomato, olive, chillies, mango, lime, lemon, bananas, ginger, turmeric etc. Spices, edible oils and other preservatives are added to the pickles for taste.

Salting or the brining methods normally adopted in vegetable and fruit pickles and the salted fish. Further addition of the sugar and heating method is used in the fruit preserves, jams, jellies, and the marmalades.

Jams, Jellies and Marmalades

Jams, jellies and marmalades are popularly grouped under the fruit jellies processing the general consistency of the jelly and made out of clear juice or pulp as the basic constituents. The quality of the product depends on the correct selection of the fruits, maturity and the time of harvesting and the method of handling, grading, and the storage prior to the harvesting. The idea fruits for the manufacture of jam are apples, plums, peaches, apricots, strawberries, pineapple mangoes etc. Marmalade is a form of the fruit jelly in which the slices of the first or fruit peels are added in a suspended manner. Lime, lemon and oranges are normally used for the preparation of marmalades.

Further marmalades are prepared by addition of the chemical preservatives such as the water soluble, salts of the chemical preservatives such as water soluble salts of the sulfur di oxide, benzoic acid, hydrogen peroxide, etc.

The basic principle followed here is to destroy the microorganism in the food and prevent the external microbial contaminations.

It also involves the altering the environment to prevent or to retard the microbial activity. Canning is the method most commonly used for the preservation.

By Fermentation

Preservation is also done through alcoholic and the acetonic fermentation as in the case of fruit wines, apple cider and the fruit vinegar.

FERMENTED BEVERAGES

Fermentation process is the beverage preparation mediated through yeast and in the process it produces a range of products such as organic acids, alcohols, Easters and the sulfurous compounds. Apple cider is prepared from apple, grape wine, perry from pears. Grapes have always been used for the wine making due to the fact that the juice is extremely rich in the natural sugars, natural association of the fermentative yeasts with the berries, high content of nitrogenous material in the promotion of growth, of yeast leading to the fermentation, high acidity of the juice favouring the yeasts and protecting against other bacterial fermentation and a very high alcohol and acid content in the fermented wine render it stable and safe for the prolonged storage.

Other Methods

A combination of other methods such as distillation, extraction, free drying and the canning on synergistic principles is also adopted.

Advanced technology of processing has great potential to expand the farm produce markets beyond the region because of the conversion of perishable produce into stable forms that can be stored and shipped to distant markets round the year extending the availability of the processed products and retaining their nutritive value and palatability.

The processing can change the horticultural produce into new and more usable forms offering better convenience to the consumers at large. The food processing industry thus takes care of the mass production, downstream activities, control of the quality of the raw produce and finished products for the better processing techniques for the desirable conversion into the more acceptable forms.

Constraints in the Horticulture Industry

The horticulture production system is highly unorganized resulting in poor yields in terms of both quantity and the quality. The backbone of an industry which is the stable production throughout the year is lacking in the industry. The fruits and vegetables should be available to the processing industries at the world market rate.

India is the second largest producer of fruits and vegetables in the world after China. Since the 1980s, the international trade in fruits and vegetables has expanded rapidly. The number of commodities as well as the number of varieties produced and traded have increased manifold during the past 25 years.

There is an overall increase in the demand for fruits and vegetables for consumption both in the fresh and the processed form. Also there is a wide diversification in production pattern globally. Income in this sector is increasing which is indeed driving the supply. In spite of being one of the largest producers of fruits and vegetables in the world, the export competitiveness among the Indian producers remains low.

But with new marketing initiatives, the post-harvest losses and the wastage due to poor infrastructure facilities, such as storage and transportation, have been reduced to a considerable extent. Yet a lot needs to be done in this sector. In an effort to overcome some of the problems associated with this sector, the case study of the successful SAFAL Market is presented in the paper.

The study has observed a shift in cropping pattern in favour of horticulture in India in the past one-and-a-half decades. Analysis of the economic feasibility of this shift away from cereals to fruits and vegetable shows that it is economically viable and beneficial to shift towards horticulture production, but this diversification needs to be planned in a systematic manner.

Certain strategies and policies are also suggested in this regards. The study confirms the changing consumption patterns and diversification, along with the outlook for the next 15-20 years in the light of shortage of supply to increased domestic demand.

The major exports from India are mango, grapes, orange, apple, banana, mosambi, onion, potato, tomato and pumpkins. The major share of India's exports of fresh fruits and vegetables go to Bangladesh, Nepal, UAE, UK and Malaysia.

The supply constraints, yield gaps and huge logistic costs affect our competitive and comparative advantage in world trade market. In this study, the nominal protection coefficient and revealed comparative advantage are computed to check on the existing status. Study also identifies the potential states for the fruits and vegetables, for which India is globally competitive and has comparative advantage in production.

These states should be targeted for enhancing the export potential of the country. The potential competing countries are also identified. Lessons from other developing countries focus on the growth of the horticulture sector through increased participation of small and marginal farmers in an organized manner and farmers being trained with entrepreneurial skills.

The horticultural production system is highly unorganized resulting in poor yields in terms of both quantity and the quality. The backbone of an industry which is the stable production throughout the year is lacking in the industry. The fruits and vegetables be available to the processing industries at the world market rate.

The processing activities are not cost effective as the technology is outmoded. Effective transportation is non-existent. To help the capacity utilization of the processing units dependent on the seasonal availability of locally grown fruits and vegetables, and fruits and vegetables grown elsewhere need to be transported to achieve the economies of the scale. Lack of transport facilities hinders this process resulting in the spoilage of large quantity of fruits and vegetables.

Suitable storage facilities like the cold storages etc. are yet to be developed.

Advances in packaging technology are way behind and the packaging materials are expensive and unsuitable for the export purposes. The cost of packaging itself amounts to around 20 per cent of the ex-factory price.

Incidence of both direct and indirect taxation on the industry over prices are relatively high, rendering it unattractive to the domestic consumers. The processing industry is subject to excise and the sales tax, on the final product. Again it has to pay similar taxes on all the inputs in the processing activity like the fruit packaging material, fuel, processing material etc. In most urban areas, octroi in the range of 4 to 8 per cent is also levied. This burden is passed on to the consumer making the product economically unattractive.

There is an absolute lack of awareness of the immense potential in the industry. Poor yields of finished products from the raw material consumption. High raw material and infrastructure cost and shortages of incentives making Indian exports non-competitive in the world markets.

The seasonal availability of fruits and vegetables requires the entire requirement of the raw material to be purchased within a short period ranging from 4 to 12 weeks and their immediate processing as a result of which, substantial amounts of the working capital are locked up in raw material and the finished products.

INDIAN FLORICULTURE INDUSTRY

Flowers and plants have always been an integral part of human living. Besides their aesthetic importance, they are also useful in improving the quality of life. Ornamental plants play a very important role in Environmental planning of urban and rural areas for abatement of pollution, social and rural forestry, wasteland development, aforestation and landscaping of outdoor and indoor spaces. Floriculture is also an important agribusiness with potential for export trade.

The area under floriculture in India has increased to nearly 40,000 hectares, which constitutes around 17 per cent of total global acreage. In spite of such a large area, production value is very low. The quality of Indian produce is poor and not acceptable in international market. The produce quality deteriorates further due to improper packaging, storage and transportation.

The floriculture market has been declared the sunrise industry in India by the Government. It is expected to witness strong growth. Exports business generates huge revenues for the market.

The report provides a brief overview of the market including the estimated market size, growth rate, production of cut flowers and loose flowers in 2007-08 and 2008-09. The market overview section also talks about the export and import market, the opportunities in the global market and covers region-wise distribution of floriculture industry.

An analysis of drivers reveals that scientific methods of flower cultivation, favourable agro-climatic conditions, social and religious events, international events and associations, growing demand from the youth population. The key challenges identified are lack of support infrastructure, high duties in the European Union, and dearth of basic inputs.

The report discusses the current market trends as players are acquiring companies in Ethiopia, setting up auction centres, PE investments and acquisitions, entry of corporate houses, players increasing their service offerings and rapid development of flower retail chains. The report provides the profile, financials of the players in the market.

Advantages of Floriculture

Floriculture has several advantages as against agriculture and horticulture.

1. Although the investment is rather high in floriculture, the returns are also proportionately high.
2. The growth rate in the industry is also high the local markets growing annually by 25-30 per cent and the global trade by 10-12 per cent.
3. There is lot of demand from foreign countries through the collaborations, joint ventures and the buyback arrangements taking advantage of the natural Indian conditions.
4. Gestation period in floriculture is comparatively less and the producers have more liquid flow of money at shorter intervals as compared to the other branches of agriculture.
5. Floriculture often requiring specialized operations provides for more employment generation per unit area.

Value Addition in the Floriculture Industry

The value addition in the floriculture industry divided into the following activities.

Product Development

There are several indigenously grown varieties of flowers and ornamentals of India which need to be promoted outside in order to get the better value for the produce. Thus, value addition will start right from the creation of the need for the particular product outside and then marketing it.

However, more important is the need to carry out the market research to identify those varieties and flowers which are popular outside and then have a systematic production program in India, entirely export oriented taking advantage of the natural climatic conditions and the adequacy of the labor. Skilled labour to carry out the appropriate cultural practices is also extremely important.

Post Harvest Methods

Suitable techniques to avoid the degradation in quality of the produce and to enhance the keeping quality has to be developed to provide value addition to the produce. Usage of the chemicals in regulated quantities should be promulgated.

Processing and Marketing

Value addition can behest implemented through the processing of the produce providing it with marketability over the place and time thus increasing the market returns.

The extracts obtained from the flowers have applications in several industries such as the perfumeries. In addition, they are also used as the most common method of flavouring the various items. Several flowers have got medicinal value and are used in locations for massages or as pure extracts for the purpose. After the extraction, the remains are again used as the fuels or as a source of manure. Systematic efforts should be made to market the produce. Greater efforts will have to be taken in the area of packaging in which India is way behind the other countries. International collaborations for the technical know-how as well as the buyback arrangements in marketing will definitely lead to better prices being received for the produce, thus bringing about the required value addition.

EXPORT TRENDS AND OPPORTUNITIES

India has been a traditional exporter of raw agricultural products like spices. Export of raw products has resulted in huge loss to Indian economy. After GATT agreement and WTO membership, processed products manufactured as per international norms only offered at competitive prices, can be exported.

However, our processed products mostly do not meet the international standards. India's share in over US$ 300 billion world trade in agricultural commodities is less than 1 per cent.

Agricultural exports used to be of the order of 30.6 per cent of the total exports during 1980-81, which came down to 19.4 per cent by 1990-91. Currently, it is at about 16 per cent due to rapid growth in other sectors as well.

Processed fruit and vegetable products have considerable export potentials and if it is properly utilized, growers, processors, traders as well as national economy will benefit. It requires correct assessment of world market, high quality of raw produce, high quality of processed product and competitive production cost.

There exists tremendous scope for the growth and development of the Indian floricultural industry through exports as the global floricultural trade is growing at a very fast pace in recent years.

Speedy development of the floriculture sector had been initiated with the setting up of the Expert group in floriculture development. Several plants, flowers and herbs suitable for export development on the basis of international markets and the environmental conditions required for growth have been identified by the expert group on horticulture both on short-term as well as long-term basis.

Large industries with the required capital base like the Tata, RPG group etc. have been encouraged to take up commercial floriculture to meet the growing demands for the floricultural products, both in domestic and in overseas markets accompanied by the tie-ups and technological collaboration with the foreign countries. The Agricultural and Processed Food Products Export Development Authority (APEDA) has been designated as the nodal agency for export promotion and the developmental activities related to floriculture and various efforts have been made in this direction.

INDIAN POULTRY INDUSTRY

Indian poultry industry has been growing at annual varying rates of 8-15 per cent and this growth in the past few decades made India fifth largest producer of eggs and ninth largest producer of poultry broiler. At present, the industry is estimated at over ₹ 30,000 crore and is expected to grow over ₹ 60,000 crore by 2010. India produces 1,400 million chickens a year, which is close to 27 million a week, of which 95 per cent is traded alive. According to a market report, the poultry production and consumption in the domestic markets is slated to grow by 66 per cent to approximately 2.3 million tons by 2010.

Meat and Poultry sector is one of the fastest growing industries of the Indian economy than any other sector contributing about $230 million to the Gross National Product. But in statistical terms, the industry has reported a loss of over ₹ 4,000 crore as an aftermath effect of the bird flu crisis.

According to Ministry of Food Processing Industry Annual Report 2007-08, India has the largest livestock population in the world. However, most animals are not bred for meat, as a vast majority of the Indian population is vegetarian. Animals are generally used in the processing of Meat and Poultry. Most of the boiled meat produced is used for domestic consumption, while beef and veal meat is also exported. The level of processing in meat is just about 6 per cent, as the Indian customers prefer fresh meat from the market than processed/frozen meat. For this reason, processing of large animal meat is usually high in exports. Also, Indian buffalo meat, due to its lean character and nearly organic in nature, is highly preferred in the export market. Poultry, with advantages of being the most economical source of animal protein, acceptability to all non-vegetarian population and with no religious taboo, is the fastest growing segment.

The animals generally used for production of meat are cattle, buffaloes, sheep, pigs and poultry. India accounts for more than half of the global buffalo population indicating a significantly high export opportunity. India ranks among the top six egg producing and among the top five chicken producing countries.

The bottleneck in Meat and Poultry segment is that there are a limited number of integrated poultry processing plants in the organized sector, though the small poultry processing units are in plenty. Per capita consumption levels of meat is very low in India, as there are religious taboos attached with consumption of beef and pork. Also, exports in poultry are hindered by the subsidies that developed countries like USA and EU provide.

Thus, apart from the huge opportunity for India in the buffalo meat export, the poultry segment with the current low per capita consumption and world-class production infrastructure and productivity offers a potential export opportunity. There is a large potential for setting up modern slaughter facilities and development of cold chains in meat and poultry processing sector. India needs to come up with strong support measures to increase its domestic consumption levels, like for example, inclusion of eggs in the mid-day meal program and a relook at the taxes including VAT for poultry segment.

The contribution of the small rural farmers points out the importance of integration of the poultry farming and the allied sector. Suguna Poultry Farm is the pioneer in poultry integration and contract poultry farming in India, with presence in nine states and membership of about 15,000 contract farmers. Suguna has set an example of integration and contract farming before the industry and has proved to be beneficial for the company. Integration could be the way forward for the entire industry towards expansion and success.

Presently, 100 per cent Foreign Direct Investment (FDI) is permitted in the food processing sector. Also FDI in food retailing, covering dairy, poultry, marine, vegetables and fruits might help the entire food processing industry grow. Poultry farming in India has transformed from a mere tool of supplementary income and nutritious food for the family to the major commercial activity generating the required revenue.

The growth of the industry with steady production of 1,800 million kg of poultry meat, 40 billion egg per year and employment generation of about 3 million people indicates the future prospects for the industry. Changing food habits, rising income of the middle class Indian, presence of private players, rising market demand of the Indian poultry produce in the export market are some of the contributing factors to the growth of the industry.

NABARD has committed to bring about rural prosperity through poultry. Meeting of sub-group of poultry has asked for funds of ₹ 1095 crore for poultry development during the 11th Plan and ₹ 30,000 crore for the entire livestock sector under various schemes of the Government of India. India has resumed egg export.

IFC (Washington based International Finance Corporation) picked up stake in Suguna Poultry farms. Suguna Poultry paves the way for North Indian expansion and introduces dial-a-chicken concept to promote value-added products. Thousands of broiler farmers will reap the benefit.

Venkateswara Hatcheries has decided to use tennis to promote their brand Venky's. Poultry farmers to get maize on concessional rate to use it as feed in poultry. Kerala livestock development board chalked out plan for poultry tourism in Myanmar.

Poultry litter to fetch carbon credit in Andhra Pradesh with 3.5 mw power plant. Godrej Agrovet Ltd. introduced wide range of processed chicken in the brand name of Godrej Real Good Chicken.

INDIAN COTTON INDUSTRY

Cotton Processing Technology

Cotton is a natural textile fibre. Traditional cotton textile industry could not face onslaught of modern high speed spinning, weaving and surface finish technologies. Small-scale textile industry supported by Swadeshi and Khadhi and Village Industries Commission face serious labour problems also. Cotton seeds are valued as feed and oilseed and the stalks are used as fuel.

However, stalks yield excellent paper and pulp, particle boards and microcrystalline cellulose (MCC). Cotton hulls also yield good particle board and furfural. Cotton willow dust can be used for production of biogas. Cotton wastes can be used for mushroom production. There is scope for income and employment generation if cotton stalks are utilized for pulp and paper making.

India Retained the Position as the Second Highest Cotton Producer in World

- With increased acreage and advent of Biotechnical (BT) cultivation, the cotton production in the country in cotton season 2009-10 had been at 295.00 lakh bales (1 bale = 170 kg) as compared to 290.00 lakh bales in the previous year. Thus, India retained its position as the second largest cotton producing country in the world, after China.

Acreage under Cotton Reached at Record Level in 2009-10

- Due to receipt of good prices for cotton as compared to other competing crops in the previous year, the cotton farmers were enthusiastic in increasing the acreage under cotton in 2009-10. As a result, the acreage under cotton in 2009-10 had reached a record level of 103.29 lakh hectares as compared to 94.06 lakh hectares in previous year.

Cotton Productivity Declined

- With unfavourable agro-climatic conditions, inadequate availability of canal water etc., the cotton productivity since last two years has been declining. In cotton season 2009-10, the cotton productivity had been 486 kgs/ha as against 524 kgs/ha in previous year.

Domestic Cotton Consumption Increased by 9 per cent

With improvement in the global economy, the demand for raw cotton and for finished products like yarn, fabrics and garments in cotton season 2009-10 has improved domestically and world over. Improvement in production across product lines has been supported by revival in the demand as well as significant additions/modernization initiatives. As a result, the domestic cotton consumption in 2009-10 had increased substantially by around 9 per cent at 250.00 lakh bales as against 229.00 lakh bales in the previous year.

Cotton Exports from the Country

Besides abundant availability of cotton, the international cotton prices in 2009-10 had been higher than domestic prices and there was good demand for Indian cotton, especially from neighbouring countries like China, Pakistan, Bangladesh etc. As a result, cotton exports from India in 2009-10 had been at 83.00 lakh bales as against 35.00 lakh bales in the previous year.

Imports of Cotton

Like previous year, cotton imports into the country had once again been limited to short supply in ELS cottons at 7.00 lakh bales as against 10.00 lakh bales during previous year.

Development of Entrepreneurship

Agriculture has always been considered to be a way of life emphasizing on subsistence farming as against an economic activity. Setting up of agro-industries is the first step towards the commercialization of agriculture and development of the entrepreneurial talents among the people.

Occupational Mobility

Agro-industries provide greater occupational mobility to the people as they can move away from the cultivation in case they are employed under the conditions of underemployment or disguised employment owing to lack of opportunities. People who are better qualified can now put their skills to better use in the field of marketing, finance, research and development and management as a whole.

Rural Institutions

Agro-processing activities very often contribute to the development of the dynamic rural institutions, both of an economic nature like cooperation and also for the provision of amenities like the schools, housing, hospitals, recreation and other welfare activities.

Dynamic Development of the Region

The agro-processing activities help in the overall development of the region through the better returns to the farmers for their produce leading to a greater percentage of savings thus enabling capital formation for the further investments through expansion and the diversification leading to the continuous ongoing dynamic development of the people in the region.

PROCESSING OF PULSES

India produced 8.4 Mt of pulses in the year 1950-51. The production grew to a level of about 14 Mt by the year 2000-2001. Starting with nearly 500 dhal mills in the country in 1950-51, there were about 15,000 dhal mills of 100-500 TPD capacity in the year 2000-2001. In a number of dhal mills, improved machinery including cleaners, graders, magnetic separators, washers, driers, polishers, colour sorters and packaging systems are being used.

With complete phasing out of hand-operated dhal chakkis, commonly used during 1950s, the technology has turned fully mechanized and more-and-more urban based. There is a need to evolve more efficient machines and processes for pre-treatment of the grain, dehusking, sorting, polishing and packaging in order to improve dhal recovery and consume less energy. Also, there is a need for product diversification and development of technology for quick cooking and ready-to-eat dal.

OILSEEDS' PROCESSING

Besides, animal based fat specifically obtained from milk and milk products, edible plant oils have been the major source of oils and fats for most of the population in the country. In the year 1950-51, the country produced 5.2 Metric tons of oilseeds. Production by the year 2000-2001 had increased to 24.5 Metric tons.

In the year 1950-51, most of the oilseeds were crushed in either bullock-operated oil ghanies or a few mechanical oil expellers. Both of these resulted in high volume of edible oil left in the cake. By the year 2000-2001, there were nearly 2.5 lakh oil ghanies, 60,000 oil expellers and 700 solvent extraction plants. Besides, there were 200 oil refining units in the country and 100 units for production of hydrogenated oil (Vanaspati).

Besides other oilseeds, soybean has gradually become an important crop of India. Its production is around 5.3 million tons. Soybean is a special legume. It has 40 per cent protein and 20 per cent oil. India has 154 solvent extraction plants and 60 soy food units. Average recovery is 17.7 per cent for oil and 82.4 per cent for meal.

Soy meal contains about 48 per cent protein. Its export has been worth ₹ 15, 000 million/ year. Soy foods are nutritious and economical and must be promoted. A strategic plan for expanded and diversified use of soybean for food and feed in India for the next 25 years should be made and implemented. This crop has a great potential to enhance nutrition and health of the people and alleviate poverty.

SUGARCANE PROCESSING INDUSTRY

Sugarcane production was 310 Mt in the year 2000-2001. About 80 per cent of the cane produced is milled, about half for the production of refined white sugar in the organized sector with the sugar mills located in the production catchments in public, private and cooperative sectors and about 42 per cent for the production of Jaggery and Khandsari. Based on sugar recovery, minimum price scheme has been introduced.

Mills have loose tie-up with the growers, some of them provide critical input support to the growers. Apparently, it is working well. But there have been cases where farmers burnt their crops in the absence of remunerative prices. For Jaggery, canes are crushed, clarified and concentrated. Gur as sweetener has better nutritional profile than white sugar. It is possible to refine the process and the product for greater competitiveness and realize export potential specially where people of Indian origin are located.

Energy efficient furnaces, concentration pans, clarificants, moulds and storage are needed for Gur. Khandsari units used open pan in place of vacuum pans for concentration and the sugar obtained is of lower quality compared to white sugar from mills. Sugar recovery in Khandsari is much lower. These units depend on grid supply or diesel generators for mechanical/electrical power or both when grid power is erratic and diesel gensets are kept as standby power sources.

This increases the cost of production of Khandsari. Bagasse, tops, dry leaves and molasses are by-products. Modern sugar mills with co-generation meet their entire energy needs, both thermal and electromechanical from these bagasse fired boilers – steam turbine units. They feed extra power to grid or save 15-20 per cent bagasse for the use as feedstock or paper making. Jaggery promotional and regulatory measures have been taken by the Government to improve quality and production. Large number of sugar mills are using outdated processes and equipment, some of them not only use entire bagasse but also use wood.

PROCESSING OF JUTE

Jute has the distinction of having ushered India into industrialization era. Both jute production and manufacture of jute-based products are highly labor intensive, concentrated mostly in Eastern India. Mini jute carding and spinning mills have now been developed which allow decentralized production of utility items from jute but these are not popular yet. For each ton of jute, 2-3 tons of jute sticks are produced. Chemically, these resemble hardwood. Sticks are traditionally used as fuelwood and low cost structural material. Jute sticks yield excellent particle boards and the technologies are now fully commercial. Jute sticks are a good feedstock for paper pulp. The sticks can also be used as fuel for steam and power generation.

PROCESSING OF ANIMAL PRODUCE

Meat and poultry production in India has been about 4.6 Mt per year with goats and sheep contributing 54 per cent, buffalo and cattle 26 per cent, poultry 13 per cent and pig 7 per cent. It is mostly used fresh. Efforts are on to develop infrastructure for export of both fresh and processed meat and poultry. Production is essentially decentralized and rural based. Poultry has done well remaining in rural sector and developing network of marketing in distant remunerative markets. Hygiene in slaughter houses and use of blood, viscera and other wastes is not satisfactory. The meat from culled birds, goats and buffaloes is tough textured, better suited for processed meat products. However, there is no tradition of using processed meat products in India.

FISH AND FISH PRODUCTS PROCESSING

India, with its 7,500 km long coastline and an exclusive economic zone of 2.02 million square km 191,024 km of rivers and canals and 4.4 million hectares of reservoirs and fresh water lakes has an enormous potential for fisheries. In 1999, the country had an estimated 1, 81,284 traditional fishing crafts; 44,578 motorized traditional crafts, 53,684 mechanized fishing boats and about 200 deep-sea vessels in operation. Fish processing in India is done almost entirely for export. Open sun dried fish and fish meal are the only major exceptions. At present, India has freezing units, cold storages, ice plants, canning units and fish meal plants.

Capacity of most of these processes and storage units is small when compared to the facilities in fish processing industry in technologically advanced countries. The total fish processing and storage facility in India grossly is inadequate compared to the potential for fish production and processing. Inland fisheries need low cost palletized feeds and special containers to transport fingerlings and fish.

More rearing ponds are needed. Techniques to reduce seepage loss of water have to be introduced. Obsolete fishing gear needs replacement with better gear. Extensive network of refrigerated handling, transport, storage and retailing has to be put in place. Also, we have to make better use of fish waste and by-products.

PROCESSING OF COMMERCIAL CROPS

The commercial crops include spices, condiments and crops such as gorgon nut (*makhana*), water chestnut, bettle leaves, tobacco etc. Post-harvest operations of these crops are highly energy intensive and there is a scope for reducing energy consumption and improvement of quality through proper cleaning, grading, drying/dehydration, milling, grinding and other operations.

India has been a leading producer, consumer and exporter of spices like black pepper, cardamom, chillies, spice oils and oleoresins. It produces about 3.0 Mt of spices valued at over ₹ 60,000 million. About 7 per cent of the total production is exported. Contribution of R&D to PHT of spices includes equipment and processes for cleaning, grading and packaging of whole spices and production of value-added products such as oleoresins and spice oils.

PROCESSING OF PLANTATION CROPS

Plantation crops contribute substantially to the national economy with export earning of ₹ 12.4 billion. Coconut alone contributed ₹ 1.72 billion by way of exports during 1996-97. However, the coconut based industry in India has been in the infancy stage. There is considerable scope of product diversification, viz., production of coconut milk and milk powder, coconut cream, shell powder, shell charcoal etc. Coconut wood utilization needs more attention. In case of other crops, financially viable technologies for product.

Diversification needs to be developed. Such products are arecanut fat, tannin, areuline, other chemicals from arecanut, honey/chocolate coated or salted kernels from cashewnuts and value-added products from by-products. The post harvest operations in these crops need to be mechanized. Though the technology has been developed for desiccated coconut, coconut cream and other products, it needs refinement.

PROCESSING OF MEDICINAL AROMATIC PRODUCTS

The plant based pharmaceuticals, herbal medicines, perfumery, cosmetics, fragrances and food flavour industries have recorded a phenomenal expansion in last 50 years and as a result, this sector figures in high annual growth rate industries in agribusiness. The market for plant based pharmaceuticals in the year 1994 was estimated to range between US$ 32-43 billion. The world essential oil production at raw materials level was estimated to be about ₹ 32 billion of which 55-60 per cent goes to food flavours, 15-20 per cent as fragrances and the remaining is broadly used as starting raw material for isolation of aromatic chemicals. In terms of market share in production value, India is sliding downwards and presently stands at sixth rank with only 6 per cent share in world trade.

APICULTURE PRODUCE PROCESSING

Bee-keeping, i.e., rearing the bees in artificial hives to produce honey and other products offers an immense potential for providing employment to rural folk in India where many evergreen and moist deciduous forests, orchards etc. constitute good bee-keeping areas. The unique feature of bee-keeping is that the capital investment required is small and unlike many other industries, it does not need raw material in usual sense as nature offers the same in the form of nectar and pollen.

The equipment required, viz., bee boxes of standard sizes, honey extractor smoker, hive tools etc. have been researched and improved in design and these can be manufactured even in small rural carpentry and blacksmith shops. Improved bee hives have been developed which make honey production much easier than the traditional long hanging hives. In general, equipment like smoker, comb foundation sheet machine, honey extractor, queen excluder, honey tank and uncapping equipment have been developed by R&D organizations.

PROCESSING OF TRADITIONAL FOODS

India has a very strong base of traditional food products, which have been developed under varied agro-climatic, geographical and socio-cultural situations over the centuries. Besides, conventional *chapaties*, these may include expended, puffed, flaked, extruded fermented products, sweets, instant mixes, breakfast foods, bakery products, beverages, health and special foods.

The production of traditional foods during 1996-97 has been estimated nearly 30 times more than that of all western style high cost processed foods in the Indian market. There is an urgent need to upgrade the conventional foods technology so that the industrial manufacturing of products can be promoted and the scope of marketing expanded.

QUALITY CONTROL AND STANDARDS

Food processing industries cover a large spectrum of products of plant and animal origin. Quality has got to be maintained for domestic as well as export markets. In this respect, a number of organizations have come up for the formulation of standards and for monitoring their quality.

These can be classified into two groups: (a) compulsory legislation and (b) voluntary standards In addition to the product specifications, which include both raw materials and final product, the Bureau of Indian Standards has brought out standards on glossary of terms for various industries and hygienic codes applicable to most of the food processing industries.

To ensure that processed foods are free from pathogenic or spoilage microorganism, limits are gradually being introduced in various specifications. In addition, separate standard methods of test for the sensory parameters have been laid down.

Containers are as important as the contents, as these may impart toxic elements to the food products and could pose potential dangers to health and safety, if they are not of the requisite quality.

Indian Standards covering 6 thermoplastics namely, polypropylene isomers and ethylene acrylic acid have been published which describe the requirement of the particular thermoplastic and necessary additive along with their limits.

SWOT ANALYSIS OF AGRO-PROCESSING INDUSTRY IN INDIA

Strengths

1. Round the year availability of raw materials.
2. Social acceptability of agro-processing as important area and support from the central government.
3. Vast network of manufacturing facilities all over the country.
4. Vast domestic market.

Weaknesses

1. High requirement of working capital.
2. Low availability of new reliable and better accuracy instruments and equipments.
3. Inadequate automation w.r.t. information management.
4. Remuneration less attractive for talent in comparison to contemporary disciplines.
5. Inadequately developed linkages between R&D labs and industry.

Opportunities

1. Large crop and material base in the country due to agro-ecological variability offers vast potential for agro-processing activities.
2. Integration of developments in contemporary technologies such as electronics, material science, Computer, biotechnology etc. offer vast scope for rapid improvement and progress.

3. Opening of global markets may lead to export of our developed technologies and facilitate generation of additional income and employment opportunities.

Threats

1. Competition from global players.
2. Loss of trained manpower to other industries and other professions due to better working conditions prevailing there may lead to further shortage of manpower.
3. Rapid developments in contemporary and requirements of the industry may lead to fast obsolescence.

PLAN AND STRATEGY

Objectives of Agro-processing Programs

— minimize product losses,
— add maximum value,
— achieve high quality standards,
— keep processing cost low,
— ensure that a fair share of added value goes to the producer.

Suggestions to Achieve these Objectives

(a) National plan for improvement and extension of agro-processing technology at farm, traditional small industry and modern industry levels should be prepared. The plan should take into account the diversity in resources and needs of different regions in the country.

It should include program details and implementation schedule for the first four or five years. The progress of plan implementation should be periodically reviewed to allow adjustments and corrective measures, and to develop program details for the years beyond the period under review.

(b) Thrust areas for research and development should be identified and medium term research and development program should be prepared and implemented to support the national plan for improvement and extension of agro-processing technology at different levels.

Treatment and utilization of effluents from agro-processing industry should be included in the R & D program.

(c) Emphasis should be put on the establishment of new agro-industrial plants in the production catchments to minimize transport cost, make use of lower cost land and more abundant water supply, create employment opportunity in the rural sector and utilize process waste and by-products for feed, irrigation and manure.

(d) Infrastructure in the production catchments selected for agro-industrial development should be improved. Because of uncertain grid power supply to rural areas, decentralized power generation using locally available resources may become an integral part of agro-industrial development.

Similarly, if the raw materials and processed products are perishable or semi-perishable in nature, cold chain will have to be established.

(e) The national plan should provide for management of agro-industrial activities in the catchment area, both by private companies and individuals as well as cooperatives.

(f) Financial incentives and support should be provided on liberal scale to promote the modernization of agro-processing industry and for establishing new such industries in production catchments.

(g) Arrangements to supply market information to the farmer and agro-processor should be put in place.

Monetary Benefits in Agro-processing System

Bulk purchases of various agricultural commodities by an agro-industrial complex results in the incurrence of lower input prices and large amount of the expenses incurred individually can be curbed through the systematic harvesting, procurement systems etc.. In the sugar factory complex, the factory itself carries out the harvesting and transportation of the different produce curtailing expenses incurred in business.

Bulk purchases of various inputs like fertilizers, agricultural implements, pesticides, etc. by the factory which is then redistributed among the members results in the imparting of a better bargaining ability leading to the reduced costs of the various inputs involved. The agro-industrial complexes being on a larger scale are able to make concentrated efforts towards marketing of the produce through specialization as compared to the individual producers. Investment on the various marketing activities like advertisement and sales promotion can also be carried out more effectively. Agro-industrial complexes also can invest more in marketing research as against individuals.

As the cost of the inputs is reduced considerably due to bulk purchases and the output prices are relatively increased due to systematic marketing effort on a wider scale, agro industrial complexes often account for a considerable increase in the productivity. The use of improved inputs and better technological practices also aid in raising the productivity. Further on account of various post-harvest and processing activities carried out by industrial complexes, there occurs greater value addition as compared to marketing of the raw materials alone.

Better facilities of grading, standardization, quality control, storage, and water housing, cold storage facilities etc. help in imparting greater value to the produce through the presentation of deterioration. Processing helps in the marketing of the produce over space and time, thus not only reducing the perishability of the produce over space and time, but also providing for better returns to the producers.

Greater employment opportunities are available to the people through off-the-farm activities like processing, packaging, maintenance of the machinery, managerial requirements, etc. thus opportunities even to those without land or the landless labourers. And several government grants and subsidies are available for the development of the agro-industrial sector. Small isolated producers are unable to make use of these very often as they are unaware of the programs and schemes are unaware of the sources and the other details concerned. Again it becomes difficult for each small producer to comply with all the required formalities of margin money etc. Industrial complexes are not only able to easily avail of these schemes but also very often efficiency in functioning enables the easy repayment of these loans.

Agro industries help in the better utilization of the resources – better the utilization of the human resources can be made of as per the skills and specializations to serve larger sections of the society as against the limited concentrations. Resources such as the warehouses and the transport can also be put to better use as there will be proper capacity utilizations where large agro-industrial complexes are concerned.

Owing to the economies of the scales of operation as well as the conversion of the perishable raw materials into sustainable finished goods will lead to better risk coverage. Greater marketing opportunities over the different areas as well as different periods of time will also help in reducing the risk. Again in case of failures also; the losses are usually manageable and the risk to individuals is reduced to a very large extent.

Welfare Benefits

Government sponsored welfare programs are also in existence which will aid the government for the diversion of funds for various welfare activities like the health, sanitation, nutrition, adult education, vocational training, housing etc. towards it, as there is need for institutionalization of various activities and effective utilization of the schemes. The entire unit can be taken up by the government as a nucleus for development.

Several non-governmental organizations also under various schemes find it easier to work towards the welfare of the people. Voluntary organizations like SEWA NGO can easily target womenfolk in the area for development. Active Self Help Groups (SHG) can also be formed to support the non-institutional form of organizational set-up for the betterment of the standard of living of the people.

Agriculture has always been considered to be a way of life, emphasizing on subsistence farming as against an economic activity. Setting up of agro-industries is the first step towards the commercialization of agriculture and the development of the entrepreneurial talents among the people. Agro industries provide greater occupational mobility to the people as they can move away from the cultivation in case they are employed under the conditions of unemployment or disguised employment owing to lack of opportunities. People who are better qualified can now put their skills to better use in the fields of marketing, finance, research and development and management as a whole.

Agro-processing activities very often contribute to the development of the dynamic rural institutions both of an economic nature like cooperatives and also for the provision of amenities like the schools, housing, hospitals, recreation and other welfare activities. The agro-processing activities help in the overall development of the region through the better returns to the farmers for their produce leading to a greater per cent of savings thus enabling capital formation for the further investments through expansion and the diversification leading to the continuous ongoing dynamic development of the people in the region.

SUMMARY

In this part you will understand uniqueness of agro industries, agro-industrial linkages, and agro industries – its overall improvement sequel to the New Industrial Policy. Further many information on elements of New Industrial Policy, Policy mix for the agro industries, various types of agro industries, right from the procurement of raw materials, quantity of the produce procured and its scheduling, constraints that are hampering the development of the industry.

Further one can understand the marketing of fruits and vegetables was facing the infrastructural constraints and over 20-40 per cent wastages witnessed earlier are now reducing because of the increasing involvement of the private sector. Contract farming is also growing because of specific requirements of quality fruit and vegetable products. The government is providing considerable support through various fiscal and monetary incentives to producers as well as traders. The government is also boosting the immense potential in this sector, so private companies are entering the market in a big way. Although the floriculture has got the status of sunrise after the economic reforms, the growth in marketing had not been very promising. As the potential for growth in floriculture lies mainly in exports, it requires very good infrastructure and technical skill at par with global standards.

India despite being the largest producer of foodgrains, fruits, vegetables, milk-meat production is processing only about 2 per cent of the total agricultural production. Basic industries such as foodgrains processing and edible oil production contributes the most to the food processing industry. Processing of fruit and vegetables and meat products are the sectors with high potential. The silk industry has very bright future in India, and internationally it has great potential as India is the second largest producer after China. The industry needs appropriate government policies to vitalize it. The Central Silk Filatures Board (CSB) was established by the Government of India to protect the industry both in terms of production as well as trade. Pisciculture is again an upcoming industry, especially for the international market. It is going to be a major source of foreign earning. The Marine Products Export Development Authority was constituted to protect the industry's vast export potential.

QUESTIONS (PART-A)

1. Elucidate functioning of various agro-processing industries.
2. What sorts of development you expect in the sector of value-added cereals processing?
3. Explain how fruits and vegetables will be processed in manufacturing value-added processed fruits and vegetables products?
4. How wastage of rice and maize would be processed to make value-added tastier processed foods?
5. What steps you suggest for starting agriculture business processing enterprises at small-scale level?

QUESTIONS (PART-B)

1. Explain the scope for agro industries under the New Economic Policy.
2. What are the unique characteristics of the agro industries?
3. What are the agro-industrial linkages? Explain their relevance to the national economy?
4. Explain the concept of value addition with respect to the horticultural industry.
5. Write short notes on: (i) Sugar industry, (ii) Role of NDDB in dairy industry, (iii) Constraints for developing fruit processing in the small-scale sector, (iv) Role of MNCs in Indian Agri-business scenario.
6. Distinguish between Agribusiness and the Indian rural economy.

OOO

CHAPTER

18

Scope for Agribusinesses in India

- Scope for Agribusiness Management in India
- Types of Small Business Units
- Forms of Business Organizations
- Importance of Personality Traits in Business
- Physical Qualities
- Mental Abilities
- Ethics
- School Qualification
- Executive Qualities
- Small-scale Industry Units (SSIs)
- Ancillary Industries Undertaking
- Tiny Enterprises
- Export Oriented Units (EOUs)
- SSI and Business Enterprises
- Village and SSI
- Characteristics
- Importance
- Advantages and Disadvantages
- Organization and Administration
- Development Commissioners' Offices
- SSI Boards
- SISI
- Some Current Problems Worrying Small Businessmen
- Causes for Business Failure
- Entrepreneurship Opportunities in Modern Agriculture
- Importance of Environmental Analysis

SCOPE FOR AGRIBUSINESSES IN INDIA

1. India is endowed with varied ago-climate, which facilitates production of temperate, sub-tropical and tropical agricultural commodities.
2. There is growing demand for agricultural inputs like feed and fodder, inorganic fertilizers, biofertilizers.
3. Biotechnology applications in agriculture have vast scope in production of seed, bio-control agents, industrial harnessing of microbes for bakery products.
4. Export can be harnessed as a source of economic growth. As a signatory of World Trade Organization, India has vast potential to improve its present position in the world trade of agricultural commodities both raw and processed form. The products line include cereals, pulses, oilseeds and oils, oil meal, spices and condiments, fruits and vegetables, flowers, medicinal plants and essential oils, agricultural advisory services, agricultural tools and implements, meat, milk and milk products, fish and fish products, ornamental fish, forest by products etc.
5. At present, processing is done at primary level only and the rising standard of living expands opportunities for secondary and tertiary processing of agricultural commodities.
6. The vast coastal line and internal water courses provides enormous opportunity for production of marine and inland fish and ornamental fish culture gaining popularity with increase in aesthetic value among the citizens of India.
7. The livestock wealth gives enormous scope for production of meat, milk and milk products, poultry products etc.
8. The forest resources can be utilized for production of by-products of forestry.
9. Beekeeping and apiary can be taken up on large scale in India.
10. Mushroom production for domestic consumption and export can be enhanced with improvement in the state-of-art of their production.
11. Organic farming has highest potential in India as the pesticide and inorganic fertilizer application are less in India compared to industrial nations of the world. The farmers can be encouraged and educated to switch over for organic farming.
12. There is wide scope for production and promotion of biopesticides and biocontrol agents for protection of crops.
13. Seeds, hybrid and genetically modified crops, have the highest potential in India in the future, since the productivity of high yielding varieties have reached a plateau.
14. Micro-irrigation systems and labour saving farm equipments have good potential for the years to come due to declining groundwater level and labour scarcity for agricultural operations like weeding, transplanting and harvesting.
15. Production of vegetables and flowers under greenhouse conditions can be taken up to harness the export market.

16. Trained human resources in agriculture and allied sciences will take on agricultural extension system due to dwindling resources of state finance and downsizing the present government agricultural extension staff as consulting services.
17. The enhanced agricultural production throws open opportunities for employment in marketing, transport, cold storage and warehousing facilities, credit, insurance and logistic support services.

TYPES OF SMALL BUSINESSES

With the exception of Government, most of the small businesses can be classified as the following types:

1. Production
2. Retailing
3. Distribution
4. Personal services
5. Professional services
6. Financial
7. Franchising

1. Production: This classification includes all types of production including agricultural production of crops and livestock, as well as forestry.

2. Distribution: This classification refers to those businesses, which do not make anything but which bring the goods and services to the consumer or user. This includes such activities as packaging, labeling, transporting, refrigerating, freezing, processing, storing, and performing any service necessary to prepare the goods or to provide the service to eventual consumer.

3. Retailing: Although often included as a phase of distribution, retailing is listed as a separate category because there are a large number of persons employed in retailing. Obviously it represents one of the best opportunities for the potential entrepreneur. Retailing is that stage of distribution, which deals with the consumers. Examples of retailers are grocers, self-service sores, florists, agricultural input retailing.

4. Personal services: Service sector is the one which do not primarily supply goods to the public, but instead perform a service. Goods may be used to perform the service but they are of secondary importance. Examples of personal service are hotels, restaurants, agro-service centers.

5. Professional services: Some type of services, in order to protect the public, requires considerable training on the part of those offering the service. Usually those professional services must have a formal education and rigid examinations before receiving licenses to offer their services to the public. Examples of those offering services are investment brokers, insurance agents etc.

6. Financial: Financial businesses are usually service-oriented but since they deal primarily with the loaning or investing of money or the equivalents of money (stocks, bonds, property rights, etc.). A separate category describes them best. Examples of financial services are commercial banks, insurance companies, thrift and loan societies etc.

7. Franchising: Franchising is a system for selectively distributing goods or services through outlets owned by the franchisee. Basically, a franchise is a patent or trademark, license, entitling the holder to market particular products or services under a brand name or trademark according to prearranged terms and conditions. The franchiser is the owner of his or her own business (the franchisee) is likely to be more diligent and strive harder for success than the hired manager of a company-owned outlet. Since franchising is form of selective distribution, the typical franchise agreement prohibits the franchise from setting up competing outlets within the franchise area. Examples of franchise services are diet services, quick-service food-drive inns like fried chicken.

FORMS OF THE BUSINESS ORGANIZATIONS

There are three basic forms of business organization methods: the sole proprietorship, the partnership, and the corporation. With only a few limited exceptions, any type of business venture one can use from these types of business organization. The factors that will affect the business form chosen are:

1. Ease of formation
2. Exposure to financial risk
3. Ability to raise capital
4. Tax treatment of income
5. Continuity of business upon the death of owner.

Entrepreneur

Many economic theories emphasize the significant role played by individual entrepreneurs as they combine talents, abilities and drive to transform resources into profitable undertakings. Joseph Schumpeter was the first major writer to highlight the human agent in the process of economic development. He believed that the economy was propelled by the activities of persons who wanted to promote new goods and new methods of productions or to exploit a new source of materials or new market not merely for profit but also for the purpose of creating. Likewise, Arthur W. Lewis contended that economic growth was bound to be slow unless there was an adequate supply of entrepreneurs looking out for new ideas, and willing to take the risk of introducing them.

The relation between self-sustained growth of an economy and entrepreneurship was further discussed by W.W. Rostow when he claimed that, "economic growth was the result of an interesting process involving the economic, social and political sectors of society, including emergence of corps of entrepreneurs who are psychologically motivated and technologically prepared regularly to lead the way in introducing new production functions in the economy". As it is, experts as have variously described the entrepreneur.

- A person who innovates
- One who allocates and manages the factors of production and bears risk
- One who has ability to perceive latent economic opportunities and devise their exploitation
- An individual, who conceives the ideas of business, design the organization of firms, accumulates capital, recruits labour, establishes relations with supplier, customers and the government and converts the conception into a functional organization.
- The supplier of resources, supervisor and coordinator and ultimate decision maker.

THE IMPORTANCE OF PERSONALITY IN BUSINESS

One of the most important assets of any business owner is a personality, which lends itself to the type of business chosen. There are many different kinds of business and innumerable types of personalities. An objective self-examination is therefore necessary for the discovery of personal strengths and weaknesses, especially as they relate to owning a particular type of business. In assessing one's own personality, the following inventory should prove helpful. Potential business owners should question themselves on each of these items, noting those areas where improvement is most needed.

A. Physical Qualities

1. Appearance
2. General health
3. Endurance
4. Vision
5. Hearing

B. Mental Abilities

1. General intelligence
2. Knowledge of business
3. Speed of reaction
4. Memory
5. Creativeness
6. Initiative
7. Insight into character

C. Ethics

1. Honesty
2. Loyalty
3. Dependability
4. Perseverance

D. Social Qualities

1. Courtesy
2. Sympathy
3. Ability to work with others
4. Cheerfulness
5. Self-confidence
6. Adaptability
7. Enthusiasm

E. Executive Qualities

1. Ability to direct others
2. Ability to organize
3. Ability to make decisions
4. Ability to take responsibility
5. Ability to accept suggestions

SMALLSCALE INDUSTRY

Small-scale Industry in the Indian Economy Development

In today's scenario, small businesses/small-scale industrial units are playing an important role in the economic development of any nation. Although it is not generally recognized, this segment of our economy includes some of the dynamic, profitable and interesting firms. In India, there are 32.25 lakh small-scale industrial units/businesses in the SSI sector, employing 177.30 lakh persons (1999-2000). The output of this sector is around ₹ 5,78,470 crores. The export amounted to ₹ 53,975 crores. SSIs contribute up to 40 per cent of gross turnover in manufacturing sector, 45 per cent of the manufacturing exports and 35 per cent of the total exports. SSI sector contributes 7 per cent of the GDP. During this era of economic liberalization, the growth of the SSI sector is rather quite perceptible.

Definition of Small-scale Industry

There is no generally accepted definition of a 'small business'. The definitions vary all the way from country to country and Government-to-Government in a country. The following are some of the definitions.

In the USA, in the Small Business Act 1953, Congress defined a small business as one that is independently owned and operated and which is not dominant in its field of operation.

In India, the Department of Small-scale and Agro and Rural Industries considered small businesses as a sector and given the following definitions.

1. Small-scale Industrial Undertaking

An industrial undertaking in which the investment in fixed assets in Plant and Machinery, whether held in ownership terms or on lease or by hire purchase, does not exceed ₹ 100 lakhs is called a Small-scale Industrial Undertaking.

2. Ancillary Industrial Undertaking

An industrial undertaking which is engaged or proposed to be engaged in the manufacture or production of parts, components, sub-assemblies, tooling or intermediates or the rendering of services and the undertaking supplies or renders or proposes to supply or render not less than 50 per cent of its production or services as the case may be to one or more other industrial undertakings and whose investment in fixed assets in Plant and Machinery, whether held on ownership terms or on lease or on by hire purchase does not exceed ₹ 100 lakhs is called an Ancillary Industrial Undertaking.

3. *Tiny Enterprises*

All small-scale units with investment limit in Plant and Machinery up to ₹ 25 lakhs irrespective of the location of the unit are called tiny enterprises.

4. *Export Oriented Units*

Units having fixed assets in Plant and Machinery not exceeding ₹ 100 lakhs and which undertake to export at least 30 per cent of its current production by the end of 3rd year from the date of its commencing of production are called Export Oriented Units (EOUs).

5. *Small-scale (Industrial-related) Service and Business Enterprises (SSSBEs)*

Industry-related Service and Business Enterprises with investment up to ₹ 5 lakhs in fixed assets excluding Land and Building are called Small-scale (Industry-related) Service and Business Enterprises (SSSBEs).

6. *Women Enterprises*

Women enterprises are those small-scale units, where one or more women entrepreneurs have not less than 51 per cent of financial holding. Such units are given more concessions and encouragement.

7. *Village and Small-scale Industries*

Modern segment – Powerlooms

Traditional segment — Khadi and Village industries, Handlooms, sericulture, handicrafts and coir units sericulture.

Objectives of a Small Business

Objectives are the ends towards which all the activities of the organization are directed.

1. Service
2. Profit
3. Community participation
4. Growth
5. Subsidiaries

Characteristics

The above definitions exhibit the following characteristics associated with small business and small-scale units.

1. Characterized by smallness
2. Involves lesser capital
3. Mostly one man venture
4. They are highly diversified – wide range of products
5. Wide dispersal geographically

Importance

There are a number of reasons why smaller firms are of importance to our economy.

1. They are the important sources of competition and challenge the economic power of larger firms.
2. They broaden the distribution of economic and political power and do not result in concentration of power.
3. They are the sources of innovation and creativity.
4. They offer career opportunities to those, who are happiest and most productive in the unstructured environment of a small company.
5. Provide the dynamism, innovation and effectiveness that leads to the productive economic system.
6. There exists vast agribusiness opportunities in developing economy of India.
7. Generating employment with minimum investment.
8. Promoting export.
9. Control over production widely distributed.
10. Develop risk takers.

Advantages

1. Less capital outlay but more employment generation
2. Does not require sophisticated technology
3. Facilitates decentralization and dispersal of business units
4. They offer a wide range of choices to consumers
5. Can serve specialized needs
6. Utilizes the resources in full without wastage

Disadvantages

1. Inadequate management ability
2. Inadequate finance
3. Poor competitive position
4. Uncertain business continuity

Organization and Administration

Organizational structure and administration for promotion of SSI in India are out lined below:

At national level, under Ministry of Industry, an exclusive Department of Small-scale and Agro and Rural industries exists since 1991 for the promotion and development of small-scale industries. The Office of Development Commissioner (Small-scale Industries) has been functioning within the Ministry of Industry since 1954 as an apex/nodal organ and provides link between the Ministry/Department and field organizations. Since 1991, it has been working as an attached office to the Department of Small-scale and Agro and Rural Industries.

Development Commissioner (Small-scale Industries)

The Small Industries Development Organization (SIDO) headed by the Additional Secretary and Development Commissioner (SSI), being an apex body for formulating policies for the development of small-scale industries in the country is playing a very constructive role for strengthening this vital sector. It functions through a network of SISIs, Branch SISIs, Regional Testing Centres, Footwear Training Centres, Production Centre, Field Testing Stations and specialized institutes. It renders services such as:

- Advising the Government in policy formulation for the promotion and development of small-scale industries.
- Providing techno-economic and managerial consultancy, common facilities and extension services to small-scale units.
- Providing facilities for technology upgradation, modernization, quality improvement and infrastructure.
- Human Resource Development through training and skill upgradation.
- Providing economic information services.
- Maintaining a close liaison with the Central Ministries, Planning Commission, State Governments, Financial Institutions and other organizations concerned with development of Small-scale Industries.
- Evolving and coordinating policies and programmes for development of small-scale industries as ancillaries to large and medium scale industries.
- Monitoring of PMRY Scheme.

Over the years, SIDO has served a very useful purpose as a catalyst of growth of small enterprises through its vast network of field organizations spread over different parts of the country.

Small-scale Industries Board

The range of development work in Small-scale Industries involves several Department/Ministries and several organizations of Central/State Governments. To facilitate coordination and inter-institutional linkage, the Small Industries Board has been constituted. It is an apex advisory body constituted to render advice to the Government on all issues pertaining to the small-scale sector. The Industry Minister of the Government of India is the Chairman and the Board comprises among others State Industry Ministers, some Members of Parliament, and Secretaries of various Departments of Government of India, financial institutions, public sector undertakings, industry associations and eminent experts in the field. The Board was last constituted on 26.9.1998 with 93 members besides the Chairman. The term of the Board is for two years.

Small Industries Service Institutes (SISIs)

There are 28 SISIs and 30 Branch SISIs set up in State capitals and other industrial cities all over the country. The main activities of these institutions are as follows:

- Assistance/Consultancy to Prospective Entrepreneurs
- Assistance/Consultancy rendered to existing units

- Preparation of State Industries Profiles
- Preparation/Updating of District Industrial Potential Surveys
- Project Profiles
- Entrepreneurship Development Programmes
- Motivational Campaigns
- Production Index
- Management Development Programmes
- Skill Development Programmes
- Energy Conservation
- Pollution Control
- Quality Control and Upgradation
- Export Promotion
- Ancillary Development
- Common Facility Workshop/Lab
- Preparation of Directory of Specific Industry
- Intensive Technical Assistance
- Coordination with DICs
- Linkage with State Government Functionaries
- Market Surveys
- Other Action Plan Activities assigned by Headquarters

SISIs and its Branches have common facility workshops in various trades. At present there are 42 such common facility workshops attached to SISIs/Branch SISIs.

Some Current Problems Worrying Small Businessmen

- Government regulation/policy in general
- Inflation
- Taxes
- Govt. paper works
- Labour unions
- High interest rates
- Environmental restrictions
- Lack of required capital
- Minimum Wage Laws
- Corruptive and bureaucratic officialdom
- Seasonality in agricultural production and interruptions in raw materials availability

- Seasonality in demand for agricultural inputs
- Lack of appropriate technology

Causes for Business Failure

- Lack of business records
- Lack of business experience
- Insufficient stock turnover
- Uncollected Accounts receivables
- Inventory shrinkage
- Poor inventory control
- Lack of finance
- Improper mark-up
- Lack of sales
- Too much left to chance
- Crucial obstacles go unnoticed through ignorance

Entrepreneurial Opportunities in Modern Agriculture

Farming	Product Marketing	Inputs Marketing	Processing Marketing	Facilitative
Crop	Wholesale	Ferilizer	Milk	Research & Development
Dairy/Poultry/ Goat	Retail	Agricultural Chemicals	Fruits	Marketing Information
Fish	Commission Agent	Seeds	Vegetables	Quality control
Rabbit	Transport	Machineries	Paddy	Insurance
Vegetables	Export	Animal feed	Sugarcane	Energy
Flowers	Finance	Poultry hatchery	Cashew	
Ornamental Plants	Storage	Vetmedicines	Coir	
Palmrosa	Consultancy	Landscaping	Poultry	
Fodder		Agricultural credit	Cattle	
Sericultue		Custom service	Tannery	
Agro-forestry		Biocontrol units	Brewery	
Beekeeping		Biotech units	P. board	
Mushroom				

There are Enterprises, Entrepreneurs and Environment. Already we discussed on the entrepreneurial personality, abilities, motives and competencies. Also we have discussed on the enterprises, opportunities and their feasibility and viability. Here onwards only those enterprises meeting the feasibility and viability will be focused and discussed for the environment in which the enterprises and entrepreneurs function.

The environment factors or forces which affect the success of business are into (1) Economic environment, (2) Demographic environment, (3) Socio-cultural environment, (4) Technological environment, (5) Political environment, and (6) Legal environment.

IMPORTANCE OF ENVIRONMENT ANALYSIS

The manager needs to be dynamic to effectively deal with the challenges of environment. The environment of business is not static. Some of the following benefits of environment scanning are as follows:

- It creates an increased general awareness of environmental changes on the part of management.
- It guides with greater effectiveness in matters relating to Government.
- It helps in marketing analysis.
- It suggests improvements in diversification and resource allocation.
- It helps firms to identify and capitalize upon opportunities rather than losing out to competitors.
- It provides a base of objective qualitative information about the business environment that can subsequently be of value in designing the strategies.

SUMMARY

Agro processing could be defined as set of techno-economic activities carried out for conservation and handling of agricultural produce and to make it usable as food, feed, fiber, fuel or industrial raw material. Hence, the scope of the agro-processing industry encompasses all operations from the stage of harvest till the material reaches the end-users in the desired form, packaging, quantity, quality and price. Ancient Indian scriptures contain vivid account of the post-harvest and processing practices for preservation and processing of agricultural produce for food and medicinal uses. Inadequate attention to the agro-processing sector in the past put both the producer and the consumer at a piquant situation and also hurting the economy of the country.

Agro-processing is now regarded as the sunrise sector of the Indian economy in view of its large potential for growth and likely socio-economic impact specifically on employment and income generation. Some estimates suggest that in developed countries, up to 14 per cent of the total workforce is engaged in agro-processing sector directly or indirectly. However, in India, only about 3 per cent of the workforce finds employment in this sector revealing its underdeveloped state and vast untapped potential for employment. Properly developed, agro-processing sector can make India a major player at the global level for marketing and supply of processed food, feed and a wide range of other plant and animal products.

QUESTIONS

1. Elucidate scope and approaches for agriculture business in India.
2. How many types of small-scale business are in operation in agribusiness?
3. What role human personality will contribute in agribusiness?
4. Explain the functions rendered by Export Oriented Units (EOUs).
5. What are the objectives of SSIs in Indian agriculture sector?
6. What are the advantages and disadvantages of SSIs in Indian agricultural sector?

UNIT - 5

CHAPTER 19

ROLE OF BANKS IN AGRICULTURE SECTOR

ROLE OF BANKS IN AGRICULTURE SECTOR

Nationalization of banks was a major step for channelising credit to various sectors of economy of which agriculture is a major sector. A dynamic and growing agricultural sector needs adequate finance through banks to accelerate the overall growth. The government has directed the banks to double their flow of credit to agriculture sector in three years commencing from the year 2004-05. With the government's keen interest and special budget allocation for agricultural in the 11th five-year plan, it is now in the hands of the farmer to reap the benefit of the schemes offered by the banks. Following is a list of offers of credit from some of the nationalized banks.

Allahabad Bank (www.allahabadbank.com)

- Kisan Shakti Yojana Scheme
- Farmers are free to utilise the loan at their own choice
- No margin is required
- 50% of the loan amount may be utilized for personal/domestic purposes including repayment of debt to moneylenders

Andhra Bank (www.andhrabank-india.com)

- Andhra Bank Kisan Green card
- Coverage under Personal Accident Insurance Scheme (PAIS)

Bank of Baroda (www.bankofbaroda.com)

- Purchase of second hand tractors scheme for dry-land farming
- Working capital needs to dealers/distributors/traders of agricultural inputs/livestock inputs
- Hiring agricultural machinery
- Development of horticulture
- Working capital for units engaged in dairy, piggery, poultry, sericulture etc.
- Financing Scheduled Caste/Scheduled Tribes for purchase of farm implements, tools, pair of bullocks, creation of irrigation facilities.

Bank of India (www.bankofindia.com)

- ***Star Bumiheen Kisan Card*** – for share croppers, tenant farmers and oral lessees
- ***Kisan Samadhan Card*** – Kisan credit card for crop production and other related investments
- ***BOI Shatabdi Krishi Vikas Card*** – electronic card for anywhere anytime banking for farmers
- Funding for contract farming in hybrid seed production, cotton industry, sugarcane industry etc.
- Special schemes for SHGs and to empower women folk
- ***Star Swarojgar Prashikshan Sansthan (SSPS)***, a new initiative to provide entrepreneurial training to farmers

- Crop loans: Upto ₹ 3 lakhs at the rate of 7 per cent per annum
- Collateral security: Loans up to ₹ 50,000, no collateral required, but for above ₹ 50,000, RBI directives are followed.

Dena Bank (www.denabank.com)

- Dena Bank is most active in Gujarat, Maharashtra, Chhattisgarh and UT of Dadra and Nagar Haveli.
- *Dena Kisan Gold Credit Card Scheme*
- Maximum credit limit up to ₹ 10 lakh
- Provision of 10 per cent towards domestic expenses including education of children
- Longer repayment period up to 9 years
- Loan is available for any type of investment in farm such as farm implements, tractors, sprinklers/drip irrigation systems, oil engine, electric pump sets, etc.
- Short term crop loan up to ₹ 3 lakhs at 7 per cent
- Disposal of loans within 15 days of application
- No collateral up to ₹ 50,000 for farm loans and up to ₹ 5 lakhs for setting up agri-clinic and agribusiness units.

Indian Bank (www.indianbank.in)

- **Production Credit:** Crop loans, Tie-up with sugar mills and Kisan Credit Card Scheme, Crop loans to tenant farmers, share croppers and oral lessees
- **Agricultural Investment Credit:** Land development, minor irrigation, micro irrigation, farm mechanization, plantation and horticulture
- **Agricultural Structured Loans:** Kisan Bike, Agri-vendors Bike, Agri-clinics and Agribusiness Centres
- **Group Lending for Agricultural Development:** Loan to joint liability groups/Self Help Groups
- **New Agricultural Avenues:** Contract farming, Organic farming, rural godowns, cold storage, medicinal and aromatic plants, biofuel crops etc.

Oriental Bank of Commerce (www.obcindia.co.in)

- Oriental Green Card (OGC) Scheme
- Composite Credit Scheme for Agricultural lending
- Setting up of cold storages/godowns
- Financing commission agents

Punjab National Bank (www.pnbkrishi.com)

- *PNB Kisan Sampuranrin Yojana*
- *PNB Kisan Icha Purti Yojana*

- Growing potatoes/fruits against pledge of cold storage receipts
- Self propelled Combine Harvestors
- Development of Forestry nursery
- Wasteland development
- Mushroom/Prawn culture and mushroom spawn production
- Purchase nad maintenance of milch animals
- *Dairy Vikas Card Scheme*
- Schemes for pisciculture, piggery, bee-keeping etc.

State Bank of Hyderabad (www.sbhyd.com)

- Crop loans and Agricultural Gold loans
- Marketing of agricultural produce
- Cold storage/private warehouse
- Minor irrigation and Dug well scheme/development of old well scheme
- Land development finance
- Purchase of tractor, power tiller and implements
- Purchase of Agricultural Land/fallow/wastelands
- Vehicle loans for farmers
- Drip irrigation and sprinklers
- Self Help Group
- Agri-clinics and Agri-business Centres
- *Yuva Krishi Plus Scheme*

State Bank of India (www.statebankofindia.com)

- Crop Loan Scheme (ACC)
- Storing produce in their own premises and renewal of loans for next season
- Kisan Credit Card Scheme
- Land Development Schemes
- Minor Irrigation Schemes
- Purchase of combine harvestor
- Kisan Gold Card Scheme
- *Krishi Plus Scheme* – for customized hiring of tractor to rural youth
- *Arthias Plus Scheme* – for Commission agents
- *Broiler Plus Scheme* – Broiler farming
- *Lead Bank Scheme*

Syndicate Bank (www.syndicatebank.com)

- Syndicate Kisan Credit card (SKCC)
- Solar Water Heater Scheme
- Agri-clinics and Agribusiness centres

Vijaya Bank (www.vijayabank.com)

- Loans to Self Help Groups
- Vijaya Kisan Card
- Vijaya Planters Card
- KVIC Margin Money Scheme for Artisans and Village Industries

SUMMARY

Nationalization of banks was a major step for channelising credit to various sectors of economy of which agriculture is a major sector. A dynamic and growing agricultural sector needs adequate finance through banks to accelerate the overall growth. The government has directed the banks to double their flow of credit to agriculture sector in three years commencing from the year 2004-05. With the government's keen interest and special budget allocation for agricultural in the 11th five-year plan, it is now in the hands of the farmer to reap the benefit of the schemes offered by the banks. Following is a list of offers of credit from some of the nationalized banks.

QUESTIONS

1. What role Indian commercial banks play in the field of Indian agriculture?
2. Elucidate which are the banks that are doing selfless service in making the life of farmers more comfortable?
3. What are the functions of State Bank of India in this endeavour?
4. What is the role of Andhra Bank and State Bank of Hyderabad in view of farmers' plight which hit the front page of all newspapers during 2009-10?

OOO

CHAPTER

20

CREDIT FACILITIES TO AGRIBUSINESS UNITS

Credit Facilities to Agriculture Business Units

Institutional Infrastructure

A. Regulatory Mechanism

Agencies for Warehousing

Schemes of APEDA

Produces under the Purview of APEDA

B. Warehousing Schemes by Public Sector

Food Corporation of India

Central Warehousing and State Warehousing Corporations

C. Other Important Organizations

Oilseeds and Vegetable Oil Board

Cotton Corporation of India Limited (CCIL)

Jute Corporation of India Limited (JCIL)

National Horticulture Board (NHB)

State Trading Corporation of India Limited (STC)

Role of NAFED

NAFED Service to Farmers

NAFED's Role in Biofertilizers

Role of NAFED in Seed Sector

Consumer Market

Market Intervention Scheme

Warehouses and Cold Storage

Other Activities

Other Public Sector Service

Development of Agriculture Marketing Infrastructure

CREDIT FACILITIES TO AGRI-BUSINESS UNITS

The progress of any economy depends to a large extent on the application of science and technology for the exploitation of agricultural raw materials into numerous consumer and industrial products, thus accelerating the process of industrialization without sacrificing agricultural development resulting in the conversion of agricultural economices to industrial economies through the agri-industry linkages.

Every primary agricultural commodity and organic residue animal by-product and waste, fishery, and forestry by-products etc. can contribute to the economic development through the development of a series of industries if the primary commodity, its by-products and waste matter are scientifically processed.

Among the uniqueness of Agro industries, few are related to agro-industrial projects because of the seasonality, perishability and the variability of the raw materials. And unlike the non-agro-industrial sector, the agro industries have to deal with supply and demand imbalances, problems of inventories production scheduling and the coordination of the production and the processing and marketing sections of the producer to the consumer chain.

Further because of the perishable nature of the biological raw materials, agro-industrial products require greater speed and care in handling and storage which can effect the nutritional quality of the products by reducing the deterioration of the produce.

Additional pressure is exerted on the agro-industrial plants' production scheduling and the quality control operations on account of the variability in the quality and the quantity of the agricultural raw materials.

As the raw materials are the major cost component of the agro industries, procurement operations fundamentally shape the economics of the operations.

INSTITUTIONAL INFRASTRUCTURE

The institutional infrastructure is available under two strategies – public sector institutions and cooperative institutions/organizations.

Public Sector Institutions

Looking at the importance of agriculture marketing for producers as well as for consumers, the government has intervened in the system since 1930 with various efforts to make the system more efficient. Various organizations are working to support the marketing of agricultural produce in the country. Some important public sector institutions/organizations working in this field are as under:

A. REGULATORY MECHANISM

Central and State Institutional Mechanism

1. Department of Agriculture and Cooperation
2. Directorate of Marketing and Inspection (DMI)
3. National Institute of Agriculture Marketing (NIAM)
4. Agriculture Produce Marketing Committees (APMC)

5. Commission for Agriculture Costs and Prices (CACP)
6. State Agricultural Marketing Boards (SAMB)
7. Council of State Agricultural Marketing Boards (COSAMB)
8. Agricultural and Processed Foods Exports Development Authority (APEDA)

Agencies for warehousing:

1. Food Corporation of India (FCI)
2. Central Warehousing Corporation (CWC)
3. State Warehousing Corporation (SWC)

Other important organizations in agricultural marketing: Government sponsored autonomous bodies:

1. Commodities Boards
2. Cotton Corporation of India Limited (CCI)
3. National Horticulture Board (NHB)
4. State Trading Corporation (STC)
5. Export Inspection Council (EIC)
6. Marine Products Exports Development Authority (MPEDA)
7. Indian Institute of Foreign Trade (IIFT)
8. Indian Institute of Packaging (IIP)
9. Export Promotion Councils (EPC)
10. Research Institutions and Agricultural Universities
11. Silk Export Promotion Council (SEPC)
12. Cashewnuts Export Promotion Council of India (CEPCI)

Regulatory Central/State Institutions for Marketing of Agricultural Products

Some important regulatory institutions/organizations in the public sector are:

I. Department of Agriculture and Cooperation:

The Department of Agriculture and Cooperation has three organizations under its administrative control dealing with marketing – the Directorate of Marketing and Inspection NIAM and Small Farmers Agri-business Consortium.

Directorate of Marketing and Inspection:

DMI has its Head office at Faridabad (Haryana) and Branch Head office at Nagpur (Maharashtra). It has eleven regional offices and twenty six sub-offices spread across the country. Besides this, it has a central AGMARK laboratory at Nagpur and sixteen regional AGMARK laboratories.

The main functions of the directorate are as follows:

- Providing advice to states/UTs on statutory regulations, development and management of agricultural produce markets

- Promoting standardizing and grading of agricultural and allied produce under the Agriculture Produce (Grading and Marking) Act, 1937
- Developing infrastructure for agricultural marketing
- Creating an efficient network for information on agricultural marketing
- Market research, surveys, and planning and extension
- Training personnel in agricultural marketing
- Constructing rural godowns

National Institute of Agricultural Marketing (NIAM)

NIAM started functioning from 8th August 1988 in Jaipur and managed by a governing body under the chairmanship of the Minister of Agriculture and an Executive Committee under the Chairmanship of the Secretary Department of Agriculture and Cooperation with following specific objectives:

(a) to impart specialized training designed specifically to develop leadership skills for the management of marketing of agricultural enterprises and services.

(b) to undertake and promote applied and operational research in the field of agricultural marketing which has direct bearing on the national economy for the government.

(c) to undertake consultancies for the appraisal of markets/marketing projects for approval and financial support by the Central Government.

(d) to formulate objective criteria and evolve a practical methodology for the application of such criteria for selective development of physical markets.

(e) to develop human resources by providing long-term need based degree diploma courses in agricultural marketing.

(f) to act as an agent to the State government to formulate strategies related to agricultural marketing and provide help to generate self-employment opportunities for the educated youth by exploiting local potential resources.

(g) To generate wide information network related to agricultural marketing for the benefit of all concerned to evolve as an efficient innovative and competitive marketing process.

(h) To work as centre of excellence by establishing liaison with international organization.

The institute has been imparting trainings by executives of the agriculture and horticulture departments, state marketing boards, agricultural produce market committees and apex level cooperatives commodity boards, export houses recognized by APEDA, agro-industries corporations, commercial banks and non-governmental organizations. Besides these clients, the NIAM also imparts training to farmers on marketing management.

II. Agricultural Produce Marketing Committees (APMC)

On the recommendation of the Royal Commission in 1928, the government of India set up DMI in 1935 under the Ministry of Food and Agriculture to regulate market practices and establish regulated markets in India to safeguard the interest of producers and eliminate malpractices in the market. As per the Model Bill circulated by DMI to the states in 1938 the Central Government advised all the State governments to enact marketing legislation to promote competitive and transparent transactional methods in order to protect the interests of the farmers.

Since 1930 some states had enacted legislation for the regulation of markets. The Agricultural Produce Markets Act (APMC) came into effect in 1939 in Bombay, Punjab and Mysore. Since then there has remarkable growth in the number of regulated markets in India. Most of the State and Union territories have enacted the APMC Act to regulate the agricultural produce market.

The **functions of APMC** in regulated markets are as follows:

(a) To supervise the method of sale (open auction or close tender) to ensure fair and competitive prices.

(b) To provide amenities at market yards.

(c) To issue, renew or withdraw licenses to functionaries operating in the markets who are supposed to ensure correct weights and measures.

(d) To ensure proper collection and dissemination of market information about price, time and date of auction.

(e) To prescribe the various market charges in a rational manner.

(f) To facilitate grading and standardizing of produce in the mandis.

(g) To settle disputes in the market among farmers, traders or functionaries of mandis.

The supervision of regulated markets is done by a supervisory committee the APMC consisting of representatives of all stakeholders, viz., farmers' traders' cooperative marketing societies banks and governments officials. The composition of the marketing committee differs from state to state.

The marketing committee gets its funds from market fees, renewal of licenses and subsidies from the government.

The number of regulated markets which was only 286 in 1950 increased to 7521 on March 31, 2005. Although considerable efforts were made by the government, the facilities are far less than required. According to the regulation of National Commission on Agriculture (1976), the facility of regulated markets should be available within a radius of 5 km but in reality each regulated markets serves an area of about 776 sq km and on an average of twenty-one villages. Supportive infrastructure and facilities existing in the markets are also insufficient as apparent from the following facts.

Objectively, the physical infrastructure required for agricultural markets is as follows:

Core Facilities:

Auction Platforms

Drying yard sanitary facilities

Platforms for automatic weighing

Loading/unloading facilities

Scientific warehousing facilities

Ripening chambers

Grading facilities

Standardization facilities

Packaging and labeling equipments

Computerized information centers with online facilities

Supportive Infrastructure

Water supply

Power

Banking

Post and telegraph

POL

Veterinary Services

Rainproofing

Repair and maintenance

Input supply and daily necessity outlets

Service Infrastructure

Parking

Sheds for animals

Rest rooms

Soil testing facilities

Drainage

Market education

Maintenance Infrastructure

Cleaning and sanitation

Garbage collection and disposal

Waste utilization

Biogas production/power

The current status of facilities in the regulated mandis is far from satisfactory.

Covered or open, auction platforms exists in only 66 per cent of the regulated markets.

Cold storage units exists in only 9 per cent of the markets.

Grading facilities are available in less than 33 per cent of the markets.

Farmers' resting facilities exists in only half the markets.

Basic facilities such as internal roads, boundary walls, electric lights, loading and unloading facilities and weighing equipment are not available in almost 20 per cent of the markets.

Prior to 2003 in the area under APMC jurisdiction, only licensed traders were allowed to carry on wholesale trading. But looking at the vast requirements of development and investment for infrastructure building in agribusiness, the amendments in APMC Act 2003 opened the door for private companies. This reform was instrumental in bringing about considerable developments in infrastructure especially in supply chain, modern market yards and retail spaces with the necessary backward and forward linkages.

III. Commission for Agricultural Costs and Prices

The Agricultural Prices Commission was set up in January 1965, and since March 1985 the Commission has been known as the Commission for Agricultural Costs and Prices. (CACP). It advises the Government on pricing policy for all major agricultural commodities and evolving a balanced and integrated price structure with a view to fulfilling the overall needs of the economy and taking care of the interests of the producers as well as the consumer.

The commission has representatives of the farming community as non-official members who have extensive field experience and are actively associated with the farming community.

On the recommendations of the CACP, the government announced the Minimum Support Prices and Procurement Prices which have been working as forward contract for the farmers. This helps the farmers to allocate their resources in an efficient manner.

Minimum Support Prices are announced for foodgrains, oilseeds, fiber crops, sugarcane and potato before the start of the sowing season. At procurement time, the Government procedure foodgrains either from the producers or traders by imposing a fixed levy. For maintaining the buffer stocks or for the Public Distribution System, procurement prices are announced before the harvesting season which is generally higher than the MSP.

IV. State Agricultural Marketing Boards

APMC were modified with the provision of establishing State Agricultural Marketing Boards (SAMBs). This SAMBs function varies from state to state with statutory. Status in some states and advisory status in others. SAMBs have been set up in twenty states and one union territory with following main functions.

- To train officers and staff in agricultural marketing
- To tender advice to the government on the functioning or improvement in agricultural marketing.
- To help APMCs by framing byelaws and supervise their operations.

V. Council of State Agricultural Marketing Boards

To coordinate the activities of SAMB especially with respect to credit mobilization and central assistance, an apex body the Council of State Agricultural Marketing Boards (COSAMB) was set up in 1988.

It was established with the following objectives:

1. To act as a common the forum at the national level to share their experience for developing a strong and efficient marketing system in country,

2. Providing assistance to credit institutions and state governments in framing norms for getting credit from banks and central assistance for developing,
3. Arranging training programmes for various functionaries.
4. Facilitating development of links between institutions, organizations, professionals, consultants, researchers and technologists and functionaries in marketing.

VI. Agricultural and Processed Food Products Export Development Authority

The Agricultural and Processed Food Products Export Development Authority (APEDA) was established in the year 1986 by the Government of India under the Ministry of Commerce to promote exports and promote the development of agricultural commodities (mostly perishables like fruits, vegetables, meat and poultry products) and processed foods. The ultimate objective of APEDA is to maximize agri-exports to earn foreign exchange earnings, value addition, increasing incomes of farmers and increasing employment.

Schemes of APEDA

APEDA provides financial assistance to promote and develop agro-exports under various schemes which are available to growers, trade associates and government agencies. Some of the activities which are eligible for financial assistances are:

(a) Supply of samples to potential importers, brand publicity etc. for export promotion, exports and market development.
(b) Assistance for studies, surveys, and research and development activities for strengthening market intelligence and database.
(c) Schemes for the development of infrastructural facilities.
(d) Quality upgradation and development/improvement of packing quality.
(e) Schemes for upgradation of meat processing facilities.

APEDA runs development programmes for promoting agro-exports through various development programmes. The programmes may include developing databases, information dissemination, product promotion and publicity in foreign countries through advisory service and support. Service is provided to traders on exports and imports, to industry and government and motivating 'best exporters' every year by distributing awards.

Products under the Purview of APEDA

- Floriculture, vegetable seeds, herbal and medicinal plants.
- Fresh fruits and vegetables- mangoes, grapes, and other fruits, dried nuts (walnuts), onions and other fresh vegetables etc.
- Processed fruits and vegetables – mango pulp, pickles, chutneys, dried and preserved vegetables and other processed fruits and vegetables (groundnut kernels, gaurgum, jaggery and confectionary and cocoa products).
- Cereals (rice) and cereal preparations (alcoholic and non-alcoholic beverages, miscellaneous preparations).

- Animal products (dairy products, poultry products, buffalos meat, sheep/goat meat, processed meat and animal castings).

B. WAREHOUSING AGENCIES IN PUBLIC SECTOR

Warehouses are scientifically constructed storage structures which protect the quality and quantity of the stored produce. Warehousing in India is currently an integrated scheme facilitating the following functions:

1. Scientific storage in warehouses helps prevent losses by protecting the quality and quantity of the stored produce from the vagaries of weather and rodents, insects and pests.
2. Warehousing of produce helps fulfill the financial needs of persons by storing the produce and providing warehouse receipts of the value of the goods stored that can be used as collateral for getting bank credit.
3. Warehouses help in regulating the supply of goods in the markets, which ultimately helps in price stabilization by balancing supply with demand.
4. Warehouses can help market intelligence by providing information about prices, supply and demand to the marketers and help them develop selling and buying strategies.

Agricultural Produce (Development and Warehousing) Corporation Act 1956

The Government of India enacted the Agricultural Produce (Development and Warehousing) Corporation Act 1956 on the recommendation of the All India Rural Credit Survey Committee of the Reserve Bank of India for the establishment of warehouses to strengthen the rural credit and marketing. The Act had the following provisions:

1. Establishment of National Cooperative Development and Warehousing Board which was set up on 1st September 1956.
2. Establishment of the CWC in 1957.
3. Establishment of SWCs in various states since 1957.
4. In 1962, the Government of India decided to bifurcate the Act of 1956 into two separate Acts.
   — The National Cooperative Development Corporation Act 1962
   — The Warehousing Corporation Act 1962

Foodgrain Storage and General Warehousing in the Public Sector

The Ministry of Food and Civil Supplies aims at providing scientific storage capacity for storing buffer stocks and operational stocks of foodgrains to run the Public Distribution System (PDS).

Efforts are also being made to improve facilities for traditional storage in rural areas. Over a period of time, sizeable scientific storage/warehousing capacity has been developed/added on by two agencies in the public sector.

FCI – Foodgrains CWC and its 17 SWCs – foodgrains and other items.

1. Food Corporation of India (FCI)

The FCI was set up in January 1965 by an Act of Parliament to accomplish its objectives:

(a) To procure the marketable surplus from primary producers at the minimum support price on behalf of Central and State governments to ensure that the primary producer gets the minimum price as a protection from the vagaries of speculative trade.

(b) To build up and maintain buffer stocks of foodgrains through the State Trading Corporation.

(c) To ensure national food security by providing foodgrains through the PDS to vulnerable sections of society.

(d) To function primarily in the purchase, movement, storage, distribution and sale of foodgrains and other foodstuffs with the objective of minimizing price fluctuation by balancing demand and supply in the country.

(e) To secure a strategic and commanding position in the trading of foodgrains in the country and intervene in the market to provide price stability.

Functions of FCI

To act as nodal agency for the procurement of wheat, paddy, rice, and coarse grains (w.e.f. April 1990) under the price support scheme in association with State governments and their agencies. Rice is procured as per the levy issued by the State government to maintain buffer stocks.

FCI imports or exports foodgrains whenever the situation arises.

To stabilize market prices through balancing of supplies according to demand and to augment the availability of stocks in the market, FCI undertakes open sales as and when directed by the central government.

FCI lifts levy sugar from various sugar mills and undertakes its movement to states against allocations made by the Central Government for distribution through PDS.

FCI maintains stocks of foodgrains for the PDS and other welfare schemes.

Stocks with FCI to meet four months' requirement for PDS are marked as optional stock and the remaining is treated as buffer stocks.

FCI generally undertakes transportation of stocks from surplus to deficit states. The bulk of the movement is done through railways. Stocks are also moved by road and river wherever necessary.

2. Central Warehousing Corporation and SWC

The Central Warehousing Corporation (CWC) is one of the biggest public warehousing agencies was established in 1957. It provides logistics services to clients of diverse groups. Through a network of 502 warehouses and about 6147 trained personnel, it provides scientific storage for more than 200 commodities including hygroscopic and perishable items. While conducting handling services, care is taken of more than 400 commodities.

Over the years, CWC has diversified its activities and as on 31.3.2006 it had:

- 500 foodgrains and industrial warehouses.
- Eighty seven custom bonded warehouses.

- Thirty-four inland clearance depots (ICD) containers freight stations (CFS) for providing import and export facilities in ports and inland stations.
- Air cargo complexes (at Amritsar, Goa and Singllur) to cater to the needs of export trade.

Functions of CWC

- To build and acquire godowns and warehouses at suitable places in India and operate them.
- To provide scientific warehousing/storage and handling facilities for more than 400 notified commodities for individuals cooperatives and other institutions.
- To facilitate the transportation of notified commodities.
- To subscribe the transportation of notified commodities
- Government's agent for clearing and forwarding, purchase/procurement, sale, storage and distribution of notified commodities.
- To carry out such other functions as may be prescribed under the Act.
- To offer consultancy services/training to different agencies for the construction of warehousing infrastructure.
- To provide disinfestations, fumigation and other ancillary services.

CWC has grown over the years in respect to storage capacity due to increase in owned capacity, while its dependence on hired warehouses has been decreased drastically from 74.79 lakh tons in 2007 to 102.20 lakh tons in 2007.

CWC's average capacity utilization of warehousing during 2005-06 has been to about 70 per cent.

State Warehousing Corporation (SCWC)

CWC has 17 associate SWCs and total investment of the CWC is 56.44 per cent shareholder in the equity capital of SWC as on 31st March 2006 and SWC paid a total dividend of ₹3.82 crore to CWC during 2004-05. The covered storage capacity available with SWC and the growth in capacity over the last four years is doubled. Its storage capacity during 2000 was 123.74 lakh tons (both owned and hired) and this figure doubled at 192.20 lakh tons during 2007.

Internal Resources

Along with seventeen associates in SWCs, the CWC has been generating internal resources which have grown significantly over the years. These are sufficient for funding its own storage construction programme as well as contributing to the SWC equity as 50 per cent shareholder.

C. OTHER IMPORTANT ORGANIZATIONS

There are many commodity boards in India which are producer controlled organizations supported by the Ministry of Commerce, while there is no control of the State governments. Each one of these boards – the Tea Board, Coffee Board, Rubber Board – deals with specific commodity. These commodity boards promote the external and internal trade of these commodities with the help and authority of the government, performing several functions related to the production, processing and marketing of the commodity and of the industry as a whole.

Other functions of these boards are supporting research related to production (varietal development, disease and pest management etc.) and extension and development programmes. One of the important functions of these boards is imparting training to producers, traders and exporters. The commodity boards are also engaged in the formulation and implementation of programmes and projects for the growth of the industry.

Some important commodity boards are the following:

1. Tea Board
2. Coffee Board
3. Coir Board
4. Rubber Board
5. Tobacco Board
6. Spices Board.
7. Coconut Board
8. Silk Board
9. Cardamom Board
10. Arecanut Board
11. Oilseeds and Vegetable Oils Board.

The Coffee Board is the oldest board under the department of Commerce. It has four regional coffee research stations, a coffee research institute, numerous regional field stations and coffee demonstration farms under it.

The Rubber Board was set up in 1947 with headquarter at Kottayam. It has five zonal offices, thirty-nine regional offices, and number of field stations, rubber development centres and regional nurseries.

The Tea Board was constituted in 1954 and it is an apex body for the tea industry in India with head office at Kolkota. It has sixteen regional and sub-regional offices in different parts of India. Apart from this network within the country, the Board has three foreign offices also.

The Tobacco Board was set up as a statutory body on 1st January 1976 under the Tobacco Act 1975 with headquarter at Guntur in AP state. The Board also has directorate of auctions at Bangalore. It is entrusted with the task of recommending minimum price to the Central government and regulates tobacco marketing in India abroad with due regard to the interests of growers.

The Spices Board was constituted as a statutory body on 26th February 1987 under the Spices Board Act, 1986. The Board has its head office at Kochi and seventeen regional offices, thirteen zonal offices, and thirty-one field units. The Board is responsible for export promotion of the fiftty-two spices mentioned in the schedule to Spices Board Act 1988.

Cotton Corporation of India Limited (CCIL)

The CCIL was set up in 1970 as PSU by the Ministry of Commerce Government of India. It is a nodal agency for procuring cotton under the support price system in all the states of India, except Maharashtra. In Maharashtra, the State Federation procures cotton to safeguard the interests of growers as well as consumers. It also undertakes the import of cotton – when needed – to control the prices and manages supplies to government and private textile mills in a sustainable manner.

Jute Corporation of India Limited (JCIL)

The JCIL set up as a PSU in 1971 by Government of India. It is responsible for procurement of Jute at MSP and sale and export/import of raw jute to maintain buffer stocks, thereby maintaining the price of jute in the market.

National Horticulture Board (NHB)

The NHB was set up as autonomous society by Government of India. The mandate of NHB is to promote integrated development in horticulture by helping in coordinating, stimulating and sustaining the production and processing of fruits and vegetables. It also envisages establishing a sound infrastructure in the field of production, processing and marketing with focus on post-harvest management to reduce losses.

***Objectives of NHB*:** Developing hubs for commercial horticulture by developing high quality horticulture farms in identified belts and making such areas vibrant with horticultural activity. Further developing the infrastructure for post-harvest management while strengthening market information systems and developing database related to horticulture. It also assists R&D programmes for developing variety-based products with improved methods and technology. Side by side, it also educates and trains farmers and processing industry personnel about new technologies related production while promoting consumption of fresh and processed fruits/vegetables.

Schemes of NHB: Development of commercial horticulture through production and post-harvest management, subsidy on capital investment for construction, modernization and expansion of cold storages for horticulture produce — development and transfer of technology for promotion of horticulture – information services for the marketing of horticulture crops and promotional services for horticulture (including terms of reference) for techno-economic feasibility studies.

State Trading Corporation (STC)

The STC, an autonomous company and premier international trading house, was set up in 1956. It has an equity base of around ₹ 30 crore of which 91 per cent is owned by the Government of India. It has developed vast expertise in handling bulk international trade with almost all countries of the world.

STC is set to become one-stop that offers specialized trade facilitation as a bulk trading agency in commodities by using its experience and contacts built over five decades. There has been a continuous spurt in the business activities of the corporation in recent years making an all-time high turnover of ₹ 10,000 crore in 2004-05 – 44 per cent higher than the target set in the MoU with the Government of India.

Among its numerous roles, STC possesses very good infrastructure and experience and therefore plays an important role in trading in India.

It arranges the import of essential items and bulk commodities for Indian consumers in accordance with the demand in the domestic markets.

It exports of a large number of agricultural commodities and manufactured products from India to all parts of the world. STC is instrumental in supplying quality products to the foreign buyer at the most competitive prices and ensure that the goods reach within the agreed delivery schedule. STC is also involved in domestic trading.

It provides market support operations to the rubber and tobacco industries.

It engages in joint ventures. And it also carries on counter trade.

Exports from India: The STC exports a diverse range of goods to a number of destinations across the world. Exports by STC vary from traditional agricultural commodities to sophisticated manufactured products.

Besides negotiating, contracting and shipping, STC seeks to introduce new products, explore new markets and undertake wide ranging ancillary functions such as product development, financing quality control, import of machinery and raw materials for export production.

STC makes purposeful use of its worldwide connections, abundant experience, up-to-date information about the market trends and long-term perspective on various commodities to ensure competitive prices and right quality. For the buyers abroad, they adhere to delivery schedules.

Principal Items of Export: Agricultural commodities — rice, wheat, sugar, tea, coffee, cashew, tobacco, rubber, extractions, opium, HPS groundnut, species, castor oil and seeds, processed foods.

Manufactured goods: Consumer products, textiles and garments, chemicals, drugs, and medical disposables, engineering and construction materials, leather ware, iron ore, steel raw materials, etc.

Imports into India: STC imports number of essential commodities whenever there are domestic shortfalls and it is instrumental in maintaining by arranging timely imports at competitive prices.

Principal Items of Imports: Agricultural commodities, edible oils, wheat, pulses, sugar, fatty acids etc.

Manufactured goods: FMCG petrochemicals, fertilizers, gold and silver, minerals, metals, scientific instruments, hospital and police equipment.

Import of Edible oils: After placement of import edible oils under Open General License (OGL) by the centre, the STC has started importing various types of edible oils on commercial account along with imports for the public-distribution system.

Services rendered while undertaking exports and imports:

To the Overseas Buyer: STC acts as an expert guide for finding the best Indian manufacturers undertakes negotiations, fixes delivery schedules and quality control for overseas buyers interested in Indian goods.

To Indian Industry: STC helps thousands of Indian manufacturers, find markets abroad for their products and assists manufacturers to use the best raw materials for their products in order to attract the buyers abroad. It also helps manufacturers in the following ways:

— Providing financial assistance on easy terms to exports.

— Exhibiting products of small-scale manufactures at international trade fairs and exhibitions.

— Importing machinery and raw materials for products to be exported.

— Assisting manufacturers in the areas of marketing, technical know-how, quality control, packaging, documentation etc.

— Supplying imported goods in small quantities as per the requirements of buyers.

Future Plans: STC has plans to expand its business and position itself by developing backward and forward integration and participating with the best international companies in industrial programmes not only for STC's requirements alone but also for the technological development in the country. It has also plans to facilitate backward integration for those who export through STC and need certain inputs as raw materials, machinery technology or assistance in developing products which might be available domestically or globally.

The corporation is also planning to enter into certain high tech areas and tie up with patent holders internationally to bring them to India and help them set up manufacturing units. The products of such units can be sold to India or exported to a third country.

Export Inspection Council (EIC)

The EIC notified under the Export (Quality Control and Inspection) Act 1963 was set up under section (3) of Export (Inspection and Quality Control) Act in 1963 in New Delhi. It is responsible for the enforcement of quality control and compulsory pre-shipment inspection of commodities meant for export. Export Inspection Agencies (EIA) located at Chennai, Delhi, Kolkata and Mumbai along with network of forty-one sub-offices and laboratories assist EIC in its functions to back up the pre-shipment inspection and certification activities.

Marine Products Exports Development Authority (MPEDA)

The MPEDA has its headquarters at Kochi, a statutory body responsible for development of the marine products industry with special focus on marine exports. MPEDA has field offices in all maritime states of India as well as Trade Promotion Offices in Tokyo and New York.

Indian Institute of Foreign Trade (IIFT)

The IIFT New Delhi has registered under Societies Registration Act 1860 was later conferred as "Deemed University" status. It has been engaged in training personnel in modern techniques of international trade, conducting market research, area and commodity surveys to foreign trade, dissemination of information arising from its research and market studies.

Indian Institute of Packaging (IIP)

IIP established in 1860 in Mumbai is registered under Societies Registration Act to stimulate consciousness of the need for good packaging. The main aim of this Institute is to undertake research of raw materials for the packaging industry and to organize training programmes on packaging technology.

Export Promotions Council (EPC)

Under the administrative control of Department of Commerce, presently there are 12 EPC and these are registered as non-profit organizations under the Companies Act/Societies Registration Act performing both advisory and executive functions. They are also the registering authorities for exporters under the Foreign Trade Policy 2004-09.

Research Institutions and Agricultural Universities

Several institutions work on marketing research of which DMI, NIAM, and SAMB, have already been studied.

The Indian Council for Agricultural Research (ICAR) is one of the most important research institutions in agriculture which sponsors research through various Central Research and State Agriculture Universities across the nation. State Agricultural Universities (SAUs) in different states also undertake research programmes for developing better techniques of better production of crops and allied sectors. These universities also develop professionals in the field of agriculture by imparting training through different programmes.

COOPERATIVE INSTITUTIONS IN AGRICULTURAL MARKETING

The cooperative movement in agriculture and allied sectors evolved with the purpose of pooling limited resources to take advantage of economies of scale. Cooperative marketing and credit societies were established prior to 1954. But since 1954, the policy has been adapted to enable cooperative societies to work with multiple purposes that could together undertake the functions of marketing and supply of credit. The cooperative societies can help farmers build backward linkages to have quality inputs and share equipments for better utilization. These societies are helping farmers and business by interlinking farming with supply of credit, marketing with elimination of most middlemen, warehousing facility of the society itself, and processing for the best advantage to farmers. Therefore, cooperatives may be the best solution for poor farmers with small holdings but most of such societies are facing problems of scarcity of resources and inefficiencies. In the current scenario of globalization and increased competition in the market, there is utmost need for reforms in policies of the cooperative societies.

At present, there is a network of over 60,000 primary cooperative marketing societies working in the country of which 3500 are special commodity marketing societies. There are 160 central marketing societies at district levels. There are twenty-nine general purpose State level Cooperative Marketing Federations. In addition, there are eight Federations State level Trade Cooperative Development Corporations.

Major sale through cooperative societies is made in foodgrains, sugarcane and cotton. The cooperatives have made good progress in sugar factories and dairy development, but in recent years the cooperatives have been developing well in the field of agricultural processing.

Amendment to the Constitution with respect to Cooperatives: The proposed amendment to the constitution is for the empowerment of cooperatives through voluntary formation, autonomous functioning, democratic control and professional management. The Constitution 106th Amendment Bill 2006 was introduced in the Lok Sabha on 22nd May 2006.

The important cooperative institutions working in the country are as follows:

1. National Cooperative Development Corporation Limited (NCDC)
2. National Dairy Development Corporation (NDDB)
3. National Agricultural Cooperative Marketing Federation Ltd. (NAFED)

4. Tribal Cooperative Marketing Development Federation Ltd. (TRIFED)
5. National Consumers Cooperative Federation Ltd (NCCF)
6. National Cooperative Tobacco Growers Federation (NTGF)
7. State Cooperative Marketing Federation (SCMF)
8. Primary Agricultural Cooperative Marketing Organizations
9. Special Commodity Cooperative Marketing Organizations (sugarcane-milk-cotton)

Some important organizations/institutes and physical infrastructure: The Public Sector and cooperative institutions are working for regulatory purposes and some in development of Infrastructures.

ROLE OF NAFED

NAFED was established in 1958 to promote cooperative marketing of agricultural produce to benefit the farmers. Farmers are the main members of the Federation who has authority as the members of the general body.

The objects of the NAFED are to organize, promote and develop marketing processing and storage of agricultural, horticultural and forest produce, undertake inter-state, import and export trade, wholesale or retail as the case may be in distribution of agricultural machinery, implements and other inputs and to act and assist for technical advice in agricultural production for the promotion and the working of its members and cooperative marketing, processing and supply societies in India. The NAFED may undertake following activities in furtherance of its objectives.

1. To promote, facilitate, coordinate the marketing and trading activities related to agricultural and other commodities articles and odds of the cooperative institutions.
2. To undertake or promote inter-state and international trade and commerce on its own or on behalf of its member institutions or the government or governmental organizations. It undertakes sale, purchase, import, export and distribution of agricultural, horticultural and forest produce, and other articles and goods from various sources for pursuing its business activities and to facilitate these activities. Wherever necessary, it open branches/sub-offices and appoint agents at required places within the country or abroad.
3. To undertake purchase, sale and supply of basic things required for agriculture production, marketing and processing, for example, seeds, fertilizers, manure, agricultural implements, and machinery, packing machinery, construction, processing machinery for agricultural commodities, forest produce, dairy, wool, and other animal products.
4. To own and construct its own godowns and cold storages to act as warehouseman under the Warehousing Act.
5. To act as an agent of government agencies or cooperative institutions for the purchase, sale, storage, and distribution of agricultural, horticultural, forest and animal husbandry produce, wool, agricultural requisites and other consumer goods.
6. To act as an insurance agent and to undertake all works that accompany this work.
7. To provide consultancy in various fields for the benefit of the cooperative institutions in general and for its members in particular.

8. To undertake research related to marketing and dissemination of market intelligence.
9. To undertake manufacture of agriculture machinery and implements, processing, packing and other production requisites and consumer articles by setting up manufacturing units either directly or in collaboration as a joint venture with any other agency. It also does imports and distribution of spare parts and components to upkeep of the machinery/implements.
10. To set up storage units for various goods and commodities by itself or in collaboration with any other organization in India or abroad.
11. For movement of goods on land, sea, air etc., it maintains transport units of its own or in collaboration with any other organ/agency in India or abroad.
12. To collaborate with any international agency or a foreign organization for the development of cooperative marketing, processing and other activities for mutual advantage in India or in abroad.
13. To subscribe to the share capital for other cooperative institutions as well as other public/joint/private sector enterprises for fulfilling the objective of the NAFED if and when considered necessary.
14. To arrange for the training of employees of cooperative societies related to marketing/processing/supply.
15. To arrange the personnel required by the marketing/processing/supply cooperative societies by maintaining common cadres/pools of managerial/technical personnel.
16. To undertake grading, packing, and standardization and to establish processing units for processing of agricultural, horticultural and forest produce and wool.
17. To acquire/sell, take/give on lease or hire, lands, buildings, fixtures and vehicles for the business of NAFED.
18. To advance loans to its members and other cooperative institutions on the security of goods or otherwise. In order to attract farmers for utilizing storage capacity of NAFED, a scheme of providing finance against storage of their produce in NAFED warehouses has been introduced with HDFC bank since February 2005.
19. To assist the development or expansion for starting any industrial undertaking in which the federation has a shareholding or financial involvement as a promoter.
20. It guarantees loans or advances or gives undertakings to any financial institution.
21. To do all other business or activities as may be accompanying or beneficial to the attainment of any or all of the above objects.

NAFED's Service for Farmers

Through the established cooperative network all over the country with active involvement of marketing societies at the mandi level, NAFED helps the farmers by procuring their produce, viz., oilseeds, foodgrains, pulses, spices, cotton produce from tribal areas, jute and jute products, eggs, fresh fruits and vegetables. Assistance to the farmers is also provided by NAFED for marketing by arranging disposal of their produce on consignment basis at terminal markets to enable them to fetch best possible price for their produce.

During 2005-06 NAFED, marketed fertilizer valued at ₹136.99 crore through NAFED's own outlets, franchises and dealers.

Role of NAFED in the Field of Biofertilizers

NAFED is engaged in manufacturing and distribution of quality biofertilizers to the farming community produced at biofertilizer plants at Indore and Bharatpur. The Bharatpur unit has also started manufacturing trichoderma, urea coating agents and composing culture. These biofertilizers have proved successful in increasing the productivity of oilseeds and pulses at lesser cost. The concept of developing and promotion liquid biofertilizer is also in line.

Role of NAFED in Seed Sector

Looking to the importance of seed in agriculture, NAFED is undertaking seed business with three tier system, i.e., seed marketing, seed multiplication programme and dealership arrangements. In seed marketing, NAFED arranges seed supplies to various State government by sourcing from the leading seed manufacturers in the market. In its seed multiplication programme, under the brand name of NAFED it took up production of seeds of soyabean in MP state and Maharashtra state and of Moong in Rajasthan.

The produced seeds are supplied to the farmers at relatively low rates than those supplied by State Seed Corporation so as to help the farmers in getting good quality of seeds at low rates with assured increased output.

Consumer Market

NAFED on behalf of the Government of India also serves the consumers' interests through supply of various essential items, such as onions, potatoes, and eggs during scarce marketing situation or when the prices of such commodities rise abnormally. About eighty institutions are presently being catered by NAFED which include clientele of leading hotels, hostels, hospitals, PSU, governmental departments, canteens, paramilitary units etc.

Market Intervention Scheme (MIS) through International Act

NAFED has been doing international trade of various agricultural and horticultural commodities since its inception for MIS as the nodal agency of Govt. of India on ad hoc scheme. The main objective of MIS is to stabilize the prices at reasonable level to sustain the production. NAFED has been doing MIS in Onion, Potato, Ginger, Malta, Nashpati, Apple, Black pepper, Red Chillies, Coriander Seed, Eggs, and oil palm bunches in different years.

Warehouses and Cold Storages

For efficient handling of agricultural and horticultural commodities, NAFED has been creating the infrastructural facilities steadily to meet its own requirements of warehouse, pre-cooling and cold storages which are being procured from the farmers. NAFED has built up capacity of general purpose warehousing to the extent of 28,000 MTs and cold storages of the capacity of 5565 MTs. In the near future, it has a plan to increase its total warehousing capacity to 57,000 MTs and cold storage to around 9600 MTs.

Other Activities

Future Trading: NAFED is one of the promoters of National Multi Commodity Exchange (NMCE) and initially took up futures trading in tuber black pepper and cardamom and intends to further expand the basket by adding other commodities including oilseeds, pulses, etc. for better risk management by hedging stock with leading commodity exchanges, viz., NCDEX, NMCE and MCX.

Insurance Business: Insurance business is one of the new activities NAFED has taken up in the last two years. During the year 2005-06, general insurance business increased manifolds.

Contract Farming: NAFED has undertaken contract farming in the MALWA region of MP state with a view to growing quality potatoes for export to Malaysia, Singapore and Sri Lanka.

Agro Service Centre: The NAFED Agro Service Centres located at Delhi, Ludhiana and Rudrapur are continuously serving the farming community by supplying the seeds, agricultural and garden hand tools, plant protection equipment, engine and spare parts.

Tribal Cooperative Marketing Federation (TRIFED): The TRIFED was established in the year 1987 to develop the system of marketing for forest produce by the tribal in the country. In the tribal dominant areas, as the product is produced in small lots and purchasers are less TRIFED arranges marketing and export of minor forest products to protect tribals from the exploitation of traders.

Objectives:

1. To secure higher earnings and generate employment opportunities for the tribal people of the country.
2. To create awareness in the interplay of market forces among tribal.
3. To provide assured markets and remunerative prices for the tribal produce and also to undertake price support operations wherever required.
4. To provide marketing and financial support to state level tribal and forest.
5. To upgrade quality of tribal products with a view to maximize unit value realization.
6. To export tribal products.
7. To provide full range of services including organization and collection of tribal produce, scientific exploitation of forest products, storage, transportation, marketing and exports.

Other Public Sector Services:

Grading and Standardization: The Agricultural Produce (Grading and Marketing) Act enacted in the year 1937 empowers the government to fix quality standards, known as AGMARK and to prescribe terms and conditions for using its seal. So far, Grade standards have been notified for 182 agricultural and allied commodities. While framing the grade standards, the purity standards under the provision of the Prevention of Food Adulteration (PFA) Act 1954 and Bureau of Indian Standards (BIS) Act 1986 are invariably taken into consideration. International Standards framed by Codex International Standards Organization (ISO) are also taken into consideration so that the Indian produce can compete in the international market.

During the year 2005-06, the final notification of Spices G & M rules 2005 is published containing standards of eleven spices. The standards of Walnut duly harmonized with the international standards have been submitted to APEDA. The final notification published in the Gazette are uploaded on the website www.agmarket.in for users.

Government's Plan for the Development of Infrastructure:

In view of the huge investment requirement for the development of infrastructure for marketing and scientific storage in the country and to induce investment in this sector, the government has implemented the following schemes:

The scheme "Construction of Rural Godowns' is being implemented through NABARD and NCDC from the year 2001. The main objectives of the scheme are creation of scientific storage capacity with the allied facilities in rural areas to meet various requirements of farmers for storing farm produce, processed produce, agricultural inputs, etc. and prevention of distress sale by creating the facility of pledge loan and marketing credit. This capital investment subsidy scheme was originally back-ended subsidy at the rate of 25 per cent of the capital cost of the project.

From October 2004, the scheme has been modified to provide subsidy at the rate of 25 per cent to farmers, agricultural graduates cooperatives and CWCs/SWCs. And around 15 per cent subsidy is provided to all other categories of individuals companies and corporations. The scheme allows subsidy for smaller godowns of 5 MT size in general and 25 MT in hilly areas. Till May 2006, around 11,583 storage projects having a capacity of 166.42 lakh tons have been sanctioned under the scheme out of which 5,00,000 tonnes capacity to be created is reserved for small farmers.

Government, under a Central Scheme for Market Research and Information Network had provided electronic connectivity to all important agricultural markets in the country, with a view to establish nationwide information network for speedy collection. And also for speedy dissemination of prices and market-related information to farmers so far, Government networked 2408 market nodes and 92 State Marketing Boards and Divisional Marketing Intelligence (DMI) offices on a single portal wherein daily prices of more than 300 commodities and about 2000 varieties are being reported. Further, it was planned to connect 2700 markets in all under this scheme during the 10th Plan.

Development of Agricultural Marketing Infrastructure

This scheme is initiated under central sector scheme of Ministry of Agriculture linked with APMC reforms of 2003 allowing setting up of competitive agricultural markets in private and cooperative sectors direct marketing and contract farming investment. Subsidy is provided at the rate of 25 per cent on the capital cost of the marketing infrastructure development project subject to a maximum of ₹ 50 lakh for each project in all states and at the rate of 33.3 per cent of capital cost subject to maximum of ₹ 60 lakh for each project in case of North Eastern States hilly areas and to SC/ST entrepreneur. There is no upper ceiling on subsidy to be provided under the scheme for the infrastructure projects of State governments/State agencies. A total number of 259 new project proposals have been provided advance subsidy of ₹ 516.30 lakh by NABARD in the states of Madhya Pradesh, Tamil Nadu, Punjab, Andhra Pradesh and Kerala.

The proposal for setting up modern terminal markets under National Horticulture Mission was approved has recently taken the initiative to promote modern terminal markets for fruits, vegetables and other perishables in important urban centers of the country envisaged to operate on "Hub-and-Spoke" format. At least ten states, viz., Bihar, Andhra Pradesh, Madhya Pradesh, Maharashtra, Orissa,

Rajasthan, Tamil Nadu, West Bengal, Nagaland and Punjab have identified more than thirty sites for setting up modern terminal markets in private sector for trading perishable products to link farmers with end users. In such ventures, the maximum equity participation for Central/State government can be 49 per cent.

The concept of Agriculture Export Zones (AEZs) were introduced in the EXIM Policy 2001 for the promotion of agriexports. There are sixty AEZs spread across the country with the investment of ₹ 1,718 crore envisaged over five years prominent AEZs are for Darjeeling Tea, Litchi, Mango, flowers, basmati rice, flowers, potato, apples, walnuts, onion, chilli, ginger, cumin, turmeric, coriander etc. The government is trying to create the infrastructure for exports by providing various fiscal reliefs to export oriented units, special economic zones, export processing units etc. This induces private investments in infrastructural development for the purpose of exports.

SUMMARY

The progress of any economy depends to a large extent on the application of science and technology for the exploitation of agricultural raw materials into numerous consumer and industrial products, thus accelerating the process of industrialization without sacrificing agricultural development resulting in the conversion of agricultural economics to industrial economies through the agri-industry linkages.

Every primary agricultural commodity and organic residue animal by-product and waste, fishery, and forestry by-products etc. can contribute to the economic development through the development of a series of industries if the primary commodity, its by-products and waste matter are scientifically processed.

Among the uniqueness of agro-industries, few are related to agro-industrial projects are unique because of the seasonality, perishability and the variability of the raw materials. And unlike the non-agro-industrial sector, the agro-industries have to deal with supply and demand imbalances, problems of inventories production scheduling and the coordination of the production and the processing and marketing sections of the producer to the consumer chain.

QUESTIONS

1. Explain how credit policy being devised periodically by RBI will facilitate the Indian farmers?
2. What regulatory mechanisms are devised by the government for creation of warehouses which are indispensable to store the produce preventing from rotting?
3. What are the functions rendered by APMC (Agriculture Produce Market Committee)?
4. What role played by Food Corporation of India in the Indian Agriculture?
5. Discuss the crucial role played by APEDA?
6. Write short notes on: CCIL-JCIL-NHB-MPEDA-EPC-EPC.
7. Discuss the role played by NAFED and elucidate how it benefits farmers?

OOO

CHAPTER 21

COOPERATIVE MARKETING AGENCIES

- Cooperative Marketing Agencies
- National Cooperative Development Organization (NCDC)
- National Dairy Development Board (NDDB)
- Procurement of Inputs/Services
- Agriculture Input Service to Consumers
- Uniformity
- Large and Diversified Input Service
- Unique Social Setup
- Input Marketing in the New Era
- On the Basis of Area Operation
- On the Basis of Degree of Competition
- On the Basis of Number of Commodities Sold in Market
- On the Basis of Types of Transaction-Channels of Marketing
- Buying and Selling Activities
- Factors Influencing the Original Retail Format
- How to Market Agriculture Products?
- How to Market Foodgrains?
- Marketing Channels through Corporates
- Other Marketing Channels
- Marketing of Cotton Products
- Cotton Corporation of India (CCI)
- Issues of Marketing
- Marketing of Fruits and Vegetable Processed Products
- Government's View
- Marketing of Floriculture Products
- Marketing of Flowers
- Marketing of Products of Animal Origin
- Milk and Milk Products Marketing
- Marketing of Ice-cream
- Features of Market Services for Milk and Milk Products
- Policy and Regulations in Milk and Milk Products Marketing
- Marketing of Milk and Milk Processed Products through Co-op. Dairies
- Government's Views
- Marketing of Processed Dairy Products
- Marketing of Dairy Whiteners
- Commercial Production of Traditional Products

COOPERATIVE MARKETING AGENCIES

A. National Cooperative Development Corporation (NCDC)

The NCDC was established in 1963 as a statutory corporation under the Ministry of Agriculture. Its functions include planning, promoting, and financing programmes for all the functions starting from production till the product reaches the consumer, viz, production, processing, marketing storage, export and import.

It deals with agricultural produce, foodstuffs and certain other notified commodities, fertilizers, insecticides, agricultural machinery, soaps, kerosene oil, textile, rubber etc. It promotes income generating activities such as poultry, dairy, fishery, sericulture, handloom, etc. Besides, it also functions for the supply of consumer goods, and collecting, processing, marketing, storage and export of minor forest produce through cooperatives.

With amendments in the NCDC Act, the area of cooperation has been broadened to assist the different types of cooperatives and to expand its financial base. NCDC will now be able to finance projects related to rural development. It advances loans and grants to State governments for financing primary and secondary level cooperative societies while for the projects whose objectives extend beyond one state, loans are advanced directly to national level and other societies.

The NCDC (Amendment) Act 2002

The NCDC Act 1962 was amended in 2002 to expand the mandate of the NDCD with following changes:

1. Inclusion of foodstuffs, livestock, industrial goods and services to the existing programmes.
2. Amendment of definition of agriculture produce to cover a wider range of activities including produce of farming, horticulture, and animal husbandry, edible and non-edible oilseeds, forestry, and cattle feed poultry, pisciculture and other allied activities.
3. The definition of industrial goods has been elaborated covering the products of allied industries and any handicrafts or rural crafts in the rural areas.
4. The definition of livestock includes all animals to be raised for milk, meat, wool, fleece, skin and other by-products.
5. Without State/Central government guarantee, NCDC will be able to provide loans directly to the cooperatives on furnishing of security to the satisfaction of NCDC.
6. Activities concerning water conservation, agricultural insurance and agricultural credit, animal care/ health, disease prevention, rural sanitation/drainage/sewerage have been declared as notified services.

B. National Dairy Development Board (NDDB)

The NDDB established in 1965 in Anand (Gujarat) with the objectives of facilitating production and marketing of milk and development of dairy cooperatives by providing them financial assistance and technical expertise. NDDB ensures reasonable prices to producers as well as the consumers. NDDB is instrumental in procurement of milk from producers in rural areas and supply of milk and other processed milk products in urban areas. Overall the NDDB supports for the development of dairy industry in India.

NATIONAL DAIRY DEVELOPMENT BOARD

Raising the genetic potential of the national milk herd is an essential element in increasing milk production, improving the productivity of cattle and buffaloes, and enhancing farmer incomes. Genetic improvement of buffaloes and crossbred cattle is a specialized field involving skilled manpower and considerable cost.

To ensure that farmers' needs are met, the National Dairy Development Board has initiated advanced programmes like Progeny Testing (PT), Embryo Transfer (ET) and Open Nucleus Breeding System (ONBS) to support ongoing cattle and buffalo breeding activities throughout the country.

Cooperative Development and Governance

The Dairy Board implements cooperative development and governance programmes across the country. The aim is to help create self-reliant and professionally managed cooperative institutions, responsive to the economic and social expectations of their members.

In addition to helping to build self-sustaining cooperatives, the NDDB is committed to serve its rural constituency by including Women's Development and Leadership Development Programmes as a central part of its activities. Need-based consultancy is provided to help evolve strategies to strengthen dairy cooperatives as well as to increase milk procurement.

The National Dairy Development Board assists in Institution Building (IB), Enhancing Women Involvement in Cooperatives (EWIC) and Strengthening Procurement Systems (SPS).

In addition to our client organizations — State Cooperative Milk Marketing Federations and Milk Producers' Cooperative Unions — NDDB's Cooperative Development and Governance services are available to non-government organizations and developmental agencies involved in working with dairy and allied cooperatives and with women's empowerment.

Product and Process Technology

As a part of its effort to add value to the business of dairy cooperatives, the Dairy Board identifies, develops, tests and transfers product and process technologies.

Regional preferences are an important basis, for developing products and their manufacturing processes. In addition, equipment has been designed and commercialized for, manufacturing indigenous milk products like *shrikhand, paneer, khoa, lassi, gulab jamun, mishti doi* and curd as well as popular western products like ice-creams and cheeses.

In developing process, product and equipment technology, emphasis is placed on maintaining high quality standards. To check milk quality, test kits have been developed. NDDB also provides services for analysis of dairy product samples.

Research and Development of Biotechnology

NDDB carries out extensive research and development activities in Biotechnology aimed at developing formulations and technologies useful for improving the productivity of milch animals. In 1979, the Dairy Board set up an Animal Disease Diagnostic Laboratory at Anand to undertake scientific research activities. NDDB has expanded its research activities to include Animal Genetics Animal Health and Animal Nutrition for supporting its Productivity Enhancement programme for dairy cooperatives.

Equipped with in-house research facilities and managed by qualified scientists, the Animal Health Section of the Laboratory is recognized as a Centre of Excellence for research on Foot and Mouth Disease and Bovine Tropical Theileriosis.

In addition to its ongoing R&D activities, NDDB offers consultancy services and training progammes to breeding organizations, cattle feed plants, disease diagnostic laboratories, vaccine manufacturing units as well as to national and international government and non-government organizations. Training is offered in the areas of cytogenetics, molecular genetics, embryo transfer, animal feed formulations, clinical diagnosis, and control of parasitic diseases and other related areas of biotechnology.

Training and Consultancy by NDDB

In today's increasingly competitive environment, the success of dairy cooperatives depends on their people. Boards, chief executives, managers, field staff, workers must all match or exceed the competence and commitment of their counterparts in investor-owned organizations. Supporting cooperatives with technical training and professional expertise has long been an NDDB priority. Over the years, the National Dairy Development Board has diversified both the physical infrastructure, machinery equipments, the operational methods and training skills that are necessary to fulfill this responsibility.

NDDB offers a variety of training programmes as well as on-demand consultancy in various technical and functional areas. The scope of training and consultancy ranges from cooperative institution building to market studies and development, from dairy plant management to feasibility and impact studies. Training programmes are designed in-house and are conducted by NDDB personnel who are specialists in the field. Most training programmes are designed exclusively for cooperative organizations. Some consultancy services and selected training programmes are also offered to other organizations.

Operation Flood's success led to NDDB evolving similar programmes for other commodities. Where potential synergies exist, NDDB has created commercial firms to exploit these for the benefit of rural producers. Some of NDDB's commercial operations include: Indian Immunologicals Limited (IIL), Hyderabad; IDMC Limited (IDMC), Anand; Mother Dairy Fruit and Vegetable Private Limited (MD F&V), Delhi and Dhara Vegetable Oil and Foods Company Limited (DOFCO), Vadodara.

In its larger interest to promote the development of cooperatives, NDDB has set up seperate units and works in close association with a number of national level institutions. Some of these include: Sabarmati Ashram Gaushala (SAG), Bidaj, Animal Breeding Centre (ABC), Salon; Institute of Rural Management (IRMA), Anand; National Cooperative Dairy Federation of India (NCDFI), Anand and Foundation for Ecological Security (FES), Anand.

In India, 1,17,575 village dairy cooperatives federated into 170 milk unions and fifteen federations indulge in procuring on average, around 21.5 million liters of milk every day with 12.4 million farmers as members of village dairy cooperatives (as on March '06). Since its inception, the NDDB has spearheaded India's dairy programmes in the hands of milk producers and professionals they employ to plan and manage their cooperatives.

The NDDB also promotes other commodity based cooperatives and allied industries with veterinary and biological infrastructure on an intensive scale and nationwide basis. In the year 1986, the NDDB has undergone structural change by registering itself as a society and got merged with a company, viz., Indian Dairy Corporation. The resulting corporate body bears the old name, i.e., NDDB and the Act has declared the Board to be an institution of national importance.

To reduce the interference of intermediaries in the marketing of products and to safeguard the interests of producer as well as consumer, the government extended the cooperative umbrella of NDDB by adding branded vegetable oils and fruits and vegetables.

Procurement of Inputs and Services:

Agri-inputs include all the inputs associated with farming, livestock rearing, fisheries, horticulture, floriculture, sericulture, and agro forestry. Use of these inputs is more complex than any other production technology as there are several climatic factors like temperature, humidity, rainfall, and wind velocity. Biological factors like insect pest attack and diseases, and natural calamities like flood, drought and cyclone, which affect the use of agri-inputs. These factors are beyond the control of the producers.

The price philosophy of agri-inputs seems to be different. Agri-input users are more quality conscious than price conscious. This is because of risk involved in using poor quality input. Consequently, promotional activities for agri-inputs carry fewer premiums, as it would be in case of non-agri-products. Distribution front is slightly complex for agri-inputs because of relatively large diverse and spread across.

Agri-input Service to Consumers:

The agri consumer is a group of millions. The total rural population in India in 2001 was 742 million and of this 77 per cent depends solely on agricultural occupation. This translates to around 585 million agri-input consumers in India. The study of this group of consumers is quite complex. This is particularly so because the typical production technology is beyond the control of the farmer and distinctive mindset of the consumer and some of the specific features of agri-input consumers are as under:

Uniformity: This group of consumers is almost similar in many respects, such as education, family, size, mindset, social strata and occupation. Therefore, this group requires different type of segmentation, primarily based on occupation (farming, dairy, fisheries, poultry and services) or land holding (small, medium and large). Not only are the consumers uniform, but the products offered as agri-input are also almost similar.

Quality conscious: Quality quantity and timeliness are the prerequisites for better productivity. Agri-input users know the consequences of using substandard quality products. Hence, they are more conscious about quality than about the price in comparison to consumers of other products. Agri-input consumers are keen to know the technical details of the products particularly when higher investment is required. For instance, the purchase of tractor. They normally consult the nearest channel partner and this makes the channel partner an important deciding factor. Therefore, this category of consumers is less responsive to promotional practices as would be in the case for other industrial products. Agri-inputs are almost homogenous required at the same time and there is little scope for value addition as compared to other industrial products.

Large and diversified: The number of prospective agri-input consumers is large, diversified, and spread across different regions. There is significant social diversity, making the marketing different. Age and income stratification is very high. In other words, special skills are required to promote homogenous product to large geographically diversified group.

Unique social set-up: Agri-input buyers are primarily from rural areas and have typical mindset, irrespective of geographical location, and usually live in joint families where the male members take all the major decisions. This suggests that the best approach would be to contact an individual or group of men for product promotion.

Distribution Channel: Relatively large and intensive distribution channels are required in the marketing of agri-input which makes the consumer channel sensitive. Large numbers of stockists, distributors, and retailers make the channel complex, and therefore needs to be monitored carefully. The channel partners sometimes act as advisors to the consumers. Because of the homogeneity of agri-input products, the role of the producers becomes very crucial.

INPUT MARKETING IN THE NEW ERA

Agri-input marketing includes supply, manufacturing and distribution. It is currently undergoing a lot of change and in future too, it is likely to undergo major structural changes. Other than physical and biological factors, here are many contemporary factors influencing input marketing. The changes are mainly because of changing consumer taste, preference, attitude, new technological advances and reframing of rules and regulations of the WTO regime. Due to WTO's influence on marketing in the input marketing arena, there is provision to regulate the grants enjoyed by agricultural producers, although agri-input subsidy in India is below the limit, and it will mean that input prices may be influenced to some extent.

The private investment in research and development and patenting of technology will change the input demand. The opening of boundaries will result in greater competition among input industries. There will be more amalgamations and acquisitions in order to survive the competition.

Trade of Outputs

There are various definitions for term market but broadly it may be defined as existence of fundamental forces of demand and supply where buyers and sellers are in free interaction with one another.

Based on different dimensions, markets may be classified into various forms as under:

1. On the basis of area of operation: Primary or local markets, Secondary or wholesale markets and Terminal or export markets

The *primary or local markets are* organized by the Village Panchayat by renting space from shopkeepers where the bulk of produce is brought by the producers for sale. These markets held once or twice in a week and one market serves an area of 8-16 sq.km. whereas a full-fledged market may cover about 459 sq.km.

Secondary or wholesale markets may be situated in producing or consuming areas also known as mandis, gangs wholesale markets. They are generally located at the tehsil headquarters, larger towns or at important trade centres. The average area covered by wholesale market in India is about 775 sq.km. varying from 168 sq.km. in Punjab to 2257 sq.km in Assam. Producers or middlemen sell the produce to the wholesaler and the wholesaler to other wholesalers and retailers. Most of the regulated mandis serve both primary and secondary markets.

Terminal markets are those where the produce is finally disposed to either consumers or processors or exported outside the country known as terminal markets. These markets may act as primary wholesale markets for one commodity and secondary markets for another. These markets are highly organized and are located in big cities like Delhi, Mumbai, Chennai and Kolkota with good warehousing and storage facilities. The service of one such terminal market may cover one or more states and are located near the sea ports and known as seaport markets from where goods are exported or imported directly and these markets have generally facilities of commodity exchange for forward trading.

2. On the basis of degree of competition: Perfect markets and Imperfect markets.

Looking at large number of buyers and sellers conceptually agricultural markets should be *perfectly competitive markets*. Practically, these markets are not so and traders as buyers are generally educated and organized with full knowledge of demand supply prices. The farmers, however, are uneducated and do not have sufficient knowledge of markets. They are unable to access the required information independently. When the prices are fixed in the open market, middlemen and traders generally cheat the farmers as they sell their produce under force or in distress. Therefore, markets of agricultural output are *imperfect markets.* The control of government on agricultural marketing reduces the freedom of markets and makes them less competitive.

3. On the basis of number of commodities sold in market: General Markets and Specialized markets.

General markets are those markets which deals with large number of commodities, viz., cereals, pulses, oilseeds, cotton, etc. In specialized markets, trading of only one or two commodities takes place, for example, flower mandi, wool mandi, fruit and vegetable mandi etc.

4. On the basis of types of transactions: Spot markets and Forward markets — wherein *spot market* goods are exchanged immediately after the exchange of ownership or sale whereas in *forward marketing* an agreement of purchase is made in advance for delivery in the future at a specified date rate and quality.

5. On the basis of channels of marketing: Government, Cooperative and Private Traders.

In our country, agriculture produce is procured from producers through mainly three channels — government, cooperative or private. In addition, in the case of certain fruit crops,a pre-harvest contractor takes the fruit gardens on contract while the fruits are still on the trees.

Government channels work actively for marketing of foodgrains. It may operate along with the cooperative or private channels. The government enters the market to buy the commodities and protect the interests of producers as well as the consumers. The *cooperative channel* is the most popularly used for milk and milk products through cooperative dairies. Now, some cooperatives are involved in the marketing of fruits and vegetables – example, SAFAL, subsidiary of MOTHER DAIRY in Delhi.

The private channel is the most popular channel and nearly 60-70 per cent of agricultural produce is sold through this channel. There are large number of intermediaries in this channel, which raises the cost of marketing and reduces the share of the consumers' rupee to the producers.

The channel of marketing is very important aspect of agricultural marketing affecting the prices paid by the consumer and the share received by the producer. A channel that provides commodities at cheaper prices to consumers and also ensures greater share to the producers is considered as the most efficient channel.

BUYING AND SELLING ACTIVITY

Traditional retailing has existed in India for centuries but is by and large unorganized, highly fragmented and predominantly small, family owned business. About 78 per cent of these businesses engage only household labour and few of them employ two or three workers only. It is low cost structure mostly owner operated has negligible real estate and labor costs and pays little or no taxes. Nearly 96 per cent of more than 5 million outlets are small with area of less than 500 sq.ft. which indicates the fact that in India the per capita retailing space is smallest (2 sq. ft.) in contrast to 16 sq. ft. in United States. And here the retail sector accounts for about 44 per cent of the total GDP. It is also the largest employer provider with 15-20 of the total workforce directly employed in retailing.

Retail sales in India account for about 69 per cent of the total consumers expenditure.

Continuing relevance and dominance of traditional retailing which runs from one generation to another – and consumers' familiarity with it, is a major advantage for the traditional retailing sector. In spite of this, marketers see great potential for organized retailing in India.

Factors Influencing Organized Retail

Economies of Scale: Large-scale operations in organized retailing would result in economies of scale in terms of space and labour efficiency.

Attractiveness: Large organized stores attract people from a wide catchments area and these formats deal in multiple product categories, offering impressive brand variants designed to draw variety seeking consumer.

Quality Service: Quality service features such as returns and adjustments delivery facilities and assistance in making purchase decisions is possible in franchised or company owned stores.

Increased brand consciousness: The modern rural customer has become more educated if not literate. This has increased brand awareness among rural consumers (80 per cent of all packaged FMCG sold in rural markets are branded) and they want to shop from reliable stores. Thus, the company owned or franchised outlets enjoy high patronage in respect of not only high involvement goods (such as agro-inputs and durables) but also in FMCGs.

Fighting fakes: To fight the danger of fake products in rural areas, companies prefer to the sell their offerings through organized retail formats. Philips uses ITC's e-choupal to sell their lighting tubes in rural India.

An overwhelming proportion of the ₹ 4,00,000 crore Indian retail market is in the unorganized segment and in the fast growing Indian economy there is tremendous growth potential for the retail business which is estimated to be about $ 12 billion (accounting for just 3 per cent of the total market). The size of organized retail is about ₹ 1,45,000 crore and the fruit and vegetable business is estimated to be about ₹ 300 crore. Fresh food accounts for 50 per cent of food and grocery bills in India, as compared to 155 in the US.

This could be a win-win situation for all the stakeholders and a study conducted by Confederation of Indian Industry – (CII) shows that the development of organized retailing will lead to increased efficiency in the agriculture sector and remove intermediaries in the food supply chain. This is because of investments in upgrading technology and agricultural practices in the entire value chain — including production, packaging, grading, storage and logistics are expected to drastically bring down the levels of wastage which is currently about 24-30 per cent.

Though organized retailing has caught the attention of economists and policymakers in the country, the government is concerned about the impact of organized retail on the 12 million small shopkeepers, 40 million hawkers and 200 million small farmers. However, industry leaders dismiss all fears of this leading to unemployment in the country.

ITC e-choupal is the pioneer effort in agri retail in the country and has become quite popular. The company has plans of increasing the number of kiosks from the current 6,.450 kiosks in 38000 villages and touching the lives of about 4 million farmers to about 20000 kiosks spread across 1,00,000 villages to serve around 10 million farmers by 2010. ITC has plans to invest about ₹ 5000 crore in e-choupal by 2012.

Godrej Agrovet has already opened thirty-three Godrej Aadhar stores across the country and is planning to open twelve more soon, concentrating mainly on inputs marketing. The other retail business comprises of fruits, vegetables, dairy and poultry through its Nature's Basket Stores.

Reliance Fresh opened its stores backing 2006 and currently has around 350 stores in thirty cities. It sells food, fruits and vegetables, household and other consumer products. Reliance Fresh faced resistance from Fruits and vegetables vendors in certain areas of UP, Orissa, and MP states. And therefore those stores have been closed. However, it is planning a new concept Reliance Mart – in the southern states. Adani Agri Fresh part of the ₹ 20,000 crore Adani group started its operation in HP state but has since been taken over by Reliance Retail.

Subiksha is a discount retail major which deals with four major product categories in its stores — fruits and vegetables, pharmaceuticals, FMCG and telecom. Subiksha started in 1997 as a single store entity in Chennai and now it has more than 800 outlets in more than sixty cities.

Bharti Retail plans to invest US$ 2-2.5 billion dollars by 2015 in its retail business operations. The company will launch its retail outlets in multiple consumer friendly formats, including hypermarkets, supermarkets and cash-and-carry stores. They will serve all regular shopping requirements of an Indian household with food and other FMCG and consumer durables. The Bharti Group is entering the retail business in India in a joint venture with US retail giant Wal-Mart for its back-end operations.

The other big players in food retailing are **Big Bazar** and **True Mart** of Pantaloon **Spencer's Retail** Limited, **Vishal Mega Mart, Big Apple and Spinach.**

HOW TO MARKET AGRI-PRODUCTS?

It is not everybody's cup of tea to market important agricultural products. Marketing of agricultural produce plays most important and crucial role in the development of agriculture sector. Efficient system of agricultural output marketing helps not only the farmers but also the entire population of the country by assuring reasonable prices of all foodstuffs. Progress in the production of foodgrains, commercial crops and horticultural products depends critically on the marketing infrastructure available to the farmers and the traders.

The marketing of agricultural outputs can be divided into farm products that include plant products and animal products and products from the food processing sector. You will also study sericulture and pisciculture. Products of pisciculture, fish and fish products and sericulture, i.e., silk are very important part of the agribusiness in India as they have good value and demand in the domestic and export markets.

Marketing of Foodgrains

Government of India during 1938 extended its directions to all State governments to protect the interests of producers and to put an end to the unfair means and malpractices in the market and to enact some viable and feasible legislations to promote competitive and healthy transactional methods for marketing methods. Since then, marketing of foodgrains being done under State's direct supervision through controlled marketing system. The main features of this system are Minimum Support System (MSP) mechanism for major agricultural commodities and procurement of the offered produce at MSP by government agencies. The wholesaling of agricultural produce was permitted only at regulated markets. This has defined an important channel through which major share of agricultural produce flows. The other channels also exists especially for retailing and after the model Act – APMC Act 2003 direct purchasing from farmers has been permitted and that has brought about revolutionary change in agricultural marketing.

The channels for all foodgrains are more or less the same except for the miller before the retailer or the consumer in the case of pulses and rice. The channels for foodgrains marketing can be mainly through four purchasers from the producers, viz., the village trader, wholesaler, government agencies and the corporates (after direct sales were allowed).

Channel through Government Agencies

Cereals: The FCI in association with State governments and their agencies procures wheat. paddy and rice for the central pool. Procurement of paddy and wheat is done under the Price Support Scheme (PSS). Rice is procured as per levy orders issued by State governments. Foodgrains are also imported and exported whenever the situation warrants. With effect from 1st April 1990, FCI also been made nodal agency for procurement of coarse grains.

After direct purchases have been allowed, NAFED also procured wheat directly from farmers on behalf of the government. During 2005-06, NAFED purchased more than 2,38,542 MT of bajra, guar, jowar, maize, paddy, rice, and wheat under the outright account and 5,99,94 MT of maize, paddy, sorghum and millet under the PPP business model.

Pulses: NAFED continues to be the nodal agency of the Government of India for the procurement of pulses under PSS. It has been successfully implementing the price support scheme in oilseeds and pulses. The objective of the scheme is to provide regular marketing support to farmers to sustain and improve the production of oilseeds and pulses. Purchases under PSS are undertaken when the prices of prescribed quality stocks of oil seeds and pulses covered under the scheme rule at or below the declared support prices.

Channel through Corporates

Corporates like ITC and Cargill procure grains either directly from the farmer or from wholesalers mainly for the purpose of processing. Contract farming is another way of procuring the desired produce from the farmers and since the last two years, it has been the most common way of procuring paddy from the farmers of Punjab for exporting rice the largest exported agri commodity from India.

MARKETING OF OILSEEDS

India is bestowed with the capability of producing various types of oilseeds and is one of the largest edible oils producing, as well as consuming countries. There are nine main oilseeds that are grown in the country. The demand of edible oils is more than the supply, resulting in large imports of edible oils. The import of edible oils is the largest of all total agricultural imports by the country. The major oilseed crops of the country are groundnut, rapeseed and mustard etc.

India is groundnut producing country in the world producing about 7-8 million tons every year. The shelf life of Indian groundnut is longer and is available throughout the year due to a two crop cycle. Groundnut is sold mostly in pod form and very small amount is sold in kernel form. In order to get better prices, grading is done on the basis of breakage of kernels before milling. The produce is mostly shelled by intermediaries before reaching the millers for oil extraction or the exporters. The varieties of Indian peanuts have a good demand in the international market.

After groundnut in the last decade, rapeseed and mustard has seen good growth. The rapeseed and mustard group contributes the largest share to the total oilseed production in India. Besides this, safflower seeds are getting more attention than ever as safflower edible oil is being used more than ever before. India is the world's largest producer of sesame seeds, contributing about one-third to the world's sesame seed production. It is grown in the black brown and white seeds varieties.

Marketing: Marketing of oilseeds is done under the APMC Act and until 2003 there was no procurement by private players. On behalf of the government, the NAFED continues to be the nodal agency for the procurement of oilseeds under the Price Support Scheme. In the mandis, the farmer sells the produce either to the wholesaler or to the processor. Of the total marketable surplus, about 70-80 per cent is taken to the market personally by the farmers. Wholesale merchants generally own shelling facilities and they advance money to village traders or farmers for sourcing the product. Banks provide finance to the farmers or traders on the basis of receipts issued by the warehouses which are pledged to the banks.

Marketing Channels

In the marketing channels for oilseeds, there may be four types of buyers and purchasing the produce from the village trader, wholesaler, government agencies and corporates. The marketing cost (packing-commission and sales-tax) is borne by the miller. The commission agents bear and arrange the transportation facilities for outstation destinations.

Oil cakes from oil extraction plant/solvent extraction unit (directly or through brokers) and deoiled cakes are either exported directly by the unit or through brokers or sold in the domestic market. Oil is extracted in village ghanis (oil presses), oil mills and solvent extraction plants. After the implementation of the Model APMC Act, some corporates are producing oilseeds directly from farmers for edible production, e.g., ITC and Cargill.

There is considerable scope for export of good quality kernels, apart from the raw edible peanuts India is also in a position to supply blanched peanuts, roasted/salted peanuts and dry roasted peanuts. India is net importer of edible oils.

Marketing of Cotton

In India, cotton alone contributes about 60 per cent of the raw material for textile industry, while at the international level it is 45 per cent. India stands third in global cotton production after USA and China. India contributes about 20 per cent of the world's production of cotton, despite this significant contribution yield of cotton in India is only 463 kg per hectare against world's average of 558 kg per hectare.

There are **some schemes** devised by eminent agriculture experts to increase the cotton yield as under:

1. **Intensive cotton production plan:** India was facing low production of cotton and the quantum of imported cotton ranged from 8-9 lakh bales per annum till 1970. After the launch of the intensive cotton production plan by the government through the Five Year Plan (FYP) by increasing the area under cotton cultivation as also the area under HYVs, the production of cotton increased around the mid 1970s. Since then, the country is self-sufficient in cotton, except for few years when cotton had to be imported either due to low production or high demand in the textile industry.
2. **Technology mission on cotton:** This programme was launched by the Government of India in February 2000 during Ninth FYP and was continued in the Tenth FYP also to bring about improvement in the productivity and quality of cotton in the country. Productivity has improved significantly through development of high-yielding varieties, appropriate transfer of technology, better farm management practices, increased area under cultivation of BT cotton hybrids etc. In order to meet the domestic and export requirements of the country, it also envisages the development of other aspects such as research, marketing and processing. All these developments have resulted in a turnaround in cotton production in the country since the last 2-3 years. The yield per hectare which was stagnant at about 300 kg/ha for more than ten years increased to 501 kg/ha in 2006-07 and the production of 270 lakh bales, up from about 150-175 lakh bales per year in 1996-97.
3. **Integrated cotton cultivation (contract farming):** There is an increasing requirement for cultivation of cotton in an integrated manner through contract farming. In order to produce

quality cotton in line with the demands of the textile industry, this scheme would be beneficial for cotton growers because of the low cost of production and high productivity. Textile mills will also benefit from the availability of quality cotton to be competitive in the world market. The Cotton Corporation of India (CCI) is signing several MoUs every year with farmers' associations in all the important cotton growing states to give a boost to cotton production through contract farming.

Cotton Corporation of India (CCI)

The CCI established in 1970s started functioning in 1971-72 and it procures cotton from domestic market and imports it when required. It aims to stabilize supplies to government and private textile millers. The objective of procurement by CCI is to provide price support to growers and stabilize prices in the long run which would be beneficial for both farmers as well as textile millers.

CCI procures kapas in open auctions and in competition with other traders and millers under the supervision of APMC officials. More than 220 centers are operating in different cotton growing states and all these purchases are made either under MSP or commercial operations. It has been able to generate confidence among the cotton growers over the period of about thirty-five years and growers like the presence of CCI representative at the kapas auctions.

The CCI procures cotton mainly from Gujarat, Andhra Pradesh, Madhya Pradesh, Punjab, Haryana, Rajasthan, Karnataka and Tamil Nadu. In Maharashtra, the State government procures cotton through the Maharashtra State Cooperative Cotton Growers Marketing Federation.

Cotton Markets: The important markets of cotton are Mumbai, Coimbatore, Ahmedabad and Kanpur.

Types of Cotton Markets (Channels):

There are three types of cotton markets in India: They are:

(i) Primary Markets – where cotton sold by grower and purchased by village trader in village.

(ii) Secondary Market – where cotton sold to important trade centres via wholesalers.

(iii) Terminal Markets – where cotton is sold to textile mills, exporters and traders.

System of Marketing: System of marketing of cotton includes starting from production in the form of cotton balls in growers' fields up to the ginning mills and then finally to the spinning mills. After packing in bales, the farmer brings the produce to the nearest market. Cotton lots are put to public auction where commission agents and wholesalers participate in handling of the produce on behalf of farmer in the presence or absence of farmer which is done by the commission agent. The market committee manages the storage space and arrangements for auction, invites tenders and announces market rates and market information. The market committee collects a cess for its services and commission agent charges his commission. The farmer gets the net amount after deduction of these various charges. Ever since the setting up of cooperative/private ginning and spinning mills in various taluks and districts, movement of cotton and lint movement to the mills of Mumbai and Surat has reduced.

Issues in Marketing

Raw materials for the textile industry are cotton and its marketing requires clear understanding of certain technical knowledge. They are packing and handling, quality of yarn, problem of contamination, and external trade of cotton in India.

The *packing and handling* is crucial aspect of cotton textile industry where cotton bales are packed in bags which are made of loosely knit Deccan or Manila hemp and can have 150-230 kgs of kapas. Bales are manually packed in bardans therefore requiring a lot of labour time. They also get exposed to dust and rain.

Quality of yarn is determined by quality of cotton yarn, the staple length (longer) ginning per cent (24-38 per cent), spinning quality (depends on staple length), fiber maturity (ripe fibre has thickened walls and good convulsion), surface friction, hydroscopic ability (water absorption capability which affects the tensile strength and elasticity), rigidity (should be less for twisting) and elasticity.

Problem of contamination is also one of the threat and challenge in the cotton textile industry. To overcome this problem in cotton, maximum quantities of cotton bales are arranged to be processed in modern ginning and pressing factories. For the packing of cotton bales, good quality grey cloth is being extensively used. In the absence of modern facilities, more labours are employed for manually removing all possible foreign materials.

External Trade of Cotton in India: From being a net cotton importer of cotton before 1970s, India has become net exporter of cotton and scenario of trade of cotton has gained momentum after the launch of the technology mission of cotton and the permission for contract farming of cotton.

MARKETING OF FRUITS AND VEGETABLES

India is bestowed with diverse agroclimatic conditions and produces a large variety of fruits. India is the largest producer of fruits and second largest producer of vegetables in the world. The important fruits grown in India are mango, apple, banana, citrus, grapes, pineapple, peach, litchi, etc. It is the largest producer of mango, banana, sapota, and acid lime in the world. It produces 46 million tons (10 per cent of the world's total production) of fruits, ranging from 4 per cent of citrus to 46 per cent of mango, but exports are very small. Potato, tomato, cauliflower and cabbage account for 60 per cent of the vegetable production in the country. India contributes to 15 per cent of world's vegetable production. The marketing of fruits and vegetables in India are adversely affected by the dominance of traders and middlemen, low and fragmented supply chain, inadequate infrastructure, high wastages (20-40 per cent) and low share of producers in consumers' prices.

Issues in developing supply chain: Extension advice through agri-professionals should be a regular feature, procuring from buyers will reduce the price spread and will benefit farmer as well as consumer. Further infrastructure needs to be supported and expanded in order to improve the supply chain. The quantity and the quality of supplies have to be ensured. The government NGO and other groups must play an active role to bring about the improvement in this critical factor of marketing.

Demand and supply of fruits and vegetables: Increased demand for Indian fruits is due to its lower prices and availability throughout the year. Increasing incomes are translating into increasing demand. Health concerns are also contributing to the increase in demand. Supply will be enhanced due to increased concern towards production technology, innovation and lower trade barriers. But the markets of fruits and vegetables are changing faster than other areas of the agri-business. Thus, there is need for creating

Region specific centres to support Public Private Partnership (PPP) scheme which will boost country's fruit and vegetable sales in future and there is wider scope for its development in days to come. The government has made several amendments in its policies to open up the market for private players.

Channels in Marketing of Fruits and Vegetables

Producer → Pre-harvest contractor

Producer → forwarding Agent → Commission Agents → Wholesaler → Retailer → Consumer.

Producer → Commission Agent/ Wholesaler → Retailer → Consumer.

Producer → Government Agency → wholesaler → Retailer → Consumer

Producer → Government Agency → Processing Unit → Retailing of processed food.

Producer → Consumer.

Corporations in the Retailing of Fruits and Vegetablest

Huge investment by leading Indian corporations is gaining momentum in organized retailing of fresh fruits and vegetables in India. Looking at the demand many modern formats of supermarkets are being promoted in large numbers in cities across the country. Some reputed retail corporates of the country who are already in the business of marketing of fruits and vegetables in different forms: They are in wholesaling, front end convenience stores, and exports with European Certification.

Other modes for fruits and vegetables, they are being imported to Bangladesh, UAE, the Netherlands, UK etc. Despite substantial production of fruits and vegetables, exports are low because of lack of exportable varieties, lack of post-harvest management, lack of scientific packing houses from farm to the ports, and high cost for obtaining certification for exports. The exports in this sector can be increased provided there is need to follow some necessary steps rigorously and then only the targeted task can be accomplished. They are adequate and efficient supply chain, economies of scale, infrastructure and storage facilities, market access, quality certification and rationalization of cost of certification. Also lack of brand image, short product life cycle, multiple safety standards, which should be at par with developed countries and technology.

Government support: The Ministry of Food Processing, National Horticultural Board, APEDA, MPEDA and Export Inspection Council are the agencies supporting the production and export of fruits and vegetables in various capacities. Special Economic Zones (SEZs), Agri Export Zones (AEZs), 100 per cent EOUs and Food Parks etc. are being provided various facilities and fiscal benefits in order to boost the production, marketing, processing and exports of fruits and vegetables and other food items.

Concept of modern terminal market: The marketing of perishable products like fruits, vegetables, flowers, aromatics, herbs, meat and poultry has special requirements. The terminal market has been conceptualized to take the producer to the market with the least number of intermediaries and to provide hasslefree, state-of-art facilities for grading, transportation, storage, domestic marketing and export at both the hub and collection centres.

Terminal markets are built, owned and operated by private players or cooperatives supported by the State governments' regulatory and legal framework and financed by the Central Government. All the functions are being carried out either by outsourcing or done by the owner. A terminal market is a hub-and-spoke arrangement, where the hub is the terminal market and the spokes are collection centres which collect produce from the States and the forward linkages may be with the whole country or world depending on the suitability.

Producer → Collection centre → Terminal market → Buyer → Consumer

Producer → Terminal market → Consumer.

Producer: A producer brings his produce to the market, either directly or through commission agents. The produce then reaches the terminal market. The producer has the facility to sell directly to an exporter, processor or retail chain network under one roof, which otherwise is not possible.

Buyer: The buyer may be a wholesaler, local retailer, retailers of hyper or supermarkets, processor, exporter etc. The buyer also has the facility of electronic auctioning.

***Collection Center*:** Collection centres are located at key production centres to establish backward linkages with the producers. The entrepreneur is free to sell the inputs, complementary services, extension services, or other complementary services, but mainly to take care of perishable commodities (could handle non-persishables up to 15 per cent and non-Fruit and vegetable perishables also up to 15 per cent). FMCG goods can also be sold at collection centres and the owner is allowed to collect fee from the user for providing all the facilities at the collection centres.

Facilities at collection centres: The infrastructural facilities: Washing, grading, sorting, weighing, multi-mode transport to Terminal Markets, plastic containers/trays, etc.

Services: Collection aggregation of produce, settlement of payments, advisory of inputs, prices quality and safety.

Facilities at terminal markets: Infrastructure and other facilities: Banking, storage (including cold storage and scientific warehousing), ripening chamber, facilities of grading and standardization, packing lines, material handling, transport facilities (with cool chain) etc.

Government's View

The installed capacity of fruits and vegetables processing industry has increased from 1.1 million tons in January 1993 to 2.1 million tons in 2006. The processing of fruits and vegetables is estimated to be around 2.2 per cent of the total production in the country. The major processed items in the fruit and vegetable segment are fruit pulps and juices, fruit based ready-to-serve beverages, canned fruits and vegetables, jams, squashes, pickles, chutneys and dehydrated vegetables. Some recent products introduced in this segment include vegetable curries in retortable pouches, canned mushroom and mushroom products, dried fruits and vegetables and fruit juice concentrates.

The fruits and vegetable processing industry is highly decentralized, and a large number of units are in the cottage, household and small-scale sector, having small capacities of up to 250 tons per annum. Since 2000, the food processing industry has seen significant growth in ready-to-serve beverages, fruit juices and pulps, dehydrated and frozen fruits and vegetable products, pickles, processed mushrooms and curried vegetables, and units engaged in these segments are export oriented.

Exporters of Fruits and Vegetables

(Quantity in Metric Ton, Value in ₹ Million)

	2001-02		2004-05		CAGR	
	Quantity	Value	Quantity	Value	Quantity	Value
Dried and Preserved Vegetables	209157.8	5371.5	351034.3	7657.5	18.8	12.5
Mango Pulp	76735.18	2413.4	90988.6	3008.6	5.8	7.6
Pickles and Chutney	38758.97	1203.4	67193.29	1205.8	20.1	0.1
Other Processed Fruits and Vegetables	61332.39	2017.4	80760.5	2755.3	9.6	10.9
Total	385984.3	11005.7	589976.7	14627.2	15.2	9.9

Source: Ministry of Food Processing Industries, Annual Report 2005-06

The domestic industry has to change its preference in favour of processed foods. Consumption of value added fruits and vegetables are low compared to the primary processed foods, fresh fruits and vegetables. The inclination towards processed foods is mostly visible in urban centres due to a high purchasing power.

A remarkable push can be given to this sector by strengthening linkages between farmers and food processors. The poor and weak linkage between farmers and markets as well as farmers and processing companies has brought about inefficiencies in the supply chain and encouraged the involvement of middlemen leading price rise to the products. The Government of India's National Agriculture Policy envisages the participation of the private sector through contract farming and landleasing arrangements which not only assures supply of raw material for processing units, but also a market for agriculture produce, accelerate technology transfer and capital inflow into the agriculture sector.

Innovative practices like contract farming in wheat practiced in Madhya Pradesh by Hindustan Lever Ltd. and by Pepsi Foods Ltd. in Punjab for tomatoes, foodgrains, spices and oilseeds are some successful examples of contract farming in India, which changed the farming landscape and promoted the cultivation of processable variety of farm produce. This will certainly power the fruits, vegetables and grain processing industry. Besides such initiatives, fiscal incentives and tax concessions will also give impetus to the sector. The five-year 100 per cent tax exemption announced by the Government in the finance year 2005 was one such incentive for upcoming fruits and vegetable processing units.

MARKETING OF FLORICULTURE PRODUCTS

In India, the area under flower crops is around 53,000 acres, out of which more than half is contributed by traditional flowers, viz., jasmine, daisy, rose, chrysanthemum, tuberose, crosssandra and aster. Entrepreneurs in the flower trade are investing larger amounts of money to develop hi tech facilities to facilitate the trade of flowers for export.

The annual growth rate of domestic trade in floriculture products is estimated to be 15-20 per cent. The liberalization of the Indian economy has shifted the focus of the floriculture industry from traditional flowers to modern cut flowers. About 60,000 hectare of area is under floriculture and produces about 2,00,000 tons of loose flowers and 500 million numbers of cut flowers.

After liberalization, the Government of India has identified floriculture as a sunrise industry and accorded it 100 per cent export oriented status. The industry is growing at rate of 20 per cent 15.5 per cent per annum. In recent years, a sharp rise in domestic demand, an unexpected and encouraging trend has been witnessed in mushrooming florists in India. Main pitfalls in the export strategy are the focus on short-term profits and switching from one market to another, resulting in loss of credibility. The niche export markets are Japan, USA and Europe.

Flowers can be categorized into two distinct categories. These categories are *traditional flowers* that are grown in larger areas, like marigold, rose, chrysanthemum, jasmine and tuberose. *Modern/ contemporary flowers* grown in small areas, viz., gladiolus, carnation, asther, gerbera, carnalius, etc. and are abundantly grown in the states of Andhra Pradesh, Karnataka, Maharashtra, Tamil Nadu, Haryana, West Bengal, and Kerala. Further this trade gave rise to floriculture industry that consists of cut flowers, cut foliage, in fresh as well as dried forms in bouquets, garlands, flower arrangements and floral baskets.

There are nurseries for the supply of propagated plant, material, for example, plants, seeds, bulbs, corns etc. Contracts for maintenance of gardens and processed forms of flowers, for example, perfume, flavours, and gulkand.

Problems of the floriculture industry

Some of the general bottlenecks associated with the development of the floriculture industry in India, are identified as follows:

1. The Indian floriculture industry is still in a nascent stage and depends on foreign technology and there is requirement of huge amounts for investment, as India is being technically strong and competitive.
2. There is need for cold supply chains to take flowers from the farm gate to the ultimate consumer especially in foreign markets. For exports, refrigerating facilities at airports and shipyards is required.
3. To boost this industry, sufficient space in air cargo and direct flights to importing countries is required.
4. Proper market information for growers and traders about export market trends, demands, prices, consumer preferences, etc. should be provided in a systematic manner.
5. The procurement cost of flowers by exporters is very high due to lack of economies of scale and proper linkages between scattered producers, processors and exporters.
6. The availability of adequate finance is problem for such a cost-intensive production process.

MARKETING OF FLOWERS

Flowers are used in a variety of ways to convey sentiments and feelings. While traditional flowers are sold all over India, and mainly in the southern states, the demand for modern flowers is more in the metropolitan cities and foreign markets. Cut flowers are an important part of the floriculture industry.

To add the value to cut flowers, florists arrange flowers in different ways. The domestic demand for cut flowers and ornamental plants is mainly met through production in the coastal areas of Kerala. The marketing of cut flowers to be sold at florists shop or for export is highly technical and requires expertise. There have been significant changes in the trade of contemporary flowers, which are fast developing in the metropolitan and big cities such as Mumbai, Delhi, Bangalore, Hyderabad, Pune, Chennai, Chandigarh, Lucknow and Kolkata.

Along with the fresh flowers, there is considerable demand for dry flowers. Since the last thirty years, arrangements of dried flowers and plants are being exported and presently India is one of the leading countries in this sector. And 75 per cent of the total produce of rose. i.e., more than 7000 tons is exported to West Asian countries in the form of dried petals. Other parts of plants like stems, pods, and seeds are used in the dry flower industry. Seeds and capsules of flowers also contribute to the total floriculture trade.

Based on a study of the Delhi flower market conducted by Yadav (2002) and Sharma (2002), an overview of simple flower mandi and a high tech at Connaught Place, New Delhi is given as follows:

Flower Mandi (Azadpur Mandi, Delhi)

The mandi operates under APMC regulations.

Open and closed auctions are eminent features of this market and 2500 licensee traders operate here.

Generally trading is done through commission agents who charge 6 per cent from the sellers and 1 per cent from the buyer to be deposited with APMC.

Here, prices are fixed according to the demand and supply.

The entire chain of commission agents and middlemen leads to an almost 100-400 per cent increase in price over actual costs.

Most of the auction is done early in the morning and two-thirds of transactions are on credit as big players provide credit facilities to their growers.

Weightage is insignificant and payment to growers is made promptly either on receipt of goods or monthly installments.

Mostly traditional flowers such as daisy, rose, tuberose, rajanigandha, marigold, chrysanthemum, chameli, kaner, mogra, dodi and exotic varieties such as carnation, gladioli, gerbera, lotus, orchids, bird of paradise and lily etc. are traded.

Hi Tech Flower Market (Connaught Place, New Delhi)

The Connaught Place flower market is regarded as a prime domestic market for high-tech flowers. Here, there is no intervention by the government. Exotic flowers (both in fresh and dry forms) and greens and accessories are traded. The majority of flowers come from Bangalore and Pune and small amounts are sourced from Kullu, Hyderabad, Shimla, and Mumbai.

Bangalore's produce/flowers are considered the best in quality. The main flowers traded are roses, carnations, anthuriums, gerbera, chrysanthemum, orchids, lily, golden torch, satis, gladiolus, limonium, etc. The dominating greens are fan palm, drysenia, ferns, arka, palm, asparagus, cycys, morphnki, dandrella, rakas a dfalas – fish palm etc. Dried flowers come mostly from Kolkata but are arranged in Delhi.

There are 20-25 big commission agents and they work on 5-12.5 per cent in magin. The rose is the most wanted and traded flower and asparagus is the most traded green. Flowers arrive at the market by bus, train, or by air. Delhi is the emerging main supply centre in the country while Bangalore is the main auction centre. Although rose is the most traded flower, the market leader is one who has the entire range of flowers. Buyers are ready to pay slightly higher prices if quality is assured.

Marketing Channel

The main marketing channel in the flower trade in India is Farmer → APMC → Auction through commission agent at 6 per cent → wholesaler → reseller/retailer → end-user.

Global Trade:

The Indian floriculture sector is successfully increasing its share in the total world trade and India has various types of climatic conditions and produces over 2000 varieties of flowers such as rose, carnation, chrysanthemum and orchid. Exports are very crucial to the flower industry and Japan has emerged as the highest market for Indian flowers. There has been an impressive growth in the export of cut flowers from ₹ 10 million to ₹ 700 million in the last few years.

After the economic reforms, a sharp growth has been witnessed in the production and demand of cut flowers for exports. The government has approved more than 191 export-oriented units (EOU) in different parts of the country, particularly around Pune, Chandigarh, Bangalore, Delhi, and Hyderabad, out of which seventy units are operational. Some of them have started production and have started exporting their products. A majority of these EOUs will have world-class setup in collaboration with foreign technology and infrastructural support.

Major flowers in the world trade: Rose, carnation, tulip, lily, gerbera, orchid, chrysanthemum.

Major exporting countries: The Netherlands (dominating the international trade of flowers) Columbia, Italy, Denmark, Belgium, Canada, USA, Ecuador, Germany, Israel, Kenya and Costa Rica etc.

Major importing countries: USA, Europe and especially Netherlands but Germany, the UK, France, Italy and Japan also have significant share.

Steps taken by the government to increase flower export are:

- APEDA is planning to enhance the exports of flowers to West Asia and make an entry into the Australian and New Zealand markets.
- The government of India is trying to get a reduction in the high import duty on cut flowers 15-20 per cent in the European Community (EC),.

- The government is working on an air freight subsidy for export of cut flowers and exemption of EOU from requirements of customs bonding.
- Subsidy on air freight has been allowed up to maximum of 25 per cent of the international freight rate for the export of tissue culture plants, and cut flowers.
- Setting up of cold storage units at international airports.
- Farmers are allowed to sell even up to 50 per cent of their produce in the domestic market.
- To increase exports, the following measures have been taken regarding export related imports.
- The Commerce Ministry is contemplating duty exemption on the import of materials for greenhouse and tissue culture labs considering the huge capital inputs.
- The quarantine procedures have been simplified for expeditious clearance for the import of seeds and planting materials.
- Import permits for flower seeds and tissue culture materials of plant origin have been waived.
- The import duty on floriculture planting material has been reduced from 55 per cent to 10 per cent.
- Import duty on seed development machinery and specified goods for green houses has been brought down from 136 per cent to 25 per cent.
- Duty on pre-cooling units and refrigerated transport units has been reduced to 25 per cent.
- Floriculture units can avail benefits of duty-free imports if they export 50 per cent of production.
- The Central Government has plans for setting up model Floriculture Regional Centre at Chennai, Bangalore, Trivandrum, Pune, Lucknow, Calcutta, Mohali, Srinagar, and Gangtok, to conserve important varieties of flower crops of the respective regions and arrange for large-scale multiplication.
- Organized training and demonstration on various aspects of floriculture and post-harvest management for farmers and entrepreneurs.

MARKETING OF PRODUCTS OF ANIMAL ORIGIN

The livestock sector plays an important role in the rural economy as a supplementary and complimentary occupation. For small and marginal farmers, and specifically for landless people, it provides subsidiary occupation thereby somewhat increasing the income of people in rural areas. About 70 per cent of the livestock market is owned by them. About 100 million tons of milk, 4.45 million tons of meat and 45 billion eggs are produced every day in India.

The share of the livestock sector in total agricultural output is 27 per cent (Economic Survey 2006-07). India has the largest livestock population in the world with about 18.5 crore heads of the cattle and 9.8 crore buffaloes (Livestock census 2003). This constitutes about 57 per cent of the world's buffaloes population. Total exports from the livestock sector was ₹ 19,234.4 million which was 0.66 per cent of total agricultural exports. Of the total exports from the livestock sector, over 70 per cent was contributed by the export of meat while dairy products contributed only 10.55 per cent.

The growth in dairy and poultry products has undergone a remarkable change in the last two decades leaving behind the growth in cereal production. This may be due to rising incomes and shifting of consumption and expenditure to more nutritive foods. China and India will become primary producers of meat and milk products in the next decade.

The states with large livestock populations are Rajasthan, Jammu and Kashmir, UP, Gujarat and hilly regions of the North and Eastern Himalayas. The major livestock animals in India are cows, buffaloes, camel, goat, sheep and pigs etc. While the production of milk is highest in India, the productivity per animal is very low. Investment in infrastructure, cooperatives, contract farming and other pro-poor market mechanisms can help increase in the productivity of the livestock sector.

The marketing of livestock products can be broadly studied under the following types:

- Milk and Milk Products
- Poultry Products
- Goat and sheep related products.

MILK AND MILK PRODUCTS

India is the largest producer of milk in the world with 91 million tons production of milk which is growing at a 4 per cent compound annual growth rate per annum. The credit for this much of production and growth goes to initiatives taken by the Operation Flood programmes in organizing milk producers into cooperatives.

MFPI and Ministry of Agriculture play a very supportive role by building necessary infrastructure for milk procurement, processing and marketing, providing financial, technical and management inputs to turn the dairy sector into viable self-sustaining organized sector in the country.

The public sector concentrates on milk supply through cooperative basis in the urban areas while private dairies concentrate on other value added products. Key players in organized dairy industry are Nestle, Mother Dairy, H.J. Heinz Limited, Paras, Vijaya Verka, Hindustan Unilever Limited, Vadilal, Cadbury, etc. and in the market they are in selling and they are in selling and marketing with various processed products of milk. Main processed products in dairy industry are packaged milk, ghee, yogurt, butter, ice-creams, milk powder, cheese, sweets etc.

Key players in the major dairy products segment in India:

Key Players	Brands	Major Dairy Products
Gujarat Coop. Milk Marketing Federation	Amul	Butter, Cheese, Chocolate
Nestle India Limited	Milkmaid, Cerelac Lactogen	Sweetened/condensed milk and Milk powder chocolates
Milkfood Limited	Milk Food	Ghee, Ice-cream
H. J. Heinz Limited	Farex, Complan. Lactose, Bonniemix Vitamilk	Infant and malted milk foods

Smithkline Beecham Limited	Horlicks	Malted milk food, ghee, butter, powdered milk, Milk based baby foods.
Cadbury	Bournvita	Malted Foods

Source: http://mofpi.nic.in/industryspecificinformation/milk/milk_players.

Ice-cream

After the opening up of the ice-cream sector to large-scale units in 1997, the sector recorded high growth rate of 15-20 per cent. Of the total market size of ₹ 15-16 billion, about 30-32 per cent is in the control of organized players. Hindustan Unilever Limited (Kwality Walls), Amul and Vadilal are the key players in the market. Vanilla, Strawberry and Chocolate, which together account for more than 70 per cent of the market are the most preferred flavours in the market followed by butter scotch and other fruit flavours.

Dairy farming has developed to a very efficient manner in all the activities related with collection, processing and distribution of milk and milk products. It contributes 65 per cent to the total livestock sector in value terms. The sector has good forward and backward market linkages and helping vulnerable groups of the society and promoting various industries, and in 2005-06. And around 97.1 million tons of milk was produced in India. The per capita availability of milk has gone up to 241 grams per day in 2005-06 from 176 grams per day in 1990-91, which is a reflection of the developments in this sector after the economic reforms (Economic Survey 2006-07,) i.e., after de-licensing of the dairy sector from the small-scale sector in 1991.

Features of Market Scenario for Milk Products

Despite being largest producer of milk, the exports are negligible as the entire amount is consumed within the country. However, there is scope of more investments in the sector for increasing supply profitably.

The perishable nature of the product is the major constraint in the marketing of milk. Being dominated by small producers and unorganized dairies, infrastructure facilities are inadequate.

Studies conducted by NDDB indicate that 45 per cent of the milk produced is consumed as liquid milk, 28 per cent as ghee, 6 per cent as butter and Khoya, 7 per cent as curd and 2.6 per cent as milk powder. The remaining milk is consumed in other forms such as paneer, ice-cream, baby foods, dairy whiteners, condensed milk and malted foods.

The major share of the milk consumers in India still prefers to purchase milk from vendors who supply it in unprocessed form at doorsteps.

Dairies in the organized sector, mostly cooperative dairies, collect the milk from surplus areas (rural areas). After processing, the milk and value-added milk products are packaged and branded and then through cold chains are distributed to different areas according to the demand.

Retail sale of milk may be done in different types of packaging such as bottles, sealed cans, tetrapacks, and aseptic paper packaging.

The price of milk depends on the type of milk (cow, buffalo, and goat), demand-supply situation, distance between the production and consumption centres and also upon the season.

There is an increasing demand for value-added and branded products. Big players have entered the market with branded milk and milk products with attractive packaging and branding, viz., AMUL, MOTHER DAIRY, MILKFED, and many other state milk producing cooperatives.

Channels of marketing of milk may be:

Producer → consumer

Producer → cooperatives/distributors/retailers → consumers

Producer → wholesaler → retailer → consumer

Producer → retailer → consumer

Policy and regulations in the milk and milk products sector

Milk production in India is regulated by the milk and milk products order which states that there is no requirement of acquiring permission from the authority appointed by the Central Government to establish units handling less than 10000 liters of liquid milk per day or milk solids up to 500 tons per annum. Up to 31 March 2006, the Central and State registering authorities have granted registration to 789 units with combined capacity of 980.50 liters of milk per day. Except for malt foods, full foreign equity participation has been allowed. Ice-cream manufacturing has been dereserved from small-scale sector and no license is now required for setting up large-scale production facilities for manufacturing ice-cream. Exports of some milk based products are freely allowed provided they satisfy BIS norms.

Cooperative Dairies

Operation Flood, which started in 1970, concluded its third phase in 1996. Science and Technology applied simply at the creation of farmer owned structures, combined with all the policies and programmes that affect production have been instrumental in the growth of dairy sector. Operation Flood revolutionized the way of the life for poor and small farmers.

A number of dairy cooperatives with a three tier structure, viz., village level primary cooperatives, district level unions and state level federations have been set up in different parts of the country under the Operation Flood Programme. For a variety of reasons, a number of these unions/federations have accumulated losses. Till 2005-06, the department has approved thirty-one rehabilitation proposals of milk missions in MP state, Chattisgarh, Karnataka, UP, Haryana, Kerala, Maharashtra, Assam, Nagaland, Punjab, West Bengal and Tamil Nadu states with total outlay of ₹ 165.34 crore. An amount of ₹ 69.64 crore had been released till 31st March 2006 and presently National Milk Grid Links 1.13 lakh village level cooperative societies spread over 265 districts and consumers of 700 towns and cities.

Government's Views

India has the highest livestock population in the world with 50 per cent of the buffaloes and 20 per cent of the world's cattle population, most of which are milch cows and milch buffaloes. India's dairy industry is considered as one of the most successful development programmes in the post-independence period. In the year 2006-07, the total milk production in the country was over 94.6 million tons with a per capita availability of 229 gms per day. The industry had been recording an annual growth of 4 per cent during the period 1993-2005, which is almost 3 times the average growth rate of the dairy industry in the world. Milk processing in India is around 35 per cent, of which the organized dairy industry account for 13 per cent of the milk produced, while the rest of the milk is either consumed at farm level, or sold as fresh, non-pasteurized milk through unorganized channels.

Dairy Cooperatives account for the major share of processed liquid milk marketed in the India. Milk is processed and marketed by 170 Milk Producers' Cooperative Unions, which federate into 15 State Cooperative Milk Marketing Federations. Over the years, several brands have been created by cooperatives like Amul (GCMMF), Vijaya (AP), Verka (Punjab), Saras (Rajasthan)., Nandini (Karnataka). Milma (Kerala) and Gokul (Kolhapur).

Uttar Pradesh, Punjab, Haryana, Rajasthan, Gujarat, Maharashtra, Andhra Pradesh, Karnataka and Tamil Nadu are the milk surplus states in India. The manufacturing of milk products is obviously high in these milk surplus States. Export of dairy products in India is growing at the rate of 25 per cent per annum in terms of quantity and 28 per cent in terms of value since 2001. Significant investment opportunities exist for the manufacturing of value-added milk products like milk powder, packaged milk, butter, ghee, cheese and ready-to-drink milk products.

India has emerged as the largest milk producing country in the world with present level of annual milk production estimated as 94.5 million tons. We expect a production level of 135 million tons by the year 2015. India has a large livestock population base constituting 278 million livestock including 180.5 million cattle, 82.8 million buffaloes, 4 million sheep and 9.2 million goats. The livestock population is projected to increase to 322 million by the year 2015.

The large livestock population is raised primarily on crop residues and grazing in the common property including basement. The forest area, which was a major source of grazing, is no longer available to livestock breeders especially landless people. As a consequence, the available feed resources fall short of the nutritional requirement. The shortfall is estimated as 59.9 million tons for the green fodder and 19.9 million tons for dry fodder. This shortfall is likely to increase by 2015 to 63.5 million tons of green fodder and 23.56 million tons of dry fodder.

The landless people are, therefore, likely to face severe shortage of resources to raise cattle and other species of livestock. There is a real danger that in the absence of resources to maintain their stock, these underprivileged rural people may give up livestock farming. This could be a serious setback to lakhs of rural families who derive income as well as employment opportunities from livestock sector.

India prepares to tackle the international market following Japan, where milk consumption today, has more than trebled to 70 kg per capita from a mere 20 kg in the sixties — the consumption of dairy products in other Asian 'tiger' nations is also growing. As a consequence, creating excellent export opportunities for India, as these nations are deficient in milk by at least 3 million tons per year. India, with some 27 per cent of Asia's population, accounts for more than half of the milk output with enough growth potential to explore foreign markets.

In anticipation of the export opportunities and in view of the post GATT scenario, India is gearing up to tackle the demands of the international market. Indian companies are preparing themselves to meet international standards and other non-tariff barriers. Planners are taking measures to meet the sanitary and phyto-sanitary specifications prescribed by Office International des Epizooties (OIE) under the auspices of the World Trade Organization (WTO) which range from the quality assurance of processed dairy products to the health status of livestock.

PROCESSED DAIRY PRODUCTS

Cheese

The organized cheese market including its variants like processed cheese, mozzarella, cheese spreads, flavoured and spiced cheese, is valued at around ₹ 4.5 billion. Processed cheese at 60 per cent of the overall market is ₹ 2.7 billion. The next most popular variant is cheese spread claiming a share of around 30 per cent of the total processed cheese market. The market is primarily an urban phenomenon and is known to be growing at around 15 per cent. The market for cheese cubes, slices and tins is growing. The flavoured cheese segment has been constantly declining.

Gujarat Cooperative Milk Marketing Federation (GCMF) with the Amul brand continues to be the main operator in the branded cheese market in India. It pioneered the market for processed, branded cheese. What GCMF did was to develop the technology to make cheese from buffalo milk. World over, it is made from cow milk.

Britannia Industries joined the fray in the cheese market in mid-1990s through an arrangement with Dynamix Dairy Industries (DDI). It was set up in 1995 by a consortium of five companies — Conwood, Indo Saigon, Hiranandani, ETA and Metro. DDI has capacity to process 500,000 litres of milk per day with an estimated investment of ₹ 1500 million. The plant designed by Valio of Finland is run on technology tie-up with Schreiber Foods of the US. Schreiber is the largest supplier of processed cheese to fast food chains in the US with expertise in sliced cheese.

Britannia's cheese is sold in tins in the form of cubes, and in individually wrapped slices in packs of fives and tens. The slices are being promoted more aggressively worldwide, and these account for a bulk of cheese consumption. These are gaining acceptance in India as well. Amul followed Britannia in launching slices. Its cheese spread in the form of paste has been well received in the market.

Britannia has been concentrating on metros and large cities. The network covers some 60,000 dairy outlets equipped with cold cabinets, refrigerators and insulated boxes. Amul covers some 500,000 retail outlets.

French cheese major, Fromageries Bel, a 10-bn French franc outfit, has entered the Indian market with La Vache Kirit or what is worldwide known as The Laughing Cow. Its target market to start with were the two metros of Delhi and Mumbai with distribution entrusted to Delhi-based Rai & Sons, distributors for premium food brands, Ferraro Rocher and Ricola.

The Bel product will be produced at Bel's facility in Poland exclusively for the Indian market. La Vache Kirit is a guaranteed vegetarian product. Fromageries Bel is expected to widen its product portfolio by launching laughing Kirit (creamy cheese in cube form) and Babybel (semi-hard with a wax coating appropriate for sandwiches).

Laughing Cow was expected to be followed by an Austrian cheese brand, Happy Cow (owned by Woerle). Woerle has entered into a licensing arrangement with Veekay Foods & Beverages in Mumbai. Nestle and Kraft have been planning to make foray in the Indian market.

Foreign brands in India include: Probolene, Colby, Mozzarella and Parmessan from Italy, Cheddar from Dutch, Gryueve. The new entrants will have to compete with well-established players such as Amul, Britannia's Milkman and Dabur's Le Bon, enjoying substantial market shares in the overall Indian cheese market. The US-based Philip Morris, which brought in its Kraft cheese brand earlier, has gained a significant presence in the market. The rest of the market is spread among Verka, Nandini, Vijaya and Vadilal.

Dabur had forayed into the dairy products market through its joint venture company, Dabon International, a 50:50 joint venture between Dabur India and French dairy products major, Bongrain. The company claimed a product range of 20 different varieties of cheese under LeBon brand. Dabon has a manufacturing facility at Noida with an installed capacity of 12,000 tons per annum. Incidentally, the government had, in a move in late April 2001, barred Dabon from marketing flavoured milk and processed cheese in the country.

Dabur was to launch speciality cheese like blue cheese and hard cheese. It had plans for developing cold chains at the distributor and retail levels in the State capitals and major towns in order to increase penetration levels.

The demand for cheese is projected to grow from about ₹ 4.50 billion in 2003-04 to ₹ 6.00 billion in 2006-07 and to over ₹ 11.00 billion by the terminal year of the projection period, 2014-15. Cheese is becoming a popular item in the menu of all relatively affluent families. Slowly but surely, it will penetrate into the rural markets.

Processed Cheese: The leading brands in this category are Amul, Vijaya, Verka, Vadilal, Kraft, Britannia.

Lead Players: The lead players in processed milk products in the market are Amul, Britannia, and others include Vijaya, Verka and Vadilal. In the category of cheese, Amul, Britannia Dabur (Le Bon) are the leading players including others like Verka, Nandini, Vijaya and Vadilal.

DAIRY WHITENERS

About 15 per cent of the total milk output in India is estimated to be processed in the organized dairy. The industry has maintained a high growth profile, especially in the wake of the Operation Flood, colloquially also termed as White Revolution, initiated in early 1980s. Today, India produces over 85 million tons of milk annually. The total milk economy is estimated at ₹ 1300 billion in terms of value.

The market for dairy whiteners (commercially known as beverage milk powders and condensed milk) and creamers is around ₹ 3,000 million. Apart from MNCs like Nestle and companies like Britannia, the Indian enterprises have also made perceptible progress. Names like Amul, Sapan, Vijaya, Mohan, Parag and several others have been seen in the marketplace with their whiteners. These are available mostly in pouches, tetrapacks, and in the near future, may be in miniportion cups.

Aseptically packed creamer in miniportions is widely used in the West, but has yet to enter the Indian market in any substantial way. Amul did make a beginning with its whitener pouches and has emerged as a leader with a market share of 45 per cent followed by Nestle's 23 per cent. Aseptically packed creamer involves techniques to impart a longer shelf life to the product. It is packed in small cups ready to be poured into a cup of tea or coffee. Creamer is fresh milk with increased fat content (upto 12 per cent) and is aseptically packed after undergoing Ultra Heat Treatment (UHT) at 140^{0}C. Its introduction will affect the existing whitener market as a natural milk product with a longer shelf life.

Britannia forayed into the dairy business as a diversification move in 1997. Its first offering, Milkman Butter, just managed a 5 per cent share. The dairy business claims a 10 per cent share in Britannia's topline. The company had drawn up plans to atleast capture 5 per cent of the overall fresh milk market estimated by Britannia at ₹ 420 billion. Extending the product portfolio beyond cheese, dairy whitener and butter, Britannia entered the fresh milk segment in 2001. In the dairy whitener, the company has managed to capture a significant market share.

Nestle India with its Everyday dairy whitener has established its brand well. It has also entered into the market with its Nestle Pure Milk and, of course, a product in its niche area, Nescafe Frappe. Having earlier launched UHT milk, Nestle is concentrating on expanding its reach. Its plans covered ₹ 800 million investment in its Moga (Punjab) facility. New product segments like butter, yoghurt and flavoured milk were also on the cards.

While Sapan characterises it as Dairy Special (instant milk mix for tea and coffee), Vijaya is the only UHT processed milk homogenised brand sold in the market in 200 ml and one litre tetrapack. All the rest, Amulya, Meadow, Mohan, Parag and Shweta dairy whiteners are in the form of powders. Mohan also markets a non-dairy whitener alongside its dairy type product.

Since India is a major consumer of tea and coffee, it would be a very large market if only the price was not a constraint. In addition to domestic consumption, the whiteners/creamers find a high level of institutional acceptance, especially by railways, hotels and restaurants, airlines, hospitals and nursing homes and corporate offices. The institutional market can be tapped first, in particular, the airlines, railways and hotels. The penetration can then be extended to the household sector. The potential for exports, especially to neighbouring countries and the countries in the Middle East, the Gulf and Africa, also exist and could be exploited.

The main thrust of proposals is on the improvement of animal health and adoption of sanitary and phyto-sanitary specifications (SPS) for dairy products. Towards this end, the Technology Mission on Dairy Development (TMDD) has initiated a wide-ranging programme.

The upsurge in milk production has thrown up challenges in milk marketing. The country is blessed with an enormous domestic market because of the following factors: large population and its continuous growth, low level of per capita milk consumption and hence large size of potential, but latent demand, increasing purchasing power, which is already in evidence, will transform the huge latent demand into real demand. The groups of dairy products offering exciting marketing opportunities are liquid milk itself, which accounts for a sizeable part of the milk consumption products, in which our dairy industry already has demonstrated considerable expertise, like milk powders, butter and ghee. The ability to manufacture the relatively new and sophisticated products like cheese and ice-cream alongside the traditional products like paneer, khoya and milk-based sweets are now being manufactured on a large scale of the total milk produced in the country, nearly 46 per cent is consumed as liquid milk and the balance converted into various dairy products, such as ghee, butter, milk powder, ice-cream, cheese, condensed milk and for making various kinds of sweetmeats having distinct regional preferences. Dairy products an estimated 54 per cent of India's milk production is converted into products, both traditional and Western. In this, the share of traditional products is about 50 per cent, accounting in 2001 for a little over 42 million tons of milk, which yields over 10 million tons of mithais and other related products per year.

COMMERCIAL PRODUCTION OF TRADITIONAL PRODUCTS

With the increase in the availability of liquid milk and Western dairy products, refinement in the marketing network and significant improvement in per capita income, there is an increased pressure for the restructuring of the indigenous milk product industry. Now, the organized sector has started showing keen interest in processes and equipment for manufacturing traditional products standardization of products, as well as refinement in packaging and improvement in safety and shelf life. Any innovation which can enable the organized sector to manufacture and market indigenous milk products on an industrial scale can have a far-reaching impact on the dairy industry as well as on the economic condition of milk producers. The market for indigenous products far exceeds that for Western dairy products like butter, milk powder and cheese. A great scope exists for further expansion of the market for indigenous milk products, provided quality and safety are ensured and the shelf life is extended to facilitate distribution over larger areas. Major innovations are needed in manufacturing, quality assurance, packaging and process engineering to adapt these products to current marketing and consumer requirements. Some commercial processes have been developed to manufacture ghee, khoya, shrikhand and gulabjamun, but much is required to be done.

SUMMARY

The NCDC was established in 1963 as a statutory corporation under the Ministry of Agriculture. Its functions include planning, promoting, and financing programmes for all the functions starting from production till the product reaches the consumer, viz., production, processing, marketing, storage, export and import.

It deals with agricultural produce, foodstuffs and certain other notified commodities, fertilizers, insecticides, agricultural machinery, soaps, kerosene oil, textile, rubber etc. It promotes income generating activities such as poultry, dairy, fishery, sericulture, handloom, etc, Besides it also functions for the supply of consumer goods, and collecting, processing, marketing, storage and export of minor forest produce through cooperatives.

With amendments in the NCDC Act, the area of cooperation has been broadened to assist the different types of cooperatives and to expand its financial base. NCDC will now be able to finance projects related to rural development. It advances loans and grants to State governments for financing primary and secondary level cooperative societies while for the projects whose objectives extend beyond one state, loans are advanced directly to national level and other societies.

QUESTIONS

1. What are the functions of Cooperative Marketing Agencies in Indian Agriculture?
2. What are the functions of different marketing channels in the marketing of food grain, cotton and floriculture products?
3. How Cooperative sector dominates the Indian Dairy Industry?
4. What are the essences of policies devised for regulation of milk and milk processed products through cooperative sector?

OOO

CHAPTER

22

Major Players in Marketing of Processed Foods

DAIRY INDUSTRY

The dairy industry in India is dominated by major players who play their key role in the cooperative sector. About 60 per cent of the installed processing capacity in the dairy products are available in the cooperative sector.

The National Dairy Development Board (NDDB) is a major player in the market with its major brand, Amul. Leading brands like Amul, Nestle, Mother Dairy and Britannia are in the race to tap the growing market.

SmithKline Beecham Consumer Healthcare, Nestlé India and Heinz India are amongst the large MNCs that dominate the high-value milk products market. Other players include Indiana Dairy Specialties, Jagatjit Industries Ltd and various other state co-operatives.

Some dairy plants have production of mithais on a commercial scale. Some national brands like Haldiram, Bikanervala, K C Das, Chitales, Ganguram, Brijwasi, Agarwal Sweets etc. are getting wide acceptance because of consistent quality. Encouraged by the growing market and cashing on brand value selected dairy companies are planning major expansion plans in various cities with new brands suited to local taste and preferences and realizing higher prices with higher sales volumes and product safety.

The milk and dairy products segment is set for upgradation of cold-storage chains for expansion. Mother Dairy, a wholly owned subsidiary of National Dairy Development Board plans to make strong presence in the market of milk and milk products under the Mother Dairy brand through retail outlets across the country in addition to its own 300 outlets with provision of cold storage and cold chains. In addition, there are areas where major thrust is required on following:

Brand image or major players need to be projected in leading international dairy trade fairs, particularly of those countries to which exports are being targeted. Another step may be to encourage technical collaboration and marketing tie-ups with leading international dairy companies.

With the liberalization and open policies of the Government and the restructuring of the economy, the dairy industry is undergoing major developments. This has brought about greater participation of the private sector. This is also consistent with global trends, which can hopefully lead to greater integration of Indian dairying with the world market for milk and milk products. India is witnessing winds of change because of improved milk availability, a changeover to market economy, globalization and the entry of the private sector in the dairy industry. The value addition and variety in the availability of milk products are on everybody's agenda. There is a consistent increasing demand for new products and processes. The major reasons are an increase in disposable incomes, changes in consumer concerns and perceptions on nutritional quality, hygiene and safety, arrival of foreign brands, increasing popularity of satellite or cable media and availability of new technologies and functional ingredients. India is the world's largest milk producer in the present scenario.

PRODUCTS FROM OTHER COMMERCIAL PRODUCTS

Coffee

Coffee bean cultivation in India is largely confined to hilly regions of the southern states of Karnataka, Tamil Nadu, and Kerala. The coffee market can be segmented into instant and filter coffee and filter coffee can further be segmented as pure and chicory blended coffee.

Every year only one-fifth of the coffee bean produce is consumed in India by consumers in domestic markets, while the rest is exported. The main importing countries are the Russian Federation, Germany, Italy and the US. The Coffee Board, which promotes coffee sales in India started emphasizing on three channels of distribution, viz., cafe chains, vending machines and ready-to-drink products.

Tea

India is not only the largest producer and consumer of tea in the world, but it also leads in global R&D in tea industry. Darjeeling tea, Assam tea, flavoured tea, and green tea. Nilgiris tea, whole leaf tea, dust tea and granular tea are some of the varieties of tea. Different regions of the country have different preferences of tea, and this tea market is experimenting with innovative packaging and flavours for the premium segment to expand its market.

Sugarcane

With 450 sugar mills, India is the largest sugar producer in the world. The marketing of sugar is also controlled by administered price policy and the sugar factories are bound to purchase cane at the price announced by the government. Sugar is sold mostly in the urbanized form. But some companies are producing it in the organized sector under their brands, such as Triveni, Balrampur Chini Mills, EID Parry, GMR and Bajaj Hindustan.

Dry Fruits

India is the world's largest cashewnut producer, consumer and exporter in the world. It is the leading cashew supplier to the US, all the major European markets, the Middle East, Russia, Eastern Europe, Australia and Japan. Other dry fruits that have a good demand in the market are walnut. Other important crops grown in India are tobacco, coconut, palm oil, oil palm and cocoa.

EXPORT OF PROCESSED FOOD PRODUCTS 2005-06

The MOFPI has been encouraging new processing capacities of agro food products through its various policy initiatives and plan schemes providing financial incentives for setting up new units and modernizing existing ones:

Items	Quantity (MT)	Value (₹ in crore)
Processed Fruits and Vegetables		
Dried and Preserved Vegetables	5,66,238	1459.17
Mango Pulp	1,34,613	364.24
Pickle and Chutney	1,35,382	260.98
Other processed Fruits and Vegetables	1,07,335	370.21
Total for Processed Fruits and Vegetables	**5,01,826**	**1359.54**
Animal Products		
Buffalo meat	4,59,938	2629.57
Sheep/Goat meat	7177.51	80.37
Poultry Products	1,45,889	167.58
Dairy Products	76.515	668.50
Animal Casings	1125.82	17.51
Processed Meat	256.04	2.43
Total for Animal products	**6,90,901**	**3566.96**
Other Processed Foods		
Groundnuts	1,90,053	513.69
Guargum	1,86,718	1049.23
Jaggery and confectionery	1,07,197	227.57
Cocoa Products	2147.09	21.83
Cereal Preparations	76,880.6	393.96
Alcoholic and Non-alcoholic Beverages	49,587.9	117.20
Miscellaneous Preparations	49,606.7	225.77
Milled Products	50,901.5	64.68
Total for other processed foods	**7,13,092**	**2613.93**
Grand Total	19,05,819	7439.43

SERICULTURE PRODUCTS

Sericulture is an agro-based industry which involves the rearing of silk worms for the production of raw silk. Silk is known as the queen of all fabrics. This is obtained from the cocoons spun by silk worms. Sericulture industry in India spearheading as profitable globally and its major activities comprises, food plant cultivation to breed the silk worms which spin silk cocoons and reeling the cocoons for the unwinding the silk filament for value added processes such as processing and weaving of high quality silk yarn and costumes for export to various countries all over the world. The country produces variety of silks named Mulberry, Tussar, Muga and Eri. These different varieties are dependent on the feeding habits of the cocoons.

This industry employs over 70,00,000 farm families and about 5.6 million farmers are dependent on the sericulture industry, of which 4.7 million are agriculturists. It is one of the most beneficial industries for agriculturists and is concentrated in Karnataka, Tamil Nadu and Andhra Pradesh and to some extent in Assam and West Bengal. More than 70 per cent of country's total silk is produced in Karnataka.

India is the largest consumer and the second largest producer of silk after China, contributing about 18 per cent of the world's total production of silk. Germany is the largest importer of Indian silk, interestingly India's requirement of raw silk is much higher than its current production growth rate of more than 10 per cent per year. Thus, there is considerable scope for stepping up production of raw silk in the country.

The key strengths of this industry are the following:

- It has a wide base of producers and consumers sustained market demand, especially from the Indian handloom sector, making it one of the most demanded products in national and international markets.
- The infrastructure created by the national sericulture project and the research and training capabilities developed by the government.

Problems of the Silk Industry in India

One of the major problems for the Indian silk industry is the cut-throat competition and flooding of cheap silk from China in Indian markets. According to the last year's records, China has produced about 69,000 metric tons of raw silk, whereas India has produced 16,000 MT far behind China's silk production.

Dumping of silk yarn by China has affected the production of silk because the rate of cocoons has come down as dealers have lost interest in buying them. This has resulted in about 49,000 hectares of mulberry trees being cut down by farmers in Karnataka state and engaging themselves in other activities.

According to estimates, India requires 12,00,000 MT of silk to meet the demands of the world market and with the better infrastructure facility the sericulture industry can improve its productivity to 15 per cent as against the current 10 per cent.

Marketing of Silk

The marketing of silk takes place in multiple steps. First, the producers rear the worm and produce cocoons. These cocoons are given different treatments for the recovery of silk thread from which the yarn is prepared. This yarn is then traded by various agencies like silk cooperatives, silk SHGs, individual producers and the Anna Silk Exchange in Kancheepuram. Many cooperatives established by the Silk Federation are engaged in the marketing of silk. These cooperatives are not only the marketing platforms for silk, but also a platform for the weavers to express their views regarding their requirements, complaints etc. From yarn, the silk is converted into number of items from sarees to furnishing materials, which is done by handloom units, exporters or individual businessmen. These readymade products are marketed by the producers and purchased by wholesalers', retailers or exporters.

According to a study, the share of income to different groups involved in silk manufacturing and marketing is as under:

+ 56.8% to the cocoon grower

+ 6.8% to the reeler

+ 9.1% to the twister

+ 10.7% to the weaver

+ 16.6% to the trade

Thus, large portion of the income goes back to the villages.

Central Silk Board

The Central Silk Board (CSB), a statutory body of the Government of India, was set up in 1949 in Bangalore. It is national organization responsible for the overall development of sericulture and the silk industry. It provides different types of services to all the stockholders in the silk industry.

Services offered by the CSB: The CSB provides high yielding varieties of silkworm food plants, season-specific package of practices for food plant cultivation and silk worming rearing, technology packages for reeling and spinning inputs to rearers and reelers to the State Sericulture Departments and NGOs.

It facilitates soil testing and soil analysis, supply of planting material for food plant cultivation and commercial silkworm seed and training to sericulturists.

It provides training and technology improvements in silkworm seed preparation, preservation and handling to seed producers.

It also provides training and improved technologies of silk reeling/spinning to silk reelers.

CSB conducts eco-testing of silk, undertakes voluntary pre-shipment inspection for ensuring the quality and content of silk products meant for exports, seed certification/phytosanitary certification for export of silk worm seed to exporters.

It provides assistance for project selection, project preparation and technical assistance and consultancy services to the entrepreneurs.

The CSB has strong infrastructure facilities for the promotion of silk and silk products. It has three Central Sericultural Research and Training Institutes, Central Sericultural Germplasm Resources Centre (Hosur, Tamil Nadu), Silkworm Seed Technology Laboratory – Bangalore. And also Seri-biotech Research Laboratory (Bangalore), Central Tasar Research and Training Institute (Ranchi), Central Muga Eri Research and Training Institute (Assam), Ten Regional Research Stations and Forty-one Research Extension Centres.

MARKETING OF PISCICULTURE PRODUCTS (FISHING)

Pisciculture is the breeding, hatching and rearing of fish. The products included are different types of fish and fish based products.

India has 8118 km of coastal line which is a great advantage for the growth of pisciculture and also provides partial or full employment to almost eleven million people. Another three million are employed in allied activities. This makes India the third largest producer of fish and the second largest producer of inland fish in the world market. Fish and fish preparations are a major source of export earnings for India following the economic reforms.

In 2005-06, the contribution of the fisheries sector was 1per cent of total GDP and its allied activities was 5.3 per cent of the total GDP from the agriculture sector. It has also become a major export earning sector in agriculture contributing $5.6 billion, and according to the Ministry of Commerce it is expected to be $4 billion by 2010. There are about 1400 fishing harbours and serve the base for 2,80,000 fishing crafts. Marine Fisheries in India cover 2.02 million sq.km. of continental shelf. The major fish exporting ports are Chennai (19 per cent), Kochi (17 per cent), JNP (16 per cent) and Vizag (15 per cent). The main importing countries are the European Unions, US, Japan and China (Indian Economy-2007).

According to the sixty-first NSS Survey, only 28 per cent of Indians consume fish which is higher in the eastern and southern region, with a national average of 0.204 kg per capita per month. The monthly per capita consumption is highest in Kerala (1913 kg) followed by West Bengal (0.768 kg) and Assam (0.631 kg). However, the per capita fish consumption in India has increased in the last two decades.

Segments of the Fisheries Industry in India:

Capture (62%)

Marine: Deep sea and coastal (60% of capture)

Inland: River, reservoirs and ponds (40% of capture)

Aquaculture (38%) in brackish water and fresh water.

Some of the main species found in Indian marine waters are mackerel, penaeid, prawn, cluepeiods, sciacnids and perches, and catla, rohu and mrigal in aquaculture.

Fish Production in India since 1980-81 (lakh tons)

Year	Marine	% of Total	Inland	% of Total	Total
1980-81	15.55	63.68	08.87	36.32	24.42
1990-91	23.00	59.96	15.36	40.04	38.36
2000-01	28.11	49.69	28.45	50.30	56.56
2004-05 (Prov.)	27.78	44.07	35.26	55.93	63.04

In the above table, it is seen that the growth in the inland fisheries has been more than in the marine fisheries business.

MARINE PRODUCTS EXPORTS DEVELOPMENT AUTHORITY (MPEDA)

The MPEDA was constituted in 1972 under the Ministry of Commerce and Industry as a nodal agency for coordinating with different Central and State governments establishment engaged in the fishery production and allied activities.

MPEDA is headquartered at Cochin and field offices are situated in all the maritime states of India for implementing its various promotional schemes. It has a trade promotion office in New Delhi which acts as a link with Central Ministries. Apart from these, there are two overseas trade promotion offices in New York and Tokyo for promoting Indian seafood.

The development schemes of the MPEDA comprehensively covers fisheries of all types, production, processing, marketing, extension, export standards and training in various aspects of the industry. The specific functions of MPEDA are:

1. Registration of infrastructural facilities for the export trade of seafood.
2. Responsibility of collection and dissemination of trade information.
3. Organization of promotional activities for the marketing of Indian marine products abroad by direct or joint participation in overseas fairs and international seafood fairs.
4. Implementation of development schemes by extending financial assistance for investment in projects related to modernization of infrastructure which is vital to the seafood industry.
5. Promotion of aquaculture and export production augmentation as aquaculture products have a high demand.
6. Promotion of deep sea fishing projects to increase efficiency in fishing.
7. Financial and related activities.

FISHERIES AND AQUA CULTURE

There is a large untapped potential in fisheries and aquaculture, which can contribute considerably to improve the livelihoods as also to the empowerment of women.

The future development of aquaculture depends on the adoption of new and innovative production technologies, management and utilization of less utilized water resources. There is a large untapped potential in fisheries and aquaculture, which can contribute considerably to improve the livelihoods as also to the empowerment of women. The future development of aquaculture depends on the adoption of new and innovative production technologies, management and utilization of less utilized water resources and proper market tie-ups.

Reservoir fisheries offer a major opportunity to enhance fish production in the country. In the marine sector, while the coastal fisheries have been fully exploited, deep-sea fisheries resources are yet to be harnessed. Diversification and high value produce could add new dimensions to the sector. Proper post-harvest handling, reduction of losses and hygienic primary processing are important to realize full potentials of the sector. Simultaneously, effective marketing arrangements are to be made to ensure adequate returns to the fishermen so that they can make available good quality fish at affordable prices to the consumers.

NATIONAL FISHERIES DEVELOPMENT BOARD (NFDB)

With these in view, National Fisheries Development Board was established to work towards a blue revolution with a focus on increasing the fish production of the country to a level of about 10 million metric tons from the present level of 6.4 million metric tons, to achieve doubling of exports and an additional direct employment to an extent of 3.5 million by extending assistance to various agencies for implementation of activities under Inland, Brackish water and Marine sectors. It is envisaged that NFDB should also be a platform for public-private partnerships for fisheries and a mechanism for an end-end approach for ensuring efficiency in the process of fish production to consumption in the country.

Objectives

- To bring activities relating to fisheries and aquaculture for focused attention and professional management.
- To coordinate activities pertaining to fisheries undertaken by different Ministries/Departments in the Central Government and also coordinate with the State/Union Territory Governments.
- To improve production, processing, storage, transport and marketing of the products of capture and culture fisheries.
- To achieve sustainable management and conservation of natural aquatic resources including the fish stocks.
- To apply modern tools of research and development including biotechnology for optimizing production and productivity from fisheries.
- To provide modern infrastructure mechanisms for fisheries and ensure their effective management and optimum utilization.
- To generate substantial employment.
- To train and empower women in the fisheries sector.
- To enhance contribution of fish towards food and nutritional security

The Vision of NFDB is to develop aquaculture in a big way by adapting new and innovative production technologies, management and utilization of less utilized water resources and with proper market tie-ups.

Mission of NFDB is to increase present level of fish production from 6.57 million tons to 10.57 million tons, contributing to food, health, economy, exports, employment and tourism in the country.

With the above Vision and Mission, National Fisheries Development Board was registered on 10th July 2006 under "Andhra Pradesh Societies Registration Act, 2001" and the Board was inaugurated on 11th September 2006 by Hon'ble Union Agriculture Minister Sri Sharad Pawar. Initially for the NFDB office, two Blocks (401 and 402) have been rented out from HUDA, Hyderabad at Maitri Vihar, HUDA commercial complex, Ameerpet, Hyderabad-500038. Govt.of Andhra Pradesh have allotted 5 acres of land on lease for 30 years for construction of NFDB office complex at Rajendranagar, Hyderabad.

Recent marketing mechanism for an end-to-end approach for ensuring proper availability and efficient marketing. A platform for public-private partnership for fisheries. Strategy for win-win situations for both producers and consumers of fishes.

ABOUT INDIAN FISHERIES

Indian fisheries and aquaculture is an important sector of food production, providing nutritional security to the food basket, contributing to the agricultural exports and engaging about fourteen million people in different activities. With diverse resources ranging from deep seas to lakes in the mountains and more than 10 per cent of the global biodiversity in terms of fish and shellfish species, the country has shown continuous and sustained increments in fish production since independence. Constituting about 4.4 per cent of the global fish production, the sector contributes to 1.1 per cent of the GDP and 4.7 per cent of the agricultural GDP.

The total fish production of 6.57 million metric tons presently has nearly 55 per cent contribution from the inland sector and nearly the same from culture fisheries. Paradigm shifts in terms of increasing contributions from inland sector and further from aquaculture are significant over the years. With high growth rates, the different facets of fishery and aquaculture industry are marine fisheries, coastal aquaculture, inland fisheries, freshwater aquaculture, coldwater fisheries to food, that will be beneficial to other sectors like health, economy, exports, employment and tourism of the country.

The country has 429 Fish Farmers Development Agencies (FFDAs) and 39 Brackishwater Fish Farmers Development Agencies (BFDAs) for promoting freshwater and coastal aquaculture. The annual crop seed production is to the tune of 20 billion and that of shrimp about 8 billion, with increasing diversification in the recent past. Along with food fish culture, ornamental fish culture and high value fish farming are gaining importance in the recent past. With over 2.4 lakh fishing crafts operating in the coast, six major fishing harbours, 40 minor fishing harbours and 151 landing centres are functioning to cater to the needs of over 3.5 million fisherfolk.

Fish and fish products have presently emerged as the largest group in agricultural exports of India, with 5.2 lakh tons in terms of quantity and ₹ 7,200 crores in value.

This accounts for around 3 per cent of the total exports of the country and nearly 20 per cent of the agricultural exports. More than 50 different types of fish and shellfish products are exported to 75 countries around the world.

There is a large number of untapped potential in fisheries and aquaculture, which can contribute considerably to improve the livelihoods as also women empowerment. The future development of aquaculture depends on adoption of new and innovative production technologies, management and utilization of less utilized water resources and proper market tie-ups.

Reservoir fisheries offers a major opportunity to enhance fish production in the country. In the marine sector, while the coastal fisheries have been fully exploited, deep-sea fisheries resources are yet to be harnessed. Diversification and high value produce could add new dimensions to the sector. Proper post-harvest handling, reduction of losses and hygienic primary processing are important to realize full potentials of the sector.

Simultaneously, effective marketing arrangements are to be made to ensure adequate returns to the fishers and the farmers as also make available good quality fish at affordable prices to the consumers. With these in view, an end-to-end approach from ensuring proper input availability to efficient marketing is contemplated, for a 'win-win' situation for both the fish producer and the consumer. Set in this background, the National Fisheries Development Board (NFDB) would seek to realize the full potentials of Indian fisheries through coordination of different agencies and public-private partnerships.

MARKETING OF FISH AND FISH PRODUCTS

The marketing of fish and fish products is affected by irregular supplies resulting in high price variations, high elasticity and seasonal nature of demand, perishable nature of the produce and traditional systems of marketing. Some other constraints that hamper the marketing of fish products are limited or inadequate infrastructural facilities in terms of availability of cold storages lack of regulated mandis and high transportation costs.

Fish, lobster, crab, prawn, and shrimp are widely accepted in the domestic market. The shrimp is a high-end product which, if positioned properly in the niche market of high class restaurants and hotels can do very well. Products that have great demand and may fetch good prices in the market are fish pickles, dried and salted fish, papads, and cutlets. The by-products of fish which are in demand are fish oils and fishmeal. Fish is usually packed with ice in baskets of wooden boxes.

The following channels are currently used in marketing fishery products:

1. Farmer → Consumer.
2. Farmer → Commission agent → Wholesaler → Retailer → Consumer.
3. Farmer → Shrimp collector → Commission agent → Processor → Export
4. Farmer → local market agent → Retailer → Consumer
5. Farmer → Vendor → Consumer.

The most common channel is the third one in which a large number of producers sell their produce to small number of buyers who are generally agents of wholesalers, who then sell it to retailers. The middlemen in the channel, i.e., commission agents and/or wholesalers provide credit to the farmers when required, thereby compelling them to sell their produce to middlemen. In this situation, producers, have little choice in terms of buyer or price. This increases the price spread in such a way that the producer as well as consumer is at loss, but the middlemen earns a large share of the price spread. The second most common channel is the first one which is adopted for local markets and in which the producer's share in the consumer's rupee is around 70 per cent.

ORGANIZED RETAILING IN FISHING TRADE

Organized retailing in this segment has not been successful to the level of that in fruits and vegetables. The main reason for this is scattered and small-scale production by a large number of producers which is not feasible for maintaining hi-tech supply chains – an important requirement for fish products. Also, the credit facility provided to producers by middlemen in the traditional channel cannot be provided by the organized retailers. Survey of supplies is also difficult in this sector because there is no insurance or compensation is available, as it is in crop production.

AQUA-CHOUPALS

In 2003 after permission for direct purchasing outside regulated mandis was granted, ITC started procuring fish though its Aqua-Choupals in AP state and in two years time its annual turnover has touched ₹ 50 crore benefiting more than 10,000 farmers spread over 100 villages of seven districts. Aqua-choupals are managed by local pratinidhis or representatives who motivate the farmers to use the laboratory and extension facilities provided by ITC and fish farmers can purchase quality inputs provided by ITC at subsidized rates. The representatives get 1 per cent of total value for his/her services. ITC procures the fish at ₹ 5 less than the market price with prompt cash payment. After procurement from farmers the fish is processed and packaged to be sold at retail outlets in metros or exported by the ITC.

Processed Products:

These include block frozen products, individual quick frozen products, minced fish products (fish sausages, cakes, cutlets, pastes, surimi), texturized products and dry fish.

Processing:

Processing of marine products in India is dominated by small-scale processors (85 per cent). Processing facilities are mainly present in Kerala, Andhra Pradesh, Gujarat, Tamil Nadu, Maharashtra and West Bengal. The marine processing is done intially in canned and frozen forms is done mostly for the export market. 60 per cent (82 per cent in value terms) of which is contributed by cultured shrimps/ freshwater prawns. Therefore, the area under shrimp production is increasing at CAGR of about 6.7 per cent in production.

Considerable improvements in infrastructure have taken place for fish processing in India. Some of the achievements (as per the Annual Report 2006-07 Ministry of Food Processing Industries) are as follows:

1. 369 freezing units with a daily processing capacity of 10,266 tons out of which 150 units are approved for export to the European Union.
2. Over 499 units are engaged in the production of frozen fish with a total storage capacity of 1,34,767 tons.
3. In addition to the above, there are twelve small units, five canning units and 473 units engaged in pre-processing and dry fish storage.
4. The quantum of marine products processed and exported and the revenue thereof during 2004-05 was 4,61,329 metric tons valued at ₹ 6,647 crore.

Export of Fish and Fish Products:

Exports of fish and fish preparations which was only ₹ 2 crore in 1950-51 rose to ₹ 893 crore in 1990-91. Since then the growth rate in the export of fish has jumped.

This figure jumped manifold with the economic reforms in place, exports rose to ₹ 6,288 crore by 2000-01 and to ₹ 7019 crore in 2005-06 attaining first place in the agricultural and allied sector.

There are 16,000 registered exporters in India out of which 773 trade directly in the international market (70 per cent small and marginal category). The export of marine products shifted from dried products to canned products in the 1980s and subsequently to frozen exporters.

Some of the leading merchant exporters in this export sector are Ruchi – Vishal Adai Aditya while Hindustan Unilever Limited Liberty and Falcan Marine are the leading producer exporters.

Export of marine products is allowed only by units which are registered with MPEDA. Fish processing projects with minimum 20 per cent value addition can be set up as 100 per cent export oriented units with foreign equity. All items can be exported freely except silver pomfrets weighing less than 300 grams.

Thus, we can say in the marketing of foodgrains and oilseeds, and all types of processed foods, the private sector is involved in procuring directly from the farmers or through wholesalers in traditional mandis. Procurement by private companies is done either for processing or selling to big retailers exporters.

The marketing of fruits and vegetables was facing various infrastructural constraints. Over 20-40 per cent wastages witnessed earlier are now reducing because of the increasing involvement of the private sector. Contract farming is also growing because of specific requirements of quality fruit and vegetable products. The government is providing considerable support through various fiscal and monetary incentives to producers as well as traders. The government is also boosting the immense potential in this sector, so private companies are entering the market in a big way.

Although the floriculture has got the status of sunrise sector after the economic reforms, the growth in marketing has not been very promising. As the potential for the growth in floriculture lies mainly in exports, it requires very good infrastructure and technical skill at par with global standards.

India, despite being the largest producer of foodgrains, fruits and vegetables, milk and meat production is processing only about 2 per cent of the total agricultural production. Basic industries such as foodgrains processing and edible oils production contributes the most to the food processing industry. Processing of fruit and vegetables and meat products are the sectors with high potential.

The silk industry has very bright future in India. Internationally, it has great potential as India is the second largest producer after China. The industry needs appropriate government policies to vitalize it. The Central Sericulture Board (CSB) was established by the government is again an upcoming industry especially for the international market. It is going to be major source of foreign exchange earning. The Marine Products Exports Development Authority was constituted to protect the industry's vast export potential.

MARKETING OF POULTRY PRODUCTS

The output from the poultry sector is more than ₹ 15,000 crore and provides employment to over three million people directly or indirectly (Economic Survey 2006-07). This sector helps increase subsidiary income and also provides nutritional security and especially to the rural poor. Andhra Pradesh, Karnataka, Tamil Nadu, Maharashtra, Gujarat, Madhya Pradesh state, Orissa and North Eastern states are the major poultry meat producing states.

With growing incomes, increasing quality consciousness and urbanization, the market for scientifically produced, hygienic poultry and meat products is expected to grow rapidly. As a result of changing lifestyle and preferences, there is growing demand for ready-to-eat processed and semi-processed meat products.

India ranks fifth in the world with an annual egg production of 1.61 million tons Indian poultry meat products have good markets in Bangladesh, Sri Lanka, Middle East, Japan, Poland, USA and Denmark. The Indian poultry sector will achieve dramatic growth over the most decade due to increasing demand which will result in changing the nature of the industry and building it into one of the India's largest food sectors.

Eggs:

According to the Indian branch of the World Poultry Science Association, the poultry industry has been growing at an annual rate of 20 per cent making it one of the fastest growing segments of Indian agriculture. The demand for eggs is expected to shoot up to 180 billion by 2015 from the current demand of 27 billion. It is expected that the demand for poultry products will increase by 16 per cent annually over the next ten years.

Both the public and private sector organizations have made their contribution to poultry output in India, making it one of the top players. The scope of foreign investments and state-of-the-art technology in the poultry industry is tremendous. In view of the growing export demand for different kinds of powders such as powders of whole egg, yolk, and albumen, the five egg powder plants in India are considered insufficient. Eggs, egg powder, frozen egg yolk and albumen in powder are exported to Europe, Japan, and other countries.

The prevailing marketing channels are:

1. Producer → Consumer
2. Producer → Processor
3. Producer → Wholesaler → retailer → Consumer
4. Producer → Retailer → consumer
5. Producer → Cooperative marketing society → Wholesaler/Retailer → Consumer.

Poultry Meat:

Over time, the poultry meat is becoming more popular and currently most of the existing players in this sector are fairly small in size, making the business less competitive. The biggest challenge for the success of this sector is in making feed available at the right price. That can be done mainly by the integration of activities, which will lead to increase in its scale, and thereby more profits.

Activity in the poultry sector needs to be enhanced rapidly to be able to cater to increasing demand due to urbanization, rising income levels, changing consumption patterns, in the future.

Marketing channels in the poultry meat sector:

Hatchery → Consumer

Hatchery → Retailer → Consumer

Hatchery → Retailer → Hotel/Restaurant → Consumer

Hatchery → Vendor → Organized retailer → (grading, labeling, packing in boxes) → Consumer

Hatchery → Organized retailer (grading, labeling, packing in boxes) → Consumer

Hatchery → Local vendor-organized retailer (leftover stock) – small shopkeeper → restaurant → Consumer.

The big players in marketing and retailing of poultry products are Venky's Suguna, R K Foodland, Prabhat, Seth and Godrej (processed meat).

During 2004-05, a new scheme the dairy/poultry venture capital fund was launched wherein there was provision to grant subsidy on interest payment was introduced. The establishment of poultry breeding farms with low input technology for duck/turkey/guinea fowl/quail/emu/ostrich/setting up of feed godowns, feed mills, feed analytical laboratories, marketing of poultry products (specialized transport vehicles, cold room storage facilities and retention sheds for birds etc).

Further egg grading packing and storage capacity for export, retail poultry dressing unit (300 birds per day) egg/broiler carts for sale of poultry products and central grower units were considered for financing under this scheme. The nodal agency for the implementation of this scheme is NABARD through nationalized commercial banks. In 2005-06, a total of 49 poultry units at a cost of ₹ 2.17 crore were approved.

Goat and Sheep Related Products

According to the Livestock Census 2003, there are about 61.47 million sheep and 124.36 million goats in the country. About five million households in the country are engaged in the rearing of small ruminants (sheep, goats, and rabbits) and other allied activities. The production of wool was 44.50 million kg during 2004-05. The expected wool production during 2005-06 stands at fifty million kg.

Meat:

The demand for meat increase on specific days of the week and on specific festivals. Mutton (goat's meat) is preferred by Indians and has good demand in the market. The market for sheep and goat meat is dominated by small and unorganized shopkeepers who are butchers and also the retailers. Consumers directly purchase the produce from these retailers. Al-Kabeer is well-known private player in the marketing of meat products.

INDIAN POULTRY AND ITS FUTURE PROSPECTS

It is believed that the Indian poultry industry is 5,000 years old, since last 4 decades it began to witness remarkable growth from backyard to poultry industry.

The organized sector of poultry industry is contributing nearly 70 per cent of the total output and the rest 30 per cent in the unorganized sector. The broiler industry is well dominated in southern states in our country with nearly 60-70 per cent total output coming from these states.

The layer industry once again is represented more in Southern states especially, Andhra Pradesh, Tamil Nadu and Maharashtra producing nearly 70 per cent of the country's egg production. India's 75 per cent of egg produce is consumed by the 25 per cent population living in urban and semi-urban areas. Presently about 800 hatcheries are operating in the country.

The Per Capita Consumption

The National Institute of Nutrition has recommended 180 eggs and 11 kg of meat per capita consumption for our country. At present, per capita availability of meat is 1.6 kg. Per capita availability of egg is 1.8 kg or 42 eggs. The average consumption of eggs in major cities is 170 eggs. Average consumption of eggs in smaller cities is 40 eggs. Average consumption of developed rural areas is 20 eggs. Average consumption of undeveloped rural areas is only 5 eggs while 20 per cent of Indian population is vegetarian.

In spite of this, with the rise of middle class and increased urbanization people prefer to go for non-vegetarian. About 3 million farmers and 15 million agrarian farmers are employed in the poultry industry that grow poultry ingredients for feed and contribute about ₹ 26,000 crore to the national income. India is the fifth largest producer of egg and ninth largest producer of poultry meat. India was positioned 17th in the world poultry production. The Indian poultry production is considered to be the cheapest in the world. Leading broiler integrators in India are as follows:

- Venkateswara Group, Pune
- Suguna Poultry Farms Ltd., Coimbatore
- Pioneer Poultry Group, Coimbatore
- Godrej Agrovet Ltd., Mumbai
- Sky Lark Group, North India
- Japfa Comfeed

These companies account for nearly 40 per cent of broiler industry integrators and contracts. Pioneer Poultry group introduced the concept of contract farming in the year 1980 and the concept of integration was introduced by Suguna Farms in 1990. Poultry farming came to be accepted as a viable activity by mid-60s and the real thrust to development came in 1971 with the establishment of Venkateswara Hatcheries Pvt. Ltd. The Central Poultry Breeding Farms laid the foundation for the development of poultry industry during 1959. Other agencies such as ICAR (CARI) contributed much in the R&D sector.

Commercial Poultry

India has emerged as the only country in the developing world a self-reliant, technology driven industry, with capability to produce every essential input for successful poultry farming including indigenous genetic resource and breeding, world-class poultry vaccines and medicines, specific pathogen free eggs (SPF), farms and hatchery automation systems, pelleted feed, egg processing, poultry processing, nationwide network of disease diagnostic laboratories and facilities for entrepreneurial development and training in both private and public sectors.

Rural Poultry Production

Rural poultry production sector constitutes important component of agricultural economy in India and in particular small poultry holder are practically capable of giving more significant contributions to alleviate malnutrition, poverty and unemployment. A spectacular progress has been made from subsistence to sustainable production system which is evident from the recent Economic Survey Reports. Indian backyard population increase is only by 16 per cent in the last 30 years from 60 to 70 million. China's 76 per cent of total egg comes from rural backyard production. India requires both mass production as well as production by masses, if it wish to supercede China.

Egg Scenario

India produces 3.6 per cent of global egg production, i.e., 61 million tons. The annual growth rate of egg is 5 per cent to 8 per cent. India has the lowest cost of egg production in the world at 2.55 US cents per egg.

Value-added Products

The introduction of new poultry products and perceptible shift in eating habits are moving people to branded food such as chicken yummiez, cold cuts, breaded and coated snacks, marinated snacks, chicken nuggets, canned chicken curry, freeze dried chicken pulao, meat soup, powder omlette and scrambled egg mixtures, sandwich, pizza, burger and dial-a-chicken and fast food joints, Kentucky Fried Chicken (KFC), McDonald's, Wimpy, Pizza Hut all these are going to change the palatability of the chicken consumer.

Medical Uses

Chicken eggs are used to produce source of molecules to treat snakebite. Duck embryos are used in manufacturing anti-rabies vaccine. Diet eggs or designer eggs are going to boost special eggs for vitamin E substitution, Omega fatty acids and antioxidant requirements. Poultry eggs and meat have got sensorial, curative, nutritive and therapeutic potential. Poultry is labour-intensive and has a potential to create 25,000 more jobs on the consumption of one more egg per capita and similarly 25,000 additional jobs on the consumption of 100 gm more chicken meat.

By the year 2010, India is expected to produce 260 million layers (77700 million eggs) and 3500 million broilers (5.9 million tons). Per capita consumption of meat will be around 3.5 to 4.5 kg and eggs will be around 65 and it is expected to contribute ₹ 60,000 crore. No agriculture sector is growing as fast as the Indian poultry, making it the most dynamic rapidly emerging sector of livestock economy.

The export of poultry meat at present is worth ₹ 150 crore and is expected to reach ₹ 1,500 crore by 2010. Indian agriculture contributes 28 per cent to the GDP of which 17 per cent is contributed by poultry. Poultry is the only industry where modern technology co-exists with the traditional poultry keeping because poultry technology is appropriate, adaptable, accessible, available and affordable both for the rich and the poor.

Recent Positive Developments of Poultry Industry

- NABARD has committed to bring about rural prosperity through poultry.
- Meeting of sub-group of poultry has asked for funds of ₹ 1095 crore for poultry development during the 11th Plan and ₹ 30,000 crore for the entire livestock sector under various schemes of the Government of India.
- India has resumed egg export.
- IFC (Washington based International Finance Corporation) picked up stake in Suguna Poultry Farms. Suguna Poultry paves the way for North Indian expansion and introduces dial-a-chicken concept to promote value-added products. Thousands of broiler farmers will reap the benefit.
- Venkateswara Hatcheries has decided to use tennis to promote their brand Venky's.
- Poultry farmers to get maize on concessional rate to use it as feed in poultry.
- Kerala Livestock Development Board chalked out plan for poultry tourism in Munnar.
- Poultry litter to fetch carbon credit in Andhra Pradesh with 3.5 mw power plant.
- Godrej Agrovet Ltd. introduced wide range of processed chicken in the brand name of Godrej Real Good Chicken.

The poultry production and consumption in the domestic market is slated to grow. Indian poultry industry has been a major contributor to the food processing sector in the country. From backyard activity to major commercial operation, the poultry sector has undergone a paradigm shift.

Indian poultry industry has been growing at annual varying rates of 8-15 per cent and this growth in the past few decades made India fifth largest producer of eggs and ninth largest producer of poultry broiler. At present, the industry is estimated at over ₹ 30,000 crore and is expected to grow over ₹ 60,000 crore by 2010.

India produces 1,400 million chickens a year, which is close to 27 million a week, of which 95 per cent is traded alive. According to a market report, the poultry production and consumption in the domestic markets is slated to grow by 66 per cent to approximately 2.3 million tons by 2010.

Poultry sector is one of the fastest growing industries of the Indian economy than any other sector contributing about $230 million to the Gross National Product. But in statistical terms, the industry has reported a loss of over ₹ 4,000 crore as an aftermath effect of the bird flu crisis.

The contribution of the small rural farmers points out the importance of integration of the poultry farming and the allied sector. Suguna Poultry Farm is the pioneer in poultry integration and contract poultry farming in India, with presence in nine states and membership of about 15,000 contract farmers. Suguna has set an example of integration and contract farming before the industry and has proved to be beneficial for the company. Integration could be the way forward for the entire industry towards expansion and success.

Presently, 100 per cent Foreign Direct Investment (FDI) is permitted in the food processing sector. Also FDI in food retailing, covering dairy, poultry, marine, vegetables and fruits might help the entire food processing industry grow. Poultry farming in India has transformed from a mere tool of supplementary income and nutritious food for the family to the major commercial activity generating the required revenue. The growth of the industry with steady production of 1,800 million kg of poultry meat, 40 billion egg per year and employment generation of about 3 million people indicates the future prospects for the industry. Changing food habits, rising income of the middle class Indian, presence of private players, rising market demand of the Indian poultry produce in the export market are some of the contributing factors to the growth of the industry.

MARKETING OF MEAT AND MEAT PRODUCTS

India ranks top in animal and cattle population. The meat and meat processing industry is still to come up. Some top players in the meat processing industry like Venkateswara Hatcheries, Godrej Agrovet, Vista Processed Food, Al Kabeer, Allanasons etc., with modern state-of-the-art slaughter and processing plants, have changed the entire scenario, making the industry grow at almost 10 per cent. There is a huge scope for expanding exports, especially in buffalo and poultry meat, eggs and dairy products.

The total meat production in India is about four million tons comprising poultry meat, beef, buffalo meat, mutton, goat meat, and pork. Beef and buffalo meat constitute 60 per cent of the total meat production. Production of poultry meat has grown at the rate of 13 per cent per annum from 1995 to 2003 to about 15,00,000 tons. Buffalo meat is the most important item in the meat industry with a production of about 1.9 MT of which 21 per cent is exported – the maximum share in meat exports from India.

Indian buffalo exports has the potential to grow significantly as it has a good demand in the international market. Mutton and lamb have lesser demand and growth potential. Poultry meat is also important and achieving high growth rate in the private sector. Future demand in meat products may include rabbit, turkey, domestic quail and emu.

A license is required under Meat Food Products Order (MFPO), 1973 for processing meat and this has been implemented by the Ministry of Food Processing Industries (MFPI) with effect from 14 May 2004. This is in line with the objectives of the Ministry's Food Processing Order, 1973, i.e., to regulate the production and sale of meat products through:

- Compulsory licensing for manufacturers enforcing hygienic and sanitary conditions prescribed for the production and processing of wholesome meat products.
- Ensuring strict quality control at all stages of production for meat products — including chilled poultry, fish products etc.

The Ministry of Food Processing Industry (MFPI) is also providing financial assistance by way of grant-in-aid to develop necessary infrastructure for the processing of meat and meat food products for the domestic as well as export/international market. In 2006-07, MFPI assisted seven projects for the manufacture of meat and meat food products.

The major players in the organzed sector of this segment are Allans (Buffalo), Venky's India Limited (poultry products), Sibaco (buffalo), Fatco (buffalo) Al-Kabeer (buffalo, sheep and goat), PML (buffalo), CDF (pork and others), APSMPC (pork), Pigpo, (pork) and MAFCO (pork).

There is an urgent need to frame a right strategy for the development of meat and poultry production in the country. This will certainly bring prosperity to millions of our rural citizens and create employment in rural India. Having achieved the Green Revolution, the White Revolution and the Blue Revolution, there is a question "Can the Pink Revolution be far behind?" Certainly this will require large investment in infrastructure, mainly in cold storages, and modern meat processing plants. Without a strong and dependable cold chain, a vital sector like meat industry, which is based mostly on perishable products, cannot survive and grow.

India ranks first in world buffalo population, with 56.5 per cent, i.e., 94.1 million of buffalo population and one-sixth of goat population in the world. India also ranks first in milk production with over 100 million tons a year. The country is also fifth in egg production with over 1.6 million tons, while it is ninth in the number of poultry. Though India tops in meat, milk and eggs production, exports are very low because of quality considerations.

The export of sheep and goat meat in terms of quantity is very small. Buffalo meat export is also not much appreciable due to lack of competitive advantage. Export is restricted to countries primarily in the Middle East, with large ethnic Indian population who prefer it. Poultry products export is also not quite good. According to APEDA, the export of buffalo meat was 343817.08 tons (value ₹ 1536.7 crore) in 2003-04, 337777.65 tons (value ₹ 1774.52 crore) in 2004-05 and 459937.63 tons (₹ 2629.57 crore) in 2005-06, 494111.48 tons(₹ 3211.70 crore) in 2006-07. The export of sheep/goat meat was 16820.53 tons (₹ 110.39 crore) in 2003-04, 9024.49 tons (₹ 81.27 crore) in 2004-05 and 7177.51 tons (₹ 80.37 crore) in 2005-06, 5481.55 tons (₹ 63.05 crore) in 2006-07. The processed meat export was 986.13 tons (₹ 7.63 crore) in 2003-04, 1359.7 tons (₹ 9.45 crore) in 2004-05 and 256.04 tons (value ₹ 2.43 crore) in 2005-06. The export of poultry products was 415228.17 tons (₹ 202.40 crore) in 2003-04, 277744.46 tons (₹ 160.79 crore) in 2004-05 and 145889 tons (₹ 167.58 crore) in 2005-06.

India produces an estimated 1.5 million tons of buffalo meat annually, of which 24 per cent is exported. Even as per the latest census of 2003, there was a growth of 7.5 per cent of buffalo livestock during the previous five years. The buffalo meat export industry has grown well. The potential for rapid growth is high, particularly if a specific time-bound plan of action between the various wings of the government and the meat export industry is drawn up. Since the growth of buffalo meat for domestic consumption is low (less than 2 per cent), the potential for export increases substantially.

India's poultry product exports are mainly confined to eggs and egg powder, which are growing due to cost competitiveness and logistical advantages. Poultry meat exports are negligible due to high costs, inadequate meat processing facilities and infrastructure bottlenecks. In recent years, some South India-based integrators have been exploring the possibility of exporting poultry meat to the Middle East and South-East Asian markets.

There are no restrictions on exports of poultry and poultry products. The government provides some transportation subsidies (₹ 3-15 per kg) for its exports. There are a number of issues that need to be addressed to fructify and ensure the growth for the current markets, industry sources expressed.

For the development of meat export from India, the industry has demanded some immediate measures like financial assistance for upgradation of export oriented abattoirs/processing plants; inclusion of buffalo meat under APEDA's Transport Assistance Scheme for new markets in Africa/CIS where freight cost from India for reefer containers is much higher than from competing countries. Restoration of DEPB rates for frozen buffalo meat and exemption from Service Tax on transportation of meat products processed for exports. This is presently applicable only for fruits, vegetables, eggs or milk even for domestic consumption.

Since 1995, production of meat and meat products has been steadily growing at a rate of 4 per cent p.a. Currently, the processing level of buffalo meat is estimated at 21 per cent, poultry 6 per cent and marine products 8 per cent. Only about 1 per cent of the total meat is converted into value-added products like sausages, ham, bacon, kababs, meatballs, etc. Production of meat is governed under local by-laws as slaughtering is a state subject. Processing of meat is licensed under the Meat Food Products Order, 1973.

In 2003 India had a livestock population of 470 million that included 205 million cattle and 90 million buffaloes. The country produces about 450 million broilers and 30 billion eggs annually. Cattle, buffaloes, sheep and goat, pigs and poultry are the types of animals, which are generally used for production of meat. Slaughter rate for cattle as a whole is 20 per cent, for buffaloes it is 41 per cent, pigs 99 per cent, sheeps 30 per cent and 40 per cent for goats. The country has 3,600 slaughterhouses, 9 modern abattoirs and 171 meat-processing units licensed under the meat products order.

The poultry industry is among the faster growing sectors rising at a rate of 8 per cent per year. Vertical integration of poultry production and marketing has lowered costs of production, marketing margins and consumer prices of poultry meat. There are eight integrated poultry processing units in the country, which hold a significant share in the industry.

	2001-02		2004-05		CAGR	
	Quantity	**Value**	**Quantity**	**Value**	**Quantity**	**Value**
Buffalo meat	243356	11444	306971	16156	8.0	12.2
Sheep/Goat meat	3915	331	8885	794	31.4	33.9
Poultry Production	19876	1301	264608	1541	137.0	5.8
Animal Casings	464	96	552	126	6.0	9.3
Processed Meat	267	13	107	16	-26.2	6.5
Total	267878	13185	581123	18633	29.5	12.2

Source: Ministry of Food Processing Industries, Annual Report 2007-08 to be compiled

Meat exports have been growing at close to 30 per cent per annum in terms of quantity, which is largely driven by poultry, buffalo, sheep and goat meat. Exports of value-added meat products are insignificant. In the domestic market, the growing number of fast food outlets in the country has had a significant impact on the meat processing industry.

WOOL

India's annual production of wool is about 45 million kg from sheep population of 52 million. India is the world's seventh largest producer of raw wool with 4.2 per cent of total sheep population and only 1.8 per cent of production facilities, which shows the low productivity (0.8 kg/sheep/year) of wool in India. The major wool producing states are Rajasthan, Jammu and Kashmir, Karnataka, Gujarat, Uttar Pradesh, Uttarakhand, Andhra Pradesh, and Haryana. The features of the wool market in India as under:

The wool industry in India is concentrated mainly in Punjab (40 per cent), Haryana (27 per cent), Rajasthan (10 per cent) and rest (23 per cent) is contributed by other states. This industry is spread evenly in the rural and urban areas and can broadly be divided into the organized and unorganized sectors.

Wool pricing depends on the quality of wool which is indicated by its staple length, fiber length, mean fiber diameter (micro value) luster, region and color. These are the major factors which govern the wool price.

Woollen products that are exported from India are RMG wool, woollen yarn, fabrics, and made-up. The export of woollens from India is increasing at about of 20 per cent per annum.

As the production of fine apparel grade wool is not enough in India, a large quantity of wool is imported from Australia, New Zealand, China, the Middle East and other countries.

China is the largest importer of raw wool followed by India and Italy.

The price and quantity are agreed upon between the buyer and seller through the intervention of indenting agents or directly from the importing country.

Woollen products in India are woollen tops, woolen yarn, worsted yarn, woollen worsted fabric, shoddy yarn, blankets, fabric, knitted goods, hand-made carpets, etc.

Other Products

Hide and skins are other products from livestock which are in good demand especially in foreign markets.

MARKETING OF FOOD PROCESSING PRODUCTS

Food processing adds value to agricultural farm producer by the increasing shelf life and or by changing the form of the produce. This includes grading, sorting, packaging and processing etc. India is the largest producer of milk, second largest producer of fruit and vegetables and third largest producer of foodgrains in the world. Only 2 per cent of fruits and vegetables, 26 per cent of marine produce, 6 per cent of poultry and 20 per cent of buffalo meat is processed.

India contributes a meager 1.5 per cent of the international food trade. There is huge scope of investment in this sector. There is immense scope of investment in this sector through massive investment and government support to improve the vital linkages and synergies between agriculture and industry which can be instrumental in increasing processing and value addition in food products.

India is the largest producer of food in the world, furthermore due to its diverse agro-climatic conditions, huge talent pool, large untapped markets with more than one billion consumers, increasing income levels with high spending on food items changing tastes and preference with changing lifestyle there is immense potential of investment in the food processing sector.

The strategies issues that require more efforts in the future are:

- Fiscal relief and incentives.
- Infrastructural development and improvement in agricultural supply chain, logistics and communication.
- Promotion of organized retailing with more investment especially in the private sector.
- Strengthening development and regulation for food safety.

Government Support:

To facilitate the growth of food processing industry, the government has taken various steps to increase value addition of food products that will result in minimizing of wastage. The policy initiatives taken by the government to support the processing of fruits and vegetables are:

- After economic liberalization, processing of food items has been exempted from licensing, except for alcoholic beverages and those reserved for the small-scale sector.
- The food processing sector has been given priority in lending by the government. NABARD refinances lending for agro-processing infrastructure and market development with a corpus of ₹ 1000 crore.
- Except alcohol beer and other items reserved for the small-scale sector subject to certain conditions, foreign equity up to 100 per cent is approved automatically for most processed food items.

- Since the budget of 2001-02, excise duty on processed fruits and vegetables has been exempted this was earlier 16 per cent.
- In the budget of 2004-05, tax holidays had been announced for certain sectors of the food processing industry.
- Excise duty has been waived on ice-cream, condensed milk, preparation of meat, fish and poultry, pudding, pasta, and yeast in the budget for 2006-07. On ready-to-eat packaged foods and instant food mixes, the excise duty has been reduced from 16 per cent to 18 per cent.
- Agro-based units can be established in special economic zones and agro-based 100 per cent EOUs are allowed to sell 50 per cent of their produce in domestic tariff areas, and import of capital goods and raw materials for such units is permitted without any import duty.
- The National Institute of Food Technology Entrepreneurship and Management has been set up by the Government to help the entrepreneurs in this field.
- Customs duty on the import of packaging machines has also been reduced from 15 per cent to 5 per cent.
- Excise duty on ready-to-eat packaged foods and instant food mixes like dosa and idli mixes has also been reduced to 8 per cent from 16 per cent.

Vision 2015 released in 2003-04 and adopted by the Ministry of Food Processing industries with expected investment of USD $24 billion envisages:

- Trebling the size of processed food sector to reach USD $300 billion by 2015.
- Increasing the level of processing of perishables from 6 per cent to 20 per cent.
- Value addition to increase from 20 per cent to 35 per cent.
- Share in the global food trade to increase from 1.5 per cent to 3 per cent.
- Increase in the share of value-added products in food consumption from the current 16 per cent to 50 per cent.

Current Trends:

1. Processing of cereals is restricted mainly to wheat and rice and the private sector companies doing well in this segment are ITC, HUL, and Cargill.
2. Among non-vegetarian items, poultry and meat are growing very fast in the organized private segment.
3. Fruit and vegetable products that are likely to see high growth in the future include pickles, fruits pulps, canned and frozen fruits and vegetables.
4. Retailing in the sale of food items is gaining momentum at a fast pace, and is estimated to grow at an annual rate of 490 per cent in the near future. This sector has attracted the attention of various Indian corporates who have already started business in this segment, viz., ITC, Bharti, Reliance, Aditya Birla Group, Subiksha and the Futures Group.

5. Organized food retailing will result in increasing awareness of farmers towards understanding consumers' demands, increased investment in infrastructures and consolidation of activities at central levels.
6. Efforts are on to increase the size of businesses to achieve economies of scale, as competition in future is going to be stiff. In this direction, some mergers have taken place and there is the possibility of many more in future. MNCs may merge/start working with Indian players by merging for specific operations. Hershey's has acquired 51 per cent stake in Godrej Foods and Beverages, Indian Hotels has acquired Amalgam Foods, Field Fresh is Bharti Group's 50-50) joint venture with Rothschild and ITC is developing its e-Choupal model for agricultural sourcing for other retailers.

While MNCs had opted for the inorganic route to enter the Indian market, others such as Danone, Fonterra and Pillsbury have preferred to enter the market organically.

A study by Federation of Indian Chambers of Commerce and Industry (FICCI) on the food and beverages market indicates that the segments which are expected to get high growths include branded flour (16 per cent), bakery products (11 per cent), biscuits (16 per cent), fruit juices, pulp and concentrates (18 per cent) and sauces/ketchups. Segments such as semi-processed/cooked ready-to-eat, ice-cream and wine products are expected to register higher growth rates.

Also India has the highest number of plans approved by the US Food and Drug Administration (FDA) outside the USA.

SUMMARY

The dairy industry in India is dominated by major players who play their key role in the cooperative sector. About 60 per cent of the installed processing capacity in the dairy products are available in the cooperative sector.

The National Dairy Development Board (NDDB) is a major player in the market with its major brand, Amul. Leading brands like Amul, Nestle, Mother Dairy and Britannia are in the race to tap the growing market.

SmithKline Beecham Consumer Healthcare, Nestlé India and Heinz India are amongst the large MNCs that dominate the high-value milk products market. Other players include Indiana Dairy Specialties, Jagatjit Industries Ltd. and various other state co-operatives.

Some dairy plants have production of mithais on a commercial scale. Some national brands like Haldiram, Bikanervala, K. C. Das, Chitales, Ganguram, Brijwasi, Agarwal Sweets etc. are getting wide acceptance because of consistent quality. Encouraged, by the growing market and cashing on brand value, select dairy companies are planning major expansion plans in various cities with new brands suited to local taste and preferences and realizing higher prices with higher sales volumes and product safety.

The milk and dairy products segment is set for upgradation of coldstorage chains for expansion. Mother Dairy, a wholly owned subsidiary of National Dairy Development Board plans to make strong presence in the market of milk and milk products under the Mother Dairy brand through retail outlets across the country in addition to its own 300 outlets with provision of cold storage and cold chains. In addition, there are areas where major thrust is required on following:

QUESTIONS

1. Who are the major players in Indian dairy industry?
2. List out different products produced by dairy industry and its value-added products.
3. List out the problems of Indian silk industry.
4. What are the process involved in marketing of Indian silk in this era of utter competition?
5. For what purpose the regulatory body Indian Central Silk Board formed?
6. What are the functions of Marine Products Exports Development Authority (MPEDA)?
7. How do you distinguish between organized retailing in fishing trade and how it differs from E-choupals and Aqua-choupals.

CHAPTER 23

MAJOR PLAYERS IN THE FOOD INDUSTRY

- Major Players in the Food Industry
- Marketing of Processed Food Products
- Products of Fresh Food Grains
- Marketing of Rice/Wheat/Maize/Barley/ Pulses
- Marketing of Edible Oils
- Marketing of Products from Fruits and Vegetables Processing
- Marketing of Spices
- Guidelines for Setting up of Units
- Minimum Requirement of Equipment and Machinery for Unit Operation
- Constraints and Drivers for Growth of Units
- Government's Incentives
- Retail in Food Processing
- Concept of Stress in Marketing
- Incentives to Corporates
- India's Untapped Marketing Potential
- Indianization of Food Processed Products
- Marketing of Milk and Dairy Products
- Investments Scenario
- Major Players in Marketing of Milk and Milk Products
- Retail Sector Pushes for Reforms in Food Processing
- Eleventh Five Year Plan Strategy
- Priority Area for Government's Intervention
- Recently Drafted Food/Banking Policy 1992
- Government's Policies and Taxation
- Initiatives for Export Promotion
- Fiscal incentives (Tax R414elief) for Food Processing Sector

Major Players in Indian Food Industry

Category	Total Size (₹. Cr)	Key Players
Edible Oils	12,000	Adani Wilmar, Ruchi Soya, Marico, Cargill Agro Tech Foods, ITC, Godrej Foods, NDDB, Markfed, Bunge
Tea	8,000	Hindustan Unilever Ltd., Tata Tea, Mcleod Russel
Bakery Products	8,000	Parle, Britania, ITC, Kellogs
Poultry	7,500	Venky's (India) Godrej, Agrovet, Vista
Branded Sugar	7,000	Triveni, Balrampur Chini, EID Parry, Bajaj Hindustan
Dairy Products	5,000	Amul, Nestle India, GalxoSmith, CHL Hatson Agro, NDDB, Mother dairy, Dynamix
Health Drinks	1,100	Nestle India, Dabur, Rasna, Heinz, GlaxoSmithkline, Amul
Culinary/Ready-to-eat Foods	2,500	MTR, Nestle India, Hindustan Unilever ITC, McCain
Branded Rice	2,000	Satnam Overseas, LT Overseas, KRBL, Lakshmi Energy, REI Agro, Amira Foods
Coffee	1,000	Hindustan Unilever, Tata Coffee, CCL, Products.
Branded Atta	500	ITC, Pilsbury, Hindustan Unilever.

Source: Article authored by Bhattacharya A. (2006) under the title "Food for Thought" appeared in Economic Times, 10-16 July 2006 and Hindu Business Line, 18 July 2006.

Food Processing Categories (Plant and Livestock Products)

1. Grain processing
2. Edible oils
3. Fruits and vegetable processing
4. Spices
5. Meat and meat processing
6. Dairy processing

MARKETING OF PROCESSED FOOD PRODUCTS

Processing of agricultural outputs is undertaken in organized as well as unorganized sectors, procuring grains either from wholesalers or directly from the producers. Direct purchase by corporates from producers is increasing through contract farming for their specific types of requirements either for processing or for exports.

PRODUCTS FROM FOODGRAINS

Grain processing is the largest segment in the food processing industry. Some of the important grains used for processing are discussed in the following sections.

Rice: Rice is the most important cereal in India. It is the most important foodgrain in the world also feeding about two-thirds of the world's population. Rice is processed from paddy and basmati variety of rice is usually sold in branded form with good packaging and advertising. It is the largest item of agricultural exports from India. Rice Bran oil, considered a healthy oil, is expected to see an increase in demand in the future.

It is the largest item of agricultural exports from India while rice bran oil considered healthy oil is expected to see an increase in demand in the future. It has good demand in Japan, Korea, and the US, where the consumers pay premium for this healthy edible oil. In India, edible oil producers are launching new brands by mixing rice bran oil with other oils, like sunflower oil, to enhance the health properties, and attracting a premium of ₹ 10 litre.

Wheat: Uttar Pradesh, Punjab, Haryana, Rajasthan, Madhya Pradesh, Gujarat and Bihar are major wheat growing states in India. Wheat and wheat flour are an important component of India's food industry. Other important processed items made of wheat are bread (₹ 38.9 billion), biscuits (₹ 13.5 billion) and pasta products (₹ 8.4 billion) contributing a total of ₹ 158.4 billion. Britannia and Modern Food Industries Limited are the only big players in the bread industry, while there are twenty-five medium and 1800 small-scale manufacturers. The industry has been fixed for the small-scale sector in 1977.

Maize: After rice and wheat, it is the maize which is the third most important crop in India, and is grown in twenty-three states. It is an important source for a large number of processed food products such as corn floor, sweet corn, baby corn, popcorn, starch, corn oil and feed for animals, and has good potential for export in different processed forms.

Barley: Barley, a hardy plant is grown mainly in Rajasthan, Madhya Pradesh, Andhra Pradesh, Orissa and Gujarat. It is widely used in the wine industry.

Pulses: India is the largest producer of pulses in the world. It is very important group for nutritional security and also important because of the fact that these crops can be grown on relatively less fertile land and with less irrigation facilities.

EDIBLE OILS

Edible oils are produced from groundnut, rapeseed, mustard, sunflower, safflower, coconut and palm. Edible oils are an important part of food processing industry in India, contributing ₹ 12,000 crore every year.

The processing for edible oil is done in local or cooperative mills or presses or by the corporate sector. Some of the corporate producing branded edible oils are Adani Wilmar, Ruchi Soya, Marico, ITC, Agro Tech, Cargill, NDDB Godrej Foods and Markfed.

PRODUCTS FROM FRUITS AND VEGETABLES

The installed capacity of the fruit and vegetable processing industry has more than doubled from 11.08 lakh tons in 1993 to 24.74 lakh tons in 2006, but still only about 2.20 per cent of the total production facility is used. Over the last few years, there has been considerable growth in the production of fruit juices and pulps, dehydrated and frozen vegetables and fruit items, soups, sauces, pickles, convenience veg-spice pastes, processed mushrooms and carried vegetables. Some important processed products from fruits and vegetables are:

- Tomato — Ketchup, paste, puree, powder
- Potato — Chips, flakes; dehydrated potato — French fries, slices etc.
- Green vegetables- Pickles, soup powder, dried and dehydrated vegetables, vegetable dyes
- Fruits — Jam, Jelly, Juice, Squash, cordial, slice, fruit bar, candy, vinegar.
- Mushroom — Processed and dried mushrooms

This sector is already an established one with many large players, yet there is much scope for development. The key players in the different categories of processed items of fruits and vegetables are as under:

Commodity	Annual Turnover (₹ in million) (Org + Unorg)	Key Players
Pickles	11,500	Nilon's Priya Desi, Praveen, Desai Bros., Cavin Care, GD Foods, Mother's Recipe
Potato Chips	5500	Pepsi
Sauce and Ketchup	5000	HUL, Mapro, Marico, Mala's
Juices/Fruit Drinks	5000	Dabur, Pepsi, Godrej, Parle, Mother Dairy
Squashes	4800	HUL, Haldiram, Mapro, Druk
Pulp/Concentrates	4000	Foods and Inns, BEC, Clean Foods, Jain Irrigations, Usha International
Jam	1300	HUL, Mapro, Marico, Mala's
Ready-to-Eat Veg.	1000	Tasty Bite, ITC, MTR, ADFC
Cooking Pastes	300	Dabur and HUL

Source: http: mofpi.nic.in/visdoc/volume2. PDF. Accessed in July 2006.

Spices:

Spices are important plant products that are extracted from various parts of the plant — bark, bud, flower, fruit, leaves, rhizome, root, stigma and style, or the entire plant top. These are used for taste, aroma, flavor, etc. In the food preparations, they are also used in ayurvedic medicines, cosmetics, perfumes, etc. Spices are used in fresh dried or ground form.

India is one of the largest producer and exporter of spices in the world. The annual production of spices in India is worth around USD $3 billion and contributes about 23 per cent to the worldwide trade in spices. In recent years, high growth in the exports of spices has opened the door for further development in spices processing. There is possibility of increasing the commercial production of oils and oleoresins of spices. It has a good demand in the export market and India meets 70 per cent of world's demand. Indian vanilla has huge potential and a significant share of Indian players can tap European markets. Ginger, turmeric and chilies are other important spices used extensively in Indian food.

GUIDELINES FOR SETTING UP OF UNIT UNDER FRUIT PRODUCTS ORDER

No person shall carry on the business of a manufacture of fruit products including synthetic syrups, synthetic vinegar and aerated sweetened beverages except under and in accordance with the terms of an effective licence granted to him under FPO.

Category-wise area requirement, annual production limit and licence fee for one terms or part thereof (Ref. Clause 5(2) and Part I(B) of the Second Schedule of Fruit Products Order, 1955)

Category	For Manufacturing Premises (in Sq. metres)	For Storage and Office Purpose (in sq. metres)	Licence Fees for One Term or Part Thereof	Annual Production Permissible per Calendar Year
Home scale 'B'	25	25	₹ 100/-	Upto 10 MT
Cottage scale	60	60	₹ 250/-	Above 10 MT but less than 50 MT.
Small scale 'A'	100	100	₹ 400/-	Above 50 MT but less than 100 MT. with installed capacity not exceeding 1 MT/ day.
Small scale 'B'	150	150	₹ 600/-	Below 250 MT with installed capacity not exceeding 2 MT per day.
Large scale	300	300	₹ 1500/	Above 250 MT with installed capacity exceeding 2 MT per day.

Note: 1. Area occupied by machinery shall not be more than 50 per cent of the manufacturing area.

2. The minimum height of the factory premises under Home Scale 'B' and Cottage Scale categories is 10 feet and for small-scale and large-scale categories 14 feet. Every manufacturer shall manufacture fruit products in conformity with the sanitary requirements and appropriate standards of quality and composition specified in the Second Schedule of FPO.

The Second Schedule

Part 1 (a): Sanitary requirements of a factory of fruit products

1. The Premises shall be adequately lighted, ventilated and cleaned by white washing/colour washing or oil painting.
2. Windows and all openings shall be well screened with wire-mesh and the doors fitted with automatic closing springs, roof shall be permanent, floor cemented.

3. The equipments and the factory premises shall not be used for manufacture of repugnant products like fish, meat, eggs etc. However, permission may be granted as a special in case, if arrangements are made for disinfections of premises after changing from meat products to fruit products (one month idle gap will be required for changeover).
4. The premises shall be located in a sanitary place with open surroundings, preferably in industrial area/estates. The premises shall not be used as or communicated directly with residence.
5. Adequate arrangements for cleaning equipments, machinery, containers tables and raw materials shall be provided.
6. Copper brass or iron equipments, containers or vessels are not permitted, in the preparation, packing or storage of fruit products, only aluminum, stainless steel, glass or tins equipment are allowed.
7. The water used shall be potable and shall be got examined chemically and bacteriologic ally by a public Health Laboratory (if no municipal water is available at the premises). The water sample should be drawn for such examination by the Public Health Authority of the area where the premises is located or should be drawn in the presence of the above authority. Free following tap water of 1 kilolitre per day shall be made available.
8. Adequate drainage system and provisions for disposal of refuse shall be made.
9. Sufficient number of latrine and urinals shall be provided for workers.
10. Wherever cooking is done on open fire, proper outlets for so smoke/steam etc. like chimney, exhaust fan etc. shall be provided.
11. The workers engaged in the factory shall be healthy and shall be medically examined, inoculated and vaccinated whenever required.
12. The workers shall be provided with aprons, head-wears/gears, gloves etc. and shall be personally neat and tidy.

Part 1(B): Qualifications of technical staff

Production shall be supervised by a person possessing one of the following qualifications:

Small scale:

1. B.Sc. with Chemistry/Agriculture as one of the subjects.
2. A Diploma or a certificate in fruit preservation or a course of at least 3 months duration from a recognized institution.

Large Scale:

(1) B.Sc. (Tech.) with Food Technology/Chemical Engineering with at least one year experience in fruit preservation factory.

(2) B.Sc. with CFTRI Diploma or Diploma of Kalamassery (Kerala Government) Polytechnic.

(3) B.Sc. with Chemistry/Agriculture with three years experience in fruit preservation factory.

Minimum Equipments and Machinery for Unit Operation

1	Washing of raw materials	Rectangular tanks with spacious bottom of not less than 20 gallons capacity
2	Washing of bottles	(i) Tanks having not less than 40 gallons capacity. (ii) Bottle washing machine, brushes (*machine, rack, trolley). (iii) Buckets (*Sterlising tanks).
3	Preparation of Fruit/ Vegetable	(i) 2-1/2 Ft. high table with aluminium/steel top having area not less than 20 sq. ft. (ii) Not less than 12 trays. (iii) Stainless less steel knives. (iv) Equip instrument for blanching.
4	Juicing, pulping and mixing	(i) Juice extractor of basket press (*Pulping machine/ hydraulic press). (ii) Steet sieve. (iii) Vessels of not less than 100 litres capacity.
5	Processing	(i) Furnace/Gas stoves (* Boiler) (ii) Vessels/Steam jacket kettle. (iii) Ladle. (iv) Thermometer, hydrometer (Refractometer). (v) Sensitive balance for weighing chemicals, colour etc.
6	Fermentation	(i) Barrels/Carboys/Earthen jars.
7	Filling and sealing	(ii) Mugs/Funnels (* Filling machine). (ii) Crown cork machine/R.O. sealing machine. (iii) Weighing balance.
8	Exhausting, processing for cans and bottles	(i) Tanks with crates/Exhaust Box. (ii) Double Seamer/Semi-automatic can sealer. (iii) Cooling tanks with crates/cranes. (iv) Pressure cooker/retorts/sterilizing equipments. (v) Incubator/pressure-cum-tester. (vi) *Pasteurizer.
9	Carbonation or aeration	(i) Power driver aerated machine or semi-automatic aerating and sealing machine.

CONSTRAINTS AND DRIVERS OF GROWTH

Changing lifestyles, food habits, organized food retail and urbanization are the key factors for processed foods in India, these are post-liberalization trends and they give boost to the sector.

There has been a notable change in consumption pattern in India. Unlike earlier, now the share and growth rates for fruits, vegetables, meats and dairy have gone higher compared to cereals and pulses.

Such a shift implies a need to diversify the food production base to match the changing consumption preferences.

Also in developed countries, it has been observed that there has been a shift from carbohydrate staple to animal sources and sugar. Going by this pattern, in future, there will be demand for prepared meals, snack foods and convenience foods and further on the demand would shift towards functional, organic and diet foods.

Key Constraints in Food Processing Industry:

- Poor infrastructure in terms of cold storage, warehousing, etc.
- Inadequate quality control and testing infrastructure
- Inefficient supply chain and involvement of middlemen
- High transportation and inventory carrying cost
- Affordability, cultural and regional preference of fresh food
- High taxation
- High packaging cost

Government's Incentives:

- Formulation of the National Food Processing Policy
- Complete delicensing, excluding for alcoholic beverages
- Declared as priority sector for lending in 1999
- 100 per cent FDI on automatic route
- Excise duty waived on fruits and vegetables processing from 2000-01
- Income tax holiday for fruits and vegetables processing from 2004-05
- Customs duty reduced on freezer van from 20 per cent to 10 per cent from 2005-06
- Implementation of Fruit Products Order
- Implementation of Meat Food Products Order
- Enactment of FSS Bill 2005
- Food Safety and Standards Bill, 2005

Apart from these Initiatives, the Centre has Requested State Governments to Undertake the Following Reforms:

- Amendment to the APMC Act
- Lowering of VAT rates
- Declaring the industry as seasonal
- Integrate the promotional structure

SWOT Analysis of FoodProcessing Industry

Strengths

- Abundant availability of raw material
- Priority sector status for agro-processing given by the Central Government
- Vast network of manufacturing facilities all over the country
- Vast domestic market

Weaknesses

- Low availability of adequate infrastructural facilities
- Lack of adequate quality control and testing methods as per international standards
- Inefficient supply chain due to a large number of intermediaries
- High requirement of working capital.
- Inadequately developed linkages between R&D labs and industry
- Seasonality of raw material

Opportunities

- Large crop and material base offering a vast potential for agro-processing activities
- Setting of SEZ/AEZ and food parks for providing added incentive to develop greenfield projects
- Rising income levels and changing consumption patterns
- Favourable demographic profile and changing lifestyles
- Integration of development in contemporary technologies such as electronics, material science, biotechnology etc. offer vast scope for rapid improvement and progress
- Opening of global markets

Threats

- Affordability and cultural preferences of fresh food
- High inventory carrying cost
- High taxation
- High packaging cost

RETAIL IN FOOD PROCESSING

The size of the Indian urban food market is estimated at ₹ 350,000 crore. The domestic market for processed food is huge and fast growing. The retail boom will create a huge demand for the food processing sector in the coming years. Little wonder that 2007 has been designated the 'Year of Food Technology'.

The private sector is yet to realize its full potential in the food retailing sector, as the market is still to explore. Though it has now started discovering the money, there is to be made in the urban food retailing market.

Assured Market

Urban centres have the potential of development process. But they do not produce food as they lack agricultural land; on contrary the rural areas do. In that sense, the urban areas provide an assured market for the food produced by farmers. The urban food marketing system thus assumes considerable importance for both feeding the urban population and helping farmers.

There are certain distinct characteristics of urban food demand. The urban population generally has a higher purchasing power. The rising average income is leading to greater demand for high-value processed food. A considerable number of urban women work, creating a demand for heat-and-serve foods.

The urban population density is high and this demands a chain or a network of retail outlets. Indian food retailing is poised for a quantum leap. Not only are newer names set to dot the retail landscape but also such new formats, as hypermarkets and supermarkets are to emerge.

The key drivers for increased demand in value-added processed food products are (a) growth in consumer class; (b) change in lifestyle characterized by expanding urban population, increased number of nuclear and dual income families; (c) change in attitudes and tastes with increasing modernization and to a lesser extent westernization of tastes, particularly, of the youth; (d) low penetration rates; and (e) ability to offset seasonal supply-and-demand effects in fresh products.

It has been estimated that during the Eleventh Plan period, an investment of ₹ 1 lakh-crore is expected in the food processing sector. Realizing the need for a regulatory framework for the retailing sector, the government has merged 16 laws relating to the food processing sector into one piece of legislation and this is expected to be put in place from the 2007-08 financial years.

Stress on Marketing

To tap into the huge market for processed foods, an efficient marketing system is necessary to bring about demand-driven production; marketing becomes the key to catalyzing agricultural development and with that fostering inclusive growth. Besides, it reduces intermediaries, increases farmers' realization and lowers consumer prices.

An efficient marketing system can reduce post-harvest losses, promote graded processing, packaging services and food safety practices, induce demand-driven production, enable high value addition and facilitate exports. Marketing reforms are needed, as they are critical to development of the potential urban food demand. The National Commission on Farmers, headed by Dr. M.S. Swaminathan, has suggested encouraging public-private partnership besides encouraging private sector investments to tap this huge potential.

At present, there are 7,521 regulated markets. Most of these lack critical infrastructure. Therefore, massive investment is needed to provide critical agricultural marketing infrastructure. It is estimated that at least ₹ 12,234 crore is needed for the regulated markets. Initiative has to be taken to promote public-private partnerships as they ensure efficient resource utilization and better management practices. There are many examples of successful public-private partnerships. Safal market in Karnataka is an instance of the modernization of wholesale markets. ITC's e-Chaupal, Haryali Kisan Bazaar, Mahindra Subh Labh, Cargil Farmgate Business and Tata Kisan Sansar are all initiatives of marketing distribution in the PPP format. Besides, commodity exchanges and futures markets have come up in the form of National Commodity and Derivative Exchange Ltd. (NCDEX) and Multi-Commodity Exchange Limited (MCX).

Incentives to Corporates

To encourage the private sector to make investments in marketing infrastructure on the required scale, a favourable regulatory environment needs to be created so as to attract large corporates.

This would include: (a) liberalized credit norms to entrepreneurs for agricultural marketing activities; (b) changes in the market regulatory framework to allow private entrepreneurs establish market yards and other regulatory facilities; (c) changes in the cooperative laws to allow farmers' cooperatives to work along corporate lines and compete with private trade; (d) review of several legal instruments to facilitate the entry of entrepreneurs in marketing activities; and (e) provisions to allow private entrepreneurs to cover price and yield risks for farmers.

The emergence of organized retailing in recent years and the creation of quality retail space have led to an increased demand for quality produce and thereby investments in supply chain infrastructure by private players.

Reliance Initiative

A visit to the fruits and vegetables stores of a leading corporate would reveal the depth and width of the market for processed foods. In fact, the company opened more than 17 such stores in one city alone. The company also plans to enter into agri-horticulture and the processed food sector. Subsequently, a subsidiary is to market agri-horticultural products across the country. Conceptually, the company is creating a virtuous circle of prosperity by bringing farmers and consumers together in a win-win partnership.

The retail business should partner with farmers, logistics operators and traders to enhance their purchasing power. A supply chain, logistics and information technology infrastructure would string the whole plan together.

Evolving System

It has taken some time but finally it seems that the evolution of organized retailing in food products is on in India. Many retail start-ups promised a lot. But failed. Through trial and error, a sustainable business model is evolving. A significant number of new businesses are poised for a major surge.

Notably, private investments in marketing of processed food for urban centres have reached the inflection point with several large corporates beginning to invest significantly. Each of these retail businesses has created a sustainable model of its own. In fact, each has developed a model unique to the Indian context. The entry of large business conglomerates is likely to attract greater investments and create a cascading effect across the SME segment of the food and agri-space.

The coming age for retailers in the organized retail sector augurs well for both consumers and farmers in India.

India's Potential Untapped

India is the world's second largest producer of food next to China, and has the potential of being the biggest with the food and agricultural sector. The processing food segment accounts for 29.4 billion, in a total estimated food market of about USD 91.7 billion. The food processing industry is one of the largest industries in India. It currently ranks fifth in terms of production, consumption, export and growth prospects.

The Confederation of Indian Industry (CII) has estimated that the food processing sector has the potential of attracting USD 33 billion of investment in 10 years and generates employment for about 9 million unemployed population. The Government has formulated and implemented several Plan Schemes to provide financial assistance for setting up and modernizing food processing units, creation of infrastructure, support for research and development and human resource development in addition to other promotional measures to encourage the growth of the processed food sector.

Though the industry is large in size, it is still at a nascent stage in terms of development. Of the country's total agriculture and food produce, only 2 per cent is processed. The highest share of processed food is in the dairy sector, where 37 per cent of the total produce is processed, of this only 15 per cent is processed by the organized sector.

India's food processing sector covers fruits and vegetables; meat and poultry; milk and milk products, alcoholic beverages, fisheries, plantation, grain processing and other consumer product groups like confectionery, chocolates and cocoa products, soya-based products, mineral water, high protein foods etc. We cover an exhaustive database of an array of suppliers, manufacturers, exporters and importers widely dealing in sectors like the food industry, dairy processing, Indian beverage industry etc. We also cover sectors like dairy plants, canning, bottling plants, packaging industries, process machinery etc.

The most promising sub-sectors includes soft-drink bottling, confectionery manufacture, fishing, aquaculture, grain-milling and grain-based products, meat and poultry processing, alcoholic beverages, milk processing, tomato paste, fast food, ready-to-eat breakfast cereals, food processing, food additives, flavours etc.

The Government of India has identified the Food Processing Industry sector as a high priority area. It has given a number of fiscal relief and incentives to encourage commercialization and value addition to agricultural produce. As per a study conducted by McKinsey and Confederation of Indian Industry (CII), the turnover of the total food market is approximately USD 69.4 billion out of which value-added food products comprise USD 22.2 billion.

The Government has also approved proposals for joint ventures; foreign collaboration, industrial licenses and 100 per cent export oriented units envisaging an investment of USD 4.80 billion during the same period. Out of this, foreign investment is over USD 18.2 billion.

India is also considering investing another USD 22.97 million in at least 10 mega food parks in the country. The move is besides working towards offering 100 per cent foreign direct investment and income-tax benefits to the sector. According to Indian Credit Rating Agency (ICRA), the processed food market accounts for 32 per cent of the total food market.

Indianization

International fast food brands spice up their plans of entering India. Many like UK brand Dixy Chicken and pizza outlet Papa John's made their foray recently, Cinnabon and Barnie's will open their first store this year and a host of other brands, including SumoSalad and Panda Express, are scouting for local partners to tempt the Indian palate.

Fast food retail chains such as KFC, McDonald's, Domino's, Pizza Hut and others are relearning marketing lessons and segmenting their product portfolio to capture Indian consumers across diverse income levels and lifestyles. The strategy is an attempt by some top retailers to tone up profit margins with a multi-layered product portfolio that addresses the aspirational need of consumers willing to splurge while meeting the basic requirement at the bottom-end.

With cut-throat competition to set up standalone outlets at busy marketplaces getting tougher, fast food chains have come up with a new recipe for success takeover and manage canteens across schools, colleges and corporate offices.

With global supermarket majors such as Wal-Mart, Tesco and Carrefour among others increasing sourcing of processed foods from the country, it makes monetary sense for local companies to enter/ expand in this arena. In fact, Food Processing Minister Subhodh Kant Sahai had said at the beginning of the year that foreign retail giants are willing to buy as much as USD 30 billion worth of processed food from the country.

Milk and Diary Products

This segment needs a special mentioning. India's milk and milk products output (milk equivalent) growth is set to outpace the growth in the global market. While world milk and milk products output is expected to grow by 2.6 per cent again in 2006, India is expected to register up to 4 per cent increase. The country will account for nearly half of the expected 5 per cent growth in Asia.

As the largest single dairy producing country in the world, India's output continues to grow strongly in the 3-4 per cent range, largely in response to internal demand growth and sustained by increasing productivity. India will account for nearly half the 226 million tons total milk output of Asia. Given recent high international prices, it has started to enter certain export markets, particularly for skimmed milk powder, and is expected to export 0.3 million ton dairy products of the total milk and milk products output of 98.9 million tons. In 2005, the country had produced 95.1 million tons of dairy products.

Amul is set to become the largest liquid milk brand in the world after the consolidation of Gujarat's milk cooperatives, which envisages bringing all district milk brands under the Amul umbrella brand. Until now, Amul's marketer GCMMF claims, it is Asia's largest milk brand.

The market of the Amul brand of liquid milk will increase by 3.6-3.8 million litre per day to 4.5-4.6 million litre a day, once the district-level milk brands are phased out. The market size for Amul milk will increase further by 200,000 litres if sales from liquid milk in paper box packs are also added to pouched milk sales.

"Meanwhile, the organized food retailing industry is likely to grow by 30 per cent in the next five years and become a USD 2.4 billion industry by 2010 from the current USD 562 million to USD 674 million", an industry expert said.

The country's seafood exports rose 11 per cent in dollar terms to USD 1.64 billion in 2005-06, helped by the increasing demand from the European Union, China and the West Asia. This is the first time seafood export from the country crossing the USD 1.5 billion mark. Last year, the exports stood at USD 1.47 billion.

Investments

The food processing sector needs investment of about USD 28-35 billion to meet the changing food demands in India, according to industry estimates. The outlay for the food processing segment has been increased from USD 19.5 million in 2004-05 to USD 41.4 million in the next year, more than twice the earlier amount.

Foreign direct investment (FDI) in the country's food sector is poised to hit the USD 3 billion mark. In the last one year alone, FDI approvals in food processing have doubled.

Add to this, the USD 55 million that has been invested in sugar and cooking oil companies, and you can see how the changing diet of upwardly mobile India along with the new mega food parks are becoming dishy to overseas investors. Foreign direct investment in food already beats the money being pumped into the far-more-glamorous hotels and tourism industry.

According to latest Industry Ministry data, the cumulative FDI inflow in food processing industry reached USD 2,804 million in March 2006. In 2005-06, the sector received approvals worth USD 41 million which shows this figure is almost double the USD 22 million as approved for 2004-2005 by Government of India.

"Foreign investors are keen in investing in the country. Recently, India has received an encouraging response from investors in the UK for establishing joint quality control testing facilities for agriculture products and establishing cold storage facilities in the country", Ministry of State for Food Processing Industries, Subodh Kant Sahai said.

Bon Appetit

The total food production in India is likely to double in the next ten years and there is an opportunity for large investments in food and food processing technologies, skills and equipment, especially in areas of Canning, Dairy and Food Processing, Specialty Processing, Packaging, Frozen Food and Refrigeration and Thermo Processing. Fruits and Vegetables, Fisheries, Milk and Milk Products, Meat and Poultry, Packaged/Convenience Foods, Alcoholic Beverages and Soft Drinks and Grains are important sub-sectors of the food processing industry. Health food and health food supplement is another rapidly rising segment of this industry, which is gaining vast popularity amongst the health conscious.

In a bid to remove constraints in the way of investments in the sector, the Ministry of Food Processing Industries (MoFPI) is set to push for creating a favourable fiscal environment to induce venture capital and mutual funds to invest in different components of supply chain or in the entire chain. This follows the recommendations of a Rabo Bank study commissioned by the Ministry to unlock investments to the tune of USD 33.4 billion in this sector over the next 10 years.

Since the sector offers immense growth potential, a large number of multinational companies (MNCs) have entered India to take advantage of the opportunity. Unilever, Nestle, Pepsi and Cadbury are some of the big, successful overseas players in India that face strife from established Indian brands.

According to a recently published report by RNCOS, Indian Food Processing (2006), "In next 3 years, the Indian food processing industry is anticipated to grow to 3 times its current size making India a key and consequential player in the food and agriculture trade. Despite being recognized as a promising growth area, the current share of Indian food processing market in the world food trade is only 2 per cent."

The food processing and bakery products sector has given the stock markets something to munch on. Stocks of major players in this slow-moving sector have been performing well on good corporate results, helpful economic conditions and good weather. Although thin margins will call for increased volumes for these companies to remain afloat two years down the line, the long-term prospects are still good because opened-up rural markets and an ever-expanding consumer base will ensure volumes.

Major Players

Godrej Foods, Reliance, Namdhari, ITC, Nestle, Ruchi Soya Industries, Tata Coffee, Tata Tea, RPG Group, Subhiksha.

Retail Sector Pushes for Reforms in Food Processing

According to The Times of India, New Delhi dated February 09, 2007, major players in the retail sector are pushing hard for abolition of or amendment to the Agricultural Produce Marketing Commission Act to speed up growth in the food processing industry, which is expected to bring in a major chunk of their moolah.

Global consultants, Dun & Bradstreet, last year estimated that India wastes roughly $13 billion worth of farm products, including dairy items, annually because of inadequate processing and cold storage facilities. A FICCI study now says that despite being the second-biggest food producer in the world after China, India's share in the $ 6.2 billion global processed food market stands at less than 1 per cent, leaving a huge scope for growth.

The study identifies the APMC Act as one of the major hurdles impeding growth as it does not allow processing units to store fruits or vegetables for more than a month. This hampers firms that deal in seasonal produce like mango or litchi. Noting that Bihar has led the growth strategy by abolishing the Act, and several other states are following suit, the study says the system of seeking licences for each item being prepared by the same unit should also be scrapped.

The study also suggests a 10-year tax holiday, excise relief, fiscal incentives for cold chain setups and a regulatory mechanism. Special incentives have been suggested for investors who enter all levels of processing industry in an integrated manner and for those providing one or more services. An excise exemption has also been sought on equipment and refrigerated trucks to attract investments and keep prices down.

Available data pegs Indian food exports in 1998 at $5.8 billion against a world total of $ 438 billion. At the start of 2000, the Indian food industry had a turnover of ₹ 140,000 crore. This indicates a vast scope for both investors and exporters. India processes only 2 per cent of the fruits and vegetables it produces annually.

ELEVENTH FIVE YEAR PLAN STRATEGY

While some of the schemes under Tenth Five Year Plan will continue during the Eleventh Five Year Plan, they need to be restructured with appropriate management/implementation arrangements in Public-Private Partnership mode, with strong Project Implementation capabilities. Also it is proposed to decentralize the Scheme for Technology Upgradation and operate it through Nodal Banks in place of State Nodal Agencies to provide back-ended credit linked subsidy. The new integrated approach not only addresses the issue of financial assistance but also the following issues:

- Skill development
- Entrepreneurship
- Investment
- Institutional Development

Providing a policy environment, that stimulates growth, the core elements of the proposed strategy are:

- Better project selection, development and implementation.
- Decentralized cluster based development, particularly for creation of infrastructure and fostering linkages to retail outlets.
- Industry-led capacity building and upgradation of standards and integrated food law and science based food standards.

Strategic intervention by government with redesigned schemes and strong implementation arrangements at the following points:

(i) Food Parks — carefully planned, cluster based, privately driven in poultry sector.

(ii) Abattoirs — publicly owned and privately managed,

(iii) Cold chains — integrated cold chain facilities and strategic distribution centres,

(iv) Street Food — upgrading quality and hygiene in the cities/towns,

(v) Wine Policy — liberalized, leveraging the agri/horticultural surpluses.

(vi) Testing and certification labs — both public and private.

Importantly, the Ministry has to be strengthened appropriately, to meet the challenges in implementing various new initiatives proposed for energizing the food processing sector in the country.

Priority Areas for Intervention

The priority areas identified for intervention therefore are:

- Infrastructure development
- The food park scheme is proposed to be modified into a scheme for an Integrated Food Zone/ Mega Food park
- Modernization of Abattoirs and setting up of National Meat Board
- Cold Chain, Value Addition and Preservation infrastructure (Cold storages, Reefer vans
- Irradiation Centres
- Research and development – Products, Technology, Quality and Skills
- Capacity Building – Human Resource Development, Research and Development, Quality, Safety, Related Infrastructure
- Implementation of Food Safety and Standards Act, 2006
- Establishment of NIFTEM
- Modernization of PPRC, Thanjayur into a National Crop Processing Center
- Upgrading safety and quality of street food and establishing food kiosks identified localities
- Wine Sector Development — Establishment of Wine Board

RECENTLY DRAFTED FINANCIAL/BANKING POLICIES

Food Processing: A Priority Sector

The following items within the food and agro-based processing sector would be eligible for classification as priority sector for lending by banks:

- Fruit and vegetable processing industry·
- Foodgrain milling industry
- Dairy products
- Processing of poultry and eggs, meat products
- Fish processing
- Bread, oilseeds, meals (edible), breakfast foods, biscuits, confectionery (including cocoa processing and chocolate), malt extract, protein isolate, high protein food, weaning food and extruded/other ready-to-eat food products
- Aerated water/soft drinks and other processed foods·
- Special packaging for food processing industries
- Technical assistance and advice to food processing industries

Based on the recommendations of an Internal Working Group, the Reserve Bank of India (RBI) has come out with revised guidelines on priority sector lending which take into account the revised definition of small and micro enterprises as per the Micro, Small and Medium Enterprises Development Act, 2006.

As per the revised guidelines, RBI will allow banks to include direct finance to companies for agriculture and allied activity of upto ₹ 1 crore as priority sector lending (PSL) exposure as against the earlier exposure of ₹ 20 lakh.

Direct finance to agriculture shall include short, medium and long term loans given for agriculture and allied activities (dairy, fishery, piggery, poultry, bee-keeping, etc.) directly to individual farmers, Self-help Groups (SHGs) or Joint Liability Groups (JLGs) of individual farmers without limit and to others (such as corporates, partnership firms and institutions) up to the limits indicated in Section I, for taking up agriculture/allied activities. Indirect finance to agriculture shall include loans given for agriculture and allied activities.

Direct finance to small enterprises shall include all loans given to micro and small (manufacturing) enterprises engaged in manufacture/production, processing or preservation of goods, and micro and small (service) enterprises engaged in providing or rendering of services, and whose investment in plant and machinery and equipment (original cost excluding land and building and such items as mentioned therein) respectively, does not exceed the amounts specified in Section I, appended.

The micro and small (service) enterprises shall include small road and water transport operators, small business, professional and self-employed persons, and all other service enterprises. Indirect finance to small enterprises shall include finance to any person providing inputs to or marketing the output of artisans, village and cottage industries, handlooms and to cooperatives of producers in this sector.

Retail Trade shall include retail traders/private retail traders dealing in essential commodities (fair price shops), and consumer cooperative stores.

Provision of credit and other financial services and products of very small amounts not exceeding ₹ 50,000 per borrower, either directly or indirectly through a SHG/JLG mechanism or to NBFC/MFI for onlending up to ₹ 50,000 per borrower, will constitute micro credit. Education loans include loans and advances granted to only individuals for educational purposes up to ₹ 10 lakh for studies in India and ₹ 20 lakh for studies abroad, and do not include those granted to institutions.

Loans up to ₹ 20 lakh to individuals for purchase/construction of dwelling unit per family, (excluding loans granted by banks to their own employees) and loans given for repairs to the damaged dwelling units of families up to ₹ 1 lakh in rural and semi-urban areas and up to ₹ 2 lakh in urban and metropolitan areas.

Source: Ministry of Food Processing Industry.

GOVERNMENT POLICIES AND INITIATIVES

IMPORTANT: The information given here may be further verified before acting upon it from primary source that is Ministry of Finance, Department of Revenue for any revision/changes.

Policy Initiatives

After liberalization, several policy measures have been taken with regard to regulation and control, export and import, fiscal policy, exchange and interest rate control taxation, export promotion and incentives to high priority industries. Food processing and agro industries have been accorded high priority with a number of important relieves and incentives. Some of the important policy changes towards food processing industry are as follows:

Regulation and Control:

- Most of the processed food items have been exempted from the purview of licensing under the Industries, Development and Regulation, Act, 1951, except items reserved for small-scale sector and alcoholic beverages.
- As per extent policy, Foreign Direct Investment up to 100 per cent is permitted under the automatic route in the food infrastructure like Food Park, Cold Chain and warehousing.
- As far as food retail is concerned the FDI policy does not permit FDI into retail sector except Single Brand Product Retailing. This policy is uniform for all retailing activity.
- FDI policy for manufacture of items reserved for the small-scale industry sector is uniform for all items so reserved and a separate dispensation for items in the food-processing sector is not contemplated.
- The policy for distillation of alcohol has been announced vide Press Note 4 (2006) according to which FDI upto 100 per cent is permitted on the automatic route for distillation and brewing of alcohol subject to licensing by the appropriate authority.
- No industrial license is required for almost all of the food and agro-processing industries except for some items like beer, potable alcohol and wines, sugarcane, hydrogenated animal fats and oils etc. and items reserved for exclusive manufacture in the small-scale sector.

Items reserved for SSI include pickles and chutneys, bread, confectionery, excluding chocolate, toffees and chewinggum etc., rapeseed, mustard, sesame and groundnut oils (except solvent extracted), ground and processed spices other than spice oil and oleoresins, sweetened cashew-nut products, tapioca sago and tapioca flour.

- Use of foreign brand names of liquors and Indian made foreign liquors now freely permitted by the government.
- MRTP (Monopolies and Restrictive Trade Practices Act) rules and FERA (Foreign Exchange Regulation Act) regulations have been relaxed and given more freedom to encourage investment and expansion by large corporates.
- Most of the items can be freely imported and exported except for items in the negative lists for imports and exports. Capital goods are also freely importable, including second hand ones in the foodprocessing sector.

Fiscal Policy and Taxation:

- Custom duty rates have been substantially reduced on food processing plant and equipments, as well as on raw materials and intermediates, especially for export production.
- Wide-ranging fiscal policy changes have been introduced progressively in food processing sector. Excise and Import duty rates have been reduced substantially. Many processed food items are totally exempt from excise duty.
- Corporate taxes have been reduced and there is a shift towards market related interest rates. There are tax incentives for new manufacturing units for certain years, except for industries like beer, wine, aerated water using flavouring concentrates, confectionery, chocolates etc.
- Indian currency, rupee, is now fully convertible on current account and convertibility on capital account with unified exchange rate mechanism is foreseen in coming years.
- Repatriation of profits is freely permitted in many industries except for some, where there is an additional requirement of balancing the dividend payments through export earnings.

Export Promotion:

- Food processing industry is one of the growing areas identified for exports. Free Trade Zones (FTZs) and Export Processing Zones (EPZs) have been set up with all infrastructures. Also, setting up of 100 per cent Export oriented units (EOU) is encouraged in other areas. They may import free of duty all types of goods, including capital foods.
- Capital goods, including spares up to 20 per cent of the CIF value of the Capital goods may be imported at a concessional rate of Customs duty subject to certain export obligations under the EPCG scheme, Export Promotion Capital Goods. Export linked duty free imports are also allowed.
- Units in EPZ/FTZ and 100 per cent Export oriented units can retain 50 per cent of foreign exchange receipts in foreign currency accounts.
- 50 per cent of the production of EPZ/FTZ and 100 per cent EOU units is saleable in domestic tariff area.

FISCAL INCENTIVES FOR FOOD PROCESSING SECTOR

Excise Duty Rates: Excise duty on condensed milk, ice-cream, preparations of meat, fish and poultry, pectins and pectates, used as a gelling agent in jams and jellies, pasta and yeast is abolished which was 16 per cent earlier.

- Excise Duty on biscuits whose retail sale price does not exceed ₹100 per kg reduced from 8 per cent to 0 per cent.
- Excise on ready-to-eat packaged food reduced from 16 per cent to 8 per cent, which is 50 per cent reduction.
- Excise Duty reduced from 8 per cent to 0 per cent on all kinds of food mixes including instant food mixes.
- Excise duty on aerated drinks has been reduced from 24 per cent to 16 per cent.
- Excise duty on meat, fish and poultry products reduced from 16 per cent to 8 per cent.
- Excise duty on Reefer Vans (refrigerated motor vehicles) reduced from 16 per cent to 8 per cent.
- Excise duty on unbranded edible preparations of oil increased from nil to 8 per cent.

Customs Duty Rates:

- Customs duty on food processing machinery and their parts is being reduced from 7.5 per cent to 5 per cent, dairy machineries are completely exempted from Central Excise Duty.
- Custom duty on Packaging Machine to be reduced from 15 per cent to 5 per cent.
- Customs duty on refrigerated vans reduced from 20 per cent to 10 per cent.

Income Tax Relief:

- Income Tax rebate is allowed, 100 per cent of profits for 5 years and 25 per cent of profits for the next 5 years, for new industries to process, preserve and package fruits and vegetables.

SUMMARY

In this chapter, we have studied about processing of agricultural outputs which is undertaken in organized as well as unorganized sectors, procuring grains either from wholesalers or directly from the producers. Direct purchase by major corporates of public and private sectors (mostly private sector) from producers is increasing through contract farming for their specific types of requirements either for processing or for exports. Grain processing is the largest segment in the food processing industry. Some of the important grains used for processing are discussed in the following sections.

In all over the world and in India in particular, Rice is the most important cereal in India. It is the most important foodgrain in the world also feeding about two-thirds of the world's population. Rice is processed from paddy and basmati variety of rice is usually sold in branded form with good packaging and advertising. It is the largest item of agricultural exports from India. Rice Bran oil, considered a healthy oil, is expected to see an increase in demand in the future.

It is the largest item of agricultural exports from India while rice bran oil considered healthy oil is expected to see an increase in demand in the future. It has good demand in Japan, Korea, and the US, where the consumers pay premium for this healthy edible oil. In India edible oil producers are launching new brands by mixing rice bran oil with other oils, like sunflower oil, to enhance the health properties, and attracting a premium of ₹ 10 litre.

Similarly wheat which is also major crop in almost developing countries in Asian region and Uttar Pradesh, Punjab, Haryana, Rajasthan, Madhya Pradesh, Gujarat and Bihar are major wheat growing states in India. Wheat and wheat flour are an important component of India's food industry. Other important processed items made of wheat are bread (₹ 38.9 billion) biscuits (₹ 13.5 billion) and pasta products (₹ 8.4 billion) contributing a total of ₹ 158.4 billion. Britannia and Modern Food Industries Limited are the only big players in the bread industry, while there are twenty-five medium and 1800 small-scale manufacturers. The industry has been fixed for the small-scale sector in 1977.

The government both at State and at Central level have also done their best to give tax incentives as sigh of relief. Excise duty on condensed milk, ice-cream, preparations of meat, fish and poultry, Pectins and Pectates, used as a gelling agent in jams and jellies, pasta and yeast is abolished which was 16 per cent earlier. Excise Duty on biscuits whose retail sale price does not exceed ₹ 100 per kg reduced from 8 per cent to 0 per cent. Excise on ready-to-eat packaged food reduced from 16 per cent to 8 per cent, which is 50 per cent reduction. Excise Duty reduced from 8 per cent to 0 per cent on all kinds of food mixes including instant food mixes. Excise duty on aerated drinks has been reduced from 24 per cent to 16 per cent Excise duty on meat, fish and poultry products reduced from 16 per cent to 8 per cent. Excise Duty on Reefer Vans (refrigerated motor vehicles) reduced from 16 per cent to 8 per cent. Excise duty on unbranded edible preparations of oil increased from nil to 8 per cent.

QUESTIONS

1. List out who are the major giants of food industry and food processed industry?
2. How marketing of processed food products takes place?
3. How marketing of processed Fruit and Vegetable products takes place?
4. Explain constraints, challenges and opportunities in the marketing of Fruit and Vegetable processed products?
5. What are the incentives devised by government at centre for corporates in the area of marketing?
6. Discuss this statement: "India's manufacturing and marketing potential of agriculture produce and value-added processed foods sector are untapped".

ooo